Updated Eighth Edition

Introduction to

Mass Communication

MEDIA LITERACY AND CULTURE

Stanley J. Baran

Bryant University

McGraw Hill Education

INTRODUCTION TO MASS COMMUNICATION: MEDIA LITERACY AND CULTURE, UPDATED, EIGHTH EDITION

Published by McGraw-Hill Education, 2 Penn Plaza, New York NY 10121. Copyright © 2015 by McGraw-Hill Education. All rights reserved. Printed in the United States of America. Previous editions © 2014, 2013, and 2012. No part of this publication may be reproduced or distributed in any form or by any means, or stored in a database or retrieval system, without the prior written consent of McGraw-Hill Education, including, but not limited to, in any network or other electronic storage or transmission, or broadcast for distance learning.

Some ancillaries, including electronic and print components, may not be available to customers outside the United States.

This book is printed on acid-free paper.

1 2 3 4 5 6 7 8 9 0 RMN/RMN 1 0 9 8 7 6 5 4

ISBN 978-0-07-750798-5
MHID 0-07-750798-3

Senior Vice President, Products & Markets: *Kurt L. Strand*
Vice President, General Manager, Products & Markets:
  Michael Ryan
Vice President, Content Production & Technology Services:
  Kimberly Meriwether David
Managing Director: *David Patterson*
Director: *Susan Gouijnstook*
Marketing Manager: *Laura Kennedy*
Director of Development: *Lisa Pinto*
Editorial Coordinator: *Jamie Daron*

Director, Content Production: *Terri Schiesl*
Content Project Manager: *Jennifer Gehl*
Senior Buyer: *Laura Fuller*
Designer: *Tara McDermott*
Cover Images: *(silhouette)* © *Getty Images/AWL Images;*
  (background) © *Getty Images/Alan Copson*
Content Licensing Specialist: *Ann Marie Jannette*
Compositor: *Aptara®, Inc.*
Typeface: *10/12 Minion*
Printer: *R. R. Donnelley*

Library of Congress Cataloging-in-Publication Data

Cataloging-in-Publication Data has been requested from the Library of Congress.

The Internet addresses listed in the text were accurate at the time of publication. The inclusion of a website does not indicate an endorsement by the authors or McGraw-Hill Education, and McGraw-Hill Education does not guarantee the accuracy of the information presented at these sites.

In loving memory of my mother,
Margaret Baran;
she gave me life;
and in honor of my wife,
Susan Baran;
she gave that life meaning.

About the Author

Stanley Baran earned his Ph.D. in communication research at the University of Massachusetts after taking his M.A. in journalism at Pennsylvania State University. He taught for four years at Cleveland State University, eventually moving to the University of Texas. He led the Department of Radio-TV-Film's graduate program for six of his nine years in Austin and won numerous teaching awards there, including the AMOCO Teaching Excellence Award as the best instructor on that 40,000-student campus, the College of Communication's Teaching Excellence Award as that college's outstanding professor, and *Utmost Magazine*'s Student Poll for best instructor. Dr. Baran moved to San Jose State University in 1987 and served nine years as chair of the Department of Television, Radio, Film, and Theatre. At SJSU he was named President's Scholar as the university's outstanding researcher. Now, he teaches at Bryant University, where he is the founding chair of that school's Communication Department. Among his other experiences shaping this book are service as a Fulbright Scholar and his many years of professional activity in audience research, writing for radio, and producing for television. Dr. Baran has published 10 books and scores of scholarly articles and sits or has sat on the editorial boards of six journals. His work has been translated into half a dozen languages. He is a skilled boater and a tenor saxophonist for the Wakefield, Rhode Island, Concert Band. He is married to Susan Baran and has two very cool children, Matt and Jordan, who grew up much faster than he wanted.

Brief Contents

Contents

PART TWO   MEDIA, MEDIA INDUSTRIES, AND MEDIA AUDIENCES   46

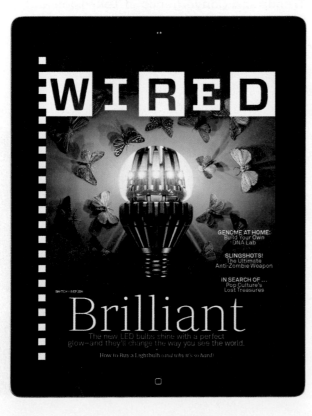

Preface

From the Author

Dear Friends,

The media, like sports and politics, are what we talk about, argue over, dissect and analyze. Those of us who teach media know that these conversations are essential to the functioning of a democratic society. We also know that what moves these conversations from simple chatting and griping to effective public discourse is media education. And regardless of what we might call the course—Introduction to Mass Communication, Introduction to Mass Media, Media and Society, or Media and Culture—media education has been part of the university for more than five decades. From the outset, the course has fulfilled these goals:

- Increasing students' knowledge and understanding of the mass communication process and the mass media industries
- Increasing students' awareness of how they interact with those industries and their content to create meaning
- Helping students become more skilled and knowledgeable consumers of media content

We now call the fulfillment of these goals *media literacy*.

A Cultural Perspective

This text's cultural orientation toward mass communication places a great deal of responsibility on media consumers. In the past, people were considered either victims of media influence or impervious to it. The cultural orientation asserts that audience members are as much a part of the mass communication process as are the media technologies and industries. As important agents in the creation and maintenance of their own culture, audience members have an obligation not only to participate in the process of mass communication but also to participate critically as better consumers of mass media.

Enriching Students' Literacy

The focus of this book, from the start, has been on media literacy and culture, and those emphases have shaped its content and its various learning aids and pedagogical features. But with this, the updated eighth edition, McGraw-Hill and I have added the digital teaching and learning environment Connect® to our arsenal of educational tools. Connect makes managing assignments easier for instructors like us and learning and studying more interactive, motivating, and efficient for our students. Assignable video and critical thinking activities in Connect support the themes and goals of *Introduction to Mass Communication*. LearnSmart™, a proven adaptive learning program, is also available in Connect; it guides students with personalized learning plans and frees up valuable class time for discussion and activities.

My Thanks to You

Thank you for teaching mass communication. There are few college courses that will mean more to our students' lives now and after they graduate than this one. Thank you, too, for considering *Introduction to Mass Communication: Media Literacy and Culture* for use in your course. I have poured the last 15 years of my career into this text and what it has to say about mass communication and the world that our interaction with the media produces. Your interest in this text confirms my passion.

—**Stanley J. Baran**

Preface

Introducing Connect Mass Communication

Connect to Success

Introduction to Mass Communication: Media Literacy and Culture is available to instructors and students in print and eBook formats, as well as within an integrated online assignment and assessment platform. These online tools, collectively called Connect Mass Communication, make managing assignments easier for instructors—and make learning and studying more motivating and efficient for students.

Assignable and Accessible Activities Instructors can deliver assignments and tests easily online, and students can practice skills related to key course challenges at their own pace and on their own schedule. Available activities include chapter pre- and post-tests, CNN and Internet video activities, and Media Literacy Worksheets. Students can review fundamental concepts, practice applying media literacy skills, and complete other activities to help them achieve success in the course.

Real-time Reports Printable, exportable reports show how well each student (or section) is performing on each course segment. Instructors can use this feature to identify students who are at risk of falling behind as well as to spot problem areas *before* they crop up on an exam.

Integrated eBook A fully loaded eBook allows students to review *Introduction to Mass Communication* anytime and anywhere. They can highlight, take notes, and quickly search for key terms and phrases.

Connect to Personalized Learning

LearnSmart, McGraw-Hill's adaptive learning system, assesses students' knowledge of course content and maps out dynamic, personalized study plans that ground students in the fundamental concepts of mass communication. Available within Connect, LearnSmart uses a series of adaptive questions to pinpoint the concepts students understand—and those they don't. The result is a proven online tool that helps students learn faster, study more efficiently, and improve their performance. LearnSmart allows instructors to focus valuable class time on higher-level concepts, activities, and discussion.

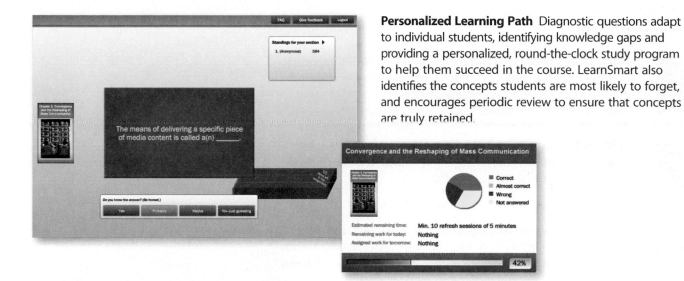

Personalized Learning Path Diagnostic questions adapt to individual students, identifying knowledge gaps and providing a personalized, round-the-clock study program to help them succeed in the course. LearnSmart also identifies the concepts students are most likely to forget, and encourages periodic review to ensure that concepts are truly retained.

Valuable Reports and Tools A personalized learning calendar shows each student her or his progress through the course. Interactive reports help students take responsibility for their own learning.

Mobile Access LearnSmart gives students the freedom to study whenever and wherever they choose. It can be accessed from any computer and via mobile devices using an app available from the iTunes store.

Preface

Key Features and Learning Aids

Students must bring media literacy—the ability to critically comprehend and actively use mass media—to the mass communication process. The updated eighth edition of *Introduction to Mass Communication: Media Literacy and Culture* includes a variety of boxed features and in-text learning aids to support student learning and enhance media literacy skills.

Boxed Features

 Using Media to Make a Difference boxes highlight interesting examples of how media practitioners and audiences use the mass communication process to further important social, political, or cultural causes.

 Cultural Forum boxes highlight media-related cultural issues that are currently debated in the mass media to help students develop their critical thinking skills.

 Media Literacy Challenge boxes, new to the updated eighth edition, build on ideas from each chapter's "Developing Media Literacy Skills" section and ask students to think critically about media content they encounter in their daily lives.

In-Text Learning Aids

▸ Chapter learning objectives and chapter-ending lists of key terms focus student learning.

▸ Historical timelines and overviews provide students with a critical foundation for understanding current issues in the media landscape.

▸ Review Points allow students to make sure they have focused on each chapter's most important material; new for the updated eighth edition, the review points are tied directly to learning objectives.

▸ Questions for Review further highlight key concepts, and Questions for Critical Thinking and Discussion encourage students to investigate their own cultural assumptions and media use and to engage one another in debate on critical issues.

▸ A comprehensive list of references is provided at the end of the book.

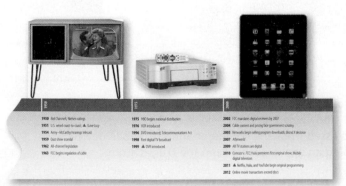

Changes to the Updated Eighth Edition: Highlights

The updated eighth edition maintains its commitment to enhancing students' critical thinking and media literacy skills. Chapters 3 through 15 include new sections dedicated to smartphones, tablets, and social networking sites. Statistics and data have been updated throughout. Additional key changes include the following:

Chapter 1 Mass Communication, Culture, and Media Literacy: Sharpened focus on the mass communication process and media literacy.

Chapter 2 Convergence and the Reshaping of Mass Communication: New discussion of the explosion of smartphones and their convergence with virtually all other electronic and print media.

Chapter 3 Books: New discussion of print-on-demand, the revival of printed books, and the spread and influence of e-readers and tablets.

Chapter 4 Newspapers: New and updated sections on how newspapers are monetizing their news and going mobile, the health of the local press, and new forms of group-funded journalism.

Chapter 5 Magazines: Updated coverage of the digital-only magazine reader, action codes (QR) and near-field communication chips (NFC), and greater reader interactivity.

Chapter 6 Film: Enhanced examination of the movement to debut movies on Facebook, Netflix, and Hulu, as well as discussion of Hollywood's resurgence.

Chapter 7 Radio, Recording, and Popular Music: Updated looks at the seeming paradox of more music (but fewer big label sales) than ever; industry concentration and its impact on artists; cloud music services and the rise of streaming services like Pandora and Spotify; and the Rush Limbaugh vs. Sandra Fluke controversy.

Chapter 8 Television, Cable, and Mobile Video: New and updated coverage of the TV Everywhere movement, network/affiliate relationships, cable cord cutting, and the growth of Facebook video.

Chapter 9 Video Games: Updated discussion of the demise of the console and the rise of smartphone and social network gaming, PlayStation Vita as counter to this trend, creation of the likes of Humble Indie Bundle as counter to "industrialized" game creation, and a look at the debate over whether games are good or bad.

Chapter 10 The Internet and the World Wide Web: New and updated material on social networking and political action (specifically Occupy Wall Street and anti-SOPA), growing privacy challenges and the Consumer Privacy Bill of Rights, the ICANN expansion of top-level domain names, the Facebook purchase of Instagram, the introduction and growth of tablets, and the rise of mobile spam.

Chapter 11 Public Relations: Examination of consumer demand for greater corporate responsibility, the rise of cause marketing (aided by smartphones and social networking, such as apps like Gripe), and new FCC rules on video news releases.

Chapter 12 Advertising: New discussion of new return on investment (ROI) and accountability measures, the explosion of advertising in "developing" markets (the BRICS and MIST, specifically China, India, and Brazil), the growth of out-of-home advertising, and neuromarketing research.

Chapter 13 Theories and Effects of Mass Communication: Updated coverage of theory and research on TV and video game violence and on social media use and friendships.

Chapter 14 Media Freedom, Regulation, and Ethics: New sections on *Brown v. EMA*, in which the Supreme Court extends First Amendment protection to violent video games; debate over whether WikiLeaks' source Bradley Manning and NSA whistle-blower Edward Snowden are traitors or free speech heroes; and examination of the question of the role of journalists—should they be truth vigilantes?

Chapter 15 Global Media: Updated discussion of the growing popularity of Al Jazeera in the United States and the American government's challenge to Chinese Internet censorship.

Teaching and Learning with *Introduction to Mass Communication*

Online Learning Center
www.mhhe.com/baran8e

The Online Learning Center for *Introduction to Mass Communication* includes comprehensive teaching resources:

▸ Instructor's Manual

▸ Test Bank

▸ PowerPoint presentations

▸ Media Literacy Worksheets

Refer to the back inside cover of the text for a list of the CNN video clips that can be found in the Connect Media Bank.

McGraw-Hill Create
http://www.mcgrawhillcreate.com

Design your own ideal course materials with McGraw-Hill's Create™. Rearrange or omit chapters, combine material from other sources, upload your syllabus or any other content you have written to make the perfect resource for your students. Search thousands of leading McGraw-Hill textbooks to find the best content for your students; then arrange it to fit your teaching style. You can even personalize your book's appearance by selecting the cover and adding your name, school, and course information. When you order a Create book, you receive a complimentary review copy. Get a printed copy in 3 to 5 business days or an electronic copy (e-Comp) via e-mail in about an hour. Register today at http://www.mcgrawhillcreate .com, and craft your course resources to match the way you teach.

CourseSmart
CourseSmart
www.coursesmart.com

CourseSmart offers thousands of the most commonly adopted textbooks across hundreds of courses from a wide variety of higher education publishers. It is the only place for faculty to review and compare the full text of a book online, providing immediate access without the environmental impact of requesting a printed exam copy. At CourseSmart, students can save up to 50 percent off the cost of a printed book, reduce their impact on the environment, and gain access to powerful web tools for learning, including full text search, notes and highlighting, and e-mail tools for sharing notes among classmates. Visit coursesmart.com to learn more or to purchase registration codes for this exciting product.

Tegrity Campus
http://tegritycampus.mhhe.com

Tegrity is a service that makes class time available around the clock. It automatically captures every lecture in a searchable format for students to review when they study and complete assignments. With a simple one-click start-and-stop process, you capture all computer screens and corresponding audio. Students replay any part of any class with easy-to-use browser-based viewing on a PC or Mac. With Tegrity Campus, students quickly recall key moments by using Tegrity Campus's unique search feature, which lets them efficiently find what they need, when they need it, across an entire semester of class recordings. Help turn all your students' study time into learning moments immediately supported by your lecture. To learn more about Tegrity, watch a two-minute Flash demo at http://tegritycampus.mhhe.com.

McGraw-Hill Campus™

McGraw-Hill Campus is a new one-stop teaching and learning experience available to users of any learning management system. This institutional service allows faculty and students to enjoy single sign-on (SSO) access to all McGraw-Hill Higher Education materials, including the award-winning McGraw-Hill Connect® platform, from directly within the institution's website. McGraw-Hill Campus provides faculty with instant access to all McGraw-Hill Higher Education teaching materials (e.g., eTextbooks, test banks, PowerPoint slides, animations, and learning objects), allowing them to browse, search, and use any instructor ancillary content in our vast library at no additional cost to instructor or students. Students enjoy SSO access to a variety of free (e.g., quizzes, flash cards, narrated presentations) and subscription-based products (e.g., McGraw-Hill Connect). With this program enabled, faculty and students will never need to create another account to access McGraw-Hill products and services.

Acknowledgements

A project of this magnitude requires the assistance of many people. For this latest edition I benefitted from several e-mails from readers—instructors and students—making suggestions and offering advice. This book is better for those exchanges.

Reviewers are an indispensable part of the creation of a good textbook. In preparing for the updated eighth edition, I was again impressed with the thoughtful comments made by my colleagues in the field. Although I didn't know them by name, I found myself in long-distance, anonymous debate with several superb thinkers, especially about some of the text's most important concepts. Their collective keen eye and questioning attitude sharpened each chapter to the benefit of both writer and reader. (Any errors or misstatements that remain in the book are of course my sole responsibility.) Now that I know who they are, I would like to thank the reviewers by name.

Lee Banville, *University of Montana*

Rick Bebout, *West Virginia University*

Bob Britten, *West Virginia University*

James Burton, *Salisbury University*

Nathan Claes, *State University of New York–Buffalo*

Helen Fallon, *Point Park University*

Ray Fanning, *University of Montana*

Richard Ganahl, *Bloomsburg University*

Paul Hillier, *University of Tampa*

Charles Marsh, *University of Kansas–Lawrence*

Susan McGraw, *Henry Ford Community College*

Bob Mendenhall, *Southwestern Adventist University*

Jensen Moore, *West Virginia University*

Timothy Pasch, *University of North Dakota*

Kenneth Ross, *Eastern Connecticut State University*

Siobhan Smith, *University of Louisville*

Jeff South, *Virginia Commonwealth University*

Richard Taflinger, *Washington State University–Pullman*

Clifford Vaughn, *Belmont University*

Kimberly Vaupel, *Henry Ford Community College*

Joe Wisinski, *University of Tampa*

Special thanks to Bob Mendenhall and Cliff Vaughn for their help in reviewing Connect activities. Thanks also to the instructors who supervised class testing of the LearnSmart modules: Cathy Bullock (Utah State University), Yolanda Cal (Loyola University, New Orleans), Daekyung Kim (Idaho State University), and Bruce Mims (Southeast Missouri State University).

I would also like to thank the reviewers of the first seven editions. **Seventh Edition Reviewers:** Kwasi Boateng, University of Arkansas at Little Rock; Mike Igoe, Buffalo State College; Joe Marre, Buffalo State College; Sonya Miller, University of North Carolina–Asheville; Yuri Obata, Indiana University–South Bend; Danny Shipka, Louisiana State University. **Sixth Edition Reviewers:** Chris Cakebread, Boston University; Cynthia Chris, College of Staten Island; Laurie Hayes Fluker, Texas State University; Jacob Podber, Southern Illinois University–Carbondale; Biswarup Sen, University of Oregon; Lisa A. Stephens, University of Buffalo; Denise Walters, Front Range Community College. **Fifth Edition Reviewers:** Jennifer Aubrey, University of Missouri; Michael Boyle, Wichita State University; Tim Coombs, Eastern Illinois University; Denise Danford, Delaware County Community College; Tim Edwards, University of Arkansas at Little Rock; Junhao Hong, State University of New York at Buffalo; Mark Kelly, University of Maine; Alyse Lancaster, University of Miami; Carol S. Lomick, University of Nebraska at Kearney; Susan Dawson-O'Brien, Rose State College; Alicia

C. Shepard, University of Texas at Austin; Tamala Sheree Martin, Oklahoma State University; Stephen D. Perry, Illinois State University; Selene Phillips, University of Louisville. **Fourth Edition Reviewers:** Kristen Barton, Florida State University; Kenton Bird, University of Idaho; Katia G. Campbell, University of Colorado; Paul A. Creasman, Azusa Pacific University; Annette Johnson, Georgia State University; James Kelleher, New York University; Polly McLean, University of Colorado; Anthony A. Olorunnisola, Pennsylvania State University; Stephen D. Perry, Illinois State University; Michael Porter, University of Missouri; Stephen J. Resch, Indiana Wesleyan University; Christopher F. White, Sam Houston State University. **Third Edition Reviewers:** Jenny L. Nelson, Ohio University; Terri Toles Patkin, Eastern Connecticut State University; Alyse Lancaster, University of Miami; Deborah A. Godwin-Starks, Indiana University–Purdue University Fort Wayne; Kevin R. Slaugher, George Mason University; Enid Sefcovic, Florida Atlantic University; David Whitt, Nebraska Wesleyan University; Roger Desmond, University of Hartford; Carol S. Lomicky, University of Nebraska at Kearney; Jules d'Hemecourt, Louisiana State University; Junhao Hong, State University of New York at Buffalo; Gary J. Wingenbach, Texas A&M University. **Second Edition Reviewers:** Rob Bellamy, Duquesne University; Beth Grobman Burruss, DeAnza College; Stephen R. Curtis, Jr., East Connecticut State University; Lyombe Eko, University of Maine; Junhao Hong, State University of New York at Buffalo; Carol Liebler, Syracuse University; Robert Main, California State University, Chico; Stephen Perry, Illinois State University; Eric Pierson, University of San Diego; Ramona Rush, University of Kentucky; Tony Silvia, University of Rhode Island; and Richard Welch, Kennesaw State University. **First Edition Reviewers:** David Allen, Illinois State University; Sandra Braman, University of Alabama; Tom Grimes, Kansas State University; Kirk Hallahan, Colorado State University; Katharine Heintz-Knowles, University of Washington; Paul Husselbee, Ohio University; Seong Lee, Appalachian State University; Rebecca Ann Lind, University of Illinois at Chicago; Maclyn McClary, Humboldt State University; Guy Meiss, Central Michigan University; Debra Merskin, University of Oregon; Scott R. Olsen, Central Connecticut State University; Ted Pease, Utah State University; Linda Perry, *Florida Today* newspaper; Elizabeth Perse, University of Delaware; Tina Pieraccini, State University of New York–College at Oswego; Michael Porter, University of Missouri; Peter Pringle, University of Tennessee at Chattanooga; Neal Robison, Washington State University; Linda Steiner, Rutgers University; and Don Tomlinson, Texas A&M University.

The updated eighth edition was written with the usual great support (and patience) of my McGraw-Hill team. The Internet may make producing a book more efficient, but it does have a big drawback—despite spending hundreds of hours "working together," I have yet to meet my teammates face-to-face. This, certainly, is my loss. Still, I have had few better colleagues than Julia Akpan, Susan Gouijnstook, Kirstan Price, Jennifer Gehl, Ann Jannette, Jennifer Gehl, Jamie Daron, and Emily Tietz. An author cannot surround himself with better people than those McGraw-Hill has given me.

Finally, my most important inspiration throughout the writing of this book has been my family. My wife, Susan, is educated in media literacy and a strong disciple of spreading its lessons far and wide—which she does with zest. Her knowledge and assistance in my writing is invaluable; her love in my life is sustaining; her fire—for improved media literacy and for our marriage—is empowering. My children—Jordan and Matthew—simply by their existence require that I consider and reconsider what kind of world we will leave for them. I've written this text in the hope that it helps make the future for them and their friends better than it might otherwise have been.

S.J.B.

Updated Eighth Edition

Introduction to
Mass Communication
MEDIA LITERACY AND CULTURE

Mass Communication, Culture, and Media Literacy

1

Learning Objectives

Mass communication, mass media, and the culture that shapes us (and that we shape) are inseparable. After studying this chapter, you should be able to

 Define *communication*, *mass communication*, *mass media*, and *culture*.

 Describe the relationships among communication, mass communication, culture, and those who live in the culture.

 Evaluate the impact of technology and economics on those relationships.

 List the components of media literacy.

 Identify key skills required for developing media literacy.

Our experiences of the world are increasingly mass mediated.

YOUR SMARTPHONE'S RADIO ALARM SINGS YOU AWAKE. It's Adele, the last few bars of "Rolling in the Deep." The laughing deejay shouts at you that it's 7:41 and you'd better get going. But before you do, he adds, listen to a few words from your friends at Best Buy electronics, home of fast, friendly, courteous service—"Buyer be happy!"

In the living room, you find your roommate has left the television on. You stop for a moment and listen: The economy is showing stronger signs of rebounding, brightening the employment picture for new college grads, several states are considering Clean Election laws to take money out of politics, democratic chaos continues to sweep across the Middle East, and you deserve a break today at McDonald's. As you head toward the bathroom, your bare feet slip on some magazines littering the floor—*Wired, Rolling Stone, People*. You need to talk to your roommate about picking up!

After showering, you quickly pull on your Levi's, lace up your Nike cross-trainers, and throw on an Under Armour jacket. No time for breakfast; you grab a Nature Valley granola bar and the newspaper and head for the bus stop. As the bus rolls up, you can't help but notice the giant ad on its side: *Transformers: Turning Toys Into Gold*. Rejecting that as a movie choice for the weekend, you sit down next to a teenager listening to music on his headphones and playing a video game. You bury yourself in the paper, scanning the lead stories and the local news and then checking out *Doonesbury* and *Dilbert*.

Hopping off the bus at the campus stop, you run into Chris from your computer lab. You walk to class together, talking about last night's *Family Guy* episode. It's not yet 9:00, and already you're involved in mass communication.

In this chapter we define *communication, interpersonal communication, mass communication, media,* and *culture* and explore the relationships among them and how they define us and our world. We investigate how communication works, how it changes when technology is introduced into the process, and how differing views of communication and mass communication can lead to different interpretations of their power. We also discuss the opportunities mass communication and culture offer us and the responsibilities that come with those opportunities. Always crucial, these issues are of particular importance now, when we find ourselves in a period of remarkable development in new communication technologies. This discussion inevitably leads to an examination of media literacy, its importance and practice.

What Is Mass Communication?

"Does a fish know it's wet?" influential cultural and media critic Marshall McLuhan would often ask. The answer, he would say, is "No." The fish's existence is so dominated by water that only when water is absent is the fish aware of its condition.

So it is with people and mass media. The media so fully saturate our everyday lives that we are often unconscious of their presence, not to mention their influence. Media inform us, entertain us, delight us, annoy us. They move our emotions, challenge our intellects, insult our intelligence. Media often reduce us to mere commodities for sale to the highest bidder. Media help define us; they shape our realities.

A fundamental theme of this book is that media do none of this alone. They do it *with* us as well as *to* us through mass communication, and they do it as a central— many critics and scholars say *the* central—cultural force in our society.

Communication Defined

In its simplest form, **communication** is the transmission of a message from a source to a receiver. For over 60 years now, this view of communication has been identified with the writing of political scientist Harold Lasswell (1948). He said that a convenient way to describe communication is to answer these questions:

- *Who*?
- Says *what*?
- Through *which* channel?
- To *whom*?
- With *what effect*?

Expressed in terms of the basic elements of the communication process, communication occurs when

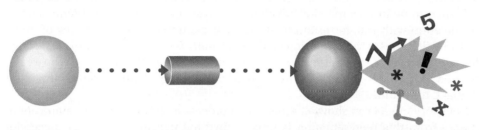

A source sends a message   through a medium   to a receiver   producing some effect.

Straightforward enough, but what if the source is a professor who insists on speaking in a technical language far beyond the receiving students' level of skill? Obviously, communication does not occur. Unlike mere message-sending, communication requires the response of others. Therefore, there must be a *sharing* (or correspondence) of meaning for communication to take place.

A second problem with this simple model is that it suggests that the receiver passively accepts the source's message. However, if our imaginary students do not comprehend the professor's words, they respond with "Huh?" or look confused or yawn. This response, or **feedback**, is also a message. The receivers (the students) now become a source, sending their own message to the source (the offending professor), who is now a receiver. Hence, communication is a *reciprocal* and *ongoing process* with all involved parties more or less engaged in creating shared meaning. Communication, then, is better defined as *the process of creating shared meaning.*

Communication researcher Wilbur Schramm, using ideas originally developed by psychologist Charles E. Osgood, developed a graphic way to represent the reciprocal nature of communication (Figure 1.1). This depiction of **interpersonal communication—**

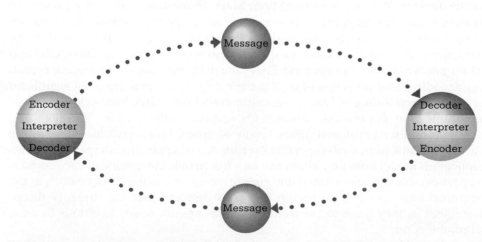

▲ **Figure 1.1** Osgood and Schramm's Model of Communication.
Source: From *The Process and Effects of Mass Communication* by Wilbur Lang Schramm, 1954. Reprinted by permission of Mary Schramm Coberly.

communication between two or a few people—shows that there is no clearly identifiable source or receiver. Rather, because communication is an ongoing and reciprocal process, all the participants, or "interpreters," are working to create meaning by **encoding** and **decoding** messages. A message is first *encoded*, that is, transformed into an understandable sign and symbol system. Speaking is encoding, as are writing, printing, and filming a television program. Once received, the message is *decoded*; that is, the signs and symbols are interpreted. Decoding occurs through listening, reading, or watching that television show.

The Osgood–Schramm model demonstrates the ongoing and reciprocal nature of the communication process. There is, therefore, no source, no receiver, and no feedback. The reason is that, as communication is happening, both interpreters are simultaneously source and receiver. There is no feedback because all messages are presumed to be in reciprocation of other messages. Even when your friend starts a conversation with you, for example, it can be argued that it was your look of interest and willingness that communicated to her that she should speak. In this example, it is improper to label either you or your friend as the source—Who really initiated this chat?—and, therefore, it is impossible to identify who is providing feedback to whom.

Not every model can show all aspects of a process as complex as communication. Missing from this representation is **noise**—anything that interferes with successful communication. Noise is more than screeching or loud music when you are trying to work online. Biases that lead to incorrect decoding, for example, are noise, as is a page torn out of a magazine story you want to read.

Encoded messages are carried by a **medium**, that is, the means of sending information. Sound waves are the medium that carries our voice to friends across the table; the telephone is the medium that carries our voice to friends across town. When the medium is a technology that carries messages to a large number of people—as newspapers carry the printed word and radio conveys the sound of music and news—we call it a **mass medium** (the plural of medium is **media**). The mass media we use regularly include radio, television, books, magazines, newspapers, movies, sound recordings, cell phones, and computer networks. Each medium is the basis of a giant industry, but other related and supporting industries also serve them and us—advertising and public relations, for example. In our culture we use the words *media* and *mass media* interchangeably to refer to the communication industries themselves. We say, "The media entertain" or "The mass media are too conservative (or too liberal)."

Mass Communication Defined

We speak, too, of mass communication. **Mass communication** is the process of creating shared meaning between the mass media and their audiences. Schramm recast his and Osgood's general model of communication to help us visualize the particular aspects of the mass communication process (Figure 1.2). This model and the original Osgood–Schramm model have much in common—interpreters, encoding, decoding, and messages—but it is their differences that are most significant for our understanding of how mass communication differs from other forms of communication. For example, whereas the original model includes "message," the mass communication model offers "many identical messages." In addition, the mass communication model specifies "feedback," whereas the interpersonal communication model does not. When two or a few people communicate face-to-face, the participants can immediately and clearly recognize the feedback residing in the reciprocal messages (our boring professor can see and hear the students' disenchantment as they listen to the lecture). Things are not nearly as simple in mass communication.

In Schramm's mass communication model, feedback is represented by a dotted line labeled delayed **inferential feedback**. This feedback is indirect rather than direct.

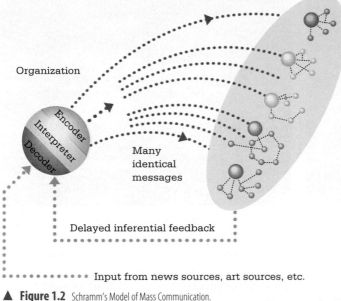

Organization

The mass audience

Many receivers, each
decoding, interpreting,
encoding

Many
identical
messages

Each connected with
a group in which the
message is reinterpreted
and often acted upon

Delayed inferential feedback

Input from news sources, art sources, etc.

▲ **Figure 1.2** Schramm's Model of Mass Communication.
Source: From *The Process and Effects of Mass Communication* by Wilbur Lang Schramm, 1954. Reprinted by permission of Mary Schramm Coberly.

Television executives, for example, must wait a day, at the very minimum, and some-times a week or a month, to discover the ratings for new programs. Even then, the ratings measure only how many sets are tuned in, not whether people liked or disliked the programs. As a result, these executives can only infer what they must do to improve programming; hence the term *inferential feedback.* Mass communicators are also subject to additional feedback, usually in the form of criticism in other media, such as a television critic writing a column in a newspaper.

The differences between the individual elements of interpersonal and mass com-munication change the very nature of the communication process. How those alter-ations influence the message itself and how the likelihood of successfully sharing meaning varies are shown in Figure 1.3. For example, the immediacy and directness of feedback in interpersonal communication free communicators to gamble, to experiment with different approaches. Their knowledge of one another enables them to tailor their messages as narrowly as they wish. As a result, interpersonal communication is often personally relevant and possibly even adventurous and challenging. In contrast, the distance between participants in the mass communica-tion process, imposed by the technology, creates a sort of "communication conser-vatism." Feedback comes too late to enable corrections or alterations in communication that fails. The sheer number of people in many mass communica-tion audiences makes personalization and specificity difficult. As a result, mass communication tends to be more constrained, less free. This does not mean, how-ever, that it is less potent than interpersonal communication in shaping our under-standing of ourselves and our world.

Media theorist James W. Carey (1975) recognized this and offered a **cultural defini-tion of communication** that has had a profound impact on the way communication scientists and others have viewed the relationship between communication and cul-ture. Carey wrote, "Communication is a symbolic process whereby reality is produced, maintained, repaired and transformed" (p. 10).

Carey's (1989) definition asserts that communication and reality are linked. Com-munication is a process embedded in our everyday lives that informs the way we per-ceive, understand, and construct our view of reality and the world. Communication is the foundation of our culture. Its truest purpose is to maintain ever-evolving, "fragile" cultures; communication is that "sacred ceremony that draws persons together in fellowship and commonality" (p. 43).

	Interpersonal Communication You invite a friend to lunch.		Mass Communication Levitan-Lloyd produces *Modern Family*	
	Nature	**Consequences**	**Nature**	**Consequences**
Message	Highly flexible and alterable	You can change it in midstream. If feedback is negative, you can offer an alternative. Is feedback still negative? Take a whole new approach.	Identical, mechanically produced, simultaneously sent Inflexible, unalterable The completed *Modern Family* episode that is aired	Once production is completed, *Modern Family* cannot be changed. If a plotline or other communicative device isn't working with the audience, nothing can be done.
Interpreter A	One person—in this case, you	You know your mind. You can encode your own message to suit yourself, your values, your likes and dislikes.	A large, hierarchically structured organization—in this case, Levitan-Lloyd Productions and the ABC television network	Who really is Interpreter A? Levitan-Lloyd Productions' executives? The writers? The director? The actors? The network and its standards and practices people? The sponsors? All must agree, leaving little room for individual vision or experimentation.
Interpreter B	One or a few people, usually in direct contact with you and, to a greater or lesser degree, known to you—in this case, your friend	You can tailor your message specifically to Interpreter B. You can make relatively accurate judgments about B because of information present in the setting. Your friend is a vegetarian; you don't suggest a steak house.	A large, heterogeneous audience known to Interpreter A only in the most rudimentary way, little more than basic demographics—in this case, several million viewers of *Modern Family*	Communication cannot be tailored to the wants, needs, and tastes of all audience members or even those of all members of some subgroup. Some more or less generally acceptable standard is set.
Feedback	Immediate and direct yes or no response	You know how successful your message is immediately. You can adjust your communication on the spot to maximize its effectiveness.	Delayed and inferential Even overnight ratings too late for this episode of *Modern Family* Moreover, ratings limited to telling the number of sets tuned in	Even if the feedback is useful, it is too late to be of value for this episode. In addition, it doesn't suggest how to improve the communication effort.
Result	Flexible, personally relevant, possibly adventurous, challenging, or experimental		Constrained by virtually every aspect of the communication situation A level of communication most likely to meet the greatest number of viewers' needs A belief that experimentation is dangerous A belief that to challenge the audience is to risk failure	

▲ **Figure 1.3** Elements of Interpersonal Communication and Mass Communication Compared.

What Is Culture?

Culture is the learned behavior of members of a given social group. Many writers and thinkers have offered interesting expansions of this definition. Here are four examples, all from anthropologists. These definitions highlight not only what culture *is* but also what culture *does*:

> Culture is the learned, socially acquired traditions and lifestyles of the members of a society, including their patterned, repetitive ways of thinking, feeling, and acting. (Harris, 1983, p. 5)

> Culture lends significance to human experience by selecting from and organizing it. It refers broadly to the forms through which people make sense of their lives, rather than more narrowly to the opera or art of museums. (Rosaldo, 1989, p. 26)

> Culture is the medium evolved by humans to survive. Nothing is free from cultural influences. It is the keystone in civilization's arch and is the medium through which all of life's events must flow. We are culture. (Hall, 1976, p. 14)

> Culture is an historically transmitted pattern of meanings embodied in symbolic forms by means of which [people] communicate, perpetuate, and develop their knowledge about and attitudes toward life. (Geertz, as cited in Taylor, 1991, p. 91)

Culture as Socially Constructed Shared Meaning

Virtually all definitions of culture recognize that culture is *learned*. Recall the opening vignette. Even if this scenario does not exactly match your early mornings, you probably recognize its elements. Moreover, all of us are familiar with most, if not every, cultural reference in it. *Family Guy*, *Rolling Stone*, McDonald's, Under Armour, *Dilbert*—all are points of reference, things that have some meaning for all of us. How did this come to be?

Creation and maintenance of a more or less common culture occurs through communication, including mass communication. When we talk to our friends; when a parent raises a child; when religious leaders instruct their followers; when teachers teach; when grandparents pass on recipes; when politicians campaign; when media professionals produce content that we read, listen to, or watch, meaning is being shared and culture is being constructed and maintained.

Functions and Effects of Culture

Culture serves a purpose. It helps us categorize and classify our experiences; it helps define us, our world, and our place in it. In doing so, culture can have a number of sometimes conflicting effects.

LIMITING AND LIBERATING EFFECTS OF CULTURE A culture's learned traditions and values can be seen as patterned, repetitive ways of thinking, feeling, and acting. Culture limits our options and provides useful guidelines for behavior. For example, when conversing, you do not consciously consider, "Now, how far away should I stand? Am I too close?" You simply stand where you stand. After a hearty meal with a friend's family, you do not engage in mental self-debate, "Should I burp? Yes! No! Arghhhh...." Culture provides information that helps us make meaningful distinctions about right and wrong, appropriate and inappropriate, good and bad, attractive and unattractive, and so on. How does it do this?

Obviously, through communication. Through a lifetime of communication we have learned just what our culture expects of us. The two examples given here are positive results of culture's limiting effects. But culture's limiting effects can be negative, such as when we are unwilling or unable to move past patterned, repetitive ways of thinking, feeling, and acting or when we entrust our "learning" to teachers whose interests are selfish, narrow, or otherwise not consistent with our own.

U.S. culture, for example, values thinness and beauty in women. How many women endure weeks of unhealthy diets and succumb to potentially dangerous surgical

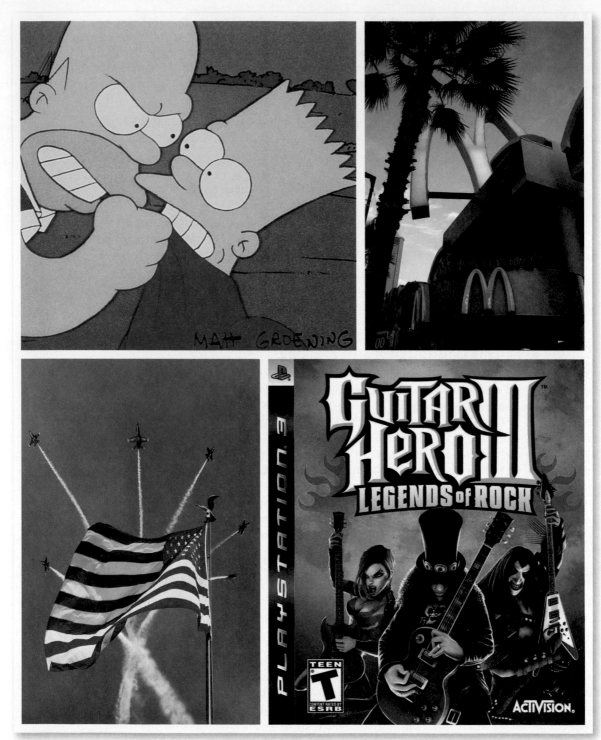

These images have meaning for all of us, meaning that is socially constructed through communication in our culture. How many can you recognize? What specific meaning or meanings does each have for you? How did you develop each meaning? How closely do you think your meanings match those of your friends? Of your parents? What value is there—if any—in having shared meaning for these things in our everyday lives?

procedures in search of a body that for most is physically unattainable? How many men (and other women) never get to know, like, or even love those women who cannot meet our culture's standards of thinness and beauty? Why do 72% of 10- to 17-year-old girls feel "tremendous pressure to be beautiful" but only 11% feel comfortable using that word, "beautiful," to describe themselves (Dove Research, 2011)? Why do 91% of all college women report dieting, with 22% dieting "always" or "often"? Why do 7 million American girls and women suffer from clinically diagnosed eating disorders? Why do 90% of American high school girls think they are overweight, up from 34% in 1995 (Brubach, 2007)? Why, when asked if they would rather be younger, thinner, richer, or smarter, do 29% of American women prefer to be thinner, while only 14% want to be smarter (Braverman, 2010)?

Now consider how this situation may have come about. Our mothers did not bounce us on their knees when we were babies, telling us that thin was good and fat was bad. Think back, though, to the stories you were told and the television shows and movies you watched growing up. The heroines (or, more often, the beautiful love interests of the heroes) were invariably tall, beautiful, and thin. The bad guys were usually mean and fat. From Disney's depictions of Snow White, Cinderella, Beauty, Tinker Bell, and Pocahontas to the impossible dimensions of most video-game heroines, the message is embedded in the conscious (and unconscious) mind of every girl and boy: You can't be too thin or too beautiful! Or as one 10-year-old girl explained to Courtney Martin (2007), author of *Perfect Girls, Starving Daughters*, "It is better to be pretty, which means thin and mean, than to be ugly, which means fat and nice. That's just how it is." And it does not help that these messages are reinforced in much advertising, for example Abercrombie & Fitch Kids' promotions for its Ashley bikinis with padded "push up triangle" tops for girls as young as 8 years old (Williams, 2011).

This message and millions of others come to us primarily through the media, and although the people who produce these media images are not necessarily selfish or mean, their motives are undeniably financial. Their contribution to our culture's repetitive ways of thinking, feeling, and acting is most certainly not primary among their concerns when preparing their communication.

Culture need not only limit. That media representations of female beauty often meet with debate and disagreement points up the fact that culture can be liberating as well. This is so because cultural values can be *contested*.

Especially in a pluralistic, democratic society such as ours, the **dominant culture** (or **mainstream culture**)—the one that seems to hold sway with the majority of people— is often openly challenged. People do meet, find attractive, like, and even love people who do not fit the standard image of beauty. In addition, media sometimes present images that suggest different ideals of beauty and success. Comedic actress Sofia Vergara; singer-actresses Queen Latifah, Jennifer Lopez, and Jennifer Hudson; and *Mad Men*'s Christina Hendricks all represent alternatives to our culture's idealized standards of beauty, and all have undeniable appeal (and power) on the big and small screens. Liberation from the limitations imposed by culture resides in our ability and willingness to learn and use *new* patterned, repetitive ways of thinking, feeling, and acting; to challenge existing patterns; and to create our own.

DEFINING, DIFFERENTIATING, DIVIDING, AND UNITING EFFECTS OF CULTURE Have you ever made the mistake of calling a dolphin, porpoise, or even a whale a fish? Maybe you have heard

▲ What is our culture's definition of beauty? Adolescence researchers argue that media offer young girls few examples of healthy beauty (Daniels, 2009). They point to the fact that female sports and athletes are woefully underrepresented in American media, appearing in only 1.6% of network television sports coverage (down from 5.6% in 2004; Kelly, 2010). Pictured here is California teen Abby Sunderland, who at 16 years old almost finished an around-the-world sail that would have made her the youngest person ever to complete a nonstop solo circumnavigation. Training from the time she was 13, she was thwarted by a dismasting in an Indian Ocean gale. Have you heard of her? Also pictured is Miley Cyrus, another American teen. The singer/actress, dubbed one of the world's 100 sexiest women by magazines like *Maxim* and *FHM*, is a frequent guest on celebrity television shows and a constant topic of Hollywood gossip. Have you heard of her? Which woman has attracted more attention from our culture? Why?

Culture can be contested. When a *New York Times* fashion writer commented unfavorably on Christina Hendricks's size, calling her a "big girl," the Internet erupted in defense of the *Mad Men* actress, forcing critic Cathy Horyn to defend herself on the paper's website (Wedemeyer, 2010). The makers of Dove soap take a different approach, contesting the culture's narrow image of beauty with its "Real Women Have Curves" campaign, placing images like this on billboards and bus stops across the country, running it in national magazines, and making it the focus of its TV commercials.

others do it. This error occurs because when we think of fish, we think "lives in the water" and "swims." Fish are defined by their "aquatic culture." Because water-residing, swimming dolphins and porpoises share that culture, we sometimes forget that they are mammals, not fish.

We, too, are defined by our culture. We are citizens of the United States; we are Americans. If we travel to other countries, we will hear ourselves labeled "American," and this label will conjure up stereotypes and expectations in the minds of those who use and hear it. The stereotype, whatever it may be, will probably fit us only incompletely, or perhaps hardly at all—perhaps we are dolphins in a sea full of fish. Nevertheless, being American defines us in innumerable important ways, both to others (more obviously) and to ourselves (less obviously).

Within this large, national culture, however, there are many smaller, **bounded cultures** (or **co-cultures**). For example, we speak comfortably of Italian neighborhoods, fraternity row, the South, and the suburbs. Because of our cultural understanding of these categories, each expression communicates something about our expectations of these places. We think we can predict with a good deal of certainty the types of restaurants and shops we will find in the Italian neighborhood, even the kind of music we will hear escaping from open windows. We can predict the kinds of clothes and cars we will see on fraternity row, the likely behavior of shop clerks in the South, and the political orientation of the suburb's residents. Moreover, the people within these cultures usually identify themselves as members of those bounded cultures. An individual may say, for example, "I am Italian American" or "I'm from the South." These smaller cultures unite groups of people and enable them to see themselves as different from other groups around them. Thus culture also serves to differentiate us from others.

In the United States, we generally consider this a good thing. We pride ourselves on our pluralism and our diversity and on the richness of the cultural heritages represented within our borders. We enjoy moving from one bounded culture to another or from a bounded culture to the dominant national culture and back again.

Problems arise, however, when differentiation leads to division. All Americans are traumatized by horrific events such as the terrorist attacks of September 11, 2001 and 2013's Boston Marathon bombing, but those tragedies are compounded for the 2.35 million Muslim Americans whose patriotism is challenged simply because they belong to a particular bounded culture. Not only does the number of cases of violence against Muslims in America remain high, but 39% of Americans want Muslims, even their fellow citizens, to carry special identification cards (Younge, 2010). And although

▲ *Pretty Little Liars*, *CSI Miami*, and *Gossip Girl*—these three television programs are aimed at different audiences, yet in each the characters share certain traits that mark them as attractive. Must people in real life look like these performers to be considered attractive? Successful? Good? The 15 people shown are all slender, tall, and young. Yes, they are just make-believe television characters, but the producers of the shows on which they appear chose these people — as opposed to others — for a reason. What do you think it was? How well do you measure up to the cultural standard of beauty and attractiveness represented here? Do you ever wish that you could be just a bit more like these people? Why or why not?

the Department of Homeland Security reports that Muslim American terrorism continues to be "a miniscule threat to public safety" and that cooperation from the Muslim American community has been essential in its efforts to investigate domestic threats (Shane, 2012), we continue to see examples of overt discrimination. For example, Lowe's Hardware, after one complaint from an anti-Muslim fringe group, pulled its advertising from the television show *All-American Muslim*, a program, ironically, designed specifically to dispel negative stereotypes of Muslims (Anderson, 2011). For these good Americans, regardless of what was in their hearts or minds, their religion, skin color, maybe even their clothing "communicate" disloyalty to the United States to many other Americans. Just as culture is constructed and maintained through communication, it is also communication (or miscommunication) that turns differentiation into division.

Yet, U.S. citizens of all colors, ethnicities, genders and gender preferences, nationalities, places of birth, economic strata, and intelligences often get along; in fact, we *can* communicate, *can* prosper, *can* respect one another's differences. Culture can divide us, but culture also unites us. Our culture represents our collective experience. We converse easily with strangers because we share the same culture. We speak the same language, automatically understand how far apart to stand, appropriately use titles or first or last names, know how much to say, and know how much to leave unsaid. Through communication with people in our culture, we internalize cultural norms and values—those things that bind our many diverse bounded cultures into a functioning, cohesive society.

DEFINING CULTURE From this discussion of culture comes the definition of culture on which the remainder of this book is based:

> Culture is the world made meaningful; it is socially constructed and maintained through communication. It limits as well as liberates us; it differentiates as well as unites us. It defines our realities and thereby shapes the ways we think, feel, and act.

Mass Communication and Culture

Because culture can limit and divide or liberate and unite, it offers us infinite opportunities to use communication for good—if we choose to do so. James Carey (1975) wrote,

> Because we have looked at each new advance in communication technology as opportunities for politics and economics, we have devoted them, almost exclusively, to government and trade. We have rarely seen them as opportunities to expand [our] powers to learn and exchange ideas and experience. (pp. 20–21)

Who are "we" in this quote? *We* are everyone involved in creating and maintaining the culture that defines us. *We* are the people involved in mass media industries and the people who compose their audiences. Together we allow mass communication not only to occur but also to contribute to the creation and maintenance of culture.

Everyone involved has an obligation to participate responsibly. For people working in the media industries, this means professionally and ethically creating and transmitting content. For audience members, it means behaving as critical and thoughtful consumers of that content. Two ways to understand our opportunities and our responsibilities in the mass communication process are to

There we are, huddled around the tribal campfire, telling and retelling the stories of our people.

▲ Storytellers play an important role in helping us define ourselves.
BALLARD STREET. By permission of Jerry Van Amerongen and Creators Syndicate, Inc.

view the mass media as our cultural storytellers and to conceptualize mass communication as a cultural forum.

Mass Media as Cultural Storytellers

A culture's values and beliefs reside in the stories it tells. Who are the good guys? Who are the bad guys? How many of your childhood heroines were chubby? How many good guys dressed in black? How many heroines lived happily ever after without marrying Prince Charming? Probably not very many. Our stories help define our realities, shaping the ways we think, feel, and act. "Stories are sites of observations about self and society," explains media theorist Hanno Hardt (2007). "These fictional accounts are the constitutive material signs of a shared conversation" (p. 476). Therefore, the "storytellers" have a responsibility to tell their stories in as professional and ethical a way as possible.

At the same time, we, the audience for these stories, also have opportunities and responsibilities. We use these stories not only to be entertained but to learn about the world around us, to understand the values, the way things work, and how the pieces fit together. We have a responsibility to question the tellers and their stories, to interpret the stories in ways consistent with larger or more important cultural values and truths, to be thoughtful, to reflect on the stories' meanings and what they say about us and our culture. To do less is to miss an opportunity to construct our own meaning and, thereby, culture.

In 2013, Procter & Gamble wanted to tell the story of its cleaning mop, the Swiffer. It could have chosen from an infinite number of images and words to craft the narrative for this ad campaign. After all, everyone has to do housework sometime. But the company's decision was to send Rosie the Riveter back to the kitchen. "To promote its new steamer, kitchen products giant Swiffer created a marketing campaign around Rosie, a World War II icon made famous by a Westinghouse poster. Rosie was a symbol of female empowerment in the workplace throughout the 1940s; in its ads, the Procter & Gamble-owned company returned the icon to household labor" (Stampler, 2013). Building off a single Tweet—"We can do it! Because cleaning kitchens is women's work"—that cleverly employed Original Rosie's slogan, people immediately took up the cause and in a cultural conversation on social media, blogs, and traditional media, rejected Procter & Gamble's simplistic telling of gender in today's America. New Rosie went into immediate retirement.

▲ The iconic Rosie. When Procter & Gamble wanted to advertise its dust mop, the Swiffer, it could have chosen from among an infinite number of characters to tell its story. It chose a female hero from World War II, Rosie the Riveter, who, with millions of other American women, helped win the war by taking on jobs long reserved for men. People complained. "We hear you," answered Procter & Gamble.

Mass Communication as Cultural Forum

Imagine a giant courtroom in which we discuss and debate our culture—what it is, and what we want it to be. What do we think about welfare? Single motherhood? Labor unions? Nursing homes? What is the meaning of "successful," "good," "loyal," "moral," "honest," "beautiful," "patriotic"? We have cultural definitions or understandings of all these things and more. Where do they come from? How do they develop, take shape, and mature?

Mass communication has become a primary forum for the debate about our culture. Logically, then, the most powerful voices in the forum have the most power to shape our definitions and understandings. Where should that power reside—with the media industries or with their audiences? If you answer "media industries," you will want members of these industries to act professionally and ethically. If you answer "audiences," you will want individual audience members to be thoughtful and critical of the media messages they consume. The forum is only as good, fair, and honest as those who participate in it.

Scope and Nature of Mass Media

No matter how we choose to view the process of mass communication, it is impossible to deny that an enormous portion of our lives is spent interacting with mass media. On a typical Sunday night, about 40 million people in the United States will tune in to a prime-time television show. Television viewing is at record levels, averaging eight and a half hours a day for a typical household. The average American watches 35.6 hours a week; kids 2 to 11 years old watch 25.8 hours a week. The average U.S. home has 2.5 sets, but 31% have 4 or more (Factsheet, 2011). U.S. households devote nearly 7% of their spending to entertainment media (Masnick & Ho, 2012), and the average American adult devotes 11 hours and 33 minutes a day to media (Friedman, 2011). Eighty-six percent of all American adults own a cell phone, but half of all Americans own a device with an advanced operating system, that is, a **smartphone**, a proportion that rises to 62% for people ages 25 to 34 (Smith, 2011c; Smith, 2012a). Worldwide, cell phone users annually download billions of **apps**, software for mobile digital devices. In December 2012, from Christmas Day to New Year's Day alone, people downloaded more than 1.76 billion apps for their iOS (Apple) and Android devices. In 2013 these billion-download weeks became routine (Farago, 2013). Moreover, because of the Internet, our interaction with the media is increasingly interactive, as every two days "we create as much digital content as we did from the dawn of civilization up until 2003." That is, every 48 hours we upload 5 billion gigabytes of data (Kirchner, 2013, p. 49).

Americans spend nearly $11 billion a year going to the multiplex, buying nearly 1.4 billion tickets (Stewart, 2013). Thirty-three percent of the world's population, 2 billion, 267 million people, regularly access the Internet, a 528% increase in the last 10 years (Internet World Stats, 2012). Global music listeners legally buy more than 1.5 billion pieces of recorded music—albums, singles, and digital tracks—a year (Masnick & Ho, 2012). If it were a country, social networking website Facebook, with its more than a billion monthly active users, would be the third largest country in the world (Delo, 2012). Two-thirds of online American adults are Facebook users, making it the country's most-visited website (Duggan & Brenner, 2013). Seventy-two percent of American households play video games (Entertainment Software Association, 2012). Figure 1.4 provides data on Americans' media preferences.

Despite the pervasiveness of mass media in our lives, many of us are dissatisfied with or critical of the media industries' performance and much of the content provided. For example, only 17% of adults feel that entertainment media provide "very good" or "excellent" value (L.D. Smith, 2011). People's evaluations of the media have become more negative over the last decade. Only 38% of the public holds a positive view of the publishing industry (down 9% from 2011); only 32% think highly of the public relations industry (down 6%); and only 39% have positive views of radio and television (down 3%; Newport, 2011). As for journalism, "negative opinions about the performance of news organizations now equal or surpass all-time highs" (Pew Research Center, 2011).

Our ambivalence—we criticize, yet we consume—comes in part from our uncertainties about the relationships among the elements of mass communication. What is the role of technology? What is the role of money? And what is *our* role in the mass communication process?

The Role of Technology

To some thinkers, it is machines and their development that drive economic and cultural change. This idea is referred to as **technological determinism**. Certainly there can be no doubt that movable type contributed to the Protestant Reformation

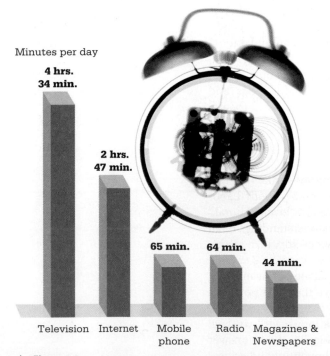

Minutes per day

4 hrs. 34 min. — Television
2 hrs. 47 min. — Internet
65 min. — Mobile phone
64 min. — Radio
44 min. — Magazines & Newspapers

▲ **Figure 1.4** Average Number of Minutes per Day a Typical Adult Spends with Selected Media, 2011.
Source: eMarketer (in Friedman, 2011).

and the decline of the Catholic Church's power in Europe or that television changed the way members of American families interact. Those who believe in technological determinism would argue that these changes in the cultural landscape were the inevitable result of new technology.

But others see technology as more neutral and claim that the way people *use* technology is what gives it significance. This perspective accepts technology as one of many factors that shape economic and cultural change; technology's influence is ultimately determined by how much power it is given by the people and cultures that use it.

This disagreement about the power of technology is at the heart of the controversy surrounding the new communication technologies. Are we more or less powerless in the wake of advances such as the Internet, the World Wide Web, and instant global audio and visual communication? If we are at the mercy of technology, the culture that surrounds us will not be of our making, and the best we can hope to do is make our way reasonably well in a world outside our control. But if these technologies are indeed neutral and their power resides in *how* we choose to use them, we can utilize them responsibly and thoughtfully to construct and maintain whatever kind of culture we want. As film director and technophile Steven Spielberg explained, "Technology can be our best friend, and technology can also be the biggest party pooper of our lives. It interrupts our own story, interrupts our ability to have a thought or daydream, to imagine something wonderful because we're too busy bridging the walk from the cafeteria back to the office on the cell phone" (quoted in Kennedy, 2002, p. 109). Or, as Dr. Ian Malcolm (Jeff Goldblum) said in Spielberg's 1997 *The Lost World: Jurassic Park*, "Oooh! Ahhh! That's how it always starts. Then later there's running and screaming."

Technology does have an impact on communication. At the very least it changes the basic elements of communication (see Figure 1.3). What technology does not do is relieve us of our obligation to use mass communication responsibly and wisely.

The Role of Money

Money, too, alters communication. It shifts the balance of power; it tends to make audiences products rather than consumers.

The first newspapers were financially supported by their readers; the money they paid for the paper covered its production and distribution. But in the 1830s a new form of newspaper financing emerged. Publishers began selling their papers for a penny—much less than it cost to produce and distribute them. Because so many more papers were sold at this bargain price, publishers could "sell" advertising space based on their readership. What they were actually selling to advertisers was not space on the page—it was readers. How much they could charge advertisers was directly related to how much product (how many readers) they could produce for them.

This new type of publication changed the nature of mass communication. The goal of the process was no longer for audience and media to create meaning together. Rather, it was to sell those readers to a third participant—advertisers.

Some observers think this was a devastatingly bad development, not only in the history of mass communication but in the history of democracy. It robbed people of their voice, or at least made the voices of the advertisers more powerful. Others think it was a huge advance for both mass communication and democracy because it vastly expanded the media, broadening and deepening communication. Models showing these two different ways of viewing mass communication are presented in the box "Audience as Consumer or Audience as Product?" Which model makes more sense to you? Which do you think is more accurate? ABC journalist Ted Koppel told the *Washington Post*, "[Television] is an industry. It's a business. We exist to make money. We exist to put commercials on the air. The programming that is put on between those commercials is simply the bait we put in the mousetrap" (in "Soundbites," 2005, p. 2). Do you think Koppel is unnecessarily cynical or is he correct in his analysis of television?

The goals of media professionals will be questioned repeatedly throughout this book. For now, keep in mind that ours is a capitalist economic system and that media

People base their judgments of media performance and content on the way they see themselves fitting into the economics of the media industry. Businesses operate to serve their consumers and make a profit. The consumer comes first, then, but who *is* the consumer in our mass media system? This is a much-debated issue among media practitioners and media critics. Consider the following models.

	PRODUCER	PRODUCT	CONSUMER
Basic U.S. Business Model	A manufacturer . . .	produces a product . . .	for consumers who choose to buy or not. The manufacturer must satisfy the consumer. Power resides here.
Basic U.S. Business Model for Cereal: Rice Krispies as Product, Public as Consumer	Kellogg's . . .	produces Rice Krispies . . .	for us, the consumers. If we buy Rice Krispies, Kellogg's makes a profit. Kellogg's must satisfy us. Power resides here.
Basic U.S. Business Model for Television (A): Audience as Product, Advertisers as Consumer	NBC . . .	produces audiences (using its programming) . . .	for advertisers. If they buy NBC's audiences, NBC makes a profit. NBC must satisfy its consumers, the advertisers. Power resides here.
Basic U.S. Business Model for Television (B): Programming as Product, Audience as Consumer	NBC . . .	produces (or distributes) programming . . .	for us, the audience. If we watch NBC's shows, NBC makes a profit. NBC must satisfy us. Power resides here.

The first three models assume that the consumer *buys* the product; that is, the consumer is the one with the money and therefore the one who must be satisfied. The last model makes a different assumption. It sees the audience, even though it does not buy anything, as sufficiently important to NBC's profit-making ability to force NBC to consider its interests above others' (even those of advertisers). Which model do you think best represents the economics of U.S. mass media?

industries are businesses. Movie producers must sell tickets, book publishers must sell books, and even public broadcasting has bills to pay.

This does not mean, however, that the media are or must be slaves to profit. Our task is to understand the constraints placed on these industries by their economics and then demand that, within those limits, they perform ethically and responsibly. We can do this only by being thoughtful, critical consumers of the media.

Mass Communication, Culture, and Media Literacy

Culture and communication are inseparable, and mass communication, as we've seen, is a particularly powerful, pervasive, and complex form of communication. Our level of skill in the mass communication process is therefore of utmost importance. This skill is not necessarily a simple one to master (it is much more than booting up the computer, turning on the television set, or flipping the pages of your favorite magazine). But it is, indeed, a learnable skill, one that can be practiced. This skill is **media literacy**—the ability to effectively and efficiently comprehend and use any form of mediated communication. But let's start with the first mass medium, books, and the technology that enabled their spread, the printing press.

The Gutenberg Revolution

As it is impossible to overstate the importance of writing, so too is it impossible to overstate the significance of Johannes Gutenberg's development of movable metal type. Historian S. H. Steinberg (1959) wrote in *Five Hundred Years of Printing*:

> Neither political, constitutional, ecclesiastical, and economic, nor sociological, philosophical, and literary movements can be fully understood without taking into account the influence the printing press has exerted upon them. (p. 11)

Marshall McLuhan expressed his admiration for Gutenberg's innovation by calling his 1962 book *The Gutenberg Galaxy*. In it he argued that the advent of print is the key to our modern consciousness, because although **literacy**—the ability to effectively and efficiently comprehend and use written symbols—had existed since the development of the first alphabets more than 5,000 years ago, it was reserved for very few, the elites. Gutenberg's invention was world-changing because it opened literacy to all, that is, it allowed *mass* communication.

THE PRINTING PRESS Printing and the printing press existed long before Gutenberg perfected his process in or around 1446. The Chinese were using wooden block presses as early as 600 C.E. and had movable clay type by 1000 C.E. A simple movable metal type was even in use in Korea in the 13th century. Gutenberg's printing press was a significant leap forward, however, for two important reasons.

Gutenberg was a goldsmith and a metallurgist. He hit on the idea of using metal type crafted from lead molds in place of type made from wood or clay. This was an important advance. Not only was movable metal type durable enough to print page after page, but letters could be arranged and rearranged to make any message possible. And Gutenberg was able to produce virtually identical copies.

In addition, Gutenberg's advance over Korean metal mold printing was one of scope. The Korean press was used to produce books for a very small, royal readership. Gutenberg saw his invention as a way to produce many books for profit. He was, however, a poor businessman. He stressed quality over quantity, in part because of his reverence for the book he was printing, the Bible. He used the highest-quality paper and ink and turned out far fewer volumes than he otherwise could have.

Other printers, however, quickly saw the true economic potential of Gutenberg's invention. The first Gutenberg Bible appeared in 1456. By the end of that century, 44 years later, printing operations existed in 12 European countries, and the continent was flooded with 20 million volumes of 7,000 titles in 35,000 different editions (Drucker, 1999).

THE IMPACT OF PRINT Although Gutenberg developed his printing press with a limited use in mind, printing Bibles, the cultural effects of mass printing have been profound.

Handwritten or hand-copied materials were expensive to produce, and the cost of an education, in time and money, had made reading an expensive luxury. However, with the spread of printing, written communication was available to a much larger portion of the population, and the need for literacy among the lower and middle classes grew. The ability to read became less of a luxury and more of a necessity; eventually literacy spread, as did education. Soldiers at the front needed to be able to read the emperor's orders. Butchers needed to understand the king's shopping list. So the demand for literacy expanded, and more (and more types of) people learned to read.

Tradespeople, soldiers, clergy, bakers, and musicians all now had business at the printer's shop. They talked. They learned of things, both in conversation and by reading printed material. As

▼ This page from a Gutenberg Bible shows the exquisite care the printer used in creating his works. The artwork in the margins is handpainted, but the text is mechanically printed.

more people learned to read, new ideas germinated and spread and cross-pollination of ideas occurred.

More material from various sources was published, and people were freer to read what they wanted when they wanted. Dominant authorities—the Crown and the Church—were now less able to control communication and, therefore, the people. New ideas about the world appeared; new understandings of the existing world flourished.

In addition, duplication permitted standardization and preservation. Myth and superstition began to make way for standard, verifiable bodies of knowledge. History, economics, physics, and chemistry all became part of the culture's intellectual life. Literate cultures were now on the road to modernization.

Printed materials were the first mass-produced product, speeding the development and entrenchment of capitalism. We live today in a world built on these changes. Use of the printing press helped fuel the establishment and growth of a large middle class. No longer were societies composed of rulers and subjects; printing sped the rise of democracy. No longer were power and wealth functions of birth. Power and wealth could now be created by the industrious. No longer was political discourse limited to accepting the dictates of Crown and Church. Printing had given ordinary people a powerful voice.

Tech writer Kevin Kelly connected printing directly to freedom and the rule of law:

> When technology shifts, it bends the culture. Once, long ago, culture revolved around the spoken word. The oral skills of memorization, recitation, and rhetoric instilled in societies a reverence for the past, the ambiguous, the ornate, and the subjective. Then, about 500 years ago, orality was overthrown by technology. Gutenberg's invention of metallic moveable type elevated writing into a central position in the culture. By means of cheap and perfect copies, text became the engine of change and the foundation of stability. From printing came journalism, science and the mathematics of libraries and law. (2008, p. 48)

The Industrial Revolution

By the mid-18th century, printing and its libraries of science and mathematics had become one of the engines driving the Industrial Revolution. Print was responsible for building and disseminating bodies of knowledge, leading to scientific and technological developments and the refinement of new machines. In addition, industrialization reduced the time necessary to complete work, and this created something heretofore unknown to most working people—leisure time.

Industrialization had another effect as well. As workers left their sunrise-to-sunset jobs in agriculture, the crafts, and trades to work in the newly industrialized factories, not only did they have more leisure time but they had more money to spend on their leisure. Farmers, fishermen, and tile makers had to put their profits back into their jobs. But factory workers took their money home; it was spendable. Combine leisure time and expendable cash with the spread of literacy and the result is a large and growing audience for printed *information* and *entertainment*. By the mid-19th century a mass audience and the means to reach it existed.

Media Literacy

Television influences our culture in innumerable ways. One of its effects, according to many people, is that it has encouraged violence in our society. For example, American television viewers overwhelmingly say there is too much violence on television. Yet, almost without exception, the local television news program that has the largest proportion of violence in its nightly newscast is the ratings leader. "If it bleeds, it leads" has become the motto for much of local television news. It leads because people watch.

So, although many of us are quick to condemn improper media performance or to identify and lament its harmful effects, we rarely question our own role in the mass communication process. We overlook it because we participate in mass communication naturally, almost without conscious effort. We possess high-level interpretive and comprehension skills that make even the most sophisticated television show, movie, or magazine story understandable and enjoyable. We are able, through a lifetime of interaction with the media, to *read media texts*.

Media literacy is a skill we take for granted, but like all skills, it can be improved. And if we consider how important the mass media are in creating and maintaining the culture that helps define us and our lives, it is a skill that *must* be improved.

Hunter College media professor Stuart Ewen (2000) emphasized this point in comparing media literacy with traditional literacy. "Historically," he wrote, "links between literacy and democracy are inseparable from the notion of an informed populace, conversant with the issues that touch upon their lives, enabled with tools that allow them to participate actively in public deliberation and social change.... Literacy was about crossing the lines that had historically separated men of ideas from ordinary people, about the enfranchisement of those who had been excluded from the compensations of citizenship" (p. 448). To Ewen, and others committed to media literacy, media literacy represents no less than the means to full participation in the culture.

Elements of Media Literacy

Media scholar Art Silverblatt (2008) identifies seven fundamental elements of media literacy. To these we will add an eighth. Media literacy includes these characteristics:

1. *A critical thinking skill enabling audience members to develop independent judgments about media content.* Thinking critically about the content we consume is the very essence of media literacy. Why do we watch what we watch, read what we read, listen to what we listen to? If we cannot answer these questions, we have taken no responsibility for ourselves or our choices. As such, we have taken no responsibility for the outcome of those choices.

2. *An understanding of the process of mass communication.* If we know the components of the mass communication process and how they relate to one another, we can form expectations of how they can serve us. How do the various media industries operate? What are their obligations to us? What are the obligations of the audience? How do different media limit or enhance messages? Which forms of feedback are most effective, and why?

3. *An awareness of the impact of media on the individual and society.* Writing and the printing press helped change the world and the people in it. Mass media do the same. If we ignore the impact of media on our lives, we run the risk of being caught up and carried along by that change rather than controlling or leading it.

4. *Strategies for analyzing and discussing media messages.* To consume media messages thoughtfully, we need a foundation on which to base thought and reflection. If we make meaning, we must possess the tools with which to make it (for example, understanding the intent and impact of film and video conventions, such as camera angles and lighting, or the strategy behind the placement of photos on a newspaper page). Otherwise, meaning is made for us; the interpretation of media content will then rest with its creator, not with us.

5. *An understanding of media content as a text that provides insight into our culture and our lives.* How do we know a culture and its people, attitudes, values, concerns, and myths? We know them through communication. For modern cultures like ours, media messages increasingly dominate that communication, shaping our understanding of and insight into our culture.

6. *The ability to enjoy, understand, and appreciate media content.* Media literacy does not mean living the life of a grump, liking nothing in the media, or always being suspicious of harmful effects and cultural degradation. We take high school and college classes to enhance our understanding and appreciation of novels; we can do the same for media texts.

Learning to enjoy, understand, and appreciate media content includes the ability to use **multiple points of access**—to approach media content from a variety of directions and derive from it many levels of meaning. Thus, we control meaning making for our own enjoyment or appreciation. For example, we can enjoy all-time global box office champion *Avatar* as an exciting, explosion-laden, action-adventure holiday blockbuster, the biggest moneymaker in cinematic history. But as movie buffs we might see it as a classic good-guy-rides-into-town movie, the OK Corral transported to Pandora. Or we might read it as an environmental allegory—don't mess with Mother Nature—or an attack on war in the Middle East, with Na'vi unobtanium substituting for Muslim oil. Maybe it's a history lesson disguised as sci-fi, reminding us of the futility of attempting to defeat a native insurgency. Or maybe it is a cool way to spend a Saturday night, entertained by the same folks who so delighted us with the *Alien* and *Terminator* movies.

In fact, television programs such as *Desperate Housewives*, *The Daily Show*, *The Simpsons*, *Grey's Anatomy*, and *Family Guy* are specifically constructed to take advantage of the media literacy skills of sophisticated viewers while providing entertaining fare for less skilled consumers. The same is true for films such as *Up*, *50/50*, *Hurt Locker*, and *Knocked Up*, magazines such as *Alarm*, and the best of jazz, rap, and rock. *Desperate Housewives* and *The Daily Show* are produced as television comedies, designed to make people laugh. But they are also intentionally produced to provide more sophisticated, media-literate viewers with opportunities to make personally interesting or relevant meaning. Anyone can laugh while watching these programs, but some people can investigate hypocrisy in suburbia (*Housewives*), or they can examine the failings and foibles of contemporary journalism (*Daily Show*).

7. *Development of effective and responsible production skills.* Traditional literacy assumes that people who can read can also write. Media literacy also makes this assumption. Our definition of literacy (of either type) calls not only for effective and efficient comprehension of content but for its effective and efficient *use.* Therefore, media-literate individuals should develop production skills that enable them to create useful media messages. If you have ever tried to make a narrative home video—one that tells a story—you know that producing content is much more difficult than consuming it. Even producing a telephone answering machine message that is not embarrassing is a daunting task for many people.

This element of media literacy may seem relatively unimportant at first glance. After all, if you choose a career in media production, you will get training in school and on

▲ *Family Guy* is a cartoon about a typical suburban family. It has all the things you would expect from a television situation comedy—an inept dad, a precocious daughter, a slacker son, a solid wife, and zany situations. Yet it also offers an intellectual dog philosopher and an evil genius, scheming baby. Why do you think the producers have gone to the trouble to populate this show with the usual trappings of a sitcom but then add other, bizarre elements? And what's going on in *Avatar*? Is it another special-effects, explosion-laden, action-adventure holiday blockbuster? A classic good-guy-rides-into-town movie—the OK Corral transported to Pandora? An environmental allegory? Commentary on war in the Middle East, with Na'vi unobtanium substituting for Muslim oil? Or maybe it is a cool way to spend a Saturday night, entertained by the same folks who created the *Alien* and *Terminator* movies.

the job. If you choose another calling, you may never be in the position of having to produce content. But most professions now employ some form of media to disseminate information: for use in training, to enhance presentations, or to keep in contact with clients and customers. The Internet and the World Wide Web, in particular, require effective production skills of their users—at home, school, and work—because online receivers can and do easily become online creators.

8. *An understanding of the ethical and moral obligations of media practitioners.* To make informed judgments about the performance of the media, we also must be aware of the competing pressures on practitioners as they do their jobs. We must

understand the media's official and unofficial rules of operation. In other words, we must know, respectively, their legal and ethical obligations. Return, for a moment, to the question of televised violence. It is legal for a station to air graphic violence. But is it ethical? If it is unethical, what power, if any, do we have to demand its removal from our screens? Dilemmas such as this are discussed at length in Chapter 14.

Media Literacy Skills

Consuming media content is simple. Push a button and you have television pictures or music on a radio. Come up with enough cash and you can see a movie or buy a magazine. Media-literate consumption, however, requires a number of specific skills:

1. *The ability and willingness to make an effort to understand content, to pay attention, and to filter out noise.* As we saw earlier, anything that interferes with successful communication is called noise, and much of the noise in the mass communication process results from our own consumption behavior. When we watch television, often we are also doing other things, such as eating, reading, or chatting on the phone. We drive while we listen to the radio. Obviously, the quality of our meaning making is related to the effort we give it.

2. *An understanding of and respect for the power of media messages.* The mass media have been around for more than a century and a half. Just about everybody can enjoy them. Their content is either free or relatively inexpensive. Much of the content is banal and a bit silly, so it is easy to dismiss media content as beneath serious consideration or too simple to have any influence.

We also disregard media's power through the **third-person effect**—the common attitude that others are influenced by media messages but that we are not. That is, we are media literate enough to understand the influence of mass communication on the attitudes, behaviors, and values of others but not self-aware or honest enough to see its influence on our lives.

3. *The ability to distinguish emotional from reasoned reactions when responding to content and to act accordingly.* Media content is often designed to touch us at the emotional level. We enjoy losing ourselves in a good song or in a well-crafted movie or television show; this is among our great pleasures. But because we react emotionally to these messages does not mean they don't have serious meanings and implications for our lives. Television pictures, for example, are intentionally shot and broadcast for their emotional impact. Reacting emotionally is appropriate and proper. But then what? What do these pictures tell us about the larger issue at hand? We can use our feelings as a point of departure for meaning making. We can ask, "Why does this content make me feel this way?

4. *Development of heightened expectations of media content.* We all use media to tune out, waste a little time, and provide background noise. When we decide to watch television, we are more likely to turn on the set and flip channels until we find something passable than we are to read the listings to find a specific program to view. When we search for online video, we often settle for the "10 most shared today." When we expect little from the content before us, we tend to give meaning making little effort and attention.

5. *A knowledge of genre conventions and the ability to recognize when they are being*

▲ The third-person effect makes it easy to dismiss media's influence on ourselves…only those other folks are affected! Media-literate people know that not only is this not the case, but even if it were, we all live in a world where people are influenced by mass communication.

David Horsey. © Tribune Media Services, Inc. All Rights Reserved. Reprinted with permission.

mixed. The term **genre** refers to the categories of expression within the different media, such as the "evening news," "documentary," "horror movie," or "entertainment magazine." Each genre is characterized by certain distinctive, standardized style elements—the **conventions** of that genre. The conventions of the evening news, for example, include a short, upbeat introductory theme and one or two good-looking people sitting at a space-age desk. When we hear and see these style elements, we expect the evening news. We can tell a documentary film from an entertainment movie by its more serious tone and the number of talking heads. We know by their appearance—the use of color and the amount of text on the cover—which magazines offer serious reading and which provide entertainment.

Knowledge of these conventions is important because they cue or direct our meaning making. For example, we know to accept the details in a documentary film about the sinking of the *Titanic* as more credible than those found in a Hollywood movie about that disaster.

This skill is also important for another reason. Sometimes, in an effort to maximize audiences (and therefore profits) or for creative reasons, media content makers mix genre conventions. Are Oliver Stone's *Nixon* and *JFK* fact or fiction? Is Geraldo Rivera a journalist, a talk show host, or a showman? Is *Bratz* a kid's cartoon or a 30-minute commercial? *Extra!* and *E! News* look increasingly like *Dateline NBC* and the *CBS Evening News*. Reading media texts becomes more difficult as formats are co-opted.

6. *The ability to think critically about media messages, no matter how credible their sources.* It is crucial that media be credible in a democracy in which the people govern because the media are central to the governing process. This is why the news media are sometimes referred to as the fourth branch of government, complementing the executive, judicial, and legislative branches. This does not mean, however, that we should believe everything they report. But it is often difficult to arrive at the proper balance between wanting to believe and accepting what we see and hear unquestioningly, especially when frequently we are willing to suspend disbelief and are encouraged by the media themselves to see their content as real and credible.

Consider the *New York Times* motto "All the News That's Fit to Print" and the title "Eyewitness News." If it is all there, it must all be real, and who is more credible than an eyewitness? But if we examine these media, we would learn that the *Times* in actuality prints all the news that fits (in its pages) and that the news is, at best, a very selective eyewitness.

7. *A knowledge of the internal language of various media and the ability to understand its effects, no matter how complex.* Just as each media genre has its own distinctive style and conventions, each medium also has its own specific internal language. This language is expressed in **production values**—the choice of lighting, editing, special effects, music, camera angle, location on the page, and size and placement of headline. To be able to read a media text, you must understand its language. We learn the grammar of this language automatically from childhood—for example, we know that when the television image goes "all woosielike," the character is dreaming.

Let's consider two versions of the same movie scene. In the first, a man is driving a car. Cut to a woman lying tied up on a railroad track. What is the relationship between the man and the woman? Where is he going? With no more information than these two shots, you know automatically that he cares for her and is on his way to save her. Now, here is the second version. The man is driving the car. Fade to black. Fade back up to the woman on the tracks. Now what is the relationship between the man and the woman? Where is he going? It is less clear that these two people even have anything to do with each other. We construct completely different meanings from exactly the same two pictures because the punctuation (the quick cut/fade) differs.

Media texts tend to be more complicated than these two scenes. The better we can handle their grammar, the more we can understand and appreciate texts. The more we understand texts, the more we can be equal partners with media professionals in meaning making.

► This television show offers all the conventions we'd expect from the news—background digital graphics, an anchor behind his desk, a well-known newsmaker as interviewee. But it also contains conventions we'd expect from a comedy program—a satirist as host and an unruly, loud audience. Why does *The Daily Show* mix the conventions of these two very different genres? Does your knowledge of those conventions add to your enjoyment of this hit cable program?

Resources for Review and Discussion

REVIEW POINTS: TYING CONTENT TO LEARNING OUTCOMES

► **Define *communication, mass communication, mass media*, and *culture*.**
- ► Communication is the process of creating shared meaning.
- ► Mass communication is the process of creating shared meaning between the mass media and their audiences.
- ► Mass media is the plural of mass medium, a technology that carries messages to a large number of people.
- ► Culture is the world made meaningful. It resides all around us; it is socially constructed and maintained through communication. It limits as well as liberates us; it differentiates as well as unites us. It defines our realities and shapes the ways we think, feel, and act.

► **Describe the relationships among communication, mass communication, culture, and those who live in the culture.**
- ► Mass media are our culture's dominant storytellers and the forum in which we debate cultural meaning.

► **Evaluate the impact of technology and economics on those relationships.**
- ► Technological determinism argues that technology is the predominant agent of social and cultural change. But it is not technology that drives culture; it is how people use technology.
- ► With technology, money, too, shapes mass communication. Audiences can be either the consumer or the product in our mass media system.

▶ **List the components of media literacy.**
  - ▶ Media literacy, the ability to effectively and efficiently comprehend and use any form of mediated communication, consists of several components:
    - Critical thinking skills enabling the development of independent judgments about media content
    - An understanding of the process of mass communication
    - An awareness of the impact of the media on individuals and society
    - Strategies for analyzing and discussing media messages
    - An awareness of media content as a "text" providing insight into contemporary culture
    - A cultivation of enhanced enjoyment, understanding, and appreciation of media content
    - The development of effective and responsible production skills
    - The development of an understanding of the ethical and moral obligations of media practitioners

▶ **Identify key skills required for developing media literacy.**
  - ▶ Media skills include
    - The ability and willingness to make an effort to understand content, to pay attention, and to filter out noise
    - An understanding of and respect for the power of media messages
    - The ability to distinguish emotional from reasoned reactions when responding to content and to act accordingly
    - The development of heightened expectations of media content
    - A knowledge of genre conventions and the recognition of their mixing
    - The ability to think critically about media messages
    - A knowledge of the internal language of various media and the ability to understand its effects

KEY TERMS

communication, 4

feedback, 5

interpersonal communication, 5

encoding, 6

decoding, 6

noise, 6

medium (pl. media), 6

mass medium, 6

mass communication, 6

inferential feedback, 6

cultural definition of communication, 7

culture, 9

dominant culture (mainstream culture), 11

bounded culture (co-culture), 12

smartphone, 16

apps, 16

technological determinism, 16

media literacy, 18

literacy, 19

multiple points of access, 22

third-person effect, 24

genre, 25

conventions, 25

production values, 25

QUESTIONS FOR REVIEW

1. What is culture? How does culture define people?
2. What is communication? What is mass communication?
3. What are encoding and decoding? How do they differ when technology enters the communication process?
4. What does it mean to say that communication is a reciprocal process?
5. What is James Carey's cultural definition of communication? How does it differ from other definitions of that process?
6. What do we mean by mass media as cultural storyteller?
7. What do we mean by mass communication as cultural forum?
8. What is media literacy? What are its components?
9. What are some specific media literacy skills?
10. What is the difference between genres and production conventions? What do these have to do with media literacy?

Mc Graw Hill connect®

For further review, go to the LearnSmart study module for this chapter.

QUESTIONS FOR CRITICAL THINKING AND DISCUSSION

1. Who were your childhood heroes and heroines? Why did you choose them? What cultural lessons did you learn from them?
2. The Gutenberg printing press had just the opposite effect from what was intended. What optimistic predictions for the cultural impact of the Internet and the World Wide

Web do you think will prove as inaccurate as Gutenberg's hopes for his innovation? What optimistic predictions do you think will be realized? Defend your answers.

3. How media literate do you think you are? What about those around you—your parents, for example, or your best friend? What are your weaknesses as a media-literate person?

Convergence and the Reshaping of Mass Communication 2

Learning Objectives

The mass media system we have today has existed more or less as we know it ever since the 1830s. It is a system that has weathered repeated significant change with the coming of increasingly sophisticated technologies—the penny press newspaper was soon followed by mass market books and mass circulation magazines. As the 1800s became the 1900s, these popular media were joined by motion pictures, radio, and sound recording. A few decades later came television, combining news and entertainment, moving images and sound, all in the home and all, ostensibly, for free. The traditional media found new functions and prospered side by side with television. Then, more recently, came the Internet, World Wide Web, and mobile technologies like smartphones and tablets. Now, because of these new technologies, all the media industries are facing profound alterations in how they are structured and do business, the nature of their content, and how they interact with and respond to their audiences. Naturally, as these changes unfold, so too will the very nature of mass communication and our role in that process. After studying this chapter you should be able to

▶ Summarize broad current trends in mass media, especially concentration of ownership and conglomeration, globalization, audience fragmentation, hypercommercialization, and convergence.

▶ Describe in broad terms how the mass communication process itself will evolve as the role of the audience in this new media environment is altered.

Louis C.K.'s *Live at the Beacon Theater*. Is it a movie? What is a movie?

"Too bad, but play fair. There have to be limits."

"It is legitimate. As I said, my favorite movie of last year is *Louis C.K.'s Live at the Beacon Theater.*"

"It's not a movie."

"Is *The Beaver* a movie?"

"Of course. It has big stars like Jodie Foster and Mel Gibson. You could see it at the movies. It made almost a million dollars at the box office."

"*Live at the Beacon* has a big star, one of the biggest in fact, Louis C.K. And it made *more* than a million dollars in its first 10 days of release."

"But it wasn't in the theaters; ergo, not a movie."

"Can you get *The Beaver* on DVD? Downloaded from iTunes? Streamed from Hulu?"

"Yes, yes, and yes. What's your point?"

"If *The Beaver* is a movie and can be viewed in any of those ways and still be a movie, then *Live at the Beacon* is a movie. You can see it all those same ways, and sure, maybe it didn't screen at the Cineplex, but it screens at its own website; ergo, a movie!"

There is a seismic shift going on in the mass media—and therefore in mass communication—that dwarfs the changes to the media landscape wrought by television's assault in the 1950s and 1960s on the preeminence of radio and the movies. Encouraged by the Internet, digitization, and mobility, new producers are finding new ways to deliver new content to new audiences. The media industries are in turmoil, and audience members, as they are confronted by a seemingly bewildering array of possibilities, are just now starting to come to terms with the new media future. Will you pay for movie downloads? How much? What will you pay for on-demand television programs? Will you be willing to view the commercials they contain if you could pay a bit less per show? Would you pay more or less for classic programming than for contemporary shows? Would you be willing to watch a movie or television show on a small screen? NBC Television's Jeff Zucker offered his solution to the upheaval, "The overall strategy is to make all our content available everywhere" (in Bing, 2006, p. 1). But will this strategy work? And remember, we're talking about *all* media. How will you listen to the radio—satellite radio or terrestrial radio or digital terrestrial radio or streamed Web radio? And what do you think of **day-and-date release**, simultaneously releasing a movie to the public in some combination of theater, video-on-demand,

▲ Day-and-date video-on-demand income for Kevin Spacey's *Margin Call* matched its theatrical box office take.

DVD, and download? Director Yann Arthus-Bertrand released his environmentally themed *Home* in all four **formats** in 127 countries on World Environment Day, 2009. Steven Soderbergh released his 2009 *The Girlfriend Experience* on cable and satellite video-on-demand a full month before he put it in theaters. In December 2011, director and feature film star Ed Burns avoided the big screen altogether, launching *Newlyweds* directly to Web downloading sites, video-on-demand services connected to 45 million homes, and iTunes. Kevin Spacey's 2011 *Margin Call* matched its $5.3 million box office take with day-and-date cable television, iTunes, and Amazon video-on-demand release. On which **platform** (the means of delivering a specific piece of media content) would you most enjoy watching these films? Can you still call it film? Would you be willing to pay more or less for the different platforms? What is the most you would be willing to pay? These are precisely the kinds of questions that audiences will be answering in the next several years. Media-literate audiences will be better equipped to do so.

Industries in Transition

Media consumer "behavior is shifting," media consultant Mike Vorhaus told industry executives at the 2009 Consumer Electronics Show, and that means media companies "have to do business differently, which is hard enough in normal times. But when you add in a deep cyclical economic situation, the result is a deep pain like they've never seen before" (in Winslow, 2009, p. 15). How much pain has been produced by the "perfect storm" of rapid technological change, shifting consumption behavior, and economic turmoil?

- Although Americans bought 1.36 billion movie tickets in 2013 and box office revenue reached $10.8 billion, in the five years from 2007 to that record year, the major movie studios lost nearly $4 billion in revenue (Friedman, 2013).

- The downward trend in annual sales of recorded music that began in the late 1990s finally stopped in 2012, which showed a .3% increase in sales to $16.5 billion. But this is still far off 1999's high of $38 billion (Pfanner, 2013).

- Fifteen years ago the four major broadcast networks commanded 61% of all television viewing. Today their share hovers around 30%. The top-rated program in 1985 was *The Cosby Show*, viewed by more than 30% of all homes watching television; today it is *American Idol*, drawing about 13% (Seabrook, 2012).

- Beginning in 2007, DVD sales have fallen dramatically—for example, as much as 20% between 2010 and 2011 (Paul, 2011). Rentals, too, are down, dropping 11% in that same time (Baar, 2012).

- Video game industry revenues from the sale and rental of both hardware and software declined 8% between 2010 and 2011, a fall that would have been steeper if it were not for the growth in mobile gaming (Epstein, 2012).

- Sales of printed books peaked in 2005 and have declined each year since (Keller, 2011).

- Daily and Sunday newspaper circulation has dropped every year since 1998, with the sharpest declines among young people under the age of 30. 2012 marked the sixth consecutive year of decline in papers' print advertising revenue (Edmonds, 2013a).

- Circulation revenues, the number of ad pages, and gross revenue growth for American consumer magazines have all been flat since 2002. Total consumer magazine advertising pages fell more than 1% from 2010 to 2011, and 152 titles disappeared in 2011 (Sass, 2011c).

- Listenership to American commercial radio has fallen steadily since 1998. Since 2008 there have been small annual upticks in the number of listeners, but in 2011 they tuned in for only 94 minutes a day, a big drop from 2008's 102 minutes (Friedman, 2011).

The Good News for Media Industries

Indeed, what this turmoil indicates is that the challenge facing the media industries today is how to capture a mass audience now fragmented into millions of niches. What has come about, according to *Variety*'s Jonathan Bing (2006), "is an unfamiliar new entertainment landscape, one in which the old rules of media consumption no longer apply" (pp. 1, 38). The "rules" of media consumption may have changed, but media consumption is at an all-time high.

Children 8 to 18 years old spend more than 10 hours and 45 minutes a day with media content, up by more than 2½ hours from 10 years ago. They amass such large amounts of consumption because they are adept at **media multitasking**, simultaneously consuming many different kinds of media (Rideout, Foehr, & Roberts, 2010). Considering all media used only at home, in 1980 Americans received about seven hours of information a day. Today they receive 11.8 hours, or more precisely, "3.6 zettabytes [a zettabyte is a billion trillion bytes]. Imagine a stack of paperback novels stacked seven feet high over the entire United States, including Alaska" (Young, 2009). The digital equivalent of all the movies ever made travels the Internet every three minutes. In 2017, more traffic will traverse global Internet networks than 1984 to 2016 combined. Globally, users will generate 3 trillion minutes of Internet video every month, which is 6 million years of video every 30 days, or more than two years' worth of video every second (Cisco, 2013). As you can see in Figure 2.1, when asked what technologies they need, nearly 93% of Americans said their cars, as you might expect. But more than 8 in 10 said broadband Internet and nearly 7 in 10 said their smartphones, both quickly becoming the primary media content delivery systems for most Americans. Large percentages of Americans also see HDTV, newspapers, Blu-Ray, and satellite radio as "necessities" (Carmichael, 2011). In fact, more than at any time in history, Americans are watching more video, listening to more music, reading more often, playing more video games, and accessing the Internet more often than ever before; they are simply doing it in new and different ways

▶ **Figure 2.1** Which Technologies Do Americans Need?
Source: Carmichael, 2011

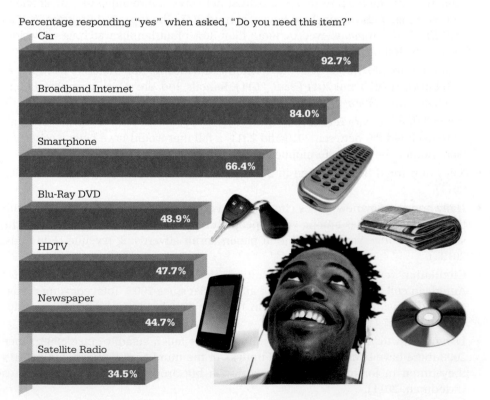

Percentage responding "yes" when asked, "Do you need this item?"

Car — 92.7%
Broadband Internet — 84.0%
Smartphone — 66.4%
Blu-Ray DVD — 48.9%
HDTV — 47.7%
Newspaper — 44.7%
Satellite Radio — 34.5%

(Masnick & Ho, 2012). For media industries, these facts offer good news—readers, viewers, and listeners are out there in ever-increasing numbers, and they value the mass communication experience. These data also offer good news for literate media consumers—their consumption choices will shape the media landscape to come and, inevitably, the mass communication process itself.

Together, media industries and media consumers face a number of challenges. Beyond fragmenting audiences and the impact of new technologies (and the **convergence**—the erosion of traditional distinctions among media—they encourage), they must also deal with three other forces that promise to alter the nature of the media industries as well as the relationship between those industries and the people with whom they interact: concentration of media ownership and conglomeration, rapid globalization, and hypercommercialization.

Changes

Concentration of Ownership and Conglomeration

Ownership of media companies is increasingly concentrated in fewer and fewer hands. Through mergers, acquisitions, buyouts, and hostile takeovers, a very small number of large conglomerates is coming to own more and more of the world's media outlets. Media observer Ben Bagdikian reported that in 1997 the number of media corporations with "dominant power in society" was 10. In 2004 columnist William Safire set the number at just 5: Comcast, Fox, Viacom, GE (NBC-Universal), and Time Warner ("Should Comcast," 2004). Since then, Comcast has grown even larger, having bought NBC-Universal from GE to become the country's largest cable company and largest residential broadband Internet provider. The conservative *New York Times* writer warned, "While political paranoids accuse each other of vast conspiracies, the truth is that media mergers have narrowed the range of information and entertainment available to people of all ideologies" (quoted in Plate, 2003, p. B4). Safire was correct; people of all ideologies feel the impact of **concentration of ownership**. FCC commissioner and Democrat Jonathan Adelstein argued, "The public has a right to be informed by a diversity of viewpoints so they can make up their own minds. Without a diverse, independent media, citizen access to information crumbles, along with political and social participation. For the sake of democracy, we should encourage the widest possible dissemination of free expression" through our media (quoted in Kennedy, 2004, p. 1). Adelstein was echoing Supreme Court Justice Hugo Black's eloquent defense of a vibrant media in his 1945 *Associated Press v. U.S.* decision: "The First Amendment rests on the assumption that the widest possible dissemination of information from diverse and antagonistic sources is essential to the welfare of the public, that a free press is a condition of a free society."

Maurice Hinchey (2006), U.S. House of Representatives member from New York, explained this concentration's threat to our democratic process:

> Changes in media ownership have been swift and staggering. Over the past two decades the number of major US media companies fell by more than one half; most of the survivors are controlled by fewer than ten huge media conglomerates. As media outlets continue to be gobbled up by these giants, the marketplace of ideas shrinks. New and independent voices are stifled. And the companies that remain are under little obligation to provide reliable, quality journalism. Stories that matter deeply to the country's well-being have been replaced by sensationalized murders and celebrity gossip. (p. 15)

As White House correspondent Julie Mason said when asked why scandal and crime dominate the media, "We are a profit-driven industry. And if you want the most eyeballs, you have to go with the thing that people are most talking about. But if you're trying to do a quality program, then maybe you have got to go with Iraq and Iran" (in Soundbites, 2011, p. 3).

Closely related to concentration is **conglomeration**, the increase in the ownership of media outlets by larger, nonmedia companies. The threat is clear, wrote veteran journalist Bill Moyers (2004):

> Media owners have businesses to run, and these media-owning corporations have enormous interests of their own that impinge on an ever-widening swath of public policy—hugely important things, ranging from campaign finance reform (who ends up with those millions of dollars spent on advertising?) to broadcast deregulation and antitrust policy, to virtually everything related to the Internet, intellectual property, globalization and free trade, even to minimum wage, affirmative action, and environmental policy. . . . In this era, when its broader and broader economic entanglements make media more dependent on state largess, the news business finds itself at war with journalism. (p. 10)

As evidence of conglomeration's influence, critics point to the March 2011 revelation that although NBC News parent company General Electric had $14.2 billion in 2010 global profits, including $5.1 billion in the United States, it paid no federal taxes and actually received a $3.2 billion refund. Given the national debate at the time over how to fix America's troubled economy, the *New York Time*'s front-page exposé was featured on all the national cable and broadcast news shows, with one exception—NBC. The story drew zero coverage on NBC's nightly news show. On the day the story broke, however, anchor Lester Holt did find time to cover the addition of the words "OMG" and "muffin top" to the Oxford English Dictionary (Farhi, 2011a).

But this conflict of interest is only one presumed problem with conglomeration. The other is the dominance of a bottom-line mentality and its inevitable degradation of media content. *Variety*'s Peter Bart (2000) explained, "Hence atop every corporation there sits a functionary who is empowered to set a number for every unit of every company. That functionary may in fact have no knowledge whatsoever of the market conditions affecting that entity and no interest in the product it produces. Nonetheless, everyone dances to his tune" (p. 95). Bart was speaking of media in general. As for journalism, former CBS anchor Dan Rather added, "The larger the entities that own and control the news operations, the more distant they become" (quoted in Auletta, 2001, p. 60). New York University law professor Burt Neuborne warned:

> The press has been subsumed into a market psychology, because they are now owned by large conglomerates, of which they are simply a piece. And they (news organizations) are expected to contribute their piece of the profit to the larger pie. You don't have people controlling the press anymore with a fervent sense of responsibility to the First Amendment. Concentrating on who's sleeping with whom, on sensationalism, is concentrating on essentially irrelevant issues. (as quoted in Konner, 1999, p. 6)

Evidence for Professor Neuborne's appraisal abounds. The Project for Excellence in Journalism revealed that while the number of foreign reporters in Washington has grown 10 times over the last 20 years, the number of U.S. newspapers with reporters covering Congress has fallen by two-thirds. The number covering Washington at all has fallen by half. The number of local television and radio stations with access to their own news bureaus in the Capitol has fallen 37% in that time, to 92 stations (MacMillan, 2009). In 2001, U.S. newspapers had 21 full-time Pentagon reporters; in 2009, amidst two ongoing wars, there were 12, and no broadcast network had a full-time correspondent in either Iraq or Afghanistan (Wasserman, 2009). As for the impact of these cuts on content, despite 2012 being Earth's hottest year on record, the nightly news shows on the three commercial television networks—ABC, CBS, and NBC—presented only 12 stories the entire year dealing with climate change (Fitzsimmons, 2013). And during the 2012 presidential election, with American economic inequality at a historic high, the country's major news outlets devoted only 0.2% of their campaign coverage to poverty ("Hard Numbers," 2012). Here is another example of the new priorities. In March 2011, CNN had 50 people covering the aftermath of the murderous Japanese earthquake and tsunami and the crisis at the Fukushima nuclear power plant. In April it assigned 400 personnel to England's royal wedding, a number that does not include correspondents in all of the British Commonwealth countries, like Australia, New Zealand, India, and

South Africa, to get reaction from locals (Chozick & Rohwedder, 2011). As the editor of a major newspaper explained, in the current news environment, "if you argue about public trust today, you will be dismissed as an obstructionist and a romantic" (Project for Excellence in Journalism, 2006). You can read more about this issue in the box titled "Concentration, Conglomeration, and Serving Democracy."

There are, however, less dire observations on concentration and conglomeration. Many telecommunications professionals argue that concentration and conglomeration are not only inevitable but necessary in a telecommunications environment that is increasingly fragmented and internationalized; companies must maximize their number of outlets to reach as much of the divided and far-flung audience as possible. If they do not, they will become financially insecure, and that is an even greater threat to free and effective mediated communication because advertisers and other well-monied forces will have increased influence over them.

Another defense of concentration and conglomeration has to do with **economies of scale**; that is, bigger can in fact sometimes be better because the relative cost of an operation's output declines as the size of that endeavor grows. For example, the cost of collecting the news or producing a television program does not increase significantly when that news report or television program is distributed over 2 outlets, 20 outlets, or 100 outlets. The additional revenues from these other points of distribution can then be plowed back into even better news and programming. In the case of conglomeration, the parallel argument is that revenues from a conglomerate's nonmedia enterprises can be used to support quality work by its media companies.

The potential impact of this **oligopoly**—a concentration of media industries into an ever smaller number of companies—on the mass communication process is enormous. What becomes of shared meaning when the people running communication companies are more committed to the financial demands of their corporate offices than they are to their audiences, who are supposedly their partners in the communication process? What becomes of the process itself when media companies grow more removed from those with whom they communicate? And what becomes of the culture that is dependent on that process when concentration and conglomeration limit the diversity of perspective and information? Or are the critics making too much of the issue? Is Clear Channel (850 radio stations) founder Lowry Mays correct when he argues, "We're not in the business of providing news and information. We're simply in the business of selling our customers' products" (quoted in Hightower, 2004a, p. 1)?

▲ CNN had 50 people covering the aftermath of the March 2011 earthquake and tsunami. It assigned more than 400 to England's royal wedding.

Globalization

Closely related to the concentration of media ownership is **globalization**. It is primarily large, multinational conglomerates that are doing the lion's share of media acquisitions. The potential impact of globalization on the mass communication process speaks to the issue of diversity of expression. Will distant, anonymous, foreign corporations, each with vast holdings in a variety of nonmedia businesses, use their power to shape news and entertainment content to suit their own ends? Opinion is divided. Some observers feel that this concern is misplaced—the pursuit of profit will force these corporations to respect the values and customs of the nations and cultures in which they operate. Some observers have a less optimistic view, arguing that "respecting" local values and customs is shorthand for pursuing profits at all costs. They point to the recent controversy surrounding the decision of Internet giants Yahoo!, Cisco, Google, and Microsoft to "respect" the local values and customs of the world's second-largest Internet population as well as its fastest-growing consumer market—China. Microsoft spokesperson Brooke Richardson explained her company's position: "Microsoft does business in many countries around the world. While different countries have different standards, Microsoft and other multinational companies have to ensure that our products and services comply with local laws, norms, and industry practices" (in Zeller, 2006, p. 4.4). Google attorney Andrew McLaughlin called it "responding to local conditions" (Bray, 2006, p. A10). But "local conditions" in this case meant censoring searches and keywords and shutting down websites on orders from China's Communist

The horrific events of September 11, 2001, put concentration and conglomeration and their effect on news squarely in the public forum. Many observers in and out of the media identified corporate-mandated cost reductions and staff cuts as the primary reason so many Americans were caught off guard. *Philadelphia Inquirer* reporter Thomas Ginsberg (2002) explained:

> From the early 1990s until September 11, 2001, the U.S. news media had subtly turned foreign news into a niche subject. By the end of the '90s, with cable TV and the Internet splintering audiences, and media conglomerates demanding news divisions make more money, broadcasters and some publications gradually changed formats to cover more scandal, lifestyle, personalities. There simply were fewer shows and pages where hard news, much less foreign news, could find a home. (p. 50)

"If we had paid more attention to Afghanistan in the '80s we might not have had 9-11," MSNBC reporter Ashleigh Banfield (2003) lectured students at Kansas State University (p. 6).

The war in Iraq added to the cultural debate. "We failed the American public by being insufficiently critical about elements of the Administration's plan to go to war," said the *New*

York Times's John Burns (quoted in Rich, 2004, p. E1). "The credulous press corps, when confronted by an Administration intent on war, sank to new depths of obsequiousness and docility," wrote *The Nation*'s Scott Sherman (2004, p. 4). But in this renewed discussion, concentration's critics identified another problem in addition to cost cutting and reductions in resources.

As in the abandonment of expensive foreign news, it is also economic—media companies' quest for profits. "Investigative reports share three things: They are risky, they upset the wisdom of the established order, and they are expensive to produce. Do profit-conscious enterprises, whether media companies or widget firms, seek extra costs, extra risk, and the opportunity to be attacked? Not in any business text I've ever read," explained BBC journalist Greg Palast (2003, p. 1). In other words, it was easier, cheaper, and safer to repeat the government's explanations than it was to investigate them. For example, reporter Judith Miller explained her unwillingness to include the views of skeptical intelligence and scientific experts in her numerous government-sourced accounts of Iraq's weapons buildup: "My job isn't to assess the government's information and be an independent

"If we had paid more attention to Afghanistan in the '80s we might not have had 9-11."

intelligence analyst myself. My job is to tell readers of the *New York Times* what the government thought of Iraq's arsenal" (quoted in Sherman, 2004, pp. 4–5). Rather than "aggressive digging for the dark facts of war," editorialized the *Columbia Journalism Review*, the public was left with "passive transmission of the Pentagon line" ("CJR Comment," 2003, p. 7).

Enter your voice in the cultural forum. Doesn't this seem a bit extreme, respected media companies placing profit and self-interest over their traditional role of serving the public? Or do you agree with media legal scholar Charles Tillinghast (2000), who wrote, "One need not be a devotee of conspiracy theories to understand that journalists, like other human beings, can judge where their interests lie, and what risks are and are not prudent, given their desire to continue to eat and feed the family" (pp. 145–146)?

Enter your voice in the cultural forum through your reaction to this oddity of our democratic life offered by media historian and reformer Robert McChesney (2007). Imagine, he suggests, that

> the federal government had issued an edict demanding that there be a sharp reduction in international journalism, or that local newsrooms be closed or their staffs and budgets slashed. Imagine if a president had issued an order that news media concentrate upon celebrities and trivia, rather than rigorously investigate and pursue scandals and lawbreaking in the White House. Had that occurred, there would have been an outcry that would have made Watergate look like a day at the beach. It would have been second only to the Civil War as a threat to the Republic.... Entire universities would have shut down in protest. Yet, when quasi-monopolistic commercial interests effectively do pretty much the same thing, and leave our country as impoverished culturally as if it had been the result of a government fiat, it passes with only minor protest. (p. 213)

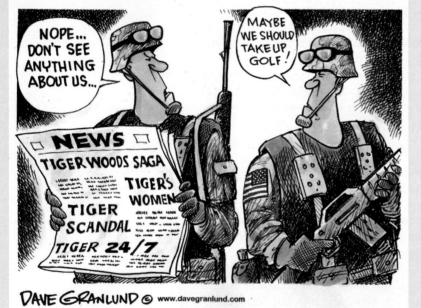

leaders. Even more distressing to critics was Yahoo!'s decision to identify one of its customers, dissident Shi Tao, as author of e-mails the Chinese government found subversive. Mr. Shi was arrested and sentenced to 10 years in prison. Would we accept this behavior from any of these companies here in the United States? How much should we accept them elsewhere in the name of "globalization"? Several groups from across the political spectrum called for protests and boycotts against Google and other tech companies that in their view go too far in meeting "local conditions" (Bray, 2006). There is much more on this conflict between localism and globalization in Chapter 15, including a discussion of Google's recent push-back against China's enforcement of local conditions.

Still, defenders of increased globalization point to the need to reach a fragmented and widespread audience—the same factor that fuels concentration—as encouraging this trend. They also cite the growing economic clout of emerging democracies (and the need to reach the people who live in them) and the increasing intertwining of the world's economies as additional reasons globalization is necessary for the economic survival of media businesses.

Audience Fragmentation

The nature of the other partner in the mass communication process is changing too. Individual segments of the audience are becoming more narrowly defined; the audience itself is less of a mass audience. This is **audience fragmentation**.

Before the advent of television, radio and magazines were national media. Big national radio networks brought news and entertainment to the entire country. Magazines such as *Life*, *Look*, and the *Saturday Evening Post* once offered limited text and many pictures to a national audience. But television could do these things better. It was radio with pictures; it was magazines with motion. To survive, radio and magazines were forced to find new functions. No longer able to compete on a mass scale, these media targeted smaller audiences that were alike in some important characteristic and therefore more attractive to specific advertisers. So now we have magazines such as *Ski* and *Internet World*, and radio station formats such as Country, Urban, and Lithuanian. This phenomenon is known as **narrowcasting**, **niche marketing**, or **targeting**.

Technology has wrought the same effect on television. Before the advent of cable television, people could choose from among the three commercial broadcast networks—ABC, CBS, NBC—one noncommercial public broadcasting station and, in larger markets, maybe an independent station or two. Now, with cable, satellite, and DVD, people have literally thousands of viewing options. The television audience has been fragmented. To attract advertisers, each channel now must find a more specific group of people to make up its viewership. Nickelodeon targets kids, for example; TV Land appeals to baby boomers; Spike aims at teen and young adult men; and Bravo seeks upper-income older people.

The new digital technologies promise even more audience fragmentation, almost to the point of audiences of one. For example, 40,000 of *Reason* magazine's 55,000 subscribers received individualized versions of the June 2007 issue. On the cover was an aerial photo of each reader's house and neighborhood. Inside were data on things like the educational levels of their neighbors and how many of the children in their zip code were being raised by grandparents. Ads were personalized as well, with appeals from public interest groups containing information on how each reader's congressperson voted on various pieces of legislation. We are living, said *Reason*'s editors approvingly, in a fragmented, *database nation* (Gillespie, 2007). Cable companies have the ability to send very specific commercials not only to specific neighborhoods but even to individual sets in individual homes. Individuated News, or I-News, is a newspaper service that delivers a completely specific, completely personalized newspaper printed at home. **Zonecasting** technology allows radio stations to deliver different commercials to specific neighborhoods, and **location-based mobile advertising** lets marketers directly send ads targeted at you wherever you are in that moment.

But if these audience-fragmenting **addressable technologies**—technologies permitting the transmission of very specific content to equally specific audience members—are changing the nature of the mass media's audiences, then the mass communication process itself must also change. What will happen as smaller, more specific audiences become better known to their partners in the process of making meaning? What will happen to the national culture that binds us as we become increasingly fragmented into demographically targeted **taste publics**—groups of people bound by little more than an interest in a given form of media content? Will there be a narrowing of our collective cultural experience, as media's storytelling function (Chapter 1) is disrupted because we are each listening to stories we individually preselect or that are preselected for us? "Maybe one day," wonders *Creativity* magazine editor Teressa Iezzi (2007), "you won't

▲ Is this our fragmented future, rocking out passionately and alone?

be able to say anything to anyone because a common language or the ability to grapple with or laugh at something outside of your comfort zone will have fallen away" (p. 11). *Time's* James Poniewozik (2004) offered his vision of our fragmented future: "Through niche media, niche foods, and niche hobbies, we fashion niche lives. We are the America of the iPod ads—stark, black silhouettes tethered by our brilliant white earbuds, rocking out passionately alone. You make your choices, and I make mine. Yours, of course, are wrong. But what do I care?" (p. 84).

There is an alternative view, however. Audience may well be fragmenting, but the interactivity encouraged and facilitated by the digital media will reconnect and reconfigure us into more numerous, more robust, more varied communities. There is a lot of, "Hey, check this out" going on. Social networks like Twitter and Facebook are places where "people can discuss their passions and discover others' on a worldwide basis" (Farhi, 2009). Technology writer Steven Johnson says, "We still have national events, but now when we have them, we're actually having a genuine, public conversation with a group that extends far beyond our nuclear family and our next-door neighbors. Some of that conversation is juvenile, of course. . . . But some of it is moving, witty, observant, subversive" (2009, p. 34).

Hypercommercialism

The costs involved in acquiring numerous or large media outlets, domestic and international, and of reaching an increasingly fragmented audience must be recouped somehow. Selling more advertising on existing and new media and identifying additional ways to combine content and commercials are the two most common strategies. This leads to **hypercommercialism**. The rise in the number of commercial minutes in a typical broadcast or cable show is evident to most viewers, as about 25% of a prime-time network television hour is devoted to commercial announcement breaks. Hypercommercialization has hit the Internet as well. In 1997 users saw 200 billion Net ads. In 2011 they endured 5 trillion, resulting in 66% of those people complaining that there are "too many digital ads" (Lunden, 2012c).

The sheer growth in the amount of advertising is one troublesome aspect of hypercommercialism. But for many observers the increased mixing of commercial and non-commercial media content is even more troubling. For example, in Chicago, WGN-Channel 9 reporters wear branded L. L. Bean clothing on air and WBBM-Channel 2 offers Honolulu weather forecasts to promote the television show *Hawaii Five-O*. In 2010, viewers saw 5,381 prime-time television product placements on the 12 largest broadcast and cable television networks, a 22% increase over 2006 (Ives, 2011a). A typical prime-time unscripted program, for example *American Idol* or *Survivor*, has more than 14 minutes of product placement and more than 15 minutes of actual commercial breaks, meaning that one-half of its hour is devoted to promotion. The typical scripted show, for example *Criminal Minds* or *Revenge*, has over four minutes of product placement and nearly 15 minutes of commercial break, resulting in one-third of its air time devoted to promotions (Kantar Media, 2011). So ubiquitous has this **product placement**—the integration, for a fee, of specific branded products into media content—become, that the Writers Guild of America, hoping to secure a piece of the annual $26 billion-and-growing industry, has demanded negotiations with television and film producers for additional compensation for writing what are, in effect, commercials (J. Hall, 2010). The producers' response is that product placement is not a commercial; rather, it represents a new form of content, **brand entertainment**—when brands are, in fact, part of and essential to the program. Pontiac's Solstice is a "character" in episodes of *The Apprentice*, and only MillerCoors beer brands are allowed to appear on programming offered by cable channels TNT and TBS. Musical artists not only take payment to include brands in their songs, some, for example Mariah Carey, now integrate brands into their CD booklets. In North Carolina, the *Charlotte Observer* and the

Raleigh News & Observer publish weekly science and technology sections sponsored by Duke Energy, headquartered in Charlotte, one of America's largest electric power companies and a strong advocate of nuclear power. Globally, marketers spend over $7 billion a year to place their products in news and entertainment content, with the U.S. leading the world at $4.26 billion a year (PQmedia, 2012).

Sometimes hypercommercialism involves direct payments of cash rather than "mere" branding. An "oral mention" on *Martha Stewart Living* can be had for $100,000. Gannett Broadcasting television stations in cities such as Atlanta, Cleveland, and Denver sell entire segments of their morning news and talk shows. For as little as $2,500, sponsors (along with their products or services) can buy not only the exclusive rights to a portion of a show but the assurance that the programs' hosts will conduct interviews with sponsors and demonstrations of their products as part of those segments (Klaassen, 2005a). Many radio stations now accept payment from record promoters to play their songs, an activity once illegal and called **payola**. It is now quite acceptable as long as the "sponsorship" is acknowledged on the air.

Again, as with globalization and concentration, where critics see damage to the integrity of the media themselves and disservice to their audiences, defenders of hypercommercialism argue that it is simply the economic reality of today's media world.

Erosion of Distinctions among Media: Convergence

Cable channel Comedy Central produces a six-show lineup exclusively for its Internet channel, *Motherload*. Movie studios make their titles available not only on DVD but for handheld video-game systems. Cable's AMC runs a slate of **webisodes**, Web-only television shows, to accompany its hit series *The Walking Dead*. Satellite provider Dish Networks offers interactive, TV remote–based play of classic video games. DVD distributor Netflix streams not only movies, but a host of new and old network television hits. The iPod Nano music player contains an FM tuner. Video game consoles not only let players download movies and television shows, surf the Internet, check their Facebook accounts, and tune in to the Weather Channel and the BBC; they also offer streaming of tens of thousands of feature films. Ken Burns unveiled his documentary series *Prohibition* on the iPad and iPhone a week before its 2011 airing on PBS, where it was simultaneously streamed over the Internet and broadcast in advance of its availability on DVD and at the iTunes store. You can subscribe to *National Geographic* and play its issue-matched video game online or on a cell phone. There are tens of thousands of U.S. commercial and noncommercial and

► Convergence killed the video store, first the mom 'n pop shops, then big chains like Blockbuster, victimized by video downloads, streaming, and online rentals—products of the convergence of movies, video, and the Internet. Convergence is strangling the bookstore as well, first the independents, then chains like Borders, victimized by online sales and downloads to portable e-readers, smartphones, and tablets—products of the convergence of print, the Internet, and smartphones.

foreign radio stations delivering their broadcasts over the Web. *Pokémon* is as much a 30-minute TV commercial for licensed merchandise as it is a cartoon.

You can read the *New York Times* or *Time* magazine and hundreds of other newspapers and magazines on your computer screen. Cell phones not only allow users to talk to other people; because they include digital camcorders, zoom and rotating lenses, and digital still cameras, complete with flash, they allow those same users to "broadcast" their "television programs" and photos. And what can "newspapers, magazines, and books," "radio and recordings," and "television and film" really mean (or more accurately, *really be*) now that people can access printed texts, audio, and moving images virtually anyplace, anytime via **Wi-Fi** (wireless Internet) and handheld devices? This erosion of distinctions among media is called *convergence*, and it is fueled, according to technology attorney Tony Kern (2005), by three elements that have come together "almost simultaneously. First is the digitization of nearly all information, which provides a common means to represent all forms of communication. Second is high-speed connectivity; networks are becoming faster and more pervasive—wired and wireless. And third is a seemingly endless advance in technology in which speed, memory, and power improvements allow a device to do more. That redefines the limits of what is possible" (p. 32).

The traditional lines between media are disappearing. Concentration is one reason. If one company owns newspapers, an online service, television stations, book publishers, a magazine or two, and a film company, it has a strong incentive to get the greatest use from its content, whether news, education, or entertainment, by using as many channels of delivery as possible. The industry calls this **synergy**, and it is the driving force behind several recent mergers and acquisitions in the media and telecommunications industries. Media giant News Corp. paid well over a billion dollars in 2005 for social networking website MySpace.com and video-game maker IGN Entertainment in order to blend its existing broadcast, film, and print media with the Net and games. In 2010, Disney bought game maker Tapulous, designer of mobile, music-based games such as *Tap Tap Revenge* with the goal of creating customized games for Disney recording and television properties like Miley Cyrus. In that same year, Google paid between $100 and $200 million for social gaming giant Zynga, makers of *Farmville* and *Texas Hold'em*, to anchor its Google Games and user-tracking platforms.

Another reason for convergence is audience fragmentation. A mass communicator who finds it difficult to reach the whole audience can reach its component parts through various media. A third reason is the audience itself. We are becoming increasingly **platform agnostic**, having no preference for where we access our media content. Will this expansion and blurring of traditional media channels confuse audience members, further tilting the balance of power in the mass communication process toward the media industries? Or will it give audiences more power—power to choose, power to reject, and power to combine information and entertainment in individual ways?

DEVELOPING MEDIA LITERACY SKILLS

Reconsidering the Process of Mass Communication

One essential element of media literacy is *having an understanding of the process of mass communication*. As we saw in Chapter 1, understanding the process—how it functions, how its components relate to one another, how it limits or enhances messages, which forms of feedback are most effective and why—permits us to form expectations of how the media industries and the process itself can serve us. But throughout this chapter we have seen that the process of mass communication is undergoing fundamental change. Media-literate individuals must understand why and how this evolution is occurring. We can do this by reconsidering its elements as described in Figure 1.3.

INTERPRETER A—THE CONTENT PRODUCER

Traditionally, the content producer, the source, in the mass communication process is a large, hierarchically structured organization—for example, Pixar Studios, the *Philadelphia Enquirer*, CBS Television. And as we saw, the typical consequence of this organizational structure is scant room for individual vision or experimentation. But in the age of the Internet, with its proliferation of **blogs** (regularly updated online journals that comment on just about everything), social-networking sites such as Facebook where users post all variety of free, personal content, and other websites, the distinction between content consumer and content provider disappears. Now, Interpreter A can be an independent musician self-releasing her music online, a lone blogger, a solitary online scrapbooker, or two pals who create digital video. Today, 37% of America's Internet users "have contributed to

▲ Convergence and the low cost of entry have made us all authors.

the creation of news, commented about it, or disseminated it via postings on social media sites" (Purcell, Rainie, Mitchell, Rosensteil, & Olmstead, 2010). Users upload 60 hours of video every minute to YouTube alone (Oreskovic, 2012). Internet domain company Go Daddy traditionally airs a viewer-created commercial during the Super Bowl. Tens of millions of producers, big and small, distribute their video fare on the Internet. Sites like Vuze, On Networks, Joost, and Blip Networks strike financial deals with producers, again big and small, for content for their own sites and for syndication to others. And what are Snapchat's 3.5 million and Instagram's 100 million users who upload 150 million and 40 million images a day, respectively, if not producers of a huge amount of sometimes very engaging content (Tsukayama, 2013)?

In the newly evolving mass communication, content providers are just as likely to be individuals who believe in something or who have something to say as they are big media companies in search of audiences and profits. Now sources themselves, they are *the people formerly known as the audience*, and it is not simply technological change that has given them voice. It is the reduction of the **cost of entry** for content production to nearly $0 that those digital technologies have wrought that has made them all creators. "Rates of authorship are increasing by historic orders of magnitude. Nearly universal authorship, like universal literacy before it, stands to reshape society by hastening the flow of information and making individuals more influential," wrote futurists Denis Pelli and Charles Bigelow. "As readers, we consume. As authors, we create. Our society is changing from consumers to creators" (2009).

What are the likely consequences of this change? Will the proliferation of content sources help mitigate the effects of concentration and conglomeration in the traditional media industries? Will the cultural forum be less of a lecture and more of a conversation? Will new and different and challenging storytellers find an audience for their narratives? Does journalist William Greider (2005), speaking specifically of the news, overstate when he says, "The centralized institutions of press and broadcasting are being challenged and steadily eroded by widening circles of unlicensed 'news' agents—from talk-radio hosts to Internet bloggers and others—who compete with the official press to be believed. These interlopers speak in a different language and from many different angles of vision. Less authoritative, but more democratic" (p. 31)?

THE MESSAGE

The message in the traditional mass communication process is typically many identical messages, mechanically produced, simultaneously sent, inflexible, and unalterable. Once CBS airs tonight's episode of *NCIS*, it has aired tonight's episode of *NCIS*. The consequence? Audiences either like it or don't like it. The program either succeeds or fails. But we've already seen that different commercial spots can be inserted into programs sent into specific homes and that thousands of issues of the same magazine can be personalized inside and on the cover. You can buy only four downloaded cuts of an artist's latest CD, add three more from an earlier release, and listen to a completely new, personally created CD. **RSS**, for **really simple syndication**, feeds are aggregators that allow Web users to create their own content assembled from the Internet's limitless supply of material. Some of the most popular are MyTimes, Blogline, Newsgator, and My Yahoo. Users tell the aggregator what sites to collect, or their issues of interest, or even their favorite writers. As soon as any new content in their preselected categories appears on the Net, it is automatically brought to their RSS file. In this way, according to journalist Robert Kuttner (2007), users can "pre-assemble an all-star Webpaper [or Webcast or Webmagazine] that no single newspaper [or radio station, cable network, television station, or magazine] can possibly duplicate" (p. 26). In other words, each RSS "message" is infinitely alterable, completely unique, and thoroughly idiosyncratic. Alternate-ending DVDs permitting viewers to "re-edit" an existing movie at home are old hat by now. But what do you think of director Steven Soderbergh's vision for a digital movie future? He said that in 5 or 10 years, when theaters convert more fully from film to digital projection (Chapter 6), he plans to exhibit multiple, different versions of the same film. "I think it would be very interesting to have a movie out in release," he said, "and then, just a few weeks later say, 'Here's version 2.0, recut, rescored.' The other version is still out there—people can see either or both" (in Jardin, 2005b, p. 257).

What will be the impact on the mass communication process when content producers no longer have to amass as large an audience as possible with a single, simultaneously distributed piece of content? When a producer can sell very specific, very idiosyncratic, constantly changing content to very specific, very idiosyncratic, constantly changing consumers, will profitability and popularity no longer be so closely linked? What will "popular" and "profitable" messages really mean when audience members can create infinitely "alterable" messages? What will happen when the mass communication process, long dependent on **appointment consumption** (audiences consume content at a time predetermined by the producer and distributor; for example, a movie time at a theater, your favorite television show at 9:00 on Tuesdays, news at the top of the hour), evolves more completely to **consumption-on-demand** (the ability to consume any content, anytime, anywhere)?

FEEDBACK AND INTERPRETER B—THE AUDIENCE

In the traditional model of the mass communication process, feedback is inferential and delayed—what is a newspaper's circulation, what were this weekend's box office numbers for that movie, what are that program's ratings? Likewise, the audience is typically seen as large and heterogeneous, known to content producers and distributors in a relatively rudimentary way, little more than basic demographics. But digital media have changed what content creators and distributors know about their audiences (Interpreter B) because they have changed how audiences talk back to those sources (feedback). Silicon Valley marketing consultant Richard Yanowitch explains, "The Internet is the most ubiquitous experimental lab in history, built on two-way, real-time interactions with millions of consumers whose individual consumption patterns can for the first time be infinitesimally measured, monitored, and molded." Adds Google advertising executive Tim Armstrong, "Traditionally, the focus has been on the outbound message. But we think the information coming back in is as important or more important than the messages going out. For years, demographics has been a religion among advertisers because it was the only information they had" (both in Streisand & Newman, 2005, p. 60).

In today's mass communication, every visit to a specific Web address (and every click of a mouse once there), every download of a piece of content, and every product bought online provide feedback to someone. But it isn't just the Internet—every selection of a channel on cable or satellite, every rental or purchase by credit card of a CD, DVD, video game, or movie ticket, and every consumer product scanned at the checkout counter is recorded and stored in order to better identify us to Interpreter A, whoever that might be. But this raises the question, Who is that? It might be content providers who want to serve us more effectively because they know us so much more thoroughly than they once did when relying solely on demographics. Or it could be those who would make less honorable use of the feedback we so willingly provide—for example, identity thieves or insurance companies that would deny us coverage because of our eating and viewing habits.

The Result

How will we use the new communication technologies? What will be our role in the new, emerging mass communication process? The world of content creators and distributors is now more democratic. Audiences, even though they may be fragmented into groups as small as one person or as large as 100 million, are better known to those who produce and distribute content and they can talk back more directly and with more immediacy. Content, the message, is now more flexible, infinitely alterable, unbound by time and space. Clearly, for content producers there is more room for experimentation in content creation and consumption. There is less risk, and possibly even great reward, in challenging audiences. The evolving mass communication process promises not only efficiency but great joy, boundless choice, and limitless access to information for all its partners. But as you might remember from Chapter 1, the technologies that help provide these gifts are in fact double-edged swords; they cut both ways, good and bad. Media-literate people, because they understand the mass communication process through which they operate, are positioned to best decide how to benefit from their potential and limit their peril.

MEDIA LITERACY CHALLENGE
The Fraction of Selection

An important part of being media literate is having critical thinking skills enabling you to develop independent judgments about media and media content. Challenge your own skill by predicting which media will survive and which will disappear as a result of the dramatic technological, economic, and audience preference turmoil currently shaking the traditional media industries. Which will change and how? The answers depend on you and your media choices. In 1954, when television was doing to movies, newspapers, magazines, and radio what the Internet and smartphones are doing to today's media, communication scholar Wilbur Schramm created the **fraction of selection** to answer the question, "What determines which offerings of mass communication will be selected by a given individual?" It looks like this:

$$\frac{\text{Expectation of Reward}}{\text{Effort Required}}$$

It suggests that you weigh the level of reward you expect from a given medium or piece of content against how much effort—in the broadest sense—you make to secure that reward. Now, consider your own media consumption. For example, how do you typically watch movies: at the theater, streamed, downloaded, on disc, wait for them to come to cable? What "data" would go in your numerator? In your denominator? Create your personal formula for other media consumption as well. News on the Internet versus the newspaper? Popular music on commercial radio versus an iPod or other MP3 player? Compare your outcomes with those of your friends. Based on your results, can you speculate on tomorrow's media winners and losers?

Resources for Review and Discussion

REVIEW POINTS: TYING CONTENT TO LEARNING OUTCOMES

▶ **Summarize broad current trends in mass media, especially concentration of ownership and conglomeration, globalization, audience fragmentation, hypercommercialization, and convergence.**

- Encouraged by the Internet and other digital technologies, content producers are finding new ways to deliver content to audiences.

- All of the traditional media have begun to see either flattening or declines in audience, yet overall consumption of media is at all-time highs.
- Five trends are abetting this situation—convenience, audience fragmentation, concentration of ownership and conglomeration, globalization, and hypercommercialism.

- Convergence is fueled by three elements—digitization of nearly all information, high-speed connectivity, and advances in technology's speed, memory, and power.

▶ **Describe in broad terms how the mass communication process itself will evolve as the role of the audience in this new media environment is altered.**
  - As a result of this change, traditional conceptions of the mass communication process and its elements must be reconsidered:
    - Content providers can now be lone individuals aided by low cost of entry.

- Messages can now be quite varied, idiosyncratic, and freed of the producers' time demands.
- Feedback can now be instantaneous and direct, and, as a result, audiences, very small or very large, can be quite well known to content producers and distributors.

KEY TERMS

QUESTIONS FOR REVIEW

1. What is convergence?
2. What is media multitasking?
3. Differentiate between concentration of media ownership and conglomeration.
4. What is globalization?
5. What is hypercommercialism?
6. What is audience fragmentation?
7. What are the two major concerns of globalization's critics?
8. What three elements are fueling today's rampant media convergence?
9. Differentiate between notions of content producers, audiences, messages, and feedback in the traditional view of the mass communication process and more contemporary understandings of these elements of the process.
10. What is the significance of low cost of entry?

⊞ connect

For further review, go to the LearnSmart study module for this chapter.

QUESTIONS FOR CRITICAL THINKING AND DISCUSSION

1. Many industry insiders attribute the recent falloff in audiences for movies, recorded music, network television, DVD, radio, newspapers, and video games to changes in technology; people are finding new ways to access content. And while this is certainly true to a degree, others say that in this age of concentrated and hypercommercialized media, audiences are simply being turned off. Would you agree with the critics? Why? Can you give examples from your own media consumption?

2. Critics of concentration of media ownership and conglomeration argue that they are a threat to democracy. What is the thrust of their concern? Do you share it? Why or why not?

3. A close reading of how the mass communication process is evolving has led some observers to argue that it is becoming less "mass" and more akin to interpersonal communication. Revisit Figure 1.3. Can you make the argument that the "result" of the process has the potential to be more "flexible, personally relevant, possibly adventurous, challenging, or experimental"?

Books

3

Learning Objectives

Books were the first mass medium and are, in many ways, the most personal. They inform and entertain. They are repositories of our pasts and agents of personal development and social change. Like all media, they mirror the culture. After studying this chapter you should be able to

▶ Outline the history and development of the publishing industry and the book itself as a medium.

▶ Describe the cultural value of books and the implications of censorship for democracy.

▶ Explain how the organizational and economic nature of the contemporary book industry shapes the content of books.

▶ Act as a more media-literate consumer of books, especially in considering their uniqueness in an increasingly mass-mediated, media-converged world.

First-time author Lena Dunham, creator of TV's *Girls*, landed a $3.7 million advance for her book *Not That Kind of Girl.*

THE VHS VIDEO BEGAN WHEN YOU HIT THE PLAY BUTTON ON THE REMOTE CONTROL. But the folks who rented the movie before you failed to rewind. So there you were, watching an arresting scene from François Truffaut's 1967 adaptation of Ray Bradbury's (1953/1981) science fiction classic *Fahrenheit 451*.

At first you couldn't make out what was happening. A group of people were wandering about, and each person was talking to him- or herself. You recognized actress Julie Christie, but the other performers and what they were saying were completely unfamiliar. You stayed with the scene. The trees were bare. Snow was falling, covering everything. Puffs of steam floated from people's mouths as they spoke, seemingly to no one. As you watched a bit more, you began to recognize some familiar phrases. These people were reciting passages from famous books! Before you could figure out why they were doing this, the film ended.

So you rewound and watched the entire video, discovering that these people *were* the books they had memorized. In this near-future society, all books had been banned by the authorities, forcing these people—book lovers all—into hiding. They hold the books in their heads because to hold them in their hands is a crime. If discovered with books, people are jailed and the books are set afire—Fahrenheit 451 is the temperature at which book paper burns.

Moved by the film, you go to the library the next day and check out the book itself. Bradbury's (1981) main character, Guy Montag, a fireman who until this moment had been an official book burner himself, speaks a line that stays with you, even today. After he watches an old woman burn to death with her forbidden volumes, he implores his ice-cold, drugged, and television-deadened wife to understand what he is only then realizing. He pleads with her to see: "There must be something in books, things we can't imagine, to make a woman stay in a burning house; there must be something there" (pp. 49–50).

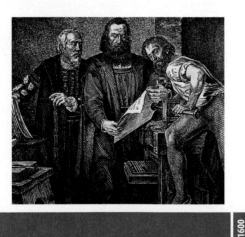

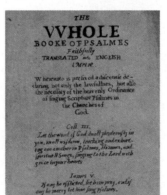

1456 ▲ First Gutenberg Bible

1638 First printing press in the Colonies

1644 ▲ *The Whole Booke of Psalms*, first book printed in the Colonies

1732 ▲ *Poor Richard's Almanack*

1765 Stamp Act

1774 Thomas Paine writes *Common Sense*

In this chapter we examine the history of books, especially in terms of their role in the development of the United States. We discuss the importance that has traditionally been ascribed to books, as well as the scope and nature of the book industry. We address the various factors that shape the contemporary economics and structures of the book industry, examining at some length the impact of convergence, concentration, and hypercommercialism on the book industry and its relationship with its readers. Finally, we discuss the media literacy issues inherent in the wild success of the *Harry Potter* books.

A Short History of Books

As we saw in Chapter 1, the use of Gutenberg's printing press spread rapidly throughout Europe in the last half of the 15th century. But the technological advances and the social, cultural, and economic conditions necessary for books to become a major mass medium were three centuries away. As a result, it was a printing press and a world of books not unlike that in Gutenberg's time that first came to the New World in the 17th century.

Books Come to Colonial North America

The earliest colonists came to America primarily for two reasons—to escape religious persecution and to find economic opportunities unavailable to them in Europe. Most of the books they carried with them to the New World were religiously oriented. Moreover, they brought very few books at all. Better-educated, wealthier Europeans were secure at home. Those willing to make the dangerous journey tended to be poor, uneducated, and largely illiterate.

1800	1900	2000
~1800 Continuous roll paper	1926 Book of the Month Club begins	2003 Project Gutenberg and *Search Inside the Book* debut
1807 John Wiley & Sons established	1935 Penguin Books (first paperbacks) established in London	2005 Google ignites controversy with plan to scan copyrighted books
1811 Steam-powered printing press	1939 Pocket Books (paperbacks) established in the U.S.	2006 Sony Reader
1817 Harper Brothers established	1953 ▲ Bradbury's *Fahrenheit 451*	2007 Final *Harry Potter* book; Amazon's Kindle
1830 Improved pulp making	1960 Paperback sales surpass hardback sales for the first time	2008 On-demand titles exceed number of traditional titles
1852 ▲ Stowe's *Uncle Tom's Cabin*	1995 Amazon.com goes online	2009 For first time, Amazon sells more e-books than hard-copy books in one day (Christmas Day). Espresso Book Machine
1860 Dime novels appear		2010 ▲ iPad
1861 U.S. achieves highest literacy rate in the world		2011 E–books outsell all print books on Amazon
1884 Linotype machine		
1885 Offset lithography		

There were other reasons early settlers did not find books central to their lives. One was the simple fight for survival. In the brutal and hostile land to which they had come, leisure for reading books was a luxury for which they had little time. People worked from sunrise to sunset just to live. If there was to be reading, it would have to be at night, and it was folly to waste precious candles on something as unnecessary to survival as reading. In addition, books and reading were regarded as symbols of wealth and status and therefore not priorities for people who considered themselves to be pioneers, servants of the Lord, or anti-English colonists. The final reason the earliest settlers were not active readers was the lack of portability of books. Books were heavy, and few were carried across the ocean. Those volumes that did make it to North America were extremely expensive and not available to most people.

The first printing press arrived on North American shores in 1638, only 18 years after the Plymouth Rock landing. It was operated by a company called Cambridge Press. Printing was limited to religious and government documents. The first book printed in the Colonies appeared in 1644—*The Whole Booke of Psalms*, sometimes referred to as the *Bay Psalm Book*. Among the very few secular titles were those printed by Benjamin Franklin 90 years later. *Poor Richard's Almanack*, which first appeared in 1732, sold 10,000 copies annually. The *Almanack* contained short stories, poetry, weather predictions, and other facts and figures useful to a population more in command of its environment than those first settlers. As the Colonies grew in wealth and sophistication, leisure time increased, as did affluence and education. Franklin also published the first true novel printed in North America, *Pamela*, written by English author Samuel Richardson. Still, by and large, books were religiously oriented or pertained to official government activities such as tax rolls and the pronouncements of various commissions.

▼ In the now not-so-distant future of *Fahrenheit 451*, people must memorize the content of books because to own a book is illegal.

The primary reason for this lack of variety was the requirement that all printing be done with the permission of the colonial governors. Because these men were invariably loyal to King George II, secular printing and criticism of the British Crown or even of local authorities was never authorized, and publication of such writing meant jail. Many printers were imprisoned—including Franklin's brother James—for publishing what they believed to be the truth.

The printers went into open revolt against official control in March 1765 after passage of the Stamp Act. Designed by England to recoup money it spent waging the French and Indian War, the Stamp Act mandated that all printing—legal documents, books, magazines, and newspapers—be done on paper stamped with the government's seal. Its additional purpose was to control and limit expression in the increasingly restless Colonies. This affront to their freedom, and the steep cost of the tax—sometimes doubling the price of a publication—was simply too much for the colonists. The printers used their presses to run accounts of antitax protests, demonstrations, riots, sermons, boycotts, and other antiauthority activities, further fueling revolutionary and secessionist sympathies. In November 1765—when the tax was to take effect—the authorities were so cowed by the reaction of the colonists that they were unwilling to enforce it.

Anti-British sentiment reached its climax in the mid-1770s, and books were at its core. Short books, or pamphlets, motivated and coalesced political dissent. In 1774 England's right to govern the Colonies was openly challenged by James Wilson's *Considerations on the Nature and Extent of the Legislative Authority of the British Parliament*, John Adams's *Novanglus Papers*, and Thomas Jefferson's *A Summary View of the Rights of British America*. Most famous of all was Thomas Paine's 47-page *Common Sense*. It sold 120,000 copies in the first three months after its release to a total population of 400,000 adults. Between 1776 and 1783, Paine also wrote a series of pamphlets called *The American Crisis*. *Common Sense* and *The American Crisis* made Paine the most widely read colonial author during the American Revolution.

THE EARLY BOOK INDUSTRY After the War of Independence, printing became even more central to political, intellectual, and cultural life in major cities like Boston, New York, and Philadelphia. To survive financially, printers also operated as booksellers, book publishers, and sometimes as postmasters who sold stationery and even groceries. A coffeehouse or tavern often was attached to the print shop. The era was alive with political change, and printer/bookshops became clearinghouses for the collection, exchange, and dissemination of information.

The U.S. newspaper industry grew rapidly from this mix, as we will see in Chapter 4. The book industry, however, was slower to develop. Books were still expensive, often costing the equivalent of a working person's weekly pay, and literacy remained a luxury. However, due in large measure to a movement begun before the Civil War, compulsory education had come to most states by 1900. This swelled the number of readers, which increased demand for books. This increased demand, coupled with a number of important technological advances, brought the price of books within reach of most people. In 1861 the United States had the highest literacy rate of any country in the world (58%), and 40 years later at the start of the 20th century, 9 out of every 10 U.S. citizens could read. Today, nearly universal literacy reigns in America.

THE FLOWERING OF THE NOVEL The 1800s saw a series of important refinements to the process of printing, most notably the **linotype** machine, a typewriter-like keyboard allowing printers to set type mechanically rather than manually, and **offset lithography**, permitting printing from photographic plates rather than from heavy, fragile metal casts. The combination of this technically improved, lower-cost printing (and therefore lower-cost publications) and widespread literacy produced the flowering of the novel in the 1800s. Major U.S. book publishers Harper Brothers and John Wiley & Sons—both in business today— were established in New York in 1817 and 1807, respectively. And books such as Nathaniel Hawthorne's *The Scarlet Letter* (1850), Herman Melville's *Moby Dick* (1851), and Mark Twain's *Huckleberry Finn* (1884) were considered by their readers to be equal to or better than the works of famous European authors such as Jane Austen, the Brontës, and Charles Dickens.

The growing popularity of books was noticed by brothers Irwin and Erastus Beadle. In 1860 they began publishing novels that sold for 10 cents. These **dime novels** were inexpensive, and because they concentrated on frontier and adventure stories, they attracted growing numbers of readers. Within five years of their start, Beadle & Company had produced over 4 million volumes of what were also sometimes called **pulp novels** (Tebbel, 1987). Advertising titles like *Malaeska: Indian Wife of the White Hunter* with the slogan "Dollar Books for a Dime!" the Beadles democratized books and turned them into a mass medium.

THE COMING OF PAPERBACK BOOKS Dime novels were "paperback books" because they were produced with paper covers. But publisher Allen Lane invented what we now recognize as the paperback in the midst of the Great Depression in London when he founded Penguin Books in 1935. Four years later, publisher Robert de Graff introduced the idea to the United States. His Pocket Books were small, inexpensive (25 cents) reissues of books that had already become successful as hardcovers. They were sold just about everywhere—newsstands, bookstores, train stations, shipping

▲ First published in 1732, Benjamin Franklin's *Poor Richard's Almanack* offered readers a wealth of information for the upcoming year.

▲ British-born writer, patriot, and revolutionary leader Thomas Paine wrote *Common Sense* and *The American Crisis* to rally his colonial compatriots in their struggle against the British.

terminals, and drug and department stores. Within weeks of their introduction, de Graff was fielding orders of up to 15,000 copies a day (Tebbel, 1987). Soon, new and existing publishers joined the paperback boom. Traditionalists had some concern about the "cheapening of the book," but that was more than offset by the huge popularity of paperbacks and the willingness of publishers to take chances. For example, in the 1950s and '60s, African American writers such as Richard Wright and Ralph Ellison were published, as were controversial works such as *Catcher in the Rye*. Eventually, paperback books became the norm, surpassing hardcover book sales for the first time in 1960. Today, more than 60% of all physical books sold in the United States are paperbacks.

Paperbacks are no longer limited to reprints of successful hardbacks. Many books now begin life as paperbacks. The John Jakes books *The Americans* and *The Titans*, for example, were issued initially as paperbacks and later reissued in hardcover. Paperbacks sell about 1 million volumes a day, and bookstores generate half their revenue from these sales.

Books and Their Audiences

The book is the least "mass" of our mass media in audience reach and in the magnitude of the industry itself, and this fact shapes the nature of the relationship between medium and audience. Publishing houses, both large and small, produce narrowly or broadly aimed titles for readers, who buy and carry away individual units. This more direct relationship between publishers and readers renders books fundamentally different from other mass media. For example, because books are less dependent than other mass media on attracting the largest possible audience, books are more able and more likely to incubate new, challenging, or unpopular ideas. As the medium least dependent on advertiser support, books can be aimed at extremely small groups of readers, challenging them and their imaginations in ways that many sponsors would find unacceptable in advertising-based mass media. Because books are produced and sold as individual units—as opposed to a single television program simultaneously distributed to millions of viewers or a single edition of a mass circulation newspaper—more "voices" can enter and survive in the industry. This medium can sustain more voices in the cultural forum than can other traditional mass media. As former head of the New York Public Library, Vartan Gregorian, explained to journalist Bill Moyers (2007), when among books, "Suddenly you feel humble. The whole world of humanity is in front of you. . . . Here it is, the human endeavor, human aspiration, human agony, human ecstasy, human bravura, human failures—all before you."

The Cultural Value of the Book

The book industry is bound by many of the same financial and industrial pressures that constrain other media, but books, more than the others, are in a position to transcend those constraints. In *Fahrenheit 451* Montag's boss, Captain Beatty, explains why all books must be burned. "Once," he tells his troubled subordinate, "books appealed to a few people, here, there, everywhere. They could afford to be different. The world was roomy. But then the world got full of eyes and elbows and mouths" (Bradbury, 1981, p. 53). Bradbury's firemen of the future destroy books precisely because they *are* different. It is their difference from other mass media that makes books unique in our culture. Although all media serve the following cultural functions to some degree (for example, people use self-help videos for personal development, and popular music is sometimes an agent of social change), books traditionally have been seen as a powerful cultural force for these reasons:

- *Books are agents of social and cultural change.* Free of the need to generate mass circulation for advertisers, offbeat, controversial, even revolutionary ideas can reach the public. For example, Andrew MacDonald's *Turner Diaries* is the ideological and how-to bible of the antigovernment militia movement in the United States. Nonetheless, this radical, revolutionary book is openly published, purchased, and discussed.

- *Books are an important cultural repository.* Want to definitively win an argument? Look it up. We often turn to books for certainty and truth about the world in which we live and the ones about which we want to know. Which countries border Chile? Find the atlas. James Brown's sax player? Look in Bob Gulla's *Icons of R & B and Soul.*

- *Books are our windows on the past.* What was the United States like in the 19th century? Read Alexis de Tocqueville's *Democracy in America.* England in the early 1800s? Read Jane Austen's *Pride and Prejudice.* Written in the times they reflect, these books are more accurate representations than are available in the modern electronic media.

- *Books are important sources of personal development.* The obvious forms are self-help and personal improvement volumes. But books also speak to us more individually than advertiser-supported media because of their small, focused target markets. For example, *Our Bodies, Ourselves,* introduced by the Boston Women's Health Book Collective in the very earliest days of the modern feminist movement, is still published today. (For more on this influential book, see the "Our Bodies, Ourselves" box.) *Dr. Spock's Baby and Child Care* has sold more than 30 million copies. J. D. Salinger's *Catcher in the Rye* was the literary anthem for the Baby Boomers in their teen years, as is William Gibson's *Neuromancer* for many Web pioneers. It is unlikely that any of these voices would have found their initial articulation in commercially sponsored media.

- *Books are wonderful sources of entertainment, escape, and personal reflection.* Suzanne Collins, John Grisham, Stephenie Meyer, and Stephen King all specialize in writing highly entertaining and imaginative novels. The enjoyment found in the works of writers Joyce Carol Oates (*On Boxing, We Were the Mulvaneys*), John Irving (*The World According to Garp, Hotel New Hampshire, A Prayer for Owen Meany*), Pat Conroy (*The Prince of Tides, Beach Music*), and J. K. Rowling (the *Harry Potter* series) is undeniable.

- *The purchase and reading of a book is a much more individual, personal activity than consuming advertiser-supported (television, radio, newspapers, and magazines) or heavily promoted (popular music and movies) media.* As such, books tend to encourage personal reflection to a greater degree than these other media. We are alone when we read a book; we are part of the tribe, as Marshall McLuhan would say, when we engage other media. As such, in the words of author Julius Lester (2002) (*Look Out, Whitey! Black Power's Gon' Get Your Mama!; Why Heaven Is Far Away*):

The mystery and miracle of a book is found in the fact that it is a solitary voice penetrating time and space to go beyond time and space, and to alight for a moment in that place within each of us which is also beyond time and space. . . . Books are the royal road that enable us to enter the realm of the imaginative. Books enable us to experience what it is to be someone else. Through books we experience other modes of being. Through books we recognize who we are and who we might become. . . . Books invite us into realms of the soul by asking us to imagine that we are someone other than who we are. Books require that we temporarily put our egos in a box by the door and take on the spirit of others. . . . This is what a book, any book, offers us the opportunity to do: confess and recognize ourselves. To confess and recognize our fantasies, our joys, and griefs, our aspirations and failures, our hopes and our fears. (pp. 26–29)

- *Books are mirrors of culture.* Books, along with other mass media, reflect the culture that produces and consumes them.

Censorship

Because of their influence as cultural repositories and agents of social change, books have often been targeted for censorship. A book is censored when someone in authority limits publication of or access to it. Censorship can and does occur in many situations

▲ Stephenie Meyer's *Twilight* series and Suzanne Collins' *Hunger Games* trilogy are hugely popular sources of entertainment, escape, and personal reflection.

USING MEDIA TO MAKE A DIFFERENCE
Our Bodies, Ourselves

Books have been central to many of the most important social and political movements in our nation's history. *Our Bodies, Ourselves*, a book for and about women, is credited with beginning the women's health movement. The profits this book generates—some 40 years after its first appearance—continue to support what has become a world-wide undertaking. How did this influential book, with more than 4 million copies sold in 18 different languages, come into being, and how does it continue to be so influential?

The story of *Our Bodies, Ourselves* begins in 1969. That year several women, aged 23 to 39, were attending a workshop on "Women and Their Bodies" at a women's liberation conference in Boston. They began exchanging "doctor stories." They readily came to the conclusion that most women were relatively ignorant about their bodies (and by extension, their sexuality) and that the male-dominated medical profession was not particularly receptive to their needs. So they gave themselves a "summer project." As explained by the women, who began identifying themselves as the Boston Women's Health Book Collective (Norsigian et al., 1999):

We would research our questions, share what we learned in our group, and then present the information in the fall as a course "by and for women." We envisioned an ongoing process that would involve other women who would go on to teach such a course in other settings. In

> "Books have been central to many of the most important social and political movements in our nation's history."

creating the course, we learned that we were capable of collecting, understanding, and evaluating medical information; that we could open up to one another and find strength and comfort through sharing some of our most private experiences; that what we learned from one another was every bit as important as what we read in medical texts; and that our experience contradicted medical pronouncements. Over time these facts, feelings, and controversies were intertwined in the various editions of *Our Bodies, Ourselves*.

How does *Our Bodies, Ourselves* continue to make a difference? One of the original Boston Women's Health Book Collective members, Jane Pincus, explains in her introduction to the 1998 edition:

Unlike most health books on the market, *Our Bodies, Ourselves for the New Century* is unique in many respects: It is based on, and has grown out of, hundreds of women's experiences. It questions the medicalization of women's bodies and lives, and highlights holistic knowledge along with conventional biomedical information. It places women's experiences within the social, political, and economic forces that determine all of our lives, thus going beyond individualistic, narrow, "self-care" and self-help approaches, and views health in the context of the sexist, racist, and financial pressures that affect far too many girls, women, and families adversely. It condemns medical corporate misbehavior driven by "bottom-line" management philosophy and the profit motive. Most of all, *Our Bodies, Ourselves* encourages you to value and share your own insights and experiences, and to use its information to question the assumptions underlying the care we all receive so that we can deal effectively with the medical system and organize for better care.... (p. 21)

You may disagree with some (or all) of the philosophy and goals of the Boston Women's Health Book Collective, but there is no argument that its book, *Our Bodies, Ourselves*, has made—and continues to make—a difference in the health of women around the world.

THE BESTSELLING CLASSIC,
INFORMING AND INSPIRING WOMEN ACROSS GENERATIONS

OUR BODIES, OURSELVES

"Within these pages, you will find the voice of a women's health movement that is based on shared experience. Listen to it—and add your own."—GLORIA STEINEM

Completely
REVISED
and
UPDATED ...

and in all media (more on this in Chapter 14). But because of the respect our culture traditionally holds for books, book banning takes on a particularly poisonous connotation in the United States.

Reacting to censorship presents a dilemma for book publishers. Publishers have an obligation to their owners and stockholders to make a profit. Yet, if responsible people in positions of authority deem a certain book unsuitable for readers, shouldn't publishers do the right thing for the larger society and comply with demands to cease its publication? This was the argument presented by morals crusader Anthony Comstock in 1873 when he established the New York Society for the Suppression of Vice. It was the argument used on the evening of May 10, 1933, in Berlin when Nazi propaganda chief Joseph

Goebbels put a torch to a bonfire that consumed 20,000 books. It was the argument made in 1953 when U.S. Senator Joseph McCarthy demanded the removal of more than 100 books from U.S. diplomatic libraries because of their "procommunist" slant. (Among them was Thomas Paine's *Common Sense*.) It is the argument made today by people like Arizona's State Superintendent of Schools John Huppenthal who, in 2012, ordered the removal of Shakespeare's *The Tempest* from all high school libraries because of its "un-American" focus on colonialism; and by the Culpeper County (Virginia) school board in 2010 when it pulled Anne Frank's diary from its curriculum after a lone parental complaint; and in that same year by the Menifee Union School District (California) when it removed *Merriam-Webster's Collegiate Dictionary* from its classrooms, again after a single complaint.

According to the American Library Association Office of Intellectual Freedom and the American Civil Liberties Union, among the library and school books most frequently targeted by modern censors are the *Harry Potter* series, Mark Twain's *The Adventures of Huckleberry Finn*, Harper Lee's *To Kill a Mockingbird*, John Steinbeck's *Of Mice and Men*, the *Goosebumps* series, Alice Walker's *The Color Purple*, and children's favorite *In the Night Kitchen* by Maurice Sendak. One readers' group's list of the 25 banned books that everyone should read is shown in Figure 3.1. With how many are you familiar? Which ones have you read? What is it about each of these books that might have brought it to the censors' attention?

Book publishers can confront censorship by recognizing that their obligations to their industry and to themselves demand that they resist censorship. The book publishing industry and the publisher's role in it are fundamental to the operation and maintenance of our democratic society. Rather than accepting the censor's argument that certain voices require silencing for the good of the culture, publishers in a democracy have an obligation to make the stronger argument that free speech be protected and encouraged. The short list of frequently censored titles in the previous paragraph should immediately make it evident why the power of ideas is worth fighting for. You can read more about censorship in the Cultural Forum box entitled "Americans Don't Burn Books."

1. *To Kill a Mockingbird* by Harper Lee
2. *American Psycho* by Bret Easton Ellis
3. *And Tango Makes Three* by Peter Parnell and Justin Richardson
4. *The Awakening* by Kate Chopin
5. *The Lord of the Rings* by J. R. R. Tolkien
6. *Candide* by Voltaire
7. *Cat's Cradle* by Kurt Vonnegut
8. *Fallen Angels* by Walter Dean Myers
9. *Forever* by Judy Blume
10. *Frankenstein* by Mary Shelley
11. *Harry Potter* series by J. K. Rowling
12. *I Know Why the Caged Bird Sings* by Maya Angelou
13. *Lady Chatterley's Lover* by D. H. Lawrence
14. *Lord of the Flies* by William Golding
15. *Of Mice and Men* by John Steinbeck
16. *Grapes of Wrath* by John Steinbeck
17. *Beloved* by Toni Morrison
18. *A Day No Pigs Would Die* by Robert Newton Peck
19. *The Adventures of Huckleberry Finn* by Mark Twain
20. *The Catcher in the Rye* by J. D. Salinger
21. *The Chocolate War* by Robert Cormier
22. *The Color Purple* by Alice Walker
23. *The Giver* by Lois Lowry
24. *The Fortunes and Misfortunes of the Famous Moll Flanders* by Daniel Defoe
25. *Ulysses* by James Joyce

▲ **Figure 3.1** Banned Books That You Should Read Today: The 25 most challenged books in America.
Source: 25 Banned, 2011

Aliteracy as Self-Censorship

Censors ban and burn books because books are repositories of ideas, ideas that can be read and considered with limited outside influence or official supervision. But what kind of culture develops when, by our own refusal to read books, we figuratively save the censors the trouble of striking the match? **Aliteracy**, wherein people possess the ability to read but are unwilling to do so, amounts to doing the censors' work for them. As Russian immigrant and writer Joseph Brodsky explained when accepting his Nobel Prize for Literature, "Since there are no laws that can protect us from ourselves, no criminal code is capable of preventing a true crime against literature; though we can condemn the material suppression of literature—the persecution of writers, acts of censorship, the burning of books—we are powerless when it comes to its worst violation: that of not reading the books. For that crime, a person pays with his whole life; if the offender is a nation, it pays with its history" (Brodsky, 1987).

The Diary of a Young Girl: The Definitive Edition and Merriam-Webster's Collegiate Dictionary were banned by school boards in 2010, each after a single parental complaint.

In 2007 the National Endowment for the Arts (NEA) released its distillation of several government and foundation studies of Americans' reading habits. *To Read or Not to Read* indicated that we are reading less and our reading proficiency is declining at troubling rates. These trends are particularly strong among older teens and young adults. For example, only 30% of 13-year-olds read almost every day. Fifteen-to-24-year-olds spend only 7 to 10 minutes a day reading anything at all, but 2½ hours a day watching television. Almost half of Americans between 18 and 24 never read books for pleasure. Forty percent of first-year college students (and 35% of seniors) read nothing at all for pleasure, while another 26% (and 28% of seniors) read for pleasure less than one hour a week (Italie, 2007; Thompson, 2007).

NEA chair Dana Gioia summed up the report's findings in four sentences: "We are doing a better job of teaching kids to read in elementary school. But once they enter adolescence, they fall victim to a general culture which does not encourage or reinforce reading. Because these people then read less, they read less well. Because they read less well, they do more poorly in school, in the job market, and in civic life." More than any other, it is the issue of quality of civic life that gives the study its subtitle, *A Question of National Consequence*. Regardless of income, reading correlates closely with quality of social life, voting, political activism, participation in culture and fine arts, volunteerism, charity work, and exercise. Gioia explained, "The habit of regular reading awakens something inside a person that

Daily reading in minutes

Books 21 23 25
Magazines 15 14 9
Newspapers 7 6 3
Online magazines and newspapers * * 2

1999
2004
2009

▶ **Figure 3.2** How Much Do 8- to 18-Year-Olds Read in a Typical Day?
Source: Rideout, Foehr, & Roberts, 2010.

*Not available

makes him or her take their own life more seriously and at the same time develops the sense that other people's lives are real." Added Timothy Shanahan, past president of the International Reading Association, "If you're low in reading ability . . . you're less likely to take part in activities like sports or church. Being low in literacy is self-isolating, tends to push you out of culture altogether" (all quoted in Thompson, 2007, p. C1).

You can see how much a typical young person reads each day in Figure 3.2. How do you account for the declines in newspaper and magazine reading? The 2 minutes a day of online reading hardly makes up for that dip. How can you explain the small rise in book reading? Do you agree with the NEA that this lack of reading for leisure has consequences for our country?

Scope and Structure of the Book Industry

More than 3 million traditional and nontraditional (print-on-demand, self-published, and niche) titles are published in North America each year; readers annually buy nearly three billion books, generating $33 billion in sales (Masnick & Ho, 2012). Today, more books than ever are being published; more people are reading books; more people are writing books. Books that would never have been published are routinely published today (Masnick, 2013).

Categories of Books

The Association of American Publishers divides books into several sales categories:

- *Book club editions* are books sold and distributed (sometimes even published) by book clubs. There are currently more than 300 book clubs in the United States. These organizations offer trade, professional, and more specialized titles—for example, books for aviation aficionados and expensive republications of classic works. The Book of the Month Club, started in 1926, is the best known; the Literary Guild and the Reader's Digest Book Club are also popular.
- *El-hi* are textbooks produced for elementary and high schools.
- *Higher education* are textbooks produced for colleges and universities.
- *Mail-order books*, such as those advertised on television by Time-Life Books, are delivered by mail and usually are specialized series (*The War Ships*) or elaborately bound special editions of classic novels.
- *Mass market paperbacks* are typically published only as paperbacks and are designed to appeal to a broad readership; many romance novels, diet books, and self-help books are in this category.
- *Professional books* are reference and educational volumes designed specifically for professionals such as doctors, engineers, lawyers, scientists, and managers.
- *Religious books* are volumes such as Bibles, catechisms, and hymnals.
- *Standardized tests* are guide and practice books designed to prepare readers for various examinations such as the SAT or the bar exam.
- *Subscription reference books* are publications such as the *Encyclopaedia Britannica*, atlases, and dictionaries bought directly from the publisher rather than purchased in a retail setting.
- **Trade books** can be hard- or softcover and include not only fiction and most nonfiction but also cookbooks, biographies, art books, coffee-table books, and how-to books.
- *University press books* come from publishing houses associated with and often underwritten by universities. They typically publish serious nonfiction and scholarly books. The University of Chicago Press and the University of California Press are two of the better-known university presses, and the Oxford University Press is the oldest publisher in the world.

Trends and Convergence in Book Publishing

Like all the media with which we are familiar, convergence is changing the nature of the book industry. In addition to convergence, contemporary publishing and its relationship with its readers are being reshaped by conglomeration, hypercommercialism and demand for profits, the growth of small presses, restructuring of retailing, and changes in readership.

Convergence

Convergence is altering almost all aspects of the book industry. Most obviously, the Internet is changing the way books are distributed and sold. But this new technology, in the form of **e-publishing**, the publication of books initially or exclusively online, offers a new way for writers' ideas to be published. Even the physical form of books is changing—many of today's "books" are no longer composed of paper pages snug between two covers. As former Random House editor Peter Osnos (2009) explained, "Unlike other printed media, books do not have advertising, so there is none to lose. They don't have subscribers, so holding on to them is not an issue either. The main challenge is to manage inventory, making books available where, when, and how readers want them. And on that score, the advances in gadgetry and the changes in popular [reading] habits over the past decade . . . have produced a major advance" (p. 38). By gadgetry, Osnos means primarily e-books, print on demand (POD), and a host of electronic reading devices.

E-BOOKS Twenty-six-year-old Amanda Hocking had written a dozen novels, mostly young adult romance stories. Rejected by several major publishing houses, the Austin, Minnesota, waitress published nine of her works in 2010 as **e-books**—books downloaded in electronic form from the Internet to computers, dedicated readers, or mobile digital devices. Within a year *My Blood Approves*, *Ascend*, and her other titles sold a million copies, earning her more than $2 million; today she sells 9,000 books a day (Saroyan, 2011). Established authors fare well, too. Stieg Larsson's best seller, *The Girl with the Dragon Tattoo*, sold 300,000 hard copies from 2008 to April 2011. In that time it also sold 1 million e-books, and his trilogy, which includes *The Girl Who Played with Fire* and *The Girl Who Kicked the Hornet's Nest*, combined, sold 3 million digital versions (Bosman, 2011).

Popular acceptance of e-books seemed in place by Christmas Day, 2009, when Amazon reported that for the first time in its history, it sold more e-books than hardcopy volumes in a single day. By summer of 2011, four short years after the introduction of the first e-book, Amazon was selling 105 e-books for every printed book, hardback and paperback ("E-book Sales," 2011). In 2012, 23% of Americans 16 and over read e-books, up from 16% in 2011. In the same timespan, those who read printed books fell from 72% to 67% (Rainie & Duggan, 2012). E-books now total one-quarter of the U.S. book sales (Owen, 2013).

Still, e-publishing's greatest impact may be on new writers. Because anyone with a computer and a novel to sell can bypass the traditional book publishers, first-time authors or writers of small, niche books now have an outlet for their work. An additional advantage of e-publishing, especially for new or small-market authors, is that e-books can be published almost instantly. Stephen King has made enough money selling his books that he can wait the one to two years it typically takes for a traditional novel to be produced once it is in the publisher's hands. Rarely can new authors afford this luxury.

Another advantage is financial. Authors who distribute through e-publishers typically get royalties of 40% to 70%, compared to the 5% to 10% offered by traditional publishers. This lets aspiring writers offer their books for as little as $3 or $4, making those works more attractive to readers willing to take a low-cost chance to find something and someone new and interesting . . . earning writers even more sales. And while traditional book publishers say their lower royalty rates are mandated by the expense of the services they provide, such as editorial assistance and marketing, not to mention the cost of production and distribution, some digital publishers offer a full range of services—copyediting, publishing, securing or commissioning artwork, jacket design, promotion, and in some cases, even hard-copy distribution to brick-and-mortar bookstores.

Print on demand (POD) is another form of e-publishing. Companies such as Xlibris, AuthorHouse, Toby Press, and iUniverse are POD publishers. They store works digitally and, once ordered, a book can be instantly printed, bound, and sent. Alternatively, once ordered, that book can be printed and bound at

▲ Amazon's Kindle, Apple's iPad, and numerous other e-readers are transforming publishing and reading.

a bookstore that has the proper technology. The advantage for publisher and reader is financial. POD books require no warehouse for storage, there are no **remainders** (unsold books returned to publishers to be sold at great discount) to eat into profits, and the production costs, in both personnel and equipment, are tiny when compared to traditional publishing. These factors not only produce less expensive books for readers but greatly expand the variety of books that can and will be published. And although a large publisher like Oxford University Press produces more than 100,000 POD volumes a year (Carnevale, 2005), smaller POD operations can make a profit on as few as 100 orders. Large commercial publishers have also found a place for POD in their business, using the technology to rush hot, headline-inspired books to readers. In 2008, for the first time, American publishers released more POD titles than new and revised titles produced by traditional methods; in 2010 the ratio was more than three to one. The availability of POD books will grow even more with the continued rollout of the Espresso Book Machine, a joint effort of several major book publishers. The devices, which can print and bind a 300-page book in four minutes, is available in hundreds of locations across the globe and has access to more than 7 million books available from self-publishers, a growing list of traditional publishing houses, and in the public domain.

Smartphones, Tablets, and e-Readers

Convergence is reshaping reading in other interesting ways. Several websites—www.fictionwise.com, www.gutenberg.org, and www.memoware.com, for example—offer e-books specifically for PDAs, smartphones, tablets, and **e-readers**, digital books with the appearance of traditional books but content that is digitally stored and accessed. Previous attempts at producing e-readers had failed, but the 2006 unveiling of the Sony Reader, dubbed the iBook after its sibling the iPod, has proven so successful that it was soon followed by several similar devices, such as Amazon's Kindle, Kindle DX, and Kindle for Blackberry, Apple's iPad, and Barnes & Noble's Nook. In addition, smartphone and tablet applications like Stanza and ScrollMotion and other e-reading alternatives such as online publisher Zinio, which makes titles available for most digital devices, and Vook, which offers video-enhanced books, also appeared. At the end of 2011, nearly one in three Americans owned at least one e-reader or tablet (Ortutay, 2012), and more than 807 million people around the world own an e-book-compatible advanced personal device (Sheehy, 2011). Issues such as the number of available titles,

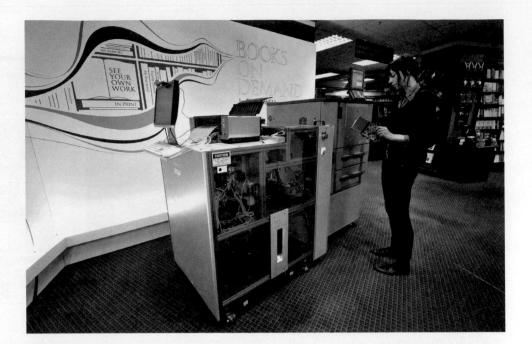

► The Espresso Book Machine—7 million titles from traditional publishers, the public domain, and self-publishers, each available in four minutes.

payment to publishers and authors, ownership of digital versus print rights, cost of digital versus hard copies, presence of advertising, and distribution of ad income are constantly debated and negotiated between the rivals, publishers, and readers.

Nonetheless, readers have welcomed the devices and publishers have understandably responded, given the industry's belief that "any business that requires a truck these days, forget it" (Thompson, 2009). Hundreds of thousands of in- and out-of-print titles are available for **platform agnostic publishing**—digital and hard-copy books available for any and all reading devices. And those reading devices themselves will continue to evolve, with advances in existing flexible screens so thin they can be rolled up and "open" e-readers that let users cut, paste, and exchange text as is routine on other computers. In anticipation of the growth of e-publishing, some traditional publishers, Dorchester Publishing, for example, have abandoned bound paper books altogether.

For readers in search of almost every book ever written or for those who want to search the contents of almost every book ever written (say, for references to the Civil War even though "Civil War" does not appear in the title), there are several developments. Online bookseller Amazon.com has scanned every page of every in-print book into its Search Inside the Book. That means anyone registered (it's free, but readers must provide a credit card number) can eventually search millions (according to Amazon) of books for just about any topic or idea. The pages cannot be downloaded, and there is a limit to how much searching a given reader can do in a specified period of time. Of course, Amazon's goal is to sell more books (you just might want to order one of the books your search has uncovered), but it is developing its own POD service that will provide, instantly, any book searched and requested. Several nonprofit organizations are also making searchable and downloadable books available online. Project Gutenberg will offer 1 million noncopyrighted classics; the Million Book Project has set as its goal 1 million government and older titles; the Open Content Alliance seeks to digitize the holdings of its many member libraries; and the International Children's Digital Library and the Rosetta Project hope to make downloadable tens of thousands of current and antique children's books from around the world.

Whereas these efforts at digitizing books have been generally well regarded, the same cannot be said for Google Print. Internet giant Google announced in late 2005 its intention to make available online 15 million books from the New York Public Library and the libraries of the University of Michigan, Stanford University, Harvard University, and Oxford University. The vast majority, 90%, would be out-of-print books not bound by copyright (see Chapter 14). The problem, however, is Google's plan to hold the entire text of all works, in and out of print, on its servers, making only small, fair-use portions of copyrighted works available to Web users. Initially, many publishers agreed to participate if the complete text of their copyrighted works could be stored on *their* servers, but Google refused. A series of lawsuits from the Author's Guild and five major publishers followed despite Google's insistence that it would protect the interests of authors and publishers as it strives to "organize the world's information and make it universally accessible and useful," in the words of the company itself. In October 2008, the parties reached an agreement in which Google set aside $125 million to establish a "Books Rights Registry" to ensure that authors are compensated for the use of their work, including payment from income earned by ads placed next to their works. Within a year Google, digitizing 1,000 pages an hour, reached the 10-million-book mark (Timpane, 2010).

Conglomeration

More than any other medium, the book industry was dominated by relatively small operations. Publishing houses were traditionally staffed by fewer than 20 people, the large majority by fewer than 10. Today, however, although more than 81,000 businesses call themselves book publishers, only a very small percentage produces four or more titles a year (Teague, 2005). The industry is dominated now by the so-called Big 5 publishing houses—Penguin Random House, Hachette, HarperCollins, Macmillan, and Simon & Schuster—and a few other large concerns, like Time Warner Publishing. Each of these giants was once, sometimes with another name, an independent book publisher. All are now part of large national or international corporate conglomerates. These major publishers control more than 80% of all U.S. book sales. Even e-publishing, heralded by some as the future of book publishing, is dominated by the big companies. Not only do all the major houses and booksellers maintain e-publishing units, but even POD sites such as Xlibris (Penguin Random House) and iUniverse (Barnes & Noble) are wholly or partly owned by these giants.

Opinion is divided on the benefit of corporate ownership. The positive view is that the rich parent company can infuse the publishing house with necessary capital, enabling it to attract better authors or to take gambles on new writers that would, in the past, have been impossible. Another plus is that the corporate parent's other media holdings can be used to promote and repackage the books for greater profitability. Neither of these benefits is insignificant, argue many industry insiders, because book publishing is more like gambling than business. Literary agent Eric Simonoff says the industry is "unpredictable . . . the profit margins are so small, the cycles (from contract to publication) are so incredibly long" and there is an "almost total lack of market research" (quoted in Boss, 2007, p. 3.6). Fiction writer James Patterson, for example, suffered 12 rejections for *The Thomas Berryman Number* before Little, Brown in 1976 accepted this first novel. Patterson has since rewarded his publisher with 51 *New York Times* best sellers, 35 of which were Number Ones. Since 2006, one out of every 17 hardcover books bought in America was written by James Patterson, and in 2009 alone he sold 14 million books in 38 different languages (Mahler, 2010). "It's guesswork," says Doubleday editor in chief Bill Thomas. "The whole thing is educated guesswork, but guesswork nonetheless. You just try to make sure your upside mistakes make up for your downside mistakes" (quoted in Boss, 2007, p. 3.6).

The negative view is that as publishing houses become just one in the parent company's long list of enterprises, product quality suffers as important editing and production steps are eliminated to maximize profits. Before conglomeration, publishing was often described as a **cottage industry**; that is, publishing houses were small operations, closely identified with their personnel—both their own small staffs and their authors. The cottage imagery, however, extends beyond smallness of size. There was a quaintness and charm associated with publishing houses—their attention to detail, their devotion to tradition, the care they gave to their façades (their reputations). The world of corporate conglomerates has little room for such niceties, as profit dominates all other considerations. Critics of corporate ownership saw profits-over-quality at play in 2007 when Simon & Schuster, owned by broadcast conglomerate CBS, announced its partnership with MediaPredict, a data collection website that uses readers' "collective judgment" to determine which book ideas to sign. Asking readers to "vote" on a proposed book's likelihood of success, they argued, is akin to the *American Idolization* of the publishing industry and a guarantee of mediocrity.

Demand for Profits and Hypercommercialism

The threat from conglomeration is seen in the parent company's overemphasis on the bottom line—that is, profitability at all costs. Unlike in the days when G. P. Putnam's sons and the Schuster family actually ran the houses that carried their names, critics fear that now little pride is taken in the content of books and that risk taking (tackling controversial issues, experimenting with new styles, finding and nurturing unknown authors) is becoming rarer and rarer.

Daniel Menaker, fiction editor for the *New Yorker*, explains, "Being a book editor is often, on balance, a rum game. The arts—high and low—have a way of moving forward, backward, or to the side which leaves their servants perpetually scrambling to catch up with and make sense of their direction and their very nature. Profit, when it gets into bed with them, doesn't like the unpredictability of the arts. It tries to rationalize them and make them financially reliable. Can't be done" (2009). As a result, Jason Epstein, longtime editor at Random House and founder of Anchor Books, writes that his is an "increasingly distressed industry" mired in "severe structural problems." Among them are a retail bookselling system that favors "brand name" authors and "a bestseller-driven system of high royalty advances." He says that contemporary publishing is "overconcentrated," "undifferentiated," and "fatally rigid" (quoted in Feldman, 2001, p. 35). To Menaker, Epstein, and other critics of conglomeration, the industry seems overwhelmed by a blockbuster mentality—lust for the biggest-selling authors and titles possible, sometimes with little consideration for literary merit. Recently, Justin Timberlake, formerly of the pop group 'N Sync, received a seven-figure advance for his first novel, *Crossover Dribble*. Michael Crichton got $40 million for a two-book deal from HarperCollins; Tom Clancy, $45 million for two books from Penguin Putnam; Mary Higgins Clark, $64 million for five books from Simon & Schuster. Random House offered Lena Dunham, creator of television's *Girls*, $3.7 million for her first book, *Not That Kind of Girl*, and Gotham Books paid a five-figure advance for *Here's the Situation* by *Jersey Shore* star, Mike "The Situation" Sorrentino. "Gossipy, inbred, lunch-dependent, and about two years behind the rest of the nation, corporate publishing is now in the business of sabotaging the very system it's supposed to keep vital," wrote Pat Holt, editor of industry website Holt Unlimited. Instead of "selecting good books" and finding a "creative, devoted, and adventurous way to sell them, the big houses continually peddle bland products that are gradually driving readers away" (quoted in "The Crisis in Publishing," 2003, p. 22). As the resources and energies of publishing houses are committed to a small number of superstar writers and blockbuster books, smaller, more interesting, possibly more serious or important books do not get published. If these books cannot get published, they will not be written. We will be denied their ideas in the cultural forum. We will see, but as we read earlier in this chapter, it is converged technologies like POD and e-books that may well be the vehicle to ensure those ideas access to the forum and us to them.

Publishers attempt to offset the large investments they do make through the sale of **subsidiary rights**, that is, the sale of the book, its contents, and even its characters to filmmakers, paperback publishers, book clubs, foreign publishers, and product producers like T-shirt, poster, coffee cup, and greeting card manufacturers. For example, based on the success of his first book, *Cold Mountain*, Charles Frazier's one-page proposal for his second novel earned his publisher $3 million for the film rights alone from Paramount Pictures. The industry itself estimates that many publishers would go out of business if it were not for the sale of these rights. Writers such as Michael Crichton (*Jurassic Park*), John Grisham (*The Client*), and Gay Talese (*Thy Neighbor's Wife*) can command as much as $2.5 million for the film rights to their books. Although this is good for the profitability of the publishers and the superstar authors, critics fear that those books with the greatest subsidiary sales value will receive the most publisher attention.

As greater and greater sums are tied up in blockbusters, and as subsidiary rights therefore grow in importance, the marketing, promotion, and public relations surrounding a book become crucial. This leads to the additional fear that only the most promotable books will be published—the stores are flooded with Martha Stewart books, celebrity picture books, unauthorized biographies of celebrities, and tell-all autobiographies from the children of famous people.

The importance of promotion and publicity has led to an increase in the release of **instant books**. What better way to unleash millions of dollars of free publicity for a book than to base it on an event currently on the front page and the television screen? Publishers see these opportunities and then initiate the projects. For example, written in 48 hours by James Clench, *William and Kate: A Royal Love Story* was in bookstores 10 days after their 2010 engagement was announced by Buckingham Palace. Lost in the wake of instant books, easily promotable authors and titles, and blockbusters, critics argue, are books of merit, books of substance, and books that make a difference.

"We have a calendar based on the book, stationery based on the book, an audiotape of the book, and a videotape of the movie based on the book, but we don't have the book."

▲ © Michael Maslin/The New Yorker Collection/ www.cartoonbank.com

Several other recent events suggest that the demand for profits is bringing even more hypercommercialism to the book business. One trend is the "Hollywoodization" of books. Potential synergies between books, television, and movies have spurred big media companies such as Viacom, Time Warner, and News Corp. to invest heavily in publishing, buying up houses big and small. Some movie studios are striking "exclusive" deals with publishers—for example, Walden Media teams with Penguin Young Readers, Focus Films with Random House, and Paramount with Simon & Schuster. In addition, in 2005 ReganBooks (owned by HarperCollins, which, in turn, is owned by News Corp.) moved its offices from New York to Los Angeles to be in a better position to develop material that has both book and film potential. In that same year, studios Warner Brothers, Columbia, Paramount, DreamWorks, Fox, New Line, Imagine, Tribeca, and Revolution Films set up operations in New York City to find books and "mine magazine articles, theater, and other properties" that can be converted to screen fare (Fleming, 2005, p. 3). In 2007 Random House and Focus Features announced that they would begin coproducing feature films based on the former's titles. Critics fear

◀ Typical of thousands of small publishing houses, Ten Speed Press offers an array of interesting, odd, or otherwise "small" books that larger publishers may ignore.

▲ *Jersey Shore* star Mike Sorrentino's treatise on GTL (gym, tan, laundry), *Here's the Situation*.

that only those books with the most synergistic potential will be signed and published. Advocates argue just the opposite—a work that might have had limited profit potential as a "mere" book, and therefore gone unpublished, just might find a home across several mutually promoting platforms. They point to *Sideways*, a small-selling book that became a best-selling book after the movie it inspired became a hit.

Another trend that has created much angst among book traditionalists is the paid product placement. Movies and television have long accepted payments from product manufacturers to feature their brands in their content, but it was not until May 2000 that the first paid-for placement appeared in a fiction novel. Bill Fitzhugh's *Cross Dressing*, published by Avon, contains what are purchased commercials for Seagram liquor. Fay Weldon followed suit in 2001, even titling her book *The Bulgari Connection*, after her sponsor, a jewelry company by the same name. *Cathy's Book*, from Perseus/Running Press, pushed Cover Girl cosmetics, but public criticism from several sources, including Consumer Alert and the *New York Times* editorial board, led the publisher to abandon product placement when the title went to paperback in 2008. As with other media that accept product placements, critics fear that content will be bent to satisfy sponsors rather than serve the quality of the work itself. For example, on contract with carmaker Ford, Carole Matthews, British writer of "edgy romantic comedy [novels] aimed at young contemporary women," penned a scene in which her heroine is "whizzing around Buckinghamshire in Imogene, my rather snazzy Ford Fiesta complete with six-CD changer, air-conditioning, and thoroughly comfy seats." Said Matthews, "I've been very pleased with Ford in that they haven't put any constraints on my writing at all." But, asks author and social critic Jim Hightower (2004b), how free was she to write something akin to "whizzing around Buckinghamshire, my snazzy Ford Fiesta sputtered and died on me again, just as the six-CD changer went on the fritz and spewed blue smoke in my face" (p. 3)?

Growth of Small Presses

The overcommercialization of the book industry is mitigated somewhat by the rise in the number of smaller publishing houses. Although these smaller operations are large in number, they account for a very small proportion of books sold. Nonetheless, as recently as seven years ago there were 20,000 U.S. book publishers. Today there are more than 81,000, the vast majority being small presses. They cannot compete in the blockbuster world. By definition *alternative*, they specialize in specific areas such as the environment, feminism, gay issues, and how-to. They can also publish writing otherwise uninteresting to bigger houses, such as poetry and literary commentary. Relying on specialization and narrowly targeted marketing, books such as Ralph Nader and Clarence Ditlow's *The Lemon Book*, published by Moyer Bell, Claudette McShane's *Warning! Dating May Be Hazardous to Your Health*, published by Mother Courage Press, and *Split Verse*, a book of poems about divorce published by Midmarch Arts, can not only earn healthy sales but also make a difference in their readers' lives. And what may seem surprising, it is the Internet, specifically Amazon, that is boosting the fortunes of these smaller houses. Because it compiles data on customer preferences (books bought, browsed, recommended to others, or wished for), it can make recommendations to potential buyers, and, quite often, those recommendations are from small publishers that the buyer might never have considered (or never have seen at a brick-and-mortar retailer). In other words, Amazon levels the book industry playing field. As Kent Sturgis, president of the Independent Book Publishers Association, explained, "All publishers are basically equal, because just about all publishers' titles are on Amazon and can be delivered to your door in a couple of days" (Gillespie, 2005, p. B2). Amazon even set up a special program in 1998, Advantage, to help smaller publishers with payment and shipping.

Restructuring of Book Retailing

There are approximately 20,000 bookstores in the United States, but the number is dwindling as small, independent operations find it increasingly difficult to compete with such chains as Barnes & Noble, Borders, and Books-A-Million. But the big chains themselves are having trouble surviving as well. As recently as 2003 the chain stores, located primarily in malls with heavy pedestrian traffic, controlled about 20% of all books sold in America. Borders alone had 1,249 stores under its own name and Waldenbooks. In 2011, however, it filed for bankruptcy and closed 200 of its remaining 642 shops (Lowrey, 2011). The remaining chains have trouble competing with online retailers like Amazon, the explosion of POD, and the rapid migration of books from paper to the electronic screens of laptops, tablet computers, e-readers, and smart phones.

Where they have prospered it is because their size enables them to purchase inventory cheaply and then offer discounts to shoppers. Because their location attracts shoppers, they can also profitably stock nonbook merchandise such as audio- and videotapes, CDs, computer games, calendars, magazines, and greeting cards for the drop-in trade. But high-volume, high-traffic operations tend to deal in high-volume books. To book traditionalists, this only encourages the industry's blockbuster mentality. When the largest bookstores in the country order only the biggest sellers, the small books get lost. When floor space is given over to Garfield coffee mugs and pop star calendars, there is even less room for small but potentially interesting books. Although big bookselling chains have their critics, they also have their defenders. At least the big titles, CDs, and cheap prices get people into bookstores, the argument goes. Once folks begin reading, even if it is trashy stuff, they might move on to better material. People who never buy books will never read books.

Indies and chains also have to deal with the discount stores such as Target, Walmart, and Costco, which together control 30% of the American book market. As a result, today there are only 1,500 independent booksellers in the United States, operating 1,900 outlets. Twenty years ago there were 4,700 independents with 5,500 storefronts (Zipp, 2013). Using their small size and independence to their advantage, the independents counter the chains and discount stores with expert, personalized service provided by a reading-loving staff, coffee and snack bars, cushioned chairs

◀ Personalized service, cushioned chairs, slow browsing, and intimate readings by favorite authors sustain today's independent booksellers. Here, adolescent literature novelist Erin Dionne reads for an adoring group of young fans.

feelings of many of our good local folk and offending everyone except like-minded racists? As the s.o.b. began to spout, the TV guys folded up their gear, the radio folks hit the off button, and I pocketed my notebook" (2010, p. 3).

Is ignoring the rants of racists responsible media practice, or is it meeting censorship with more censorship?

Few acts of protest are as universally reviled in America as book burning. "We have gone to war with people who do burn books," wrote author James Boyce, "Adolph Hitler comes to mind. Stalin. Pol Pot. There are others. Our military graveyards are full of the men and women who protected us, who gave their lives for us. Not one soldier has ever died so we could burn books" (2010). Americans don't burn books. Such a fundamental truth about our democracy would seem beyond debate, but book burning blazed across the cultural forum in 2011 when Florida Pastor Terry Jones torched a kerosene-soaked Koran, the Muslim holy book. Jones leads the Dove World Outreach Center, a church with a membership short of 50, yet his eight-minute mock "trial" and "conviction" of the Koran for "crimes against humanity" drew national media attention. In response, protestors in Afghanistan killed 10 United Nations workers (Thorp, 2011).

Enter your voice. Why did an abhorrent act committed by a fringe pastor of a tiny church attract the attention of the major American broadcast, cable, and print news organizations? Was it that the act itself—book burning—is so repellant that it warranted coverage? Was it because it was the Koran, a Muslim book? What if it had been the Christian Bible? The Jewish Torah? What is it about books—as opposed to other forms of media—that generate this kind of emotion? How much blame do you put on Jones for the death of those

> "Not one soldier has ever died so we could burn books."

people in Afghanistan? How much blame do you put on the media? Might the country have been better served if the media had ignored Jones? Consider veteran reporter Tom Gardner's recounting of how he covered a Ku Klux Klan "press conference" in 1980s Alabama. Caucusing with other reporters, he asked "if any of them thought this was a news story worth covering. Nope. Then why would we cover this non-event, letting this racist jerk hurt the

and sofas for slow browsing, and intimate readings by favorite authors. In fact, so successful have these devices been that the big stores now are copying them. Barnes & Noble, for example, sponsors a program it calls Discover to promote notable first novels, and Borders does the same with Original Voices. Not only do these efforts emulate services more commonly associated with smaller independents, but they also help blunt some of the criticism suffered by the chains, specifically that they ignore new and smaller-selling books. Still, the big operations cannot or will not emulate some strategies. Specialization is one. Religious, feminist, and animal-lover bookstores exist. The in-store book club for children or poetry fans, for example, is another small-store strategy.

Another alternative to the big mall chain store is buying books online. Amazon.com is the best known of the online book sales services. Thorough, fast, and well stocked, Amazon boasts low overhead, and that means better prices for readers. In addition, its website offers book buyers large amounts of potentially valuable information. Once online, customers can identify the books that interest them, read synopses, check reviews from multiple sources, read sample pages from a book, and see comments not only from other readers but sometimes from the authors and publishers as well. Of course, they can also order books. The Seattle company controls more than half of the U.S. book business across all formats and 60% of the e-book market (Auletta, 2012). It promises to dominate even more with innovations such as the sale of used e-books and self-publishing platforms Kindle Single (for short e-books selling for $2.99) and Kindle Worlds, an outlet for original fan fiction self-publishing.

DEVELOPING MEDIA LITERACY SKILLS

The Lessons of Harry Potter

The excitement surrounding the release in July 2007 of the seventh and final installment of J. K. Rowling's series on youthful British sorcerer Harry Potter offers several important lessons for the media-literate person. Publication of *Harry Potter and the Deathly Hallows* highlighted several elements of media literacy and called into play a number of media literacy skills. For example, its huge appeal to young people can be used to examine one element of media literacy, understanding content as a text providing insight into our culture and lives. Just why have these books resonated so strongly with young readers? The controversy surrounding the numerous efforts to have the series banned from schools and libraries as antireligious and anti-Christian and its status as the "most challenged" (censored) children's literature in the United States call into play the particular media literacy skill of developing the ability and willingness to effectively and meaningfully understand content.

The publishing industry classifies the *Harry Potter* books as juvenile literature. But their phenomenal reception by readers of all ages suggests these works not only have broader appeal but are in themselves something very special. The initial U.S. printing of a *Harry Potter* book is about 14 million copies—100 times that of a normal best seller. Although *Deathly Hallows* was not available for sale until July 21, 2007, by the first week of February—23 weeks before its release—it reached the Number One spot on Amazon's best-seller list. The seven *Harry Potters* combined have sold more than 450 million copies worldwide, and two-thirds of all American children have read at least one edition. The *Potter* series has been published in over 67 languages (including Greek, Latin, and "Americanized English") in more than 200 countries. *Potter* books occupy spots 1, 2, 3, and 4 on the all-time fastest-selling booklist.

What has been Harry Potter's impact on reading? In 1963 the Gallup polling organization found that fewer than half of all Americans said they had read a book all the way through in the previous year. But soon after the release of *The Prisoner of Azkaban* in 1999, that number was 84% (Quindlen, 2000). Nobody would claim that Harry alone was responsible, but *Newsweek*'s Anna Quindlen speculated that he had helped "create a new generation of inveterate readers" (p. 64). Fright master Stephen King agreed, writing, "If these millions of readers are awakened to the wonders and rewards of fantasy at 11 or 12 . . . well, when they get to age 16 or so, there's this guy named King" (as quoted in Garchik, 2000, p. D10). Caroline

▼ Harry Potter, the little wizard who launched a million readers.

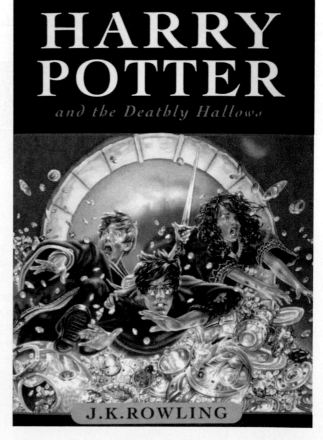

Ward, president of the American Library Association's Services to Children, said, "It's hard to believe that one series of books could almost turn an entire nation back to reading, but that is not an exaggeration," and Diane Roback, children's book editor at *Publishers Weekly*, cited "'the Harry Potter halo effect,' in which children come into stores and libraries asking for books that resemble the Rowling series" (*USA Today*, 2000, p. E4). A Scholastic Books survey of 500 *Harry Potter* readers aged 5 to 7 indicated that 51% said they did not read books for fun until they started reading the series. Three-quarters said Harry had made them interested in reading other books (Rich, 2007), and they did, as data from 2008 and 2009 show that sales of juvenile books were the strongest of any category in those years (Lowman, 2010).

One element of media literacy is the development of an awareness of the impact of media, and the *Harry Potter* series has amply demonstrated its influence. But its wild success is used by many media critics to castigate both media professionals who underestimate their audiences *and* audience members who encourage that underestimation. In other words, the success (and profitability) of this well-written, thoughtful, high-quality content stood in stark contrast to what critics contend is a steady decline in quality in other media, particularly advertiser-supported media such as radio and television. The argument is simple: Broadcasters, especially the major national television networks, respond to falling viewership not by improving content but by lowering its intelligence and worth. Whereas the *Harry Potter* books get better (and longer; *Deathly Hallows* fills 759 pages) in response to reader enthusiasm, network television dumbs down, giving its audience *Fear Factor*, *Here Comes Honey Boo Boo*, and other so-called reality programming.

And radio, as you will see in Chapter 6, has responded to years of declining levels of listenership and the loss of interest among its young core audience not with new, imaginative programming but with more homogenization, automation, and the disappearance of local programming and news. The pressures on advertiser-supported media are somewhat different from those on books and film; with the latter two, readers and moviegoers express their desires and tastes directly through the purchase of content (the books themselves and tickets, respectively). But media-literate people must ask why their exodus from a particular medium is not more often met with the presentation of better fare. Harry Potter shows that an audience that develops heightened expectations can and will have those expectations met.

MEDIA LITERACY CHALLENGE
Literacy: Limiting Access to Books in School

The *Harry Potter* books have been best sellers, but they have also been the frequent target of people wanting to censor them from school libraries. You may never have read any of these works, but consider the possible reasons that parents might not want their children to read certain books without their knowledge and then answer the following questions. To do so will call into play important components of media literacy, *the development of an understanding of the ethical and moral obligations of those who make (and dispense) media content and the awareness of media content as "texts" that provide insight into our culture*. Two media literacy skills are also involved, *the ability to distinguish emotional from reasoned reactions when responding to content* and *the ability to think critically about media messages*.

Your challenge is to answer these questions. Is it ever okay for groups outside the school, parents or concerned citizens for example, to choose not to allow certain books in their schools? Why or why not? If you think it is appropriate to ask (or even insist) that movies, TV, video games, and recordings used in schools have warning labels or that parents who object to their children's exposure to that content be allowed to "opt out," would you hold books to those same controls? Should other in-school media be subject to greater control than books? Why or why not? Is it better to have children reading controversial books as long as it encouraged them to read or would it be better if those children were not reading at all? Which is the greater "evil"? You can approach this challenge as either an opportunity for personal reflection, committing your thoughts to paper, or you can set it up as a debate, for example the No Limits versus the Some Limits versus the Strong Limits.

Resources for Review and Discussion

REVIEW POINTS: TYING CONTENT TO LEARNING OUTCOMES

▶ **Outline the history and development of the publishing industry and the book itself as a medium.**

- ► Although the first printing press came to the Colonies in 1638, books were not central to early colonial life, but books and pamphlets were at the heart of the colonists' revolt against England in the 1770s.
- ► Developments in the 18th and 19th centuries, such as improvements in printing, the flowering of the American novel, and the introduction of the paperback, helped make books a mass medium.

▶ **Describe the cultural value of books and the implications of censorship for democracy.**

- ► Books have cultural value because they are agents of social and cultural change; important cultural repositories; windows on the past; important sources of personal development; sources of entertainment, escape, and personal reflection; mirrors of culture; and because the purchase and reading of a book is a much more individual, personal activity than consuming advertiser-supported or heavily promoted media.
- ► Censorship, both formal and in the form of people's own aliteracy, threatens these values, as well as democracy itself.

▶ **Explain how the organizational and economic nature of the contemporary book industry shapes the content of books.**

- ► Convergence is reshaping the book industry as well as the reading experience itself through advances such as e-publishing, POD, e-books, e-readers, smartphones and tablets, and several different efforts to digitize most of the world's books.
- ► Conglomeration affects the publishing industry as it has all media, expressing itself through trends such as demand for profit and hypercommercialization.
- ► Demand for profit and hypercommercialization manifest themselves in the increased importance placed on subsidiary rights, instant books, "Hollywoodization," and product placement.
- ► Book retailing is undergoing change; large chains dominate the business but continue to be challenged by imaginative, high-quality independent booksellers. Much book buying has also gravitated to the Internet.

▶ **Act as a more media-literate consumer of books, especially in considering their uniqueness in an increasingly mass-mediated, media-converged world.**

- ► The wild success of the *Harry Potter* series holds several lessons for media-literate readers, not the least of which is that people value quality media content.

KEY TERMS

linotype, 51	trade books, 57	e-reader, 59
offset lithography, 51	e-publishing, 58	platform agnostic publishing, 60
dime novels, 51	e-book, 58	cottage industry, 61
pulp novels, 51	print on demand (POD), 59	subsidiary rights, 62
aliteracy, 55	remainders, 59	instant book, 63

QUESTIONS FOR REVIEW

1. What were the major developments in the modernization of the printing press?
2. Why were the early colonists not a book-reading population?
3. What was the Stamp Act? Why did colonial printers object to it?
4. What factors allowed the flowering of the American novel, as well as the expansion of the book industry, in the 1800s?
5. Who developed the paperback in England? In the United States?
6. Name six reasons books are an important cultural resource.
7. What are the major categories of books?
8. What is the impact of conglomeration on the book industry?
9. What are the products of increasing hypercommercialism and demands for profit in the book industry?
10. What are e-books, e-readers, and e-publishing?

connect

For further review, go to the LearnSmart study module for this chapter.

QUESTIONS FOR CRITICAL THINKING AND DISCUSSION

1. Do you envision books ever again having the power to move the nation as they did in Revolutionary or antislavery times? Why or why not?
2. Are you proud of your book-reading habits? Why or why not? This chapter mentioned someone named Mark Twain. Who is this?
3. Under what circumstances is censorship permissible? Whom do you trust to make the right decision about what you should and should not read? If you were a librarian, under what circumstances would you pull a book?

Newspapers 4

Learning Objectives

Newspapers were at the center of our nation's drive for independence and have a long history as the people's medium. The newspaper was also the first mass medium to rely on advertising for financial support, changing the relationship between audience and media from that time on. After studying this chapter you will be able to

▶ Outline the history and development of the newspaper industry and the newspaper itself as a medium.

▶ Identify how the organizational and economic nature of the contemporary newspaper industry shapes the content of newspapers.

▶ Describe the relationship between the newspaper and its readers.

▶ Explain changes in the newspaper industry brought about by converging technologies and how those alterations may affect the medium's traditional role in our democracy.

▶ Apply key newspaper-reading media literacy skills, especially in interpreting the relative placement of stories and use of photos.

Has reading the newspaper become old-fashioned?

YOU STRUGGLE OVER YOUR APPLICATION. The last time you had to do something like this was four years ago when you were in high school; still, here you are, filling out paperwork, hoping to get into graduate school. What's making it especially tough, though, is your friends' constant teasing. Grad school, they say, isn't such a bad idea, but *journalism* grad school!? Aren't newspapers dying? Didn't the Internet kill journalism?

But you know better. Yes, your friends are half right; thousands of newspaper journalists have lost their jobs in the last decade (Edmonds, Guskin & Rosenstiel, 2011). But you did your research. You also know that the Bureau of Labor Statistics reports that by 2016, entry-level positions for journalists will increase by 2% and the need for experienced writers and editors will grow by 10%. You also know that applications to journalism graduate programs are exploding (Herskowitz, 2011) because newspapers are not dead, they're simply undergoing *disruptive transition* (remember to use that in your essay!). "Many young people seem to be excited by the turmoil in journalism and see it as an opportunity to get in on something new, rather than as a threat," wrote one journalism school dean. "The main problem in journalism today lies on the supply side, not the demand side" (Lemann, 2009, p. B8). He's right; people are reading more news than ever before, maybe not on paper, but they're reading it; someone's got to write it (remember to use this, too!).

And despite your friends' skepticism, your research also showed you that most American newspapers remain financially healthy, many not just surviving, but thriving (Edmonds, 2013b). So j-school it is. You want to be on the inside as the daily paper finds its new place in the tumultuous media environment. *Disruptive transition*, man, that's good!

In this chapter we examine that disruptive transition and what it means for the relationship between the newspaper and its readers. We start with a look at the medium's roots, beginning with the first papers, following them from Europe to colonial America, where many of the traditions of today's free press were set. We study the cultural changes that led to the creation of the penny press and to competition between these mass circulation dailies that gave us "yellow journalism."

We then review the modern newspaper in terms of its size and scope. We discuss different types of newspapers and the importance of newspapers as an advertising

1600	1700

100 B.C.E. ▲ Acta Diurna in Caesar's Rome

1620 Corantos

~1625 Broadsides

1641 Diurnals

~1660 "Newspaper" enters the language

1665 *Oxford Gazette*

1690 ▲ *Publick Occurrences Both Foreign and Domestick*

1704 *Boston News-Letter*

1721 *New-England Courant's* James Franklin jailed for "scandalous libels"

1729 ▲ Benjamin Franklin's *Pennsylvania Gazette*

1734 The Zenger Trial

1765 Stamp Act

1791 The First Amendment to the Constitution

1798 The Alien and Sedition Acts

medium. The wire and feature services, important providers of newspaper content, are also highlighted.

We then detail how the relationship between medium and audience is shifting as a result of the loss of competition within the industry, hypercommercialism in the guise of commercial pressure on papers' editorial content, the positive and negative impacts of new and converging technology, the rise of online newspapers, and changes in the nature of newspaper readership. Finally, we test our media literacy skill through a discussion of how to read the newspaper—for example, interpreting the relative positioning of stories.

A Short History of Newspapers

The opening vignette makes an important point about contemporary newspapers—they are in a state of disruption, but they are working hard to secure new identities for themselves in an increasingly crowded media environment. As a medium and as an industry, newspapers are poised at the edge of a significant change in their role and operation. The changing relationship between newspapers and readers is part of this upheaval. And while it's not uncommon to read or hear comments such as this one from Microsoft CEO Steve Ballmer, "There will be no media consumption left in 10 years that is not delivered over IP [Internet Protocol] network. There will be no newspapers, no magazines that are delivered in paper form. Everything gets delivered in an electronic form" (in Dumenco, 2008, p. 48), newspapers have faced similar challenges more than once in the past and have survived.

The Earliest Newspapers

In Caesar's time Rome had a newspaper. The **Acta Diurna** (actions of the day), written on a tablet, was posted on a wall after each meeting of the Senate. Its circulation was one, and there is no reliable measure of its total readership. However, it does show that people have always wanted to know what was happening and that others have helped them do so.

1800	1900	2000
1827 The first African American newspaper, *Freedom's Journal*	**1905** ▲ *Chicago Defender*	**2003** Readership Institute circulation study
1828 *Cherokee Phoenix*	**1907** United Press International	**2007** Murdoch buys *Wall Street Journal*
1833 The penny press	**1908** *Christian Science Monitor*	**2009** *Christian Science Monitor* ceases daily publication; *Rocky Mountain News* shuttered; Internet overtakes paper as news source
1844 Introduction of the telegraph	**1909** International News Service	
1847 Frederick Douglass's *North Star*	**1970** Newspaper Preservation Act	**2011** ▲ Apple's Newsstand
1856 The New York Associated Press	**1982** *USA TODAY*	**2012** Association of Alternative Newsweeklies becomes Association of Alternative Newsmedia
1883 Pulitzer's *New York World*, yellow journalism		
1889 ▲ *Wall Street Journal*		

The newspapers we recognize today have their roots in 17th-century Europe. **Corantos**, one-page news sheets about specific events, were printed in English in Holland in 1620 and imported to England by British booksellers who were eager to satisfy public demand for information about Continental happenings that eventually led to what we now call the Thirty Years' War.

Englishmen Nathaniel Butter, Thomas Archer, and Nicholas Bourne eventually began printing their own occasional news sheets, using the same title for consecutive editions. They stopped publishing in 1641, the same year that regular, daily accounts of local news started appearing in other news sheets. These true forerunners of our daily newspaper were called **diurnals**, but by the 1660s the word *newspaper* had entered the English language (Lepore, 2009).

Political power struggles in England at this time boosted the fledgling medium, as partisans on the side of the monarchy and those on the side of Parliament published papers to bolster their positions. When the monarchy prevailed, it granted monopoly publication rights to the *Oxford Gazette*, the official voice of the Crown. Founded in 1665 and later renamed the *London Gazette*, this journal used a formula of foreign news, official information, royal proclamations, and local news that became the model for the first colonial newspapers.

COLONIAL NEWSPAPERS In Chapter 3 we saw how bookseller/print shops became the focal point for the exchange of news and information and how this led to the beginning of the colonial newspaper. It was at these establishments that **broadsides** (sometimes referred to as **broadsheets**), single-sheet announcements or accounts of events imported from England, would be posted. In 1690 Boston bookseller/printer (and coffeehouse owner) Benjamin Harris printed his own broadside, *Publick Occurrences Both Foreign and Domestick*. Intended for continuous publication, the country's first paper lasted only one day. Harris had been critical of local and European dignitaries, and he had also failed to obtain a license.

More successful was Boston postmaster John Campbell, whose 1704 *Boston News-Letter* survived until the Revolution. The paper featured foreign news, reprints of articles from England, government announcements, and shipping news. It was dull, and it was also expensive. Nonetheless, it established the newspaper in the Colonies.

The *Boston News-Letter* was able to survive in part because of government subsidies. With government support came government control, but the buildup to the Revolution helped establish the medium's independence. In 1721 Boston had three papers. James Franklin's *New-England Courant* was the only one publishing without authority. The *Courant* was popular and controversial, but when it criticized the Massachusetts governor, Franklin was jailed for printing "scandalous libels." When released, he returned to his old ways, earning himself and the *Courant* a publishing ban, which he circumvented by installing his younger brother Benjamin as nominal publisher. Ben Franklin soon moved to Philadelphia, and without his leadership the *Courant* was out of business in three years. Its lasting legacy, however, was in proving that a newspaper with popular support could indeed challenge authority.

In Philadelphia, Benjamin Franklin established a print shop and later, in 1729, took over a failing newspaper, which he revived and renamed the *Pennsylvania Gazette*. By combining the income from his bookshop and printing businesses with that from his popular daily, Franklin could run the *Gazette* with significant independence. Even though he held the contract for Philadelphia's official printing, he was unafraid to criticize those in authority. In addition, he began to develop advertising support, which also helped shield his newspaper from government control by decreasing its dependence on official printing contracts for survival. Ben Franklin demonstrated that financial independence could lead to editorial independence. It was not, however, a guarantee.

In 1734 *New York Weekly Journal* publisher John Peter Zenger was jailed for criticizing that colony's royal governor. The charge was seditious libel, and the verdict was based not on the truth or falsehood of the printed words but on whether they had been printed. The criticisms had been published, so Zenger was clearly guilty.

▼ The first daily newspaper to appear in the 13 Colonies, *Publick Occurrences Both Foreign and Domestick*, lasted all of one edition.

But his attorney, Andrew Hamilton, argued to the jury, "For the words themselves must be libelous, that is, false, scandalous and seditious, or else we are not guilty." Zenger's peers agreed, and he was freed. The case of Peter Zenger became a symbol of colonial newspaper independence from the Crown, and its power was evident in the refusal by publishers to accept the Stamp Act in 1765 (see Chapter 3).

NEWSPAPERS AFTER INDEPENDENCE After the Revolution, the new government of the United States had to determine for itself just how free a press it was willing to tolerate. When the first Congress convened under the new Constitution in 1790, the nation's founders debated, drafted, and adopted the first 10 amendments to the Constitution, called the **Bill of Rights**. The **First Amendment** reads:

> Congress shall make no law respecting an establishment of religion, or prohibiting the free exercise thereof; or abridging the freedom of speech, or of the press; or the right of the people peacefully to assemble, and to petition the Government for a redress of grievances.

But a mere eight years later, fearful of the subversive activities of foreigners sympathetic to France, Congress passed a group of four laws known collectively as the **Alien and Sedition Acts**. The Sedition Act made illegal writing, publishing, or printing "any false scandalous and malicious writing" about the president, Congress, or the federal government. So unpopular were these laws with a people who had just waged a war of independence against similar limits on their freedom of expression that they were not renewed when Congress reconsidered them two years later in 1800. We will examine in detail the ongoing commitment to the First Amendment, freedom of the press, and open expression in the United States in Chapter 14.

▲ Benjamin Franklin published America's first political cartoon—"Join, or Die," a rallying call for the Colonies—in his *Pennsylvania Gazette* in 1754.

▼ Volume 1, Number 1 of Benjamin Day's *New York Sun*, the first of the penny papers.

The Modern Newspaper Emerges

At the turn of the 19th century, New York City provided all the ingredients necessary for a new kind of audience for a new kind of newspaper and a new kind of journalism. The island city was densely populated, a center of culture, commerce, and politics, and especially because of the wave of immigrants that had come to its shores, demographically diverse. Add to this growing literacy among working people, and conditions were ripe for the **penny press**, one-cent newspapers for everyone. Benjamin Day's September 3, 1833, issue of the *New York Sun* was the first of the penny papers. Day's innovation was to sell his paper so inexpensively that it would attract a large readership, which could then be "sold" to advertisers. Day succeeded because he anticipated a new kind of reader. He filled the *Sun*'s pages with police and court reports, crime stories, entertainment news, and human interest stories. Because the paper lived up to its motto, "The Sun shines for all," there was little of the elite political and business information that had characterized earlier papers.

Soon there were penny papers in all the major cities. Among the most important was James Gordon Bennett's *New York Morning Herald*. Although more sensationalistic than the *Sun*, the *Herald* pioneered the correspondent system, placing

reporters in Washington, D.C., and other major U.S. cities as well as abroad. Correspondents filed their stories by means of the telegraph, invented in 1844. Horace Greeley's *New York Tribune* was an important penny paper as well. Its nonsensationalistic, issues-oriented, and humanitarian reporting established the mass newspaper as a powerful medium of social action.

THE PEOPLE'S MEDIUM People typically excluded from the social, cultural, and political mainstream quickly saw the value of the mass newspaper. The first African American newspaper was *Freedom's Journal*, published initially in 1827 by John B. Russwurm and the Reverend Samuel Cornish. Forty others soon followed, but it was Frederick Douglass who made best use of the new mass circulation style in his newspaper *The Ram's Horn*, founded expressly to challenge the editorial policies of Benjamin Day's *Sun*. Although this particular effort failed, Douglass had established himself and the minority press as a viable voice for those otherwise silenced. Douglass's *North Star*, founded in 1847 with the masthead slogan "Right is of no Sex—Truth is of no Color—God is the Father of us all, and we are all Brethren," was the most influential African American newspaper before the Civil War.

The most influential African American newspaper after the Civil War, and the first black paper to be a commercial success (its predecessors typically were subsidized by political and church groups), was the *Chicago Defender*. First published on May 5, 1905, by Robert Sengstacke Abbott, the *Defender* eventually earned a nationwide circulation of more than 230,000. Especially after Abbott declared May 15, 1917, the start of "the Great Northern Drive," the *Defender*'s central editorial goal was to encourage southern black people to move north.

"I beg of you, my brothers, to leave that benighted land. You are free men. . . . Get out of the South," Abbott editorialized (as quoted in Fitzgerald, 1999, p. 18). The paper would regularly contrast horrific accounts of southern lynchings with northern African American success stories. Within two years of the start of the Great Drive, more than 500,000 former slaves and their families moved north. Within two more years, another 500,000 followed.

Native Americans found early voice in papers such as the *Cherokee Phoenix*, founded in 1828 in Georgia, and the *Cherokee Rose Bud*, which began operation 20 years later in Oklahoma. The rich tradition of the Native American newspaper is maintained today around the country in publications such as the Oglala Sioux *Lakota Times* and the Shoshone–Bannock *Sho-Ban News*, as well as on the World Wide Web. For example, the *Cherokee Observer* is at www.cherokeeobserver.org; the *Navajo Times* is at navajotimes.com; and *News from Indian Country* can be found at www.indiancountrynews.com.

Throughout this early period of the popularization of the newspaper, numerous foreign-language dailies also began operation, primarily in major cities in which immigrants tended to settle. Sloan, Stovall, and Startt (1993) report that in 1880 there were more than 800 foreign-language newspapers publishing in German, Polish, Italian, Spanish, and various Scandinavian languages. As you'll see later in this chapter, the modern foreign language press and its close cousin, the alternative press, are enjoying significant success in today's era of flat or falling readership for more mainstream papers.

THE FIRST WIRE SERVICES In 1848, six large New York papers, including the *Sun*, the *Herald*, and the *Tribune*, decided to pool efforts and share expenses collecting news from foreign ships docking at the city's harbor. After determining rules of membership and other organizational issues, in 1856 the papers established the first news-gathering (and distribution) organization, the New York Associated Press. Other domestic **wire services** followed—the Associated Press in 1900, the United Press in 1907, and the International News Service in 1909.

This innovation, with its assignment of correspondents to both foreign and domestic bureaus, had a number of important implications. First, it greatly expanded the breadth and scope of coverage a newspaper could offer its readers. This was a boon to dailies wanting to attract as many readers as possible. Greater coverage of distant domestic news helped unite an expanding country while encouraging even more expansion. The United States was a nation of immigrants, and news from people's homelands drew more readers. Second, the nature of reporting began to change. Reporters could now produce stories by rewriting—sometimes a little, sometimes a lot—the actual on-the-spot coverage of others. Finally, newspapers were able to reduce expenses (and increase profits) because they no longer needed to have their own reporters in all locations.

YELLOW JOURNALISM In 1883 Hungarian immigrant Joseph Pulitzer bought the troubled *New York World*. Adopting a populist approach to the news, he brought a crusading, activist style of coverage to numerous turn-of-the-century social problems—growing slums, labor tensions, and failing farms, to name a few. The audience for his "new journalism" was the "common man," and he succeeded in reaching readers with light, sensationalistic news coverage, extensive use of illustrations, and circulation-building stunts and promotions (for example, an around-the-world balloon flight). Ad revenues and circulation figures exploded.

Soon there were other new journalists. William Randolph Hearst applied Pulitzer's successful formula to his *San Francisco Examiner*, and then in 1895 he took on Pulitzer himself in New York. The competition between Hearst's *Morning Journal* and Pulitzer's *World* was so intense that it debased newspapers and journalism as a whole, which is somewhat ironic in that Pulitzer later founded the prize for excellence in journalism that still bears his name.

Drawing its name from the Yellow Kid, a popular cartoon character of the time, **yellow journalism** was a study in excess—sensational sex, crime, and disaster news; giant headlines; heavy use of illustrations; and reliance on cartoons and color. It was

◀ Several of yellow journalism's excesses—dramatic graphics, bold headlines, the reporting of rumor—are evident in this front page from Joseph Pulitzer's *New York World*. Many historians believe that the sinking of the *Maine* was engineered by yellow journalist William Randolph Hearst, publisher of the *New York Morning Journal*, in order to create a war that his papers could cover as a way to build circulation.

successful at first, and other papers around the country adopted all or part of its style. Although public reaction to the excesses of yellow journalism soon led to its decline, traces of its popular features remain. Large headlines, big front-page pictures, extensive use of photos and illustrations, and cartoons are characteristic even of today's best newspapers.

The years between the era of yellow journalism and the coming of television were a time of remarkable growth in the development of newspapers. From 1910 to the beginning of World War II, daily newspaper subscriptions doubled and ad revenues tripled. In 1910 there were 2,600 daily papers in the United States, more than at any time before or since. In 1923, the American Society of Newspaper Editors issued the "Canons of Journalism and Statement of Principles" in an effort to restore order and respectability after the yellow era. The opening sentence of the Canons was, "The right of a newspaper to attract and hold readers is restricted by nothing but considerations of public welfare." The wire services internationalized. United Press International started gathering news from Japan in 1909 and was covering South America and Europe by 1921. In response to the competition from radio and magazines for advertising dollars, newspapers began consolidating into **newspaper chains**—papers in different cities across the country owned by a single company. Hearst and Scripps were among the most powerful chains in the 1920s. For all practical purposes, the modern newspaper had now emerged. The next phase of the medium's life, as we'll soon see, begins with the coming of television.

Newspapers and Their Audiences

Nearly 46 million newspapers are sold daily in the United States, and 44% of Americans report reading a paper or its website every day, 69% at least once a week (Newspaper Association of America, 2011). The industry that serves those readers looks quite different from the one that operated before television became a dominant medium. There are now fewer papers. There are now different types of papers. They deliver the news on different platforms, and more newspapers are part of large chains.

The advent of television at the end of World War II coincided with several important social and cultural changes in the United States. Shorter work hours, more leisure, more expendable cash, movement to the suburbs, and women joining the workforce in greater numbers all served to alter the newspaper–reader relationship. When the war ended, circulation equaled 1.24 papers per American household per day; today that figure is 0.37 per household per day (Gitlin, 2013).

Today, Americans may well buy 46 million papers every day, but in 1970, they bought 62.1 million. The number of daily newspapers also continues to fall. There were more than 1,600 in 1990; the current total is around 1,500. In 2008, the *Baltimore Examiner, New York Sun, Albuquerque Tribune, Cincinnati Post, Kentucky Post,* and *Birmingham Post-Herald* closed shop. In 2009 Denver's 150-year-old *Rocky Mountain News* folded and the 146-year-old *Seattle Post-Intelligencer* converted to Web-only. The 101-year-old *Christian Science Monitor* also shut down its print operation to become an online daily and a weekend newsmagazine. Circulation has suffered 10 consecutive years of decline, and ad revenues are falling at a double-digit pace. Today's newspapers are buffeted by technological and economic change like no other traditional medium.

Scope and Structure of the Newspaper Industry

Today there are more than 9,800 newspapers operating in the United States. Of these, 15% are dailies and the rest are weeklies (77%) and semiweeklies (8%). They have a combined circulation of nearly 130 million. **Pass-along readership**—readers who did not originally purchase the paper—brings 104 million people a day in touch with a

Journalist Chris Hedges wrote, "The death of newsprint represents the end of an era. And news gathering will not be replaced by the Internet. Journalism, at least on the large scale of old newsrooms, is no longer commercially viable. Reporting is time-consuming and labor-intensive. It requires going out and talking to people. It means doing this every day. It means looking constantly for sources, tips, leads, documents, informants, whistle-blowers, new facts and information, untold stories and news. Reporters often spend days finding little or nothing of significance. The work can be tedious and is expensive. And as the budgets of large metropolitan dailies shrink, the very trade of reporting declines." Another reporter, Gary Kamiya, explained why the Internet is not a worthy substitute, "What is really threatened by the decline of newspapers and the related rise of online media is reporting—on-the-ground reporting by trained journalists who know the

> "The papers still must cover their markets; they need content."

subject, have developed sources on all sides, strive for objectivity, and are working with editors who check their facts, steer them in the right direction, and are a further check against unwarranted assumptions, sloppy thinking and reporting, and conscious or unconscious bias" (2009). And yet although "one third of the newspaper newsrooms in America have disappeared," said Charles Lewis of the Investigative Reporting Workshop, "the papers still must cover their markets; they need content" (in Herskowitz, 2011, p. 58).

Over the last several years, hundreds of nonprofit newsrooms—staffed by veteran and newly minted professional journalists—have sprung up to fill the void, hoping to make a difference. Some are funded by foundations, some by voluntary payments from their for-profit media partners, and some, Spot.us for example, practice **crowdfunded journalism**, where journalists pitch stories to readers who contribute small amounts of money to those they want to see completed. Large investigative reporting nonprofits ProPublica and the Center for Public Integrity are backed by major philanthropies like the Ford and Knight Foundations. And while some nonprofit newsrooms are small and serve local communities and local media—for example Backyard News, serving six Harrisburg, Pennsylvania, suburbs, and GrossePointToday.com in Michigan—many maintain partnerships with major national media. The *New York Times* uses the work of nonprofit newsrooms in Chicago, San Francisco, and other locations to strengthen its reporting in those locales. In addition to the *Times*,

major media outlets such as *60 Minutes*, National Public Radio, *Salon*, *USA Today*, NBC-owned television stations, the *Los Angeles Times*, *Bloomberg Businessweek*, and the *Washington Post* make regular use of several nonprofits' investigative reporting on controversial and expensive investigations into issues like natural gas drilling, abuse of federal stimulus dollars, and the failure of many of the nation's coroner and medical examiner offices. Have nonprofit newsrooms made a difference? "We can get to do the kind of investigative and enterprise stories we wouldn't be able to singularly," says public radio's Bill Davis (in Rainey, 2011). The Center for Public Integrity "has won over 40 national journalism awards. ProPublica has won two Pulitzer Prizes, and they've been around only since 2008. The Center for Investigative Reporting, started in '77, has also won dozens of national journalism awards" (Herskowitz, 2011, p. 61). Columbia *Journalism Review* maintains a list of more than 200 nonprofit newsrooms at www.cjr.org/the_news_frontier_database/.

▲ ProPublica, started in 2008, has won two Pulitzer Prizes.

daily and 200 million a week in touch with a weekly. But as we've seen, overall print circulation is falling despite a growing population. Therefore, to have success and to ensure their future, newspapers have had to adjust.

Types of Newspapers

We've cited statistics about dailies and weeklies, but these categories actually include many different types of papers. Let's take a closer look at some of them.

NATIONAL DAILY NEWSPAPERS We typically think of the newspaper as a local medium, our town's paper. But two national daily newspapers enjoy large circulations and significant social and political impact. The older and more respected is the *Wall Street Journal*, founded in 1889 by Charles Dow and Edward Jones. Today, as then, its focus is on the world of business, although its definition of business is broad. The *Journal* has a circulation of 1.5 million, and an average household income of its readers of $150,000 makes it a favorite for upscale advertisers. In 2007 it became part of Rupert Murdoch's News Corp. media empire.

The other national daily is *USA Today*. Founded in 1982, it calls itself "The Nation's Newspaper," and despite early derision from industry pros for its lack of depth and apparent dependence on style over substance, "it shed its lightweight 'McPaper' persona in the 1990s, becoming a serious national paper and luring topflight talent from places like the *Washington Post*" (Smolkin, 2004, p. 20). Today, the paper's daily circulation of 1.4 million suggests that readers welcome its mix of short, lively, upbeat stories; full-color graphics; state-by-state news and sports briefs; and liberal use of easy-to-read illustrated graphs and tables.

LARGE METROPOLITAN DAILIES To be a daily, a paper must be published at least five times a week. The circulation of big-city dailies has dropped over the past 30 years, with the heavy losses of the evening papers offsetting increases for the morning papers. Dailies continue to lose circulation at a rate approaching 10% a year (Rosenstiel & Mitchell, 2011). Many old, established papers, including the *Philadelphia Bulletin* and the *Washington Star*, have stilled their presses in recent years. When the *Chicago Daily News* closed its doors, it had the sixth-highest circulation in the country.

As big cities cease to be industrial centers, homes, jobs, and interests have turned away from downtown. Those large metropolitan dailies that are succeeding have used a number of strategies to cut costs and to attract and keep more suburban-oriented readers. Some publish **zoned editions**—suburban or regional versions of the paper—to attract readers and to combat competition for advertising dollars from the suburban papers. But once-customary features like these zoned editions (*Providence Journal*), stand-alone book review sections (*Chicago Tribune, Washington Post*), weekly magazines (*Los Angeles Times*), classified sections (*Cincinnati Enquirer, Boston Globe*), even daily home delivery (*Cleveland Plain Dealer*) are disappearing as papers big and small battle declining ad revenue and rising production and distribution costs.

The *New York Times* is a special large metropolitan daily. It is a paper local to New York, but the high quality of its reporting and commentary, the reach and depth of both its national and international news, and the solid reputations of its features (such as the weekly *Times Magazine* and the *Book Review*) make it the nation's newspaper of record. Its print circulation hovers between 700,000 and 800,000 a day.

SUBURBAN AND SMALL-TOWN DAILIES As the United States has become a nation of transient suburb dwellers, so too has the newspaper been suburbanized. Since 1985 the number

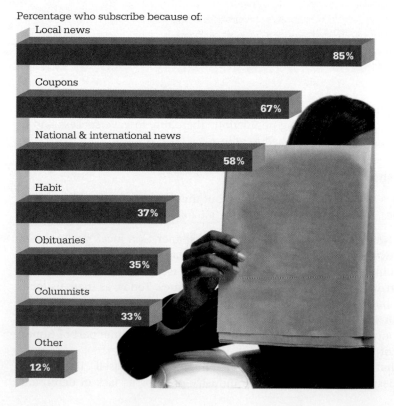

Percentage who subscribe because of:

Local news — 85%
Coupons — 67%
National & international news — 58%
Habit — 37%
Obituaries — 35%
Columnists — 33%
Other — 12%

▶ **Figure 4.1** Reasons People Subscribe to Their Local Paper.
Source: Data Page, 2011b.

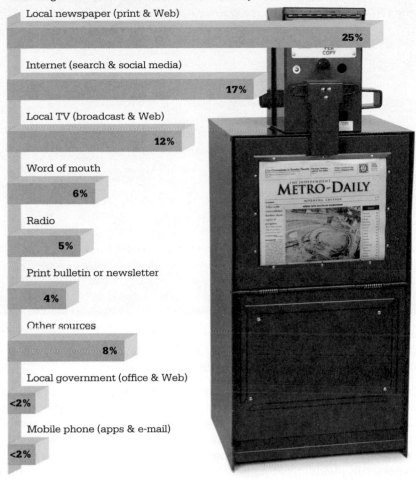

Percentage who learn about their local community from:

Local newspaper (print & Web)
25%

Internet (search & social media)
17%

Local TV (broadcast & Web)
12%

Word of mouth
6%

Radio
5%

Print bulletin or newsletter
4%

Other sources
8%

Local government (office & Web)
<2%

Mobile phone (apps & e-mail)
<2%

◀ **Figure 4.2** How People Learn about Their Local Community.
Source: Edmonds, Guskin, & Rosenstiel (2011).

of suburban dailies has increased by 50%, and one, Long Island's *Newsday*, is the 11th largest paper in the country, with a print circulation of 265,782.

Small-town dailies operate much like their suburban cousins if there is a nearby large metropolitan paper; for example, the *Lawrence Eagle-Tribune* publishes in the shadow of Boston's two big dailies. Its focus is the Merrimack River Valley in Massachusetts, 25 miles northwest of Boston. If the small-town paper has no big-city competition, it can serve as the heart of its community. Figure 4.1 details the reasons people subscribe to their local paper.

WEEKLIES AND SEMIWEEKLIES Many weeklies and semiweeklies have prospered because advertisers have followed them to the suburbs. Community reporting makes them valuable to those people who identify more with their immediate environment than they do with the neighboring big city. Suburban advertisers like the narrowly focused readership and more manageable advertising rates.

In fact, the thriving newspapers mentioned in this chapter's opening are primarily the suburban and small-town dailies and weeklies. Readers looking for national and international news have hundreds of online sources for that information. But those looking for local and regional news as well as the "holy trinity" of local information—high school sports, obituaries, and the police blotter—do not (Muller, 2011). Figure 4.2 graphically presents the importance of the local paper in keeping people in touch with

▼ High school sports, part of the "holy trinity" of local news buoying community papers' bottom lines.

their communities, and you can read about the how and why of smaller papers' success in the box entitled "Smaller Is (Sometimes) Better."

THE ETHNIC PRESS One hundred and thirty U.S. cities are served by at least one Spanish-language publication. This number remains constant as publications backed by English-language papers, such as the Tribune Company's *Hoy* (in several cities) and the *Dallas Morning News*'s *Al Día*, join more traditional weekly and semiweekly independent Spanish-language papers, such as the nation's several *La Voz Hispana* papers. This phenomenal stability is a result of three factors. First, the big dailies have realized, as have all media, that to be successful (and, in this case, to reverse long-standing declines in circulation) they must reach an increasingly fragmented audience. Second, at more than 18% of the population, self-described Hispanic or Latino people represent not only a sizable fragment of the overall audience but America's fastest-growing minority group. Third, because the newspaper is the most local of the mass media, and nonnative speakers tend to identify closely with their immediate locales, Spanish-language papers—like most foreign-language papers—command a loyal readership, one attractive to advertisers who have relatively few other ways to reach this group.

African American papers, as they have for a century and a half, remain a vibrant part of this country's **ethnic press**. African Americans represent about 12% of the total population. But because English is their native language, African Americans typically read mainstream papers. In fact, after whites, they represent the second-largest group of newspaper readers in the country. Still, 250 dailies, weeklies, and semiweeklies aim specifically at African Americans. And papers like the *Amsterdam News* in New York, the *Philadelphia New Observer*, and the *Michigan Citizen* in Detroit specialize in urban-based journalism unlike that found in the traditional mainstream dailies.

A robust ethnic press exists beyond Spanish-language and African American papers. For example, New York City is home to foreign-language papers serving nationalities speaking 50 different languages—in the *B*s alone there are Bangladeshi, Bosnian, Bulgarian, Brazilian, and Byelorussian. The *I*s have Indian, Iranian, Irish, Israeli, and Italian. In addition, the United States is home to more than 200 other foreign language papers.

THE ALTERNATIVE PRESS Another type of paper, most commonly a weekly and available at no cost, is the **alternative press**. The offspring of the underground press of the 1960s antiwar, antiracism, pro-drug culture, these papers have redefined themselves. The

Like dozens of papers across the country, the *Birmingham Eccentric*, serving the Detroit suburb of Birmingham, was going to die. That put the value of small papers squarely into the cultural forum.

Founded in 1878 and purchased in 2005 by the Gannett chain, the *Eccentric*'s new owners were prepared to let the two-times-a-week, 7,000 circulation paper expire. But local residents, "shocked at the idea of losing a touchstone of their community, began an ongoing effort to save their paper" (Dellamere, 2009). Several thousand new readers subscribed at $52 a year, and local merchants, who spend the lion's share of their advertising dollars on print and did not want to lose their primary advertising vehicle, recommitted themselves to the paper.

The *Eccentric* survived, but that came as no surprise to longtime journalist-turned-media-critic Ben Bagdikian (2004) who, early in newspapers' current slide, wrote,

Newspapers have a unique social function that their media competitors do not. They are crucial to American local civic life, which In turn, is a unique part of the U.S. political system. No other industrial democracy leaves to each community the control of its local schools, police, land use, and most taxes. In other countries these are national functions. Thus, every American city and town has voters involved in the performance of the school system in which their children are educated, in the taxes they pay on their property, even the behavior of the local sheriff's department. They vote on these on election day, and the only medium that informs them on these matters in any detail is the printed newspaper. (p. 70)

Recent industry research supports Mr. Bagdikian's esteem for local papers. In communities served by small papers (circulation under 15,000), 74% of the adults read the paper every week, spending nearly 40 minutes poring over it; 73% read "most or all" of it; 44% keep it around the house for 6 or more days; on average, they share it with more than 2.33 friends; and, a full 94% pay for their papers (Survey, 2011; Muller, 2011).

Now enter your voice in the cultural forum. Is the newspaper so vital to the functioning of your local community that you can never see yourself without it? Do, or can, other media serve this function? But what about "local schools, police, land issues, and most taxes"? Can

▶ Is there an *Eccentric* in your life? To what lengths would you go to save it?

you get these elsewhere? Do you even care? What if there really were no local newspapers? How different would your life be? Ask your parents and then your grandparents these same questions. How similar are their responses to your own? Why do you think you have differences or similarities?

> "Every American city and town has voters involved in the performance of the school system in which their children are educated, in the taxes they pay on their property, even the behavior of the local sheriff's department. They vote on these on election day, and the only medium that informs them on these matters in any detail is the printed newspaper."

most successful among them—the *Village Voice*, the *L.A. Weekly*, the *Chicago Reader*, and the *Seattle Weekly*—succeed by attracting upwardly mobile young people and young professionals, not the disaffected counterculture readers who were their original audiences. Their strategy of downplaying politics and emphasizing events listings, local arts advertising, and eccentric personal classified ads has permitted the country's 125 alternative weeklies to attract 25 million hard-copy and online readers a week. But this figure masks the fact that the number of hard-copy readers is in decline, as content once considered "alternative" and therefore not suited for traditional newspapers is quite at home on the Web. In response, most alternative papers have a Web presence, and there are now Web-only alternative "papers," leading the industry trade group, the Association of Alternative Newsweeklies, to change its name in 2011 to the Association of Alternative Newsmedia (Anderson, Guskin, & Rosenstiel, 2012).

COMMUTER PAPERS Modeled after a common form of European newspaper, free dailies designed for commuters are becoming commonplace in America's biggest cities. Like the most successful Spanish-language papers, they represent the major dailies' effort to reach a segment of the audience not likely to buy the parent papers' product. Here, though, the target is young readers (who are already used to getting free media from the alternative press and the Internet) and the goal is twofold. First, these readers represent a valuable demographic, one especially attractive to local advertisers, the newspaper's bread-and-butter financial base. Second, the big dailies hope these young readers will develop the daily newspaper-reading habit and will become regular newspaper readers. Typical of the successful **commuter papers** are the *Washington Post*'s *Express* and the Tribune Company's *amNewYork*.

The Newspaper as an Advertising Medium

The reason we have the number and variety of newspapers we do is that readers value them. When newspapers prosper financially, it is because advertisers recognize their worth as an ad medium. Nonetheless, the difficult truth for newspapers is that print advertising revenues fell from nearly $50 billion in 2005 to $22 billion in 2012. The $3 billion in online advertising papers sold in 2012 hardly compensated for that precipitous decline, especially as this was a period of increases in overall ad spending across all media (Sass, 2013b). Still, $25 billion in annual sales suggests that advertisers find newspapers' readers an attractive audience. One reason is papers' reach. Nearly 70% of all Americans read a print or online paper every week, four out of 10 every day, or the equivalent of a daily Super Bowl broadcast. A second reason is good demographics. Newspaper readers tend to be white-collar employed adults, to be college graduates, and to have household incomes over $100,000 (Sigmund, 2010). Finally, newspapers are local. Supermarkets, car dealers, department stores, movie theaters, and other local merchants who want to announce a sale or offer a coupon or circular automatically turn to the local paper. As a result, when asked which media most influence their product purchases, 57% said their local daily or Sunday printed paper, compared to 33.3% who said local television news and 28.1% who said local radio stations (Advertising Mediums, 2011).

The News and Feature Services

Much of the 35% of the newspaper that is not advertising space is filled with content provided by outside sources, specifically the news and feature services. News services, as we've already seen, collect news and distribute it to their members. (They are no longer called "wire" services because they no longer use telephone wires. Today material is more likely to come by computer network or satellite.) Unlike the early days of the wire services, today's member is three times more likely to be a broadcast outlet than a newspaper. These radio and television stations receive voice and video, as well as written copy. In all cases, members receive a choice of material, most commonly national and international news, state and regional news, sports, business news, farm and weather reports, and human interest and consumer material.

The feature services, called **feature syndicates**, do not gather and distribute news. Instead, they operate as clearinghouses for the work of columnists, essayists, cartoonists, and other creative individuals. Among the material provided (by wire, by computer, or physically in packages) are opinion pieces such as commentaries by Ellen Goodman or Garrison Keillor; horoscope, chess, and bridge columns; editorial cartoons, such as the work of Scott Willis and Ben Sergeant; and comics, the most common and popular form of syndicated material. Among the major syndicates, the best known are the *New York Times* News Service, King Features, Newspaper Enterprise Association (NEA), the *Washington Post* News Service, and United Feature Syndicate.

Trends and Convergence in Newspaper Publishing

Loss of competition within the industry, hypercommercialism, convergence, and the evolution of newspaper readership are altering not only the nature of the medium but also its relationship with its audiences.

Loss of Competition

The newspaper industry has seen a dramatic decline in competition. This has taken two forms: loss of competing papers and concentration of ownership. In 1923, 502 American cities had two or more competing (having different ownership) dailies. Today, fewer than 20 have separate competing papers. With circulation and advertising revenues leveling out for urban dailies, very few cities can support more than one paper. Congress attempted to reverse this trend with the 1970 Newspaper Preservation Act, which allowed **joint operating agreements (JOAs)**. A JOA permits a failing paper to merge most aspects of its business with a successful local competitor as long as their editorial and reporting operations remain separate. The philosophy is that it is better to have two more or less independent papers in one city than to allow one to close. Six cities, including Detroit and Charleston, WV, currently have JOAs.

The concern behind the creation of JOAs was editorial diversity. Cities with only one newspaper have only one newspaper editorial voice. This runs counter to two long-held American beliefs about the relationship between a free press and its readers:

• Truth flows from a multitude of tongues.
• The people are best served by a number of antagonistic voices.

These are the same values that fuel worry over concentration as well. What becomes of political, cultural, and social debate when there are neither multiple nor antagonistic (or at least different) voices? Media critic Robert McChesney (1997) offered this answer: "As ownership concentrated nationally in the form of chains, journalism came to reflect the partisan interests of owners and advertisers, rather than the diverse interests of any given community" (p. 13). Today, five chains—Gannett (88 papers), Tribune (9), New York Times (20), Advance Publications (59), and Media News Group (54)—receive 54% of all newspaper industry revenue (Morrison, 2011).

Chains are not new. Hearst owned several big-city papers in the 1880s, but at that time most cities enjoyed significant competition between papers. Now that most communities have only one paper, nonlocal chain or conglomerate control of that voice is more problematic. Additional concern is raised about chain ownership when the chain is also a media conglomerate, owning several different types of media outlets, as well as other nonmedia companies. Will the different media holdings speak with one corporate voice? Will they speak objectively, and will they cover at all the doings of their nonmedia corporations?

Chains do have their supporters. Although some critics see big companies as more committed to profit and shareholder dividends, others see chains such as McClatchy (77 papers), winner of numerous Pulitzer prizes and other awards, as turning expanded economic and journalistic resources toward better service and journalism. Some critics see outside ownership as uncommitted to local communities and issues, but others see balance and objectivity (especially important in one-paper towns). Ultimately, we must recognize that not all chains operate alike. Some operate their holdings as little more than profit centers; others see profit residing in exemplary

▲ The *Miami Herald*, a McClatchy paper. Even though newspaper chains have their critics, defenders point to the McClatchy papers as an example of one chain that uses its size to good journalistic ends.

service. Some groups require that all their papers toe the corporate line; others grant local autonomy. Gannett, for example, openly boasts of its dedication to local management control.

Conglomeration: Hypercommercialism, Erosion of the Firewall, and Loss of Mission

As in other media, conglomeration has led to increased pressure on newspapers to turn a profit. This manifests itself in three distinct but related ways—hypercommercialism, erasure of the distinction between ads and news, and ultimately, loss of the journalistic mission itself.

Many papers, such as *USA Today*, the *New York Times*, the *Orange County Register*, and Michigan's *Oakland Press* and *Macomb Daily*, sell ad space on their front pages, once the exclusive province of news. Other papers, Rhode Island's *Providence Journal*, for example, take this form of hypercommercialism halfway, affixing removable sticker ads to their front pages. Many papers now permit (and charge for) the placement of pet obituaries alongside those of deceased humans. The *Southeast Missourian* sells letters-to-the-editor placement to those who want to support political candidates.

A second product of conglomeration, say critics, is that the quest for profits at all costs is eroding the *firewall*, the once inviolate barrier between newspapers' editorial and advertising missions. Although they find the position of "advertorial editor" at the *Fairbanks* (Alaska) *Daily News-Miner*—whose salary is split equally between the newsroom and advertising department—strikingly inappropriate, most papers of all sizes face the same problem. For example, newsroom staff at the *Daytona Beach News Journal*, including reporters and editors, are asked to sell advertising in order to earn cash rewards for successful sales (Jackson, 2012). The *Long Beach* (CA) *Beachcomber* seldom sends reporters and/or photographers to staged events, but may do so, in the words of editor Jeff Beeler, if they are "very newsworthy" or organized by "an advertiser in our newspaper [who] contribute(s) to the expense of those reporters and photographers" (Romenesko, 2012).

"There's definitely more interaction as newspapers have come under more financial pressure," said Steve Proctor, deputy managing editor for sports and features at the *Baltimore Sun*. "It used to be if you had a newspaper in town you were able to make a steady profit. Now, like so many other things in the world, newspapers are more at the whim of the opinions of Wall Street analysts. There's a lot more pressure to increase the profit margin of the paper, and so that has led to a lot more interplay between the newsroom and the business side of the paper" (quoted in Vane, 2002, pp. 60–61). Entrepreneur Mark Cuban, who made his fortune in the Internet's early days, concurs: "The minute you have to run your business for share prices, you've lost. . . . What [newspapers] should do is step back and ask, 'What makes us special?'" (Cuban Knows, 2006, p. 10).

Newspapers will die, say conglomeration's critics, because they will have abandoned their traditional democratic mission, a failure all the more tragic because despite falling circulation, more newspapers might have remained financially healthy had they invested rather than cut when times were good. William Falk (2005), editor in chief of newsmagazine *The Week*, wrote that the medium's demise

> will be suicide. . . . The mammoth corporations that now run newspapers have responded to the new competitive challenge (of digital technologies) in the stupidest way possible: by cutting quality. They're eliminating foreign bureaus, investigative-reporting teams, and experienced editors, and filling their pages with shallow filler and bland features. Ambitious reporting and edgy writing are disappearing. Once-great newspapers . . . are now flat and generic; their authority is leaking away. The corporate guys, who think only of pleasing Wall Street, keep cutting costs and boosting profits—and wringing their hands in puzzlement when circulation keeps going down. Guess what guys? People stop buying newspapers when there's nothing in them that they don't already know. (p. B7)

In the era of record revenues and record profits, papers were laying off staff, closing state and regional bureaus, hiring younger and less experienced reporters, and shrinking their newsholes. Newspaper owners were so focused on profit margins that the editors who worked for them were distracted from finding and running great stories. For example, in 1995, at the time the *Baltimore Sun* closed its 85-year-old, 86,000-circulation afternoon edition, it was achieving 37% profit margins. Nonetheless, it fired nearly 100 editors and reporters. "In the years before the Internet deluge, [these] men and women who might have made *The Sun* a more essential vehicle for news and commentary—something so strong that it might have charged for its product online—were being ushered out the door so that Wall Street could command short-term profits in the extreme," wrote press critic John Nichols (2009, p. C5). The *Sun*'s owners, the Tribune Company, filed for bankruptcy protection in 2008. Says Bill Marimow, two-time Pulitzer Prize–winning investigative reporter and former editor of the *Sun*, "When editors become focused on accounting rather than journalism, you have a problem for democracy" (in Outing, 2005).

Convergence with the Internet

Why so much talk about money? You and the new digital technologies are the two answers. *Barron's* online columnist Howard Gold explained, "A crisis of confidence has combined with a technological revolution and structural economic change to create what can only be described as a perfect storm. Print's business model is imploding as younger readers turn toward free tabloids and electronic media to get news" (in Farhi, 2005, p. 52). It is the fear that the newspaper industry will fail to successfully weather the storm—Gold's "crisis of confidence"—that drives owners and their investors to cut out those characteristics—especially good journalism—that once defined newspapers.

The Internet has proven most directly financially damaging in its attack on newspapers' classified advertising business. Before the Internet, classified advertising was the exclusive domain of local newspapers. Today, the Net challenges newspapers' one-time dominance through commercial online classified advertising sites (for example, eBay, cars.com, and traderonline.com), advertisers connecting directly with customers on their own sites and bypassing newspapers altogether, and communitarian-minded (that is, free community-based) sites. Craigslist, for example, originating in San Francisco in 1995, is now in more than 500 cities across 50 different countries. More than half of all adult Americans now visit online classified sites (Zickuhr, 2010). Advertising losses are most striking in employment and auto sales classifieds (more than 50% in both categories at many papers). To counter career sites like Monster.com, about one-third of the papers across the country created their own national service, CareerBuilder, which rivals Monster's number of listings but not income. Two hundred dailies also have an affiliation with Yahoo!'s HotJobs service. Another 75 work with competitor-turned-partner Monster.com. To counter online auto sales classified sites, as well as real estate and general merchandise sites, virtually every newspaper in the country now maintains its own online classified pages. These efforts, however, have done little to save newspapers' one-time classified dominance.

The problem of the loss of classified ad income is magnified by the exodus of young people, that highly desirable demographic, from print to electronic news sources. Only 12% of American newspaper readers between 10 and 34 years old read the printed paper, while another 79% access newspaper content online, on mobile devices, and on e-readers (Data Page, 2011c). Not only do the Internet and the World Wide Web provide readers with more information and more depth, and

▼ One of the more successful online newspapers. *The Atlanta Journal-Constitution*, © September 7, 2010 Cox Newspapers. All rights reserved. Used by permission and protected by the copyright laws of the United States. The printing, copying, redistribution, or retransmission of the material without express written permission is prohibited. www.ajc.com

with greater speed, than the traditional newspaper, but they empower readers to control and interact with the news, in essence becoming their own editors in chief. As a result, the traditional newspaper is reinventing itself by converging with these very same technologies.

The marriage of newspapers to the Web has not yet proved financially successful for the older medium. The problem is replacing *analog dollars* with *digital dimes.* In other words, despite heavy traffic on newspaper websites—average Americans spend more than half of their time online reading news, and over 111 million people a month click in to a newspaper site—online readers simply are not worth as much as print readers (Sass, 2011a; Hendricks, 2012). In fact, to date, papers have been able to earn only one digital dime for every one analog (print) dollar they lose (Edmonds, Guskin, Rosenstiel, & Mitchell, 2012). Still, there are encouraging signs. And, in fact, the newspaper industry recognizes that it must accept economic losses while it is building online readers' trust, acceptance, and above all regular and frequent use.

The Internet Public Library lists and provides Web links to thousands of online newspapers for every state in the union and most foreign countries. These papers have adopted a variety of strategies to become "relevant on the Internet." The *Washington Post*, for example, has joined with *Newsweek* magazine, cable television channel MSNBC, and television network NBC to share content among all the parties' websites and to encourage users to link to their respective sites. Others have adopted just the opposite approach, focusing on their strength as local media. The *Boston Globe*, for example, offers readers Boston.com, the *Miami Herald* Miami.com, and the *Kansas City Star* KansasCity.com. Each offers not only what readers might expect to find in these sites' parent newspapers but also significant additional information on how to make the most of the cities they represent. These sites are as much city guides as they are local newspapers.

The local element offers several advantages. Local searchable and archivable classified ads offer greater efficiency than do the big national classified ad websites such as Monster.com and Cars.com. No other medium can offer news on crime, housing, neighborhood politics, zoning, school lunch menus, marriage licenses, and bankruptcies—all searchable by street or zip code. Local newspapers can use their websites to develop their own linked secondary sites, thus providing impressive detail on local industry. For example, the *San Jose Mercury News*'s SiliconValley.com focuses on the digital industries. Another localizing strategy is for online papers to build and maintain message boards and chat groups on their sites that deal with important issues. One more bow to the power of the Web—and users' demands for interactivity— is that most papers have begun their own blog sites, inviting readers and journalists to talk to one another.

Despite all this innovation and the readership it generates ("Newspapers don't have a demand problem," said former Google CEO Eric Schmidt, "they have a business-model problem"; in Fallows, 2010, p. 48), papers still face two lingering questions about their online success. The first, as we've seen, is how they will earn income from their Web operations. Internet users expect free content, and for years newspapers were happy to provide their product for free, simply to establish their presence on the Net. "The central economic challenge of a newspaper is printing and delivering the newspapers," explains journalist and media executive Steven Brill. "Chopping down all these trees and printing and distributing is by far the biggest cost a newspaper has. So the Internet should have let newspapers get rid of their major cost. Instead, they decided to be online but do it for free, so they still do the newspaper, which they charge for, but not as many people want to buy it, because they can get it for free online" (in Thornton, 2009, p. 2). So, newspapers have to fix themselves.

Among those "fixes" are papers that rely on advertising for their online revenue. Many continue to provide free access, hoping to attract more readers and, therefore, more advertising revenue. Some papers even offer free online classifieds to draw people to their sites (and their paid advertisers). Other papers, recognizing that the Internet surpassed print papers as a source of news in 2009 (Mindlin,

2009), are experimenting with variations of a **paywall**, that is, making all or some of their content available only to those visitors willing to pay. Many papers, large and small, have strict paywalls; readers gain access only by paying for it. The *Wall Street Journal* and the *Newport* (RI) *Daily News* employ this method. The *New York Times* offers a *metered system*. Print subscribers get all online content for free, but nonsubscribers are limited to a specified number of free stories before they have to pay. The metered system is the most common form of paywall. In all, about 30% of American papers have some form of paywall; and in 2012, for the first time in a decade, newspapers actually showed an increase in circulation revenue (James, 2013).

All this activity, however, is taking place in the face of two realities of online news. First, if the story or information is available elsewhere on the Net for free, people are unlikely to pay anything, even a dime. Therefore, whatever is behind the wall has to be unique. Second, 77% of Internet users say they will *never* pay to read online newspapers (Whitney, 2010). Online newspaper optimists point out, however, that 23% of North America's hundreds of millions of Internet users, each paying $5 to $10 a month, would provide significant revenue for papers' Web operations, and industry research indicates that many papers' pre-paywall "fears of precipitous drops in traffic just haven't materialized" (Mitchell, 2011).

This raises a second question faced by online newspapers, How will circulation be measured? In fact, if visitors to a newspaper's website are added to its hard-copy readership, newspapers are more popular than ever; that is, they are drawing readers in larger numbers than ever before. Therefore, if many online papers continue to rely on a free-to-the-user, ad-supported model to boost their "circulation," how do they quantify that readership for advertisers, both print and online? Industry insiders have called for a new metric to more accurately describe a paper's true reach. "Circulation," they say, should be replaced by **integrated audience reach**, the total number of readers of the print edition plus those unduplicated Web readers who access the paper only online or via a mobile device. This is not insignificant given the heavy traffic enjoyed by newspaper websites.

Smartphones, Tablets, and e-Readers

We saw in Chapter 3 that nearly one in three Americans owns at least one e-reader or tablet. In addition, as 2012 opened, more than half of all U.S. mobile phone owners carried a smartphone, and industry predictions were that by the end of that year that proportion would be 90% (Fischer, 2011). Data such as these have added to the newspaper industry's optimism about its digital future. For example, 56% of tablet and e-reader owners and 51% of smartphone owners use their devices to read the news (Olmstead, Sasseen, Mitchell, & Rosenstiel, 2012), and when doing so they spend more time, visit more pages, and return more frequently than when reading on conventional computers (Mitchell, Rosenstiel, & Christian, 2012). "There will always be improvements in technology, but it's hard to beat a lightweight, portable and highly legible, multimedia-driven delivery vehicle," said American Society of News Editors president Ken Paulson, speaking specifically about tablets, "It's a newspaper amplified" (in Johnson, 2012, p. 20).

The industry shares Mr. Paulson's enthusiasm. Eighty-eight percent of U.S. newspapers make their content available for mobile devices, up from just about half in 2009, and many predict that mobile platforms "will become the dominant form of reading the news within three years" (Audit Bureau of Circulations, 2011; Edmonds, Guskin, & Rosenstiel, 2011). In fact, some papers, the *Philadelphia Inquirer* and the *Philadelphia Daily News*, for example, have begun subsidizing their readers' purchase of tablets. These mobile technologies are of great interest to newspapers because they are especially attractive to young readers who otherwise have abandoned print. In fact, when *all* technologies are considered, young adults rival their parents in the amount of news they consume (Ellis, 2012).

Access to newspapers on tablets and smartphones increased dramatically in late 2011 with the arrival of Apple's Newsstand, a preinstalled folder on iPhones and iPads that allows users to stock its shelves with the apps of free and subscription publications which are then automatically delivered daily. Within a week of its introduction, the

New York Times's iPhone app was downloaded 1.8 million times, compared to 21,000 the week before; its iPad app was downloaded 189,000 times, a sevenfold increase over the previous week (Palser, 2011). iPad users alone spend more than $70,000 a day on newsstand papers and magazines (Yarow, 2012).

Changes in Newspaper Readership

Newspaper publishers know well that newspaper readership in the United States is least prevalent among younger people. A declining number of young people reads a daily paper. "Newspaper readers are heading into the cemetery," explained investment genius Warren Buffett, "while newspaper nonreaders are just getting out of college" (in Ambrose, 2007, p. B5). Look at Figure 4.3. Note the decline in newspaper readership, print and online, as people get younger. How do you feel about the fact that so few young people read the paper? The problem facing newspapers, then, is how to lure young people (readers of the future) to their pages. Online and free commuter papers might be two solutions, but the fundamental question remains: Should newspapers give these readers what they *should* want or what they *do* want?

Some newspapers confront this problem directly. They add inserts or sections directed toward, and sometimes written by, teens and young people. This is good business. But traditionalists disagree with another youth-targeted strategy—altering other, more serious (presumably more important) parts of the paper to cater to the infrequent and non-newspaper reader. As more newspaper professionals adopt a market-centered approach in their pursuit of what media ethicist Jay Black (2001, p. 21) calls (fairly or unfairly?) the "bifurcating, self-indulgent, highly transient, and significantly younger audiences whose pocketbooks are larger than their attention spans"—using readership studies, focus groups, and other tests of customer satisfaction to design their papers—they increasingly find themselves criticized for "cheapening" both the newspaper as a medium and journalism as an institution.

What happens to journalistic integrity, critics ask, to community service, to the traditional role of newspapers in our democracy, when front pages are given over to reports of starlets' affairs, sports heroes' retirements, and full-color photos of plane wrecks because this is what younger readers want? As topics of interest to

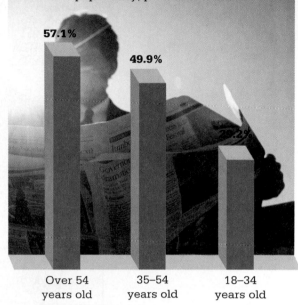

Percentage of Americans who read the paper daily, print and/or online

57.1% — Over 54 years old
49.9% — 35–54 years old
18–34 years old

▲ **Figure 4.3** Newspaper Audience by Age, 2011.
Source: Newspaper Association of America (2011).

◀ Young readers have abandoned print, but their consumption of news rivals that of their parents thanks to mobile communication devices.

the 18- to 35-year-old reluctant reader and nonreader are emphasized, what is ignored? What happens to depth, detail, and precision as stories get shorter and snappier? What kind of culture develops on a diet of **soft news** (sensational stories that do not serve the democratic function of journalism) rather than **hard news** (stories that help citizens to make intelligent decisions and keep up with important issues of the day)? Molly Ivins offered a pessimistic answer. The late columnist suggested that newspapers aren't dying; they're committing suicide. "This is the most remarkable business plan," she told *Editor & Publisher*. "Newspaper owners look at one another and say, 'Our rate of return is slipping a bit; let's solve the problem by making our product smaller and less helpful and less interesting'" (in Nichols, 2007, p. 14).

The "softening" of newspapers raises a potential media literacy issue. The media-literate person has an obligation to be aware of the impact newspapers have on individuals and society and to understand how the text of newspapers offers insight into contemporary culture. We might ask ourselves: Are we getting what we asked for? What do we as a people and as individuals want from our newspaper? Do we understand the role newspapers play in our democratic process? Are we fully aware of how newspapers help shape our understanding of ourselves and our world?

In a 1787 letter, Thomas Jefferson wrote to a colleague, "Were it left to me to decide whether we should have a government without newspapers or newspapers without government, I should not hesitate to prefer the latter." Would he write that about today's newspaper, a newspaper increasingly designed to meet the wants, needs, and interests of younger, occasional newspaper readers or those who do not read at all?

There is another view, however—that there is no problem here at all. Ever since the days of the penny press, newspapers have been dominated by soft news. All we are seeing today is an extension of what has always been. Moreover, nonreaders are simply going elsewhere for the hard news and information that were once the sole province of newspapers. They're going online, to television, and to specifically targeted sources, including magazines and newsletters.

DEVELOPING MEDIA LITERACY SKILLS

Interpreting Relative Placement of Stories

Newspapers tell readers what is significant and meaningful through their placement of stories in and on their pages. Within a paper's sections (for example, front, leisure, sports, and careers), readers almost invariably read pages in order (that is, page 1, then page 2, and so on). Recognizing this, papers place the stories they think are most important on the earliest pages. Newspaper jargon for this phenomenon has even entered our everyday language. "Front-page news" means the same thing in the living room as in the pressroom.

The placement of stories on a page is also important (Figure 4.4). English readers read from top to bottom and from left to right. Stories that the newspaper staff deems important tend to be placed above the fold and toward the left of the page. This is an important aspect of the power of newspapers to influence public opinion and of media literacy. As you'll see in Chapter 13, relative story placement is a factor in **agenda setting**—the way newspapers and other media influence not only what we think but what we think about.

A media-literate newspaper reader should be able to make judgments about other layout decisions. The use of photos suggests the importance the editors assign to a story, as do the size and wording of headlines, the employment of *jumps* (continuations to other pages), and placement of a story in a given section. A report of a person's death on the front page, as opposed to the international section or in the obituaries, carries a different meaning, as does an analysis of an issue placed on the front page as opposed to the editorial page.

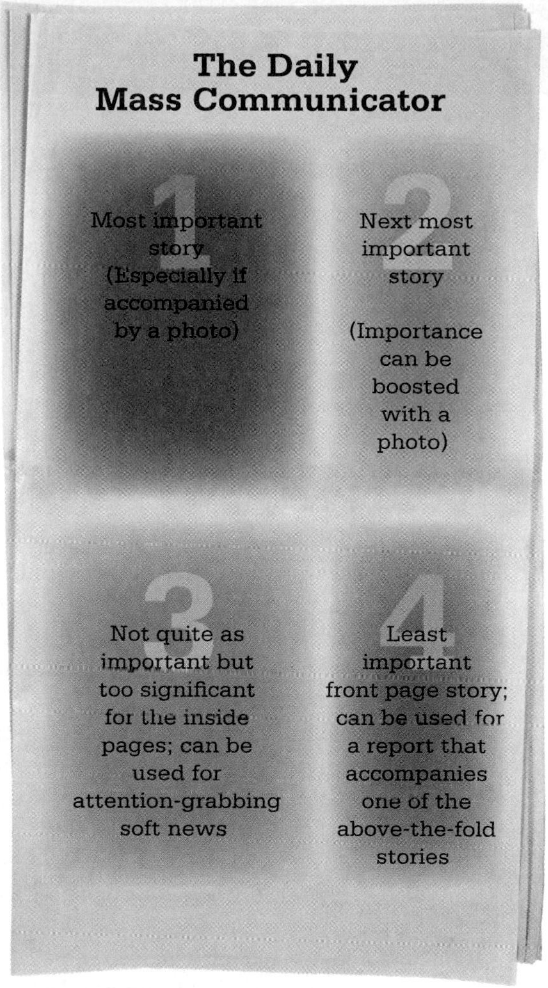

The Daily Mass Communicator
1
Most important story (Especially if accompanied by a photo)
2
Next most important story
(Importance can be boosted with a photo)
3
Not quite as important but too significant for the inside pages; can be used for attention-grabbing soft news
4
Least important front page story; can be used for a report that accompanies one of the above-the-fold stories

▲ **Figure 4.4** Placement of Stories on a Typical Front Page.

MEDIA LITERACY CHALLENGE

Reading the Newspaper: Hard Copy vs. Online vs. Mobile

Two elements of media literacy are *critical thinking skills enabling the development of independent judgments about media content* and *strategies for analyzing and discussing media messages.* Both are involved in this challenge.

Find the Web version of a newspaper with which you are familiar, its app-enabled version for your smartphone or tablet, and its dead-tree version, all from the same day. Compare the three. What content is common to all three? What content exists online or on mobile technology that is unavailable in the printed newspaper?

How would you characterize the Web-specific content? The mobile-specific content? That is, are there specific types of content that seem to appear online and on mobile devices as opposed to appearing in the hard-copy version? Can you speculate why this might be?

How similar or different are the advertisers in the two electronic versions from those in the printed version? Do the Web and mobile versions have different advertisers? Can you speculate on why the similarities and differences you found exist? Describe your experience reading the online and mobile newspapers. What did you like about it? What did you dislike? Do the same for the printed version. Despite the demographic trends that might suggest otherwise, do you think you could ever become a regular reader of the hard-copy newspaper? Why or why not?

Resources for Review and Discussion

REVIEW POINTS: TYING CONTENT TO LEARNING OUTCOMES

▶ **Outline the history and development of the newspaper industry and the newspaper itself as a medium.**
- ▸ Newspapers have been a part of public life since Roman times, prospering in Europe, and coming to the Colonies in the 1690s.
- ▸ The newspaper was at the heart of the American Revolution, and, as such, protection for the press was enshrined in the First Amendment.
- ▸ The penny press brought the paper to millions of "regular people," and the newspaper quickly became the people's medium.

▶ **Identify how the organizational and economic nature of the contemporary newspaper industry shapes the content of newspapers.**
- ▸ There are several types of newspapers, including national dailies; large metropolitan dailies; suburban and small-town dailies; weeklies and semiweeklies; ethnic and alternative papers; and free commuter papers.
- ▸ Despite falling hard-copy readership, newspapers remain an attractive advertising medium.
- ▸ The number of daily newspapers is in decline, and there are very few cities with competing papers. Chain ownership has become common.
- ▸ Conglomeration is fueling hypercommercialism, erosion of the firewall between the business and editorial sides of the newspaper, and the loss of the newspaper's traditional journalistic mission.

▶ **Describe the relationship between the newspaper and its readers.**
- ▸ Newspaper readership is changing—it is getting older, as young people abandon the paper for the Net or for no news at all. How newspapers respond will define their future.
- ▸ Localism, that is, providing coverage of material otherwise difficult to find on the Internet, has proven successful for many papers.

▶ **Explain changes in the newspaper industry brought about by converging technologies and how those alterations may affect the medium's traditional role in our democracy.**
- ▸ Newspapers have converged with the Internet. Although most people read news online, still unanswered are questions of how to charge for content and how to measure readership.
- ▸ The industry has found new optimism in the success of their mobile—smartphone, tablet, and e-reader—offerings.

▶ **Apply key media literacy skills, especially in interpreting the relative placement of stories and use of photos.**
- ▸ Where content appears—factors such as what page a story is on, where on the page it appears, and the presence of accompanying photos—offers significant insight into the importance a paper places on that content.
- ▸ This relative placement of stories has influence on what readers come to see as the important news of the day.

KEY TERMS

Acta Diurna, 73

corantos, 74

diurnals, 74

broadsides (broadsheets), 74

Bill of Rights, 75

First Amendment, 75

Alien and Sedition Acts, 75

penny press, 75

wire services, 76

yellow journalism, 77

newspaper chains, 78

pass-along readership, 78

crowdfunded journalism, 79

zoned editions, 80

ethnic press, 82

alternative press, 82

commuter papers, 84

feature syndicates, 85

joint operating agreement (JOA), 86

paywall, 90

integrated audience reach, 90

soft news, 92

hard news, 92

agenda setting, 93

QUESTIONS FOR REVIEW

1. What are Acta Diurna, corantos, diurnals, and broadsheets?

2. What is the significance of *Publick Occurrences Both Foreign and Domestick*, the *Boston News-Letter*, the *New-England Courant*, the *Pennsylvania Gazette*, and the *New York Weekly Journal*?

3. What factors led to the development of the penny press? To yellow journalism?

4. What are the similarities and differences between wire services and feature syndicates?

5. When did newspaper chains begin? Can you characterize them as they exist today?

6. What are the different types of newspapers?

7. Why is the newspaper an attractive medium for advertisers?

8. How has convergence affected newspapers' performance?

9. What is the firewall? Why is it important?

10. How do online papers succeed?

McGraw Hill **connect**®

For further review, go to the LearnSmart study module for this chapter.

QUESTIONS FOR CRITICAL THINKING AND DISCUSSION

1. Where do you stand on the debate over chains? Are they good or bad for the medium?

2. Do you read an online newspaper? How would you describe your experience?

3. Compare your local paper and an alternative weekly. Choose different sections, such as front page, editorials, and classified ads. How are they similar; how are they different? Which one, if any, speaks to you and why?

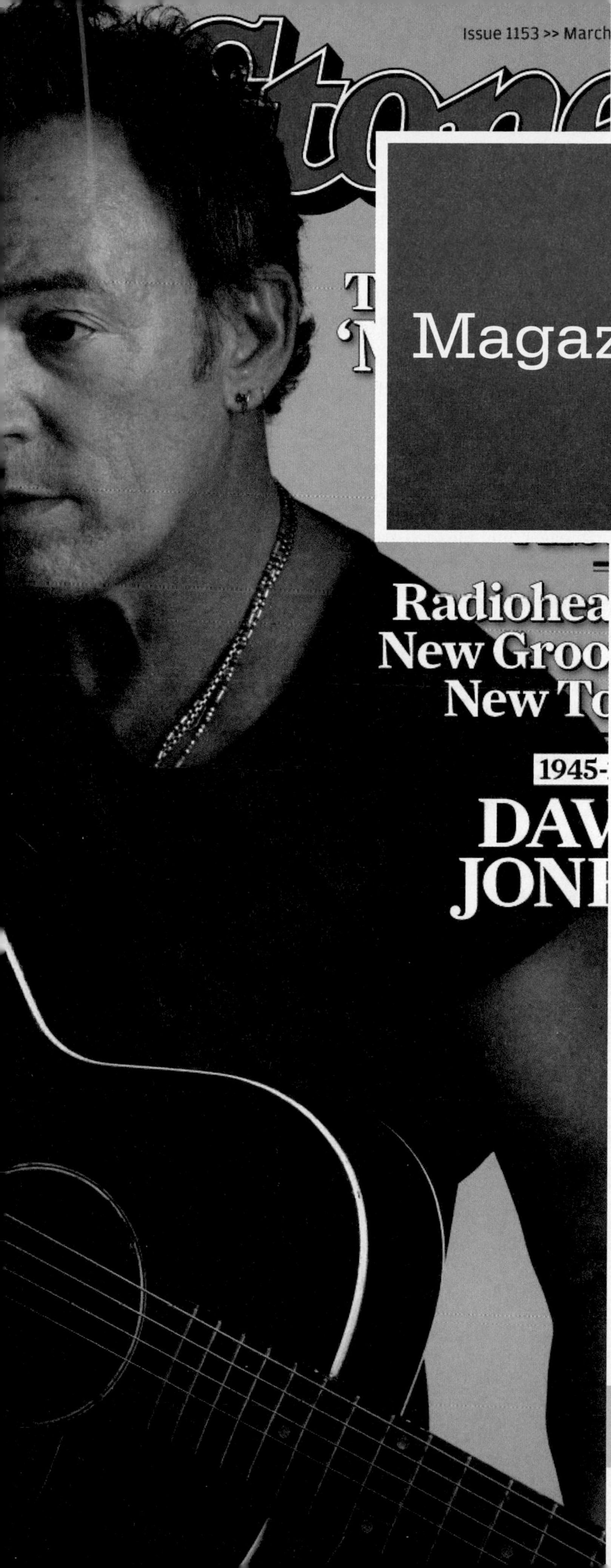

Magazines

5

Radiohea
New Groo
New To

1945-
DAV
JONE

Learning Objectives

Magazines were once a truly national mass medium, the television of their time. But changes in the nature of American society and the economics of mass media altered their nature. They are the medium that first made specialization a virtue, and they prosper today by speaking to even more narrowly defined groups of readers. After studying this chapter you should be able to

▶ Describe the history and development of the magazine industry and the magazine itself as a medium.

▶ Identify how the organizational and economic nature of the contemporary magazine industry shapes the content of magazines.

▶ Describe the relationship between magazines and their readers.

▶ Explain convergence of magazines with the Internet and mobile technologies.

▶ Apply key magazine-reading media literacy skills.

Magazines survive, even prosper, by meeting readers' varied tastes.

GOURMET, THE CROWN JEWEL OF THE CONDÉ NAST MAGAZINE EMPIRE. You had arrived, working at one of the biggest and best of America's consumer publications. It wasn't an easy road, not by any stretch. Right out of college you went to work at *Men's Vogue*, the company's prized new companion to *GQ*. When it closed in January 2009, Condé Nast moved you, primarily because you were young, eager, and inexpensive, to *Domino*, one of its shelter, or home, magazines, always a sure thing—people need homes. But when *Domino* died in March 2009 you were shuttled to the company's experiment in high-end, extra-slick magazine publishing, *Portfolio*. Launched in 2007, it would prove that upscale readers would pay for quality content. This was the kind of opportunity you had always dreamed of. When *Portfolio* shut down in April 2009 you were moved to *Cookie*, the company's offering for moms with disposable income. When *Cookie* was put to rest in November 2009 you landed at *Gourmet*. Safe at last. This venerable book has been around since 1941, longer than your parents, maybe even your grandparents!

You were shocked, then, when you left the meeting. Condé Nast was closing *Gourmet* and relying on sister publication *Bon Appétit* as its entry in the cooking category. *Gourmet* had a higher circulation, you were told, but *Bon Appétit*, focusing on food and entertainment, was less expensive to produce and sold more ad pages. Not to worry; you were still young, eager, and inexpensive, so the company would find you a spot with one of its magazines' Web divisions. CEO Charles Townsend assured you that the company was committed to developing digitized content across all its assets. "We expect to reach mostly new consumers with this digitized content, consumers who have historically not selected magazines as their vehicle of choice for information and entertainment services," he said ("Condé Nast Says," 2010). But after this blow, do you really want to stay in the magazine business? It's been a rough few years for the magazine biz. One hundred and fifty-two magazines closed in 2011, another 176 in 2010, and a disastrous 596 in 2009 (Sass, 2011e). There were some pretty big titles among the departed—*Brides*, *Cosmo Girl*, *Playgirl*, *Country Home*, *Teen*. But maybe a magazine website would be a wonderful experience. Is that the future? *Advertising Age*'s Bob Garfield (2007) thinks so, because you are entering a

1800

1850

1729 Ben Franklin's *Pennsylvania Gazette*

1741–1794 45 new American magazines appear

1741 ▲ *American Magazine, or a Monthly View of the Political State of the British Colonies* and *General Magazine, and Historical Chronicle, for All the British Plantations in America*, the first American magazines

1821 ▲ *Saturday Evening Post*

1850 ▲ *Harper's*

1857 *Atlantic Monthly*

1879 Postal Act

"post-apocalyptic media world . . . in which Canadian trees are left standing and broadcast towers aren't" (p. 1). The fallen TV towers don't bother you, but those living trees mean dead magazines. Maybe the Web *is* the way to go. But even there the data are mixed. The first (and best) Web-only magazines, *Slate* and *Salon*, have only recently reached profitability, and newer Web-only titles like *U.S. News Weekly* are too new to give you any clue. On the other hand, maybe print magazines have a future. Forbes just released *ForbesLife*; Time Warner launched *Style & Design*; Bloomberg introduced *Pursuits*; McGraw-Hill started a quarterly design magazine, *HQ*. All are from big-time operations, and all had warm receptions from readers. You just have to be good and patient.

Still, young people are increasingly consuming all media online, and in 2006 Internet advertising revenues surpassed those of magazines for the first time (Ives, 2006b). So online it is! No, wait! There will always be a place for magazines! Like Time Inc. senior vice president John Squires said, "The tactile quality of a magazine, the 'for me' time that magazines represent, the ability to take it wherever you want, the ability to not have a screen blinking at you, I don't think that's easily substituted" (in Ives, 2007a, p. 44).

In this chapter we examine the dynamics of the contemporary magazine industry—paper and online—and its audiences. We study the medium's beginnings in the Colonies, its pre–Civil War expansion, and its explosive growth between the Civil War and World War I. This was the era of great mass circulation magazines, but it was also the era of powerful writers known as muckrakers.

Influenced by television and by the social and cultural changes that followed World War II, the magazine took on a new, more narrowly focused nature, which provided

▲ *Salon*'s home page.

Salon.com screenshot featuring Jonathan Bernstein, "Dems Desert the Left." http://www.salon.com/2012/04/27/dems_desert_the_left. This article first appeared in *Salon.com*, at http://www.Salon.com An online version remains in the Salon archives. Reprinted with permission.

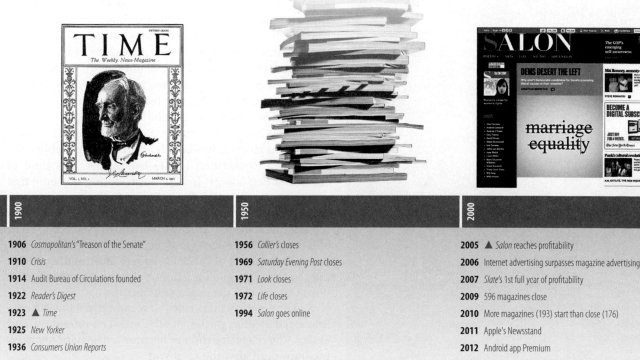

1900	1950	2000
1906 *Cosmopolitan's* "Treason of the Senate"	**1956** *Collier's* closes	**2005** ▲ *Salon* reaches profitability
1910 *Crisis*	**1969** *Saturday Evening Post* closes	**2006** Internet advertising surpasses magazine advertising
1914 Audit Bureau of Circulations founded	**1971** *Look* closes	**2007** *Slate's* 1st full year of profitability
1922 *Reader's Digest*	**1972** *Life* closes	**2009** 596 magazines close
1923 ▲ *Time*	**1994** *Salon* goes online	**2010** More magazines (193) start than close (176)
1925 *New Yorker*		**2011** Apple's Newsstand
1936 *Consumers Union Reports*		**2012** Android app Premium
1939 NBC unveils TV at World's Fair		**2012** Audit Bureau of Circulations renamed Alliance for Audited Media

the industry with a growing readership and increased profits. We detail the various categories of magazines, discuss circulation research, and look at the ways the industry protects itself from competition from other media and how advertisers influence editorial decisions. The influence of convergence runs through all these issues. Finally, we investigate some of the editorial decisions that should be of particular interest to media-literate magazine consumers.

A Short History of Magazines

Magazines were a favorite medium of the British elite by the mid-1700s, and two prominent colonial printers hoped to duplicate that success in the New World. In 1741 in Philadelphia, Andrew Bradford published *American Magazine, or a Monthly View of the Political State of the British Colonies*, followed by Benjamin Franklin's *General Magazine, and Historical Chronicle, for All the British Plantations in America*. Composed largely of reprinted British material, these publications were expensive and aimed at the small number of literate colonists. Without an organized postal system, distribution was difficult, and neither magazine was successful. *American Magazine* produced three issues; *General Magazine*, six. Yet between 1741 and 1794, 45 new magazines appeared, although no more than three were published in the same time period. Entrepreneurial printers hoped to attract educated, cultured, moneyed gentlemen by copying the successful London magazines. Even after the Revolutionary War, U.S. magazines remained clones of their British forerunners.

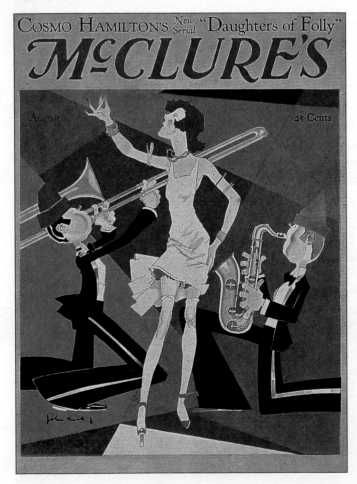

▼ This *McClure's* cover captures the spirit of the Roaring Twenties as well as the excitement of the burgeoning magazine industry.

The Early Magazine Industry

In 1821 the *Saturday Evening Post* appeared; starting life as Ben Franklin's *Pennsylvania Gazette* in 1729, it was to continue for the next 148 years. Among other successful early magazines were *Harper's* (1850) and *Atlantic Monthly* (1857). Cheaper printing and growing literacy fueled expansion of the magazine as they had the book (see Chapter 3). But an additional factor in the success of the early magazines was the spread of social movements such as abolitionism and labor reform. These issues provided compelling content, and a boom in magazine publishing began. In 1825 there were 100 magazines in operation; by 1850 there were 600. Because magazine articles increasingly focused on matters of importance to U.S. readers, magazines such as the *United States Literary Gazette* and *American Boy* began to look less like London publications and more like a new and unique product. Journalism historians John Tebbel and Mary Ellen Zuckerman (1991) called this "the time of significant beginnings" (p. 13); it was during this time that the magazine developed many of the characteristics we associate with it even today. Magazines and the people who staffed them began to clearly differentiate themselves from other publishing endeavors (such as books and newspapers). The concept of specialist writers took hold, and their numbers rose. In addition, numerous and detailed illustrations began to fill the pages of magazines.

Still, these early magazines were aimed at a literate elite interested in short stories, poetry, social commentary, and essays. The magazine did not become a true national mass medium until after the Civil War.

The Mass Circulation Era

The modern era of magazines can be divided into two parts, each characterized by a different relationship between medium and audience.

Mass circulation popular magazines began to prosper in the post–Civil War years. In 1865 there were 700 magazines publishing; by 1870 there were 1,200; by 1885 there were 3,300. Crucial to this expansion was the women's magazine. Suffrage—women's right to vote—was the social movement that occupied its pages, but a good deal of content could also be described as how-to for homemakers. Advertisers, too, were eager to appear in the new women's magazines, hawking their brand-name products. First appearing at this time are several magazines still familiar today, including *Ladies' Home Journal* and *Good Housekeeping*.

There were several reasons for this phenomenal growth. As with books, widespread literacy was one reason. But the Postal Act of 1879, which permitted mailing magazines at cheap second-class postage rates, and the spread of the railroad, which carried people and publications westward from the East Coast, were two others. A fourth was the reduction in cost. As long as magazines sold for 35 cents—a lot of money for the time—they were read largely by the upper class. However, a circulation war erupted between giants *McClure's*, *Munsey's Magazine*, and the *Saturday Evening Post*. Soon they, as well as *Ladies' Home Journal*, *McCall's*, *Woman's Home Companion*, *Collier's*, and *Cosmopolitan*, were selling for as little as 10 and 15 cents, which brought them within reach of many working people.

This 1870s price war was made possible by the newfound ability of magazines to attract growing amounts of advertising. As we'll see in Chapter 12, social and demographic changes in the post–Civil War era—urbanization, industrialization, the spread of roads and railroads, and development of consumer brands and brand names—produced an explosion in the number of advertising agencies. These agencies needed to place their messages somewhere. Magazines were the perfect outlet because they were read by a large, national audience. As a result, circulation—rather than reputation, as had been the case before—became the most important factor in setting advertising rates. Magazines kept cover prices low to ensure the large readerships coveted by advertisers. The fifth reason for the enormous growth in the number of magazines was industrialization, which provided people with leisure and more personal income.

Magazines were truly America's first *national* mass medium, and like books they served as an important force in social change, especially in the **muckraking** era of the first decades of the 20th century. Theodore Roosevelt coined this label as an insult, but the muckrakers wore it proudly, using the pages of *The Nation*, *Harper's Weekly*, the *Arena*, and even mass circulation publications such as *McClure's* and *Collier's* to agitate for change. Their targets were the powerful. Their beneficiaries were the poor.

The mass circulation magazine grew with the nation. From the start there were general interest magazines such as the *Saturday Evening Post*, women's magazines such as *Good Housekeeping*, pictorial magazines such as *Life* and *Look*, and digests such as *Reader's Digest*, which was first published in 1922 and offered condensed and tightly edited articles for people on the go in the Roaring Twenties. What these magazines all had in common was the size and breadth of readership. They were mass market, mass

▲ The first issue of *Time*.

▼ Much respected today, *Harper's* gave early voice to the muckrakers and other serious observers of politics and society.

▶ A wide array of specialized magazines exists for all lifestyles and interests. Here are some of the 7,300 special interest consumer magazines available to U.S. readers.

circulation publications, both national and affordable. As such, magazines helped unify the nation. They were the television of their time—the dominant advertising medium, the primary source for nationally distributed news, and the preeminent provider of visual, or photo, journalism.

Between 1900 and 1945, the number of families who subscribed to one or more magazines grew from 200,000 to more than 32 million. New and important magazines continued to appear throughout these decades. For example, African American intellectual W. E. B. DuBois founded and edited the *Crisis* in 1910 as the voice of the National Association for the Advancement of Colored People (NAACP). *Time* was first published in 1923. Its brief review of the week's news was immediately popular (it was originally only 28 pages long). It made a profit within a year. The *New Yorker*, "the world's best magazine," debuted in 1925.

The Era of Specialization

In 1956 *Collier's* declared bankruptcy and became the first mass circulation magazine to cease publication. But its fate, as well as that of other mass circulation magazines, had actually been sealed in the late 1940s and 1950s following the end of World War II. Profound alterations in the nation's culture—and, in particular, the advent of television—changed the relationship between magazines and their audience. No matter how large their circulation, magazines could not match the reach of television. Magazines did not have moving pictures or visual and oral storytelling. Nor could magazines match television's timeliness. Magazines were weekly, whereas television was continuous. Nor could they match television's novelty. In the beginning, *everything* on television was of interest to viewers. As a result, magazines began to lose advertisers to television.

The audience changed as well. As we've seen, World War II changed the nature of American life. The new, mobile, product-consuming public was less interested in the traditional Norman Rockwell world of the *Saturday Evening Post* (closed in 1969) and more in tune with the slick, hip world of narrower interest publications such as *GQ* and *Self*, which spoke to them in and about their new and exciting lives. And because

A change in people's tastes in magazines reflects some of the ways the world changed after World War II. Norman Rockwell's America was replaced by that of *GQ*, *Self*, and *People*.

World War II had further urbanized and industrialized America, people—including millions of women who had entered the workforce—had more leisure and more money to spend. They could spend both on a wider array of personal interests *and* on magazines that catered to those interests. Where there were once *Look* (closed in 1971) and the *Saturday Evening Post*, there were now *Flyfishing*, *Surfing*, *Ski*, and *Easyrider*. The industry had hit on the secret of success: specialization and a lifestyle orientation. We saw in Chapter 1 that all media have moved in this direction in their efforts to attract an increasingly fragmented audience, but it was the magazine industry that began the trend. In fact, as the editors of the Project for Excellence in Journalism (2004, p. 1) wrote,

> Magazines often are harbingers of change. When large social, economic, or techno-logical shifts begin to reshape the culture, magazines frequently are the first media to move, and the structure of the industry is one reason. Unlike newspapers, most maga-zines are not so tied to a specific geographic area, but are instead centered on interests or niches. Writers are looking for trends. Publishers can more quickly than in other media add and subtract titles aimed at specific audience segments or interests. Adver-tisers, in turn, can take their dollars to hot titles of the moment aimed at particular demographics.

Magazines and Their Audiences

Exactly who are the audiences for magazines? Magazine industry research indicates that among people with at least some college, 94% subscribe to at least one magazine. Overall, 93% of all American adults read a magazine, a proportion that's even higher, 96%, for the attractive 18- to 35-year-old demographic. All adults read on average 7.7 issues a month (8.3 issues for the 18 to 35 age group), and they spend 42 minutes on each issue. And magazine readers are attentive, as they are much less likely to consume other media or to engage in non-media activities than are users of television, radio, or the Internet (Association of Magazine Media, 2012a).

How people use magazines also makes them an attractive advertising medium. Magazines sell themselves to potential advertisers based not only on the number and demographic desirability of their readers, but on readers' engagement with and affin-ity for magazine advertising. Ed Kelly, CEO of American Express Publishing, explains *engagement*: "The power of magazines is a personal experience. When I pick up a magazine to read, I choose a certain magazine because it covers topics that interest me, so everything in the issue speaks to me—including the ads." Adds Hearst Magazines' chief marketing officer Michael Clinton, "Unlike a lot of media, consum-ers pay for magazines. They are spending their good old-fashioned dollars to buy the product. That is an engagement in itself in terms of how they are involved with the magazine" (both in "The New Imperative," 2005, p. M24). *Affinity* for magazine adver-tising is demonstrated by industry research that shows that more than all other com-mercial media, magazine advertising ranks first in making a positive impression and second, behind only video games, in people's assertion that they continue to enjoy the content at the time they see the ad. More American adults (48%) trust magazine advertising than they do television or Internet advertising (40%; Association of Magazine Media, 2012a).

Scope and Structure of the Magazine Industry

In 1950 there were 6,950 magazines in operation. The number now exceeds 20,000, some 7,300 of which are general interest consumer magazines. Of these, 800 produce three-fourths of the industry's gross revenues. In 2012 alone, 227 new magazines were started, and that's on top of 2011's 239 new launches (Sass, 2012). Contemporary magazines are typically divided into three broad types:

- *Trade, professional,* and *business magazines* carry stories, features, and ads aimed at people in specific professions and are distributed either by the professional organizations themselves (*American Medical News*) or by media companies such as Whittle Communications and Time Warner (*Progressive Farmer*).
- *Industrial, company,* and *sponsored magazines* are produced by companies specifically for their own employees, customers, and stockholders, or by clubs and associations specifically for their members. *Friendly Exchange,* for example, is the magazine of the Fireman's Fund insurance company. *AARP The Magazine* is the magazine for members of the American Association of Retired Persons (AARP).
- *Consumer magazines* are sold by subscription and at newsstands, bookstores, and other retail outlets, including supermarkets, garden shops, and computer stores. *Sunset* and *Wired* fit here, as do *Road & Track, US, TV Guide,* and the *New Yorker* (Figure 5.1).

Categories of Consumer Magazines

The industry typically categorizes consumer magazines in terms of their targeted audiences. Of course, the wants, needs, interests, and wishes of those readers determine the content of each publication. Although these categories are neither exclusive (where do *Chicago Business* and *Sports Illustrated for Women* fit?) nor exhaustive (what do we do with *Hot Rod* and *National Geographic*?), they are at least indicative of the cascade of options. Here is a short list of common consumer magazine categories, along with examples of each type.

Alternative magazines: *Mother Jones,* the *Utne Reader*
Business/money magazines: *Money, Black Enterprise*
Celebrity and entertainment magazines: *People, Entertainment Weekly*
Children's magazines: *Highlights, Ranger Rick*
Computer magazines: *Internet, PC World*
Ethnic magazines: *Hispanic, Ebony*
Family magazines: *Fatherhood, Parenting*
Fashion magazines: *Bazaar, Elle*
General interest magazines: *Reader's Digest, Life*
Geographical magazines: *Texas Monthly, Bay Area Living*
Gray magazines: *AARP The Magazine*
Literary magazines: *Atlantic Monthly, Harper's*
Men's magazines: *GQ, Field & Stream, Playboy*
Newsmagazines: *Time, U.S. News & World Report*
Political opinion magazines: *The Nation, National Review*
Sports magazines: *Sport, Sports Illustrated*
Sunday newspaper magazines: *Parade, USA Weekend*
Women's magazines: *Working Woman, Good Housekeeping, Ms.*
Youth magazines: *Seventeen, Tiger Beat*

Magazine Advertising

Magazine specialization exists and succeeds because the demographically similar readership of these publications is attractive to advertisers. Advertisers want to target ads for their products and services to those most likely to respond to them. Despite a 30% tumble

Magazine title, rank, and circulation (in millions)

Rank	Magazine	Circulation
1	Better Homes and Gardens	7.65
2	Game Informer	5.95
3	Reader's Digest	5.65
4	National Geographic	4.45
5	Good Housekeeping	4.34
6	Woman's Day	3.86
7	Family Circle	3.83
8	People	3.56
9	Time	3.38
10	Ladies Home Journal	3.27
11	Taste of Home	3.24
12	Sports Illustrated	3.21
13	Cosmopolitan	3.03
14	Prevention	2.90
15	Southern Living	2.83
16	Maxim	2.53
17	O, the Oprah Magazine	2.46
18	Glamour	2.30
19	Parenting	2.23
20	Parents	2.22

▶ **Figure 5.1** Top 20 U.S. Magazines by Circulation, 2011.
Source: Association of Magazine Media, 2012a.

in the number of ad pages sold in American magazines from 2006 to 2011 (Sass, 2011a), this remains a lucrative situation for the magazine industry. There are about 360 million magazines sold in the United States every year, and their average editorial-to-advertising-page ratio is 53% to 47%. The industry takes in more than $30 billion a year in revenue, about half of that amount generated by advertising. Magazines command 6% of all the dollars spent on advertising in this country (Sass, 2011b). (But for a look at a magazine with no advertising at all, see the essay, "No Ads? No Problem: *Consumer Reports*.") How advertising dollars are spread among different types of advertisers is shown in Figure 5.2.

Magazines are often further specialized through **split runs**, special versions of a given issue in which editorial content and ads vary according to some specific demographic or regional grouping. *Time*, for example, has at least eight regional editions, more than 50 state editions, and eight professionally oriented editions. Magazines work to make themselves attractive to advertisers in other ways, especially as the country and industry deal with tough economic conditions. One strategy is *single sponsor magazines*—having only one advertiser throughout an entire issue. Health publication *Walk It Off* uses this technique exclusively, and even

Rank	Category
1	Toiletries and Cosmetics
2	Drugs and Remedies
3	Food and Food Products
4	Apparel and Accessories
5	Retail
6	Media
7	Direct Response Companies
8	Automotive
9	Home Furnishings and Supplies
10	Financial, Insurance, and Real Estate

▲ **Figure 5.2** Top 10 Magazine Advertiser Categories, 2011.
Source: Association of Magazine Media, 2012b.

◀ Like many media companies, Meredith offers accountability guarantees.

No Ads? No Problem:
Consumer Reports

Consumer Reports, first published in 1936 as *Consumer Union Reports* and boasting an initial circulation of 400, charges for access to its Web version. Its 3.3 million online subscribers pay the same rate as its 4.5 million print readers. Nonetheless, its Web readership is the highest of any online magazine in the world, and its print circulation is higher than that of all but a few major magazines, exceeding that of titles like *Ladies' Home Journal* (3.3 million subscribers), *Time* (3.4 million), and *People* (3.6 million).

There is a discount for subscribing to both, but because the two versions appeal to distinctly different groups of readers, only about 600,000 avail themselves of this option.

Very few magazines survive today without accepting advertising. Those that are ad-free insist that freedom from commercial support allows them to make a greater difference in the lives of their readers. *Ms.*, for example, cannot advocate development of strong, individual females if its pages carry ads that suggest beauty is crucial for women's success. *Ms.* began life in 1972 as a Warner Communications publication and has gone through several incarnations as both a for-profit and a not-for-profit publication. Today it is published four times a year, maintains an online version, carries no advertising, and remains committed to advancing the cause of women and feminism on a global scale. But it is *Consumer Reports* that makes the no-advertising case most strongly—it must be absolutely free of outside influence if its articles about consumer products are to maintain their well-earned reputation for fairness and objectivity. As its editors explain on the magazine's website, their mission is to "test, inform, and protect. To maintain our independence and impartiality, Consumers Union [the magazine's parent organization] accepts no outside advertising, no free test samples, and has no agenda other than the interests of consumers." So protective is the magazine of that independence that it refuses to let its ratings be used in any advertising of the products and services it evaluates, even those that it judges superior.

> "Very few magazines survive today without accepting advertising. Those that are ad-free insist that freedom from commercial support allows them to make a greater difference in the lives of their readers."

Print readers typically want to be "generally well-informed consumers," explains Giselle Benatar, editor in chief of the online version. "But on the Web site, we're attracting very transaction-minded consumers. They're shoppers. They're looking for a product, they want ratings, they want recommendations, and they want it now, not once a month" (in Perez-Pena, 2007, p. C1). The Web version does offer a good deal of free information, especially when evaluated products may cause health and safety problems. Also occasionally available for free is special content, such as an ongoing series of media literacy videos examining the persuasive appeals used in consumer drug advertising. But

venerable titles like the *New Yorker* (Target stores) and *Time* (Kraft foods) publish single-sponsor issues on occasion. Another strategy is to make *accountability guarantees. The Week*, for example, promises that independent testing will demonstrate that its readers recall, to an agreed-upon level, a sponsor's ad; if they do not, the advertiser will receive free ad pages until recall reaches that benchmark. Many of the large publishers, Meredith and Time, Inc. for example, also offer similar guarantees.

Types of Circulation

Magazines price advertising space in their pages based on **circulation**, the total number of issues of a magazine that are sold. These sales can be either subscription or single-copy sales. For the industry as a whole, about 68% of all sales are subscription. Some magazines, however—*Woman's Day, TV Guide*, and *Penthouse*, for example—rely heavily on single-copy sales. Subscriptions have the advantage of an ensured ongoing readership, but they are sold below the cover price and have the additional burden of postage included in their cost to the publisher. Single-copy sales are less reliable, but to advertisers they are sometimes a better barometer of a publication's value to its readers. Single-copy readers must consciously choose to pick up an issue and they pay full price for it.

A third form of circulation, **controlled circulation**, refers to providing a magazine at no cost to readers who meet some specific set of advertiser-attractive criteria. Free airline and hotel magazines fit this category. Although they provide no subscription or single-sales revenue, these magazines are an attractive, relatively low-cost advertising vehicle for companies seeking narrowly defined, captive audiences. The magazine with the wealthiest readers, in fact, is United Airlines' *Hemisphere*. Its 4.5 million readers have a median household income of $129,487—double, for example, *Vogue*'s $67,024 (Ives, 2011a). These **custom publishing** magazines are discussed in more detail later in this chapter.

subscribers have access to much more. For example, there are videos of front and side impact tests on just about every vehicle sold in this country. The Web *Consumer Reports* maintains a searchable archive of all tests and their results as well as up-to-the-minute evaluations of new products.

Because the electronic version has no paper, printing, trucking, or mailing expenses, it actually makes more money than its print sibling. To increase profits on its print version, *Consumer Reports* is produced on less expensive paper rather than the glossy stock used by most magazines, and as a nonprofit group, it pays lower postage rates than other consumer magazines.

Another magazine that, like *Ms.* and *Consumer Reports*, eschews advertising because it sees it as inimical to its larger mission of making a difference with its particular category of reader is *Adbusters*. Founded in 1989, *Adbusters* boasts a worldwide circulation of 50,000 and won the *Utne Reader* Award for General Excellence three times in its first six years of operation. It aims to help stem the erosion of the world's physical and cultural environments by what it views as greed and commercial forces. Its online version allows users to download spoofs of popular ad campaigns and other anticonsumerism spots for use as banner ads on their own sites.

▶ *Consumer Reports*, hard copy and online.

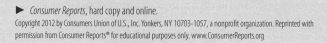

Measuring Circulation

Regardless of how circulation occurs, it is monitored through research. The Audit Bureau of Circulations (ABC) was established in 1914 to provide reliability to a booming magazine industry playing loose with self-announced circulation figures. In 2012, recognizing that "circulation" should include digital editions and apps, the ABC became platform agnostic and renamed itself the Alliance for Audited Media (AAM). The AAM provides reliable circulation figures, as well as important population and demographic data. Circulation data are often augmented by measures of *pass-along readership*, which refers to readers who neither subscribe nor buy single copies but who borrow a magazine or read one in a doctor's office or library. *Handguns*, for example, has a paid circulation of 114,000, but its pass-along readership is 5.4 million (Ives, 2007b).

This traditional model of measurement, however, is under increasing attack. As advertisers demand more precise assessments of accountability and return on their investment (Chapter 12), new metrics beyond circulation are being demanded by professionals inside and outside the industry. "We live in a very short-term measurement world," says advertising sales executive Steve Lanzano. "I need answers now. The time lag hurts [magazines] because everybody wants immediate turnaround. It has been the same measurement system for 25 years. To get the attention of ad agencies, they need to come up with a whole different model" (in Ives, 2006a, p. S-2). Speed is only one issue. Others argue that it is one thing for magazine publishers to boast of engagement and affinity, but how are they measured? As a result, the advertising and magazine industries are investigating "a whole different model." In 2006, audience assessment firm McPheters & Co. rolled out a new measurement service, Readership.com, designed to provide near real-time information on magazine distribution, readership, and engagement. It tallies not only the number of people a magazine reaches but the effect

▲ Controlled circulation magazines like Amtrak's *Arrive* (train), Delta's *Sky* (airplane), and *WebMD, the Magazine* (doctor's office) take advantage or readers' captivity.

its ads have on brand awareness, readers' intent to buy, and actual actions taken. If this new model wins enough supporters, measuring "mere" circulation will become a thing of the past.

Several magazines, most prominently *Time*, already offer advertisers the option of choosing between *total audience* and paid circulation when setting advertising rates. Akin to newspapers' integrated audience except that it totals all readers, not only unique readers, total audience combines print and Web readership. In *Time*'s case, for example, circulation jumps from under 4 million to a total audience of five times that size. The goal is to attract advertisers to the *Time* brand rather than to *Time*, the magazine.

Trends and Convergence in Magazine Publishing

Even though the number of ad pages has been declining, total readership of American consumer magazines, both print and digital, continues to grow, reaching 1.23 billion editions read in 2013 (Sass, 2013a). Nonetheless, the forces that are reshaping all the mass media are having an impact on magazines. Alterations in how the magazine industry does business are primarily designed to help magazines compete with television and the Internet in the race for advertising dollars. Convergence, too, has its impact.

Online Magazines

Online magazines have emerged, made possible by convergence of magazines and the Internet. Most magazines, 83%, now produce online editions offering special interactive features not available to their hard-copy readers (Audit Bureau of Circulations, 2011). Different publications opt for different payment models, but most provide online-only content for free and charge nonsubscribers for access to print magazine content that appears online. This strategy encourages readers who might otherwise go completely digital (and drop print) to renew their subscriptions. This is important to publishers and their advertisers because ads in hard-copy magazines are more effective and therefore more valuable: 60% of readers 14 and older say they pay more attention to print advertising in magazines than any type of online advertising. Eight in 10 who have online access to their favorite magazine say they prefer reading the printed version; 70% admit that they enjoy reading print magazines even though they know they can find most of the same information online; and 55% of Web magazine readers continue to subscribe to the printed version (Deloitte, 2011). Nonetheless, more than half of magazine readers access their favorite publications electronically, and 75% say that the digital content they find there complements rather than substitutes for the printed content (Association of Magazine Media, 2012a).

Several strictly online magazines have been attempted. In 1996, former *New Republic* editor Michael Kinsley moved from Washington, D.C., to Washington State to publish the exclusively online magazine *Slate* for Microsoft. The Washington Post Company bought *Slate* from Microsoft in 2004 to increase its online presence. Two years earlier, several staffers from the *San Francisco Chronicle*, armed with $100,000 in start-up money from Apple Computer, went online with *Salon*. Both *Salon* and *Slate* wanted to do magazine journalism—a mix of breaking news, cultural criticism, political and social commentary, interviews—at the Internet's speed with the Internet's interactivity and instant feedback.

Although both pioneers regularly draw roughly 2 million unique monthly visitors, they only recently reached profitability, *Salon* in 2005 and *Slate* in 2007. One reason is that as opposed to sites produced by paper magazines, purely online magazines must generate original content, an expensive undertaking, yet they compete online for readers and advertisers as equals with those subsidized by paper magazines. In addition, these sites must compete with all other websites on the Internet. They are but one of an infinite number of choices for potential readers, and they do not enjoy the security of readers' loyalty to a parent publication.

▲ *Slate's* home page.

Smartphones, Tablets, and e-Readers

As with books and newspapers, mobile digital media are reshaping the relationship between magazines and readers. Time-Warner CEO Jeff Bewkes quickly moved his company's 21 publications to mobile, saying, "For digital magazines to take off we need to offer consumers the flexibility of purchasing single-copy digital issues, having digital-only subscriptions, and having a content-everywhere approach that allows us to offer dual print and digital subscriptions" (in Matsa, Rosenstiel, & Moore, 2011). Particularly successful, especially after the introduction of Apple's Newsstand (see Chapter 3) are *The Economist*, whose app has been downloaded by more than 3 million readers, and *National Geographic*, which saw its app-based subscriptions increase fivefold (Smith, 2011b; Palser, 2011). *Popular Science*, which was averaging 75 new digital subscriptions a day before Newsstand saw 3,900 people sign on in the first six days of Newsstand's debut (Matsa, Sasseen & Mitchell, 2012). Newsstand's success prompted a consortium of major magazine publishers to create its own version, Unlimited, an app designed for Android tablets that gives readers access to a wide variety of titles.

Readers have enthusiastically responded to mobile magazines. Fifty-three percent of e-book owners read magazines on their devices, and among the 18- to 34-year-olds, more than 40% have downloaded magazine apps to their tablets and smartphones (Association of Magazine Media, 2012a). Among readers with mobile devices, 90% report that since acquiring that technology, they are consuming just as much—if not more—magazine content; 66% plan to consume more digital magazines; and 63% want even more magazine content in digital form. Readers (55%) especially like to access digital back issues of titles; 83% are interested in archiving an article or an entire issue; and 86% want to be able to share issues or articles (Association of Magazine Media, 2011).

▲ Quick response codes have reached near ubiquity in the magazine industry.

And interestingly, smartphones and tablets now make hard-copy magazines more attractive to readers and advertisers now that **QR codes**, **quick response codes**, appear on virtually all consumer magazines. When readers use their mobile devices to capture the image of these small, black-and-white squares, they are instantly directed to a publisher's or marketer's website, increasing engagement. Even easier to use are **NFC (near-field communication) chips**, tags embedded in magazines that connect readers to advertisers' digital content when they simply hold their smartphones near an ad; no need to have the correct app or to take a picture of the QR code.

Custom Magazines

Another trend finds its roots in the magazine industry's response to an increasingly crowded media environment. Custom publishing is the creation of magazines specifically designed for an individual company seeking to reach a very narrowly defined audience, such as favored customers or likely users or buyers. *WebMD*, the medical information website, for example, distributes free to 85% of all American doctors' offices a magazine of the same name with a circulation of 1.3 million—rivaling that of the *New Yorker* and *PC World*, and exceeding that of *BusinessWeek*. Naturally, such specifically targeted magazines take advantage of readers' engagement with and affinity for magazine advertising.

There are two broad categories of custom publishing. A **brand magazine** is a consumer magazine, complete with a variety of general interest articles and features, published by a retail or other business for readers having demographic characteristics similar to those of consumers with whom it typically does business. These publications carry ad pages not only for the products of their parent business, but for others as well. Energy drink maker Red Bull publishes *Red Bulletin*, for example, and among others, Dodge, Hallmark, Bloomingdale's, Saks Fifth Avenue, Crunch Fitness, and Sea Ray

▲ The professional organization, The Custom Content Council, produces its own publication, the high-quality *Content* magazine.

boats all have successful brand magazines. This new form of magazine recognizes two important contemporary realities of today's media environment: (a) The cost of retaining existing customers is significantly lower than that of recruiting new ones, and (b) marketers must "find ways to stand out from the quantity and clutter of commercial messages and to connect with an increasingly cynical and suspicious public" (Virgin, 2004, p. E1).

Closely related is the **magalogue**, a designer catalog produced to look like a consumer magazine. Abercrombie & Fitch, J. Crew, Harry Rosen, and Diesel all produce catalogs in which models wear for-sale designer clothes. Magalogues "cut to the chase," says J. Crew's Margot Brunelle; they bring "a fresh point of view, an immediacy and ease of use that quite frankly has been missing from a lot of magazines." Advertising buyer David Verklin agrees, "People have been ripping pages out of magazines and putting them in their purse forever. These magazines are taking it one step further by showing pages of the products and having a point of view" (both in Carr, 2004, p. C1).

Every *Fortune* 500 company and every major retailer either already engages in custom publishing or plans to do so in the very near future. There are more than 100,000 different brand magazines and magalogues in America, representing over 34 billion individual annual copies. Ninety-three percent of adults are familiar with at least one, and large numbers of readers find them useful (68%) and have bought something they saw (63%) in one of them (Sass, 2009).

Meeting Competition from Cable Television

As we've seen, the move toward specialization in magazines was forced by the emergence of television as a mass-audience, national advertising medium. But television again—specifically cable television—eventually came to challenge the preeminence of magazines as a specialized advertising medium. Advertiser-supported cable channels survive using precisely the same strategy as magazines—they deliver to advertisers a relatively large number of consumers who have some important demographic trait in common. Similar competition also comes from specialized online content providers such as ESPN's several sports-oriented sites and The Discovery Channel Online. Magazines are well positioned to fend off these challenges for several reasons.

First is internationalization, which expands a magazine's reach, making it possible for magazines to attract additional ad revenues for content that, essentially, has already been produced. Internationalization can happen in one of several ways. Some magazines, *Time* and *Monthly Review*, for example, produce one or more foreign editions in English. Others enter cooperative agreements with overseas companies to produce native-language versions of essentially U.S. magazines. For example, Hearst and the British company ITP cooperate to publish British and Middle Eastern editions of *Esquire*, two of the 18 international versions of the men's magazine. ITP and Hearst also team up on the Dubai version of the fashion magazine *Harper's Bazaar* and 75 other titles in the Middle East and India. Often, American publishers prepare special content for foreign-language editions. *Elle* has 42 local language versions of its magazine, including countries like Argentina, Serbia, Poland, Thailand, and Turkey. *Vogue* offers 19 in locales such as China, Greece, and Portugal. The internationalization of magazines will no doubt increase as conglomeration and globalization continue to have an impact on the magazine industry as they have on other media businesses.

Second is technology. Computers and satellites now allow instant distribution of copy from the editor's desk to printing plants around the world. The result—almost immediate delivery to subscribers and sales outlets—makes production and distribution of even more narrowly targeted split runs more cost-effective. This is an efficiency that cable television has yet to match.

▼ The look alone of this magazine's cover makes it clear that it is the German version of what we know in the United States as *Psychology Today*.

In early 2013, the online edition of the *Atlantic* ran a long, laudatory article on the Church of Scientology and its leader, David Miscavige. For several reasons, including the publication of a best-selling book critical of the religion, Scientology had been much in the news at the time, so the magazine's decision to do the story made good journalistic sense. But controversy erupted when it was discovered that the piece was actually an advertorial, written not by the *Atlantic*'s journalists but by the Church of Scientology itself. The resulting explosion of criticism put **sponsored content**, online articles paid for by advertisers, into the public forum.

There are many names for the practice, including branded content, native advertising, brand journalism, and content marketing, but whatever the label, **the strategy of permitting advertisers to pay for or even create articles that look like traditional editorial content is now common as publishers try to find new sources of income.** Sometimes the material is written by the magazine's journalists; other times it is provided by the sponsor or its advertising agency. In either case, the story typically looks in tone and design like content usually found on the magazine's site. "The reason sponsored content is so attractive to advertisers and marketers," explains media critic Andrew Leonard, "is that, done well, it's very difficult to tell what is actually news content and what is just a commercial" (2013).

Many reputable and well-established online magazines engage in the practice. *Business Insider,* for example, attaches sponsored slide shows to stories written by its own people. *Atlantic* maintains a team of writers, Atlantic Marketing, that produces content "on behalf of its advertising partners" (Atlantic, 2013). *Forbes* publishes pieces written by its sponsors. An article by a FedEx employee, for example, might focus on small business. But, according to the magazine, participating brands are not allowed to make direct commercial pitches to readers. "It is, in fact, content," explains *Forbes*'s Michael Perlis. "It's not advertising. It's about big issues that relate to thought leadership" (in Vega, 2013, p. B1).

Journalism professor Jeff Jarvis disagrees: "The reader must never be confused about the source of content. Confusing the audience is clearly the goal of native-sponsored-brand-

> **"The reader must never be confused about the source of content."**

content-voice-advertising. And the result has to be a dilution of the value of news brands. Some say those brands are diminishing anyway. So sponsored content is just another way to milk the old cows as they die. Lately I've been shocked to hear some executives at news organizations, as well as some journalism students and even teachers, shrug at the risk. If I'm the guy who argues that news must find new paths to profitability, then what's my problem?" (2013). Blogger Andrew Sullivan, who once wrote for the *Atlantic*, offers his answer to that question: "The very phrases—'sponsored content,' 'native advertising'—are as accurate as 'enhanced interrogation.' It's either an advertisement or your media company is producing content. Creating editorial content for advertisers for money, rather than for readers for its own

---

Third is the sale of subscriber lists and a magazine's own direct marketing of products. Advertisers buy space in specialized magazines to reach a specific type of reader. Most magazines are more than happy to sell those readers' names and addresses to those same advertisers, as well as to others who want to contact readers with direct mail pitches. Many magazines use their own subscriber lists and Web visitors' details for the same purpose, marketing products of interest to their particular readership. Some magazines meet television's challenge by becoming television themselves. Fox Television Studios, for example, produces Web-based programs based on Hearst publications *CosmoGirl* and *Popular Mechanics.*

Advertorials

Publishers and advertisers increasingly use advertorials as a means of boosting the value of a magazine as an advertising medium. **Advertorials** are ads that appear in magazines and take on the appearance of genuine editorial content. Sometimes they are a page or less, sometimes inserts composed of several pages. They frequently carry the disclaimer "Advertisement," but it is usually in small print. Sometimes the disclaimer is no more than the advertiser's logo in a page corner. The goal is to put commercial content before readers, cloaked in the respectability of editorial content. Advertorial-generated revenue in the magazine industry more than doubled in the 1990s, as did the number of ad pages given over to their use. Advertorials now account

sake, is a major shift in this industry. There is an obvious solution. It is to make the advertorials look more different from editorial than they now do and slap a clear word ADVERTISEMENT on top of them. If that ethical labeling ruins your business model, it's proof that your business model isn't ethical" (2013).

Enter your voice. Do you find this practice problematic, even if the sponsored content is clearly labeled? Is Mr. Sullivan correct, that having writers create content for advertisers is a fundamental alteration of journalism itself? Professor Jarvis worries "about journalists who spend one day writing to serve the public and the next writing to serve sponsors." When do journalists become copywriters? Should we care that they sometimes do?

Or are critics like Sullivan and Jarvis just old, traditional media types who don't understand that boosting revenues by whatever means is the only way that magazines can survive in the new world of online journalism? *Atlantic*'s publisher, Jay Lauf, seems to get it, explaining, "I would love to eliminate banners [static online ads] because I think most of them don't work. There's a need for scalable solution for certain advertisers. What I'm advocating is more relevant, engaging content. . . . A lot of people worry about crossing editorial and advertising lines, but I think it respects readers more. It's saying, 'You know what you're interested in.' It's more respectful of the reader that way" (in Sternberg, 2012). Do you accept Mr. Lauf's assertion that he is showing you respect by publishing sponsored content? Do you accept the argument that the magazine industry must loosen its standards, even if only a little and even if only online, in order to compete in a tough media environment? Why or why not?

▲ An *Atlantic* story paid for by the controversial Church of Scientology brought sponsored content quite dramatically into the cultural forum.

for over 10% of all magazine advertising income. The question for media-literate magazine readers is clear: Is an item journalism or is it advertising?

Critics of advertorials argue that this blurring of the distinction between editorial and commercial matter is a breach of faith with readers (see the essay "Sponsored Content: Corrupting or Necessary?"). Moreover, if the intent is not deception, why is the disclaimer typically small; why use the editorial content format at all? Defenders contend that advertorials are a well-entrenched aspect of contemporary magazines. The industry considers them not only financially necessary in an increasingly competitive media market but proper as well. No one is hurt by advertorials. In fact, they often deliver useful information. Advertisers are free in America to use whatever legal and truthful means are available to sell their products. Magazines always label the paid material as such. And readers aren't idiots, defenders claim. They know an ad when they see one.

Advertiser Influence over Magazine Content

Sometimes controversial, too, is the influence that some advertisers attempt to exert over content. This influence is always there, at least implicitly. A magazine editor must satisfy advertisers as well as readers. One common way advertisers' interests shape content is in the placement of ads. Airline ads are moved away from stories about plane crashes. Cigarette ads rarely appear near articles on lung cancer. In fact, it is an accepted industry practice for a magazine to provide advertisers with a heads-up, alerting them

that soon-to-be-published content may prove uncomfortable for their businesses. Advertisers can then request a move of their ad, or pull it and wait to run it in the next issue. Magazines, too, often entice advertisers with promises of placement of their ads adjacent to relevant articles.

But **complementary copy**—content that reinforces the advertiser's message, or at least does not negate it—is problematic when creating such copy becomes a major influence in a publication's editorial decision making. This happens in a number of ways. Editors sometimes engage in self-censorship, making decisions about how stories are written and which stories appear based on the fear that specific advertisers will be offended. Some magazines, *Architectural Digest*, for example, identify companies by name in their picture caption copy only if they are advertisers. But many critics inside and outside the industry see increased crumbling of the wall between advertising demands and editorial judgment.

This problem is particularly acute today, say critics, because a very competitive media environment puts additional pressure on magazines to bow to advertiser demands. For example, a Sears marketing executive suggested that magazines needed to operate "in much less traditional ways" by allowing advertisers to "become a part of the storyline" in their articles (Atkinson, 2004). Lexus, for example, asks the magazines it advertises in to use its automobiles in photos used to illustrate editorial content. But most troubling are advertisers who institute an **ad-pull policy**, the demand for an advance review of a magazine's content, with the threat of pulled advertising if dissatisfied with that content. The advertising agencies for oil giant BP and financial services company Morgan Stanley shocked the magazine industry by demanding just that—in the case of BP, insisting that it be informed "in advance of any news text or visuals magazines plan to publish that directly mention the company, a competitor, or the oil-and-energy industry" (Sanders & Halliday, 2005). Events like this moved *Advertising Age* to editorialize, "Shame on BP. And shame on Morgan Stanley and General Motors and any other advertisers involved in assaults on editorial integrity and independence. By wielding their ad budget as weapons to beat down newsrooms, these companies threaten the bond that media properties have with their audiences, the very thing that gives media their value to advertisers to begin with" ("Shame on BP," 2005). This concern is overwrought, say many industry people. When the American Society of Magazine Editors announced it would "revise its guidelines for protecting editorial integrity" in 2008, there was significant push-back. "As long as it's interesting to the reader, who cares?" argued one editor. "This ivory-tower approach that edit[orial] is so untouchable, and what they're doing is so wonderful and can't be tainted by the stink of advertising just makes me sick" (in Ives, 2008).

The critics' question, however, remains, "How can a magazine function, offering depth, variety, and detail, when BP and Morgan Stanley are joined by dozens of other advertisers, each demanding to preview content, not for its direct comment on matters of importance to their businesses, but for controversy and potential offensiveness? What will be the impact on the ideals of a free press and of free inquiry?"

DEVELOPING MEDIA LITERACY SKILLS

Recognizing the Power of Graphics

Detecting the use of and determining the informational value of advertorials is only one reason media literacy is important when reading magazines. Another necessary media literacy skill is the ability to understand how graphics and other artwork provide the background for interpreting stories. Some recent incidents suggest why.

The notorious June 27, 1994, *Time* O. J. Simpson cover—for which artists altered Simpson's facial tones on an L.A. police department mug shot—is one controversial example of how graphics are used to create meaning. The magazine said it wanted to show the "real" O. J., free of the glamour and hype that usually surround him. Critics claimed that darkening Simpson's face was designed to play to the ugly stereotype of African Americans as criminals. Media-literate readers might also ask, "How does changing what was a 'real' photograph make the subject seem more real?"

More recent examples of digital fakery raise a different question. *Glamour* digitally "reduced" television's *Ugly Betty*, America Ferrera, two dress sizes in October 2007, leading to industry calls for an investigation of the practice. Then there is the September 2009 *Self* cover photo of Kelly Clarkson that pitted her fans against the magazine's editors. The Kelly Clarkson who graced that cover, like America Ferrera on the front of *Glamour*, was much thinner than in real life. That was bad enough for some, but editor Lucy Danzinger's response to critics set off a firestorm of Internet protest. Editor Danzinger explained that even though the singer possessed "the truest beauty . . . the kind that comes from within" and that Kelly "doesn't care what people think of her weight," *Self* altered the image because it wanted to present the *American Idol* winner, "the picture of confidence [that she] truly is," as looking "her personal best" (in Williams, 2009). In other words, to show the *real* Kelly Clarkson, *Self* had to show the *unreal* Kelly Clarkson.

The American Medical Association found the practice sufficiently harmful that at its 2011 annual meeting it voted to encourage magazine industry efforts to discontinue its use. "Advertisers commonly alter photographs to enhance the appearance of models' bodies, and such alterations can contribute to unrealistic expectations of appropriate body image—especially among impressionable children and adolescents," wrote the AMA. "A large body of literature links exposure to media-propagated images of unrealistic body image to eating disorders and other child and adolescent health problems" (in Ives, 2011c).

An additional media literacy issue here has to do with maintaining the confidence of audience members. As digital altering of images becomes more widespread—and its occurrence better known—will viewers and readers come to question the veracity of even unaltered images and the reports that employ them? "With new technology, faking or doctoring photographs has never been simpler, faster, or more difficult to detect," explains *American Journalism Review*'s Sherry Ricchiardi. "Skilled operators truly are like magicians, except they use tools like

▼ In October 2007, *Glamour*'s editors shaved at least two dress sizes from America Ferrera's body in an effort, in their eyes, to make her a less Ugly Betty. This not only put the alteration of magazine graphics squarely into the cultural forum, but it led the American Society of Magazine Editors to convene an industry committee to discuss possible rule changes regarding alteration of images.

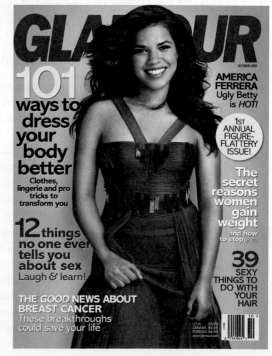

Photoshop . . . to create their illusions." "The public is losing faith in us. Without credibility, we have nothing; we cannot survive," adds John Long, chair of the ethics and standards committee of the National Press Photographers Association (both in Ricchiardi, 2007, pp. 37–38).

What do you think? Did you see any of these images? Did you know they had been altered? If you did, would that have changed your reading of the stories or events that they represented? Does the fact that major media outlets sometimes alter the images they present to you as news lead you to question their overall performance? Do you believe that media outlets that use altered images have an obligation to inform readers and viewers of their decision to restructure reality? How does it feel to know that almost all of the images that we see in our daily newspapers and news magazines today are digitized?

MEDIA LITERACY CHALLENGE
Identifying Digital Alteration

Media-literate magazine readers are *critical thinkers who make independent judgments about content*, they *think critically about media messages*, and they *have heightened expectations of the content they read*. You'll have to have all these skills to complete this challenge.

Choose your favorite magazine and find all the pages, editorial and advertising, that show images of people. Identify those that have been digitally enhanced or changed. Critics and proponents alike acknowledge that just about every image appearing in a consumer magazine has been altered. How many did you find? What were your clues? How do you feel about the practice, and do you think the magazine had the right to make these alterations? What do your answers say about your understanding and respect for the power of media messages, your expectations of magazine content, and your ability to think critically about the messages in magazines? You may want to meet this challenge individually, using your favorite publication, or make it a competition. You can have different people examining the same magazine to see who can find the greatest number of alterations, or you can have teams compete against one another looking at an array of titles.

Resources for Review and Discussion

REVIEW POINTS: TYING CONTENT TO LEARNING OUTCOMES

▶ **Describe the history and development of the magazine industry and the magazine itself as a medium.**
- ▶ Magazines, a favorite of 18th-century British elite, made an easy transition to colonial America.
- ▶ Mass circulation magazines prospered in the post–Civil War years because of increased literacy, improved transportation, reduced postal costs, and lower cover prices.
- ▶ Magazines' large readership and financial health empowered the muckrakers to challenge society's powerful.

▶ **Identify how the organizational and economic nature of the contemporary magazine industry shapes the content of magazines.**
- ▶ Television changed magazines from mass circulation to specialized media; as a result, they are attractive to advertisers because of their demographic specificity, reader engagement, and reader affinity for the advertising they carry.

- ▶ The three broad categories of magazines are trade, professional, and business; industrial, company, and sponsored; and consumer magazines.
- ▶ Magazine circulation comes in the form of subscription, single-copy sales, and controlled circulation. Advertiser demands for better measures of readership and accountability may render circulation an outmoded metric.

▶ **Describe the relationship between magazines and their readers.**
- ▶ Custom publishing, in the form of brand magazines and magalogues, is one way that magazines stand out in a cluttered media environment.
- ▶ Magazines further meet competition from other media, especially cable television, through internationalization, technology-driven improvements in distribution, and the sale of subscriber lists and their own direct marketing efforts.

- Explain the convergence of magazines with the Internet and mobile technologies.
  - Virtually all magazines have online equivalents, although they employ different financial models.
  - Readers are overwhelmingly positive about electronic magazines.
  - They are equally enthusiastic about accessing magazines from mobile devices.
- Apply key magazine-reading media literacy skills.
  - A number of industry revenue-enhancing practices pose different challenges to media-literate readers:
    - Advertorials are commercial content designed to appear like genuine editorial material.

- Interruptive ads are ad copy that weaves in and around editorial content.
- Complementary copy is editorial content that reinforces an advertiser's message.
- Ad-pull policies are advertiser demands, on threat of removal of its ads, for an advance view of a magazine's content.
- Heavy reliance on digitally altered graphics is regularly employed in both advertising and editorial content and is highly controversial.

KEY TERMS

muckraking, 101

split runs, 107

circulation, 108

controlled circulation, 108

custom publishing, 108

QR (quick response) codes, 112

NFC (near-field communication) chips, 112

brand magazine, 112

magalogue, 113

sponsored content, 114

advertorial, 114

complementary copy, 116

ad-pull policy, 116

QUESTIONS FOR REVIEW

1. How would you characterize the content of the first U.S. magazines?
2. What factors fueled the expansion of the magazine industry at the beginning of the 20th century?
3. What factors led to the demise of the mass circulation era and the development of the era of specialization?
4. What are the three broad types of magazines?
5. Why do advertisers favor specialization in magazines?
6. What are engagement and affinity? Why are they important to advertisers?
7. In what different ways do magazines internationalize their publications?

8. Why is the magazine industry optimistic about the effects of new mobile technologies on its relationship with readers?
9. What is an advertorial? What is its function?
10. What is complementary copy? Why does it trouble critics?

McGraw Hill connect

For further review, go to the LearnSmart study module for this chapter.

QUESTIONS FOR CRITICAL THINKING AND DISCUSSION

1. Can you think of any contemporary crusading magazine or muckraking writers? Compared with those of the progressive era, they are certainly less visible. Why is this the case?
2. Which magazines do you read? Draw a demographic profile of yourself based only on the magazines you regularly read.

3. Are you troubled by the practice of altering photographs? Can you think of times when it might be more appropriate than others?

Film

6

Learning Objectives

The movies are our dream factories; they are bigger than life. With books, they are the only mass medium not dependent on advertising for their financial support. That means they must satisfy you, because you buy the tickets. This means that the relationship between medium and audience is different from those that exist with other media. After studying this chapter you should be able to

▶ Outline the history and development of the film industry and film itself as a medium.

▶ Describe the cultural value of film and the implications of the blockbuster mentality for film as an important artistic and cultural medium.

▶ Summarize the three components of the film industry—production, distribution, and exhibition.

▶ Explain how the organizational and economic nature of the contemporary film industry shapes the content of films.

▶ Describe the promise and peril of convergence and the new digital technologies to film as we know it.

▶ Understand how production is becoming more expensive and, simultaneously, less expensive.

▶ Apply film-watching media literacy skills, especially in interpreting merchandise tie-ins and product placements.

Academy Award nominee *The Help*. Amid the blockbusters, Hollywood can still produce mature, serious movies.

PARIS IS COLD AND DAMP ON THIS DECEMBER NIGHT, THREE DAYS AFTER CHRISTMAS IN 1895. But you bundle up and make your way to the Grand Café in the heart of the city. You've read in the morning paper that brothers Auguste and Louis Lumière will be displaying their new invention that somehow makes pictures move. Your curiosity is piqued.

Tables and chairs are set up in the basement room of the café, and a white bedsheet is draped above its stage. The Lumières appear to polite applause. They announce the program: *La Sortie des usines Lumière (Quitting Time at the Lumière Factory)*; *Le Repas de bébé*, featuring a Lumière child eating; *L'Arroseur arrosé*, about a practical-joking boy and his victim, the gardener; and finally *L'Arrivée d'un train en gare*, the arrival of a train at a station.

The lights go out. Somewhere behind you, someone starts the machine. There is some brief flickering on the suspended sheet and then . . . you are completely awe-struck. There before you—bigger than life-size—photographs are really moving. You see places you know to be miles away. You spy on the secret world of a prankster boy, remembering your own childhood. But the last film is the most impressive. As the giant locomotive chugs toward the audience, you and most of the others are convinced you are about to be crushed. There is panic. People are ducking under their chairs, screaming. Death is imminent!

The first paying audience in the history of motion pictures has just had a lesson in movie watching.

The Lumière brothers were excellent mechanics, and their father owned a factory that made photographic plates. Their first films were little more than what we would now consider black-and-white home movies. As you can tell from their titles, they were simple stories. There was no editing; the camera was simply turned on, then turned off. There were no fades, wipes, or flashbacks. No computer graphics, no dialogue, and no music. And yet much of the audience was terrified by the oncoming cinematic locomotive. They were illiterate in the language of film.

We begin our study of the movies with the history of film, from its entrepreneurial beginnings, through the introduction of its narrative and visual language, to its

1800

1850

1720s Early efforts using chemical salts to capture temporary photographic images

1793 ▲ Niépce begins experimenting with methods to set optical images

1816 Niépce develops photography

1839 ▲ Daguerreotype introduced; Talbot's calotype (paper film)

1877 ▲ Muybridge takes race photos

1887 Goodwin's celluloid roll film

1888 Dickson produces kinetograph

1889 Eastman's easy-to-use camera

1891 Edison's kinetoscope

1895 Lumière brothers debut cinématographe

1896 Edison unveils Edison Vitascope

◀ The Lumières' *L'Arrivée d'un train en gare*. As simple as early films were, their viewers did not have sufficient film literacy to properly interpret, understand, and enjoy them. This scene supposedly sent people screaming and hiding to avoid being crushed by the oncoming train.

establishment as a large, studio-run industry. We detail Hollywood's relationship with its early audiences and changes in the structure and content of films resulting from the introduction of television. We then look at contemporary movie production, distribution, and exhibition systems and how convergence is altering all three, the influence of the major studios, and the economic pressures on them in an

1900

1950

2000

1902 Méliès's *A Trip to the Moon*

1903 Porter's *The Great Train Robbery* (montage)

1908 Motion Picture Patents Company founded

1915 Lincoln Motion Picture Company; Griffith's *The Birth of a Nation*

1922 Hays office opens

1926 ▲ Sound comes to film

1934 Motion Picture Production Code issued

1939 Television unveiled at World's Fair

1947 HUAC convenes

1948 Paramount Decision Cable TV introduced

1969 ▲ Indie film *Easy Rider*

1976 VCR introduced

1996 ▲ DVD introduced

2007 *Purple Violets* released directly to iTunes

2009 ▲ *Avatar*

2011 27 sequels released, the most ever in one year

2012 For first time, more money spent on online movies than on DVD

increasingly multimedia environment. We examine the special place movies hold for us and how ever-younger audiences and the films that target them may affect our culture. Recognizing the use of product placement in movies is the basis for improving our media literacy skill.

A Short History of the Movies

We are no longer illiterate in the grammar of film, nor are movies as simple as the early Lumière offerings. Consider the sophistication necessary for filmmakers to produce a computer-generated movie such as *Rango* and the skill required for audiences to read *Inception*'s shifts in time and space, unconventional camera angles, and other twists and turns. How we arrived at this contemporary medium–audience relationship is a wonderful story.

Early newspapers were developed by businesspeople and patriots for a small, politically involved elite that could read, but the early movie industry was built largely by entrepreneurs who wanted to make money entertaining everyone. Unlike television, whose birth and growth were predetermined and guided by the already well-established radio industry (see Chapter 7), there were no precedents, no rules, and no expectations for movies.

Return to the opening vignette. The audience for the first Lumière movies did not "speak film." Think of it as being stranded in a foreign country with no knowledge of the language and cultural conventions. You would have to make your way, with each new experience helping you better understand the next. First you'd learn some simple words and basic customs. Eventually, you'd be able to better understand the language and people. In other words, you'd become increasingly literate in that culture. Beginning with that Paris premiere, people had to become film literate. They had to develop an understanding of cinematic alterations in time and place. They had to learn how images and sound combined to create meaning. But unlike visiting in another culture, there was no existing cinematic culture. Movie creators and their audiences had to grow up together.

The Early Entrepreneurs

In 1873 former California governor Leland Stanford needed help winning a bet he had made with a friend. Convinced that a horse in full gallop had all four feet off the ground, he had to prove it. He turned to well-known photographer Eadweard Muybridge, who worked on the problem for four years before finding a solution. In 1877 Muybridge arranged a series of still cameras along a stretch of racetrack. As the horse sprinted by, each camera took its picture. The resulting photographs won Stanford his bet, but more important, they sparked an idea in their photographer. Muybridge was intrigued by the appearance of motion created when photos are viewed sequentially. He began taking pictures of numerous kinds of human and animal action. To display his work, Muybridge invented the **zoopraxiscope**, a machine for projecting slides onto a distant surface.

When people watched the rapidly projected, sequential slides, they saw the pictures as if they were in motion. This perception is the result of a physiological phenomenon known as **persistence of vision**, in which the images our eyes gather are retained in the brain for about 1/24 of a second. Therefore, if photographic frames are moved at 24 frames a second, people perceive them as actually in motion.

Muybridge eventually met the prolific inventor Thomas Edison in 1888. Edison quickly saw the scientific and economic potential of the zoopraxiscope and set his top scientist, William Dickson, to the task of developing a better projector. But Dickson correctly saw the problem as one of developing a better system of *filming*. He understood that shooting numerous still photos, then putting them in sequential order, then redrawing the images they held onto slides was inherently limiting. Dickson combined

▲ Muybridge's horse pictures. When these plates were placed sequentially and rotated, they produced the appearance of motion.

Hannibal Goodwin's newly invented celluloid roll film with George Eastman's easy-to-use Kodak camera to make a motion picture camera that took 40 photographs a second. He used his **kinetograph** to film all types of theatrical performances, some by unknowns and others by famous entertainers such as Annie Oakley and Buffalo Bill Cody. Of course, none of this would have been possible had it not been for photography itself.

THE DEVELOPMENT OF PHOTOGRAPHY The process of photography was first developed by French inventor Joseph Nicéphore Niépce around 1816. Although there had been much experimentation in the realm of image making at the time, Niépce was the first person to make practical use of a camera and film. He photographed natural objects and produced color prints. Unfortunately, his images would last only a short time.

Niépce's success, however, attracted the attention of country-man Louis Daguerre, who joined with him to perfect the process. Niépce died before the 1839 introduction of the **daguerreotype**, a process of recording images on polished metal plates, usually copper, covered with a thin layer of silver iodide emulsion. When light reflected from an object passed through a lens and struck the emulsion, the emulsion would etch the image on the plate. The plate was then washed with a cleaning solvent, leaving a positive or replica image.

In the same year as Daguerre's first public display of the daguerreotype, British inventor William Henry Fox Talbot introduced a paper film process. This process was more important to the development of photography than the metal film system, but the daguerreotype received widespread attention and acclaim and made the public enthusiastic about photography.

▼ Typical of daguerreotypes, this plate captures a portrait. The method's long exposure time made all but the most stationary subjects impossible to photograph.

The **calotype** (Talbot's system) used translucent paper, what we now call the negative, from which several prints could be made. In addition, his film was much more sensitive than Daguerre's metal plate, allowing for exposure times of only a few seconds as opposed to the daguerreotype's 30 minutes. Until calotype, virtually all daguerreotype images were still lifes and portraits, a necessity with long exposure times.

The final steps in the development of the photographic process necessary for true motion pictures were taken, as we've just seen, by Goodwin in 1887 and Eastman in 1889 and were adapted to motion pictures by Edison scientist Dickson.

THOMAS EDISON Edison built the first motion picture studio near his laboratory in New Jersey. He called it Black Maria, the common name at that time for a police paddy wagon. It had an open roof and revolved to follow the sun so the performers being filmed would always be illuminated.

The completed films were not projected. Instead, they were run through a **kineto-scope**, a sort of peep show device. Often they were accompanied by music provided by another Edison invention, the phonograph. Patented in 1891 and commercially available three years later, the kinetoscope quickly became a popular feature in penny arcades, vaudeville halls, and big-city Kinetoscope parlors. This marked the beginning of commercial motion picture exhibition.

THE LUMIÈRE BROTHERS The Lumière brothers made the next advance. Their initial screenings demonstrated that people would sit in a darkened room to watch motion pictures projected on a screen. The brothers from Lyon envisioned great wealth in their ability to increase the number of people who could simultaneously watch a movie. In 1895 they patented their **cinématographe**, a device that both photographed and projected action. Within weeks of their Christmastime showing, long lines of enthusiastic moviegoers were waiting for their makeshift theater to open. Edison recognized the advantage of the cinématographe over his kinetoscope, so he acquired the patent for an advanced projector developed by U.S. inventor Thomas Armat. On April 23, 1896, the Edison Vitascope premiered in New York City, and the American movie business was born.

The Coming of Narrative

The Edison and Lumière movies were typically only a few minutes long and showed little more than filmed reproductions of reality—celebrities, weight lifters, jugglers, and babies eating. They were shot in fixed frame (the camera did not move), and there was no editing. For the earliest audiences, this was enough. But soon the novelty wore thin. People wanted more for their money. French filmmaker Georges Méliès began making narrative motion pictures, that is, movies that told a story. At the end of the 1890s he was shooting and exhibiting one-scene, one-shot movies, but soon he began making stories based on sequential shots in different places. He simply took one shot, stopped the camera, moved it, took another shot, and so on. Méliès is often called the "first artist of the cinema" because he brought narrative to the medium in the form of imaginative tales such as *A Trip to the Moon* (1902).

Méliès had been a magician and caricaturist before he became a filmmaker, and his inventive movies showed his dramatic flair. They were extravagant stage plays in which people disappeared and reappeared and other wonders occurred. *A Trip to the Moon* came to America in 1903, and U.S. moviemakers were quick not only to borrow the idea of using film to tell stories but also to improve on it.

Edwin S. Porter, an Edison Company camera operator, saw that film could be an even better storyteller with more artistic use of camera placement and editing. His 12-minute *The Great Train Robbery* (1903) was the first movie to use editing, intercutting of scenes, and a mobile camera to tell a relatively sophisticated tale. It was also the first Western. This new narrative form using **montage**—tying together two separate but related shots in such a way that they took on a new, unified meaning—was

an instant hit with audiences. Almost immediately hundreds of **nickelodeons**, some having as many as 100 seats, were opened in converted stores, banks, and halls across the United States. The price of admission was one nickel, hence the name. By 1905 cities such as New York were opening a new nickelodeon every day. From 1907 to 1908, the first year in which there were more narrative than documentary films, the number of nickelodeons in the United States increased tenfold. With so many

exhibition halls in so many towns serving such an extremely enthusiastic public, many movies were needed. Literally hundreds and hundreds of new **factory studios**, or production companies, were started.

Because so many movies needed to be made and rushed to the nickelodeons, people working in the industry had to learn and perform virtually all aspects of production. There was precious little time for, or profitability in, the kind of specialization that marks contemporary filmmaking. Writer, actor, and camera operator D. W. Griffith perfected his craft in this environment. He was quickly recognized as a brilliant director. He introduced innovations such as scheduled rehearsals before final shooting and production based on close adherence to a shooting script. He lavished attention on otherwise ignored aspects of a film's look—costume and lighting—and used close-ups and other dramatic camera angles to transmit emotion.

All his skill came together in 1915 with the release of *The Birth of a Nation*. Whereas Porter had used montage to tell a story, Griffith used it to create passion, move emotions, and heighten suspense. The most influential silent film ever made, this three-hour epic was six weeks in rehearsal and nine weeks in shooting, cost $125,000 to produce (making it the most expensive movie made to that date), was distributed to theaters complete with an orchestral music score, had a cast of thousands of humans and animals, and had an admission price well above the usual 5 cents—$3. It was the most popular and profitable movie made and remained so until 1939, when it was surpassed by *Gone with the Wind*. With other Griffith masterpieces, *Intolerance* (1916) and *Broken Blossoms* (1919), *The Birth of a Nation* set new standards for the American film. They took movies out of the nickelodeons and made them big business. At the same time, however, *The Birth of a Nation* represented the basest aspects of U.S. culture because it included an ugly, racist portrayal of African Americans and a sympathetic treatment of the Ku Klux Klan. The film inspired protests in front of theaters across the country and criticism in some newspapers and magazines, and African Americans fought back with their own films (see the essay, "African American Response to D. W. Griffith: The Lincoln and Micheaux Film Companies"). Nevertheless, *The Birth of a Nation* found acceptance by the vast majority of people.

▶ The Ku Klux Klan was the collective hero in D. W. Griffith's *The Birth of a Nation*. This cinematic masterpiece and groundbreaking film employed production techniques never before used; however, its racist theme mars its legacy.

The African American community did not sit passively in the wake of D. W. Griffith's 1915 cinematic but hateful wonder, *The Birth of a Nation*. The NAACP fought the film in court and on the picket line, largely unsuccessfully. But other African Americans decided to use film to combat *Birth*. The first was Emmett J. Scott, a quiet, scholarly man. He sought money from the country's Black middle class to produce a short film showing the achievements of African Americans. His intention was to attach his film, *Lincoln's Dream*, as a prologue to screenings of the Griffith film. Together with screenwriter Elaine Sterne, Scott eventually expanded the project into a feature-length movie. He approached Universal Studios with his film but was rejected.

> "They might not be able to convince White America of Griffith's error, but they could reassure African Americans that their views could find expression."

With independent backing from both Black and White investors, the film was released in 1918. Produced by an inexperienced cast and crew working on a production beset by bad weather and technical difficulties, the retitled *The Birth of a Race* filled 12 reels of film and ran more than three hours. Its publicity hailed it as "The Greatest and Most Daring of Photoplays . . . The Story of Sin . . . A Master Picture Conceived in the Spirit of Truth and Dedicated to All the Races of the World" (Bogle, 1989, p. 103). It was an artistic and commercial failure. Scott, however, had inspired others.

Even before *The Birth of a Race* was completed, the Lincoln Motion Picture Company was incorporated, in Nebraska in 1916 and in California in 1917, by brothers Noble P. and George Johnson. Their tack differed from Scott's. They understood that their Black films would never be allowed on "White" screens, so they produced movies designed to tell Black-oriented stories to Black audiences. They might not be able to convince White America of Griffith's error, but they could reassure African Americans that their views could find expression. Lincoln's first movie was *The Realization of a Negro's Ambition*, and it told the story of Black American achievements. The Johnson brothers turned U.S. racism to their advantage. Legal segregation in the South and de facto segregation in the North had led to an explosion of Black theaters. These movie houses needed content. Lincoln helped provide it by producing 10 three-reelers between 1916 and 1920.

Another notable film company soon began operation, hoping to challenge, at least in Black theaters, Griffith's portrayals. Oscar Micheaux founded the Micheaux Film and Book

Company in 1918 in Chicago and soon produced *The Homesteader*, an eight-reel film based on the autobiographical novel he'd written three years earlier. It was the story of a successful Black homestead rancher in South Dakota. But Micheaux was not content to boost Black self-esteem. He was determined to make "racial photoplays depicting racial life" (as quoted in Sampson, 1977, p. 42). In 1920 he released *Within Our Gates*, a drama about the southern lynching of a Black man. Censored and denied a screening in dozens of cities both North and South, Micheaux was undeterred. In 1921 he released the eight-reeler *The Gunsaulus Mystery*, based on a well-known murder case in which a Black man was convicted.

These early film pioneers used their medium to make a difference. They challenged the interpretation of history being circulated by the most popular movie in the world, and they provided encouragement and entertainment to the African American community.

▶ A scene from *The Realization of a Negro's Ambition*.

The Big Studios

In 1908 Thomas Edison, foreseeing the huge amounts of money that could be made from movies, founded the Motion Picture Patents Company (MPPC), often simply called the Trust. This group of 10 companies under Edison's control, holding the patents to virtually all existing filmmaking and exhibition equipment, ran the production and distribution of film in the United States with an iron fist. Anyone who wanted to make or exhibit a movie needed Trust permission, which typically was not forthcoming. In addition, the MPPC had rules about the look of the movies it would permit: They must be one reel, approximately 12 minutes long, and must adopt a "stage perspective"; that is, the actors must fill the frame as if they were in a stage play.

Many independent film companies sprang up in defiance of the Trust, including Griffith's in 1913. To avoid MPPC scrutiny and reprisal, these companies moved to

California. This westward migration had other benefits. Better weather meant longer shooting seasons. Free of MPPC standards, people like Griffith who wanted to explore the potential of films longer than 12 minutes and with imaginative use of the camera were free to do so.

The new studio system, with its more elaborate films and big-name stars, was born, and it controlled the movie industry from California. Thomas H. Ince (maker of the William S. Hart Westerns), Griffith, and comedy genius Mack Sennett formed the Triangle Company. Adolph Zukor's Famous Players in Famous Plays—formed when Zukor was denied MPPC permission to distribute one of his films—joined with several other independents and a distribution company to become Paramount. Other independents joined to create the Fox Film Company (soon called 20th Century Fox) and Universal. Although films were still silent, by the mid-1920s there were more than 20,000 movie theaters in the United States, and more than 350,000 people were making their living in film production. More than 1,240,000 feet of film was shot each year in Hollywood, and annual domestic U.S. box office receipts exceeded $750 million.

The industry prospered not just because of its artistry, drive, and innovation but because it used these to meet the needs of a growing audience. At the beginning of the 20th century, generous immigration rules, combined with political and social unrest abroad, encouraged a flood of European immigrants who congregated in U.S. cities where the jobs were and where people like themselves who spoke their language lived. American farmers, largely illiterate, also swarmed to the cities as years of drought and farm failure left them without home or hope. Jobs in the big mills and factories, although unpleasant, were plentiful. These new city dwellers had money and the need for leisure activities. Movies were a nickel, required no ability to read or to understand English, and offered glamorous stars and wonderful stories from faraway places.

Foreign political unrest proved to be a boon to the infant U.S. movie business in another way as well. In 1914 and 1915, when the California studios were remaking the industry in their own grand image, war raged in Europe. European moviemaking, most significantly the influential French, German, and Russian cinema, came to a halt. European demand for movies, however, did not. American movies, produced in huge numbers for the hungry home audience, were ideal for overseas distribution. Because so few in the domestic audience could read English, few printed titles were used in the then-silent movies. Therefore, little had to be changed to satisfy foreign moviegoers. Film was indeed a universal language, but more important, the American film industry had firmly established itself as the world leader, all within 20 years of the Lumière brothers' first screening.

Change Comes to Hollywood

As was the case with newspapers and magazines, the advent of television significantly altered the movie–audience relationship. But the nature of that relationship had been shaped and reshaped in the three decades between the coming of sound and the coming of television.

THE TALKIES The first sound film was one of three films produced by Warner Brothers. It may have been *Don Juan* (1926), starring John Barrymore, distributed with synchronized music and sound effects. Or perhaps Warner's more famous *The Jazz Singer* (1927), starring Al Jolson, which had several sound and speaking scenes (354 words in all) but was largely silent. Or it may have been the 1928 all-sound *Lights of New York*. Historians disagree because they cannot decide what constitutes a sound film.

There is no confusion, however, about the impact of sound on the movies and their audiences. First, sound made possible new genres—musicals, for example. Second, as actors and actresses now had to really act, performance aesthetics improved. Third, sound made film production a much more complicated and expensive proposition. As a result, many smaller filmmakers closed shop, solidifying the hold of the

▲ Al Jolson, in blackface, and May McAvoy starred in the 1927 *The Jazz Singer*, one of three claimants to the title of first sound movie.

big studios over the industry. In 1933, 60% of all U.S. films came from Hollywood's eight largest studios. By 1940, they were producing 76% of all U.S. movies and collecting 86% of the total box office. As for the audience, in 1926, the year of *Don Juan*'s release, 50 million people went to the movies each week. In 1929, at the onset of the Great Depression, the number had risen to 80 million. By 1930, when sound was firmly entrenched, the number of weekly moviegoers had risen to 90 million (Mast & Kawin, 1996).

SCANDAL The popularity of talkies, and of movies in general, inevitably raised questions about their impact on the culture. In 1896, well before sound, *The Kiss* had generated a great moral outcry. Its stars, John C. Rice and May Irwin, were also the leads in the popular Broadway play *The Widow Jones*, which closed with a climactic kiss. The Edison Company asked Rice and Irwin to re-create the kiss for the big screen. Newspapers and politicians were bombarded with complaints from the offended. Kissing in the theater was one thing; in movies it was quite another! The then-newborn industry responded to this and other calls for censorship with various forms of self-regulation and internal codes. But in the early 1920s more Hollywood scandals forced a more direct response.

In 1920 "America's Sweetheart" Mary Pickford obtained a questionable Nevada divorce from her husband and immediately married the movies' other darling, Douglas Fairbanks, himself newly divorced. In 1920 and 1921 comedian Fatty Arbuckle was involved in police problems on two coasts. The first was apparently hushed up after a $100,000 gift was made to a Massachusetts district attorney, but the second involved a murder at a San Francisco hotel party thrown by the actor. Although he was acquitted in his third trial (the first two ended in hung juries), the stain on Arbuckle and the industry remained. Then, in 1922, actor Wallace Reid and director William Desmond

▲ Screwball comedies like *Bringing Up Baby* helped Americans escape the misery of the Great Depression.

Taylor both died in what the newspapers referred to as "a mysterious fashion" in which drugs and sex were thought to have played a part. The cry for government intervention was raised. State legislatures introduced more than 100 separate pieces of legislation to censor or otherwise control movies and their content.

Hollywood responded in 1922 by creating the Motion Picture Producers and Distributors of America (MPPDA) and appointing Will H. Hays—chair of the Republican Party, a Presbyterian church elder, and a former postmaster general—president. The Hays Office, as it became known, undertook a vast effort to improve the image of the movies. Stressing the importance of movies to national life and as an educational medium, Hays promised better movies and founded a committee on public relations that included many civic and religious leaders. Eventually, in 1934, the Motion Picture Production Code (MPPC) was released. The MPPC forbade the use of profanity, limited bedroom scenes to married couples, required that skimpy outfits be replaced by more complete costumes, delineated the length of screen kisses, ruled out scenes that ridiculed public officials or religious leaders, and outlawed a series of words from "God" to "nuts," all enforced by a $25,000 fine.

NEW GENRES, NEW PROBLEMS By 1932 weekly movie attendance had dropped to 60 million. The Great Depression was having its effect. Yet the industry was able to weather the crisis for two reasons. The first was its creativity. New genres held people's interest. Feature documentaries such as *The Plow That Broke the Plains* (1936) spoke to audience needs to understand a world in seeming disorder. Musicals such as *42nd Street* (1933) and screwball comedies like *Bringing Up Baby* (1938) provided easy escapism. Gangster movies such as *Little Caesar* (1930) reflected the grimy reality of Depression city streets and daily newspaper headlines. Horror films such as *Frankenstein* (1931) articulated audience feelings of alienation and powerlessness in a seemingly uncontrollable time. Socially conscious comedies such as *Mr. Deeds Goes to Town* (1936) reminded moviegoers that good could still prevail, and the **double feature** with a **B-movie**—typically a less expensive movie—was a welcome relief to penny-pinching working people.

The movie business also survived the Depression because of its size and power, both residing in a system of operation called **vertical integration**. Using this system, studios produced their own films, distributed them through their own outlets, and exhibited them in their own theaters. In effect, the big studios controlled a movie from shooting to screening, guaranteeing distribution and an audience regardless of quality.

When the 1930s ended, weekly attendance was again over 80 million, and Hollywood was churning out 500 pictures a year. Moviegoing had become a central family and community activity for most people. Yet the end of that decade also brought bad news. In 1938 the Justice Department challenged vertical integration, suing the big five studios—Warner Brothers, MGM, Paramount, RKO, and 20th Century Fox—for restraint of trade; that is, they accused the studios of illegal monopolistic practices. The case would take 10 years to decide, but the movie industry, basking in the middle of its golden age, was under attack. Its fate was sealed in 1939 when the Radio Corporation of America (RCA) made the first public broadcast of television from atop the Empire State Building. The impact of these two events was profound, and the medium would have to develop a new relationship with its audience to survive.

TELEVISION When World War II began, the government took control of all patents for the newly developing technology of television as well as of the materials necessary for its production. The diffusion of the medium to the public was therefore halted, but its technological improvement was not. In addition, the radio networks and advertising agencies, recognizing that the war would eventually end and that their futures were in television, were preparing for that day. When the war did end, the movie industry found itself competing not with a fledgling medium but with a technologically and economically sophisticated one. The number of homes with television sets grew from 10,000 in 1946 to more than 10 million in 1950 and 54 million in 1960. Meanwhile, by 1955 movie attendance was down to 46 million people a week, fully 25% below even the worst attendance figures for the Depression years.

THE PARAMOUNT DECISION In 1948, 10 years after the case had begun, the Supreme Court issued its Paramount Decision, effectively destroying the studios' hold over moviemaking. Vertical integration was ruled illegal, as was **block booking**, the practice of requiring exhibitors to rent groups of movies, often inferior, to secure a better one. The studios were forced to sell off their exhibition businesses (the theaters). Before the Paramount Decision, the five major studios owned 75% of the first-run movie houses in the United States; after it, they owned none. Not only did they no longer have guaranteed exhibition, but other filmmakers now had access to the theaters, producing even greater competition for the dwindling number of movie patrons.

RED SCARE The U.S. response to its postwar position as world leader was fear. So concerned were some members of Congress that communism would steal the people's rights that Congress decided to steal them first. The Hollywood chapter of the virulent anticommunism movement we now call McCarthyism (after the Republican senator from Wisconsin, Joseph McCarthy, its most rabid and public champion) was led by the House Un-American Activities Committee (HUAC) and its chair, J. Parnell Thomas (later imprisoned for padding his congressional payroll). First convened in 1947, HUAC had as its goal to rid Hollywood of communist influence. The fear was that communist, socialist, and leftist propaganda was being secretly inserted into entertainment films by "Reds," "fellow travelers," and "pinkos." Many of the industry's best and brightest talents were called to testify before the committee and were asked, "Are you now or have you ever been a member of the Communist Party?" Those who came to be known as the Hollywood 10, including writers Ring Lardner Jr. and Dalton Trumbo and director Edward Dmytryk, refused to answer the question, accusing the committee, by its mere existence, of being in violation of the Bill of Rights. All were jailed. Rather than defend its First Amendment rights, the film industry abandoned those who were even mildly critical of the "Red Scare," jettisoning much of its best talent at a time when it could least afford to do so. In the fight against television, movies became increasingly tame for fear of being too controversial.

The industry was hurt not only by its cowardice but also by its shortsightedness. Hungry for content, the television industry asked Hollywood to sell it old features for broadcast. The studios responded by imposing on themselves the rule that no films could be sold to television and no working film star could appear on "the box." When it could have helped to shape early television viewer tastes and expectations of the new medium, Hollywood was absent. It lifted its ban in 1958.

FIGHTING BACK The industry worked mightily to recapture audiences from television using both technical and content innovations. Some of these innovations remain today and serve the medium and its audiences well. These include more attention to special effects, greater dependence on and improvements in color, and CinemaScope (projecting on a large screen two and one-half times wider than it is tall). Among the forgettable technological innovations were primitive 3-D and smellovision (wafting odors throughout the theater).

Innovation in content included spectaculars with which the small screen could not compete. *The Ten Commandments* (1956), *Ben Hur* (1959), *El Cid* (1960), and *Spartacus* (1960) filled the screen with many thousands of extras and lavish settings. Now that television was catering to the mass audience, movies were free to present challenging fare for more sophisticated audiences. The "message movie" charted social trends, especially alienation of youth (*Blackboard Jungle*, 1955; *Rebel Without*

a Cause, 1955) and prejudice (*12 Angry Men*, 1957; *Imitation of Life*, 1959; *To Kill a Mockingbird*, 1962). Changing values toward sex were examined (*Midnight Cowboy*, 1969; *Bob and Carol and Ted and Alice*, 1969), as was the new youth culture's rejection of middle-class values (*The Graduate*, 1967; *Goodbye Columbus*, 1969) and its revulsion/attraction to violence (*Bonnie and Clyde*, 1967). The movies as an industry had changed, but as a medium of social commentary and cultural impact, they may have grown up.

Movies and Their Audiences

We talk of Hollywood as the "dream factory," the makers of "movie magic." We want our lives and loves to be "just like in the movies." The movies are "larger than life," and movie stars are much more glamorous than television stars. The movies, in other words, hold a very special place in our culture. Movies, like books, are a culturally special medium, an important medium. In this sense the movie–audience relationship has more in common with that of books than with that of television. Just as people buy books, they buy movie tickets. Because the audience is in fact the true consumer, power rests with it in film more than it does in television.

For better or worse, today's movie audience is increasingly a young one. The typical moviegoer in the United States is a teenager or young adult. These teens and 20-somethings, although making up less than 20% of the total population, represent more than 30% of the tickets bought. It's no surprise, then, that new screens sprout at malls, where teens and even younger people can be dropped off for a day of safe entertainment. Many movies are aimed at kids—*Alvin and the Chipmunks*, *Ice Age*, *Lilo & Stitch*, and *Scooby-Doo*; all the *Toy Story*, *Rush Hour*, and *American Pie* films; all the movies based on television shows, computer games, and comic books. Look at the top 20 worldwide box office hits of all time in Figure 6.1. With the exception of *Titanic* (1997), a special-effects showcase itself, all are fantastic adventure films that appeal to younger audiences. The question asked by serious observers of the relationship between film and culture is whether the medium is increasingly dominated by the wants, tastes, and needs of what amounts to an audience of children. What becomes of film as an important medium, one with something to say, one that challenges people?

What becomes of film as an important medium, say the movies' defenders, is completely dependent on us, the audience. "It's the public," explains popular and distinguished actor John Malkovich. "The public gets the kind of politics, movies, and culture it deserves. The current state of affairs [in American filmmaking] is the result of the

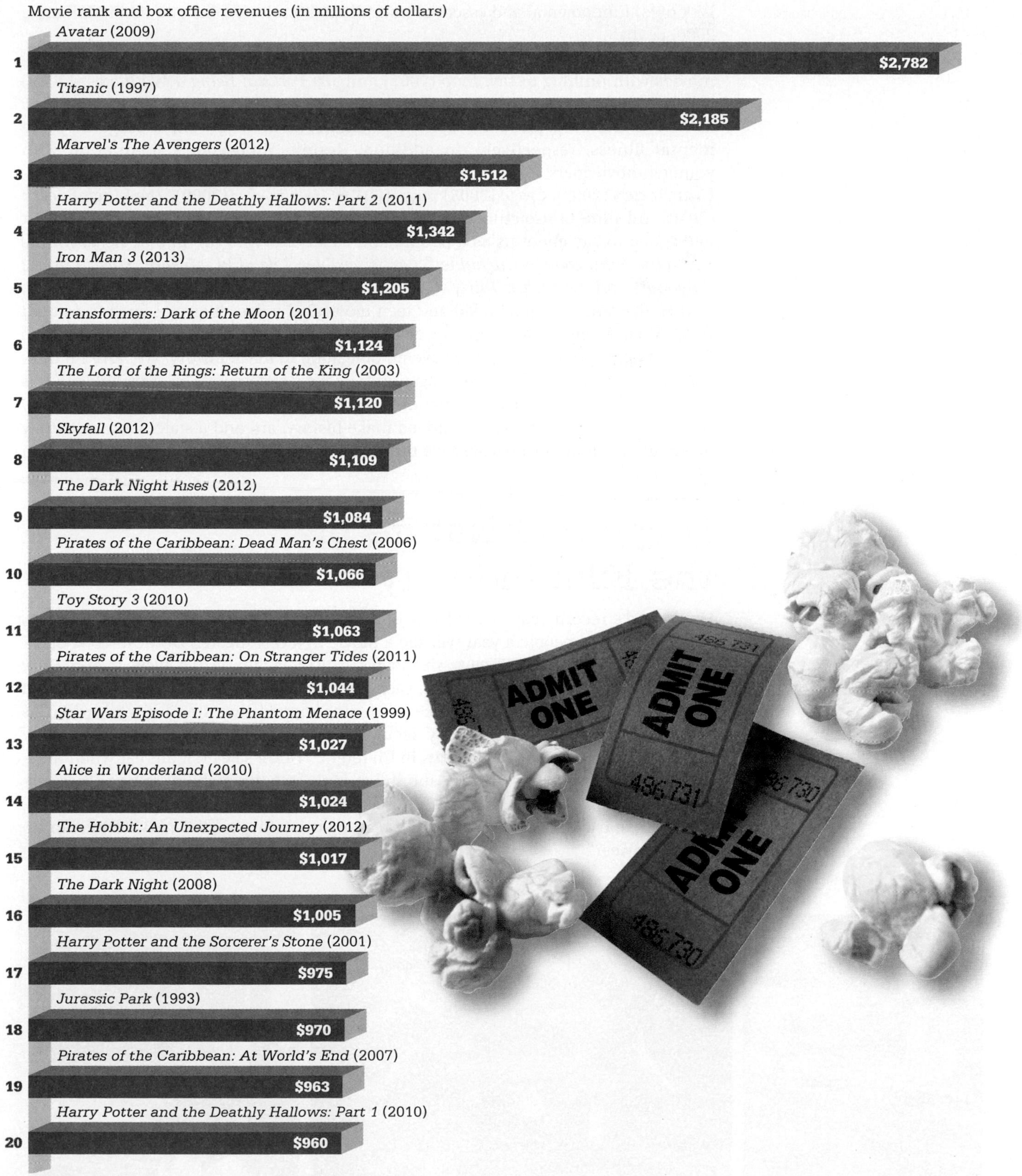

Movie rank and box office revenues (in millions of dollars)

Rank	Movie	Revenue
1	Avatar (2009)	$2,782
2	Titanic (1997)	$2,185
3	Marvel's The Avengers (2012)	$1,512
4	Harry Potter and the Deathly Hallows: Part 2 (2011)	$1,342
5	Iron Man 3 (2013)	$1,205
6	Transformers: Dark of the Moon (2011)	$1,124
7	The Lord of the Rings: Return of the King (2003)	$1,120
8	Skyfall (2012)	$1,109
9	The Dark Night Rises (2012)	$1,084
10	Pirates of the Caribbean: Dead Man's Chest (2006)	$1,066
11	Toy Story 3 (2010)	$1,063
12	Pirates of the Caribbean: On Stranger Tides (2011)	$1,044
13	Star Wars Episode I: The Phantom Menace (1999)	$1,027
14	Alice in Wonderland (2010)	$1,024
15	The Hobbit: An Unexpected Journey (2012)	$1,017
16	The Dark Night (2008)	$1,005
17	Harry Potter and the Sorcerer's Stone (2001)	$975
18	Jurassic Park (1993)	$970
19	Pirates of the Caribbean: At World's End (2007)	$963
20	Harry Potter and the Deathly Hallows: Part 1 (2010)	$960

▲ **Figure 6.1** Top 20 All-Time Worldwide Box Office Hits (in millions).
Source: imdb.com

lack of [a] fundamental and essential trait, which is curiosity" (as quoted in McKenna, 2000, p. 70).

Industry defenders argue that films aimed at young people aren't necessarily movies with nothing to say. *Juno* (2007) and *The Perks of Being a Wallflower* (2012) are "teen films" offering important insight into American society and youth culture, as well as into the topics they explicitly examine, namely, unwanted pregnancy and mental illness, respectively. In addition, despite Hollywood's infatuation with younger moviegoers, it still produces scores of movies of merit for a wider audience—*Gran Torino* (2009), *Crash* (2005), *Argo* (2012), *Hurt Locker* (2009), *The King's Speech* (2010). All nine best-picture nominees in 2012 were adult, important movies that had much to say about us as a people and as a culture: *Argo*, *Amour*, *Beasts of the Southern Wild*, *Django Unchained*, *Les Misérables*, *Life of Pi*, *Lincoln*, *Silver Linings Playbook*, and *Zero Dark Thirty*.

If Hollywood is fixated on kid and teen movies, why does it give us such treasures? True, Michael Eisner, as president of Paramount Pictures and then CEO of Disney, wrote in an internal memo, "We have no obligation to make history. We have no obligation to make art. We have no obligation to make a statement. Our only obligation is to make money" (as quoted in "Friend," 2000, p. 214). Nevertheless, the movie industry continues to produce films that indeed make history, art, and a statement while they make money. It does so because we buy tickets to those movies.

Scope and Nature of the Film Industry

Hollywood's record year of 1946 saw the sale of more than 4 billion tickets. Today, about 1.6 billion people a year will see a movie in a U.S. theater. Domestic box office in 2012 was $10.8 billion. Twenty-six movies in 2012, including *The Avengers*, *The Dark Knight Rises*, and *The Hunger Games*, each taking in more than $400 million, exceeded $100 million in U.S.–only box office. Fifty-nine topped that amount worldwide. As impressive as these numbers may seem, like other media people, movie industry insiders remain nervous, as you saw in Chapter 2. Ticket sales remain flat when measured against population growth, and much of the relative stability in box office revenues is attributable to higher ticket prices. The question they ask about the future, one you can try to answer yourself after reading the essay, is "Will We Continue to Go to the Movies?"

▲ Critics assailed *Titanic* for its weak story line and two-dimensional characters—the real stars of the world's first billion-dollar box office hit were the special effects. But grand special effects are no guarantee of success. FX-laden *Mars Needs Moms* was an all-time box office stinker, costing $150 million to make and earning only $39 million worldwide in 2011, while 2009's *Paranormal Activity*, devoid of technical legerdemain and made in seven days for $15,000, earned $170 million in global box office that year.

The data tell a troubling tale. 2012's 1.6 billion movie attendees, while impressive, represents the first time in a decade that the number has been that high; also, the $10.8 billion in ticket sales is lower than 2002's $11 billion. The ups and downs of the movie business are in the news, but the issue that roils the cultural forum is, "Will people keep going to the movies?" As you might imagine, there is no shortage of answers.

1. *The last several years have seen too many bad movies.* Only big-budget sequels and higher-priced tickets for 3-D movies saved box office totals from even greater declines. These made up for flops like *Land of the Lost, Mars Needs Moms,* and *The Three Musketeers.* Many critics even saw Hollywood's 2010 announcement that beginning with 2009's crop of films, there would be 10 nominees for a "Best Picture" Academy Award instead of the usual 5 as a cynical attempt to double the number of "acclaimed best pictures," not double the number of actual good movies.

2. Not unrelated, *fewer good movies* mean that not as many people are making it to the theater in the first place, denying them the opportunity to see trailers for and get excited about other films.

3. If there are good films, people go the movies; if not, they go less frequently and they tend to forget about the movies as an option when looking for entertainment. *Ad Age* critic T. L. Stanley (2005) calls this *out of sight, out of mind* (p. 20).

4. This problem is further complicated by people's skepticism about just what they will see should they go to the movies. Stanley calls this *what you see is not what you get.* In other words, desperate studios over-hyping every new movie as an event or something special or out of the ordinary eventually turns off inevitably disappointed fans.

5. But what faces fans when they do arrive at the movies? A very *expensive* outing. The average ticket price has increased at twice the rate of inflation in the last 15 years, to $7.96, up from $4.69 in 1998 (Barnes, 2013). Add to this the cost of the overpriced Goobers, popcorn, and soda plus the cost of gas to get there plus the price of a trustworthy baby-sitter (if necessary), and "catching a flick" becomes quite costly.

6. And what happens when people get to their seats? Chatty neighbors—that is, *an increasingly loud and rude environment,* especially cell phone users, crying babies, and antsy children at age-inappropriate movies.

7. But surely once the house goes dark, all is well. Well, no. People who have just paid handsomely to be at the movies are then faced with *full-length commercials before the trailers.* Most of the screens in the United States run these commercials.

> "People's reliance on sophisticated in-home technologies poses an additional threat to the film industry because it presages a generational shift away from movies. It is precisely those young people who will be tomorrow's seat-fillers who are leaving the movie experience with the least regret."

Audiences notice, and anecdotal evidence suggests they're unhappy. Film critic Richard Roeper argues, "If someone's waiting through 20 minutes of commercials, you've got people behind your seat and talking on cell phones, don't you think a lot of people might say, 'You know what? I've got a great sound system, I've got a 50-inch plasma screen. I'm just going to wait two months until the DVD comes out'?" (in Germain, 2005).

8. This, in fact, is the industry's greatest fear, *new digital technologies,* especially wired homes (with video-on-demand; high-definition, big-screen TVs; pay-per-view movies); increasingly sophisticated DVDs (that are not only packed with extra features but now released within weeks of the film's big-screen premiere); dollar-DVD kiosks at supermarkets, McDonalds, and gas stations (more than 33,000); and easy-to-use and inexpensive Internet movie downloads.

9. People's reliance on sophisticated in-home technologies poses an additional threat to the film industry because it presages a generational *shift away from movies.* It is precisely those young people who will be tomorrow's seat-fillers who are abandoning the theater experience with the least regret. Even though males between 13 and 25 years old still constitute the largest single moviegoing demographic, when box office dips, moviegoing among these valuable fans drops even more than other groups because they have ready access to and greater facility with attractive and inexpensive options, specifically video games and the Internet.

Enter your voice. Do you go to the movies as much as you once did? If not, why not? If you remain a regular moviegoer, why? What makes the "moviegoing experience" worth the effort? Many exhibitors are adding "perks," such as video arcades and wine and martini bars. Would moves such as these "improve" the experience for you?

◀ Will outlandish snack prices keep you from going to the movies?

Three Component Systems

There are three component systems in the movie industry—production, distribution, and exhibition. Each is undergoing significant change in the contemporary digital, converged media environment.

PRODUCTION Production is the making of movies. About 700 feature-length films are produced annually in the United States, a large increase over the early 1980s, when, for example, in 1985, 288 features were produced. As we'll see later in this chapter, significant revenues from home video are one reason for the increase, as is growing conglomerate ownership that demands more product for more markets.

Technology, too, has affected production. Most Hollywood films are now shot digitally. The industry was slow to make the change from film, citing the "coldness" of digital's look and digital's roots in technology rather than art. But the success of digitally shot movies big (all-time box office champ, 2009's *Avatar*, George Lucas's 2012 *Red Tails*) and small (1999's *Blair Witch Project*, made for $35,000, earning $220 million worldwide; 2009's *Paranormal Activity*, shot in seven days for $15,000, earning $170 million) has moved even more filmmakers to greater use of digital capture—on videotape, disc, or memory chip—as a primary shooting format.

Another influence of technology can be seen in the three top-grossing movies of 2012, *The Avengers*, *The Dark Knight Rises*, and *The Hunger Games*, all rich in special effects. Digital filmmaking has made grand special effects not only possible but expected. Stunning special effects, of which *Titanic* (1997) and *Avatar* are fine examples, can make a good movie an excellent one. The downside of computer-generated special effects is that they can greatly increase production costs. *Titanic* cost more than $200 million to make; *Avatar* more than $300 million. The Motion Picture Association of America (MPAA) reports that the *average* cost of producing and marketing a Hollywood feature is $112 million, a figure inflated, in large part, by the demands of audience-expected digital legerdemain. Many observers see this large increase in production costs as a major reason studios are less willing to take creative chances in a big-budget film.

DISTRIBUTION Distribution was once as simple as making prints of films and shipping them to theaters. Now it means supplying these movies to television networks, cable and satellite networks, makers of videodiscs, and Internet streaming companies. In all, a distributor must be able to offer a single movie in as many as 250 different digital formats worldwide to accommodate the specific needs of the many digital retailers it must serve (Ault, 2009). The sheer scope of the distribution business ensures that large companies (most typically the big studios themselves) will dominate. In addition to making copies and guaranteeing their delivery, distributors now finance production and take responsibility for advertising and promotion and for setting and adjusting release dates. The advertising and promotion budget for a Hollywood feature usually equals 50% of the production costs. Sometimes, the ratio of promotion to production costs is even higher. *Avatar* may have cost $300 million to produce, but its studio, Fox, spent another $200 million in marketing and promotion, bringing the total to half a billion dollars, the most expensive movie ever made (Hampp, 2010). Was it worth it? *Avatar* took only 39 days from the day of its release to become the highest-grossing movie of all time ($1.86 billion), accounting for 56 million tickets in the United States alone. Within another month, it had increased that take to $2.36 billion (Cieply, 2010; Hampp, 2010). So spending $25 million to $50 million to tout a Hollywood movie (the industry average; Graser, 2011) is not uncommon, and the investment is seen as worthwhile, if not necessary. In fact, so important has promotion become to the financial success of a movie that studios such as Universal and MGM include their advertising and marketing people in the **green light process**, that is, the decision to make a picture in the first place. These promotion professionals can say yes or no to a film's production, and they

must also declare how much money and effort they will put behind the film if they do vote yes.

Another important factor in a film's promotion and eventual financial success is the distributor's decision to release it to a certain number of screens. One strategy, called the **platform rollout**, is to open a movie on a few screens and hope that critical response, film festival success, and good word-of-mouth reviews from those who do see it will propel it to success. Naturally, the advantage of this approach for the distributor is that it can greatly reduce the cost of promotion. The Weinstein Company opened *The King's Speech* on four screens in 2010, awaiting the rush of critical acclaim that was sure to follow. It went into wide release—2,553 screens—a month later after winning scores of awards, including 12 Oscar nominations, 1 for Best Picture. Films likely to suffer at the hands of critics or from poor word-of-mouth—for example, *The Rite* (2011, 2,553 screens) and *After Earth* (2013, 3,401 screens)—typically open in thousands of theaters simultaneously. However, it is not uncommon for a potential hit to open on many screens, as *Avatar* did in 2009—on more than 18,300 worldwide.

EXHIBITION There are currently over 40,000 movie screens in the United States spread over 6,000 sites. More than 80% of theaters have two or more screens and average 340 seats in front of each. One-half of all screens are owned by a studio. For example, Sony owns more than 3,000 under the names Sony/Loews, Sony IMAX, Magic Johnson, and Loews-Star Theaters. Screens not owned by a studio are typically part of larger chains, for example, National Cinemas with 10,000 screens. The seven largest chains, including those owned by studios, control 80% of all U.S. ticket sales.

It is no surprise to any moviegoer that exhibitors make much of their money on concession sales of items that typically have an 80% profit margin, accounting for 40% of a theater's profits. This is the reason that matinees and budget nights are attractive promotions for theaters. A low-priced ticket pays dividends in overpriced popcorn and Goobers. This, too, is why many exhibitors present more than movies to keep seats filled and concessions flowing. "Live simulcasts of sporting events or whatever won't displace the first week of *Harry Potter*," said Landmark Theater's Ted Mundorff, "but they might displace the fifth week" (in Barnes, 2008, p. A1). So, too, might stand-up comedians, the NFL and NBA in 3-D, live opera performances, big-name musical concerts, and classic TV show marathons, especially when augmented by the wine bars and restaurants exhibitors are now adding to their cineplexes.

The Studios

Studios are at the heart of the movie business and increasingly are regaining control of the three component systems of the industry. There are major studios, corporate independents, and independent studios. The majors, who finance their films primarily through the profits of their own business, include Warner Brothers, Columbia, Paramount, 20th Century Fox, Universal, MGM/UA, and Disney. The **corporate independents** (so named because they produce movies that have the look and feel of independent films) include Sony Classics, New Line Cinema (Warner), Fox Searchlight, and Focus Features (Universal). These companies are in fact specialty or niche divisions of the majors, designed to produce more sophisticated—but less costly—fare to (1) gain prestige for their parent studios and (2) earn significant cable and DVD income after their critically lauded and good word-of-mouth runs in the theaters. Focus Features, for example, was responsible for *Tinker Tailor Soldier Spy* (2011) and *Moonrise Kingdom* (2012); Fox Searchlight was home to Oscar nominees *Black Swan* (2010), *Tree of Life* (2011), and *The Descendants* (2011); New Line Cinema released *Hall Pass* (2011) and *Valentine's Day* (2010); Sony Classics screened Oscar nominee *Midnight In Paris* (2011) and *The Skin I Live In* (2011).

Together, the majors and their specialty houses account for roughly 80% of annual U.S. box office revenues, although they produce only about one-fifth of each year's feature films ("Seismic," 2013). The remainder come from independent studios, companies that raise money outside the studio system to produce their films. Lionsgate and Weinstein Company are two of the few remaining true independents in Hollywood, producing films like *The Hunger Games*, the *Twilight Saga*, and the *Saw* and Tyler Perry movies (Lionsgate) and *Silver Linings Playbook*, *The King's Speech*, and the *Halloween* movies (Weinstein). But countless other independents continue to churn out films, often with the hope of winning a distribution deal with one of the Hollywood studios. For example, *Paranormal Activity* was distributed by Paramount, which paid $300,000 for the rights; 2005 Oscar-winner for Best Picture, *Crash*, from Stratus Films, was distributed by Lionsgate; and the 2004–2005 $100 million box office hit *Million Dollar Baby*, from independent Lakeshore, was distributed by Warner Brothers.

Independent films tend to have smaller budgets. Often this leads to much more imaginative filmmaking and more risk taking than the big studios are willing to undertake. The 1969 independent film *Easy Rider*, which cost $370,000 to produce and made over $50 million in theater rentals, began the modern independent film boom. *My Big Fat Greek Wedding* (2002) cost $5 million to make and earned over $300 million in global box office receipts. Some independent films with which you might be familiar are *Magic Mike* (2012), *Before Midnight* (2013), Oscar-winners for Best Screenplay *Pulp Fiction* (1994) and *The Pianist* (2002), *Crouching Tiger, Hidden Dragon* (2000), *Traffic* (2000), *Best Exotic Marigold Hotel* (2012), and Best Picture Oscar-winner *Hurt Locker* (2009).

▶ Corporate indie Sony Classics' *Midnight in Paris* earned its parent company an Academy Award best-picture nomination and a $155 million box office take.

Trends and Convergence in Moviemaking

Stagnant box office, increased production costs largely brought about by digital special effects wizardry, and the "corporatization" of the independent film are only a few of the trends reshaping the film industry. There are several others, however, including some that many critics see as contributors to Hollywood's changing future.

Conglomeration and the Blockbuster Mentality

Other than MGM, each of the majors is a part of a large conglomerate. Paramount is owned by Viacom, Warner Brothers is part of the huge Time Warner family of holdings, Disney is part of the giant conglomerate formed in the 1996 Disney/Capital Cities/ABC union, and Universal was bought by NBC's parent company, General Electric, in 2004 and became part of cable TV giant Comcast in 2009. Much of this conglomeration takes the form of international ownership. Columbia is owned by Japanese Sony and Fox by Australia's News Corp. According to many critics, this combination of conglomeration and foreign ownership forces the industry into a **blockbuster mentality**—filmmaking characterized by reduced risk taking and more formulaic movies. Business concerns are said to dominate artistic considerations as accountants and financiers control more decisions once made by creative people. "Once you start to make crucial decisions by committee and each member of that committee is extremely anxious about his or her job," explains actor Ben Kingsley, "then you're not going to have the right decisions made. You're going to have decisions that are fear-based, you are going to have decisions based on what they think they should say, or what they think their boss needs to hear, rather than going out on a limb and being actually creative" ("Stars Diss Hollywood," 2012). The common outcomes of this blockbuster mentality are several.

CONCEPT MOVIES The marketing and publicity departments of big companies love **concept films**—movies that can be described in one line. *Twister* is about a giant, rogue tornado. *The Lost World* is about giant, rogue dinosaurs. *King Kong* (2005) is about a giant, rogue ape who comes to New York.

International ownership and international distribution contribute to this phenomenon. High-concept films that depend little on characterization, plot development, and dialogue are easier to sell to foreign exhibitors than are more sophisticated films. *Fantastic Four* and *300* play well everywhere. Big-name stars also have international appeal. That's why they can command huge salaries. The importance of foreign distribution cannot be overstated. Only 2 in 10 U.S. features make a profit on U.S. box office. Much of their eventual profit comes from overseas sales. For example, 2011's *Green Hornet* disappointed at home ($99 million) but earned $129 million overseas. Likewise, *Resident Evil: Afterlife* nearly quadrupled its domestic $60 million, making $236 million in foreign box office. And it's not just domestic disappointments that do well overseas. *Titanic* doubled its 2009 $601 million U.S. box office, earning $1.2 billion elsewhere. *Avatar* did the same. *Harry Potter and the Deathly Hallows: Part 2* tripled its domestic take, as did *Transformers: Dark of the Moon*; and *Pirates of the Caribbean: On Stranger Tides* more than quadrupled its $241 million domestic box office. Overseas box office accounts for 70% of a studio movie's total ticket sales (Soderbergh, 2013).

AUDIENCE RESEARCH Before a movie is released, sometimes even before it is made, its concept, plot, and characters are subjected to market testing. Often multiple endings are produced and tested with sample audiences by companies such as National Research Group and Marketcast. Despite being "voodoo science, a spin of the roulette wheel," says *Chicago Reader* film critic Jonathan Rosenbaum, audience testing is "believed in like a religion at this point. It's considered part of filmmaking" (quoted in Scribner, 2001, p. D3). This testing produced the "lowest scores in studio history" for *Pulp Fiction* (1994), which went on to earn more than $200 million, and "the highest scores in studio history" for *Akeelah and the Bee* (2006), which made $19 million (Friend, 2009). If the voodoo is so unreliable, ask film purists, what is to become of the filmmaker's genius? What separates these market-tested films from any other commodity? *Variety* film writer Dade Hayes (2003) explains the dilemma facing blockbuster-driven Hollywood, "Testing contributes to the sameness of the movies, and feeds into audience expectations of comfortable patterns and makes them uneasy if a film diverges from that formula. . . . [B]ut there cannot be much creative freedom with a $200 million **tentpole**" (an expensive blockbuster around which a studio plans its other releases; pp. 1, 53).

SEQUELS, REMAKES, AND FRANCHISES Nothing succeeds like success. How many *Batman*s have there been? *Indiana Jones*es? *Legally Blonde*s? *Lethal Weapon*s? *American Pie*s, and *Terminator*s? Johnny Depp's *Charlie and the Chocolate Factory* (2005) is a remake of Gene Wilder's 1971 classic *Willie Wonka and the Chocolate Factory*. The Titans clashed in 1981 and again in 2010. We passed *The Last House on the Left* in 1972 and

▼ *Footloose* danced across the silver screen in 1984 and again in 2011.

again in 2009. *The Birds* flew in 1963 and in 2011. *Dune* (2010), *Fame* (2010), and *Total Recall* (2012) are other recent remakes. Hollywood, too, is making increasing use of **franchise films**, movies that are produced with the full intention of producing several more sequels. The first James Bond film (1962) has had 22 sequels; *Star Wars* (1977), 5. *Harry Potter* (2001) had 7. There were 27 sequels among Hollywood's 2011 releases, and the top 7 moneymakers of that year were franchise installments, giving credence to the old industry saying, "Nobody ever got fired for green-lighting a sequel." Revisit Figure 6.1. With the exception of *Avatar*, *Titanic*, and *Alice in Wonderland*, every other top 20 all-time box office champion is a sequel or part of a franchise. *Marvel's The Avengers* itself stars a collection of characters from a number of other Marvel Comics movie franchises.

"What do I do? I'm a film remaker."

▲ Remakes and sequels are two products of Hollywood's blockbuster mentality.
© Alex Gregory/The New Yorker Collection/www.cartoonbank.com

TELEVISION, COMIC BOOK, AND VIDEO-GAME REMAKES Nothing succeeds like success. That, and the fact that teens and preteens still make up the largest proportion of the movie audience, is the reason so many movies are adaptations of television shows, comic books, and video games. In the last few years *Inspector Gadget*, *Dudley Do-Right*, *The Flintstones*, *My Favorite Martian*, *The Fugitive*, *The Saint*, *Mission: Impossible*, *George of the Jungle*, *The Dukes of Hazzard*, *Speed Racer*, *Charlie's Angels*, *Beavis and Butthead*, *X-files* (twice), *The Brady Bunch*, *Bewitched*, and *Get Smart* have moved from small to big screen. *The Addams Family*, *Dennis the Menace*, *Richie Rich*, *Spider-Man*, *Batman*, and *Superman* have traveled from the comics, through television, to the silver screen. *Sin City*, *30 Days of Night*, *X-Men*, *Road to Perdition*, *Whiteout*, *300*, *The Lost Squad*, *Men in Black*, *Fantastic Four*, *The Hulk*, and *The Crow* have moved directly from comics to movies. *Tomb Raider*, *Resident Evil*, *Mortal Kombat*, and *Final Fantasy* went from game box to box office. Movies from comics and video games are especially attractive to studios because of their built-in merchandise tie-in appeal.

MERCHANDISE TIE-INS Films are sometimes produced as much for their ability to generate interest for nonfilm products as for their intrinsic value as movies. Kids' 2012 hit *Lorax* had more than 70 "product partners." Hollywood makes close to $200 billion a year from merchandise tie-ins to its movie and television shows. Disney, for example, earned $2.8 billion from *Toy Story 3* in 2010. Its 2006 *Cars* generated $10 billion in global merchandise sales, making the studio $2.5 billion in licensing fees. According to a Disney executive, *Cars* is less a movie than a "lifestyle brand for young boys . . . the male answer to the Disney Princess marketing push" (in Forbes, 2011). And as almost all of us know, it is nearly impossible to buy a meal at McDonald's, Burger King, or Taco Bell without being offered a movie tie-in product. Studios often believe it is riskier to make a $7 million film with no merchandising potential than a $100 million movie with greater merchandising appeal.

PRODUCT PLACEMENT Many movies are serving double duty as commercials. We'll discuss this phenomenon in detail later in the chapter as a media literacy issue.

Convergence Reshapes the Movie Business

So intertwined are today's movie and television industries that it is often meaningless to discuss them separately. As much as 70% of the production done by the studios is for television. But the growing relationship between **theatrical films**—those produced originally for theater exhibition—and television is the result of technological changes in the latter. The convergence of film with satellite, cable, video-on-demand, pay-per-view, DVD, and Internet streaming has provided immense distribution and exhibition opportunities for the movies. For example, in 1947 box office receipts accounted for 95% of the studios' film revenues. Now they make up about one-quarter. Today's distributors make three times as much from domestic home entertainment (DVD, network and cable television, downloads, and streaming) as they do from rentals to movie houses. DVD sales remain a lucrative business as well, but unfortunately for the movie industry, not as lucrative as in the past. Until quite recently, DVD sales represented 50% of a studio's profit, but that once reliable income has dropped by as much as 25% for some producers. In fact, in 2012 Americans spent more downloading online movies than they did buying and renting discs (O'Malley, 2012). Where a solid box office performer—*The Hangover* (2009), for example—could once sell 10 million discs in its first six months of release, today's movies are far more likely to be downloaded for a few dollars on VOD rather than purchased as a disc for $15. This change has forced studios into even heavier dependence on big-ticket, star-driven movies likely to be attractive to international audiences and those with built-in "pre-awareness"—that is, sequels and titles based on comic books, TV shows, and video games. There is less "cash that [once] fueled competitive commerce, gut calls, or real movies, the extra spec script purchase, the pitch culture," writes producer Lynda Obst. "We're running on empty, searching for sources of new revenue" (2013).

The convergence of film with digital technologies is beginning to reshape production, distribution, *and* exhibition. Two factors have combined to encourage the rollout of digital distribution and exhibition. The first is the convenience of digital movies. Nearly 90% of North America's 40,000 screens have been converted to digital exhibition. Digital exhibition's savings in money and labor to both exhibitor and distributor are dramatic. Rather than making several thousand film prints to be physically transported to individual theaters in metal cans, the satellite distribution of digital movies costs under $100 per screen for the entire process (Stewart & Cohen, 2013). The second factor encouraging digital conversion is the growing number of successful movies shot with digital equipment.

The surprise 1999 hit *The Blair Witch Project* is considered the start of the growing **microcinema** movement, through which filmmakers using digital video cameras and desktop digital editing machines are finding audiences, both in theaters and online, for their low-budget (sometimes as little as $10,000) features. The success of *Paranormal Activity* has reinforced interest in microcinema, leading the major studios to create their own in-house microcinema divisions—for example, Paramount's Insurge Pictures. Microcinema has also been boosted by the willingness of A-list talent to get involved with these "small" pictures; for example, Rashida Jones (*Parks and Recreation*), Andy Samberg (*Saturday Night Live*), and Elijah Wood (*Harry Potter*) teamed up on *Celeste and Jesse Forever* (2012). Website Kickstarter, which allows filmmakers to appeal directly to fans for financing of their movies, has been a boon as well, funding 2013 Oscar nominee *Buzkashi Boys*.

As digitization and convergence are changing exhibition and production, they are also changing distribution. Although slowed by fears of piracy, the online distribution of feature films has taken hold. The typical American home with Internet and cable access has at least 100,000 full-length movies and television shows to choose from on any given day (Whitney, 2011). Netflix, which originally was a company that delivered DVDs to people's homes by mail, has discontinued that service in every country other than the United States. Now focusing on streaming movies, it operates in 45 countries, bringing its subscriber total to nearly 30 million. In fact, Netflix-streamed content is the single largest component of American Internet traffic (Manjoo, 2011). And Netflix is not the only source for streamed movies; Internet giants Google Movies and Amazon Instant Video and the Comcast cable operation are only three of the scores of sites offering fans everything from classic and niche films to the latest box office hits. And not to be outdone, studios like Disney, Sony, Universal, Warner Brothers, and Lionsgate stream their films via YouTube. Paramount has even experimented with direct-to-consumer streaming, offering big hits like its Transformers movies. There are industry analysts, however, who say direct-to-home digital distribution of movies is even more robust than described here because of two new technologies that free downloads from the computer screen. The first allows downloads directly to TV set-top boxes, avoiding the computer altogether (Netflix and LG Electronics offer one version; Amazon and TiVo another). The second, for example Apple TV, transmits computer-downloaded movies to any electronic device in the home. Much more will be said about Internet distribution of film and video content in Chapter 10.

But a potentially bigger alteration to traditional movie distribution resides in the efforts of studios like IFC Entertainment, directors like Steven Soderbergh, and exhibitors such as billionaire Mark Cuban's Landmark Theaters. All plan for the simultaneous release of movies to theaters, DVD, cable video-on-demand, and streaming. Disney has publicly committed to considering this model of distribution as well. Director Soderbergh predicts that once digital production, distribution, and exhibition are firmly in place, "in five or ten years, you're going to see name filmmakers self-distributing" (in Jardin, 2005b, p. 257). In fact, this is already taking place. We've already seen in Chapter 2 that actor-director Ed Burns (*Purple Violets, Newlyweds*), routinely skips the big screen and comedian Louis CK self-produces and distributes his concert films. Director Kevin Smith self-distributed his 2011 *Red State*, personally taking it from city to city for screening (and to build word-of-mouth) in advance of releasing it to DVD, VOD, and streaming. These changes will eventually force significant alterations in the economics of Hollywood, argues *Washington Post* media writer Steven Pearlstein (2005). "The studios will be indifferent about how you choose to get a movie—their profit will be the same whether you see it in a theater, rent it, or order it up from Comcast." He sees this as an improvement over the way Hollywood currently operates, forcing studios to become more competitive, efficient, and audience-driven. Studios will no longer be able to rely as heavily on blockbusters and big-name superstars as they do now. Successful studios will be those producing a wide "range of well-done movies for a variety of niche audiences reached through targeted marketing and distribution channels" (p. D1).

Smartphones, Tablets, and Social Networking Sites

Studios are also distributing their movies via the social networking site Facebook. Fans not only can get Miramax, Paramount, Universal, and Warner Brothers films, they can use Facebook's many features to "like" and share quotations, scenes, and other parts of the movie they enjoy with their friends. This utilization of social networking is fueled by the migration of movie streaming to smartphones and tablets. Movies available for online streaming or download can be accessed on any advanced Android or Apple operating system device containing the proper apps. Fans are open to watching movies on their smartphones and tablets—nearly 300 million people a month access some form of mobile video content ("Online Video," 2011). The industry, however, sees this advance as a mixed blessing. Yes, studios and distributors have many more ways to get content to audiences, but as fans, especially young people already comfortable with relatively small, mobile screens, increasingly watch movies in places other than theaters, what happens to what we have called "the movies" for more than a century?

DEVELOPING MEDIA LITERACY SKILLS

Recognizing Product Placements

Transformers (the toy) may have been the star of the 2007 movie of the same name, but there were enough General Motors cars, especially the Chevy Camaro, sprinkled throughout the movie that GM's sales were up 2.7% in the three months following the film's debut (Brodesser-Akner, 2008). 2012's *The Vow* stars Rachael McAdams, Channing Tatum, and nearly 39 "brand partners." Before it sold a single ticket, 2013's *Man of Steel* had already earned $160 million in promotional support, much of it coming from Superman's co-stars: the National Guard, Gillette, Sears, Chrysler, Hardee's, International House of Pancakes, and Nokia, among others. Its more than 100 "global promotional partners" made it the most commercially branded movie of all time (Morrison, 2013). In another 2013 summer movie, *The Internship*, co-stars Vince Vaughn and Owen Wilson play interns who compete for full-time jobs at the headquarters of Internet giant Google. They are judged on their "Googliness," as the film explains, that "intangible stuff that made a search engine into an engine for doing good." People at the company work long hours, movie-goers are told, because Google "makes people's lives just a little bit better." To the dismay of many critics, Google's public relations department had full veto power over the script (Depillis, 2013).

The practice of placing brand-name products in movies is not new; Katharine Hepburn throws Gordon's gin into the river in the 1951 *The African Queen*, and Spencer Tracy is splashed with Coca-Cola in the 1950 *Father of the Bride*. But in today's movie industry, product placement has expanded into a business in its own right. About 100 product placement agencies are operating in Hollywood, and there's even an industry association, the Entertainment Resources and Marketing Association (ERMA). The attraction of product placements for sponsors is obvious. For one flat fee paid up front, a product that appears in a movie is in actuality a commercial that lives forever—first on the big screen, then on television and cable, and then on purchased and rented discs and downloads. The commercial is also likely to have worldwide distribution.

Many people in and outside the movie industry see product placement as inherently deceptive. "Why not identify the ads for what they are?" they ask. From a media literacy standpoint, the issue is the degree to which artistic decisions are being placed second to obligations to sponsors. Scripts are altered and camera angles are chosen to accommodate paid-for placements. "The average viewer probably doesn't know, for example, about the kind of wrangling that goes on behind the scenes to get those products into movies—that strong-arming can occur during shooting to ensure that you see a certain brand of soda at just the right time," writes film critic Christy Lemire. "Artistic integrity? Whatever," responds *Rush Hour* director Brett Ratner (both in Lemire, 2011, p. D3). Equally unconcerned is *Transformer* director Michael Bay, "There are products in everything in everyday life. Do people think there shouldn't be brand names or something? Everything is branded. I hate [entertainment content] when they take logos off of stuff. It's not real life" (in Fagbire, 2007).

Knowing how media content is funded and how that financial support shapes content is an important aspect of understanding the mass communication process. Therefore, an awareness of the efforts of the movie industry to maximize income from its films is central to good film literacy.

Consider, for example, the following product placements. If you saw these two recent movies, did you recognize the placements?

| *Valentine's Day* | 1-800-Flowers, adidas, American Airlines, American Express, Apple, BlackBerry, Blazer, Cadillac, Cadillac Escalade, Cartier, Chanel, Chevrolet, Chicago Cubs, Christian Louboutin, Craigslist, Discovery Channel, ESPN, evite.com, Facebook, FedEx, Ford, Ford Mustang, Gatorade, Hollywood Forever Cemetary (sic), Indiana University, International Creative Management, Los Angeles Dodgers, Mapquest, Marc Jacobs, |

	Moët & Chandon, Nike, Nokia, Northwestern University, Polaroid, Porsche, PUMA, Quiksilver, Range Rover, Retin-A, Scope, Sharpie, Sony, Southwest Airlines, Stanford University, The BLVD (Los Angeles), The Lawrence Foundation, Toyota, Tufts University, US Army, USPS, Versace, Victoria's Secret, Volkswagen Beetle, Walt Disney Concert Hall, Yale, York
The Social Network	adidas, Apache, Apple, Arm & Hammer, Boston University, Brooks Brothers, Cadillac, Cambridge University, Columbia University, Cornell University, Dell, Disney, Exeter Academy, Facebook, Friendster, Gap, Google, Harvard University, LiveJournal, London School of Economics, Macy's, match .com, Microsoft, Mountain Dew, MySpace, Napster, Network Solutions, New England Patriots, NFL, Nike, Oxford University, Patagonia, Philips, Polaroid, Polo Ralph Lauren, Porsche, Range Rover, Red Bull, Samsung, Sony VAIO, Stairmaster, Stanford University, The Harvard Crimson, The North Face, The Unlimited, Thirsty Scholar, Tower Records, Ty Nant, Under Armour, Victoria's Secret, Yale University

Does it trouble you that content is altered, even if sometimes only minimally, to allow for these brand identifications? To what extent would script alterations have to occur to accommodate paid-for messages before you find them intrusive? Do you think it is fair or honest for a moviemaker who promises you film content in exchange for your money to turn you into what amounts to a television viewer by advertising sponsors' products? At least in television, by law, all commercial messages must be identified as such, and the sponsors of those messages must be identified. Do you think such a rule ought to apply to movies?

Literate film consumers may answer these questions differently, especially as individuals hold film in varying degrees of esteem—but they should answer them. And what do you make of the latest Hollywood product placement trend, **branding films**, the sponsor-financing of movies to advance a manufacturer's product line. Unilever (Dove soap) co-financed *The Women*, Chrysler underwrote *Blue Valentine*, and Gatorade co-financed *Gracie*. Universal Studios and Hasbro have a four-picture deal in which the world's second-largest toymaker agreed to co-finance a picture a year based on its popular board games such as Candy Land and Monopoly. Burger King has announced that it will produce its own movies. *Variety*'s Peter Bart (2007) asks, "Would *Waitress* be the same edgy movie had Applebee's decided to finance it? How would the script of *Bug* been altered had it been funded by Raid? Good movies are hard enough to make without worrying about the branding needs of consumer companies or the script notes of marketing gurus" (p. 58).

MEDIA LITERACY CHALLENGE
Product Placement in Movies

Choose two films. Try for variation, for example, a big-budget blockbuster and a romantic comedy, your choice. List every example of product placement that you can find. In which instances do you believe the film's content was altered, however minimally, to accommodate the placement? Product placement proponents argue that this is a small price to pay for the "reality" that using real brands brings to a film. Do you agree or disagree? Explain your answer in terms of your *expectations of movies' content* and your *ability to recognize when advertising and movie genre conventions are being mixed*. Tackle this one individually, committing your findings to writing, or make it a challenge against one or more classmates.

Resources for Review and Discussion

REVIEW POINTS: TYING CONTENT TO LEARNING OUTCOMES

▶ **Outline the history and development of the film industry and film itself as a medium.**

- ▸ Film's beginnings reside in the efforts of entrepreneurs such as Eadweard Muybridge and inventors like Thomas Edison and William Dickson.
- ▸ Photography, an essential precursor to movies, was developed by Hannibal Goodwin, George Eastman, Joseph Nicéphore Niépce, Louis Daguerre, and William Henry Fox Talbot.
- ▸ Edison and the Lumière brothers began commercial motion picture exhibition, little more than representations of everyday life. George Méliès added narrative; Edwin S. Porter added montage; and D. W. Griffith developed the full-length feature film.
- ▸ Movies became big business at the turn of the 20th century, one dominated by big studios, but change soon came in the form of talkies, scandal, and control, and new genres to fend off the Depression.

▶ **Describe the cultural value of film and the implications of the blockbuster mentality for film as an important artistic and cultural medium.**

- ▸ Conglomeration and concentration affect the movie industry, leading to an overreliance on blockbuster films for its success.
- ▸ Debate exists over whether film can survive as an important medium if it continues to give its youth-dominated audience what it wants.
- ▸ The annual roster of adult, important movies suggests that film can give all audiences what they want.

▶ **Summarize the three components of the film industry—production, distribution, and exhibition.**

- ▸ Production is the making of movies, increasingly using digital technology.
- ▸ Distribution is supplying movies to television and cable networks, DVD makers, Internet streaming and downloading services, and even to individual viewers.
- ▸ Exhibition is showing movies in a theater, increasingly using digital technologies.

▶ **Explain how the organizational and economic nature of the contemporary film industry shapes the content of its films.**

- ▸ Studios are at the heart of the movie business and are increasingly in control of the three component systems.
- ▸ There are major, corporate independent, and independent studios.

▶ **Describe the promise and peril of convergence and the new digital technologies to film as we know it.**

- ▸ Convergence is reshaping the industry, promising to alter its structure and economics, especially as new distribution models fueled by the Internet and related mobile technologies become even more common than they are now.

▶ **Understand how production is becoming more expensive and, simultaneously, less expensive.**

- ▸ Distribution is becoming more complex, getting more movies to more people over more platforms.
- ▸ Exhibition is increasingly out-of-theater and mobile, but is it still "the movies"?

▶ **Apply film-watching media literacy skills, especially in interpreting merchandise tie-ins and product placements.**

- ▸ The financial benefits of merchandise tie-ins and product licensing are factors in the industry's overreliance on big budget, youth-oriented movies (and the relative scarcity of more adult films).
- ▸ The inclusion of product placements in films often shapes their scripts and production practices, either for better or worse.

KEY TERMS

QUESTIONS FOR REVIEW

1. What are the kinetograph, kinetoscope, cinématographe, daguerreotype, calotype, and nickelodeon?

2. What were Méliès's, Porter's, and Griffith's contributions to film as a narrative medium?

3. What was the Motion Picture Patents Company, and how did it influence the content and development of the movie industry?

4. What societal, technical, and artistic factors shaped the development of movies before World War II?

5. What are the three component systems of the movie industry?

6. What are major and corporate independent studios? What is an independent?

7. What are concept films? Product tie-ins? Product placement?

8. What is platform rollout? When and why is it used?

9. How are digitization and convergence reshaping exhibition? Distribution? Production?

10. How will distribution change as the industry becomes more fully digital?

For further review, go to the LearnSmart study module for this chapter.

QUESTIONS FOR CRITICAL THINKING AND DISCUSSION

1. What do you think of the impact of the blockbuster mentality on movies? Should profit always be the determining factor in producing movie content? Why or why not?

2. Are you a fan of independent movies? When you are watching a movie, how can you tell that it's an independent? If you are an indie fan, do you welcome the micro-cinema movement? Why or why not?

3. Most industry-watchers see the new distribution model promised by digitization of the three component systems as inevitably changing the economics of Hollywood. Some, though, think it will produce better movies. Do you agree or disagree? Why?

7

Radio, Recording, and Popular Music

Learning Objectives

Radio was the first electronic mass medium; it was the first national broadcast medium. It produced the networks, program genres, and stars that made television an instant success. But for many years radio and records were young people's media; they gave voice to a generation. As such, they may be our most personally significant mass media. After studying this chapter you should be able to

▶ Outline the history and development of the radio and sound recording industries and radio and sound recording themselves as media.

▶ Describe the importance of early financing and regulatory decisions regarding radio and how they have shaped the nature of contemporary broadcasting.

▶ Explain how the organizational and economic natures of the contemporary radio and sound recording industries shape the content of both media.

▶ Identify new and converging radio and recording technologies and their potential impact on music, the industries themselves, and listeners.

▶ Apply key radio-listening media literacy skills, especially in assessing the cultural value of shock jocks.

Homemade YouTube videos brought the then 12-year-old Justin Bieber to music industry attention and then fame.

"CAN WE LISTEN TO THE RADIO?"

"We are listening to the radio."

"I mean something other than this."

"You want music?"

"Yes, please, anything but public radio. Too much talk."

"OK. Here."

"What! That's the classical music station!"

"What's wrong with that?"

"Nothing . . . much."

"What's that supposed to mean, 'Nothing . . . much'?"

"Nothing . . . much. Let me choose."

"OK. You find a station."

"Fine. Here."

"What's that?!"

"It's the New Hot One. KISS 100. All the hits all the time."

"That's not music."

"You sound like my parents."

"I don't mean the stuff they play isn't music, I mean the DJ is yammering away."

"Hang on. A song is coming up. Anyway, this is funny stuff."

"I don't find jokes about minority wheelchair races funny."

"It's all in fun."

"Fun for whom?"

1900		1925
1844 Samuel Morse's telegraph	**~1900** Tesla and Marconi file radio patents	**1926** NBC, first radio network
1860 Scott's phonautograph	**1903** ▲ Marconi sends first wireless signal across the Atlantic	**1927** Radio Act; Federal Radio Commission
1876 Alexander Graham Bell's telephone	**1905** Columbia Phonograph Company develops two-sided disc	**1934** Communications Act; Federal Communications Commission
1877 ▲ Edison patents "talking machine"	**1906** Fessenden makes first public broadcast of voice and music; DeForest invents audion tube	**1939** Television introduced at World's Fair; FM goes on air
1896 Marconi sends wireless signal over 2 miles	**1910** Wireless Ship Act of 1910	**1946** GIs return from Germany with tape recorder
1899 Marconi sends wireless signal across the English Channel	**1912** Radio Act of 1912	**1947** Columbia Records introduces 33⅓ rpm disc
	1916 Sarnoff sends Radio Music Box Memo	**1949** ▲ Development of the DJ
	1919 Radio Corporation of America formed	
	1920 KDKA goes on air	
	1922 First radio commercial	

"What's *your* problem today?"

"Nothing, I just don't find that kind of stuff funny. Here, I'll find something."

"What's that?"

"The jazz station."

"Give me a break. How about Sports Talk?"

"Nah. How about All News?"

"No way. How about the All Talk station?"

"Why, you need another fix of insulting chatter?"

"How about silence?"

"Yeah, how about it?"

In this chapter we study the technical and social beginnings of both radio and sound recording. We revisit the coming of broadcasting and see how the growth of regulatory, economic, and organizational structures led to the medium's golden age.

The heart of the chapter covers how television changed radio and produced the medium with which we are now familiar. We review the scope and nature of contemporary radio, especially its rebirth as a local, fragmented, specialized, personal, and mobile medium. We examine how these characteristics serve advertisers and listeners. The chapter then explores the relationship between radio, the modern recording industry, popular music, and the way new and converging technologies serve and challenge all three. The popularity of shock jocks inspires our discussion of media literacy.

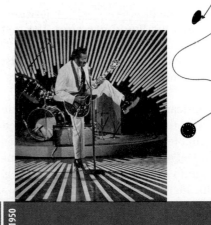  

1950	1975	2000

1951 Car radios exceed home sets	**1983** ▲ CD introduced	**2001** Satellite radio begins
Mid-50s Network affiliation halved	**1987** MP3 developed	**2002** Terrestrial digital radio
1955 ▲ DJ Freed brings R&B to New York	**1996** Telecommunications Act	**2003** ▲ iTunes
Late-50s National billings drop nearly 80%		**2004** Podcasting
		2005 *MGM v. Grokster* P2P decision
		2007 Imus fired
		2008 Sony BMG lifts copy protection from downloads; Imus back on the air
		2009 iTunes becomes DRM free
		2010 10 billionth iTunes download sold
		2011 Digital music sales surpass physical sales
		2012 Limbaugh "slut" controversy

A Short History of Radio and Sound Recording

The particular stations you disagree about may be different, but almost all of us have been through a conversation similar to the one in the opening vignette. Radio, the seemingly ubiquitous medium, matters to us. Because we often listen to it alone, it is personal. Radio is also mobile. It travels with us in the car, and we take it along in our iPods and smartphones. Radio is specific as well. Stations aim their content at very narrowly defined audiences. But these are characteristics of contemporary radio. Radio once occupied a very different place in our culture. Let's see how it all began.

Early Radio

Because both applied for patents within months of one another in the late 1890s, there remains disagreement over who "invented" radio, Eastern European immigrant Nikola Tesla, or Guglielmo Marconi, son of a wealthy Italian businessman and his Irish wife. Marconi, however, is considered the "Father of Radio" because not only was he among the first to send signals through the air, he was adroit at gaining maximum publicity for his every success. His improvements over earlier experimental designs allowed him to send and receive telegraph code over distances as great as two miles by 1896. His native Italy was not interested in his invention, so he used his mother's contacts in Great Britain to find support and financing there. England, with a global empire and the world's largest navy and merchant fleets, was naturally interested in long-distance wireless communication. With the financial and technical help of the British, Marconi successfully transmitted across the English Channel in 1899 and across the Atlantic in 1901. Wireless was now a reality. Marconi was satisfied with his advance, but other scientists saw the transmission of *voices* by wireless as the next hurdle, a challenge that was soon surmounted.

In 1903 Reginald Fessenden, a Canadian, invented the **liquid barretter**, the first audio device permitting the reception of wireless voice transmissions. His 1906 Christmas Eve broadcast from Brant Rock, a small New England coastal village, was the first public broadcast of voices and music. His listeners were ships at sea and a few newspaper offices equipped to receive the transmission.

▼ Guglielmo Marconi (seated).

Later that same year American Lee DeForest invented the **audion tube**, a vacuum tube that improved and amplified wireless signals. Now the reliable transmission of clear voices and music was a reality. But DeForest's second important contribution was that he saw radio as a means of *broadcasting*. The early pioneers, Marconi included, had viewed radio as a device for point-to-point communication—for example, from ship to ship or ship to shore. But in the 1907 prospectus for his radio company DeForest wrote, "It will soon be possible to distribute grand opera music from transmitters placed on the stage of the Metropolitan Opera House by a Radio Telephone station on the roof to almost any dwelling in Greater New York and vicinity. . . . The same applies to large cities. Church music, lectures, etc., can be spread abroad by the Radio Telephone" (as quoted in Adams, 1996, pp. 104–106). Soon, countless "broadcasters" went on the air. Some broadcasters were giant corporations, looking to dominate the medium for profit; some were hobbyists and hams, playing with the medium for the sheer joy of it. There were so many "stations" that havoc reigned. Yet the promise of radio was such that the medium continued to mature until World War I, when the U.S. government ordered "the immediate closing of all stations for radio communications, both transmitting and receiving."

Early Sound Recording

The late 1800s have long been considered the beginning of sound recording. However, the 2008 discovery in a Paris archive of a 10-second recording by an obscure French tinkerer, Edouard-Leon Scott de Martinville, has some audio historians rethinking recording's roots. Scott recorded a folk song on a device he called a phonautograph in 1860, and he always thought that Thomas Edison had stolen credit that should have been his ("Edison Not," 2008). Nonetheless, in 1877 prolific inventor Edison patented his "talking machine," a device

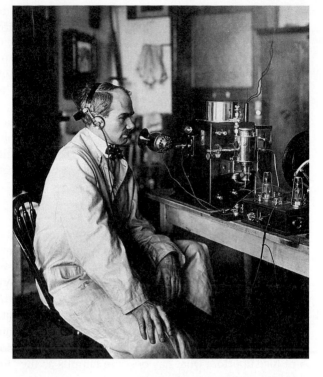

for replicating sound that used a hand-cranked grooved cylinder and a needle. The mechanical movement caused by the needle passing along the groove of the rotating cylinder and hitting bumps was converted into electrical energy that activated a diaphragm in a loudspeaker and produced sound. The drawback was that only one "recording" could be made of any given sound; the cylinder could not be duplicated. In 1887 that problem was solved by German immigrant Emile Berliner, whose gramophone used a flat, rotating, wax-coated disc that could easily be copied or pressed from a metal master. Two equally important Berliner contributions were development of a sophisticated microphone and later (through his company, RCA Victor Records) the import from Europe of recordings by famous opera stars. Now people had not only a reasonably priced record player but records to play on

◀ In 1887 Emile Berliner developed the flat disc gramophone and a sophisticated microphone, both important to the widespread public acceptance of sound recordings for the home. Nipper, the trademark for his company, RCA Victor, is on the scene even today.

it. The next advance was introduction of the two-sided disc by the Columbia Phonograph Company in 1905. Soon there were hundreds of phonograph or gramophone companies, and the device, by either name, was a standard feature in U.S. homes by 1920. More than 2 million machines and 107 million recordings were sold in 1919 alone. Public acceptance of the new medium was enhanced even more by development of electromagnetic recording in 1924 by Joseph P. Maxwell at Bell Laboratory.

The parallel development and diffusion of radio and sound recording is significant. For the first time in history, radio allowed people to hear the words and music of others who were not in their presence. On recordings they could hear words and music that may have been created days, months, or even years before.

The Coming of Broadcasting

The idea of broadcasting—that is, transmitting voices and music at great distances to a large number of people—predated the development of radio. Alexander Graham Bell's telephone company had a subscription music service in major cities in the late 1800s, delivering music to homes and businesses by telephone wires. A front-page story in an 1877 edition of the *New York Daily Graphic* suggested the possibilities of broadcasting to its readers. The public anticipated and, after DeForest's much publicized successes, was eager for music and voices at home. Russian immigrant David Sarnoff, then an employee of American Marconi, recognized this desire and in 1916 sent his superiors what has become famous as the "Radio Music Box Memo." In this memo Sarnoff wrote of

a plan of development which would make radio a "household utility" in the same sense as the piano or phonograph. The idea is to bring music into the house by wireless. . . . The receiver can be designed in the form of a simple "Radio Music Box" and arranged for several different wavelengths, which should be changeable with the throwing of a single switch or pressing of a single button. (Sterling & Kitross, 1990, p. 43)

▼ This cover of an 1877 newspaper proved prophetic in its image of speakers' ability to "broadcast" their words.

The introduction of broadcasting to a mass audience was delayed in the first two decades of the 20th century by patent fights and lawsuits. DeForest and Fessenden were both destroyed financially by the conflict. Yet when World War I ended, an enthusiastic audience awaited what had become a much-improved medium. In a series of developments that would be duplicated for television at the time of World War II, radio was transformed from an exciting technological idea into an entertainment and commercial giant. To aid the war effort, the government took over the patents relating to radio and continued to improve radio for military use. Thus, refinement and development of the technical aspects of radio continued throughout the war. Then, when the war ended in 1919, the patents were returned to their owners—and the bickering was renewed.

Concerned that the medium would be wasted and fearful that a foreign company (British Marconi) would control this vital resource, the U.S. government forced the combatants to merge. American Marconi, General Electric, American Telephone & Telegraph, and Westinghouse (in 1921)—each in control of a vital piece of technology—joined to create the Radio Corporation of America (RCA). RCA was a government-sanctioned monopoly, but its creation avoided direct government control of the new medium. Twenty-eight-year-old David Sarnoff, author of the Radio Music Box Memo, was made RCA's commercial manager. The way for the medium's popular growth was paved; its success was guaranteed by a public that, because of the phonograph, was already attuned to music in the home and, thanks to the just-concluded war, was awakening to the need for instant, wide-ranging news and information.

On September 30, 1920, a Westinghouse executive, impressed with press accounts of the number of listeners who were picking up broadcasts from the garage radio station of company engineer Frank Conrad, asked him to move his operation to the Westinghouse factory and expand its power. Conrad did so, and on October 27, 1920, experimental station 8XK in Pittsburgh, Pennsylvania, received a license from the Department of Commerce to broadcast. On November 2 this station, KDKA, made the first commercial radio broadcast, announcing the results of the presidential election that sent Warren G. Harding to the White House. By mid-1922, there were nearly 1 million radios in American homes, up from 50,000 just a year before (Tillinghast, 2000, p. 41).

The Coming of Regulation

As the RCA agreements demonstrated, the government had a keen interest in the development, operation, and diffusion of radio. At first government interest focused on point-to-point communication. In 1910 Congress passed the Wireless Ship Act, requiring that all ships using U.S. ports and carrying more than 50 passengers have a working wireless and operator. Of course, the wireless industry did not object, as the legislation boosted sales. But after the *Titanic* struck an iceberg in the North Atlantic in 1912 and it was learned that hundreds of lives were lost needlessly because other ships in the area had left their radios unattended, Congress passed the Radio Act of 1912, which not only strengthened rules regarding shipboard wireless but also required that wireless operators be licensed by the Secretary of Commerce and Labor.

The Radio Act of 1912 established spheres of authority for both federal and state governments, provided for allocating and revoking licenses and fining violators, and assigned frequencies for station operation. The government was in the business of regulating what was to become broadcasting, a development that angered many operators. They successfully challenged the 1912 act in court, and eventually President Calvin Coolidge ordered the cessation of government regulation of radio despite his belief that chaos would descend on the medium.

He proved prophetic. The industry's years of flouting the 1912 act had led it to the brink of disaster. Radio sales and profits dropped dramatically. Listeners were tired of the chaos. Stations arbitrarily changed frequencies, power, and hours of operation, and there was constant interference between stations, often intentional. Radio industry leaders petitioned Commerce Commissioner Herbert Hoover and, according to historian Erik Barnouw (1966)—who titled his book on radio's early days *A Tower in Babel*—"encouraged firmness" in government efforts to regulate and control the competitors. The government's response was a series of four National Radio Conferences involving industry experts, public officials, and government regulators. These conferences led to the Radio Act of 1927. Order was restored, and the industry prospered. But the broadcasters had made an important concession to secure this saving intervention. The 1927 act authorized them to *use* the channels, which belonged to the public, but not to *own* them. Broadcasters were thus simply the caretakers of the airwaves, a national resource.

The act further stated that when a license was awarded, the standard of evaluation would be the *public interest, convenience, or necessity*. The Federal Radio Commission (FRC) was established to administer the provisions of the act. This **trustee model** of regulation is based on two premises (Bittner, 1994). The first is the philosophy of **spectrum scarcity**. Because broadcast spectrum space is limited and not everyone who wants to

▼ The wireless-telegraphy room of the *Titanic*. Despite the heroic efforts of wireless operator Jack Philips, scores of people died needlessly in the sinking of that great ocean liner because ships in its vicinity did not monitor their receivers.

broadcast can, those who are granted licenses to serve a local area must accept regulation. The second reason for regulation revolves around the issue of influence. Broadcasting reaches virtually everyone in society. By definition, this ensures its power.

The Communications Act of 1934 replaced the 1927 legislation, substituting the Federal Communications Commission (FCC) for the FRC and cementing its regulatory authority, which continues today.

Advertising and the Networks

While the regulatory structure of the medium was evolving, so were its financial bases. The formation of RCA had ensured that radio would be a commercial, profit-based system. The industry supported itself through the sale of receivers; that is, it operated radio stations in order to sell radios. The problem was that once everybody had a radio, people would stop buying them. The solution was advertising. On August 22, 1922, New York station WEAF accepted the first radio commercial, a 10-minute spot for Long Island brownstone apartments. The cost of the ad was $50.

The sale of advertising led to establishment of the national radio networks. Groups of stations, or **affiliates**, could deliver larger audiences, realizing greater advertising revenues, which would allow them to hire bigger stars and produce better programming, which would attract larger audiences, which could be sold for even greater fees to advertisers. RCA set up a 24-station network, the National Broadcasting Company (NBC), in 1926. A year later it bought AT&T's stations and launched a second network, NBC Blue (the original NBC was renamed NBC Red). The Columbia Broadcasting System (CBS) was also founded in 1927, but it struggled until 26-year-old millionaire cigar maker William S. Paley bought it in 1928, making it a worthy competitor to NBC. The fourth network, Mutual, was established in 1934 largely on the strength of its hit Western *The Lone Ranger*. Four midwestern and eastern stations came together to sell advertising on it and other shows; soon Mutual had 60 affiliates. Mutual differed from the other major national networks in that it did not own and operate its own flagship stations (called **O&Os**, for owned and operated). By 1938 the four national networks had affiliated virtually all the large U.S. stations and the majority of smaller operations as well. These corporations grew so powerful that in 1943 the government forced NBC to divest itself of one of its networks. It sold NBC Blue to Life Saver candy maker Edward Noble, who renamed it the American Broadcasting Company (ABC).

The fundamental basis of broadcasting in the United States was set:

- Radio broadcasters were private, commercially owned enterprises, rather than government operations.
- Governmental regulation was based on the public interest.
- Stations were licensed to serve specific localities, but national networks programmed the most lucrative hours with the largest audiences.
- Entertainment and information were the basic broadcast content.
- Advertising formed the basis of financial support for broadcasting.

The Golden Age

The networks ushered in radio's golden age. Although the 1929–1939 Great Depression damaged the phonograph industry, with sales dipping to as few as 6 million records in 1932, it helped boost radio. Phonographs and records cost money, but once a family bought a radio, a whole world of entertainment and information was at its disposal, free of charge. The number of homes with radios grew from 12 million in 1930 to 30 million in 1940, and half of them had not one but two receivers. Ad revenues rose from $40 million to $155 million over the same period. Between them, the four national networks broadcast 156 hours of network-originated programming a week. New genres became fixtures during this period: comedy (*The Jack Benny Show, Fibber McGee and Molly*), audience participation (*Professor Quiz, Truth or Consequences, Kay Kyser's Kollege of Musical Knowledge*), children's shows (*Little Orphan Annie, The Lone Ranger*),

soap operas (*Oxydol's Own Ma Perkins, The Guiding Light*), and drama (Orson Welles's *Mercury Theater of the Air*). News, too, became a radio staple.

RADIO AND SOUND RECORDING IN WORLD WAR II The golden age of radio shone even more brightly after Pearl Harbor was bombed by the Japanese in 1941, propelling the United States into World War II. Radio was used to sell war bonds, and much content was aimed at boosting the nation's morale. The war increased the desire for news, especially from abroad. The war also caused a paper shortage, reducing advertising space in newspapers. No new stations were licensed during the war years, and the 950 existing broadcasters reaped all the broadcast advertising revenues, as well as additional ad revenues that otherwise would have gone to newspapers. Ad revenues were up to $310 million by the end of World War II in 1945.

Sound recording benefited from the war as well. Prior to World War II, recording in the United States was done either directly to master metal disc or on wire recorders, literally magnetic recording on metal wire. But GIs brought a new technology back from occupied Germany, a tape recorder that used an easily handled paper tape on a reel. Then, in 1947, Columbia Records introduced a new 33⅓ rpm (rotations-per-minute) long-playing plastic record perfected by Peter Goldmark. A big advance over the previous standard of 78 rpm, it was more durable than the older shellac discs and played for 23 rather than 3⅓ minutes. Columbia offered the technology free to all other record companies. RCA refused the offer, introducing its own 45 rpm disc in 1948. It played for only 3⅓ minutes and had a huge center hole requiring a special adapter. Still, RCA persisted in its marketing, causing a speed war that was settled in 1950 when the two giants compromised on 33⅓ as the standard for classical music and 45 as the standard for pop. And it was the 45, the single, that sustained the music business until the mid-1960s, when the Beatles not only ushered in the "British invasion" of rock 'n' roll but also transformed popular music into a 33⅓ album-dominant cultural force, shaping today's popular music and helping reinvent radio.

▼ The Iowa radio station that bought space on the cover of industry "bible" *Broadcasting/Telecasting* wanted readers to believe that all was well in radio-land in 1953. It wasn't.

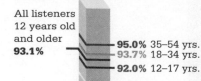

Percentage who listen every week
(by age)

All listeners
12 years old
and older
93.1%

95.0% 35–54 yrs.
93.7% 18–34 yrs.
92.0% 12–17 yrs.

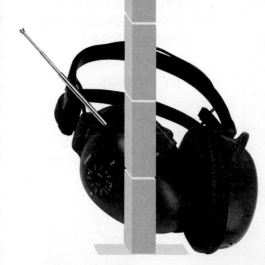

▲ **Figure 7.1** Percentage of Americans Who Listen to the Radio Every Week by Age. *Source:* Radio, 2011.

TELEVISION ARRIVES When the war ended and radio licenses were granted again, the number of stations grew rapidly to 2,000. Annual ad revenues reached $454 million in 1950. Then came television. Network affiliation dropped from 97% in 1945 to 50% by the mid-1950s, as stations "went local" in the face of television's national dominance. National radio advertising income dipped to $35 million in 1960, the year that television found its way into 90% of U.S. homes. If radio were to survive, it would have to find new functions.

Radio and Its Audiences

Radio more than survived; it prospered by changing the nature of its relationship with its audiences. The easiest way to understand this is to see pretelevision radio as television is today—nationally oriented, broadcasting an array of recognizable entertainment program formats, populated by well-known stars and personalities, and consumed primarily in the home, typically with people sitting around the set. Posttelevision radio is local, fragmented, specialized, personal, and mobile. Whereas pretelevision radio was characterized by the big national networks, today's radio is dominated by formats, a particular sound characteristic of a local station.

Who are the people who make up radio's audience? In an average week, more than 242 million people, 93.1% of all Americans 12 and over, will listen to the radio ("Radio Broadcasters Attract," 2011). Broadcast radio's audience growth, however, is stagnant. That 93.1% figure is in fact a decline from the 95.6% who listened regularly in 2009. And while the audience's *size* has remained relatively constant for the last few years, *time spent listening* has fallen, dropping several minutes in that span (Walsh, 2011). But most troubling to radio professionals is that time listening *among teenagers* is in decline, as it is with college graduates (Sass, 2010). You can see a demographic breakdown of listeners in Figure 7.1. Note it is teens who listen the least. The industry itself attributes this situation to dissatisfaction with unimaginative programming, hypercommercialization—on average about 12 minutes of commercials an hour—and the availability of online music sources and mobile technologies like MP3 players and smartphones. Today, 38% of Americans now listen to audio on digital devices, a proportion that is expected to double by 2015 (Santhanam, Mitchell, & Rosenstiel, 2012).

Scope and Nature of the Radio Industry

There are 14,952 broadcast radio stations operating in the United States today: 4,766 commercial AM stations, 6,542 commercial FM stations, and 3,644 noncommercial FM stations. These are joined on the dial by 838 **Low Power FM (LPFM)** stations. There are more than two radios for every person in the United States. The industry as a whole sells more than $17 billion a year of ad time, and radio remains people's primary means of consuming audio content.

FM, AM, and Noncommercial Radio

Although FMs constitute 58% of all commercial stations (to AMs' 42%), they attract over 75% of all radio listeners. This has to do with the technology behind each. The FM (frequency modulation) signal is wider, allowing the broadcast not only of stereo but also of better fidelity to the original sound than the narrower AM (amplitude modulation) signal. As a result, people attracted to music gravitate toward FM. People favoring news, sports, and information tend to find themselves listening to the AM dial. AM signals travel farther than FM signals, making them perfect for rural parts of the country. But rural areas tend to be less heavily populated, and most AM stations serve fewer listeners. The FCC approved stereo AM in

1985, but relatively few people have AM stereo receivers. There seems to be little demand for news, sports, and information in stereo.

Many of today's FM stations are noncommercial—that is, they accept no advertising. When the national frequency allocation plan was established during the deliberations leading to the 1934 Communications Act, commercial radio broadcasters persuaded Congress that they alone could be trusted to develop this valuable medium. They promised to make time available for religious, children's, and other educational programming. No frequencies were set aside for noncommercial radio to fulfill these functions. At the insistence of critics who contended that the commercial broadcasters were not fulfilling their promise, in 1945 the FCC set aside all FM frequencies between 88.1 and 91.9 megahertz for noncommercial radio. Today these noncommercial stations not only provide local service, but many also offer national network quality programming through affiliation with National Public Radio (NPR) and Public Radio International (PRI) or through a number of smaller national networks, such as Pacifica Radio.

Radio Is Local

No longer able to compete with television for the national audience in the 1950s, radio began to attract a local audience. Because it costs much more to run a local television station than a local radio station, advertising rates on radio tend to be much lower than on television. Local advertisers can afford radio more easily than they can television, which increases the local flavor of radio.

Radio Is Fragmented

Radio stations are widely distributed throughout the United States. Virtually every town—even those with only a few hundred residents—has at least one station. The number of stations licensed in an area is a function of both population and proximity to other towns. Small towns may have only one AM or FM station, and a big city can have as many as 40 stations. This fragmentation—many stations serving many areas—makes possible contemporary radio's most important characteristic, its ability to specialize.

Radio Is Specialized

When radio became a local medium, it could no longer program the expensive, star-filled genres of its golden age. The problem now was how to program a station with interesting content and do so economically. A disc jockey playing records was the best solution. And stations soon learned that a highly specialized, specific audience of particular interest to certain advertisers could be attracted with specific types of music. **Format** radio was born. Of course, choosing a specific format means accepting that many potential listeners will not tune in. But in format radio the size of the audience is secondary to its composition.

Radio ratings service Arbitron annually recognizes 60 different formats, from the most common, which include Country, Top 40, Album-Oriented Rock, and All Talk, to the somewhat uncommon, for example, World Ethnic. Many stations, especially those in rural areas, offer **secondary services** (formats). For example, a country station may broadcast a religious format for 10 hours on Saturday and Sunday. Figure 7.2 shows Arbitron's 60 formats.

Format radio offers stations many advantages beyond low-cost operations and specialized audiences that appeal to advertisers. Faced with falling listenership or declining advertising revenues, a station can simply change disc jockeys (DJs) and discs. Neither television nor the print media have this content flexibility. When confronted with competition from a station with a similar format, a station can further narrow its audience by specializing its formula even more.

Music format radio requires a disc jockey. Someone has to spin the discs and provide the talk. The modern DJ is the invention of Todd Storz, who bought KOHW in Omaha, Nebraska, in 1949. He turned the radio personality/music formula on its head.

80s Hits	New Country
Active Rock	News/Talk/Information
Adult Contemporary	Nostalgia
Adult Hits	Oldies
Adult Standards/MOR	Other
Album Adult Alternative	Pop Contemporary Hit Radio
Album Oriented Rock	Religious
All News	Rhythmic AC
All Sports	Rhythmic Contemporary Hit Radio
Alternative	Rhythmic Oldies
Blues	Smooth Adult Contemporary
Children's Radio	Soft Adult Contemporary
Christian AC	Southern Gospel
Classical	Spanish Adult Hits
Classic Country	Spanish Contemporary
Classic Hits	Spanish Contemporary Christian
Classic Rock	Spanish Hot Adult Contemporary
Contemporary Christian	Spanish News/Talk
Contemporary Inspirational	Spanish Oldies
Country	Spanish Religious
Easy Listening	Spanish Sports
Educational	Spanish Tropical
Family Hits	Spanish Variety
Gospel	Talk/Personality
Hot Adult Contemporary	Tejano
Jazz	Urban Adult Contemporary
Latino Urban	Urban Contemporary
Mexican Regional	Urban Oldies
Modern Adult Contemporary	Variety
New Adult Contemporary/Smooth Jazz	World Ethnic

▲ **Figure 7.2** Arbitron's Radio Formats.
Source: Arbitron, 2012.

Before Storz, radio announcers would talk most of the time and occasionally play music to rest their voices. Storz wanted more music, less talk. He thought radio should sound like a jukebox—the same few songs people wanted to hear played over and over again. His Top 40 format, which demanded strict adherence to a **playlist** (a predetermined sequence of selected records) of popular music for young people, up-tempo pacing, and catchy production gimmicks, became the standard for the posttelevision popular music station. Gordon McClendon of KLIF in Dallas refined the Top 40 format and developed others, such as Beautiful Music, and is therefore often considered, along with Storz, one of the two pioneers of format radio.

Radio Is Personal

With the advent of television, the relationship of radio with its audience changed. Whereas families had gathered around the radio set to listen together, we now listen to the radio alone. We select personally pleasing formats, and we listen as an adjunct to other personally important activities.

Radio Is Mobile

The mobility of radio accounts in large part for its personal nature. We can listen anywhere, at any time. We listen at work, while exercising, while sitting in the sun. By 1947 the combined sale of car and alarm clock radios exceeded that of traditional living-room receivers, and in 1951 the annual production of car radios exceeded that of home receivers for the first time. Today, two-thirds of all traditional radio listening occurs away from home (Santhanam, Mitchell, & Rosenstiel, 2012).

The Business of Radio

The distinctive characteristics of radio serve its listeners, but they also make radio a thriving business.

Radio as an Advertising Medium

Advertisers enjoy the specialization of radio because it gives them access to homogeneous groups of listeners to whom products can be pitched. Income earned from the sale of airtime is called **billings**. Local time and national spots (for example, Prestone Antifreeze buys time on several thousand stations in winter areas) account for 92% of all billings; network time makes up the rest (Television Bureau of Advertising, 2011). The cost of time is based on the **ratings**, the percentage of the total available audience reached.

Radio is an attractive advertising medium for reasons other than its delivery of a homogeneous audience. Radio ads are inexpensive to produce and therefore can be changed, updated, and specialized to meet specific audience demands. Ads can also be specialized to different times of the day. For example, a hamburger restaurant may have one version of its commercial for the morning audience, in which its breakfast menu is touted, and a different version for the evening audience driving home, dreading the thought of cooking dinner. Radio time is inexpensive to buy, especially when compared with television. An audience loyal to a specific format station is presumably loyal to those who advertise on it. Radio is the listeners' friend; it travels with them and talks to them personally.

▲ Fans debate whether Todd Storz or Gordon McClendon first invented the DJ. But there is no dispute that Alan Freed, first in Cleveland and then in New York, established the DJ as a star. Freed, here in a 1958 photo, is credited with introducing America's white teenagers to rhythm 'n' blues artists like Chuck Berry and Little Richard and ushering in the age of rock 'n' roll.

Deregulation and Ownership

The business of radio is being altered by deregulation and changes in ownership rules. To ensure that there were many different perspectives in the cultural forum, the FCC had long limited the number of radio stations one person or company could own to one AM and one FM locally and seven AMs and seven FMs nationally. These numbers were revised upward in the late 1980s, and controls were almost totally eliminated by the Telecommunications Act of 1996. Now, thanks to this **deregulation**, there are no national ownership limits, and one person or company can own as many as eight stations in one market, depending on the size of the market. This situation has allowed **duopoly**—one person or company owning and managing multiple radio stations in a single market—to explode. Since the passage of the 1996 act, more than 10,000 radio stations have been sold, and there are now 1,100 fewer station owners, a 30% decline. The vast majority of these sales have been to already large radio groups such as Clear Channel and Cumulus, with 850 and 525 stations, respectively. As a result, in 25 of the 50 largest radio markets, three companies claim 80% of all listeners. In 43 different cities, one-third of the radio stations are owned by a single company, making radio "the most consolidated industry in the media" (Morrison, 2011). Whereas all of Boston's 15 FMs and 14 of Seattle's 17 FMs are owned by four companies, each of the 12 FMs in Toronto, Canada, has a different owner.

This concentration is a source of concern for many radio professionals. Local public affairs shows now make up less than one-half of 1 percent of all commercial broadcast time in the United States. "There is a crisis," said FCC Commissioner Michael Copps (2011), "when more than one-third of our commercial

▲ What small increase there is in the size of radio's audience is attributed to "noncorporate" programming like public radio, sports-talk, and Spanish-language stations. Pictured here is Miami's Javier Ceriani.

broadcasters offer little to no news whatsoever to their communities of license. America's news and information resources keep shrinking and hundreds of stories that could inform our citizens go untold and, indeed, undiscovered. Where is the vibrancy when hundreds of newsrooms have been decimated and tens of thousands of reporters are walking the street in search of a job instead of working the beat in search of a story?" As for the music, in 2011, when Clear Channel and Cumulus collectively laid off "dozens to hundreds" of DJs in a move toward "more automated or national syndicated programming" (Sass, 2011b), veteran Los Angeles rock DJ Jim Ladd said, "It's really bad news. It was people in my profession that first played Tom Petty, first played the Doors. But the people programming stations now are not music people—they're business people" (in Knopper, 2011, p. 19). Does it surprise you, then, that the biggest audience increases over the last 10 years come from stations—public radio (up 31%), sports talk (up 25%), and Spanish-language (up 54%)—unlikely to receive playlists from Corporate Central (Stevenson, 2008)? Low Power FM, 10- to 100-watt nonprofit community radio stations with a reach of only a few miles, are one response to radio concentration. As a result of the Local Community Radio Act of 2005, which enjoyed wide bipartisan support in Congress, 838 LPFM stations, serving all 50 states, now offer opportunities for additional radio voices to serve their local listenerships. The FCC reports that it receives "tens of thousands of inquiries annually from groups and individuals wishing to start a low power radio station" (Federal Communications Commission, 2012).

Scope and Nature of the Recording Industry

When the DJs and Top 40 formats saved radio in the 1950s, they also changed for all time popular music and, by extension, the recording industry. Disc jockeys were color-deaf in their selection of records. They introduced record buyers to rhythm 'n' blues in the music of African American artists such as Chuck Berry and Little Richard. Until the mid-1950s the work of these performers had to be **covered**—rerecorded by White artists such as Perry Como—before it was aired. Teens loved the new sound, however, and it became the foundation of their own subculture, as well as the basis for the explosion in recorded music. See the essay, "Rock 'n' Roll, Radio, and Race Relations," for more on rock's roots.

Today more than 5,000 U.S. companies annually release around 100,000 new albums on thousands of different labels. Customers in America annually buy one-third of the world's recorded music in more than 1.5 billion individual transactions, up from 845 million in 2000 (Masnick & Ho, 2012).

The Major Recording Companies

Three major recording companies control 75% of the global recorded music market. Two (Sony and Universal) control 50% of the world's $17 billion global music market. Two of the three are foreign-owned:

- Sony, controlling about 22% of the world music market, is co-owned by two global media conglomerates, Japan's Sony and Germany's Bertelsmann. Its labels include Columbia, Epic, RCA, and Arista.
- New York–based Warner Music Group, controlling about 25%, is owned by billionaire Len Blavatnik's Access Industries and several private investors. Its labels include Atlantic, Electra, and Warner Brothers.
- Universal Music Group, controlling about 28%, is owned by French conglomerate Vivendi Universal and controls labels such as MCA, Capitol, and Def Jam Records.

Critics have long voiced concern over conglomeration and internationalization in the music business, a concern that centers on the traditional cultural value of music, especially for young people. Multibillion-dollar conglomerates typically are not rebellious in their cultural tastes, nor are they usually willing to take risks on new ideas. These duties have fallen primarily to the independent labels, companies such as Real

World Records and Epitaph. Still, problems with the music industry–audience relationship remain and have contributed to its current turmoil.

Cultural homogenization is the worrisome outcome of virtually all the world's influential recording being controlled by a few profit-oriented giants. If bands or artists cannot immediately deliver the goods, they aren't signed. So derivative artists and manufactured groups dominate—for example, Justin Bieber and Hannah Montana.

The *dominance of profit over artistry* worries many music fans. When a major label must spend millions to sign a bankable group such as R.E.M. ($80 million) or Mariah Carey ($80 million), it typically pares lesser-known, potentially more innovative artists from its roster.

Critics and industry people alike see the ascendance of profits over artistry as a problem for the industry itself, as well as for the music and its listeners. As we saw in Chapter 2, record industry sales have dropped consistently over the past decade, with the steepest fall-off coming in more recent years. As a result, EMI let 2,000 employees go in 2008, only months after Warner cut loose 400 people of its own. Staff at the other major labels faced the same fate (Garside & Power, 2008). The reason for this state of affairs, say many music critics, is not Internet piracy, as asserted by the recording industry, but the industry itself. As music critic John Seabrook (2003) explains, "The record industry has helped to create these thieving, lazy, and disloyal fans. By marketing superficial, disposable pop stars, labels persuade fans to treat the music as superficial and disposable." He quotes legendary music producer Malcolm McLaren: "The amazing thing about the death of the record industry is that no one cares. If the movie industry died, you'd probably have a few people saying, 'Oh, this is too bad—after all, they gave us Garbo and Marilyn Monroe.' But now the record industry is dying, and no one gives a damn" (p. 52). What kept the red ink from flowing even faster was strong sales in **catalogue albums** (more than 30% of all discs sold), albums more than three years old. However, sales of **recent catalogue albums**, that is, those that have been out for 15 months to three years, have fallen dramatically over the last five years, further damaging the industry's bottom line. "Recent catalogue" cannot become "catalogue" unless a label stays with an artist, allowing him or her to grow, possibly through three or four albums. Look at the names of the best-selling albums and artists in Figure 7.3.

▼ **Figure 7.3** The Top 10 Best-selling Albums and Artists of All Time, U.S. Sales Only. *Source:* Recording Industry Association of America (www.riaa.com).

Best-selling artists (units sold in millions)

1	Beatles	177.0
2	Elvis Presley	134.5
3	Garth Brooks	128.0
4	Led Zeppelin	111.5
5	Eagles	100.0
6	Billy Joel	81.5
7	Pink Floyd	74.5
8	Elton John	72.0
9	Barbra Streisand	71.5
10	AC/DC	71.5

Best-selling albums

1. *Thriller* (Michael Jackson)
2. *Eagles/Their Greatest Hits* (Eagles)
3. *Led Zeppelin IV* (Led Zeppelin)
4. *The Wall* (Pink Floyd)
5. *Greatest Hits Volumes I & II* (Billy Joel)
6. *Back in Black* (AC/DC)
7. *Double Lives* (Garth Brooks)
8. *Come on Over* (Shania Twain)
9. *Beatles* (The Beatles)
10. *Rumours* (Fleetwood Mac)

USING MEDIA TO MAKE A DIFFERENCE
Rock 'n' Roll, Radio, and Race Relations

After World War II African Americans in the United States refused to remain invisible. Having fought in segregated units in Europe and proven their willingness to fight and die for freedom abroad, they openly demanded freedom at home. Some Whites began to listen. President Harry Truman, recognizing the absurdity of racial separation in the self-proclaimed "greatest democracy on earth," desegregated the armed forces by executive order in 1948. These early stirrings of equality led to a sense among African Americans that anything was possible, and that feeling seeped into their music. What had been called cat, sepia, or race music took on a new tone. While this new sound borrowed from traditional Black music—gospel, blues, and sad laments over slavery and racial injustice—it was different, much different. Music historian Ed Ward said that this bolder, more aggressive music "spoke to a shared experience, not just to Black (usually rural Black) life," and it would become the "truly biracial popular music in this country" (Ward, Stokes, & Tucker, 1986, p. 83).

Hundreds of small independent record companies sprang up to produce this newly labeled rhythm and blues (R&B), music focusing on Americans' shared experience, and sex and alcohol were part of life for people of all colors. With its earthy lyrics and thumping dance beat, R&B very quickly found an audience in the 1950s, one composed largely of urban Blacks (growing in number as African Americans increasingly fled the South) and White teenagers.

The major record companies took notice, and rather than sign already successful R&B artists, they had their White artists cover the Black hits. The Penguins' "Earth Angel" was covered by the reassuringly named Crew Cuts, who also covered the Chords' "Sh-Boom." Chuck Berry's "Maybellene" was covered by both the Johnny Long and Ralph Marterie orchestras. Even Bill Haley and the Comets' youth anthem "Shake, Rattle and Roll" was a cover of a Joe Turner tune.

But these covers actually served to introduce even more White teens to the new music, and these kids demanded the original versions. This did not escape the attention of Sam Phillips, who in 1952 founded Sun Records in an effort to bring Black music to White kids ("If

I could find a White man who had the Negro sound, I could make a billion dollars," he is reported to have mused ["Why Elvis Still Lives," 2002]). In 1954 he found that man: Elvis Presley.

The situation also caught the attention of Cleveland DJ Alan Freed, whose nationally distributed radio (and later television) show featured Black R&B tunes, never covers. Freed began calling the music he played rock 'n' roll (to signify that it was Black and White youth music), and by 1955, when Freed took his show to New York, the cover business was dead. Black performers were recording and releasing their own music to a national audience, and people of all colors were tuning in.

Now that the kids had a music of their own, and now that a growing number of radio stations were willing to program it, a youth culture began to develop, one that was

> "R&B and rock 'n' roll did not end racism. But the music made a difference, one that would eventually make it possible for Americans who wanted to do so to free themselves from racism's ugly hold."

antagonistic toward their parents' culture. The music was central to this antagonism, not only because it was gritty and nasty but also because it exposed the hypocrisy of adult culture.

For young people of the mid-1950s and 1960s, the music of Little Richard, Fats Domino, Ray Charles, and Chuck Berry made a lie of all that their parents, teachers, and government leaders had said about race, the inferiority of African Americans, and Blacks' satisfaction with the status quo.

Ralph Bass, a producer for independent R&B label Chess Records, described the evolution to historian David Szatmary. When he was touring with Chess's R&B groups in the early 1950s, "they didn't let whites into the clubs. Then they got 'white spectator tickets' for the worst corner of the joint. They had to keep the white kids out, so they'd have white nights sometimes, or they'd put a rope across the middle of the floor. The blacks on one side, the whites on the other, digging how the blacks were dancing and copying them. Then, hell, the rope would come down, and they'd all be dancing together. Salt and pepper all mixed together" (Szatmary, 2000, p. 21).

How many recent or current artists and albums do you think will ever join these ranks? Critics of the ascendance of profits over artistry argue that the industry simply lacks the patience to develop careers.

Promotion overshadows the music, say the critics. If groups or artists don't come across well on television or are otherwise a challenge to promote (for example, they do not fit an easily recognizable niche), they aren't signed. Again, the solution is to create marketable artists from scratch. Promoting tours is also an issue. If bands or artists do not have corporate sponsorship for their tours, there is no tour. If musicians do not tour, they cannot create an enthusiastic fan base. But if they do not have an enthusiastic fan base, they cannot attract the corporate sponsorship necessary to mount a tour. This makes radio even more important for the introduction of new artists and forms of music, but radio, too, is increasingly driven by profit-maximizing format narrowing and is therefore dependent on the major labels' definition of playable artists. As a result, when the Internet began to undermine a complacent industry's long-profitable business model, it was ill prepared to meet the challenges that came its way.

▲ The music of Chuck Berry, Bo Diddley, and Little Richard may have been covered by White performers, but its passion and soul soon attracted young listeners of all races, making a lie of their parents' racial intolerance.

R&B and rock 'n' roll did not end racism. But the music made a difference, one that would eventually make it possible for Americans who wanted to do so to free themselves of racism's ugly hold. Rock music (and the radio stations that played it) would again nudge the nation toward its better tendencies during the antiwar and civil rights movements of the late 1960s. And it is against this backdrop, a history of popular music making as real a difference as any piece of official legislation, that contemporary critics lament the homogenizing of popular music. Music can and has made a difference. Can and will it ever again? they ask.

Trends and Convergence in Radio and Sound Recording

Emerging and changing technologies have affected the production and distribution aspects of both radio and sound recording.

The Impact of Television

We have seen how television fundamentally altered radio's structure and relationship with its audiences. Television, specifically cable channel MTV, changed the recording industry, too. MTV's introduction in 1981 helped pull the industry out of its disastrous 1979 slump, but at a price. First, the look of concerts has changed. No longer is it sufficient to pack an artist or group into a hall or stadium with a few thousand screaming fans. Now a concert must be an extravagant multimedia event approximating the sophistication of an MTV video. This means that fewer acts take to the road, changing

the relationship between musicians and fans. Second, the radio-recording industry relationship has changed. Even as MTV began to program fewer and fewer music videos, record companies grew even more reliant on television to introduce new music. *American Idol* contestants, for example, accounted for 60 Number One hits and 14 platinum (over a million sales) albums in the first seven years after the show's 2002 debut. Labels now time record releases to artists' television appearances, and new and old tunes alike find heavy play on television shows like *Gossip Girl* and *Glee*. "TV is the new radio," says Leonard Richardson, vice president for music at the CW television network. "People say that all the time, but it's definitely true" (in Littleton & Schneider, 2009, p. 62). Internet video has also become "the new radio." Not only did YouTube serve as the career launch pad for pop star Justin Bieber, who in 2008 used a series of homemade videos of his 12-year-old self singing in the mirror and around his hometown to catch the eye of the star-hungry record industry, but two-thirds of U.S. teens listen to music on YouTube, more than on any other medium (Sisario, 2012).

▶ TV is the new radio. Labels time record releases to tunes' presence on shows like *Glee*.

These artists (from left to right)—the Pussycat Dolls, Arcade Fire, Aimee Mann, and My Chemical Romance—are finding new ways to prosper in a rapidly changing music industry while still engaging fans.

Satellite and Cable

The convergence of radio and satellite has aided the rebirth of the radio networks. Music and other forms of radio content can be distributed quite inexpensively to thousands of stations. As a result, one "network" can provide very different services to its very different affiliates. Citadel, for example, maintains the Rick Dees Weekly Top 40 and ESPN networks. Westwood One, through its **syndication** operations, delivers its more than 300 varied network and program syndication services to almost every commercial station in the country. The low cost of producing radio programming, however, makes the establishment of other, even more specialized networks possible. Satellites, too, make access to syndicated content and formats affordable for many stations. Syndicators can deliver news, top 10 shows, and other content to stations on a market-by-market basis. They can also provide entire formats, requiring local stations, if they wish, to do little more than insert commercials into what appears to listeners to be a local broadcast.

Satellite has another application as well. Many listeners now receive "radio" through their cable televisions in the form of satellite-delivered **DMX (Digital Music Express)**. Direct satellite home, office, and automobile delivery of audio by **digital audio radio service (DARS)** brings Sirius XM Radio to more than 25 million subscribers (32 million total listeners) by offering hundreds of commercial channels—primarily talk, sports, and traffic—and commercial-free channels—primarily music. Those numbers will likely grow because the company has arrangements with every major carmaker in the country to offer its receivers as a factory-installed option.

Satellite radio's true impact on the radio and recording industries, however, may be more than simply offering a greater variety of listening options. Because despite the fact that traditional radio station operators continue to dismiss satellite radio for its relatively small audience, those same operators have begun to change the sound of their stations in response to the new technology. They are reducing the number of commercials they air, adding hundreds of new songs and artists to their playlists, and introducing new formats. Many are also beefing up their local news operations. Both radio and popular music should be better for the change.

Terrestrial Digital Radio

Since late 2002, thousands of radio stations have begun broadcasting **terrestrial** (land-based) **digital radio**. Relying on digital compression technology called **in-band-on-channel (IBOC)**, terrestrial digital radio allows broadcasters to transmit not only their usual analog signal, but one or more digital signals using their existing spectrum space. And although IBOC also improves sound fidelity, making possible high-definition radio, most stations using the technology see its greatest value in pay services—for example, subscription data delivery. IBOC proponents optimistically predict that terrestrial digital radio will completely replace analog radio by 2017.

Web Radio and Podcasting

Radio's convergence with digital technologies is nowhere more pronounced and potentially profound than in **Web radio**, the delivery of "radio" directly to individual listeners over the Internet, and in **podcasting**, recording and downloading of audio files stored on servers, or, in the words of *Fortune* technology writer Peter Lewis (2005), "Simultaneously a rebellion against the blandness of commercial radio, a demonstration of time shifting for radio, just as TiVo allows time shifting for television, and a celebration of the Internet's power to let individuals offer their own voices to a global audience" (p. 204).

First, Web radio. Tens of thousands of "radio stations" exist on the Web in one of two forms. *Radio simulcasts* are traditional, over-the-air stations transmitting their signals online. Some simply re-create their original broadcasts, but more often, the simulcast includes additional information, such as song lyrics or artists' biographical information and concert dates.

Bitcasters, Web-only radio stations, can be accessed only online. There are narrowly targeted bitcasts, such as Indie 103.1, a Los Angeles alternative rock station, and allworship.com, a Christian station Webcasting from Birmingham, Alabama. But the most dramatic evidence of the popularity of bitcasting exists in the success of two **streaming** services that allow the simultaneous downloading and accessing of music. Pandora is platform agnostic, available on virtually every new digital device, not only the obvious like smartphones, televisions, and car radios, but also the less-so, for example WiFi-enabled refrigerators. Listeners, who log more than 1 billion hours a month (Walsh, 2012b), can pay a small monthly fee to hear the service absent commercials, but the vast majority of its 75 million subscribers tune in for free and hear demographically and taste-specific commercials. Pandora accomplishes this ad specificity by coupling it with its Music Genome Project. After listeners tell Pandora what artists they like, the Genome Project, according to the company, "will quickly scan its entire world of analyzed music, almost a century of popular recordings—new and old, well known and completely obscure—to find songs with interesting musical similarities to your choice." Listeners can create up to 100 unique "stations," personally refining them even more if they wish, and at any time, they can purchase the tune they are hearing with a simple click.

With more than 10 million subscribers worldwide, Spotify came to the U.S. in 2011. Using a "freemium model," it offers listeners more than 15 million songs. They can listen for free, hearing commercials and living with limits on how much music they can stream, or they can pay a small monthly fee for premium limitless, commercial-free listening. Including other streaming services such as Slacker, Rdio, Apple's iRadio, Microsoft's game console–based Xbox Music, Clear Channel's iHeart Radio, and Yahoo Music, nearly half of U.S. Internet users stream music, and this online radio is the country's fastest-growing way to listen to music (Walsh, 2012c).

Podcasts, however, because they are posted online, do not require streaming software. They can be downloaded, either on demand or automatically (typically by subscription), to any digital device that has an MP3 player, including PCs, laptops, and smartphones. Nearly 27,000 podcasters are now online, and they cover every conceivable topic on which an individual or organization cares to comment. And while podcasting was begun in earnest in 2004 by individual techies, audio bloggers, and DJ-wannabes, within a year they were joined by "professional" podcasters such as record companies, commercial and public radio stations, and big media companies like ESPN, CNN, Bravo, and Disney. Listenership has also exploded as iPods and other MP3 devices have become ubiquitous and as more people have broadband Internet access. Twenty-five percent of Americans listen to podcasts, more than double the proportion who listened in 2006. In fact, including all forms, more than 56% of Americans 12 and older listen to Internet radio, averaging nearly 10 hours of listening a week (Edison Research, 2011).

Smartphones, Tablets, and Social Networking Sites

One of radio's distinguishing characteristics, as we've seen, is its portability. Smartphones and tablets reinforce that benefit. For example, more than half of all Pandora listening is mobile, and it is the leading audio app on the iPhone and iPad. Eleven percent of smartphone owners listen to streamed music while driving by connecting their devices to their cars' sound systems, and 19% download music from other devices to their smartphones for listening-on-the-go (Santhanam, Mitchell, & Rosenstiel, 2012).

Much smartphone and tablet listening occurs via social networking sites' streaming services such as MySpaceMusic and Facebook's free music links to sites such as Spotify, Pandora, and turntable.fm. Digital technology, so much a threat to the traditional recording industry business model, has also helped the labels' balance sheets in an unlikely manner—the sale of music to mobile phones. Ringtone downloads, people downloading recorded music to serve as the alerting sound on their phones, is already a global $10 billion business. For the record labels, this income is equivalent to "found money," as it is generated from fragments of already existing recordings (see Figure 7.4).

▲ **Figure 7.4** Units of Recorded Music Shipped by Major Format, 2012.
Source: Adapted from Record Industry Association of America (www.riaa.com).

Digital Technology

In the 1970s the basis of both the recording and radio industries changed from analog to **digital recording**. That is, sound went from being preserved as waves, whether physically on a disc or tape or through the air, to conversion into 1s and 0s logged in millisecond intervals in a computerized translation process. When replayed at the proper speed, the resulting sound was not only continuous but pristine—no hum, no hiss. The CD, or compact disc, was introduced in 1983 using digital coding on a 4.7-inch disc read by a laser beam. In 1986 *Brothers in Arms* by Dire Straits became the first million-selling CD. In 1988 the sale of CDs surpassed that of vinyl discs for the first time, and today CDs account for 11.7% of all music sales.

Convergence with computers and the Internet offers other challenges and opportunities to the radio and recording industries. The way the recording industry operates has been dramatically altered by the Internet. Traditionally, a record company signs an artist, produces the artist's music, and promotes the artist and music through a variety of outlets but primarily through the distribution of music to radio stations. Then listeners, learning about the artist and music through radio, go to a record store and buy the music. But this has changed. Music fans are now "in a new century and floating free with more sounds than ever," writes music critic Gabriel Boylan (2010, p. 34). Head of Country Music Television, Brian Philips, explains, "The old logic of just get something played a lot on the radio and it will sell seems less and less to be predictably true. . . . The winners these days are people who can imagine beyond the narrow limitations of the old system" (in Klaassen, 2005b, p. 12). Those "narrow limitations" are indeed being overcome, as you can read in the essay, "The Future of the Music Business?"

Artists themselves are using the Internet for their own production, promotion, and distribution, bypassing radio and the recording companies altogether. Musicians are using their own sites, social networking sites, and sites designed specifically to feature new artists, such as purevolume.com, to connect directly with listeners. Fans can hear (and in some cases, even download) new tunes for free, buy music downloads, CDs, and merchandise, get concert information and tickets, and chat with artists and other fans. You may never have heard of the bands Hawthorne Heights, Pomplamoose, or Nicki Bluhm and the Gamblers, but using the Internet they have created "a new middle class of popular music: acts that can make a full-time living selling only a modest number of discs, on the order of 50,000 to 500,000 per release" (Howe, 2005a, p. 203). Big-name artists, too, are gravitating to the Web. Public Enemy released *There's a Poison Going On* exclusively online; Lady Gaga made her 2011 album *Born This Way* available for streaming a week in advance of its hard copy release, and she and artists like Kanye West and Jay-Z have exclusive deals with digital stores like Amazon and iTunes.

The Internet and the Future of the Recording Industry

The Internet music revolution began with the development of **MP3** (for MPEG-1, Audio Layer 3), compression software that shrinks audio files to less than a tenth of their original size. Originally developed in 1987 in Germany by computer scientist Dieter Seitzer, it began to take off in the early 1990s as more users began to hook up to the Net with increasingly faster **modems**. This **open source software**, or freely downloaded software, permits users to download recorded music. Today, half of all American homes have at least one MP3 player (Edison Research, 2011).

The crux of the problem for recording companies was that they sold music "in its physical form," whereas MP3 permitted music's distribution in a nonphysical form. First discussed as "merely" a means of allowing independent bands and musicians to post their music online where it might attract a following, MP3 became a headache for the recording industry when music from the name artists they controlled began appearing on MP3 sites, making **piracy**, the illegal recording and sale of copyrighted material and high-quality recordings, a relatively simple task. Not only could users listen to their downloaded music from their hard drives, but they could make their own CDs from MP3 files and play those discs wherever and whenever they wished.

Rather than embrace MP3, the Recording Industry Association of America (RIAA), representing all of the United States' major labels, responded to the threat by developing their own "secure" Internet technology, but by the time it was available for release it was too late: MP3, driven by its availability and ease of use, had become the technology of choice for music fans already unhappy with the high cost of CDs and the necessity of paying for tracks they didn't want in order to get the ones they did. "The record labels had an opportunity to create a digital ecosystem and infrastructure to sell music online, but they kept looking at the small picture instead of the big one," explained one-time EMI and Warner music executive Ted Cohen. "They wouldn't let go of CDs" (in Mnookin, 2007, pp. 209–210). But the CD is quickly going the way of the vinyl record. It has been replaced by the download. Downloading occurs in two forms: industry-approved and **P2P** (peer-to-peer).

Industry-Approved Downloading

Illegal file sharing proved the popularity of downloading music from the Internet. So the four major labels combined to offer "approved" music download sites. None did well. They offered downloads by subscription, that is, so many downloads per month for a set fee. In addition, they placed encrypted messages in the tunes that limited how long the song would be playable and where the download could be used and copied. As a result, illegal file sharing continued. But it was Apple's 2003 introduction of its iPod and iTunes Music Store that suggested a better strategy. Fans could simply buy and own albums and individual songs for as little as 99 cents. Apple controlled only 5% of the PC market, yet it sold over a million tunes in its first week of operation. This activity led Warner Brothers CEO Tom Whalley to enthuse, "This is what the people who are willing to pay for music have been looking for all along" (quoted in Oppelaar, 2003, p. 42). For many observers, CEO Whalley's comments signaled the industry's recognition of the inevitability of the cyber revolution. Still, the major labels insisted that their music be downloaded with copy protection built in. But when Sony became the last of the major labels to relent, announcing in 2008 that it would allow the sale of much of its catalog free of copy protection, the distribution and sale of music by Internet became standard, aided by the 2009 announcement from the world's leading music retailer, iTunes (it sold its 10 billionth download in February 2010; Plambeck, 2010), that it would sell downloads from its 10-million-title catalog without antipiracy restrictions. There are now hundreds of legally licensed music sites on the Net selling tens of millions of different music tracks. Digital music sales surpassed physical sales for the first time in 2011, and the CD's 11.7% share of sales is a far cry from its dominance of 60 to 70% of all sales just a few years ago. This rise in downloading has also been fueled by **cloud-music services**, subscription sites that allow users to store their digital music online and stream it to any computer or digital device anywhere. Amazon Cloud, iTunes Match, and Google Music offer this service, sometimes called *digital lockers*. Not coincidentally, the number of brick-and-mortar record stores in America has been halved since 2003, their function—that which hasn't been displaced by the Internet—taken over by retail giants like Wal-Mart and Target that account for a majority of all physical music retail sales (Hogan, 2011).

P2P Downloading

Illegal downloading still occurs. Illegal downloads account for 95% of all music pulled from the Internet (Morrissey, 2011). The vast majority of the 1.1 billion songs downloaded from file-sharing sites every month are shared illegally, but ironically

The recording industry has seen a $55 billion decline in revenue in the last decade (Pollack, 2011); that is a fact. But how it, artists, and fans will shape the future of the music business is less certain. Legendary recording executive David Geffen explained, "The music business, as a whole, has lost its faith in content. Only 10 years ago, companies wanted to make records, presumably good records, and see if they sold. But panic has set in, and now it's no longer about making music, it's all about how to sell music. And there's no clear answer about how to fix that problem." Columbia Records head Rick Rubin added, "Fear is making the record companies less arrogant. They're more open to ideas" (both in Hirschberg, 2007, pp. 28–29). There is, in fact, no shortage of ideas, and they are being debated in the cultural forum.

Talking Heads leader David Byrne (2008a) wrote, "What is called the music business today is not the business of producing music. At some point it became the business of selling CDs in plastic cases, and that business will soon be over. But that's not bad news for music, and it's certainly not bad news for musicians" (p. 126). He detailed six ideas for reshaping the relationship between the recording industry, musical artists, and fans:

1. *The 360 deal* (sometimes called an equity or multiple rights deal) renders artists brands. Every aspect of their careers—recording, merchandising, marketing, touring—is handled by the label. Because artists and their music are "owned" by the label, that company, freed from the tyranny of the hit CD, will ostensibly take a long-term perspective in its artists' careers. The Pussycat Dolls have a 360 deal with Interscope Records. Madonna left Warner after 25 years with that label to sign a $120 million 360 deal with concert promoter Live Nation.

2. *The standard distribution deal* is how the music business operated for decades. The label underwrites the recording, manufacturing, distribution, and promotion of its artists' music. The label owns the copyright to the music and artists earn their percentage of profits only after all the recording, manufacturing, distribution, and promotion costs have been recouped by the label.

3. *The license deal* is the same as a standard distribution arrangement except that artists retain the copyright to their music and ownership of the master recordings, granting the rights to both to a label for a specified period of time, usually seven years. After that, artists are free to do with their music what they wish. Canadian rockers Arcade Fire have such an arrangement with indie label Merge Records.

> "Fear is making the record companies less arrogant. They're more open to ideas."

4. *The profit-sharing deal* calls for a minimal advance from a label, and as such, it agrees to split all profits with the artist before deducting its costs. Artists maintain ownership of the music, but because the label invests less in them than it might otherwise, they may sell fewer records. Both sides benefit, however. The label takes a smaller risk; the artist receives a greater share of the income. Byrne's Talking Heads has a profit-sharing arrangement with label Thrill Jockey for its album *Lead Us Not Into Temptation*.

▼ Apple had one answer to piracy: cheap, permanent, go-anywhere downloads.

it is illegal file sharers who spend the most money on legal downloads (Shields, 2009). Sites such as Gnutella, Freenet, LimeWire, Morpheus, and BearShare use P2P technologies, that is, peer-to-peer software that permits direct Internet-based communication or collaboration between two or more personal computers while bypassing centralized servers. P2P allows users to visit a constantly and infinitely changing network of machines through which file sharing can occur. The record companies (and movie studios) challenged P2P by suing the makers of its software. In 2005, the Supreme Court, in *MGM v. Grokster*, unanimously supported industry arguments that P2P software, because it "encouraged" copyright infringement, rendered its makers liable for that illegal act. The industry's next challenge, then, is **BitTorrent**, file-sharing software that allows anonymous users to create "swarms" of data as they simultaneously download and upload "bits" of a given piece of content from countless, untraceable servers. BitTorrent now accounts for 20 to 40% of all data sent across the Net and has more than 150 million monthly users (BitTorrent, 2012). Its critics accuse it of facilitating more than half of the world's illegal file-sharing.

No matter what model of music production and distribution eventually results from this technological and financial tumult, serious questions about the Net's impact on **copyright** (protecting content creators' financial interest in their product) will remain. There is much more on copyright in Chapter 14.

5. *A manufacturing and distribution deal* requires artists to undertake every aspect of the process except manufacturing and distribution. They retain ownership and rights to their music, but assume all other costs, for example, recording, marketing, and touring. Big labels avoid these deals because there is little profit in it for them. Smaller labels benefit from association with well-known artists, such as Aimee Mann, and artists have the benefit of artistic freedom and greater income (although they take on greater risk).

6. *The self-distribution model* grants artists the greatest freedom. They play, produce, market, promote, and distribute the music themselves. Byrne (2008a) calls this "freedom without resources—a pretty abstract sort of independence" (p. 129), but many artists big and small, aided by the Internet, have opted for this model. Musicians are using their own sites, social networking sites, and sites designed specifically to feature new artists to connect directly with listeners. Fans can hear and download new tunes for free; buy downloads, CDs, and merchandise; get concert information and tickets; and chat with artists and other fans. My Chemical Romance is one of the thousands of musical artists using the Internet to self-distribute and connect with fans.

Enter your voice. After all, the success of any or all of these different ideas depends on your willingness to buy the music that they produce. Which of these models do you think will dominate music's future, if any? The first, a 360 deal, gives musicians the least artistic freedom, but the greatest guarantee of success. The last, self-distribution, grants the greatest freedom, but the smallest guarantee of success. Which, including those in between, would you choose? Why? Might different models work better for different kinds of acts or for artists at different levels of notoriety? In which form would you be most comfortable buying your favorite music? If it were "up to you," what would you pay for a download of your favorite artist's latest release? Why? Byrne thinks the upheaval in the music business is "not bad news for music, and it's certainly not bad news for musicians." Do you agree? Will independence from the big labels and their demand for profitable hits free artists to make the music they want? Will there be more or less music of interest to you?

▲ Madonna is one of the many big-name artists experimenting with new models of artist/recording industry relationships.

DEVELOPING MEDIA LITERACY SKILLS

Listening to Shock Jocks

The proliferation of shock jocks—outrageous, rude, crude radio personalities—offers an example of the importance of media literacy that may not be immediately apparent. Yet it involves four different elements of media literacy: development of an awareness of media's impact, cultivation of an understanding of media content as a text that provides insight into our culture and our lives, awareness of the process of mass communication, and an understanding of the ethical demands under which media professionals operate (Chapter 1). Different media-literate radio listeners judge the shock jocks differently, but they all take time to examine jocks' work and their role in the culture.

The literate listener asks this question of shock jocks and the stations that air them: "At what cost to the culture as a whole, and to individuals living in it, should a radio station program an offensive, vulgar personality to attract listeners and, therefore, profit?" Ours is a free society, and freedom of expression is one of our dearest rights. Citing their First Amendment rights, as well as strong listener interest, radio stations have made Howard Stern and other shock jocks like Rush Limbaugh and Don Imus the fashion of the day. Stern, for example, took poorly rated WXRX in New York to Number One, and, as Infinity Broadcasting's top attraction, he was syndicated throughout the country where he was free to pray for cancer to kill public officials he did not like, joke constantly about sexual and other bodily functions, make sexist, homophobic, and misogynistic comments, and insult guests and callers. But when Infinity began pulling Stern from the air in response to an FCC anti-indecency crusade, Stern moved his show to satellite radio provider SiriusXM.

Self-proclaimed inventor of the shock jock, Don Imus, created a well-known ruckus. On the air for 30 years, *Imus in the Morning* was cancelled in April 2007 by CBS Radio. Host Imus had referred to the Rutgers University women's basketball team, then playing for a national championship against the University of Tennessee, as a bunch of "nappy-headed hos," a term Gwen Ifill (2007) called "a shockingly concise sexual and racial insult" (p. A21). Ifill, an African American who before moving to public television had covered the White House for the *New York Times* and Capitol Hill for NBC, had herself been called a "cleaning lady" by Imus in 1993. That racist slur passed, but the insult to the Rutgers women did not. Imus was fired.

But it is Rush Limbaugh's 2012 attack on Georgetown University law student Sandra Fluke that recently energized the media literacy discussion about shock jocks' value. After she testified before Congress on the need for employers' insurance plans to offer coverage for women's contraception for both reproductive and broader medical reasons, Limbaugh attacked the 30-year-old by name 46 times over three straight days, offering commentary such as "Can you imagine if you were her parents how proud . . . you would be? Your daughter . . . testifies she's having so much sex she can't afford her own birth control pills . . . What does that make her? It makes her a slut, right? It makes her a prostitute. She wants to be paid to have sex . . . She wants you and me and the taxpayers to pay her to have sex . . . [Ms. Fluke] is having so much sex, it's amazing she can still walk . . . [Fluke] is a woman who is happily presenting herself as an immoral, baseless, no-purpose-to-her life woman. She wants all the sex in the world whenever she wants it, all the time, no consequences. No responsibility for her behavior."

Public reaction was immediate and fierce. Not only had Limbaugh misrepresented Ms. Fluke's testimony (for example, employees and their employers, not taxpayers, pay for insurance and Mr. Limbaugh seemed not to understand how the pill works), but he was seen to have attacked a private citizen doing nothing more than exercising her right as a citizen to comment on an important issue of the day. More than 50 sponsors quickly pulled their spots from Limbaugh's show; within a week it was practically devoid of paid advertisements (Mirkinson, 2012), and Premiere Networks, which distributes the program, sent an e-mail to stations listing 98 corporations that had requested their ads appear only on "programs free of content that you know are deemed to be offensive or controversial" (in Avlon, 2012).

"Censorship," cried Limbaugh's supporters. "This is not censorship," replied his critics, "The government is not involved; in fact, it is the market at work. Advertisers listened to their customers." As journalist Hank Kalet said at the time of the Imus affair,

► Rush Limbaugh's attacks on law student Sandra Fluke tested people's media-literate listening skills.

this was an example of "repugnant speech being met with more speech . . . It was the powerful . . . a host who has been rubbing shoulders with presidential candidates and power-brokers, a host who has made his reputation by shocking for shock's sake and belittling the powerless in the process—being held to account" (2007, p. 21).

But it's all in fun, say shock jock defenders. Can't you take a joke; what are you, the thought police? Why not just turn the dial? These questions do indeed pose a problem for media-literate listeners. Literacy demands an understanding of the importance of freedom not only to the operation of our media system but to the functioning of our democracy. Yet literacy also means that we can't discount the impact of the shock jocks. Nor can we assume that their expression does not represent a distasteful side of our culture and ourselves.

Media-literate listeners also know that Imus, Stern, Limbaugh, and the other shock jocks exist because people listen to them. All three are on the air—radio and television— and enjoy large followings. Are their shows merely a place in which the culture is contested (Chapter 1)? Are they a safe place for the discussion of the forbidden, for testing cultural limits? In fact, a literate listener can make the argument, as do shock jocks' fans, that they serve the important cultural function of "hypocrisy-buster . . . truth-teller . . . scatological sage" (Cox, 2005, p. 101).

MEDIA LITERACY CHALLENGE
Listening to Shock Jocks with a Media-Literate Ear

Find a local shock jock. Most major markets have at least one or more. Why did you put him (it's almost always a man) in that category? If you can't find a local jock in your radio market, use syndicated Don Imus or Sirius XM Howard Stern for this challenge. After listening, answer these questions. What did you hear that some people might find shocking? Do you think the jock is absolutely serious about believing all of these statements or are some of them uttered to provoke listeners? What influence do these statements really have? Do the listeners respond blindly to the host's leading? As a media-literate radio listener you should *develop an understanding of the ethical and moral obligations of those who produce the material you listen to*; therefore, do you think it ethical for the station to allow these statements on the air? If not, are there other voices on the air who present the opposing views, and is this a sufficient remedy? Does the text from these "shock jocks" *provide context and insight into our culture*? How? Having *heightened expectations of media content,* will you continue to listen? Why or why not?

Resources for Review and Discussion

REVIEW POINTS: TYING CONTENT TO LEARNING OUTCOMES

▶ **Outline the history and development of the radio and sound recording industries and radio and sound recording themselves as media.**

- ▶ Guglielmo Marconi's radio allowed long-distance wireless communication; Reginald Fessenden's liquid barretter made possible the transmission of voices; Lee DeForest's audion tube permitted the reliable transmission of voices and music broadcasting.
- ▶ Thomas Edison developed the first sound-recording device, a fact now in debate; Emile Berliner's gramophone

improved on it as it permitted multiple copies to be made from a master recording.

▶ **Describe the importance of early financing and regulatory decisions regarding radio and how they have shaped the nature of contemporary broadcasting.**

- ▶ The Radio Acts of 1910, 1912, and 1927 and the Communications Act of 1934 eventually resulted in the FCC and the trustee model of broadcast regulation.

- Advertising and the network structure of broadcasting came to radio in the 1920s, producing the medium's golden age, one drawn to a close by the coming of television.

▶ **Explain how the organizational and economic natures of the contemporary radio and sound recording industries shape the content of both media.**
- Radio stations are classified as commercial and non-commercial, AM and FM.
- Radio is local, fragmented, specialized, personal, and mobile.
- Deregulation has allowed concentration of ownership of radio into the hands of a relatively small number of companies.
- Three major recording companies control 59% of the world's recorded music market.

▶ **Identify new and converging radio and recording technologies and their potential impact on music, the industries themselves, and listeners.**
- Convergence has come to radio in the form of satellite and cable delivery of radio, terrestrial digital radio, Web

radio, podcasting, and music streaming from a number of different types of sites.
- Digital technology, in the form of Internet creation, promotion, and distribution of music, legal and illegal downloading from the Internet, and mobile phone downloading, promises to reshape the nature of the recording industry.
- Personal technologies such as smartphones and tablets reinforce radio's mobility and expand its audience.

▶ **Apply key radio-listening media literacy skills, especially in assessing the cultural value of shock jocks.**
- Shock jocks pose a vexing problem for media-literate listeners—are they signs of our culture's coarseness or a forum for the contesting of culture?

KEY TERMS

liquid barretter, 154	deregulation, 163	bitcasters, 170
audion tube, 154	duopoly, 163	streaming, 170
trustee model, 157	cover, 164	digital recording, 171
spectrum scarcity, 157	catalogue albums, 165	MP3, 172
affiliates, 158	recent catalogue albums, 165	modem, 172
O&O, 158	syndication, 169	open source software, 172
Low Power FM (LPFM), 160	DMX (Digital Music Express), 169	piracy, 172
format, 161	digital audio radio service (DARS), 169	P2P, 173
secondary services, 161	terrestrial digital radio, 169	cloud-music service, 173
playlist, 162	in-band-on-channel (IBOC), 169	BitTorrent, 174
billings, 163	Web radio, 170	copyright, 174
ratings, 163	podcasting, 170	

QUESTIONS FOR REVIEW

1. Who were Guglielmo Marconi, Nikola Tesla, Reginald Fessenden, and Lee DeForest?

2. How do the Radio Acts of 1910, 1912, and 1927 relate to the Communications Act of 1934?

3. What were the five defining characteristics of the American broadcasting system as it entered the golden age of radio?

4. How did World War II and the introduction of television change radio and recorded music?

5. What does it mean to say that radio is local, fragmented, specialized, personal, and mobile?

6. What are catalogue albums? Recent catalogue albums?

7. How have cable and satellite affected the radio and recording industries? Computers and digitization?

8. Is the size of radio's audience in ascendance or in decline? Why?

9. What is streaming audio?

10. What is P2P technology?

Mc Graw Hill **connect**

For further review, go to the LearnSmart study module for this chapter.

QUESTIONS FOR CRITICAL THINKING AND DISCUSSION

1. Would you have favored a noncommercial basis for our broadcasting system? Why or why not?

2. What do you think of the argument that control of the recording industry by a few multinational conglomerates inevitably leads to cultural homogenization and the ascendance of profit over music?

3. How much regulation do you believe is necessary in U.S. broadcasting? If the airwaves belong to the people, how can we best ensure that license holders perform their public service functions?

Television, Cable, and Mobile Video

8

Learning Objectives

No one is neutral about television. We either love it or hate it. Many of us do both. The reason is that it is our most ubiquitous and socially and culturally powerful mass medium. Recent and on-the-horizon technological advances promise to make it even more so. After studying this chapter you should be able to

▶ Outline the history and development of the television and cable television industries and television itself as a medium.

▶ Describe how the organizational and economic nature of the contemporary television and cable industries shapes the content of television.

▶ Explain the relationship between television in all its forms and its viewers.

▶ Identify new and converging video technologies and their potential impact on the television industry and its audience.

▶ Describe the digital and mobile television revolution.

▶ Apply key television-viewing media literacy skills.

HBO's *Game of Thrones*. Innovative, challenging cable programming helps improve the quality of all television.

"WHAT ARE YOU WATCHING? Is that *The Sopranos*? Boy, I love old shows on Hulu; TV on the Internet is the best!"

"Slow down. Yes, it's the Net; it's Netflix, but not *The Sopranos*."

"But that's Silvio Dante, Steven Van Zandt, *Sopranos*."

"Yes, it's Steven Van Zandt, but this is *Lilyhammer*. Van Zandt's still a mobster, but he ends up in the witness protection program and goes to Norway and because he can't make it as an unemployed immigrant, he returns to a life of crime."

"I don't remember *Lilyhammer*. Is it really old or something?"

"Nope, brand new. Netflix's doing it as an original series."

"Netflix, the Internet movie site? You're kidding?"

"Again, nope. And later I'm going to watch another new series, Kevin Spacey in *House of Cards*, and then I'll go to Hulu for *Battleground* . . . yes, Hulu, and yes, like I said, Netflix."

"No way."

"Way. Television is changing, my friend, more than you realize."

Indeed it is. Netflix outbid established video giants HBO and AMC for *House of Cards*, ordering two seasons, 26 episodes, for over $100 million. In early 2011, YouTube committed $100 million to commission original programming designed exclusively for its planned 20 new channels. Machinima, its video gaming channel, gets more than a billion views a month (Whitney, 2012). A few years before these developments, in 2007, the first television series produced specifically for smartphones debuted simultaneously on those devices and the Internet. Each of *Afterworld*'s 130 episodes ran just over two minutes. Producer Stan Rogow explained why he resisted the SciFi Channel's request that he produce it as a traditional series television show, opting for phones and the Web: "I think this is where the TV industry is heading, and I also think that at the end of the day it will not necessarily be the end of network television, but I think it's going to be a different form of network television that will offer the experience on multiple platforms" (in Moses, 2007). Mr. Rogow was prescient. Today, 188 million Americans a month watch online television—38 billion individual pieces of content (Lardinois, 2012). And it's not just short clips; 60% of *total viewing time* is *premium video*, or "real"

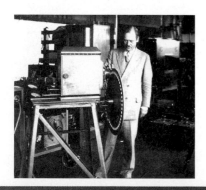

1900

1925

1884 ▲ Nipkow invents his disc

1923 ▲ Zworykin demonstrates electronic iconoscope tube

1927 Farnsworth demonstrates electronically scanned television images

1928 ▲ Baird transmits mechanical video image across Atlantic

1939 Sarnoff introduces regular television broadcasting at World's Fair

1941 First two commercial stations approved

1948 Television freeze; Walson begins CATV

television shows (Friedman, 2012). Yes, television is changing, and this chapter details that change, from early experiments with mechanical scanning to the electronic marvel that sits in our homes to the mobile video screens we carry in our pockets. We trace the rapid transformation of television into a mature medium after World War II and examine how the medium, the entire television industry, in fact, was altered by the emergence and success of cable and satellite television. But significant change is once again remaking what we currently know as television. The changes just mentioned reflect only a small part of the coming transformation. **Nonlinear TV**—watching television on our own schedules, not on some cable or broadcast programmer's—is here right now. Even more dramatic evolution is in the offing.

The remarkable reach of television—in all its forms—accounts for its attractiveness as an advertising medium. We discuss this reach, and we explore the structure, programming, and economics of the television and cable industries. We consider new technologies and their convergence with television and how they promise to change the interaction between the medium and its audiences. Finally, we discuss media literacy in terms of the practice of recognizing news staging.

▲ Political thriller *Battleground* is an early entry in Hulu's push into original programming.

A Short History of Television

Television has changed the way teachers teach, governments govern, religious leaders preach and the way we organize the furniture in our homes. Television has changed the nature, operation, and relationship to their audiences of books, magazines, movies, and radio. The Internet, with its networking abilities, may eventually overtake television

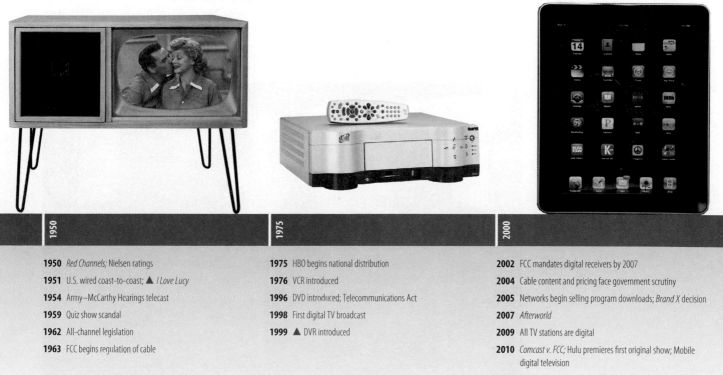

1950

1975

2000

1950 *Red Channels;* Nielsen ratings	**1975** HBO begins national distribution	**2002** FCC mandates digital receivers by 2007
1951 U.S. wired coast-to-coast; ▲ *I Love Lucy*	**1976** VCR introduced	**2004** Cable content and pricing face government scrutiny
1954 Army–McCarthy Hearings telecast	**1996** DVD introduced; Telecommunications Act	**2005** Networks begin selling program downloads; *Brand X* decision
1959 Quiz show scandal	**1998** First digital TV broadcast	**2007** *Afterworld*
1962 All-channel legislation	**1999** ▲ DVR introduced	**2009** All TV stations are digital
1963 FCC begins regulation of cable		**2010** *Comcast v. FCC;* Hulu premieres first original show; Mobile digital television
		2011 ▲ Netflix, Hulu, and YouTube begin original programming
		2012 Online movie transactions exceed discs

as a medium of mass communication, but television defines even its future. Will the promise of the Web be drowned in a sea of commercials? Can online information services deliver faster and better information than television? Even the computer screens we use look like television screens, and we sign up for Internet video, online video conferencing, and the new and improved online video game. Before we delve deeper into the nature of this powerful medium and its relationship with its audience, let's examine how television developed as it did.

Mechanical and Electronic Scanning

In 1884 Paul Nipkow, a Russian scientist living in Berlin, developed the first workable device for generating electrical signals suitable for the transmission of a scene that people could see. His **Nipkow disc** consisted of a rotating scanning disc spinning in front of a photoelectric cell. It produced 4,000 **pixels** (picture dots) per second, producing a picture composed of 18 parallel lines. Although his mechanical system proved too limiting, Nipkow demonstrated the possibility of using a scanning system to divide a scene into an orderly pattern of transmittable picture elements that could be recomposed as a visual image. British inventor John Logie Baird was able to transmit moving images using a mechanical disc as early as 1925, and in 1928 he successfully sent a television picture from London to Hartsdale, New York.

Electronic scanning came either from another Russian or from a U.S. farm boy; historians disagree. Vladimir Zworykin, an immigrant living near Pittsburgh and working for Westinghouse, demonstrated his **iconoscope tube**, the first practical television camera tube, in 1923. In 1929 David Sarnoff lured him to RCA to head its electronics research lab, and it was there that Zworykin developed the **kinescope**, an improved picture tube. At the same time, young Philo Farnsworth had moved from Idaho to San Francisco to perfect an electronic television system, the design for which he had shown his high school science teacher when he was 15 years old. In 1927, at the age of 20, he made his first public demonstration—film clips of a prize fight, scenes from a Mary Pickford movie, and other graphic images. The "Boy Wonder" and Zworykin's RCA spent the next decade fighting fierce patent battles in court. In 1939 RCA capitulated, agreeing to pay Farnsworth royalties for the use of his patents.

In April of that year, at the World's Fair in New York, RCA made the first true public demonstration of television in the form of regularly scheduled two-hour NBC broadcasts. These black-and-white telecasts consisted of cooking demonstrations,

▶ A Nipkow disc.

singers, jugglers, comedians, puppets—just about anything that could fit in a hot, brightly lit studio and demonstrate motion. People could buy television sets at the RCA Pavilion at prices ranging from $200 for the 5-inch screen to $600 for the deluxe 12-inch-screen model. The FCC granted construction permits to the first two commercial stations in 1941, but World War II intervened. But as was the case with radio during World War I, technical development and improvement of the new medium continued.

The 1950s

In 1952, 108 stations were broadcasting to 17 million television homes. By the end of the decade, there were 559 stations, and nearly 90% of U.S. households had televisions. In the 1950s more television sets were sold in the United States (70 million) than there were children born (40.5 million) (Kuralt, 1977). The technical standards were fixed, stations proliferated and flourished, the public tuned in, and advertisers were enthusiastic. The content and character of the medium were set in this decade as well:

- Carried over from the radio networks, television genres included variety shows, situation comedies, dramas (including Westerns and cop shows), soap operas, and quiz shows.

- Two new formats appeared: feature films and talk shows. Talk shows were instrumental in introducing radio personalities to the television audience, which could see its favorites for the first time.

- Television news and documentary remade broadcast journalism as a powerful force in its own right, led by CBS's Edward R. Murrow (*See It Now*, 1951) and NBC's David Brinkley and Chet Huntley. Huntley and Brinkley's 1956 coverage of the major political conventions gave audiences an early glimpse of the power of television to cover news and history in the making.

- AT&T completed its national **coaxial cable** and **microwave relay** network for the distribution of television programming in the summer of 1951. The entire United States was now within the reach of the major television networks, and they came to dominate the medium.

Four other events from the 1950s would permanently shape how television operated: the quiz show scandal, the appearance of *I Love Lucy*, McCarthyism, and the establishment of the ratings system. Another, in 1948, would permanently *reshape* the television industry. That development, as you'll soon see, was cable television.

THE QUIZ SHOW SCANDAL AND CHANGES IN SPONSORSHIP Throughout the 1950s the networks served primarily as time brokers, offering airtime and distribution (their affiliates) and accepting payment for access to both. Except for their own news and sports coverage, the networks relied on outside agencies to provide programs. An advertising agency, for example, would hire a production company to produce a program for its client. That client would then be the show's sponsor—*The Kraft Television Theatre* and *Westinghouse Studio One* are two examples. The agency would then pay a network to air the program over its national collection of stations. This system had enriched the networks during the heyday of radio, and they saw no reason to change.

► Running from 1947 until 1958, NBC's *Kraft Television Theatre* aired some of the golden age's most respected live anthology dramas. *Top left*, Richard Kiley and Everett Sloane; *lower left*, Ossie Davis; *lower right*, Walter Matthau and Nancy Walker.

But in 1959 the quiz show scandal, enveloping independently produced, single-advertiser-sponsored programs, changed the way the networks did business. When it was discovered that popular shows like *The $64,000 Question* had been fixed by advertisers and producers to ensure desired outcomes, the networks, mindful of their reputations, were determined to take control of their schedules. They, themselves, began commissioning or buying the entertainment fare that filled their broadcast days and nights. Now, rather than selling blocks of time to ad agencies and sponsors, the networks paid for the content they aired through **spot commercial sales** (selling individual 60-second spots on a given program to a wide variety of advertisers).

As a result, the content of television was altered. Some critics argue that this change to spot sales put an end to the golden age of television. When sponsors agreed to attach their names to programs, *Alcoa Presents* or the *Texaco Star Theater*, for example, they had an incentive to demand high-quality programming. Spot sales, with network salespeople offering small bits of time to a number of different sponsors, reduced the demand for quality. Because individual sponsors were not identified with a given show, they had no stake in how well it was made—only in how many viewers it attracted. Spot sales also reduced the willingness of the networks to try innovative or different types of content. Familiarity and predictability attracted more viewers and, therefore, more advertisers.

◄ *I Love Lucy* was significant for far more than its comedy. Thanks to Lucille Ball's shrewd business sense, it became the foundation for the huge off-network syndicated television industry.

There is a counterargument, however. Once the financial well-being of the networks became dependent on the programming they aired, the networks themselves became more concerned with program quality, lifting television from its dull infancy (remembered now as the golden age only by those small, early audiences committed to serious character-driven televised drama). Different historians and critics offer arguments for both views.

I LOVE LUCY AND MORE CHANGES In 1951 CBS asked Lucille Ball to move her hit radio program, *My Favorite Husband*, to television. Lucy was willing but wanted her real-life husband, Desi Arnaz, to play the part of her video spouse. The network refused (some historians say the network objected to the prime-time presentation of an interracial marriage—Desi Arnaz was Cuban—but CBS denies this). But Lucy made additional demands. Television at the time was live: Images were typically captured by three large television cameras, with a director in a booth choosing among the three available images. Lucy wanted her program produced in the same manner—in front of a live audience with three simultaneously running cameras—but these cameras would be *film* cameras. Editors could then review the three sets of film and edit them together to give the best combination of action and reaction shots. Lucy also wanted the production to take place in Hollywood, the nation's film capital, instead of New York, the television center at the time. CBS was uncertain about this departure from how television was typically produced and refused these requests as well.

Lucy and Desi borrowed the necessary money and produced *I Love Lucy* on their own, selling the broadcast rights to CBS. In doing so, the woman now best remembered as "that zany redhead" transformed the business and look of television:

- Filmed reruns were now possible, something that had been impossible with live television, and this, in turn, created the off-network syndication industry.

- The television industry moved from New York, with its stage drama orientation, to Hollywood, with its entertainment film mind-set. More action, more flash came to the screen.

- Weekly series could now be produced relatively quickly and inexpensively. A 39-week series could be completed in 20 or 24 weeks, saving money on actors, crew, equipment, and facilities. In addition the same stock shots—for example, certain exterior views—could be used in different episodes.

MCCARTHYISM: THE GROWING POWER OF TELEVISION The Red Scare that cowed the movie business also touched television, aided by the publication in 1950 of *Red Channels: The Report of Communist Influence in Radio and Television*, the work of three former FBI agents operating a company called American Business Consultants. Its 200 pages detailed the alleged pro-Communist sympathies of 151 broadcast personalities, including Orson Welles and journalist Howard K. Smith. Advertisers were encouraged to avoid buying time from broadcasters who employed these "Red sympathizers." Like the movie studios, the television industry caved in. The networks employed security checkers to look into people's backgrounds, refused to hire suspect talent, and demanded loyalty oaths from performers. In its infancy television had taken the safe path. Many gifted artists were denied not only a paycheck but also the opportunity to shape the medium's content.

Ironically, it was this same Red Scare that allowed television to demonstrate its enormous power as a vehicle of democracy and freedom. Joseph McCarthy, the Republican junior senator from Wisconsin whose tactics gave this era its name, was seen by millions of viewers as his investigation of Reds in the U.S. Army was broadcast by all the networks for 36 days in 1954. Daytime ratings increased 50% (Sterling & Kittross, 1990). At the same time, Edward R. Murrow used his *See It Now* to expose the senator's lies and hypocrisy. As a consequence of the two broadcasts, McCarthy was ruined; he was censured by his Senate colleagues and later died a lonely alcoholic's death. Television had given the people eyes and ears—and power—where before they had had little. The Army–McCarthy Hearings and Murrow's challenge to McCarthyism are still regarded as two of television's finest moments.

THE NIELSEN RATINGS The concept of computing ratings was carried over from radio (see Chapter 7) to television, but the ratings as we know them today are far more sophisticated. The A. C. Nielsen Company began in 1923 as a product-testing company, but soon branched into market research. In 1936 Nielsen started reporting radio ratings and was doing the same for television by 1950.

To produce the ratings today, Nielsen selects 37,000 households thought to be representative of the entire U.S. viewing audience. To record data on what people in those TV households are watching, Nielsen employs the **personal peoplemeter**. It requires each member of a television home to press buttons to record his or her individual viewing. The information recorded is sent to Nielsen by telephone lines, and the company can then determine the program watched, who was watching it, and the amount of time each viewer spent with it. But convergence is changing how ratings data will be gathered and computed. The company now reports the **Total Audience Measurement Index (TAMi)**, a measure of all viewing of a single television episode across all platforms—television, DVR, Internet, and mobile video. To improve TAMi's accuracy, Nielsen will replace the peoplemeter with the **Global Television Audience Metering meter (GTAM meter)**, which will actively (requiring viewer input) and passively (automatically reading digital codes embedded in video content) measure viewing as people, with increasing mobility, consume video on a growing array of technologies.

To draw a more complete picture of the viewing situation and to measure local television viewing, Nielsen conducts diary surveys of viewing patterns four times a year. These **sweeps periods** are in February, May, July, and November. During sweeps, diaries are distributed to thousands of sample households in selected markets. Viewers are asked to write down what they're watching and who is watching it. The diary data are then combined with the peoplemeter data to help stations set their advertising rates for the next three months. The company announced in June 2006, however, that it would eventually abandon paper diaries and move to completely electronic measurement.

Sweeps, too, may soon be a thing of the past. These quarterly extravaganzas of heavily promoted network programming and titillating local news (High School Binge Drinking? Story and Shocking Video at 6!) are likely to disappear for two reasons. First, the rhythm of broadcast television scheduling is changing because of competition with cable. Cable introduces new shows and big movies throughout the year, rendering such concepts as "The Fall Season" and "Premiere Week" obsolete. Fox has long had year-round premieres, and NBC announced in 2008 that it would follow suit. CBS's *Survivor*

Ratings and shares can be computed using these formulas:

$$\text{Rating} = \frac{\text{Households tuned in to a given program}}{\text{All households with television}}$$

$$\text{Share} = \frac{\text{Households tuned in to a given program}}{\text{All households tuned in to television at that time}}$$

Here's an example. Your talk show is aired in a market that has 1 million television households; 400,000 are tuned in to you. Therefore,

$$\frac{400,000}{1,000,000} = .40, \text{ or a rating of } 40.$$

At the time your show airs, however, there are only 800,000 households using television. Therefore, your share of the available audience is

$$\text{Share} = \frac{400,000}{800,000} = .50, \text{ or a share of } 50.$$

If you can explain why a specific program's share is always higher than its rating, then you understand the difference between the two.

▲ **Figure 8.1** Computing Ratings and Shares.

and NBC's *Fear Factor* both debuted in summer, formerly network television's programming graveyard. With the basic structure of the programming year disrupted, broadcasters can no longer afford to save their best or biggest programming for sweeps weeks. Second, the personal peoplemeter delivers detailed viewing and demographic data every day of the year, making the four-times-a-year, data-intensive ratings periods unnecessary.

A second, more important measure of television's audience is its **share**, which is a direct reflection of a particular show's competitive performance. Share doesn't measure viewers as a percentage of *all* television households (as do the ratings). Instead, the share measures a program audience as a percentage of the *television sets in use* at the time it airs. It tells us what proportion of the *actual* audience a program attracts, indicating how well a particular program is doing on its given night, in its time slot, against its competition (Figure 8.1). For example, *Late Show with David Letterman* normally gets a rating of around 4—terrible by prime-time standards—but because it's on when fewer homes are tuned in, its share of 15 (15% of the homes with sets in use) is very high.

There is a third audience measure, the **C3 rating**, but it is not a program rating. Because people might view a specific program on a number of platforms, Nielsen counts audiences on three screens—TV (original airing plus DVR), Internet, and mobile video. The "3" represents not screens, but the viewing of the *commercials* that appear in that specific program *within three days* of its premiere telecast in order to capture DVR playback and Internet viewing. In 2012, in an attempt to mollify advertisers still dissatisfied with audience metrics in a multiscreen, time-shifting television world, Nielsen offered to boost C3 to C7, measuring an entire week's viewing. The ad industry, wanting more precision, not more time, was unimpressed (see Chapter 12).

The Coming of Cable

Mahanoy City, Pennsylvania, appliance sales representative John Walson was having trouble selling televisions in 1948. The Pocono Mountains sat between his town and Philadelphia's three new stations. But Walson was also a powerline worker, so he convinced his bosses to let him run a wire from a tower he erected on New Boston Mountain to his store. As more and more people became aware of his system, he began wiring the homes of customers who bought his sets. In June of that year, Walson had 727 subscribers for his **community antenna television (CATV)** system (Chin, 1978). Although no one calls it CATV anymore, cable television was born.

The cable Walson used was a twin-lead wire, much like the cord that connects a lamp to an outlet. To attract even more subscribers, he had to offer improved picture quality. He accomplished this by using *coaxial cable* and self-manufactured boosters (or amplifiers). Coaxial cable—copper-clad aluminum wire encased in plastic foam insulation, covered by an aluminum outer conductor, and then sheathed in plastic—had more bandwidth than did twin-lead wire. As a result, it allowed more of the original signal to pass and even permitted Walson to carry a greater number of channels.

As Walson continued to expand his CATV business, Milton Jerrold Shapp, later to become Pennsylvania's governor, noticed thousands of antennas cluttering the roofs of department stores and apartment buildings. Seeing Walson's success, he set up master antennas and connected the sets in these buildings to them, employing a signal booster he had developed. This was the start of **master antenna television (MATV)**.

With expanded bandwidth and the new, powerful Jerrold boosters, these systems began experimenting with the **importation of distant signals**, using wires not only to provide improved reception but also to offer a wider variety of programming. They began delivering independent stations from as far away as New York to fill their then-amazing 7 to 10 channels. By 1962, 800 systems were providing cable television to more than 850,000 homes.

The industry today is composed of 7,143 individual cable systems serving 59.8 million homes subscribing to at least basic cable; 78.4% receive digital cable. The industry generates revenues of $97.6 billion, with $27.2 billion of that amount earned through advertising (NCTA, 2012).

▲ John Walson.

Television and Its Audiences

The 1960s saw some refinement in the technical structure of television, which influenced its organization and audience. In 1962 Congress passed **all-channel legislation**, which required that all sets imported into or manufactured in the United States be equipped with both VHF and UHF receivers. This had little immediate impact; U.S. viewers were now hooked on the three national networks and their VHF affiliates. Still, UHF independents and educational stations were able to at least attract some semblance of an audience. The UHF independents would have to wait for the coming of cable to give them clout. Now that the educational stations were attracting more viewers, they began to look less educational in the strictest sense of the word and began programming more entertaining cultural fare (see the essay "The Creation of *Sesame Street*"). The Public Broadcasting Act of 1967 united the educational stations into an important network, the Public Broadcasting Service (PBS), which today has nearly 400 member stations.

The 1960s also witnessed the immense social and political power of the new medium to force profound alterations in the country's consciousness and behavior. Particularly influential were the Nixon–Kennedy campaign debates of 1960, broadcasts of the aftermath of Kennedy's assassination and funeral in 1963, the 1969 transmission of Neil Armstrong's walk on the moon, and the use of television at the end of the decade by civil rights and anti–Vietnam War leaders.

The 1960s also gave rise to a descriptive expression often used today when television is discussed. Speaking to the 1961 convention of the National Association of Broadcasters, John F. Kennedy's new FCC chair, Newton Minow, invited broadcasters to

> sit down in front of your television set when your station goes on the air and stay there without a book, magazine, newspaper, profit and loss sheet, or ratings book to distract you, and keep your eyes glued to that set until the station signs off. I can assure you that you will observe a **vast wasteland**.

Whether or not one agrees with Minow's assessment of television, then or now, there is no doubt that audiences continue to watch:

- There are 114.7 million television households in the United States, 97% of all U.S. homes.
- A television is on for an average of 59 hours 28 minutes a week in each of those households.
- The average American watches 34 hours 12 minutes a week.
- Television reaches more adults each day than any other medium, and those people spend more time with television than with any other medium.
- Even among regular Internet users, 71% say that watching television is their "favorite media-related activity."
- Television provides 31.1% of Americans' news and information; 71% say it's their leading source for national and international news and 64% say the same for local news (Nielsen, 2011; eMarketer, 2010).

USING MEDIA TO MAKE A DIFFERENCE
The Creation of *Sesame Street*

In 1968 a public affairs program producer for Channel 13 in New York City identified a number of related problems that she believed could be addressed by a well-conceived, well-produced television show.

Joan Ganz Cooney saw that 80% of 3- and 4-year-olds and 25% of 5-year-olds in the United States did not attend any form of preschool. Children from financially disadvantaged homes were far less likely to attend preschool at these ages than their better-off peers. Children in these age groups who did go to preschool received little academic instruction; preschool was the equivalent of organized recess. Large numbers of U.S. children, then, entered first grade with no formal schooling, even though education experts had long argued that preschool years were crucial in children's intellectual and academic development. In addition, the disparity in academic preparedness between poor and other children was a national disgrace.

What did these children do instead of going to preschool? Cooney knew that they watched television. But she also knew that "existing shows for 3- through 5-year-old

children . . . did not have education as a primary goal" (Ball & Bogatz, 1970, p. 2). Her idea was to use an interesting, exciting, visually and aurally stimulating television show as an explicitly educational tool "to promote the intellectual and cultural growth of preschoolers, particularly disadvantaged preschoolers," and to "teach children how to think as well as what to think" (Cook et al., 1975, p. 7).

Cooney established a nonprofit organization, the Children's Television Workshop (CTW), and sought funding for her program. Several federal agencies, primarily the Office of Education, a number of private foundations including Carnegie and Ford, and public broadcasters contributed $13.7 million for CTW's first four years.

After much research into producing a quality children's television show and studying the best instructional methods for teaching preschool audiences, CTW unveiled *Sesame Street*

> "Did Cooney and her show make a difference? Several national studies demonstrated that academic performance in early grades was directly and strongly correlated with regular viewing of *Sesame Street*."

during the 1969 television season. It was an instant hit with children and parents. The *New Republic* said, "Judged by the standards of most other programs for preschoolers, it is imaginative, tasteful, and witty" (cited in Ball & Bogatz, 1970, p. 3). Originally scheduled for one hour a day during the school week, within months of its debut *Sesame Street* was being programmed twice a day on many public television stations, and many ran the entire week's schedule on Saturdays and Sundays. Today, nearly 45 years after its debut, *Sesame Street* still airs 26 new episodes a year.

Did Cooney and her show make a difference? Several national studies demonstrated that academic performance in early grades was directly and strongly correlated with regular viewing of *Sesame Street*. The commercial networks began to introduce educational fare into their Saturday morning schedules. ABC's *Grammar Rock*, *America Rock* (on U.S. history), and *Multiplication Rock* were critical and educational successes at the time, and a traditional children's favorite, CBS's *Captain Kangaroo*, started airing short films influenced by *Sesame Street* on a wide variety of social and personal skills. By the time of its 40th birthday in 2009, *Sesame Street* had won 122 Emmy Awards and had been adapted for 120 countries around the world, including troubled lands like Kosovo and the Palestinian territories (Gardner, 2009).

◄ The *Sesame Street* gang.

There can be no doubt, either, that television is successful as an advertising medium:

- Total annual billings for television are around $70 billion, with approximately two-thirds generated by broadcast and one-third by cable television. Together they collected 40% of all U.S. ad spending.

- The average 30-second prime-time network television spot costs $100,000 (on *American Idol* ads have gone as high as $705,000, and the 2010 *Lost* finale had several $900,000 spots).

- Prime ad time on the February, 2013 Ravens–49ers Super Bowl broadcast cost $4 million for 30 seconds. (And viewers prefer the ads to the game itself, 39% to 28%; Lukovitz, 2013.)

- Eighty-six percent of American consumers see television as the most influential ad medium; 78%, the most persuasive; 61%, the most authoritative; and 83%, the most exciting.
- A 30-second local spot can fetch up to $30,000 on a top-rated special in a major market (all statistics from www.tvb.org).

Scope and Nature of the Broadcast Television Industry

Today, as it has been from the beginning, the business of broadcast television is dominated by a few centralized production, distribution, and decision-making organizations. These **networks** link affiliates for the purpose of delivering and selling viewers to advertisers. The large majority of the 1,390 commercial stations in the United States are affiliated with a national broadcasting network: ABC, NBC, and CBS each have over 200 affiliates and Fox has close to that number. Many more stations are affiliated with the CW Network, often referred to as a "weblet." Although cable has introduced us to dozens of popular cable networks—ESPN, MTV, Comedy Central, and A&E, to name a few—most programs that come to mind when we think of television were either conceived, approved, funded, produced, or distributed by the broadcast networks.

Local affiliates carry network programs (they **clear time**). Until quite recently, affiliates received direct payment for carrying a show, called compensation, and the right to keep all income from the sale of local commercials on that program. But loss of network audience and the rise of cable have altered this arrangement. Now networks receive **reverse compensation**, a fee paid by the local station for the right to be that network's affiliate. It is typically based on the amount of money the local cable operation pays to the station to carry its signal, called **retransmission fees**.

The Networks and Program Content

Networks control what appears on the vast majority of local television stations, but they also control what appears on non-network television, that is, when affiliates program their own content. In addition, they influence what appears on independent stations and on cable channels. This non-network material not only tends to be network-*type* programming but most often is programming that originally aired on the networks themselves (called **off-network** programs).

Why do network and network-type content dominate television? *Availability* is one factor. There is 65 years' worth of already successful network content available for airing on local stations. A second factor is that the *production and distribution* mechanisms that have long served the broadcast networks are well established and serve the newer outlets just as well as they did NBC, CBS, and ABC. The final reason is us, the audience. The formats we are most comfortable with—our television tastes and expectations—have been and continue to be developed on the networks.

How a Program Gets on the Air

The national broadcast networks look at about 4,000 proposals a year for new television series. Many, if not most, are submitted at the networks' invitation or instigation. Of the 4,000, about 100 will be filmed as **pilots**, or trial programs, at a cost of $3 million for a 30-minute pilot to $7 million for an hour drama (the pilot for *Lost* cost $10 million; Guthrie, 2010). Perhaps 20 to 30 will make it onto the air. Only 12 of these (1 in 10) will last a full broadcast season. In a particularly good year, at most three or four will succeed well enough to be called hits. The networks spend over $500 million to suffer this process. For this reason, they prefer to see ideas from producers with established track records and financial and organizational stability—for example, Jerry

Two of syndication's biggest winners, *The Big Bang Theory* and *Friends*.

Bruckheimer is the source of *CSI*, *CSI*: *Miami*, *CSI*: *NY*, *The Amazing Race*, *Cold Case*, and *Without a Trace* in addition to 12 other prime time series aired in the last 10 years.

The way a program typically makes it onto the air differs somewhat for those who have been asked to submit an idea and for producers who bring their concepts to the networks. First, a producer has an *idea*; or a network has an idea and asks a proven producer to propose a show based on it (possibly offering a **put**, a deal that guarantees the producer that the network will order at least a pilot or it has to pay a hefty penalty). The producer must then *shop* the idea to one of the networks; naturally, an invited producer submits the proposal only to the network that asked for it. In either case, if the network is persuaded, it *buys the option* and asks for a written *outline* in which the original idea is refined. If still interested, the network will order a full *script*.

If the network approves that script, it will order the production of a pilot. Pilots are then subjected to rigorous testing by the networks' own and independent audience research organizations. Based on this research, networks will often demand changes, such as writing out characters who tested poorly or beefing up story lines that test audiences particularly liked.

If the network is still interested, that is, if it believes that the show will be a hit, it orders a set number of episodes and schedules the show. In television's early days, an order might be for 26 or 39 episodes. Today, however, because of escalating production costs, the convention is at first to order six episodes. If these are successful, a second order of nine more is placed. Then, if the show is still doing well, a final nine episodes (referred to as *the back nine*) will be commissioned. Few shows make it that far.

The reason television program producers participate in this expensive enterprise is that they can make vast amounts of money in syndication, the sale of their programs to stations on a market-by-market basis. Even though the networks control the process from idea to scheduling and decide how long a show stays in their lineups, producers continue to own the rights to their programs. Once enough episodes are made (generally about 50, which is the product of four years on a network), producers can sell the syndicated package to the highest bidder in each of the 210 U.S. television markets, keeping all the revenues for themselves. This is the legacy of Lucille Ball's business genius. The price of a syndicated program depends on the market size, the level of competition between the stations in the market, and the age and popularity of the program itself. The station buys the right to a specified number of plays, or airings.

Dr. Phil is among the more successful first-run syndicated programs.

After that, the rights return to the producer to be sold again and again. A program that has survived at least four years on one of the networks has proven its popularity, has attracted a following, and has accumulated enough individual episodes so that local stations can offer weeks of daily scheduling without too many reruns. The program is a moneymaker. Paramount has already earned more than $2 billion from its syndication of *Frasier*; Warner Brothers collected more than $5.8 million an episode from its original syndication of *Friends* and gets $4 million an episode for *The Big Bang Theory*, although it is still in its network run.

So attractive is syndication's income potential, especially when coupled with the promise of profits from digital downloads and sales of DVD collections of television shows, that the networks themselves have become their own producers (and therefore syndicators). In fact, the major broadcast networks now produce 82% of all the prime-time programming on their own and the top 20 cable networks (McAdams, 2010).

It is important to note that there is another form of syndicated programming. **First-run syndication** is programming produced specifically for sale into syndication on a market-by-market basis. It is attractive to producers because they don't have to run the gauntlet of the network programming process, and they keep 100% of the income.

Satellites have improved the distribution process for first-run syndicated series, increasing the number and variety of available programs. Game and talk shows, staples of the business in the past, have proliferated and been joined by programs such as *Judge Judy* and *Judge Joe Brown*, court shows distributed daily by satellite to hundreds of stations. They are inexpensive to make, inexpensive to distribute, and easily **stripped** (broadcast at the same time five evenings a week). They allow an inexhaustible number of episodes with no repeats and are easy to promote ("Watch the case of the peeping landlord. Tune in at 5:30.").

In whatever form, the process by which programs come to our screens is changing because the central position of networks in that process has been altered. In 1978 ABC, CBS, and NBC drew 92% of all prime-time viewers. In 1988 they collected 70%. In 2002 their share fell "to an historic low: 47%. Not only is it a record low, but it's the first time the four-network share has dropped below 50%, a benchmark broadcasters dreaded to fall beneath" (McClellan, 2002, p. 6). In fact, the much-anticipated *Friends* finale had a rating of just under 30, not even coming close to being one of the most-watched programs (Figure 8.2). New technologies—cable, VCR, DVD, digital video recorders, satellite, the Internet and digitization, and even the remote control—have upset the long-standing relationship between medium and audience. Convergence is also reshaping that relationship.

Top 10 Most-Watched Nonsports Television Broadcasts

Rank	Program	Rating/Share
1	*M*A*S*H* (final episode), 1983	60.2/77
2	*Dallas* ("Who Shot JR?"), 1980	53.3/76
3	*Roots* (Part VIII), 1977	51.1/71
4	*Gone with the Wind* (Part 1), 1976	47.7/65
5	*Gone with the Wind* (Part 2), 1976	47.4/64
6	*Bob Hope Christmas Show*, 1970	46.6/64
7	*The Day After* (movie), 1983	46.0/62
8	*The Fugitive* (last episode), 1967	45.9/72
9	*Roots* (Part VI), 1977	45.9/66
10	*Roots* (Part V), 1977	45.7/71

CBS — ABC — NBC

▲ **Figure 8.2** Top 10 Most-Watched Nonsports Television Broadcasts.

Source: Television Bureau of Advertising (www.tvb.org).

Cable and Satellite Television

John Walson's brainchild reshaped the face of modern television. During cable's infancy, many over-the-air broadcasters saw it as something of a friend. It extended their reach, boosting both audience size and profits. Then, in November 1972, Sterling Manhattan Cable launched a new channel called Home Box Office. Only a handful of homes caught the debut of what we now call HBO, but broadcasters' mild concern over this development turned to outright antagonism toward cable in 1975, when new HBO owner Time Inc. began distributing the movie channel by satellite. Now **premium cable** was eating into the broadcasters' audience by offering high-quality, nationally produced and distributed content. The public enthusiastically embraced cable and

▲ Satellites like this one made national distribution of HBO possible in 1975. Television was then changed for all time.

▲ Revenues of cable shopping network QVC exceed those of traditional television networks ABC and NBC.

that, coupled with the widespread diffusion of **fiber optic** cable (the transmission of signals by light beam over glass, permitting the delivery of hundreds of channels), brought the medium to maturity.

Programming

We've already seen that cable's share of the prime-time audience exceeded that of the Big Four broadcast networks for the first time in 2002. Its total audience share has exceeded that of ABC, CBS, NBC, and Fox every year since. What attracts these viewers is programming, a fact highlighted by two pieces of recent industry data: *cable shows annually earn 50%* of all prime-time Academy Awards nominations, and cable viewing exceeds network viewing for every single American age demographic. Even home-shopping channels such as QVC (whose annual revenues of over $7 billion exceed those of traditional networks ABC and NBC) have made their mark.

As we've seen, cable operators attract viewers through a combination of basic and premium channels, as well as with some programming of local origin. There are more than 560 national cable networks and scores of regional cable networks. We all know national networks such as CNN, Lifetime, HBO, and the History Channel. Regional network North-West Cable News serves Washington, Oregon, Idaho, Montana, northern California, and parts of Alaska; New England Cable News serves the states that give it its name; and several regional sports-oriented channels serve different parts of the country. The financial support and targeted audiences for these program providers differ, as does their place on a system's **tiers**, groupings of channels made available to subscribers at varying prices.

BASIC CABLE PROGRAMMING In recognition of the growing dependence of the public on cable delivery of broadcast service as cable penetration increased, Congress passed the Cable Television Consumer Protection and Competition Act of 1992. This law requires operators to offer a truly basic service composed of the broadcast stations in their area and their access channels. Cable operators also offer another form of basic service, **expanded basic cable**, composed primarily of local broadcast stations and services with broad appeal such as TBS, TNT, the USA Network, and Comedy Central. These networks offer a wide array of programming not unlike that found on the traditional, over-the-air broadcast networks. The 20 cable networks with the largest numbers of subscribers appear in Figure 8.3. All rank in the top 20, not necessarily because they are the most watched, but because they all sit on cable's basic tiers. Naturally, that is the place to be because advertisers covet those large potential audiences. This is the dispute, for example, at the heart of the NFL Network's long-running fight with the nation's cable operators. Most operators want to put the network on a for-pay tier. NFL Network wants placement on basic cable. Sports channel MSG Network and Time Warner have been embroiled in a similar dispute for some time.

Because of concentration, operators are increasingly choosing to carry a specific basic channel because their owners (who have a financial stake in that channel) insist that they do. **Multiple system operators (MSOs)** are companies that own several cable franchises. Time Warner, Liberty, and Cablevision own truTV. Comcast has an interest in numerous prime channels. Viacom owns BET. Naturally, these networks are more likely to be carried by systems controlled by the MSOs that own them and less likely to be carried by other systems. This pattern also holds true for MSO-owned premium channels such as HBO and Showtime.

The long-standard concept of different pricing for different packages or tiers of channels is currently under attack by the FCC and some members of Congress. Concerns over viewers' accidental access to unwanted, offensive content and rising cable prices (at twice the rate of inflation) are leading to calls for **à la carte pricing**—that is, paying

Rank and network subscribers (in millions)

Rank	Network	Subscribers
1	TBS	102.1
2	Discovery	101.9
3	ESPN	101.4
4	CNN	101.3
4	USA Network	101.3
4	Food Network	101.3
7	Weather Channel	100.9
7	TLC	100.9
7	ESPN2	100.9
7	C-Span	100.9
7	HGTV	100.9
12	MTV	100.5
13	Spike TV	100.4
13	TNT	100.4
13	Fox News	100.4
13	Nickelodeon	100.4
17	Disney Channel	100.2
17	Comedy Central	100.2
19	A&E	100.1
20	ABC Family	99.9
20	CNBC	99.9
20	Cartoon Network	99.9
20	Lifetime Television	99.9

▲ Sports channel MSG Network's feud with Time Warner Cable over carriage denied millions of basketball fans their chance to see Jeremy Lin's spectacular 2012 entry into the NBA.

for cable on a channel-by-channel basis. The industry itself is split on the issues, system operators versus programmers. You can read more about the dispute in the box entitled, "Bundle or À la Carte?"

PREMIUM CABLE As the FCC lifted restrictions on cable's freedom to import distant signals and to show current movies, HBO grew and was joined by a host of other satellite-delivered pay networks. Today, the most familiar and popular premium cable networks are HBO, Showtime, the Spice Channel, the Sundance Channel, and Cinemax.

In addition to freedom from regulatory constraint, two important programming discoveries ensured the success of the new premium channels. After television's early experiments with over-the-air **subscription TV** failed, many experts believed people simply would not pay for television. So the first crucial discovery was that viewers would indeed pay for packages of contemporary, premium movies. These movie packages could be sold less expensively than could films bought one at a time, and viewers were willing to be billed on a monthly basis for the whole package rather than pay for each viewing.

The second realization boosting the fortunes of the premium networks was the discovery that viewers not only did not mind repeats (as many did with over-the-air television) but welcomed them as a benefit of paying for the provider's slate of films. Premium channel owners were delighted. Replaying content reduced their programming costs and solved the problem of how to fill all those hours of operation.

Premium services come in two forms: movie channels (HBO, Starz!, and Encore, for example) that offer packages of new and old movies along with big sports and other special events—all available for one monthly fee—and pay-per-view channels, through which viewers choose from a menu of offerings (almost always of very new movies and very big sporting events) and pay a fee for the chosen viewing.

People enjoy premium channels in the home for their ability to present unedited and uninterrupted movies and other content not usually found on broadcast channels—for example, adult fare and championship boxing and wrestling. Increasingly, however, that "content not usually found on broadcast channels" consists not of movies and sports but high-quality serial programming—content unencumbered by the need to attract the largest possible audience possessing a specific set of demographics. Premium cable series such as *The Sopranos*, *Game of Thrones*, *Curb Your Enthusiasm*, *Spartacus*, *Dexter*, *The Wire*, *Weeds*, and *Girls* attract large and loyal followings.

The other dominant multichannel service is direct broadcast satellite (DBS). First available to the public in 1994, it has brought cable's subscriber growth to a near standstill because from the viewer's perspective, what is on a DBS-supplied screen differs little from what is on a cable-supplied screen.

DBS in the United States is dominated by two companies, DirecTV (owned by Rupert Murdoch's News Corporation) and Dish Network (owned by EchoStar, a publicly traded company). DirecTV has 19.8 million subscribers; Dish Network, 13.9 million. And these two companies, along with Verizon's fiber optic FiOS-TV and its 4 million subscribers, have recently been peeling away subscribers from cable. Look at the list of the 10 largest cable MSOs in Figure 8.4. Note that Dish, DirecTV, and FiOS are all among that group. Cable's ever-increasing monthly rates encourage this move to DBS. But DBS providers, like other MSOs, face the troubling problem of **cord-cutting**, viewers leaving cable and DBS altogether and relying on Internet-only television viewing. A million subscribers bolted in 2012 alone, and **zero-TV homes**, those with sets that receive neither over-the-air nor cable/satellite television, now account for 5% of all U.S. TV homes (Friedman, 2013c).

Viewers and critics agree that much of television's most sophisticated (and enjoyable) programming is available on premium cable. Unafraid of offending advertisers, cable networks can present challenging, often controversial content. Can you match the title with the image? *The Newsroom, Spartacus, Girls, Homeland.*

Rank and subscribers (in millions)

Rank	Provider	Subscribers
1	Comcast	22.4
2	DirecTV	19.8
3	Dish Network	13.9
4	Time Warner	12.1
5	Cox	4.8
6	Charter	4.4
7	Verizon	4.0
8	AT&T	3.6
9	Cablevision	3.3
10	Bright House	2.1

◀ **Figure 8.4** Top 10 Cable MSOs, 2011.
Source: NCTA, 2012.

The debate over how to price a cable subscription has entered the cultural forum because of a perfect storm of concern. Many consumers are upset over rising subscription rates, likely to top $200 a month by 2020 (Tharp, 2012). Some politicians worry about people accidentally seeing material they find offensive, and more than a few MSOs are chafing under big hikes in what they have to pay for the channels they carry. For them, programming costs have escalated between 6% and 10% a year for the last decade, and for popular channels like ESPN, for example, MSOs must pay $4.69 for each of their cable households (Schechner & Peers, 2011). The solution to meeting these different concerns is to let the market (meaning viewers) decide, that is, à la carte pricing. That way, consumers wouldn't have to pay for unwatched channels (92% of cable subscribers would prefer à la carte; Wallenstein, 2012); there would be reduced risk of exposure to unwanted content; and MSOs wouldn't have to pay programming costs for all its subscribing households, just for those deciding to watch a specific channel.

But, argue cable network programmers like Disney and Viacom, our costs have escalated dramatically as well. ESPN spends more than $5 billion a year on programming (up 50% from five years ago); TNT spends $1.1 billion (up 55%); the History Channel spends over $283 million (a 50% rise; James, 2011). Viewers have decided, say the programmers, and this expensive content is what they want. In fact, they argue, à la carte would actually raise consumers' costs because those expensive popular channels make possible the smaller, niche channels. There might be a lot of people willing to pay $4 for ESPN, but how many viewers would pay for C-Span, or a foreign-language channel, or a religious channel, and how much would they be willing to pay? À la carte means the menu gets much, much smaller. And besides, continues the programmers'

> "Would you be happier paying for only the 15 channels you watch, or do you find value in having a lot of options, even if you don't take advantage of them all the time?"

position, people are already comfortable with bundles. Newspapers and magazines are bundles—we buy the whole publication, not individual stories. Subscription channels like HBO and Cinemax are bundles—we pay for all their programs, not just the ones we watch (and of course, HBO and Cinemax are themselves already available à la carte from MSOs). Even amusement parks are bundles—one price gets us in and we can ride all, some, or even none of the rides.

Enter your voice, à la carte or bundle? Would you be happier paying for only the 15 channels you watch, or do you find value in having a lot of options, even if you don't take advantage of them all the time? And what about *serendipitous viewing*, running across something you might not have thought to watch, but it catches your eye? Isn't this one of the great gifts of cable? Have you ever become a fan of something you inadvertently saw?

◀ Rising rates help fuel the argument over à la carte pricing for cable channels.
© Dave Granlund and politicalCartoons.com

Trends and Convergence in Television and Cable

The long-standing relationship between television and its audiences is being redefined. Nielsen's chief technology officer, Bob Luff, explained: "Radio is going on the Web, TV is going on cellphones, the Web is going on TV, and everything, it seems, is moving to video-on-demand and quite possibly the iPod and PlayStation Portable. Television and media will change more in the next three to five years than they've changed in the past 50" (in Gertner, 2005, p. 34). This profound change, initially wrought by cable and satellite, has been and is being driven by other new technologies as well—VCR, DVD, DVR, the Internet, digitization, and even the smartphone.

VCR

Introduced commercially in 1976, videocassette recorders (VCRs) quickly became common in American homes, but they are now disappearing as newer video technologies giving people even more control over viewing choices have emerged. Still, their introduction further eroded the audience for traditional over-the-air television, as people could now watch rented and purchased videos. VCR also allowed **time-shifting**, taping a show for later viewing, and **zipping**, fast-forwarding through taped commercials. As a result, people became comfortable with, in fact came to expect, more control over when, what, and how they watched television.

DVD

In March 1996 **digital video disc (DVD)** went on sale in U.S. stores. Using a DVD, viewers can stop images with no loss of fidelity; can subtitle a movie in a number of languages; can search for specific scenes from an on-screen picture menu; and can access information tracks that give background on the movie, its production, and its personnel. Scenes and music not used in the theatrical release of a movie are often included on the disc.

Innovations such as these made DVD at the time of its introduction the fastest-growing consumer electronic product of all time. Sales of DVD players exceeded those of VCRs for the first time in September 2001. Machines now sit in 85% of U.S. homes. Because of the many viewing options now available, DVD sales and rentals have fallen dramatically for the last several years (delia Cava, 2012), and in 2012, the number of online movie transactions (sales and rentals) exceeded the number of physical, that is disc, transactions for the first time, 3.4 billion to 2.4 billion (Smith, 2012b).

DVR

In March 1999 Philips Electronics unveiled the **digital video recorder (DVR)**. It contains digital software that puts a significant amount of control over content in viewers' hands. They can "rewind" and play back portions of a program while they are watching and recording it without losing any of that show. They can digitally record programs by simply telling the system their titles. By designating their favorite shows, viewers can instruct DVR to automatically record and deliver not only those programs but all similar content over a specified period of time. This application can even be used with the name of a favorite actor. Punch in Adam Sandler, and DVR will automatically record all programming in which he appears.

DVR does not deliver programming the way broadcasters, cablecasters, and DBS systems do. Rather, it is employed *in addition to* these content providers. All DBS providers and almost every MSO now offer low-cost DVR as part of their technology platform, significantly hastening its diffusion into American homes. Today, about half of all TV households have DVR. Naturally, traditional broadcast and ad-supported cable networks find the rapid diffusion of DVR troubling, and while it is true that DVR is dramatically changing television viewing as we have known it, it has not had as negative an effect on those traditional programming sources as originally anticipated. In DVR homes, 21% of all viewing is in DVR playback, totaling 2 hours and 9 minutes, often adding as many as 7.9 ratings points to prime-time viewing. In fact, DVR homes watch more prime-time programming than do non-DVR homes. In addition, DVR viewers watch 45% of all recorded advertising, and in total, DVR viewing of time-shifted commercials increases their viewership, on average, by 16% (Nielsen, 2011; Loechner, 2011a).

Video on the Internet

Television on the Internet was slow to take off because of copyright and piracy concerns, and because few viewers had sufficient **bandwidth**, space on the wires bringing content into people's homes. So for several years the most typical video fare on the Net was a variety of short specialty transmissions such as movie trailers, short independent films, music videos, and news clips. But the development of increasingly sophisticated video compression software and the parallel rise of homes with **broadband** Internet connections (66.3% of American adults have broadband at home; Neilsen, 2011) have changed that. Because broadband offers greater information-carrying capacity (that is, it increases bandwidth), watching true television on the Internet is now common. Much of that viewing is of content that originated on network and cable television, but much is also Web-only video (*most* if the number of streamed videos is the measure).

But as we saw in this chapter's opening, the distinction between Web-only and broadcast/cable programming is disappearing. Internet video sites Netflix, Hulu, and YouTube commission original content. Among YouTube's many channels are *Life and Times*, focusing on musician Jay-Z's cultural interests; *Dance On*, a dance channel from Madonna; the *Smart Girls at the Party* channel from *Parks and Recreation*'s Amy Poehler; several sports channels, and a number of news channels from print operations like the *Wall Street Journal* and Hearst. In 2013 online retailer Amazon commissioned 14 pilots, offering them free to viewers, who then voted on which should be produced as full series for its new video channel. Fans chose two comedies and three kids' shows. This variety is similar to what we find on cable and its advertising support akin to what we have come to accept from network television.

It's fitting that YouTube should be leading the evolution of Internet video from its short-clips era to that of long-form programming, because it was YouTube that originally made video on the Internet a success. Attracting as few as 600,000 unique monthly visitors in 2005, today it draws nearly 160 million unique visitors who watch 4 billion videos a day and upload 60 hours of new content every minute (Online Video Market, 2011; Oreskovic, 2012).

There are many other successful, more narrowly targeted Internet video sites. Blip .tv, for example, is a springboard for high-quality original Web series like *Fred* and *iJustine* that it eventually distributes across the Web, and Atom.com focuses on comedy and airs a cable version on Comedy Central. This wealth of Internet video is starting to alter viewing habits, especially among young people. While overall television viewing is at an all-time high, there has been a steady decline among 18- to 34-year-olds, as much as nine minutes a day (Stelter, 2012). You can see where Internet users watch video in Figure 8.5, but be aware; the small percentage that now watches Net content on home sets will soon explode, as by 2016 more than 100 million North Americans and Western Europeans will own Internet-connected home televisions (Chmielewski, 2012). Because Net-connected television encourages cord-cutting and zero-TV homes, the MSOs suffer most, so they are scrambling to make their set-top boxes Internet-friendly. But they face challenges on several fronts, including video on Facebook. Already America's third-most-visited website, accounting for 1 in every 11 visits to the Internet and 1 in every 5 page views (Dougherty, 2012), Facebookers watch nearly 200 million videos a month (Online Video Market, 2011).

Ultimately, the convergence of the Internet and television will be even more seamless as there are several new technologies further discouraging the distinction between the two. Slingbox, for example, allows users to "sling" television content to their computers and cell phones. Viewers can buy the device as a stand-alone, and several cable and satellite companies are investigating making it available to their subscribers. Viewers can also sling video in the other direction with devices such as AppleTV, Boxee, and Roku that send Web video to home sets. In addition, Internet-enabled HDTVs that can directly stream any video available on the Web are currently in stores, and sales are expected to reach 80 million by 2013. Including video-game consoles (Chapter 9), one-third of all U.S. homes already have Web-to-TV connections (Poggi, 2012).

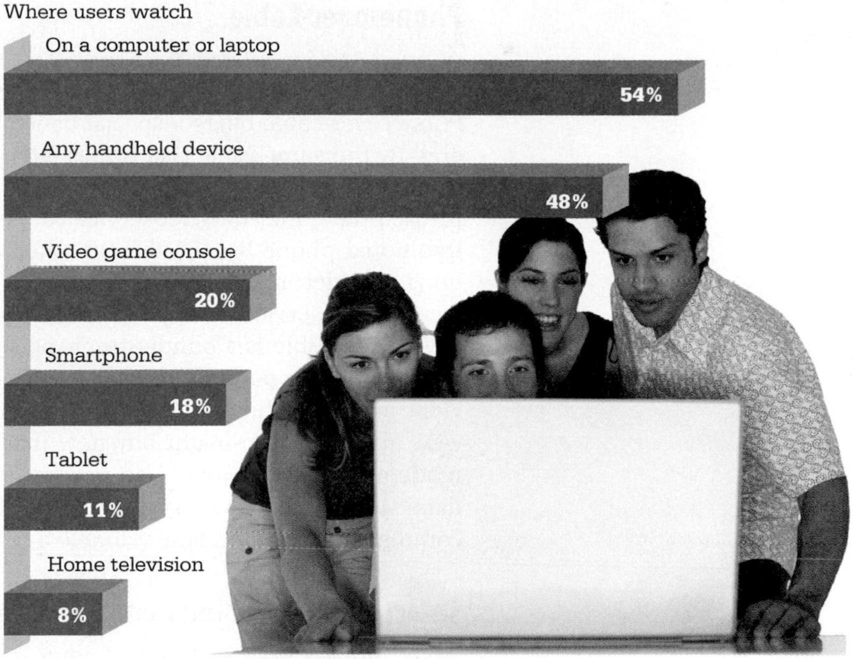

Where users watch
On a computer or laptop — 54%
Any handheld device — 48%
Video game console — 20%
Smartphone — 18%
Tablet — 11%
Home television — 8%

▲ **Figure 8.5** Where Adult Internet Users Watch Video.
Source: Online Video Business, 2012.

Interactive Television

The Internet is not the only technology that permits interactivity. Cable and satellite also allow viewers to "talk back" to content providers. But it is **digital cable television**, the delivery of digital images and other information to subscribers, that offers the truest form of interactive television. There are 45.7 million digital cable subscribers in the United States. Many digital cable subscribers also use their cable connections to access the Internet. Currently, there are also 46.4 million users with cable modems connecting their computers to the Net via a specified Internet service provider, or ISP (NCTA, 2012). As a result, "must-carry" has taken on new meaning in the Internet age, as Congress and the courts debate cable's power to grant or limit access to its wires to outside service and content providers and those providers' right to demand that access.

Cable's digital channels permit multiplexing, carrying two or more different signals over the same channel. This, in turn, is made possible by *digital compression*, which "squeezes" signals to permit multiple signals to be carried over one channel. Digital compression works by removing redundant information from the transmission of the signal. For example, the set behind two actors in a movie scene might not change for several minutes. So why transmit the information that the set is there? Simply transmit the digital data that indicate what has changed in the scene, not what has not.

This expanded capacity makes possible *interactive cable*, that is, the ability of subscribers to talk back to the system operator (extra space on the channel is used for this back talk). And *this* permits the following services, many of which you already use: **video-on-demand (VOD)**, one-click shopping (you see it, you click on it, you buy it), local information on demand (news, traffic, and weather), program interactivity (choose a camera angle, learn more about an actor's career, play along with game show contestants), interactive program guides, and as you'll read more about in Chapter 9, video games. But it is video-on-demand—the ability to access pay-per-view movies and other content that can be watched at any time—that best shows the economic advantage of putting more control into viewers' hands. The VOD business earns the MSOs nearly $1.7 billion a year, a figure destined to grow as today's 53 million VOD households expand to a predicted 71 million—nearly 60% of all U.S. television homes—by 2016 (Marich, 2011; Steinberg, 2011).

Phone-over-Cable

Another service offered by many MSOs is phone service over cable wires. Currently there are 25 million cable-delivered residential telephone subscribers (NCTA, 2012). Phone-over-cable offers a special benefit to MSOs. If telephone service can be delivered by the same cable that brings television into the home, so too can the Internet. And what's more, if the cable line is broadband capable of handling digitally compressed data, that Internet service can be even faster than the service provided over traditional phone lines. Cable, in other words, can become a one-stop communications provider: television, VOD, audio, high-speed Internet access, long-distance and local phone service, multiple phone lines, and fax. This is **bundling**.

How valuable is a bundle-receiving subscriber to an MSO? Add together the bills you're probably paying right now—basic or premium cable, your Internet service provider, and your phone bill. What does that total? Now speculate on how much pay-per-view and VOD you might buy now that you have broadband and a superfast cable modem. And what would you pay for home delivery of real-time sports or financial data? And the MSO would collect each time you accessed an interactive classified or commercial ad. That's how valuable a bundled subscriber will be.

Smartphones, Tablets, and TV Everywhere

We've already seen that 48% of adult Internet users watch video on mobile devices, and teens are its heaviest consumers, watching more than seven hours a month, even paying attention to the commercials (58%; Loechner, 2011b). Smartphones and tablets, just as they have for other media, have made television watching an anywhere, anytime activity. But so have two other developments. The first is the popularity of handheld gaming devices like Nintendo's Game Boy Advance and Sony's PlayStation Portable and Vita, all of which can stream video and play video discs or cartridges (Chapter 9). The second is the TV Everywhere Initiative, content providers' ongoing efforts to make digital on-demand programming available to all mobile devices. Slowed by concerns over pricing, advertising models, audience measurement, and release-of-content strategies, its participants include MSOs like Comcast, Dish, and Verizon and broadcast networks like Fox and CBS. In addition, 900 over-the-air commercial and public broadcasters, through the Open Mobile Video Coalition, are working to bring their signals to TV Everywhere. At of the start of 2012, more than 120 stations were providing mobile digital signals to their viewers, a 70% jump from a year earlier (Open Mobile, 2012).

This mobile viewing activity promises to alter the television/viewer relationship in a way other than mobility. Time with mobile devices is slowly replacing time with the television set. Already, mobile device users spend more time with those devices than in front of a television screen (27% of their media time vs. 22%) and 39% use their mobile devices while watching television (Patel, 2012). In fact, when asked if they would rather give up their smartphone or their television, 58% said they would eliminate television (Edison Research, 2011).

DEVELOPING MEDIA LITERACY SKILLS

Recognizing Staged News

For years, studies have shown that a majority of the American public turns to television as the source of most of its news and that viewers rank it as the most believable news source. Television news can be immediate and dramatic, especially when events being covered lend themselves to visual images. But what if they don't? News may be journalism, but television news is also a television *show*, and as such it must attract viewers. Television newspeople have an obligation to truthfully and accurately inform the public, but they also have an obligation to attract a large number of people so their station or network is profitable.

Even the best television journalists cannot inform a public that does not tune in, and the public tunes in to see pictures. Television professionals, driven to get pictures, often walk the fine ethical line of **news staging**—that is, re-creating some event that is believed to or could have happened. Sometimes news staging takes simple forms; for example, a reporter may narrate an account of an event he or she did not witness while video of that event is played. The intended impression is that the reporter is on the scene. What harm is there in this? It's common practice on virtually all U.S. television news shows. But how much of a leap is it from that to ABC News splicing together several different pieces of video to create the appearance of reporter Brian Ross at the wheel of an out-of-control Toyota (Cook, 2010)?

The broadcasters' defense is, "This is not staging in the sense that the *event* was staged. What does it matter if the reporter was not actually on the spot? What was reported actually did happen." If you accept this view (the event *did* happen, therefore it's not news staging), how would you evaluate Fox News's Geraldo Rivera's 2002 reporting from "sacred ground," the scene of a battle in Afghanistan in which U.S. forces suffered heavy losses, even though he was miles from the actual spot? And if you accept digital alteration of news scenes to place network reporters at the scene, how would you evaluate CBS's common practice of digitally inserting its network logo on billboards and buildings that appear behind its reporters and anchors? If this staging is acceptable to you, why not okay the digital enhancement of fires and explosions in the news?

Some media-literate viewers may accept the-event-did-happen argument, but another form of news staging exists that is potentially more troublesome—re-creation. In 2011, a Rhode Island station asked golfers to re-create for its cameras the last hole of a tournament while its reporter narrated as if the play was in real time (Busbee, 2011). Here the defense is that the re-creation is a true representation of what had occurred. Watching video coverage of an Air Force bombing action in Iraq in 2003 from the relative safety of his hotel in Erbil, combat reporter Ashley Gilbertson was struck by the sight of a Fox News correspondent "crouching in front of sandbags, wearing a flak jacket and a helmet. He was supposedly on the front lines, reporting via a scratchy video phone. He had to whisper, he said." But Gilbertson soon recognized the "distinctive architecture of our hotel." The correspondent "was reporting live" from a foxhole that had been "re-created" in his hotel room. The angry Gilbertson called the Fox reporter on his in-room phone and hung up so all could hear that this was a staged report (in Genoways, 2007, pp. 80–81). This staging was justified with the claim that it "could have happened."

Where do media professionals draw the line? What happens to the public's trust in its favorite news source as the distinctions between fact and fiction, reality and illusion, what is and what is not digital, and reporting and re-creating disappear?

If you see a televised news story labeled as a re-creation or simulation, what leads you to trust the re-creator's or simulator's version? Media-literate people develop strategies to analyze content, deciding where *they* draw the line and rejecting staged news that crosses it. The news producer must balance service to the public against ratings and profit, but viewers must balance their desire for interesting, stimulating visuals against confidence that the news is reported rather than manufactured.

Why do broadcasters feel compelled to stage the news?

▼ Did Geraldo Rivera engage in permissible or impermissible news staging when he reported from "sacred ground" although he was miles from the actual spot?

There are two possible explanations. One is the need to meet television audience demands for visuals. The second explanation is the assumption, widely held by television professionals, that people are incapable of reading, accepting, interpreting, and understanding important issues unless they are presented in a manner that meets viewers' expectations of the news. If this is accurate, media-literate viewers must reconsider their expectations of the medium. If this assumption about viewers is incorrect, media-literate people must make that clear to those who produce the news, either by choosing news programs that avoid staging or by protesting to those that do.

MEDIA LITERACY CHALLENGE
No Video for a Week

There is no better way to *become aware of the impact of the media on you and society* than to do without them. As a media-literate individual, you can test for yourself just how free you are of the power of one specific medium, video. See if you control your viewing or if your viewing controls you. To start, pick a five-day period and simply stop watching. No television. No videos on the Internet or your smartphone. No video games. Simply put: Don't watch or even look at any video screen anywhere for five entire days. If you are adventurous, enlist one or more friends, family members, or roommates.

Simply changing your routine viewing behavior will not do very much for you unless you reflect on its meaning. Ask yourself (and any confederates you may have enlisted) these questions. How easy or difficult is it for you to break away from all video? Why or why not? What did you learn about your video consumption habits? How did you use the freed-up time? Were you able to find productive activity, or did you spend your time longing for a screen? Be sure to describe how not watching affected your other life habits (eating, socializing with family and friends, news gathering, and the like). Describe your interactions with other people during this week. Did your conversations change? That is, were there alterations in duration, depth, or subject matter? If you were unable to complete the week of nonviewing, describe why. How easy or difficult was it to come to the decision to give up? Do you consider it a failure to have resumed watching before the five days were up? Why or why not? Once you resume your normal video habits, place yourself on a scale of 1 to 10, with 1 being I-Control-Video and 10 being Video-Controls-Me. Explain your self-rating.

Resources for Review and Discussion

REVIEW POINTS: TYING CONTENT TO LEARNING OUTCOMES

▶ **Outline the history and development of the television and cable television industries and television itself as a medium.**

- ▶ In 1884 Paul Nipkow developed the first device for transmitting images. John Logie Baird soon used this mechanical scanning technology to send images long distance. Vladimir Zworykin and Philo Farnsworth developed electronic scanning technology in the 1920s, leading to the public demonstration of television in 1939.
- ▶ In the 1950s, the quiz show scandal, the business acumen of Lucille Ball, McCarthyism, and the ratings system shaped the nature of broadcast television. Cable, introduced in 1948, would soon effect even more change.
- ▶ Cable, designed initially for the importation of distant signals, became a mature medium when it began offering movies and other premium content.

▶ **Describe how the organizational and economic nature of the contemporary television and cable industries shapes the content of television.**

- ▶ Cable, dominated by large MSOs, offers programming in tiers that include basic, expanded basic, and premium cable. Some favor a new pricing scheme, à la carte.
- ▶ Direct broadcast satellite is the primary multichannel competitor to cable, now joined by fiber optic systems like FiOS.

▶ **Explain the relationship between television in all its forms and its viewers.**

- ▶ Once described as a vast wasteland, it is the leading source of news for a large majority of Americans.
- ▶ Viewers rate television as their most influential, persuasive, authoritative, and exciting ad medium.

▶ **Identify new and converging video technologies and their potential impact on the television industry and its audience.**

▶ A host of technologies influence the television-viewer relationship, including VCR, DVD, DVR, video on the Internet, and interactive television.

▶ **Describe the digital and mobile television revolution.**

▶ Mobile video-over smartphones, tablets, and other portable video devices are now common, aided by the idea of TV Everywhere and the rise of video via social networking site.

▶ **Apply key television-viewing media literacy skills.**

▶ Staged news raises several questions for media-literate people about broadcaster integrity and respect for viewers.

KEY TERMS

nonlinear TV, 183

Nipkow disc, 184

pixel, 184

iconoscope tube, 184

kinescope, 184

coaxial cable, 185

microwave relay, 185

spot commercial sales, 187

personal peoplemeter, 189

Total Audience Measurement Index (TAMi), 189

Global Television Audience Metering meter (GTAM meter), 189

sweeps periods, 189

share, 190

C3 rating, 190

community antenna television (CATV), 190

master antenna television (MATV), 191

importation of distant signals, 191

all-channel legislation, 191

vast wasteland, 191

network, 193

clear time, 193

reverse compensation, 193

retransmission fees, 193

off-network, 193

pilot, 193

put, 194

first-run syndication, 195

stripping, 195

premium cable, 195

fiber optics, 196

tiers, 196

expanded basic cable, 196

multiple system operator (MSO), 196

à la carte pricing, 196

subscription television, 198

cord-cutting, 198

zero-TV homes, 198

time-shifting, 201

zipping, 201

digital video disc (DVD), 201

digital video recorder (DVR), 201

bandwidth, 202

broadband, 202

digital cable television, 203

video-on-demand (VOD), 203

bundling, 204

news staging, 205

QUESTIONS FOR REVIEW

1. What is the importance of each of the following to the history of television: Paul Nipkow, John Logie Baird, Vladimir Zworykin, Philo Farnsworth, and Newton Minow?

2. What was the impact on television of the quiz show scandal, *I Love Lucy*, McCarthyism, and the Nielsen ratings?

3. How are the ratings taken? What are some complaints about the ratings system?

4. How does a program typically make it to the air? How does syndication figure in this process?

5. How have cable, VCR, DVD, DVR, and DBS affected the networks?

6. What are some of the changes in television wrought by cable?

7. Explain the difference between basic cable, expanded basic cable, premium cable, pay-per-view, and à la carte pricing.

8. What are importation of distant signals, premium cable, and fiber optics? How are they related? What do they have to do with cable's maturity as a medium?

9. In what ways can viewers access video on the Internet? Via mobile devices? What kinds of content are available on these platforms?

10. What is news staging?

Mc Graw Hill connect

For further review, go to the LearnSmart study module for this chapter.

QUESTIONS FOR CRITICAL THINKING AND DISCUSSION

1. As an independent producer, what kind of program would you develop for the networks? How immune do you think you could be from the pressures that exist in this process?

2. Are you a cable subscriber? Why or why not? At what level? Would you prefer à la carte pricing? Why or why not?

3. Is news staging ever permissible? If not, why not? If yes, under what conditions? Have you ever recognized a report as staged when it was not so identified? Describe what you saw.

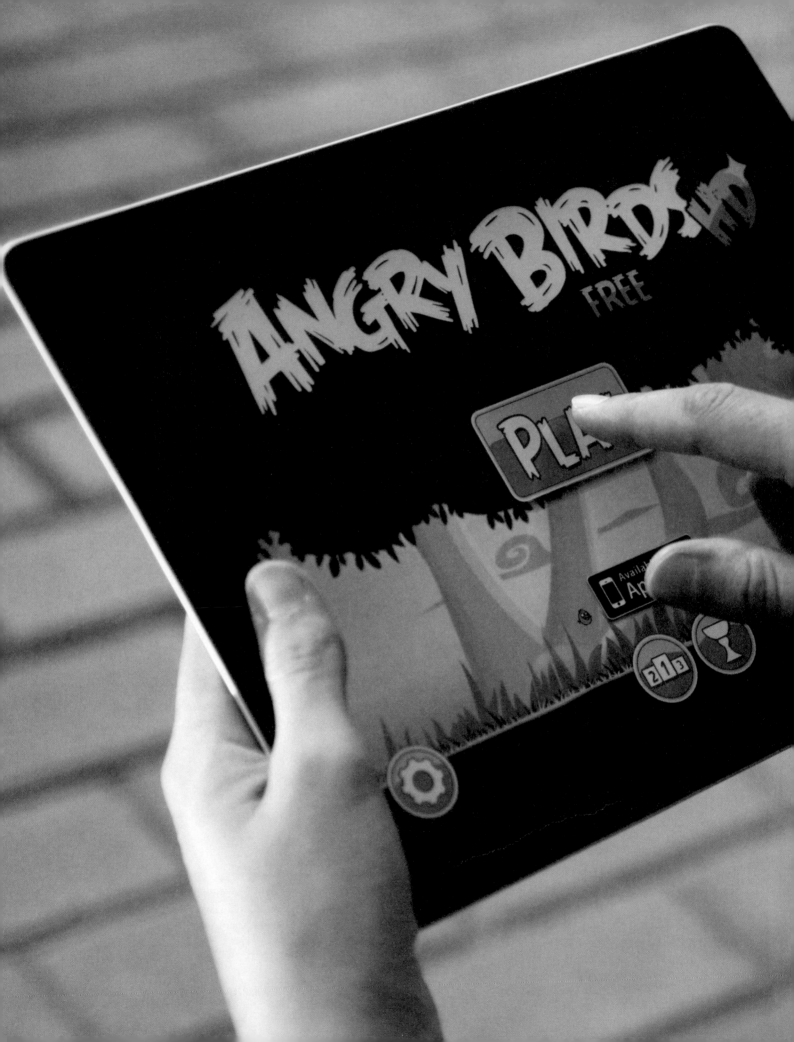

Video Games

9

Learning Objectives

Video games are accelerating the five trends reshaping mass communication and the mass media industries. They are the product of a highly concentrated industry; they are luring people from the more traditional media (audience fragmentation); they are used as and filled with advertising (hypercommercialization); they know no borders (globalization); and they are played on numerous technologies, from game consoles to personal computers to the Internet to cell phones (convergence). And even though the game industry grosses nearly twice as much as Hollywood does every year, mass communication experts are only now taking this medium seriously. After studying this chapter you should be able to

▶ Outline the history and development of games and the gaming industry.

▶ Describe how the organizational and economic nature of the contemporary gaming industry shapes the content of games.

▶ Explain the relationship between games and their players.

▶ Identify changes in the game industry brought about by new and converging technologies.

▶ Apply key game-playing media literacy skills.

The casual game *Angry Birds* had 42 million downloads in its first year.

"WHY ARE YOU PLAYING VIDEO GAMES? Don't you have homework or a paper due or something?"

"This is more important. And anyway, what are you, my mother?"

"Nope, I just don't want to have to dig up another roommate, that's all."

"Glad to know you care. And anyway, it may look like I'm playing video games, but I'm really doing research for my global politics class. Check it out. This is a game that the U.S. Navy put out, MMOWGLI. It stands for Massively Multiplayer Online Wargame Leveraging the Internet, and the idea is to combat Somali pirates."

"A game from the government about thwarting Somali pirates?"

"That's this one. There are others, depending on what problem the Office of Naval Research wants help with. They created a game environment where players like us and experts on all kinds of issues can share new ideas and collaborate with other players. We earn points to win the game."

"Why does the Navy care what you think?"

"It doesn't, not really. But it cares about what all of us think. It's Web-based, so MMOWGLI lets the Navy strategize with way more people than it could ever assemble face-to-face. Navy people know Navy stuff; Africa experts know Africa stuff. Other people like us know other stuff. So we all go online and **crowdsource** different solutions and unimagined possibilities, you know, let a whole network of people, the crowd, get involved in the process. Wanna play?"

"No thanks. If I'm going to play games, I'd like to kill bad guys with a vast array of magnificent weapons and be able to leap tall buildings in a single bound."

In this chapter we examine games played on a variety of electronic, microprocessor-based platforms. But before we get deeper into our discussion of the sophisticated, entertaining, and sometimes (as you can tell from our opening vignette) not very playful games that abound today, let's look at their roots in the convergence of pinball machines and military simulators. This is fitting, because as with other media, possibly even more so, converging technologies define video games' present and future.

1931 ▲ *Baffle Ball*, first mass-produced arcade game

1933 *Contact*, first electric pinball game

1940

1947 ▲ Flippers come to pinball

1951 Japanese playing-card company Marufuku changes its name to Nintendo

1955

1961 Russell creates *Spacewar*

1964 Sega formed

1966 Sega exports *Periscope* to United States and Europe; first amusement game export; ▲ 25 cents per play established as arcade game standard

1968 Baer patents interactive television game

A Short History of Computer and Video Games

Carnival man David Gottlieb invented the first mass-produced arcade game, *Baffle Ball*, in 1931. A small wooden cabinet, it had only one moving part, a plunger. Players would launch a ball into the playing field, a slanted surface with metal "pins" surrounding "scoring holes." The object was to get the ball into one of the holes. Gottlieb was soon manufacturing 400 cabinets a day. Just as quickly, he had many imitators. One, Harry Williams, invented *Contact*, the first electric pinball game. Williams was an engineer, and his 1933 gaming innovations were electronic scoring (*Baffle Ball* players had to keep their scores in their heads) and scoring holes, or pockets, that threw the ball back into the playing field (in *Baffle Ball*, when a ball dropped into a hole, it dropped into a hole). The popularity of arcade games exploded, and players' enthusiasm was fueled even more when slot-machine makers entered the field, producing games with cash payouts. With the Depression in full force in the 1930s, however, civic leaders were not much in favor of this development, and several locales, most notably New York City, banned the games. Pinball was considered gambling.

David Gottlieb had the answer. Games of skill were not gambling. And games that paid off in additional games rather than cash were not gambling. In 1947, he introduced *Humpty Dumpty*, a six-flipper game that rewarded high-scorers with replays. Bans were lifted, pinball returned to the arcades, even more players were attracted to the skills-based electronic games, and the stage was set for what we know today as video and computer games. As Steven Baxter of the *CNN Computer Connection* wrote, "You can't say that video games grew out of pinball, but you can assume that video games wouldn't have happened without it. It's like bicycles and the automobile. One industry leads to the other and then they exist side-by-side. But you had to have bicycles to one day have motor cars." Games writer Steven Kent adds, "New technologies

1970 | 1985 | 2000

1971 ▲ *Computer Space*, first arcade computer game	
1972 *Odyssey* released; Atari formed, develops *Pong*	
1975 *Home Pong* debuts; *Gunfight*, first game to use a microprocessor	
1976 *Channel F*, first programmable, cartridge-based home game	
1977 First handheld video game	
1979 First handheld programmable game system	
1980 Home *Space Invaders*; first arcade game for home systems / *Pac-Man*	
1981 *Donkey Kong*	

1985 Nintendo's NES introduced	
1986 *Legend of Zelda*	
1987 PC games introduced	
1989 ▲ Game Boy	
1990 *Super Mario Bros. 3*	
1993 *Doom* released	
1994 ESRB ratings established; *Myst* released	
1995 PlayStation in United States	

2000 ▲ Xbox	
2001 Game Cube	
2003 *Second Life* launched	
2004 *Halo 2* released; PlayStation Portable introduced	
2006 Nintendo Wii	
2012 Xbox entertainment use surpasses gaming	
2013 Wii U, PlayStation 4, Xbox One	

▶ Gottlieb's *Baffle Ball* and *Humpty Dumpty*.

do not simply spring out of thin air. They need to be associated with familiar industries or ideas. People may have jokingly referred to the first automobiles as 'horseless carriages,' but the name also helped define them. The name changed them from nebulous, unexplainable machines to an extension of an already accepted mode of transportation" (both quotes from Kent, 2001, pp. 1–2).

Today's Games Emerge

Throughout the late 1950s and 1960s, computers were hulking giants, filling entire rooms (see Chapter 10). Most displayed their output on paper in the form of teletype. But the very best, most advanced computers, those designed for military research and analysis, were a bit sleeker and had monitors for output display. Only three universities—MIT, the University of Utah, and Stanford—and a few dedicated research installations had these machines. At MIT, a group of self-described nerds, the Tech Model Railroad Club (TMRC), began writing programs for fun for a military computer. Club members would leave their work next to the computer so others could build on what had come before. One member, Steve Russell, decided to write the ultimate program, an interactive game. It took him 200 hours over six months to produce the first interactive computer game, *Spacewar*, completed in 1961. This version featured toggle switches that controlled the speed and direction of two spaceships and the torpedoes they fired at each other. His final version, completed the next year, had an accurate map of the stars in the background and a sun with a mathematically precise gravitational field that influenced play. Russell and his club-mates even built remote control units with switches for every game function, the first game pad. "We thought about trying to make money off it for two or three days but concluded that there wasn't a way that it could be done," said Russell (quoted in Kent, 2001, p. 20).

▼ This is the universe navigated by *Spacewar* gamers, simple by today's standards, but a dramatic beginning for the medium.

But another college student, Nolan Bushnell, thought differently (DeMaria & Wilson, 2004, p. 16). For two years after the completion of Russell's game, the TMRC distributed it to other schools for free. Bushnell, who worked in an arcade to pay for his engineering studies at the University of Utah, played *Spacewar* incessantly. After graduation he dedicated himself to developing a coin-operated version of the game that had consumed so much of his time. He knew that to make money, it would have to attract more than computer enthusiasts, so he designed

a futuristic-looking fiberglass cabinet. The result, *Computer Space*, released in 1971, was a dismal failure. It was far too complicated for casual play, doing good business near college campuses but bombing in bowling alleys and beer halls. Yet Bushnell was undeterred. With two friends and investments of $250 each, he quit his engineering job and incorporated Atari in 1972.

Long before this, in 1951, Ralph Baer, an engineer for a military contractor charged with developing "the best TV set in the world," decided a good set should do more than receive a few channels (remember, this was before cable's rise). He suggested building games into the receivers. His bosses were unimpressed. Fifteen years later Baer was working for another defense contractor when he drafted the complete schematics for a video-game console that would sell for about $20. He patented it in 1968 and licensed his device to Magnavox, which, in 1972, marketed the first home video-game system as *Odyssey* and sold it for $100.

Odyssey was a simple game offering two square spots to represent two players (or paddles), a ball, and a center line. It had six plug-in cartridges and transparent, colored screen overlays producing 12 games, all very rudimentary. Its high cost and Magnavox's decision to sell it through its television set dealers—leading to the incorrect perception that it could be played only on Magnavox sets—limited its success. Only 100,000 units were sold. But with *Odyssey* and Atari,

▼ Original *Pong*.

> the stage was set for the introduction of a new art form, and a new industry. The technological foundation was built. The earliest pioneers had seen farther than any others and had made their tentative steps along the path. The world was in flux, as new politics, new music, and new social consciousness began to spread throughout the United States and Europe. The 60s were over. A generation of young people dreamed new dreams and broke down the status quo. It was into that world that first Ralph Baer and then Nolan Bushnell made their humble offerings, and changed the world in ways no one could have foreseen. (DeMaria & Wilson, 2004, p. 17)

The spark that set off the game revolution was *Pong*, Atari's arcade ping-pong game, introduced in 1972. Bushnell had seen *Odyssey* at an electronics show and set his people to creating a coin-operated version (Atari later agreed to pay a licensing fee

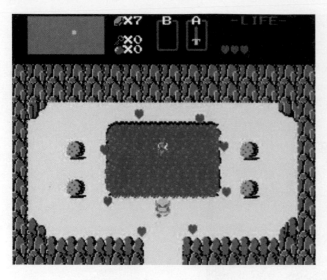

▲ *Legend of Zelda*, 1986, introduced open structure play, now standard in modern games.

to Magnavox). The two-player game was an overnight hit, selling 100,000 units in its first year—and twice as many knockoffs (Burnham, 2001, p. 61). Players poured quarters into games looking remarkably like *Pong*, including Harry Williams's *Paddle-Ball*, Rally's *For-Play*, and then in an effort to head off what Nolan Bushnell called "the jackals," Atari's own *Pong Doubles*, *Super Pong*, and *Quadrapong* (Sellers, 2001).

Rapid-Fire Developments

What followed, partly as a result of the swift advance of the microchip and computer industries (and a healthy dose of technological genius from a thriving game industry in Japan), was a rapid-fire succession of innovation and development. In 1975 Atari, by marketing *Home Pong* through Sears, made its first steps toward bringing arcade games into the home. Its 1980 release of home *Space Invaders* cemented the trend. Also in 1975, Midway began importing *Gunfight* from Japanese manufacturer Taito. *Gunfight* was significant for two reasons. Although Sega, with *Periscope*, began importing arcade games into the United States in 1966, *Gunfight* was the first imported video game, and in fact, it was the first game to use a computer microprocessor. In 1976, Fairchild Camera and Instrument introduced *Channel F*, the first programmable, cartridge-based home game. Mattel Toys brought true electronic games to handheld devices in 1977, with titles like *Missile Attack, Auto Race,* and *Football* played on handheld, calculator-sized **LED**, or **light-emitting diode**, and **LCD**, or **liquid crystal display**, screens. In 1979 Milton Bradley released Microvision, the first programmable handheld game system. Two Japanese arcade imports, Namco's *Pac-Man* in 1980 and Nintendo's *Donkey Kong* in 1981, become instant classics, all-time best sellers, and with the introduction of Nintendo's groundbreaking game console NES in 1985, home-version successes. The Japanese company further advanced gaming with its 1986 release of home console game *Legend of Zelda*, revolutionary because it introduced open structure play—that is, players could go wherever they wanted and there were multiple routes to winning, now standard in modern games.

Arcade games, handheld systems, and home game consoles were joined by personal computer games, beginning with the 1987 release of NEC's hybrid PC/console in Japan. Now, with games being played on microprocessor-based consoles, producing them for microprocessor-based PCs was a simple matter. By the early 1990s, CD-ROM-based computer games were common and successful. *Doom* (1993) and *Myst*

▶ All-time classics *Pac-Man* and *Donkey Kong*.

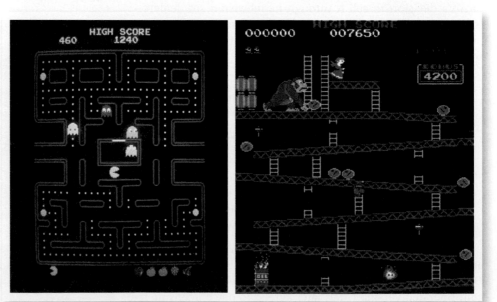

▲ Two of the first interactive games, *Doom* and *Myst*.

(1994) were among the first big personal computer game hits. *Doom* hinted at a development soon to come in games because it could be played over **LANs**, or **local area** computer **networks**, typically in a single building; that is, it was an interactive game played by several people over a computer network. It was also the first **first-person perspective** shooting **game**; gamers "carried" the weapon, and all action in the game was seen through their eyes.

Games and Their Players

Two-thirds of all Americans, 211.5 million people, play video games (Snider, 2012). But before we look at these people a bit more closely, we need to define exactly what constitutes a video game.

◀ Regardless of the platform, a game is a video game if the action takes place interactively on-screen.

The video-game industry has reached a level of legitimacy and respectability equal to that of other mass media. Now it is being asked the same questions regarding content as they are: What is the impact on kids? What regulations should be imposed? How is the medium used? And just as important, how can we use the medium to make a positive difference?

Game industry professionals, social scientists, educators, and parents regularly examine this last question. Their efforts focus on the use of games for policy change, training, and learning. Their products include initiatives such as Cisco Systems' *Peter Packet Game and Challenge*, designed to confront poverty, and the work of nonprofit Global Kids Inc., which has teamed with organizations such as Lego, Microsoft, and PBS in an effort to encourage kids to create their own educational video games. Persuasive Games is yet another example of a provider building electronic games designed for instruction and activism, as is P.O.V. Interactive, which uses interactive games in coordination with PBS documentaries to explore environmental and other issues. The National Academy of Sciences is funding game development by the Federation of American Scientists, designed to build enthusiasm for science as a discipline and a career.

One of the most successful games-for-good efforts is Games for Health, a community of game developers, researchers, and health care and medical professionals who maintain an ongoing "best practices" conversation—online and in annual conferences—to share information about the impact existing and original games can have on health care and policy. Japanese game maker Konami's *Dance Dance Revolution*, for example, is an existing **exergame** that invites people to exercise while they play. Players follow cascading arrows on a video screen, mimicking their movements on a large footpad attached by a cable to a game console. Sony and Nike teamed up to produce another beneficial exergame, *EyeToy Kinetic*, that encourages users to kickbox, practice yoga, or engage in a number of other physical activities in a variety of simulated environments. Other existing games—just about anything played on a handheld console—are frequently used to reduce children's anxiety before anesthesia, dialysis, or chemotherapy. Research has shown that time on a portable game relaxes preoperative children even more than do their parents.

> "These efforts are examples of the gamification of society, using video game skills and conventions to solve real-world problems in medicine, health, public policy, personal responsibility, in fact, any issue that humans face."

New games, too, are developed specifically to meet people's health needs. Nintendo developed *GlucoBoy*, an original game to help children manage their diabetes, and *Dr. Mario*, to aid patients in managing their own diabetic needs. We saw in the chapter opener that the Navy developed MMOWGLI, but it also created a virtual reality game to help soldiers returning from the Middle East deal with post-traumatic stress disorder. A therapist controls the game to re-create troubling events, helping the player/patient slowly revisit the scene of the trauma. And it should come as no surprise, but Atari founder Nolan Bushnell has also tried his hand at games-for-good. His *Anti-Aging Games* website offers older folks several games intended to improve short-term memory, focus, and concentration.

These efforts are examples of the **gamification** of society, using video game skills and conventions to solve real-world problems in medicine, health, policy, personal responsibility, in fact, any issue that humans face. In this sense, gamification is the ultimate use of games for good.

◀ Nolan Bushnell's Anti-Aging Games offers seniors several games designed to improve short-term memory, focus, and concentration.
© 2010–2011 Anti-Aging Games, LLC. Anti-Aging Games® is a trademark of Anti-Aging Games, LLC. Reprinted by permission.

What Is a Video Game?

As technologies converge, the same game can be played on an increasing number of platforms. *Myst*, for example, was originally a computer game written for Macintosh computers, then IBM PCs, then external CD-ROM drives, then video-game consoles such as PlayStation. Now it can be played online. Versions of *Donkey Kong* can be played in arcades and on consoles, on the Internet, on Macs and PCs, and on handheld players. *Q*bert* can be played on arcade machines and on collectable Nelsonic wristwatch gameplayers. Thousands of games can be played on smartphones and tablets. For our purposes, then, a game is a **video game** when the action of the game takes place interactively on-screen. By this definition, an online text-based game such as a

▲ The skinny, sun-deprived teen boy gamer stereotype may persist, but it doesn't reflect the reality.
GET FUZZY: © Darby Conley/Distributed by United Feature Syndicate, Inc.

MUD, or **multiuser dimension**, which has no moving images, is a video game, but the home version of *Trivial Pursuit*, employing a DVD to offer video hints to those playing the board game, is not.

That takes care of the technologically based half of the word (*video*), but what is a *game*? For our purposes, a video game is a game when a player has direct involvement in the on-screen action to produce some desired outcome. In a MUD, for example, players use text—words—to create personalities, environments, even worlds in which they interact with others toward some specific end. That's a game. But what about *Mario Teaches Typing*, a cartridge-based learning aid? Even though its goal is teaching, because it has gamelike features (in this case, the famous Super Mario and the manipulation of on-screen action to meet a particular end), it's a game. The essay titled "Using Games for Good" looks at games that function as more than entertainment.

Who Is Playing?

What do we know about the 211.5 million regular American video-game players? For one thing, they are not necessarily the stereotypical teenage boys gaming away in their parents' basements, as you can see in Figure 9.1 and from these data (Entertainment Software Association, 2013).

- The average game player is 30 years old; 37% of Americans over 36 play.
- Adult women represent a larger proportion of the game-playing population (30%) than boys under 18 (18%).
- Fifty-one percent of U.S. households own a dedicated game console, and those that do own an average of two.

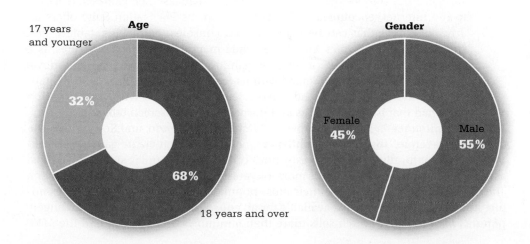

◀ **Figure 9.1** Game Players' Demographics, 2011.
Source: Entertainment Software Association, 2013.

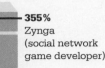

Percentage company growth, 2009–2010

355%
Zynga
(social network
game developer)

116%
Facebook
(social network
website)

Take-Two
(video game
developer &
publisher)

Ubisoft
(video game
developer &
publisher)

37%

39%

28%
Gray Television
(owner of local
TV stations)

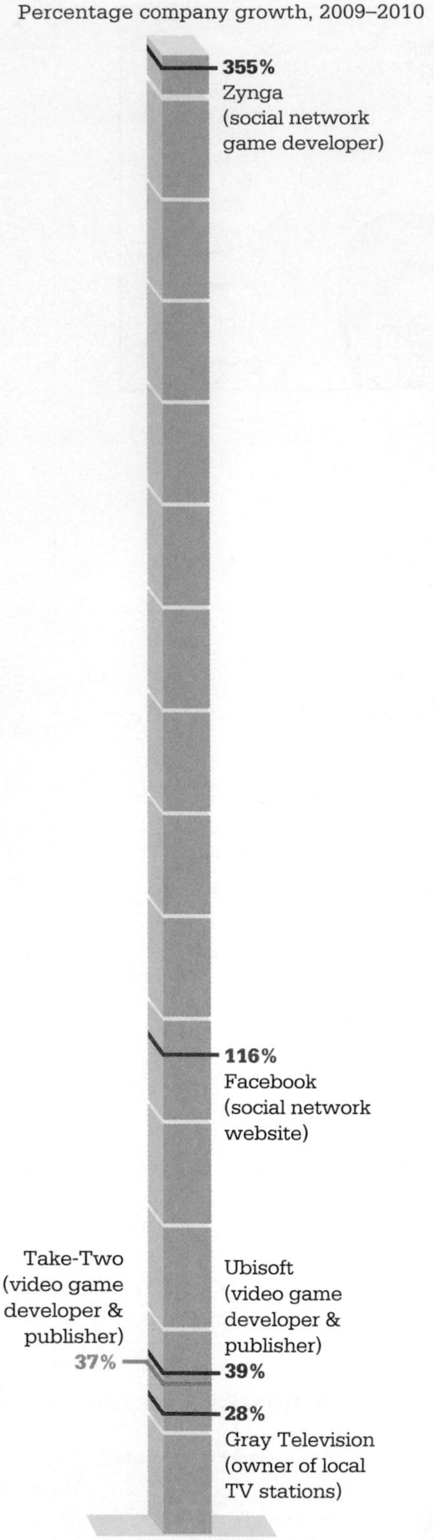

▲ **Figure 9.2** Fastest-Growing Media
Companies, 2010.
Source: Johnson, 2011a.

- The global gamer population has exploded from 250 million to 1.5 billion in that same time (Masnick & Ho, 2012).
- Thirty-five percent of parents of gamers play weekly with their children; 78% say games are a good opportunity to socialize with their kids.

Scope and Nature of the Video-Game Industry

The United States accounts for about half of the approximately $72 billion worldwide video-game industry market. Half of this total is spent on software (in 2008 surpassing for the first time the annual amount expended on DVDs), more than 3 billion individual game purchases (Masnick & Ho, 2012). Note in Figure 9.2 that three of the fastest-growing media companies in the world are video game businesses. The 2011 release of *Call of Duty: Modern Warfare 3* made over $400 million in its first 24 hours, and its $1 billion in 16 days topped by one day the movie *Avatar*'s record of fastest popular culture title to a billion dollars (Masnick & Ho, 2012).

As is the case with every media industry we've studied so far, concentration and globalization are the rule in gaming. Game console sales are the sole province of three companies—the United States' Microsoft, best known for Xbox and Kinect, and two Japanese companies, Nintendo (Wii) and Sony (PlayStation). Versions of PlayStation and Xbox have long dominated sales and time-of-play. But Wii, introduced in 2006 to appeal specifically to new, nontraditional gamers, has gained significant popularity, primarily because it permits full-body, interactive play using a variety of control wands rather than the typical game's button-laden controller. In 2010 Microsoft met Wii's challenge with Kinect, a motion-sensitive game that reads players' body movements without controllers or wands of any kind. Equipped with facial- and voice-recognition capabilities, Kinect is the fastest-selling consumer electronics device in history, selling 8 million units in its first 60 days of availability (besting former champs iPhone and iPad; Kato, 2012).

Nintendo's cartridge-based Game Boy Advance, multimedia DSi (released in 2009), and glasses-free 3-D, Internet-capable 3DS (2011) dominate handheld devices. Sony counters with PlayStation Portable (2004), offering Internet access for multiplayer gaming, and Wi-Fi–capable PlayStation Vita (2012), boasting the power and graphics of a console and video streaming from partners such as Netflix. But note that all these consoles and handhelds were recently released in relatively rapid succession. Why? Because hardware makers are struggling to recapture players' loyalty as gamers increasingly abandon consoles and handhelds for smartphones and tablets. Thus, in addition to the frequent upgrades of their mobile devices, all three manufacturers introduced powerful new consoles in 2013. Sony's PlayStation 4 lets players broadcast their games in real time to the Internet, encouraging friends to join in. Its PlayStation Suite offers an array of games that can be played across consoles, handhelds, tablets, and smartphones. Microsoft's Xbox One, while maintaining Kinect's features, is a home entertainment hub, integrating gaming, television, Internet, and movie and music services. When joined with its SmartGlass application, players' tablets become second game and video screens. Nintendo's Wii U comes with a gamepad that is, for all intents and purposes, a touchscreen tablet.

Their dominance in hardware provides Microsoft, Nintendo, and Sony with more than sales revenue. **Third-party publishers**, companies that create games for existing systems, naturally want their best games on the most popular systems. And just as naturally, better games attract more buyers to the systems that support them. Third-party publishers produce their most popular titles for all systems. For example, Activision's *Call of Duty* is available for all consoles and Mac and PC; the hugely popular *Madden NFL*, which sells more than 5 million copies a year, and the *MVP*

Baseball series come from EA Sports; *Metal Gear* is from Konami, *Tony Hawk* from Activision, *Elder Scrolls* is from Bethesda Softworks, and *Batman* from Warner Bros. Interactive. Conversely, Codemaster's *MTV Music Generator* is available only for PlayStation and Xbox, and several third-party publishers produce Wii-only software—for example, Ubisoft and EA's Headgate division. Console makers do produce their own titles. Nintendo has the *Pokémon, Super Mario*, and *Pikmin* series. Sony publishes the *Gran Turismo* line, and Microsoft offers titles such as *XNS Sports* and *Halo*. Concentration exists in the game software business just as it does on the hardware side. Atari owns several game makers, including Infogrames, and EA controls nearly 50% of all video game sales. In mid-2011 EA further increased its dominance of the content side of the industry with its purchase of casual game developer PopCap, source of some of the most popular free online games such as *Bejeweled* and *Plants vs. Zombies*. In an effort to counter this trend, however, a number of websites for independent game designers has sprung up. Most notable is Humble Indie Bundle. Small developers who cannot afford to distribute and market their games on the scale of the big companies upload their games to its website, free of copy- and other theft-protection. Games are designed for all platforms and, once bundled with other games, are for sale at whatever price a player wishes to pay, with a portion of the proceeds going to charity. In its first two years of operation it earned more than $11 million for the site operators, game designers, and charity, and *PC Gamer* magazine named the Humble Indie Bundle its 2011 community heroes for its support of the indie game development market (Francis, 2011).

▲ Will video game players carry a handheld system, even one as powerful as the PlayStation Vita, in addition to a smartphone?

A serious problem faced by third-party game creators is that, as in the more traditional media, especially film, production and marketing costs are skyrocketing. Not only has the production technology itself become more sophisticated and therefore expensive, but games, like movie stars, build followings. Given that, the creative forces behind them can demand more recognition and compensation. In 2001, the average game cost $5 million to produce and $2 million to promote. Today, the cost of development *alone* is between $15 and $25 million, and a blockbuster like *Grand Theft Auto IV* costs $100 million to produce and tens of millions more to promote. Again, as with film, industry insiders and fans are expressing concern over the industry's reliance on sequels of franchises and licensed content, including movie- and television-based games. For example, there are over 65 different *Mario* games, and money is increasingly diverted to paying to license properties like *James Bond 007* and *Spider-Man*. And while industry research indicates that a majority of players want game makers to rely less on licensed content and sequels, those wants are in conflict with three important realities of the contemporary game industry—production, promotion, and distribution costs are soaring; 50% of all games introduced to the market fail; and every one of the

▲ Two very popular titles from third-party publishers, *Madden NFL* and *360 Call of Duty*.

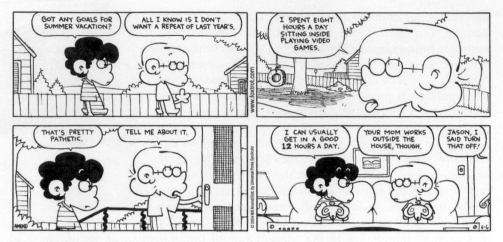

top 10 best-selling games in 2011 and 2012 was either a sequel to a franchise or a licensed title. Buffeted by difficult economic times like other media, the game industry wants to mitigate its risks, and when franchise titles such as *Call of Duty* and *Grand Theft Auto* can top $500 million in sales in their first few days of availability, insiders see sequels a reasonable strategy.

Trends and Convergence in the Video-Game Industry

Like every media industry we've studied, the game industry is experiencing significant change, most of it driven by convergence and hypercommercialism.

Convergence Everywhere

Cable television giants Comcast and Cox each offer fee-based game services for their broadband customers; both DBS providers also offer interactive game services. Most Internet service providers (see Chapter 10) provide some form of online interactive game playing. AOL's iPlay, for example, offers scores of games from designers such as EA Sports, TryMedia, and Funkitron. The service is free for AOL subscribers, and its

▼ Social networking site games like *Happy Aquariums* and *Farmville* attract tens of millions of daily, primarily female, players.

goal is to keep existing broadband users while attracting new ones. The game site of another ISP, Yahoo!, draws nearly 5 million unique monthly visitors. Many game makers, too, offer online interactive gaming. EA's Pogo.com has 9 million subscribers competing in board, puzzle, word, casino, sports, and card games, some for free and some for a fee.

We've already seen that the new generation of handheld game devices is Internet capable. And in an obvious bow to convergence, all three new consoles are designed to perform a wide range of game and nongame functions, including playing DVDs, burning music CDs, and providing Internet access with music and video streaming capability, all in widescreen HDTV and digital multichannel sound. For example, Clear Channel's iHeart Radio brings more than 800 live concert broadcast and digital-only radio stations to Xbox users who, if they have Kinect, can control their listening through voice and body movements. Xbox users can also access Slacker's personal radio service and its tens-of-millions of music tracks, and if they subscribe to Microsoft's SmartGlass service, they can stream any and all content from their smartphones and tablets to their televisions through their gaming consoles. Manufacturer Samsung sells television sets that connect viewers directly to its cache of games housed on its distant, dedicated servers (see *cloud computing* in Chapter 10). Cable companies Verizon and Comcast and program providers like HBO, Epix, Netflix, and Hulu stream content via game consoles. In fact, people with home game consoles spend 22% of their time with those devices watching streamed video (Friedman, 2013b) and in 2012, for the first time, entertainment usage passed multiplayer game usage on the Xbox, that is, users spent more time with online video and music than playing games (Tsukayama, 2012b).

Home computer users, able to interact with other gamers for decades via MUDs, have been joined by console players in flocking to **massively multiplayer online role-playing games** (**MMO**) such as *Ultima Online, World of Warcraft, EverQuest*, and *Second Life*. Thirty million people worldwide play more than 80 **virtual worlds games**, and one, the hugely popular *World of Warcraft*, earns close to $1 billion a year in monthly subscriptions and other revenues (Dibbell, 2007).

Technology and players' comfort with it are two reasons for this wave of convergence—games can be played on cable television, on a dedicated console, on a handheld gamer, online through an ISP or social networking site, online from a game developer's website, online through a game console, online through a tablet or smartphone, and online through a home or office personal computer.

TECHNOLOGY As smaller, faster, more powerful microprocessors were developed and found their way into game consoles, the distinction between games and personal computers began to disappear. A game console with high-speed microprocessors attached to a television set is, for all intents and purposes, a computer and monitor.

COMFORT WITH TECHNOLOGY As the distinction between the technologies on which games are played has diminished, players' willingness to play games on different platforms has grown. Demographics help account for this trend. Speaking at the 10th E^3, the game industry's annual trade show, Entertainment Software Association president Douglas Lowenstein (2005) explained, "Looking ahead, a child born in 1995, E^3's inaugural year, will be 19 years old in 2014. And according to Census Bureau data, by the year 2020, there will be 174 million Americans between the ages of 5 and 44. That's 174 million Americans who will have grown up with PlayStations, Xboxes, and GameCubes from their early childhood and teenage years. . . . What this means is that the average gamer will be both older and, given their lifetime familiarity with playing interactive games, more sophisticated and discriminating about the games they play" (p. 4).

No better evidence of people's comfort with playing games across a variety of technologies exists than that which resides in the smartphone you most probably already use.

Smartphones, Tablets, and Social Networking Sites

Smartphones and tablets are revolutionizing the video game industry. Ninety-two percent of smartphone and tablet owners play games at least once a week; 45% play daily (Baar, 2011). In fact, tablets are now players' preferred platform for gaming—30% of tablet owners say they are playing less on consoles; 36% are playing less on handhelds. And it's not simply tablets' mobility that gamers find attractive; more than 80% of their owners' gameplay is at home (Smith, 2013a). Independent game developers are moving to tablets and smartphones as well. Citing the huge investment in time and money required for developing console games and the growing market for mobile play, more than half say they now create games specifically for tablets and smartphones (Smith, 2013b).

Much, if not most, of today's mobile gaming takes the form of **casual games**—classic games such as card games (poker, cribbage, solitaire), table games (checkers, pool), matching games, and word and trivia games. *Angry Birds*, which lets players fling birds at smug pigs, was downloaded 700 million times in its first three years of existence, and players spend 200 million minutes with the game every day (Anderson, 2012). Casual games can be played in spurts and are easily accommodated by the cell phone's small screen. To be sure, however, casual games are a hit among Internet players as well, with more than 100 million online casual game players regularly visiting sites such as gametap.com, realarcade.com, and pogo.com. They are joined by the tens of millions of gamers, primarily female, playing at social networking sites such as Facebook. *Farmville*, from game publisher Zynga, has more than 80 million active players who, with users of Zynga's other Facebook games like *Mafia Wars*, *Cityville*, and *Draw Something*, total 232 million regular players, accounting for 12% of the social networking site's total $3.7 billion revenue in 2011, income made through players' spending on virtual goods and Facebook ads sold alongside the games (Franzen, 2012). In fact, casual gamers spend more than half their time (56%) on social networking sites playing games, and 51% log in specifically to play (PopCap, 2011). You can see how casual gamers spend their social networking time in Figure 9.3.

Hypercommercialism

Hypercommercialism has come to all media. Advertisers' desire to find new outlets for their messages and avoid the advertising clutter in traditional media has combined with gamers' attractive, segmented demographics to make video games particularly appealing vehicles for many types of commercial and other persuasive campaigns. Advertisers have come to think of games as much like magazines.

Different titles attract different demographics—*Mortal Kombat* and *Grand Theft Auto* draw different players than do *Spider-Man* and MSN Games' *Outsmart Jennifer*

▼ *Crazy Taxi* and *Arena Football* are replete with brands and logos.

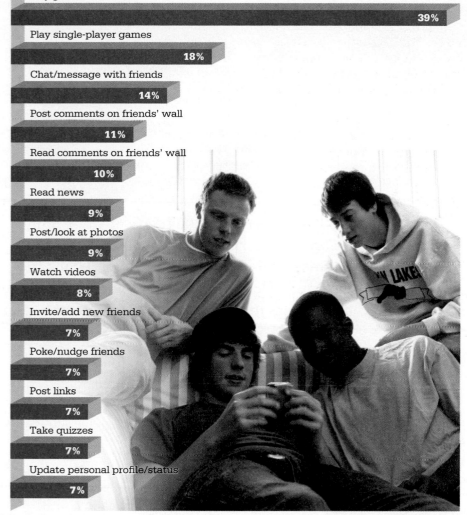

Percentage participating in the activity

Play games with others — 39%

Play single-player games — 18%

Chat/message with friends — 14%

Post comments on friends' wall — 11%

Read comments on friends' wall — 10%

Read news — 9%

Post/look at photos — 9%

Watch videos — 8%

Invite/add new friends — 7%

Poke/nudge friends — 7%

Post links — 7%

Take quizzes — 7%

Update personal profile/status — 7%

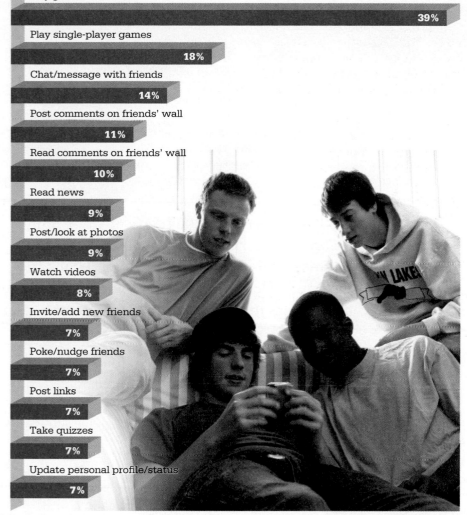

◀ **Figure 9.3** What Casual Gamers Do on Social Networking Sites.
Source: PopCap, 2011.

Lopez. Another reason advertisers are attracted to online games is that they are **sticky**. Players tend to stay (stick) with a game site longer than with other websites. Visitors to EA's pogo.com, for example, spend 25 million hours a month playing games on the site (Traffic Stats, 2010). Regardless of the platform, industry research indicates the average gamer spends two to four hours playing a single game in a single sitting. Sponsors use games to reach their targets in four ways—product placement, freemium games, advergaming, and advocacy gaming.

PRODUCT PLACEMENT Advertisers like product placement for several reasons. First, a product used in a game is there forever—every time the game is played, the advertiser's brand not only appears but is used. Second, the placement is not only permanent, it's Tivo-proof; it can't be skipped. Third, a brand's association with a game renders it "cool," but equally important, games' interactivity creates a stronger emotional connection and therefore a more positive association for players to brands—more so, for example, than simply viewing a TV spot. Fourth, players seem not to mind the ads and even welcome them if it means a game costs less or can be played online for free (Vorhaus, 2009). Fifth, they are effective, and that effectiveness can be measured because the response, clicking through to the sponsor, can be precisely measured. And finally, where in-game ads were once static—a billboard atop a building or a logo on the side of a race car—today's ads are dynamic, that is, a

"The single biggest misconception about games is that they're an escapist waste of time. But more than a decade's worth of scientific research shows that gaming is actually one of the most productive ways we can spend time." With those words expressing the theme of her 2011 book, *Reality Is Broken: Why Games Make Us Better and How They Can Change the World*, Jane McGonigal thrust the value of games into the cultural forum. Although a game developer with success in the games-for-good movement, McGonigal was making the argument that games—period—were good for humanity. Yes, kids may play 100,000 hours of video games before they turn 21, but it's not wasted time. By giving them a sense of accomplishment, meaning, and productivity, game play is producing a new generation of "super-empowered hopeful individuals." For example, networked games like *LittleBigPlanet* teach collaboration; games with rewards like *Foursquare* teach motivation; pro-social games like *Super Mario Sunshine* teach altruism. She points to the more than 6 million cumulative years people have spent in the *World of Warcraft*, just about the same amount of time since humans first walked upright. These gamers, she argues, aren't just enjoying themselves, they're literally evolving in real time.

But, counters tech writer Dave Gilson, "Never mind that Americans watch nearly 29 million years of TV every single year, yet no one suggests our living rooms are a modern-day Olduvai Gorge [the Cradle of Mankind]" (2011, p. 56). And social scientists are equally skeptical of games' purity of purpose. Craig Anderson and his colleagues demonstrated a causal relationship between playing violent games like *Grand Theft Auto* and both short- and long-term aggression (Anderson et al., 2003). Another group of psychologists found a causal link between more than two hours a day of game playing and attention disorders in kids that persist into early adulthood (Swing et al., 2010). Still another team of researchers discovered that 8.5% of American youth who play video games show multiple signs of behavioral addiction, including "spending increasing amounts of time and money on video games to feel the same level of excitement; irritability

> "Kids may play 100,000 hours of video games before they turn 21, but it's not wasted time. By giving them a sense of accomplishment, meaning, and productivity, game play is producing a new generation of 'super-empowered hopeful individuals.'"

or restlessness when play is scaled back; escaping problems through play; skipping chores or homework to spend more time at the controller; lying about the length of playing time; and stealing games or money to play more" (in St. George, 2009).

But, answers video game industry group Entertainment Software Association (2012), if there is a problem with game playing, it's up to people, especially parents, to monitor their own play. The ESA notes that 45% of parents play games with their children at least once a week; 68% believe that game play provides mental stimulation or education; 57% say games encourage family time; and 54% think games help their kids connect with friends. Not only do parents seem to agree with Jane McGonigal about the benefits of gaming, but industry sales data suggest that the "bad" games identified by those social scientists are a small minority of all games sold, only 17%.

Enter your voice. Games, good or bad? Of course, you know it's a much more complicated matter than that. Games do have negative effects on some people, and they clearly can be a good in people's lives. So where do you stand, given the information provided here? Revisit your answer after you read the scientific evidence demonstrating the effects of media on attitudes and behaviors in Chapter 13 and officials' ability to regulate those media in Chapter 14.

◄ Critics argue that there can be little good in scenes like this from *Grand Theft Auto*.

sponsor can alter them remotely and on-the-fly, tailoring them to specific locations and times-of-day.

But why, beyond the cash they earn, do game designers want product placements in their creations, a practice begun in the 1980s when Sega put Marlboro banners in its arcade racing games? First, brand names add a bit of realism to the game's virtual world, presumably enhancing the player's enjoyment. Second, advertisers and game makers frequently engage in cross-promotion. For example, Sprite billboards highlight Activision's *Street Hoops* and the soda maker pushes the game on its cans and in its ads. Champs Sports, featured everywhere in EA's *Arena Football*, encourages shoppers in its 600 stores to play the game on specially designed kiosks in order to win Champs merchandise.

So mutually beneficial has game product placement become that placements, which can cost more than $1 million in a popular game, are frequently bartered for free; that is, the game maker and the brand advertiser exchange no money. The brand image is provided to the designer (for realism) and the sponsor gets placement (for exposure). Industry estimates are that by 2014 in-game advertising will generate $1 billion in revenues for game makers (Entertainment Software Association, 2012).

FREEMIUM GAMES Even more deeply integrating products into games are **freemium games**, in which advertising serves as in-game virtual currency. Freemiums happen in a number of ways. In some games, in exchange for watching a commercial, players can obtain virtual goods, like weapons or armor, rather than work to earn the credits necessary to buy them (most players given this option take it). In others, choosing to use a brand-name product imbues players with special in-game attributes unavailable to players content with generic products. Online game site Outspark's snowboarding game, for example, gives players opting to wear Rocawear ski apparel magical trick-performing powers that earn them extra points.

ADVERGAMING Product placement in games has proven so successful that, in many instances, brands have become the games themselves in **advergames**. Advergaming typically occurs in two ways, on CD-ROM and via the Internet to either consoles or mobile devices; and online advergaming typically takes the form of brand-specific sites and game sites unaffiliated with a single sponsor but offering brand-based games. The auto industry, for example, makes good use of CD-ROM advergames. Chrysler distributes free games and has even set up gaming kiosks in some dealerships. Its Jeep game encourages players to take a Jeep anywhere, do anything. Crashes are okay—a click does the necessary bodywork. Half of all recipients of an advergame will play it for an average of 25 minutes (Entertainment Software Association, 2012).

Brand-specific game websites are sometimes downloadable from the Net, sometimes played while connected. Either way, their goal is to produce an enjoyable experience for players while introducing them to the product and product information. Volkswagen, for example, distributes a free iPhone game app called *Real Racing GTI*. Players compete against other drivers for a chance to win a real car and can communicate with them via Twitter. Particularly exciting laps can be uploaded to *Real Racing*'s YouTube channel. Payment card network Visa Inc. opts for a different approach,

▼ Volkswagen's *Real Racing GTI* and Visa's *Financial Soccer* represent two of gaming's most successful advergames.
Financial Soccer, © 2010 Visa. All rights reserved. Reprinted with permission. *Financial Soccer* is part of *Practical Money Skills for Life*, Visa's free, award-winning, financial education program. *Financial Soccer* is a fast-paced, multiple-choice question video game, testing players' knowledge of financial management skills as they advance down field, and try to score goals.

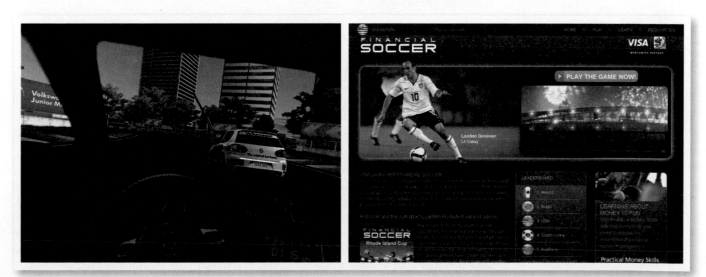

▲ *Fatworld* is an advocacy game exploring the relationships between obesity, nutrition, and socioeconomics in the United States.
ITVS Interactive, "Online Video Game, Fatworld", Public Broadcasting Service-Independent Lens, http://www.fatworld. org. © 2006 Persuasive Games, LLC. All Rights Reserved. Reprinted by permission.

partnering with FIFA to sponsor a World Cup soccer educational video game on its website created specifically to foster financial literacy. Cable television's Hallmark Channel goes in even another direction, establishing its own game site, *Fun & Games*, which offers more than 1,000 online and downloadable games, all coincidentally designed to promote its basic cable programming.

Unaffiliated game sites that offer brand-specific games, however, have raised the question of fairness. Critics argue that embedding brand characters and logos in non-brand-specific games masks the true intent of those games. Neopets.com, for example, calls itself "the greatest Virtual Pet Site on the Internet." It explains to its primarily preteen players, "With your help, we have built a community of over 70 million virtual pet owners across the world! Neopets has many things to offer including over 160 games, trading, auctions, greetings, messaging, and a tree with a giant brain. Best of all, it's completely FREE!" The games, however, include the *Lucky Charms Super Search Game*, the *Nestlé Ice Cream Frozen Flights* game, the *Pepperidge Farms Goldfish Sandwich Snacks* game, *McDonald's: Meal Hunt* game, and visits to the Disney or General Mills theaters where points are awarded for watching commercials. The company assures parents that all sponsored content is clearly labeled, but critics respond that little kids don't know the difference between an ad campaign and a game, even if it is is so identified.

ADVOCACY GAMING Companies or organizations wanting to get their noncommercial messages out are also turning to **advocacy games**, primarily on the Web and for mobile devices. Many national political candidates are "supported" by advocacy games. Particularly popular among college-age voters is the still-playable arcade game *Obama Race for the White House Game*. Dr. Ian Bogost, who created the genre with his 2004 release of the still-playable *Howard Dean for Iowa Game*, said, "I didn't get into games because I wanted to reach a demographic, I did it because I think games can communicate political concepts and processes better than other forums" (quoted in Erard, 2004, p. G1).

Supporters of political advocacy games see three significant strengths. First, the games are relatively inexpensive. A good political game can be created in about three weeks for about $20,000, well under the cost of television time. Second, like other advergames, they are sticky and the message is reinforced with each play (broadcast ads are fleeting). Finally, they are interactive, making them a powerful means of communicating with potential voters, especially younger ones. More traditional forms of advocacy messaging, such as radio and television ads and campaign fliers, passively engage voters with their campaign rhetoric. But games encourage potential voters to interact with the message.

Not all advocacy games are about politics, however. There are games advocating the use of energy alternatives to oil (*Oiligarchy*), religious freedom (*Faith Fighter*), a more flexible application of copyright (*The Free Culture Game*), and improving kids' nutrition (*Fatworld*).

DEVELOPING MEDIA LITERACY SKILLS

Using the ESRB Ratings

The link between games and antisocial behavior has been at issue ever since there have been games, finding particular urgency after dramatic events like those in Jonesboro and at Columbine High. In 1998, 13-year-old Mitchell Johnson and 11-year-old Andrew Golden of Jonesboro, Arkansas, heavy players of the shooting game *GoldenEye 007*, set off fire alarms at their middle school and shot at students and teachers as they fled the building. In 1999, *Doom* fans 18-year-old Eric Harris and 17-year-old Dylan Klebold killed 12 students and one teacher and wounded 23 at Columbine High School in Colorado. In each instance, the teens' "addiction" to games was prominently noted. The Columbine shooters had even created a custom *Doom* to represent the shooting of their classmates.

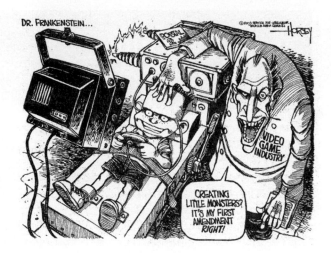

Congress first investigated the effects of video games in 1993, the same year that *Doom* was released for home computers. In an effort to head off government restrictions, in 1994 the industry established the Entertainment Software Ratings Board (ESRB) rating system. It has six ratings (a seventh, RP for Rating Pending, is the equivalent of "this film has not yet been rated"):

EC	Early Childhood	ages 3 and up
E	Everyone	ages 6 and up
E10+		ages 10 and up
T	Teen	ages 13 and up
M	Mature	ages 17 and up
AO	Adults Only	ages 18 and up

Like the movie rating system, the ESRB system requires that games offer content descriptors somewhere on the front or back of the game package explaining why a particular rating was assigned. Although the Federal Trade Commission has lauded the ESRB ratings as the most comprehensive of the three industries' (games, recordings, movies), media-literate gamers (or friends and parents of gamers) should understand the strengths and weaknesses of this system. Depending on your perspective, this self-regulation is either a good thing because it keeps government's intrusive hand out of people's lives and protects game makers' First Amendment rights, or a bad thing because it is self-serving and rarely enforced. The value of the content descriptors, too, is in dispute. All a game maker is required to list is *any one* of the descriptors that has led to a given rating—for example, *strong lyrics*. For some, this is useful information. For others, it masks potential problems. First, according to the ESRB system, if this content is sufficient to give the game an M rating, no other content that might have contributed to that rating, such as *mature sexual themes* and *violence*, need be listed. Second, *strong lyrics* might apply to song lyrics about sex, violence, alcohol, or drug use. Only when the game is played will the player identify the reason for the rating and descriptor.

An additional concern over the rating system is that it is poorly enforced. A National Institute on Media and the Family study showed that 87% of boys and 46% of girls played M-rated games. Their average age was 13.5 years old. More than half the parents did not understand the system, and the Federal Trade Commission discovered that 69% of children under 17 who attempted to buy an M-rated game succeeded (Meehan, 2004). One solution, in voluntary use in Canada, is the Retail Council of Canada's "Commitment to Parents" program. Participating game outlets hang posters and distribute brochures explaining the ESRB ratings. Many have installed automatic cash register prompts that alert salespeople when M-rated games are being rented or bought. You can read the box entitled "Are Games Good or Bad?" to get additional background on why many people think rating video games is a good idea.

Select five games that feature both male and female characters. For each of those people list the first three descriptors that come to mind as you look at them. Are there common traits among the men? Among the women? If so, why do you think they exist? How realistic are the portrayals of the men? Of the women? Can you explain your findings and your reactions to those findings in terms of these media literacy skills: Your *ability and willingness to pay attention to and understand video game content*; your *respect for the power of games' messages*; and your *ability to distinguish emotional from reasoned reactions when playing video games*?

Media-literate game players have *an understanding of the ethical and moral obligations of those who design the games they play*. Keep this in mind as you read what Entertainment Software Association President Douglas Lowenstein had to say about video game content, "It is one thing to say a product is protected speech, which it is, or that it is rated and parents need to accept responsibility for what their kids play, which they do. But it is quite another thing to say we have no larger responsibility for shaping the quality and values of the culture we live in" (2005). Given what you've learned in this exercise about games' portrayal of men and women, can you address the question of the ethics of gender representation in video games?

Resources for Review and Discussion

REVIEW POINTS: TYING CONTENT TO LEARNING OUTCOMES

▶ **Outline the history and development of games and the gaming industry.**
  - ▸ While the pinball games developed by David Gottlieb and Harry Williams are the precursors to video games, Steve Russell, Nolan Bushnell, and Ralph Baer are most responsible for what we now call electronic video games.
  - ▸ A game is a video game when a player has direct involvement in some on-screen action to produce a desired outcome.

▶ **Describe how the organizational and economic nature of the contemporary gaming industry shapes the content of games.**
  - ▸ Games are most frequently played on game consoles (home and portable), PCs, and the Internet, but increasingly smartphones are serving as a popular game platform.
  - ▸ Game consoles are the sole province of Microsoft, Nintendo, and Sony.
  - ▸ Third-party publishers design games for the most popular systems.
  - ▸ Rising costs in the production of games have led to hypercommercialism and a reliance on blockbusters, franchises, and sequels.
  - ▸ Hypercommercialism in games takes the form of product placement and advertising.

▶ **Explain the relationship between games and their players.**
  - ▸ The demographics of America's 135 million gamers closely match the demographics of all Americans.
  - ▸ Adult women represent a larger proportion of the game-playing population than boys under 18, primarily because of the growth of casual games.

▶ **Identify changes in the game industry brought about by new and converging technologies.**
  - ▸ Convergence, driven by more powerful technology and people's comfort with it, has overtaken gaming, as games can be played on a host of platforms.
  - ▸ Wi-Fi-capable handheld devices, smartphones, and tablets have not only freed games from the console, but have fueled the rise of casual games and swelled the ranks of female and adult players.
  - ▸ Social networking sites like Facebook further encourage these changes.

▶ **Apply key game-playing media literacy skills.**
  - ▸ The ESRB game-rating system is much admired but still raises important questions for media-literate game players; for example, how reliable are they, and whose obligation is it to ensure responsible game play?

KEY TERMS

QUESTIONS FOR REVIEW

1. Who are David Gottlieb and Harry Williams? What were their contributions to the development of pinball?

2. How did *Pong* affect the development of video gaming?

3. What makes a video game a *video game*?

4. What are the most frequently employed platforms for game playing?

5. What is a third-party publisher?

6. What determines whether a third-party publisher creates a game for a given platform?

7. How does product placement occur in games?

8. What are the different forms of advergaming?

9. What is advocacy gaming?

10. What are the levels of the ESRB rating system?

connect

For further review, go to the LearnSmart study module for this chapter.

QUESTIONS FOR CRITICAL THINKING AND DISCUSSION

1. What is your favorite game platform? Why? Do you think different types of players gravitate toward different platforms? Why or why not?

2. Does advergaming, especially where children are the players, bother you? Do you find advergaming inherently deceptive for these young players? Why or why not?

3. Have you ever played an advocacy game? If so, what was it? Was it from a group with which you were sympathetic? What would it take to get you to play a game from a site with which you disagree?

The Internet and the World Wide Web

10

Learning Objectives

It is not an overstatement to say that the Internet and World Wide Web have changed the world, not to mention all the other mass media. In addition to being powerful communication media themselves, the Net and the Web sit at the center of virtually all the media convergence we see around us. After studying this chapter you should be able to

▶ Outline the history and development of the Internet and World Wide Web.

▶ Explain the potential cultural value of the Internet and World Wide Web.

▶ Describe how the organizational and economic nature of the contemporary Internet and World Wide Web industries shapes their content.

▶ Identify alterations in the nature of mass communication made possible by the Internet, the World Wide Web, and their convergence with all media.

▶ Analyze social and cultural questions posed by the Internet, World Wide Web, and related emerging technologies.

▶ Describe the relationship between these new media and their various users and audiences.

▶ Apply key Internet and World Wide Web media literacy skills, especially in protecting your privacy and reflecting on the Net's double edge of (potentially) good and troublesome change.

The Internet was and is at the heart of the Middle East democracy movement.

WILLIAM GIBSON AND MARSHALL MCLUHAN HAVE BEEN TWO OF YOUR INTELLECTUAL HEROES EVER SINCE YOU STARTED COLLEGE. Gibson is called the godfather of cyberspace, originator of the term, and is the author of *Neuromancer* and *Johnny Mnemonic*. McLuhan is the author of *Understanding Media: The Extensions of Man* and originator of some of your favorite expressions such as "hot and cool media" and "the medium is the message." But now, as you see it, Gibson and McLuhan are in conflict.

For example, another of McLuhan's famous expressions is "the global village." You understood this to mean that as media "shrink" the world, people will become increasingly involved in one another's lives. As people come to know more about others who were once separated from them by distance, they will form a new, beneficial relationship, a global village.

Then you saw Gibson interviewed on television. His vision of technology's impact on the globe was anything but optimistic. He said, "We're moving toward a world where all the consumers under a certain age will . . . identify more with their consumer status or with the products they consume than they would with an antiquated notion of nationality. We're increasingly interchangeable" (as cited in Trench, 1990).

Maybe you were wrong about McLuhan's ideas. He did his influential writing a long time ago. Where was it you read about the global village? In a magazine interview? You look it up at the library to confirm that you understood him correctly. There it is, just as you thought: "The human tribe can become truly one family and man's consciousness can be freed from the shackles of mechanical culture and enabled to roam the cosmos" ("A Candid Conversation," 1969, p. 158).

McLuhan's global village is an exciting place, a good place for people enjoying increased contact and increased involvement with one another aided by electronic technology. Gibson's nationless world isn't about involving ourselves in one another's lives and experiences. It's about electronic technology turning us into indistinguishable nonindividuals, rallying around products. We are united by buyable things,

1885 ▲ Babbage designs "computer"

1940s British develop Colossus and binary code

1946 ▲ ENIAC

1950 UNIVAC

1951 Census Bureau makes first successful commercial use of computers

1957 ▲ *Sputnik* launched

1960 Licklider's *Man–Computer Symbiosis*; IBM mainframe technology

1962 ARPA commissions Baran to develop computer network

1964 McLuhan's *Understanding Media*

1969 ARPAnet goes online

identifying not with others who share our common culture but with those who share common goods. McLuhan sees the new communication technologies as expanding our experiences. Gibson sees them more negatively. You respect and enjoy the ideas of both thinkers. How can you reconcile the disagreement you have uncovered?

We begin this chapter with an examination of the **Internet**, the "new technology" that helped bring Gibson to prominence and gave renewed life to Marshall McLuhan's ideas. We study the history of the Internet, beginning with the development of the computer, and then we look at the Net as it exists today. We examine its formats and its capabilities, especially the popular World Wide Web. The number and nature of today's Internet users are also discussed.

Many of the issues discussed here will be familiar to you. Given the fundamental role that the Internet plays in encouraging and permitting convergence, concentration, audience fragmentation, globalization, and hyper-commercialism, you should not be surprised that we've "met" the Internet and the Web before now in discussing the more traditional media.

The Web and Net are significantly reshaping the operation of those media, and as the media with which we interact change, the role they play in our lives and the impact they have on us and our culture will likewise be altered. We will look at the new technology's double edge (its ability to have both good and bad effects), the Internet's ability to foster greater freedom of expression, efforts to control that expression, changes in the meaning of and threats to personal privacy, and the promise and perils of practicing democracy online.

Finally, our discussion of improving our media literacy takes the form of an examination of the five Internet freedoms. But first, the Internet.

▲ William Gibson.

1970	**1985**	**2000**
1972 ▲ E-mail	**1990** ▲ HTTP developed	**2000** U.S. women pass men as users
1974 Internet emerges	**1992** Internet society chartered	**2004** ▲ Facebook launched
1975 Gates develops PC operating system	**1994** Spam appears; First banner ad	**2006** Twitter
1977 Jobs and Wozniak develop Apple II	**1995** Classmates.com	**2007** Laptops outsell desktops; Apple app store opens
1979 BITNET		**2009** Internet surpasses newspapers as news source; Social networking surpasses e-mail for person-to-person communication
1981 IBM PC introduced		**2010** First popular tablet computer
		2012 25th billion app download from Apple app store; Facebook buys Instagram; Mobile becomes top e-mail platform
		2013 Tablets outsell laptops; smartphones outsell cellphones

A Short History of the Internet

There are conflicting versions about the origins of the Internet. In the words of media historian Daniel J. Czitrom (2007), they involve "the military and the counterculture, the need for command and control and the impulse against hierarchy and toward decentralization" (p. 484). The more common story—the command-and-control version—is that the Net is a product of the Cold War. In this version, the air force in 1962, wanting to maintain the military's ability to transfer information around the country even if a given area was destroyed in an enemy attack, commissioned leading computer scientists to develop the means to do so. But many researchers and scientists dispute this "myth that [has] gone unchallenged long enough to become widely accepted as fact," that the Internet was initially "built to protect national security in the face of nuclear attack" (Hafner & Lyon, 1996, p. 10).

In the second version, the decentralization version, as early as 1956 psychologist Joseph C. R. Licklider, a devotee of Marshall McLuhan's thinking on the power of communication technology, foresaw linked computers creating a country of citizens "informed about, and interested in, and involved in, the process of government" (as quoted in Hafner & Lyon, 1996, p. 34). He foresaw "home computer consoles" and television sets connected in a nationwide network. "The political process would essentially be a giant teleconference," he wrote, "and a campaign would be a months-long series of communications among candidates, propagandists, commentators, political action groups, and voters. The key," he added, "is the self-motivating exhilaration that accompanies truly effective interaction with information through a good console and a good network to a good computer" (p. 34).

In what many technologists now consider to be the seminal essay on the potential and promise of computer networks, *Man–Computer Symbiosis*, Licklider, who had by now given up psychology and devoted himself completely to computer science, wrote in 1960, "The hope is that in not too many years, human brains and computing machines will be coupled . . . tightly, and the resulting partnership will think as no human brain has ever thought and process data in a way not approached by the information handling machines we know today" (as quoted in Hafner & Lyon, 1996, p. 35). Scores of computer experts, enthused by Licklider's vision (and many more who saw networked computers as a way to gain access to the powerful but otherwise expensive and unavailable computers just beginning to become available), joined the rush toward the development of what we know today as the **Internet**, a global network of interconnected computers that communicate freely and share and exchange information.

Development of the Computer

The title "originator of the computer" resides with Englishman Charles Babbage. Lack of money and unavailability of the necessary technology stymied his plan to build an Analytical Engine, a steam-driven computer. But in the mid-1880s, aided by the insights of mathematician Lady Ada Byron Lovelace, Babbage did produce designs for a "computer" that could conduct algebraic computations using stored memory and punch cards for input and output. His work provided inspiration for those who would follow.

Over the next 100 years a number of mechanical and electromechanical computers were attempted, some with success. But Colossus, developed by the British to break the Germans' secret codes during World War II, was the first electronic **digital computer**. It reduced information to a **binary code**—that is, a code made up of the digits 1 and 0. In this form information could be stored and manipulated. The

▲ Marshall McLuhan.

▼ Joseph C. R. Licklider envisioned a national system of interconnected home computers as early as 1956.

first "full-service" electronic computer, ENIAC (Electronic Numerical Integrator and Calculator), based on the work of Iowa State's John V. Atanasoff, was introduced by scientists John Mauchly and John Presper Eckert of the Moore School of Electrical Engineering at the University of Pennsylvania in 1946. ENIAC hardly resembled the computers we know today: 18 feet tall, 80 feet long, and weighing 60,000 pounds, it was composed of 17,500 vacuum tubes and 500 miles of electrical wire. It could fill an auditorium and ate up 150,000 watts of electricity. Mauchly and Eckert eventually left the university to form their own computer company, later selling it to the Remington Rand Corporation in 1950. At Remington they developed UNIVAC (Universal Automatic Computer), which, when bought for and used by the Census Bureau in 1951, became the first successful commercial computer.

The commercial computer explosion was ignited by IBM. Using its already well-entrenched organizational system of trained sales and service professionals, IBM helped businesses find their way in the early days of the computer revolution. One of its innovations was to sell rather than rent computers to customers. As a result of IBM's success, by 1960 the computer industry could be described as "IBM and the Seven Dwarfs"—Sperry, Control Data, Honeywell, RCA, NCR, General Electric, and Burroughs (Rosenberg, 1992, p. 60).

Military Applications

In 1957 the Soviet Union launched *Sputnik*, Earth's first human-constructed satellite. The once-undisputed supremacy of the United States in science and technology had been usurped, and U.S. scientists and military officials were in shock. The Advanced Research Projects Agency (ARPA) was immediately established to sponsor and coordinate sophisticated defense-related research. In 1962, as part of a larger drive to promote the use of computers in national defense (and giving rise to one of the stories of the Net's origins), ARPA commissioned Paul Baran of the Rand Corporation to produce a plan that would enable the U.S. military to maintain command over its missiles and planes if a nuclear attack knocked out conventional means of communication. The military thought a decentralized communication network was necessary. In that way, no matter where the bombing occurred, other locations would be available to launch

CHAPTER 10 The Internet and the World Wide Web **235**

▲ The Soviet Union's 1-foot-in-diameter, 184-pound *Sputnik* was not only the first human-made satellite to orbit Earth; it sent shudders throughout the American scientific and military communities.

a counterattack. Among Baran's plans was one for a "packet switched network." He wrote,

> Packet switching is the breaking down of data into datagrams or packets that are labeled to indicate the origin and the destination of the information and the forwarding of these packets from one computer to another computer until the information arrives at its final destination computer. This (is) crucial to the realization of a computer network. If packets are lost at any given point, the message can be resent by the originator. (As cited in Kristula, 1997, p. 1)

The genius of the system Baran envisioned is twofold: (1) common communication rules (called **protocols**) and common computer languages would enable any type of computer, running with any operating system, to communicate with another; and (2) destination or delivery instructions embedded in all information sent on the system would enable instantaneous "detours" or "rerouting" if a given computer on the network became unavailable.

Using Honeywell computers at Stanford University, UCLA, the University of California, Santa Barbara, and the University of Utah, the switching network, called ARPAnet, went online in 1969 and became fully operational and reliable within one year. Other developments soon followed. In 1972 an engineer named Ray Tomlinson created the first e-mail program (and gave us the ubiquitous @). In 1974 Stanford University's Vinton Cerf and the military's Robert Kahn coined the term "the Internet." In 1979 a graduate student at the University of North Carolina, Steve Bellovin, created Usenet and, independent of Bellovin, IBM created BITNET. These two networking software systems enabled virtually anybody with access to a Unix or IBM computer to connect to others on the growing network. By the time the Internet Society was chartered and the World Wide Web was released in 1992, there were more than 1.1 million **hosts**—computers linking individual personal computer users to the Internet. Today there is an ever-expanding number of

► A 1960s-vintage IBM mainframe computer. The personal computer in your home probably carries more computing power than this giant machine.

hosts, close to one hundred million and growing, serving more than 2.3 billion users across the globe, or 33% of the world's population (Internet World Stats, 2012).

The Personal Computer

A crucial part of the story of the Internet is the development and diffusion of personal computers. IBM was fantastically successful at exciting businesses, schools and universities, and other organizations about computers. But IBM's and other companies' **mainframe** and **minicomputers** employed **terminals**, and these stations at which users worked were connected to larger, centralized machines. As a result, the Internet at first was the province of the people who worked in those settings.

When the semiconductor (or integrated circuit, or chip) replaced the vacuum tube as the essential information processor in computers, its tiny size, absence of heat, and low cost made possible the design and production of small, affordable **personal** or **microcomputers (PCs)**. This, of course, opened the Net to anyone, anytime. Laptop computers, which outsold desktop models for the first time in 2007, extended that reach to anywhere. The tablet computer was first introduced in 2006 by Microsoft. It remained a niche computer favored by medical professionals. But the 2010 introduction of the iPad, with its integrated flat screen and operated not by keyboard but by touch screen, not only continued the expansion of computing to anyone, anywhere, it made it even more convenient. In 2013 tablets outsold laptops for the first time and were on schedule to outsell laptops *and* PCs by 2015 (Molina & Swartz, 2013).

The leaders of the personal computer revolution were Bill Gates and the duo of Steve Jobs and Stephen Wozniak. As a first-year college student in 1975, Gates saw a magazine story about a small, low-powered computer, the MITS Altair 8800, that could

▼ The desktop computer opened the Net to anyone, anytime. The laptop extended that reach to anywhere. The tablet made anytime, anywhere more convenient.

be built from a kit and used to play a simple game. Sensing that the future of computing was in these personal computers and that the power of computers would reside not in their size but in the software that ran them, Gates dropped out of Harvard University and, with his friend Paul Allen, founded Microsoft Corporation. They licensed their **operating system**—the software that tells the computer how to work—to MITS. With this advance, people no longer had to know sophisticated operating languages to use computers. At nearly the same time, in 1977, Jobs and Wozniak, also college dropouts, perfected Apple II, a low-cost, easy-to-use microcomputer designed specifically for personal rather than business use. It was immediately and hugely successful, especially in its development of **multimedia** capabilities—advanced sound and image applications. IBM, stung by its failure to enter the personal computer business, contracted with Microsoft to use the Microsoft operating system in its IBM PC, first introduced in 1981. All of the pieces were now in place for the home computer revolution.

The Internet Today

The Internet is most appropriately thought of as a "network of networks" that is growing at an incredibly fast rate. These networks consist of LANs (local area networks), connecting two or more computers, usually within the same building, and **WANs (wide area networks)**, connecting several LANs in different locations. When people access the Internet from a computer in a university library, they are most likely on a LAN. But when several universities (or businesses or other organizations) link their computer systems, their users are part of a WAN.

As the popularity of the Internet has grown, so has the number of **ISPs (Internet service providers)**, companies that offer Internet connections at monthly rates depending on the kind and amount of access needed. There are hundreds of ISPs operating in the United States, including some of the better known such as America Online, EarthLink, and Quest. Americans increasingly find that their ISP and video (cable or FiOS) provider are one and the same—for example, Comcast and Verizon. Half of all U.S. Internet users are served by the five largest ISPs. Through providers, users can avail themselves of numerous services, among them e-mail and VoIP.

With an Internet **e-mail** account, users can communicate with anyone else online, any place in the world. Each person online has a unique e-mail address that works just like a telephone number. There are even online "Yellow Pages" and "White Pages" to help users find other people by e-mail. You may be surprised that 250 billion e-mails are sent each day. But if you are a regular e-mail user, you aren't surprised to learn that another 200 billion unsolicited commercial e-mails, 90% of all global e-mail traffic, are also sent daily, much of this **spam** originating overseas (Elias, 2010). **Instant messaging**, or **IM**, is the real-time version of e-mail, allowing two or more people to communicate instantaneously and in immediate response to one another. IM can also be used for downloading text, audio, and video files and for gaming.

Voice over Internet Protocol (VoIP), pronounced "voyp," is telephone whereby calls are transferred in digital packets over the Internet rather than on circuit-switched telephone wires. Think of it as "voice e-mail." This transformative technology "means any corporation with a network or any individual with a $30-a-month broadband connection can make calls without paying the phone company" ("Finally, 21st Century Phone," 2004, p. 1). Today, one-fourth of American Internet users, 19% of the adult population, have made an online phone call, up from 8% in 2007 (Raine, 2011).

The World Wide Web

Another way of accessing information files is on the Internet via the **World Wide Web** (usually referred to as "the Web"). The Web is not a physical place, or a set of files, or even a network of computers. The heart of the Web lies in the protocols that define its use. The World Wide Web (WWW) uses hypertext transfer protocols (HTTP) to transport files from one place to another. Hypertext transfer was developed in the early

1990s by England's Tim Berners-Lee, who was working at CERN, the international particle physics laboratory near Geneva, Switzerland. Berners-Lee gave HTTP to the world for free. "The Web is more a social creation than a technical one," he wrote. "I designed it for a social effect—to help people work together—and not as a technical toy. The ultimate goal of the Web is to support and improve our web-like existence in the world" (Berners-Lee & Fischetti, 1999, p. 128).

The ease of accessing the Web is a function of a number of components: hosts, URLs, browsers, search engines, and home pages.

HOSTS (COMPUTERS CONNECTED TO THE INTERNET) Most Internet activity consists of users accessing files on remote computers. To reach these files, users must first gain access to the Internet through "wired-to-the-Net" hosts. These hosts are often called servers.

Once users gain access to a host computer on the Internet, they then have to find the exact location of the file they are looking for *on* the host. Each file or directory on the Internet (that is, on the host computer connected to the Internet) is designated by a **URL (uniform resource locator)**. A URL is, in effect, a site's official address. But as any user of the Web knows, sites are more commonly recognized by their **domain names**. The last part of a site's address, the *.com* or *.org*, is its Top Level Domain Name, so we know that .com is a business and .org is a nonprofit. But in 2012 the Internet Corporation for Assigned Names and Numbers, or ICANN, authorized the use of a virtually unlimited number of generic Top-Level Domains to include almost any word or name, for example *.defibrillator* or *.newyorkcity*. It also permits, for the first time, the use of non-Latin language scripts, such as Arabic, Chinese, and Cyrillic. The number of individual domains, or websites, changes by the minute, but in July 2008, two Google software engineers counted more than 1 trillion unique URLs operating on the Internet at the same time (Alpert & Hajaj, 2008). You can see the most heavily trafficked sites in Figure 10.1.

BROWSERS Software programs loaded onto the user's computer and used to download and view Web files are known as **browsers**. Browsers take separate files (text files, image files, and sound files) and put them all together for viewing. Netscape and Internet Explorer are two of the most popular Web browsers.

SEARCH ENGINES Finding information on the Web is simple thanks to **search engines**, software that allows users to navigate the Net simply by entering a search word and pointing and clicking at the resulting on-screen menus. Among the better known are Ask and Bing. Globally, users make more than 113 billion searches a month on scores of search engines, but the best known and most frequently used—69% of all searches worldwide—is Google, which produces its results with technology that uses the collective intelligence of the Web itself; that is, search results are presented and ranked based on how frequently a given site is linked to others ("Digital Fast Facts," 2012).

HOME PAGES Once users reach the intended website, they are greeted by a **home page**— the entryway to the site itself. It not only contains the information the site's creators want visitors to know but also provides **hyperlinks** to other material in that site, as

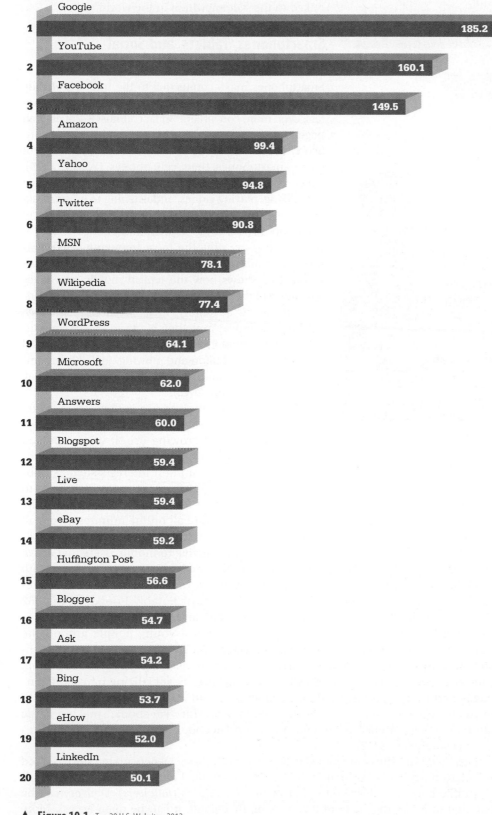

Rank and monthly visitors (in millions)

Rank	Website	Visitors
1	Google	185.2
2	YouTube	160.1
3	Facebook	149.5
4	Amazon	99.4
5	Yahoo	94.8
6	Twitter	90.8
7	MSN	78.1
8	Wikipedia	77.4
9	WordPress	64.1
10	Microsoft	62.0
11	Answers	60.0
12	Blogspot	59.4
13	Live	59.4
14	eBay	59.2
15	Huffington Post	56.6
16	Blogger	54.7
17	Ask	54.2
18	Bing	53.7
19	eHow	52.0
20	LinkedIn	50.1

▲ **Figure 10.1** Top 20 U.S. Websites, 2012.
Source: Quantcast, 2012.

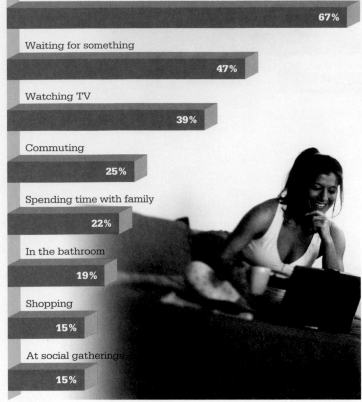

Percent Who Use Mobile While...

Lying in bed
67%

Waiting for something
47%

Watching TV
39%

Commuting
25%

Spending time with family
22%

In the bathroom
19%

Shopping
15%

At social gatherings
15%

▲ **Figure 10.2** When Mobile Device Users
Access the Internet, 2012.
Source: Patel, 2012.

well as to material in other sites on other computers linked to the Net anywhere in the world.

Smartphones, Tablets, and Social Networking Sites

Smartphones make connecting to the Internet, already an anytime/anywhere activity thanks to laptops and tablets, even more convenient. In fact, almost 8% of all Web page views occur on smartphones and tablets (comScore, 2012). In 2013, for the first time, users bought more smartphones than cell phones (Walsh, 2013), which is not surprising, as after browsing the Net, social networking, playing games, and listening to music, making phone calls is only the fifth most frequent use of smartphones (O2, 2012). In fact, smartphones—not PCs, not laptops—are now the most frequently used platform for sending and receiving e-mail (Walsh, 2012a). Figure 10.2 shows how the typical mobile user takes advantage of the technologies' convenience. Spammers, too, are taking advantage of smartphones' mobility, catching users away from their home and office computers. The number of mobile spam messages has doubled since 2009, to 4.5 billion and growing, fueled by unlimited texting plans and mobile carriers' relatively weak spam filters (Oremus, 2012).

Of course, much mobile use is devoted to social networking. Where e-mail was long the Net's most common and fastest-growing use, it was surpassed in 2009 by **social networking sites**, websites that function as online communities of users. These communities are often defined by common interests such as hobbies, professions, or schools, but as the name suggests, users usually visit them to socialize; once there, however, people can gravitate toward groups, more specific categories of interest-bound socializers. Nearly 17% of all online minutes across all platforms is devoted to social networking sites (comScore, 2012), and it was Facebook's specific desire to make itself even more attractive to mobile users that drove the company in 2012 to buy two-year-old, purely mobile photo start-up Instagram for $1 billion. Classmates.com's 1995 launch began the social networking movement, and it was soon followed by similar sites, most notably Friendster in 2002 and LinkedIn in 2003. MySpace, launched in 2003 and hipper and more feature-filled than these earlier efforts, became a favorite of young people around the world until it was unseated by Facebook, Harvard University–specific at birth in 2004, becoming global in 2006. By 2012 the number of Facebookers was 845 billion, more than one-third of the world's Internet population, socializing in over 40 languages and racking up more than 1 trillion page views a month (Marche, 2012). Fourteen percent of all U.S. Internet searches are for "Facebook," making it the country's most searched term, and American Facebook users average 20 minutes a visit (Dougherty, 2012).

These "old line" sites were joined in 2006 by Twitter, a social networking site designed for "micro-blogging," posts of up to 140 characters (called *tweets*) displayed on a sender's profile page and delivered to her or his subscribers (*followers*). Delivery can be restricted to a specific circle of followers or, by default, it can be open access. More than 300 million Internet users are on Twitter, and while much of the activity is innocuous (actor Ashton Kutcher has more than 4 million followers, as does Britney Spears), much of it is serious. As he geared up for his 2012 reelection run, President Barack Obama had 12.8 million followers, and the first—and for a long time, the only—images available to the world of the 2008 Mumbai massacre and the 2010 Haiti earthquake were tweets. Twitter is also at the heart of the ongoing push for democracy in the Middle East, as you'll see in detail in Chapter 15.

The Internet and Its Users

We typically think of people who access a medium as audience members, but the Internet has *users*, not audience members. At any time—or even at the same time—a person may be both *reading* Internet content and *creating* content. E-mail and chat rooms are obvious examples of online users being both audience and creators, but others exist as well. For example, MMOs (Chapter 9) enable entire alternative realities to be simultaneously constructed and engaged, and computer screens that have multiple open windows enable users to "read" one site while creating another, sometimes using the just-read material. With ease we can access the Web, link from site to site and page to page, and even build our own sites. As we saw in Chapter 2, the Internet makes us all journalists, broadcasters, commentators, critics, filmmakers, and advice columnists.

It is almost impossible to tell exactly how many users there are on the Internet. People who own computers are not necessarily linked to the Internet, and people need not own computers to use the Net. Some users access the Net through machines at school, a library, or work. Current best estimates indicate that there are at least 2.5 billion users worldwide—35% of Earth's population and a 566% increase since 2000. Eighty percent of Americans use the Net, a 39% increase (Internet World Stats, 2013). The Net's demographics have undergone a dramatic shift in the last several years. In 1996, for example, 62% of U.S. Internet users were men. In 2000, women became the Net's majority gender for the first time (Hamilton, 2000). Today, women in every age group use the Internet more than do men, and not surprisingly, the younger a person, the greater the likelihood he or she has access to the Net.

Changes in the Mass Communication Process

In Chapter 2 we saw how concentration of ownership, globalization, audience fragmentation, hypercommercialism, and convergence were influencing the nature of the mass communication process. Each redefines the relationship between audiences and media industries. For example, elsewhere in this text we have discussed the impacts of concentration on newspaper readership; of globalization on the type and quality of films available to moviegoers; of audience fragmentation on the variety of channel choices for television viewers; of convergence on the music industry's reinvention; and of hypercommercialism on all media.

The Internet is different from these more traditional media. Rather than changing the relationship between audiences and industries, the Net changes the *definition* of the different components of the process and, as a result, changes their relationship. As you read in Chapter 2, we are the people formerly known as the audience, and many—soon to be most—of us are **digital natives**, people who have never known a world without the Internet. On the Net a single individual can communicate with as large an audience as can the giant, multinational corporation that produces a network television program. That corporation fits our earlier definition of a mass communication source—a large, hierarchically structured organization—but the Internet user does not. Feedback in mass communication is traditionally described as inferential and delayed, but online feedback can be, and very often is, immediate and direct. It is more similar to feedback in interpersonal communication than to feedback in mass communication.

This Internet-induced redefinition of the elements of the mass communication process is refocusing attention on issues such as freedom of expression, privacy, responsibility, and democracy.

▲ Technology, even one with as much potential as the Internet, is only as good as the uses we make of it.

DILBERT: © Scott Adams/Dist. by United Feature Syndicate, Inc.

The Double Edge of Technology

The solution to the McLuhan–Gibson conflict in the opening vignette is one of perspective. McLuhan was writing and thinking in the relative youth of the electronic media. When *Understanding Media* was published in 1964, television had just become a mass medium, the personal computer wasn't even a dream, and Paul Baran was still envisioning ARPAnet.

Gibson, writing much later in the age of electronic media, was commenting from a more experienced position and after observing real-world evidence. McLuhan was optimistic because he was speculating on what electronic media *could do*. Gibson was pessimistic because he was commenting on what he had seen electronic media *doing*.

Still, neither visionary is completely right or completely wrong. Technology alone, even the powerful electronic media that fascinated both, cannot create new worlds or new ways of seeing them. *We* use technology to do these things. This is why technology is a double-edged sword. Its power—for good and for bad—resides in us. The same aviation technology that we use to visit relatives halfway around the world can also be used to destroy the World Trade Center. The same communication technologies used to create a truly global village can be used to dehumanize and standardize the people who live in it.

McLuhan's Renaissance

Marshall McLuhan's ideas are in vogue again. The Canadian English professor was at the center of the early intellectual debate over electronic media. His books—especially *The Gutenberg Galaxy* (1962), *Understanding Media: The Extensions of Man* (1964), and *The Medium Is the Massage* (McLuhan & Fiore, 1967)—generated heated comment and earned McLuhan much criticism. His ideas satisfied almost no one. Critics from the humanities castigated him for wasting his time on something as frivolous as television. True culture exists in "real" literature, they argued. McLuhan fared just as badly among mass communication theorists. Social scientists committed to the idea of limited media effects (see Chapter 13) simply disagreed with his view of powerful media technologies, however optimistic. Others who were convinced of media's potential negative influence dismissed him as blindly in love with technology and overly speculative. Social scientists demanded scientific verification of McLuhan's ideas. Labeled the "High Priest of Popcult," the "Metaphysician of Media," the "Oracle of the Electronic Age," McLuhan may simply have been ahead of his time.

What has returned McLuhan to the forefront of the cultural discussion surrounding the mass media is the Internet. (Remember, some tech historians trace the Net's genesis to a McLuhan acolyte, Joseph C. R. Licklider.) McLuhan's ideas resonate with those who believe the new medium can fulfill his optimistic vision of an involved, connected global village. Those who think the potential of the Internet, like that of television before it, will never fulfill McLuhan's predictions are forced to explain their reasoning in terms of his

▲ The books that put Marshall McLuhan at the center of the debate over electronic communication.

ideas. McLuhan is back, and, as before, he is controversial. *Wired* magazine, the self-proclaimed "Bible of Cyberspace," has anointed McLuhan its patron saint. But as we saw in the opening vignette, not everyone in the cyberworld trusts the technology as much as he did. Two of his concepts, however—the global village and media as extensions of our bodies—are receiving renewed discussion precisely because of the Net.

THE GLOBAL VILLAGE Many concepts survive McLuhan's 1980 death and serve as his legacy. None is more often quoted than the **global village**, the idea that the new communication technologies will permit people to become increasingly involved in one another's lives. Skeptics point out that McLuhan, with this notion, reveals his unrealistic, utopian infatuation with technology. But McLuhan himself never said all would be tranquil in the global village. Yes, he did believe electronic media would permit "the human tribe" to become "one family," but he also realized that families fight:

> There is more diversity, less conformity under a single roof in any family than there is with the thousands of families in the same city. The more you create village conditions, the more discontinuity and division and diversity. The global village absolutely insures maximal disagreement on all points. (McLuhan & Stearn, 1967, p. 279)

Involvement does not mean harmony, but it does mean an exchange of ideas. As McLuhan said, the global village is "a world in which people encounter each other in depth all the time" (p. 280).

MEDIA AS EXTENSIONS OF OUR BODIES Central to McLuhan's view of how media and cultures interact is the idea that media do not *bring* the world to us but rather permit us to experience the world with a scope and depth otherwise impossible. Media, then, are extensions of our bodies. Just as clothes are an extension of our skin, permitting us to wander farther from our warm caves into the cold world; just as the automobile is an extension of our feet, enabling us to travel farther than we could ever walk; television extends our vision and hearing and computers extend our central nervous system. With television we can see and hear around the world, beyond the galaxy, into the future, and into the past. Computers process, sort, categorize, reconfigure, and clarify. McLuhan's message here is not unlike Carey's (1975) ritual view of mass communication. Communication technologies do not deliver or transmit information; they fundamentally alter the relationship between people and their world, encouraging us to construct new meanings for the things we encounter with and through them. Again, McLuhan, "We shape our tools and afterwards our tools shape us" (in Carr, 2011, p. 10).

Reconceptualizing Life in an Interconnected World

What happens to people in the global village? What becomes of audiences and users as their senses are extended technologically? How free are we to express ourselves? Does greater involvement with others mean a loss of privacy? These are only a few of the questions confronting us as we attempt to find the right balance between the good and the bad that come from the new communication technologies.

The Internet and Freedom of Expression

By its very nature the Internet raises a number of important issues of freedom of expression. There is no central location, no on-and-off button for the Internet, making it difficult for those who want to control it. For free expression advocates, however, this freedom from control is the medium's primary strength. The anonymity of its users provides their expression—even the most radical, profane, and vulgar—great protection, giving voice to those who would otherwise be silenced. This anonymity, say advocates of strengthened Internet control, is a breeding ground for abuse. But opponents of control counter that the Net's affordability and ease of use make it our most democratic medium. Proponents of control argue that this freedom brings with it responsibilities that those who create content for other media understand but are ignored by many online. Internet freedom-of-expression issues, then, fall into two broad categories. The first is the Net's potential to make the First Amendment's freedom-of-the-press guarantee a reality for greater numbers of people. The second is the problem of setting boundaries of control.

▶ Activists at MoveOn.org protested a war and rallied millions of people worldwide to their cause. Reprinted by permission of www.moveon.org.

Freedom of the Press for Whom?

Veteran *New Yorker* columnist A. J. Liebling, author of that magazine's "Wayward Press" feature and often called the "conscience of journalism," frequently argued that freedom of the press is guaranteed only to those who own one. Theoretically, anyone can own a broadcast outlet or cable television operation. But the number of outlets in any community is limited, and they are unavailable to all but the richest people and corporations. Theoretically, anyone can own a newspaper or magazine, but again the expense involved makes this an impossibility for most people. Newsletters, like a soap-box speaker on a street corner, are limited in reach, typically of interest to those who already agree with the message,

▲ OccupyWallStreet protesters were self-organizing and hyper-networked.

and relatively unsophisticated when compared with the larger commercial media.

The Net, however, turns every user into a potential mass communicator. Equally important, on the Internet every "publisher" is equal. The websites of the biggest government agency, the most powerful broadcast network, the newspaper with the highest circulation, the richest ad agencies and public relations firms, the most far-flung religion, and the lone user with an idea or cause figuratively sit side by side. Each is only as powerful as its ideas.

In other words, the Net can give voice to those typically denied expression. Writing for the alternative press news service AlterNet, activist L. A. Kauffman said, "The Internet is an agitator's dream: fast, cheap, far-reaching. And with the planetary reach of the World Wide Web, activist networks are globalizing at nearly the pace of the corporate order they oppose" (in Cox, 2000, p. 14). AlterNet's Brad deGraf (2004) later added, "If a paradigm shift from industrial- to information-age and from hierarchies to networks is happening, it will naturally favor those who want that shift to happen. In that sense, it threatens the two-party system in general, Republicans and Democrats alike, because they can't control the game rules as they have in the past, and the 'barrier to entry' just went from 'establishing a third party' to 'self-organizing a movement'" (p. 3).

This paradigm shift is dramatically demonstrated by **flash mobs** (sometimes called **smart mobs**), "large, geographically dispersed groups connected only by thin threads of communications technology . . . drawn together at a moment's notice like schools of fish to perform some collective action" (Taylor, 2003, p. 53). The 5-million-member MoveOn .org is the best-known site for the coordination of flash mobs and, as it has matured, online political action. Using e-mail and instant messaging, MoveOn led the February 15, 2003, worldwide antiwar protest, gathering 400,000 people in New York and 10 million more across the globe to protest the impending war in Iraq. But a website need not be an "activist" site to connect people moved to action. In mid-2011, anticonsumer activists at Adbusters.com sent their subscribers an e-mail suggesting a protest on Wall Street similar to those fueling the Middle East democracy movement. The idea quickly spread via Twitter, Facebook, and image-based Tumblr, and soon there were Occupy Wall Street protests in more than 900 cities around the world, sustaining a movement that had the support of a majority of Americans and that shaped the national political debate for the next year (Garofoli, 2012). "What's really revolutionary about all these gatherings," wrote *Wired* senior editor Bill Wasik, "is the way they represent a disconnected group getting connected, a mega-underground casting off its invisibility to embody itself, formidably, in physical space" (2012, p. 112). Modern political action, he argued is "self-organizing" and "hyper-networked." In other words, the best way to move people to action—to get them away from their computers—is through the computer. You can read about online organizing that unlike Occupy Wall Street, remained very successfully online in the essay entitled "Shutting Down the Internet to Save the Internet."

The Internet also offers expanded expression through Weblogs, or blogs. Before September 11, 2001, blogs were typically personal online diaries. But after that horrible day, possibly because millions of people felt that the mainstream press had left them unprepared and clueless about what was really going on in the world, blogs changed. *Blog* now refers to regularly updated online journals of commentary, often containing links to their commentary. Internet research company Technocrati regularly tracks more than 100 million active blogs worldwide. Technology writer and conservative activist Andrew Sullivan argues that "blogging is changing the media world and could foment a revolution in how journalism functions in our culture," not only because individual bloggers have earned their readers' respect, but because their "personal touch is much more in tune with our current sensibilities than (are) the opinionated magazines and newspapers of old. Readers increasingly doubt the authority of the *Washington Post* or *National Review*" (Sullivan, 2002, p. 43).

Sullivan, former editor of the *New Republic,* says this "means the universe of permissible opinions will expand, unconstrained by the prejudices, tastes or interests of the old-media elite" (quoted in Seipp, 2002, p. 43). In other words, because bloggers in effect own their own presses, they have freedom of the press. And people are taking advantage of that freedom. Revisit Figure 10.1 and you'll see that the 9th, 12th, and 16th most visited U.S. websites exist specifically to house and/or facilitate blogging. Blogs can also be more agile than the traditional media. More so than these older, more cumbersome media they encourage citizen action in a newly *see-through society.* For example, millions of bloggers constantly and in real time fact-check candidates. Some track the flow of money to politicians, connecting it to how they vote on important public issues. They remind the powerful that "little brother" is watching. Images caught by chance on a video-capable cell phone, arcane public data that goes otherwise unexamined, citizen video taken at official events, all make their way to the Internet and to the people. Whistle-blowers distrustful of mainstream outlets can distribute secret or confidential content on Wikileaks.org with total assurance of anonymity. As Web activist Micah Sifry explained, "Even without central direction, the crowd is sourcing the world for interesting news and

▶ The Internet's freedom may give lies great reach. But the Net has a way of dealing with them. Snopes, the self-proclaimed "definitive Internet reference source for urban legends, folklore, myths, rumors, and misinformation," is one of the best. Reprinted by permission of Snopes.com

On January 18, 2012, more than 13 million people joined an online protest that included 115,000 websites going dark or otherwise altering their home-pages in support. Wikipedia, for example, blocked access to all its English-language pages, greeting 162 million visitors with the message, "Imagine a World Without Free Knowledge." Google, too, did its part, placing a censor's black bar over its logo and advising users to call their representatives.

What had inspired Internet users to shut down the Internet were two pieces of legislation—the Stop Online Piracy Act (SOPA) and the Protect Intellectual Property Act (PIPA)—that the movie, television, and music industries said were essential to combating illegal downloading. So important were these bills that those

> "Tens of millions of people who make the Internet what it is joined together to defend their freedoms. The network defended itself."

industries had 241 lobbyists working the halls of Congress on their behalf, spending more than $280 million on the effort (Aguilar, 2012; Scola, 2011).

Opponents, however, saw something much more sinister in these two bills that would have, upon a single complaint from a content owner, empowered the U.S. Justice Department,

without a court order, to demand that American search engines, ISPs, advertising networks, and payment services block foreign-based websites suspected of copyright infringement. The prob-lem, explained the Electronic Frontier Foundation, is that "the legislation would grant the government and private parties unprecedented power to in-terfere with the Internet's underlying infrastructure. The government would be able to force ISPs and search engines to block users' attempts to reach certain websites' URLs . . . Broad immunity provisions (combined with a threat of litigation) would encourage service providers to overblock innocent users or even block websites voluntarily. This gives content companies every incentive to create unofficial blacklists of websites, which service providers would be under pressure to block without regard to the First Amendment" (Electronic Frontier Foundation, 2012).

Did the "collective flexing of Internet muscle" make a difference? Anti-SOPA/PIPA orga-nization Fight for the Future had an answer, "Tech companies and users teamed up. Geeks took to the streets. Tens of millions of people who make the Internet what it is joined to-gether to defend their freedoms. The network defended itself. Whatever you call it, we changed the politics of interfering with the Internet forever—there's no going back" (in Forbes, 2012). And to what extent did the protest change the politics? Three representatives who had co-sponsored SOPA withdrew their support; seven senators who had cosponsored PIPA did the same, and 19 more publicly repudiated it. Both chambers of Congress tabled the legislation. Even the Obama White House was moved to comment, saying it supports action to fight online piracy, but "does not support legislation that reduces freedom of expression . . . or undermines the dynamic, innovative global Internet" (in Tsukayama, 2012a).

◄ Thousands of people in the street and millions more online shut down the Internet to save it.

sharing tidbits constantly" (in Melber, 2008). This is no small matter as the Internet has surpassed newspapers as Americans' primary news source (Mindlin, 2009).

Blogs are not without their critics. *Advertising Age* media writer Simon Dumenco (2006) calls them little more than writers "with a cooler name," referring to membership in the ranks of bloggers of voices from just about every mainstream media outlet and *Fortune* 500 company (p. 18). Whole Foods CEO John Mackey, for example, was outed as the author of a blog he maintained under a pseudonym in which he boosted his supermarket chain as well as himself, and there are companies such as PayPerPost that pay bloggers for mentioning their clients whether they use those clients' products and services or not. All a blogger has to do is log on to view the available "opportunities." A blogger, in other words, is just as likely to be an "insider" as an "outsider." More troubling to blogs' detractors is that bloggers are responsible to no one. Media critic Eric Alterman (2005) says that for political blogs, "The very act of weighing evidence, or even presenting any, is suspect. The modus operandi is accuse, accuse, accuse and see what sticks" (p. 10). Additionally, argue critics, corporate bloggers are often little more than fronts set up to attack competitors. "Bloggers are more of a threat than people realize, and they are only going to get more toxic. This is the new reality," explains Peter Blackshaw, chief marketing officer of a company that polices blogs for commercial clients such as Procter & Gamble and Ford. He estimates that 50% to 60% of the online attacks his clients endure come not from independent bloggers but from competitors (in Lyons, 2005, p. 130).

Controlling Internet Expression

Abuses of the Net's freedom such as these are behind the argument for greater control of the Internet. The very same medium that can empower users who wish to challenge those more powerful than themselves can also be used to lie and cheat. The Internet does not distinguish between true and false, biased and objective, trivial and important. Once misinformation has been loosed on the Net, it is almost impossible to catch and correct it.

The *smear forward* has plagued countless people and organizations. Procter & Gamble was victimized by stories that its cleaners killed pets. Starbucks was falsely accused of refusing to provide coffee to Marines serving in Iraq. Other Internet-sustained falsehoods can have far more damaging real-world effects, such as the scientifically discredited belief that vaccines cause autism, leading many parents to deny their children potentially life-saving vaccinations. Actress Jenny McCarthy, who "has become the public face of the anti-vaccination movement, boasts that much of her knowledge about the harms of vaccination comes from 'the University of Google.' She regularly shares her 'knowledge' about vaccination with her nearly half-million Twitter followers" (Morozov, 2012).

Lies have always been part of human interaction; the Internet only gives them greater reach. "Never has there been a medium as perfectly suited to the widespread anonymous diffusion of misinformation as e-mail," commented *In These Times* editor Christopher Hayes (2007, p. 12). But there is little that government can do to control this abuse. Legal remedies already exist in the form of libel laws and prosecution for fraud. Users can help by teaching themselves to be more attentive to return addresses and by ignoring messages that are sent anonymously or that have suspicious origins. There is an Internet-based solution as well. Hoaxbusters.org maintains an exhaustive, alphabetically organized list and debunking of the Internet's biggest lies. Also of value is Snopes.com, the self-proclaimed "definitive Internet reference source for urban legends, folklore, myths, rumors, and misinformation."

Pornography on the World Wide Web

Most efforts at controlling the Internet are aimed at indecent or pornographic Web content. We will see in Chapter 14 that indecent and pornographic expression is protected. The particular concern with the Internet, therefore, is shielding children.

The Child Pornography Prevention Act of 1996 forbade online transmission of any image that "appears to be of a minor engaging in sexually explicit conduct." Proponents argued that the impact of child porn on the children involved, as well as on society, warranted this legislation. Opponents argued that child pornography per se was already illegal, regardless of the medium. Therefore they saw this law as an unnecessary and overly broad intrusion into freedom of expression on the Net. In April 2002 the Supreme Court sided with the act's opponents. Its effect would be too damaging to freedom of expression. "Few legitimate movie producers or book publishers, or few other speakers in any capacity, would risk distributing images in or near the uncertain reach of this law," wrote Justice Anthony Kennedy. "The Constitution gives significant protection from over-broad laws that chill speech within the First Amendment's vast and privileged sphere" (in "Justices Scrap," 2002, p. A3). Kennedy cited the antidrug film *Traffic*, Academy Award–winning *American Beauty*, and Shakespeare's *Romeo and Juliet*, all works containing scenes of minors engaged in sexual activity, as examples of expression that would disappear from the Net.

The primary battleground, then, became protecting children from otherwise legal content. The Net, by virtue of its openness and accessibility, raises particular concerns. Children's viewing of sexually explicit material on cable television can theoretically be controlled by parents. Moreover, viewers must specifically order this content and typically pay an additional fee for it. The purchase of sexually explicit videos, books, and magazines is controlled by laws regulating vendors. But computers sit in homes, schools, and libraries. Children are encouraged to explore their possibilities. A search for the novel *Little Women*, for example, might turn up any number of pornographic sites.

Proponents of stricter control of the Net liken the availability of smut on the Internet to a bookstore or library that allows porn to sit side by side with books that children *should* be reading. In actual, real-world bookstores and libraries, professionals, whether book retailers or librarians, apply their judgment in selecting and locating material, ideally striving for appropriateness and balance. Children are the beneficiaries of their professional judgment. No such selection or evaluation is applied to the Internet. Opponents of control accept the bookstore/library analogy but argue that, as troubling as the online proximity of all types of content may be, it is a true example of the freedom guaranteed by the First Amendment.

The solution seems to be in technology. Filtering software, such as Net Nanny, can be set to block access to websites by title and by the presence of specific words and images. Few free speech advocates are troubled by filters on home computers, but they do see them as problematic when used on more public machines—for example, in schools and libraries. They argue that software that can filter sexual content can also be set to screen out birth control information, religious sites, and discussions of racism. Virtually any content can be blocked. This, they claim, denies other users—adults and mature teenagers, for example—their freedoms.

Congress weighed in on the filtering debate, passing the Children's Internet Protection Act in 2000, requiring schools and libraries to install filtering software. But First Amendment concerns invalidated this act as well. A federal appeals court ruled in June 2002 that requiring these institutions to install filters changes their nature from places that provide information to places that unconstitutionally restrict it. Nonetheless, in June 2003 a sharply divided Supreme Court upheld the Children's Internet Protection Act, declaring that Congress did indeed have the power to require libraries to install filters.

Copyright (Intellectual Property Ownership)

Another freedom-of-expression issue that takes on a special nature on the Internet is copyright. Copyright protection is designed to ensure that those who create content are financially compensated for their work (see Chapter 14). The assumption is that more "authors" will create more content if assured of monetary compensation from those who use it. When the content is tangible (books, movies, videotapes, magazines, CDs), authorship and use are relatively easy to identify. But in the cyberworld, things become a bit more complex. John Perry Barlow (1996), a cofounder of the Electronic Frontier Foundation, explained the situation relatively early in the life of the Internet:

> The riddle is this: If our property can be infinitely reproduced and instantaneously distributed all over the planet without cost, without our knowledge, without its even leaving our possession, how can we protect it? How are we going to get paid for the work we do with our minds? And, if we can't get paid, what will assure the continued creation and distribution of such work? (p. 148)

Technically, copyright rules apply to the Internet as they do to other media. Material on the Net, even on electronic bulletin boards, belongs to the author, so its use, other than fair use, requires permission and possibly payment. But because material on the Internet is not tangible, it is easily, freely, and privately copied. This renders it difficult, if not impossible, to police those who do copy.

Another confounding issue is that new and existing material is often combined with other existing material to create even "newer" content. This makes it difficult to assign authorship. If a user borrows some text from one source, combines it with images from a second, surrounds both with a background graphic from a third, and adds music sampled from many others, where does authorship reside?

To deal with these thorny issues, in 1998 the U.S. Congress passed the Digital Millennium Copyright Act. Its primary goal was to bring U.S. copyright law into compliance with that of the World Intellectual Property Organization (WIPO), headquartered in Geneva, Switzerland. The act does the following:

- Makes it a crime to circumvent antipiracy measures built into commercial software
- Outlaws the manufacture, sale, or distribution of code-breaking devices used to illegally copy software
- Permits breaking of copyright protection devices to conduct encryption research and to test computer security systems
- Provides copyright exemptions for nonprofit libraries, archives, and educational institutions under certain circumstances
- Limits the copyright infringement liability of Internet service providers for simply transmitting information over the Internet, but ISPs are required to remove material from users' websites that appears to constitute copyright infringement
- Requires webcasters (Chapter 7) to pay licensing fees to record companies
- States explicitly that **fair use**—instances in which copyrighted material may be used without permission or payment, such as taking brief quotes from a book (see Chapter 14)—applies to the Internet

What the debate over Internet copyright represents—like concern about controlling content that children can access and efforts to limit troublesome or challenging expression—is a clash of fundamental values that has taken on added nuance with the coming of computer networks. Copyright on the Internet is discussed more fully in Chapter 14.

Privacy

The issue of privacy in mass communication has traditionally been concerned with individuals' rights to protect their privacy from invasive, intrusive media (see Chapter 14). For example, should newspapers publish the names of rape victims and juvenile offenders? When does a person become a public figure and forfeit some degree of privacy? In the global village, however, the issue takes on a new character. Whereas Supreme Court Justice Louis Brandeis could once argue that privacy is "the right to be left alone," today privacy is just as likely to mean "the right to maintain control over our own data." Privacy in the global village has two facets. The first is protecting the privacy of communication we wish to keep private. The second is the use (and misuse) of private, personal information willingly given online.

PROTECTING PRIVACY IN COMMUNICATION The 1986 Electronic Communication Privacy Act guarantees the privacy of our e-mail. It is a criminal offense to either "intentionally [access] without authorization a facility through which an electronic communication service is provided; or intentionally [exceed] an authorization to access that facility." In addition, the law "prohibits an electronic communications service provider from knowingly divulging the contents of any stored electronic communication." The goal of this legislation is to protect private citizens from official abuse; it gives e-mail "conversations" the same protection that phone conversations enjoy. If a government agency wants to listen in, it must secure permission, just as it must get a court order for a telephone wiretap.

If a person or company feels that more direct protection of communication is necessary, encryption is one solution, but it is controversial. **Encryption** is the electronic coding or masking of information that can be deciphered only by a recipient with the decrypting key. According to the FBI and many other government officials, however, this total privacy is an invitation for terrorists, drug lords, and mobsters to use the Net to threaten national security. As such, in early January 2000 the Clinton administration proposed "relaxed" rules—relaxed from initial plans to allow the government to hold the key to *all* encryption technologies. The new rules require makers of encryption software to turn over a copy of their code to a designated third party. The government may access it only with a court order.

"Authorized" interception of messages is another problem for privacy. Courts have consistently upheld employers' rights to intercept and read their employees' e-mail. Employers must be able to guarantee that their computer systems are not abused by the people who work for them. Thoughtful companies solve the problem by issuing clear and fair guidelines on the use of computer networks. Therefore, when they do make unannounced checks of employees' electronic communication, the employee understands that these checks do occur, why they occur, and under what circumstances they can lead to problems.

PROTECTING PRIVACY OF PERSONAL INFORMATION Every online act leaves a "digital trail," making possible easy **dataveillance**—the massive collection and distillation of consumer data. Ironically, we participate in this intrusion into our privacy. Because of computer storage, networking, and cross-referencing power, the information we give to one entity is easily and cheaply given to countless, unknown others.

One form of dataveillance is distributing and sharing personal, private information among organizations other than the one for whom it was originally intended. Information from every credit card transaction (online or at a store), credit application, phone call, supermarket or other purchase made without cash (for example, with a check, debit card, or "club" card), newspaper and magazine subscription, and cable television subscribership is digitally recorded, stored, and most likely sold to others. The increased computerization of medical files, banking information, job applications, and school records produces even more salable data. Eventually, anyone who wants to know something about a person can simply buy the necessary information—without that person's permission or even knowledge. These data can then be used to further invade people's privacy. Employers can withhold jobs for reasons unknown to applicants. Insurance companies can selectively deny coverage to people based on data about their grocery choices. According to the international human rights group Privacy International's Global Privacy Index, the United States ranks in the lowest category, "endemic surveillance societies." Considering such factors as lack of legal protection, degree of enforcement, amount of data sharing, frequency of use of biometrics, and ubiquity of closed-circuit cameras, among America's neighbors in the endemic surveillance societies were Malaysia, Russia, and China (Lawless, 2008).

Recognizing the scope of data collection and the potential problems that it raises, Congress passed the 1974 Federal Privacy Act, restricting *governments'* ability to collect and distribute information about citizens. The act, however, expressly exempted businesses and other nongovernmental organizations from control. As a result, the average Internet user has 736 pieces of personal data collected every day, and companies retain this information for as long as they like. This is like "a third party owning nearly four years of your life" (Popova, 2012). And people are starting to notice. Seventy-one percent of Americans have concerns about companies distributing their information without permission, and 56% say they have similar concerns about companies that hold onto data "even when the companies don't need it anymore." Smartphone users are concerned as well; 65% say they worry about apps that can access their contacts, photos, location, and other data (Tsukayama, 2012c). A recent ad industry study discovered that people "are more worried about loss of personal privacy than they are about most other issues, including rising terrorism, climate change and the growing number of pandemics" (McClellan, 2011).

The Internet industry and the federal government have responded in 2012 with a "Consumer Privacy Bill of Rights," voluntary guidelines asking sites to place a "do not track" button on their Web pages. Critics contend that these guidelines are insufficient protection, as not all sites will comply, and even those with the button may still collect and hold users' personal data for their own market research. They object to the idea that websites should provide us that security only if we specifically ask for it, called **opt-out**. But, asks *Vanity Fair* editor Henry Alford, "When did privacy become a choice rather than a given?" and why does "figuring out how to activate a site's privacy control settings sometimes feel as if it requires a graduate degree in tiny print" (2012, p. ST2). Instead, sites should have to get our permission before they collect and disseminate

▲ In spite of his look of surprise, this consumer willingly gave away the personal information that is now stored and distributed by computers.

Signe Wilkinson Editorial Cartoon used with the permission of Signe Wilkinson, the Washington Post Writers Group and the Cartoonist Group. All rights reserved.

our personal data, that is, we should be able to **opt in**, as is the case in Europe. European Union privacy law not only requires Internet companies to get explicit user consent before using their data, it also grants all citizens the "right to be forgotten," that is, the right to ask to have all their collected personal data deleted forever. Privacy advocates ask the question, "If we have legislation to bring our copyright laws into compliance with those of other nations, why shouldn't we do the same with our privacy laws?" You can read about Facebook's fight with privacy advocates in the box entitled, "My 873 Friends and I Would Like to Be Alone, Please: Facebook & Privacy."

Three new technological advances—**radio frequency identification (RFID) chip**, **augmented reality (AR)**, and **cloud computing**—pose additional privacy problems. RFID, already used by many retailers, is a grain-of-sand-sized microchip and antenna embedded in consumer products that transmits a radio signal. The advantage to retailers is greater inventory control and lower labor costs. The retailer has an absolute, up-to-the-minute accounting of how many boxes of widgets are on the shelf, and consumers simply walk out the door with their boxes while the RFID sends a signal charging the correct amount to the proper credit card; no checkout personnel needed. The fear of privacy advocates should be clear. That signal keeps on sending. Now marketers, the government, and others will know where you and your box of widgets are at all times, how quickly you go through your box of widgets, and where you are when you run out of widgets. How soon until the phone starts ringing with offers of widgets on sale? What if a burglar could use an RFID reader from outside your house to preview its contents? What happens when these data are networked with all your other personal information? What if you buy a case of beer rather than a box of widgets? Will your employer know? What if your tastes run to sugared snacks? Should your insurance company know?

Introduced in 2009 and available in smartphones containing the program Layar, augmented reality (AR) permits users to point their phones at a real-world location, person, or scene and be instantly linked to hundreds of websites containing information about those things, superimposed over the screen image. Very cool, say proponents—instant restaurant reviews, nearby flu-shot locations, related Flickr photos, and the names of relatives you might know in the area. Very scary, say privacy advocates: "Fold in facial-recognition [already extant] and you could point your phone at Bob from accounting, whose visage is now 'augmented' with the information that he has a gay son and drinks Hoegaarden" (Walker, 2009, p. 32). In other words, everything that exists on the Internet is linkable. When anyone and everyone can access these data by simply pointing a phone at someone, privacy, already on life support, dies.

The third advance worrying privacy advocates is the growing use of cloud computing, the storage of computer data, including personal information and system-operating software, on off-site, third-party environments that offer on-demand access. Google, Microsoft, and several independent providers offer cloud computing, and advocates tout the increased power and memory of the cloud, arguing that even if your laptop is lost or destroyed, you lose nothing. But privacy advocates counter that "data stored online has less privacy protection both in practice and under the law. . . . Before, the bad guys usually needed to get their hands on people's computers to see their secrets; in today's cloud all you need is a password." Rented or purchased music downloads or e-books are at risk of reclamation should the vendor go out of business or unilaterally change the terms of service, as happened in 2009 when Amazon erased e-versions of *1984* from users' readers because of a copyright dispute. Harvard's Jonathan Zittrain sums up these worries: "If you entrust your data to others, they can let you down or outright betray you" (2009, p. A19).

Another form of dataveillance is the electronic tracking of the choices we make when we are on the Web, called our **click stream**. Despite the anonymity online users think they enjoy, every click of a key can be, and often is, recorded and stored. This happens whether or not the user actually enters information—for example, a credit card number to make a purchase or a Social Security number to verify identity. This tracking is made possible by **cookies**, an identifying code added to a computer's hard drive by a visited website. Normally, only the site that has sent the cookie can read it—the next time you visit that site it "remembers" you. But some sites bring "third-party" cookies to your computer. Maintained by big Internet advertising networks like DoubleClick and Engage, these cookies can be read by any of the thousands of websites also belonging to that network, whether you've visited them or not, and without your knowledge. As a result, this software is more commonly referred to as **spyware**, identifying code placed on a computer by a website without permission or notification. Spyware not only facilitates tracking by sites and/or people unknown (those "third parties"), but opens a computer to unwanted pop-up ads and other commercial messages.

At any given time, a regular Web user will have dozens of cookies on his or her hard drive, but most commercial browsers come equipped with the capacity to block or erase them. The Anti-Spyware Coalition offers information and assistance on how to deal with cookies and spyware. In addition, users can purchase cookie-scrubbing software. Commercial firms such as Anonymizer sell programs that not only block and erase spyware but also allow users to surf the Web in anonymity.

Virtual Democracy

The Internet is characterized by freedom and self-governance, which are also the hallmarks of true democracy. It is no surprise, then, that computer technology is often trumpeted as the newest and best tool for increased democratic involvement and participation. Since the 2008 presidential election, all major and even minor candidates have made extensive use of the Internet. In fact, experts attribute increases in voter registration and voting among Americans under 30 in that contest to the Internet. Political scientist Daniel Shea says "young voters are paying attention. They're online. They're blogging. They're talking about the election" (in Mieszkowski, 2008).

This enthusiasm for a technological solution to what many see as increased disenchantment with politics and the political process mirrors that which followed the introduction of radio and television. A September 3, 1924, *New Republic* article, for example, argued that the high level of public interest in the radio broadcast of the 1924 political party conventions brought "dismay" to "the most hardened political cynic" (in Davis, 1976, p. 351). In 1940 NBC founder and chairman David Sarnoff predicted that television would enrich democracy because it was "destined to provide greater knowledge to larger numbers of people, truer perception of the meaning of current events, more accurate appraisals of men in public life, and a broader understanding of the needs and aspirations of our fellow human beings" (in Shenk, 1997, p. 60).

Some critics argue that the Internet will be no more of an asset to democracy than have been radio and television because the same economic and commercial forces that have shaped the content and operation of those more traditional media will constrain just as rigidly the new. They point to the endless battles to keep the Internet open and free. Recall the fight over SOPA and PIPA. And there are the ongoing legal and legislative battles over **network neutrality**, the requirement that all ISPs, including cable MSOs, allow the free and equal flow of all Web traffic. Their pessimism also resides in part in concentration and conglomeration of the Internet—2005's News Corp. purchase of hugely popular (and democratic) MySpace; 2006's Google acquisition of hugely popular (and democratic) YouTube; Microsoft's 2011 purchase of Internet video phone company Skype; Facebook's purchase of photo-sharing site Instagram, Google's acquisition of smartphone maker Motorola, and Microsoft's takeover of social networking site Yammer, all in 2012; and Yahoo's 2013 purchase of blogging service Tumblr.

THE TECHNOLOGY GAP An important principle of democracy is "one person, one vote." But if democracy is increasingly practiced online, those lacking the necessary technology and skill will be denied their vote. This is the **technology gap**—the widening disparity between the communication technology haves and have-nots. Even with its rapid diffusion, 20% of the people in the United States do not use the Internet. The "democratization" of the Net still favors those who have the money to buy the hardware and software needed to access the Net as well as to pay for that connection. This leaves out many U.S. citizens—those on the wrong side of the **digital divide**.

The digital divide describes the lack of technological access among specific groups of Americans. And it is controversial. When asked in 2001 about his plans to bridge the divide, then-FCC chair Michael Powell told reporters that the expression itself is "dangerous in the sense that it suggests that the minute a new and innovative technology is introduced in the market, there is a divide among every part of society, and that is just an unreal understanding of an American capitalistic system. . . . I'm not meaning to be completely flip about this—I think it's an important social issue—but it shouldn't be used to justify the notion of, essentially, the socialization of deployment of the infrastructure. . . . You know, I think there's a Mercedes divide. I'd like to have one; I can't afford one" (in Jackson, 2001, p. 9). Critics pointed out that as the Internet becomes increasingly essential for full membership in America's economic and cultural life, those on the wrong side of the divide will be further disenfranchised. And, in the event that the Net becomes even more essential to the practice of democracy than it already may be, say, through widespread online voting, those on the wrong side of the divide will be denied their basic democratic rights.

How real is the digital divide? Although 80% of all Americans regularly access the Internet, usage rates lag for the less educated, people with disabilities, lower-income and rural homes, and Hispanic and African American households (Zickuhr & Smith, 2012). You can see the divide represented graphically in Figure 10.3. These data led the Knight Commission on the Information Needs of Communities in a Democracy to declare that there are two Americas, one wired, one not very well, producing disparities in literacy, political knowledge, and social participation (Tessler, 2010).

THE INFORMATION GAP Another important principle of democracy is that self-governing people govern best with full access to information. This is the reason our culture is so suspicious

▼ **Figure 10.3** The Digital Divide, 2010.
Source: *Pew Internet and American Life Project*, Raine, 2010.

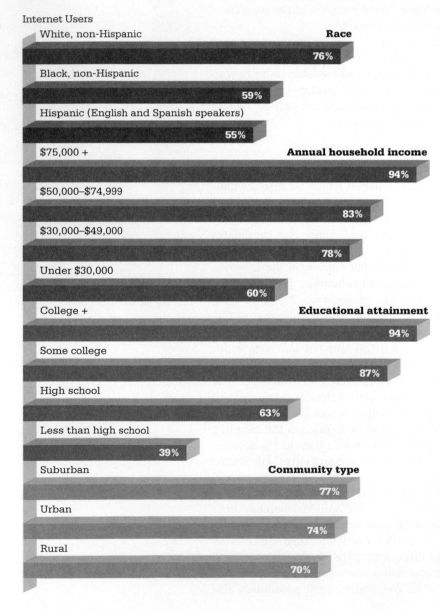

Internet Users

White, non-Hispanic — Race — 76%
Black, non-Hispanic — 59%
Hispanic (English and Spanish speakers) — 55%
$75,000 + — Annual household income — 94%
$50,000–$74,999 — 83%
$30,000–$49,000 — 78%
Under $30,000 — 60%
College + — Educational attainment — 94%
Some college — 87%
High school — 63%
Less than high school — 39%
Suburban — Community type — 77%
Urban — 74%
Rural — 70%

As 2011 came to a close, Facebook found itself uncomfortably in the news, and as a result, the issue of the privacy of our personal information was thrust firmly into the cultural forum. First, Austrian law student Max Schrems requested that Facebook turn over all the personal data it had on him from his three years using the site. According to European Union law the company had to comply, and it did—it sent him a CD containing 1,222 pages of data, including chats he had deleted more than a year earlier, "pokes" (friends saying "hello") dating back to 2008, invitations to which he had never responded, and hundreds of other details; most of these data were held in violation of European privacy laws (Eddy, 2011). The story, naturally, sped around the world on the Internet.

Then came news of trouble with the Federal Trade Commission. In spite of Facebook's assurances that it "does not provide advertisers with information about its users," the FTC found that, "in truth and in fact . . . Facebook has provided advertisers with information about its users." That information was so specific, ruled the FTC, that it included data that could be used to determine a user's real name. Facebook advertisers, the FTC said, could then "combine the user's real name with any targeted traits used for the ad the user clicked" (in Dumenco, 2011). Facebook was censured, but paid no other penalty.

What is the real controversy here? Is it that Facebook says one thing and does another, or is it the mere fact that this kind of dataveillance happens at all? Before you enter your voice in the Facebook vs. users' privacy debate, consider these data: Eleven percent of social network site users have posted content they later regret (Madden, 2012) and 70% of U.S. recruiters and human resources professionals admit having rejected job candidates based on

information they found online. Moreover, 93% of Americans favor the right to opt-in before an online company can use their personal data, and 69% want the federal government to adopt a law giving them the right to learn everything a website knows about them (Andrews, 2012). Now read Facebook founder Mark Zuckerberg's explanation of why you should welcome tracking, "We help you share information, and when you do that, you're more

> "Seventy percent of U.S. recruiters and human resources professionals admit having rejected job candidates based on information they found online."

engaged on the site, and then there are ads on the side of the page. The more you're sharing, the more—the model all just works out" (in Bazelon, 2011, p. 16).

Enter your voice. The sharing of your personal information may work for Facebook—it makes over $2 billion a year in ad revenues—but does it work for college-age users like you—94% of whom report having shared personal information that they had not intended to make public (in Bazelon, 2011)?

◀ Matt Davies. © Tribune Media Services, Inc. All Rights Reserved. Reprinted with permission.

of censorship. The technology gap feeds a second impediment to virtual democracy, the **information gap**. Those without the requisite technology will have diminished access to the information it makes available. In other words, they will suffer from a form of technologically imposed censorship.

Critics of the information gap point to troubling examples of other media failures to deliver important information to all citizens. Cable television subscribership is lowest among urban working-class and poor people. Many newspapers, uninterested in these same people because they do not possess the demographic profile coveted by advertisers, do not promote their papers in the neighborhoods in which they live and, in some large cities, do not even deliver there. For the same reason, there are precious few consumer magazines aimed at less well-off people. If the computer technology gap creates an even wider information gap than already exists between these audiences and other citizens, democracy will surely suffer from what social scientists call the **knowledge gap**, growing differences in knowledge, civic activity, and literacy between better-informed and less-informed Americans.

DEVELOPING MEDIA LITERACY SKILLS

The Five Internet Freedoms

At a talk he gave in 2004 to telecommunication industry professionals, then-FCC Chair Michael Powell spelled out the Four Internet Freedoms. He called his speech "Preserving Internet Freedom: Guiding Principles for the Industry." The Four Freedoms, he said, were:

- *Freedom to Access Content.* First, consumers should have access to their choice of legal content. Consumers have come to expect to be able to go where they want on high-speed connections.
- *Freedom to Use Applications.* Consumers should be able to run applications of their choice. As with access to content, consumers have come to expect that they can generally run whatever applications they want.
- *Freedom to Attach Personal Devices.* Consumers should be permitted to attach any devices they choose to the connection in their homes. Because devices give consumers more choice, value, and personalization with respect to how they use their high-speed connections, they are critical to the future of broadband.
- *Freedom to Obtain Service Plan Information.* Consumers should receive meaningful information regarding their service plans. . . . Providers have every right to offer a variety of service tiers with varying bandwidth and feature options. Consumers need to know about these choices as well as whether and how their service plans protect them against spam, spyware, and other potential invasions of privacy.

In 2009, recognizing that even if the Internet industry committed itself to these four freedoms it would mean little if they could control the flow of content, new FCC Commissioner Michael Copps proposed a fifth freedom, *nondiscrimination*, which in fact was a reaffirmation of the principle of network neutrality (which Chair Powell opposed during his tenure at the FCC). Service providers, Copps said, could not prioritize, privilege, or degrade content carried over their lines (Eggerton, 2009).

These five freedoms are important. As media-literate Internet users, we should know what freedoms we should enjoy when dealing with our service providers. But we should also recognize that there are two very important aspects of the Internet–user relationship that are absent, even with Commissioner Copps's addendum. The first is that these are promises that the industry makes to us as consumers, not as citizens. If the Internet is a necessity, a life-sustaining utility, shouldn't we hold expectations that rise to a level somewhat above those of a business's customers?

But the more glaring absence is that of *our promise*. If we are guaranteed unfettered access to this most powerful communication tool, what promises do we make? What are our obligations as media-literate Internet users? Heather Havrilesky of *Salon*, one of the first online ventures, undertaken when hopes for the Internet were at their highest and risk the greatest, writes that we have already failed: "Let's see, so the digital revolution led us all to this: a gigantic, commercial, high school reunion/mall filthy with insipid tabloid trivia, populated by perpetually distracted, texting, tweeting demi-humans. Yes, the information age truly is every bit as glorious and special as everyone predicted it would be!" (2010).

But technology expert Clay Shirky argues that it is not too late, that we hold the power to make the Internet what we want it to be. The decision is ours. "Given what we have today," he wrote, "the Internet could easily become Invisible High School, with a modicum of educational material in an ocean of narcissism and social obsessions. We could, however, also use it as an Invisible College, the communicative backbone of real intellectual and civic change, but to do this will require more than technology. It will require that we adopt norms of open sharing and participation" (2010). It will require, in other words, our commitment to meet the industry's promises of accessibility with our own promise of responsibility.

It is important to remember that culture is neither innate nor inviolate. *We* construct culture—both dominant and bounded. Increasingly, we do so through mass communication, and the Internet has given us voice once unimaginable. So before we can enter the forum in which those cultures are constructed and maintained, we must understand where we stand and what we believe. We must be able to defend our positions. The hallmarks of a media-literate individual are analysis and self-reflection. Reread the five promises. Does your provider meet them? Were you aware that several ISPs, notably Comcast, Frontier Communications, and Time Warner Cable, have either tried or announced they would begin **metering** of Internet use? That is, they would begin charging users "by the byte"—heavier users would pay more, more modest users pay less. Is this consistent with the promise of full access? Reread the Havrilesky and Shirky quotes. Who's correct? If it's too late, what was your contribution to the Internet's failure to meet its potential? If it's not, what will you do to make better, more meaningful, more enjoyable use of the Internet?

MEDIA LITERACY CHALLENGE
A Cost/Benefit Analysis of Twitter

Novelist Jonathan Franzen offered this opinion of Twitter to the audience at one of his book readings: "Twitter is unspeakably irritating. Twitter stands for everything I oppose . . . it's hard to cite facts or create an argument in 140 characters . . . it's like if Kafka had decided to make a video semaphoring *The Metamorphosis*. Or it's like writing a novel without the letter 'P' . . . It's the ultimate irresponsible medium. People I care about are readers . . . these are my people. And we do not like to yak about ourselves" (in Attenberg, 2012). Mr. Franzen may not care for Twitter, but as a media-literate Internet user you should *be aware of its impact on individuals and society* and, like it or not, you know that Twitter *content is a text providing insight into contemporary culture.* So undertake this challenge to your media literacy with the award-winning writer's critique in mind. Survey three non-college-student adults about their Twitter use. Ask them how many Tweets they get and send each day. Ask them what percentage of those Tweets (both sent and received) they consider important. Ask them how much time they spend on Twitter. Ask them any other questions you consider important. Do the same with three college students. Then, based on the responses from your survey and your own experience, answer these questions in either a short essay or a brief oral presentation: Is Twitter just people "yakking" about themselves? In what ways has Twitter improved people's ability to communicate and receive information? What trade-offs, if any, are required in terms of the negative aspects of Twitter in order to get these benefits?

Resources for Review and Discussion

REVIEW POINTS: TYING CONTENT TO LEARNING OUTCOMES

▶ **Outline the history and development of the Internet and World Wide Web.**
- ▶ The idea for the Internet came either from technological optimists like Joseph C. R. Licklider or from the military, hoping to maintain communication networks in time of enemy attack—or from both.
- ▶ Paul Baran devised a packet-switching network, the technological basis for the Internet, to be used on powerful computers developed by John V. Atanasoff, John Mauchly, and John Presper Eckert.
- ▶ The personal computer was developed by Bill Gates and the team of Steve Jobs and Stephen Wozniak.

▶ **Explain the potential cultural value of the Internet and World Wide Web.**
- ▶ Questions about the double edge of Internet technology have given rise to renewed interest in Marshall McLuhan, creator of concepts such as the global village and media as extensions of our bodies.

▶ **Describe how the organizational and economic natures of the contemporary Internet and World Wide Web industries shape their content.**
- ▶ The Internet facilitates e-mail, VoIP, social networking, and the World Wide Web, all greatly facilitated by the rapid diffusion of smartphones and tablets.
- ▶ The Web relies on a system of hosts, browsers, and search engines to bring users to websites, characterized by URLs and home pages.

▶ **Identify alterations in the nature of mass communication made possible by the Internet, the World Wide Web, and their convergence with all media.**

▶ **Analyze social and cultural questions posed by the Internet, World Wide Web, and related emerging technologies.**
- ▶ The Internet makes freedom of expression a reality for anyone linked to it. But abuse of that freedom has led to calls for greater control.
- ▶ Restrictions on access to pornography, protection of copyright, and threats to identity are primary battlegrounds for opponents and proponents of control.

▶ **Describe the relationship between these new media and their various users and audiences.**
- ▶ The Internet's potential contributions to participatory democracy are also in debate, as problems such as the technology and information gaps and the digital divide have yet to be resolved.

▶ **Apply key Internet and World Wide Web media literacy skills, especially in protecting your privacy and reflecting on the Net's double edge of (potentially) good and troublesome change.**
- ▶ The Internet and Web, especially with their power to reshape all the mass media, raise multiple issues for media-literate users hoping to effectively make their way in an interconnected world, guidance for which can be found in the five Internet freedoms:
  - ▶ Freedom to Access Content
  - ▶ Freedom to Use Applications
  - ▶ Freedom to Attach Personal Devices
  - ▶ Freedom to Obtain Service Plan Information
  - ▶ From discrimination, that is, network neutrality

KEY TERMS

QUESTIONS FOR REVIEW

1. What is the importance of each of these people to the development of the computer: Charles Babbage, John Atanasoff, John Mauchly, and John Presper Eckert?

2. What were the contributions of Joseph C. R. Licklider, Paul Baran, Bill Gates, Steve Jobs, and Stephen Wozniak to the development and popularization of the Internet?

3. What are digital computers, microcomputers, and mainframe computers?

4. What factors have led to the popularity of the World Wide Web?

5. What are the differing positions on Internet copyright?

6. Why is there renewed interest in Marshall McLuhan? What does he mean by the global village and media as extensions of our bodies?

7. What are the two primary privacy issues for online communication? What are some of the new technological threats?

8. What is a blog? How might blogs alter journalism?

9. What are some of the arguments supporting the idea that the Internet will be a boost to participatory democracy? What are some of the counterarguments?

10. What are the technology and information gaps? What do they have to do with virtual democracy or cyberdemocracy? What is the digital divide?

McGraw Hill connect®

For further review, go to the LearnSmart study module for this chapter.

QUESTIONS FOR CRITICAL THINKING AND DISCUSSION

1. What controls should be placed on blogs, if any? Do you see them as a way of distributing power in the culture between traditional media outlets and ordinary individuals? Why or why not?

2. Do you ever make personal information available online? If so, how confident are you of its security? Do you take steps to protect your privacy?

3. Do you believe the new communication technologies will improve or damage participatory democracy? Why? Can you relate a personal experience of how the Net increased or limited your involvement in the political process?

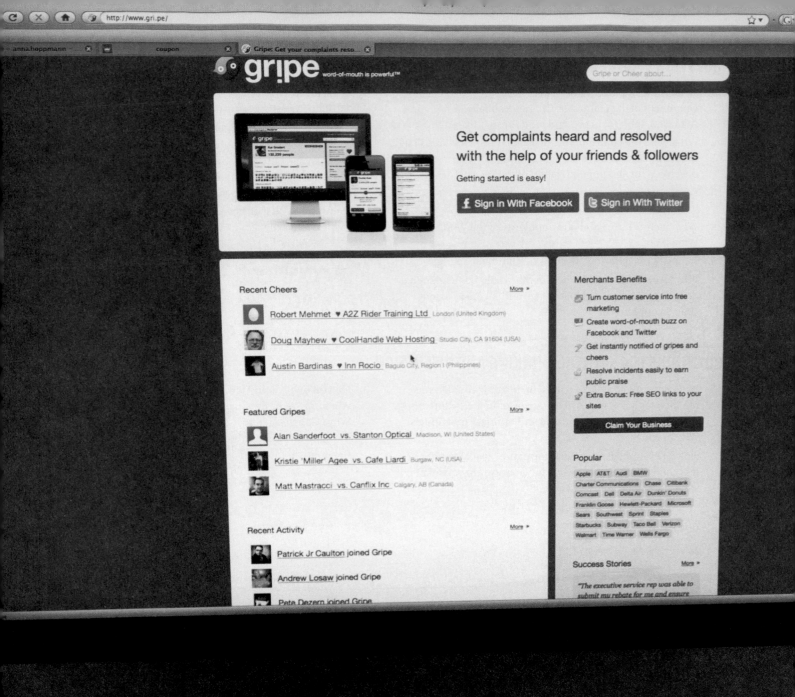

Public Relations

11

Learning Objectives

It is no small irony that PR has such poor PR. We criticize the flacks who try to spin the truth because PR is most obvious when used to reclaim the reputation of someone or some organization in need of such help. But public relations is essential for maintaining relationships between organizations and their publics. In fact, much PR is used for good. After studying this chapter you should be able to

▶ Outline the history and development of the public relations industry.

▶ Describe how the organizational and economic nature of the contemporary public relations industry shapes the messages with which publics interact, especially in an increasingly converged media environment.

▶ Identify different types of public relations and the different publics each is designed to serve.

▶ Explain the relationship between public relations and its various publics.

▶ Apply key media literacy skills when consuming public relations messages, especially video news releases.

Apps like Gripe enrich the relationship between organizations and their publics.
Reprinted by permission of Gri.pe

"WHAT'S WITH THE SNICKERS? I thought you were on a diet."

"I am."

"O.K., but why are you watching TV? I thought you had a term paper due tomorrow."

"Well, my babysitter, if you must know I'm helping fight hunger. Snickers provides food to people who don't have enough to eat. I just have to type the code on the wrapper and the company will donate two meals to a family in need. The more candy I eat, the more people get fed. Snickers wants to 'bar hunger,' get it?"

"I do. And TV?"

"I'm watching the races. See car 18, that's Kyle Busch, and see the logo . . . Bar Hunger. He's supporting the effort, so I'm supporting him. You sure you get the bar hunger pun?"

"Yes, I get it. But I still don't get you."

More than likely what your curious friend doesn't get is the relationship between auto racing, candy bars, and alleviating hunger. You, however, know that Mars Chocolate, the makers of Snickers, like thousands of other companies, has teamed up with a public service organization to do good for the community while burnishing its corporate image, not unimportant at a time when confidence in the corporate world is a bit shaky. Hoping to reduce the suffering of at least some of the nearly 40 million Americans who go to bed hungry every night, Mars assembled celebrities like actor David Arquette and rockers Benji and Joel Madden from Good Charlotte, magazines like *GQ* and *Rolling Stone*, and athletes like Mr. Busch; used Facebook, Twitter, and a dedicated Web page; and teamed up with Feeding America, the nation's largest hunger-relief charity with more than 200 individual food banks across the country. The Bar Hunger campaign is the company's quite visible public participation public relations effort.

In this chapter we investigate the public relations industry and its relationship with mass media and their audiences. We first define public relations. Then we study its history and development as the profession matured from its beginnings in hucksterism to a full-fledged, communication-based industry. We see how the needs and interests

1800

1850

1773 ▲ Boston Tea Party

1833 ▲ Andrew Jackson hires Amos Kendall, first presidential press secretary

1896 ▲ William Jennings Bryan and William McKinley launch first national political campaigns

1889 Westinghouse establishes first corporate public relations department of the profession's various publics became part of the public relations process. We also define exactly who those publics are. The scope and nature of the industry are detailed. Types of public relations activities and the organization of a typical public relations operation are described. We study trends such as globalization and specialization, as well as the impact of new, converging communication technologies on the industry. Finally, we discuss trust in public relations. As our media literacy skill, we learn how to recognize video news releases.

Defining Public Relations

Feeding America, like Mothers Against Drunk Driving, Save Venice, Handgun Control Incorporated, the National Environmental Trust, and countless other nonprofit organizations, is an interest group that uses a variety of public relations tools and strategies to serve a variety of publics. It wants to use public relations to do good. The companies that sponsor its activities also want to do good—do good for their communities *and* for themselves. Even the most cynical person must applaud their efforts on behalf of feeding people in need.

But for many people, efforts such as these serve to demonstrate one of the ironies of public relations, both as an activity and as an industry: Public relations has terrible public relations. We dismiss information as "just PR." Public relations professionals are frequently equated with snake oil salespeople, hucksters, and other willful deceivers. They are referred to both inside and outside the media industries as **flacks**. Yet virtually every organization and institution—big and small, public and private, for-profit and volunteer—uses public relations as a regular part of its operation. Many have their own public relations departments. The term "public relations" carries such a negative connotation that most independent companies and company departments now go by the name "public affairs," "corporate affairs," or "public communications."

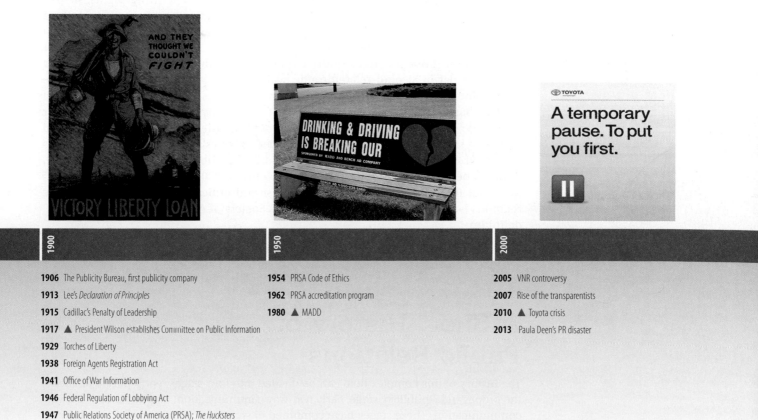

▲ Snickers and racecar driver Kyle Busch team up with Feeding America to help alleviate hunger for millions of Americans.

The problem rests, in part, on confusion over what public relations actually is. There is no universally accepted definition of public relations because it can be and is many things—publicity, research, public affairs, media relations, promotion, merchandising, and more. Much of the contact media consumers have with public relations occurs when the industry defends people and companies who have somehow run afoul of the public. China sought help from Ogilvy Public Relations when it was discovered that the toys it was exporting to the United States were coated with dangerous lead paint and the toothpaste it was sending here was tainted with diethylene glycol, a toxin. Washington PR giant Qorvis's representation of repressive Middle Eastern regimes Yemen and Bahrain led to a much-publicized walk-out by a third of its partners. At the height of the recent tumultuous debate over reforming the American health care system, Get Health Reform Right was caught paying online gamers virtual currency (Chapter 9) to send prewritten, antireform e-mails to Congress. The group was actually an **astroturf** (a fake grassroots organization) public relations outfit funded by 10 of the country's largest insurers. In summer 2013, as celebrity cook Paula Deen saw her television and cookbook businesses threatened by lawsuit revelations of racist language, she turned to the Rose Group, a firm specializing in repairing scandal-damaged reputations.

Yet when seven people died from cyanide poisoning after taking tainted Tylenol capsules in 1982, a skilled and honest public relations campaign by Johnson & Johnson (makers of Tylenol) and its public relations firm, Burson-Marsteller, saved the brand and restored trust in the product. In 2010 when Toyota, famed for its safety record, was struck by a series of recalls surrounding sudden involuntary acceleration in several of its models, its direct and aggressive campaign to identify and eliminate the problem, going so far as to close down several manufacturing plants, helped save the brand and thousands of jobs. The public relations campaign by Mothers Against Drunk Driving (MADD) led directly to passage of tougher standards in virtually every state to remove drunk drivers from the road and to provide stiffer sentences for those convicted of driving under the influence. Dramatic reductions in the number of alcohol-related traffic accidents resulted from this effort (see the essay, "The MADD Campaign").

"P.R. has a P.R. problem," says Syracuse University public relations professor Brenda Wrigley. "We have to get our own house in order. . . . We are advocates and there's no shame in that as long as it's grounded in ethics and values." Public Relations Society of America president Judy Phair adds, "For public relations to be effective, it has to be built on public trust" (both in O'Brien, 2005, p. 3.1). Accepting, therefore, that public relations should be honest and ethical, our definition of public relations is drawn from the Public Relations Society of America's "widely accepted" definition:

"Public relations is a strategic communication process that builds mutually beneficial relationships between organizations and their publics" (PRSA, 2012b).

A Short History of Public Relations

The history of this complex field can be divided into four stages: early public relations, the propaganda–publicity stage, early two-way communication, and advanced two-way communication. These stages have combined to shape the character of this industry.

After her child was killed in a drunk-driving accident in 1980, Candy Lightner sought out others like herself, mothers who had lost children to the volatile mix of cars and alcohol. She hoped they could provide one another with emotional support and campaign to ensure that other parents would never know their grief. Thus, Mothers Against Drunk Driving (MADD) was born.

Among MADD's publics are teenagers. With its parallel organization, Students Against Destructive Decisions (SADD), MADD targets this high-risk group through various educational campaigns and in the media that attract teen audiences. The organization also conducts public information campaigns aimed at adult

the Victim's Crime Act of 1984, making compensation from drunk drivers to victims and their families federal law.

"MADD's cultural impact shows most strongly in the way people treat drunk drivers. It is no longer cool to talk about how smashed we got at the party, or how we can't believe we made it home. Almost every evening out with a group of friends includes a designated driver. Drunk drivers are considered nearly as despicable as child molesters."

There are two even more dramatic examples of how successful Lightner's group has been. According to the U.S. Department of Transportation, the number of alcohol-related auto fatalities in the 30 years following MADD's founding has fallen to record low levels (Phillips, 2010). But MADD's cultural impact shows most strongly in the way people treat drunk drivers. It is no longer cool to talk about how smashed we got at the party, or how we can't believe we made it home. Almost every evening out with a group of friends includes a designated driver. Drunk drivers are considered nearly as despicable as child molesters. Many in public relations, traffic safety, and law enforcement credit MADD's public relations efforts with this change.

drivers and repeat drunk drivers, often in conjunction with state and other authorities. It also assists legislators in their efforts to pass drunk-driving legislation. Two more of MADD's publics are public servants such as police and paramedics who must deal with the effects of drunk driving, and the families and friends who have lost loved ones in alcohol- or drug-related driving accidents.

Has MADD made a difference? Since 1988, numerous prime-time television programs have featured episodes about the dangers of drunk driving. MADD's professional staff has served as script advisors to these programs. MADD was instrumental in passage of the federal Drunk Driving Prevention Act of 1988, offering states financial incentives to set up programs that would reduce alcohol- and drug-related automobile fatalities. This legislation also made 21 the national minimum legal drinking age. MADD successfully campaigned for

► MADD reaches its various publics in a variety of ways.

Early Public Relations

Archaeologists in Iraq have uncovered a tablet dating from 1800 B.C.E. that today we would call a public information bulletin. It provided farmers with information on sowing, irrigating, and harvesting their crops. Julius Caesar fed the people of the Roman Empire constant reports of his achievements to maintain morale and to solidify his reputation and position of power. Genghis Khan would send "advance men" to tell stories of his might, hoping to frighten his enemies into surrendering.

Public relations campaigns abounded in colonial America and helped create the Colonies. Merchants, farmers, and others who saw their own advantage in a growing colonial population used overstatement, half-truths, and lies to entice settlers to the New World. *A Brief and True Report of the New Found Land of Virginia*, by John White, was published in 1588 to lure European settlers. The Boston Tea Party was a well-planned media event organized to attract public attention for a vital cause. Today we'd call it a **pseudo-event**, an event staged specifically to attract public attention. Benjamin

A temporary pause. To put you first.

⏸

Why we've temporarily stopped some of our plants:

As you may have heard, in rare cases, sticking accelerator pedals have occurred in some of our vehicles. We believe we are close to announcing an effective remedy. And we've temporarily halted production at some of our North American plants to focus on the vehicles we've recalled. Why have we taken this unprecedented action? Because it's the right thing to do for our customers.

To find out if your Toyota is affected and to get the very latest information about the recall, please visit:

toyota.com

▲ Toyota's powerful public relations campaign, going as far as to close down manufacturing plants, helped save the brand's reputation and thousands of its employees' jobs.

Franklin organized a sophisticated campaign to thwart the Stamp Act, the Crown's attempt to limit colonial press freedom (Chapter 3), using his publications and the oratory skills of criers. *The Federalist Papers* of John Jay, James Madison, and Alexander Hamilton were originally a series of 85 letters published between 1787 and 1789, which were designed to sway public opinion in the newly independent United States toward support and passage of the new Constitution, an early effort at issue management. In all these examples, people or organizations were using communication to inform, to build an image, and to influence public opinion.

The Propaganda–Publicity Stage

Mass circulation newspapers and the first successful consumer magazines appeared in the 1830s, expanding the ability of people and organizations to communicate with the public. In 1833, for example, Andrew Jackson hired former newspaper journalist Amos Kendall as his publicist and the country's first presidential press secretary in an effort to combat the aristocrats who saw Jackson as too common to be president.

Abolitionists sought an end to slavery. Industrialists needed to attract workers, entice customers, and enthuse investors. P. T. Barnum, convinced that "there's a sucker born every minute," worked to lure them into his shows. All used the newspaper and the magazine to serve their causes.

Politicians recognized that the expanding press meant that a new way of campaigning was necessary. In 1896 presidential contenders William Jennings Bryan and William McKinley both established campaign headquarters in Chicago from which they issued news releases, position papers, and pamphlets. The modern national political campaign was born.

It was during this era that public relations began to acquire its deceitful, huckster image. PR was associated more with propaganda than with useful information. A disregard for the public and the willingness of public relations experts to serve the powerful fueled this view, but public relations began to establish itself as a profession

▶ The December 16, 1773, Boston Tea Party was one of the first successful pseudo-events in the new land. Had cameras been around at the time, it would also have been a fine photo op.

during this time. The burgeoning press was its outlet, but westward expansion and rapid urbanization and industrialization in the United States were its driving forces. As the railroad expanded to unite the new nation, cities exploded with new people and new life. Markets, once small and local, became large and national.

As the political and financial stakes grew, business and government became increasingly corrupt and selfish—"The public be damned" was William Vanderbilt's official comment when asked in 1882 about the effects of changing the schedule of his New York Central Railroad. The muckrakers' revelations badly tarnished the images of industry and politics. Massive and lengthy coal strikes led to violence and more anti-business feeling. In the heyday of the journalistic exposé and the Progressive movement (Chapter 5), government and business both required some good public relations.

In 1889 Westinghouse Electric established the first corporate public relations department, hiring a former newspaper writer to engage the press and ensure that company positions were always clear and in the public eye. Advertising agencies, including N. W. Ayer & Sons and Lord and Thomas, began to offer public relations services to their clients. The first publicity company, The Publicity Bureau, opened in Boston in 1906 and later expanded to New York, Chicago, Washington, St. Louis, and Topeka to help the railroad industry challenge federal regulations that it opposed.

The railroads also had other problems, and they turned to *New York World* reporter Ivy Lee for help. Beset by accidents and strikes, the Pennsylvania Railroad usually responded by suppressing information. Lee recognized, however, that this was dangerous and counterproductive in a time when the public was already suspicious of big business, including the railroads. Lee escorted reporters to the scene of trouble, established press centers, distributed press releases, and assisted reporters in obtaining additional information and photographs.

When a Colorado coal mine strike erupted in violence in 1913, the press attacked the mine's principal stockholder, New York's John D. Rockefeller, Jr., blaming him for the shooting deaths of several miners and their wives and children. Lee handled press relations and convinced Rockefeller to visit the scene to talk (and be photographed) with the strikers. The strike ended, and Rockefeller was soon being praised for his sensitive intervention. Eventually Lee issued his *Declaration of Principles*, arguing that public relations practitioners should be providers of information, not purveyors of publicity.

Not all public relations at this time was damage control. Henry Ford began using staged events such as auto races to build interest in his cars, started *Ford Times* (an in-house employee publication), and made heavy use of image advertising.

Public relations in this stage was typically one-way, from organization to public. Still, by the outbreak of World War I, most of the elements of today's large-scale, multifunction public relations agency were in place.

Early Two-Way Communication

Because the U.S. public was not particularly enthusiastic about the nation's entry into World War I, President Woodrow Wilson recognized the need for public relations in support of the war effort (Zinn, 1995, pp. 355–357). In 1917 he placed former newspaper journalist George Creel at the head of the newly formed Committee on Public Information (CPI). Creel assembled opinion leaders from around the country to advise the government on its public relations efforts and to help shape public opinion. The committee sold Liberty Bonds and helped increase membership in the Red Cross. It engaged in public relations on a scale never before seen, using movies, public speakers, articles in newspapers and magazines, and posters.

About this time public relations pioneer Edward Bernays began emphasizing the value of assessing the public's feelings toward an organization. He would then use this knowledge as the basis for the development of the public relations effort. Together with Creel's committee, Bernays's work was the beginning of two-way communication in public relations—that is, public relations talking to people and, in return, listening to them when they talked back. Public relations professionals began

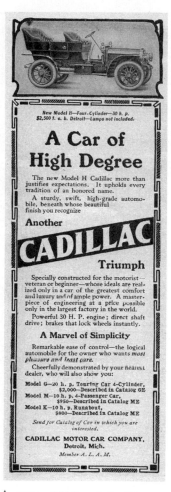

▲ 1906 Car of High Degree Cadillac. This campaign was an early but quite successful example of image advertising—using paid ads to build goodwill for a product.

AND THEY THOUGHT WE COULDN'T FIGHT

VICTORY LIBERTY LOAN

▲ World War I brought government into large-scale public relations. Even today, the CPI's posters—like this one encouraging citizens to support the war effort through war bonds—are recognized.

representing their various publics to their clients, just as they represented their clients to those publics.

There were other advances in public relations during this stage. During the 1930s, President Franklin D. Roosevelt, guided by advisor Louis McHenry Howe, embarked on a sophisticated public relations campaign to win support for his then-radical New Deal policies. Central to Roosevelt's effort was the new medium of radio. The Great Depression that plagued the country throughout this decade once again turned public opinion against business and industry. To counter people's distrust, many more corporations established in-house public relations departments; General Motors opened its PR operation in 1931. Public relations professionals turned increasingly to the newly emerging polling industry, founded by George Gallup and Elmo Roper, to better gauge public opinion as they constructed public relations campaigns and to gather feedback on the effectiveness of those campaigns. Gallup and Roper successfully applied newly refined social science research methods—advances in sampling, questionnaire design, and interviewing—to meet the business needs of clients and their publics.

The growth of the industry was great enough and its reputation sufficiently fragile that the National Association of Accredited Publicity Directors was founded in 1936. The American Council on Public Relations was established three years later. They merged in 1947, creating the Public Relations Society of America (PRSA), the principal professional group for today's public relations professionals.

World War II saw the government undertake another massive campaign to bolster support for the war effort, this time through the Office of War Information (OWI). Employing techniques that had proven successful during World War I, the OWI had the additional advantage of public opinion polling, fully established and powerful radio networks and their stars, and a Hollywood eager to help. Singer Kate Smith's war bond radio telethon raised millions, and director Frank Capra produced the *Why We Fight* film series for the OWI.

During this era both public relations and Ivy Lee suffered a serious blow to their reputations. Lee was the American public relations spokesman for Germany and its leader, Adolf Hitler. In 1934 Lee was required to testify before Congress to defend himself against the charge that he was a Nazi sympathizer. He was successful, but the damage had been done. As a result of Lee's ties with Germany, Congress passed the Foreign Agents Registration Act in 1938, requiring anyone who engages in political activities in the United States on behalf of a foreign power to register as an agent of that power with the Justice Department.

Advanced Two-Way Communication

Post–World War II U.S. society was confronted by profound social change and expansion of the consumer culture. It became increasingly important for organizations to know what their clients were thinking, what they liked and disliked, and what concerned and satisfied them. As a result, public relations turned even more decidedly toward integrated two-way communication, employing research, advertising, and promotion.

As the public relations industry became more visible, it opened itself to closer scrutiny. Best-selling novels such as *The Hucksters* and *The Man in the Gray Flannel Suit* (and the hit movies made from them) painted a disturbingly negative picture of the industry and those who worked in it. Vance Packard's best-selling book *The Hidden Persuaders*, dealing with both public relations and advertising, further eroded PR esteem. As a result of public distrust of the profession, Congress passed the Federal Regulation of Lobbying Act in 1946, requiring, among other things, that those who deal with federal employees on behalf of private clients disclose those relationships. And as the industry's conduct and ethics came under increasing attack, the PRSA responded with a code of ethics in 1954 and an accreditation program in 1962. Both, with modification and improvement, stand today.

The modern era of public relations is characterized by other events as well. More people buying more products meant that greater numbers of people were coming into contact with a growing number of businesses. As consumer markets grew in size, the basis for competition changed. Texaco, for example, used advertising to sell its gasoline. But because its products were not all that different from those of other oil companies, it also sold its gasoline using its good name and reputation. Increasingly, then, advertising agencies began to add public relations divisions. This change served to blur the distinction between advertising and PR.

▲ Better known for hits such as *Mr. Smith Goes to Washington* and *It's a Wonderful Life*, director Frank Capra brought his moviemaking talents to the government's efforts to explain U.S. involvement in World War II and to overcome U.S. isolationism. His *Why We Fight* documentary series still stands as a classic of the form.

Women, who had proved their capabilities in all professional settings during World War II, became prominent in the industry. Anne Williams Wheaton was associate press secretary to President Eisenhower; Leone Baxter was president of the powerful public relations firm Whitaker and Baxter. Companies and their executives and politicians increasingly turned to television to burnish their images and shape public opinion. Nonprofit, charitable, and social activist groups also mastered the art of public relations. The latter used public relations especially effectively to challenge the PR power of targeted businesses. Environmentalist, civil rights, and women's rights groups and safety and consumer advocate organizations were successful in moving the public toward their positions and, in many cases, toward action.

Shaping the Character of Public Relations

Throughout these four stages in the development of public relations, several factors combined to shape the identity of public relations, influence the way the industry does its job, and clarify the necessity for PR in the business and political world.

Advances in technology. Advances in industrial technology made possible mass production, distribution, and marketing of goods. Advances in communication technology (and their proliferation) made it possible to communicate more efficiently and effectively with ever-larger and more specific audiences.

Growth of the middle class. A growing middle class, better educated and more aware of the world around it, required information about people and organizations.

Growth of organizations. As business, organized labor, and government grew bigger after World War II, the public saw them as more powerful and more remote. As a result, people were naturally curious and suspicious about these forces that seemed to be influencing all aspects of their lives.

Better research tools. The development of sophisticated research methodologies and statistical techniques allowed the industry to know its audiences better and to better judge the effectiveness of public relations campaigns.

Professionalization. Numerous national and international public relations organizations helped professionalize the industry and clean up its reputation.

Public Relations and Its Audiences

Virtually all of us consume public relations messages on a daily basis. Increasingly, the video clips we see on the local evening news are provided by a public relations firm or the PR department of some company or organization. The content of many of the stories we read online or hear on local radio news comes directly from PR-provided press releases. As one media relations firm explained in a promotional piece sent to prospective clients, "The media are separated into two categories. One is content and the other is advertising. They're both for sale. Advertising can be purchased directly from the publication or through an ad agency, and the content space you purchase from PR firms" (quoted in Jackson & Hart, 2002, p. 24). In addition, the feed-the-hungry campaign we support, the poster encouraging us toward safer sex, and the corporation-sponsored art exhibit we attend are all someone's public relations effort. Public relations professionals interact with seven categories of publics, and a **public** is any group of people with a stake in an organization, issue, or idea:

Employees. An organization's employees are its lifeblood, its family. Good public relations begins at home with company newsletters, social events, and internal and external recognition of superior performance.

Stockholders. Stockholders own the organization (if it is a public corporation). They are "family" as well, and their goodwill is necessary for the business to operate. Annual reports and stockholder meetings provide a sense of belonging as well as information.

Communities. An organization has neighbors where it operates. Courtesy, as well as good business sense, requires that an organization's neighbors be treated with friendship and support. Information meetings, company-sponsored safety and food drives, and open houses strengthen ties between organizations and their neighbors.

Media. Very little communication with an organization's various publics can occur without the trust and goodwill of professionals in the mass media. Press packets, briefings, and facilitating access to organization newsmakers build that trust and goodwill.

Government. Government is "the voice of the people" and, as such, deserves the attention of any organization that deals with the public. From a practical perspective, governments have the power to tax, regulate, and zone. Organizations must earn and maintain the goodwill and trust of the government. Providing information and access through reports, position papers, and meetings with personnel keeps government informed and builds its trust in an organization. The government is also the target of many PR efforts, as organizations and their lobbyists seek favorable legislation and other action.

Investment community. Corporations are under the constant scrutiny of those who invest their own money, invest the money of others, or make recommendations on investment. The value of a business and its ability to grow are functions of the investment community's respect for and trust in it. As a result, all PR efforts that build an organization's good image speak to that community.

Customers. Consumers pay the bills for companies through their purchase of products or services. Their goodwill is invaluable. That makes good PR, in all its forms, invaluable.

Scope and Structure of the Public Relations Industry

Today some 275,200 people identify themselves as working in public relations, and virtually every major U.S. company has a public relations department, some housing as many as 400 employees. There are over 7,000 public relations firms in the United States, the largest employing as many as 2,000 people. Most, however, have fewer, some as few as four employees. American PR firms had $5.7 billion in revenue in 2010, a sum expected to reach nearly $11 billion in 2015 (PRSA, 2012a). Figure 11.1 shows the 10 largest public relations firms in the United States.

Net fees in millions of dollars by firm rank and headquarters

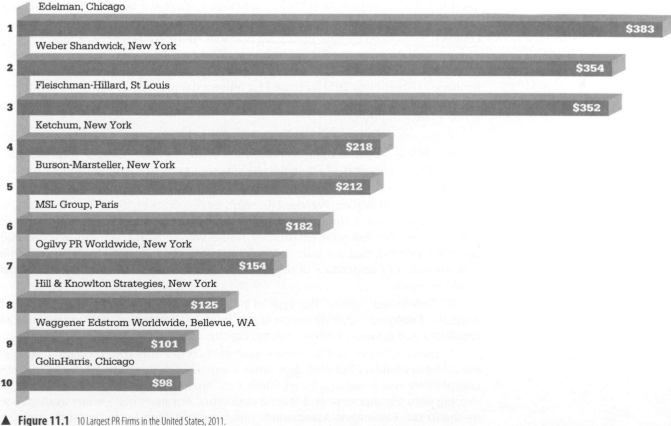

Rank	Firm	Net fees
1	Edelman, Chicago	$383
2	Weber Shandwick, New York	$354
3	Fleischman-Hillard, St Louis	$352
4	Ketchum, New York	$218
5	Burson-Marsteller, New York	$212
6	MSL Group, Paris	$182
7	Ogilvy PR Worldwide, New York	$154
8	Hill & Knowlton Strategies, New York	$125
9	Waggener Edstrom Worldwide, Bellevue, WA	$101
10	GolinHarris, Chicago	$98

▲ **Figure 11.1** 10 Largest PR Firms in the United States, 2011.
Source: Agency Report, 2012b.

There are full-service public relations firms and those that provide only special services. Media specialists for company CEOs, Web commentary monitoring services, and makers of video news releases are special service providers. Public relations firms bill for their services in a number of ways. They may charge an hourly rate for services rendered, or they may be on call, charging clients a monthly fee to act as their public relations counsel. Hill and Knowlton, for example, charges a minimum fee of several thousand dollars a month. Third are **fixed-fee arrangements**, wherein the firm performs a specific set of services for a client for a specific and prearranged fee. Finally, many firms bill for **collateral materials**, adding a surcharge as high as 17.65% for handling printing, research, and photographs. For example, if it costs $3,000 to have a poster printed, the firm charges the client $3,529.50 ($3,000 + [$3,000 × .1765] = $3,000 + $529.50).

Public Relations Activities

Regardless of the way public relations firms bill their clients, they earn their fees by offering all or some of these 14 interrelated services:

1. *Community relations.* This type of public affairs work focuses on the communities in which the organization exists. If a city wants to build a new airport, for example, those whose property will be taken or devalued must be satisfied. If they are not, widespread community opposition to the project may develop.

2. *Counseling.* Public relations professionals routinely offer advice to an organization's management concerning policies, relationships, and communication with its various publics. Management must tell its publics "what we do." Public relations helps in the creation, refinement, and presentation of that message.

3. *Development/fund-raising.* All organizations, commercial and nonprofit, survive through the voluntary contributions in time and money of their members, friends, employees, supporters, and others. Public relations helps demonstrate the need for those contributions. These activities sometimes take the form of **cause marketing**—work in support of social issues and causes—and their importance to clients is evidenced by data indicating that 83% of Americans believe that "companies need to do more good, not just less bad" and 77% say that "brands and corporations have a responsibility to improve the local communities in which they do business" (Greenberg, 2011). Figure 11.2 offers a deeper look at the value of informing the public about clients' efforts at cause marketing and other forms of corporate social responsibility.

4. *Employee/member relations.* Similar to the development function in that the target public is employees and members, this form of public relations responds specifically to the concerns of an organization's employees or members and its retirees and their families. The goal is maintenance of high morale and motivation.

5. *Financial relations.* Practiced primarily by corporate organizations, financial PR is the enhancement of communication between investor-owned companies and their shareholders, the financial community (for example, banks, annuity groups, and investment firms), and the public. Much corporate strategy, such as expansion into new markets and acquisition of other companies, is dependent upon good financial public relations.

6. *Government affairs.* This type of public affairs work focuses on government agencies. **Lobbying**—directly interacting to influence elected officials or government regulators and agents—is often a central activity.

7. *Industry relations.* Companies must interact not only with their own customers and stockholders but also with other companies in their line of business, both competitors and suppliers. In addition, they must also stand as a single voice in dealing with various state and federal regulators. For example, groups as disparate as the Texas Restaurant Association, the American Petroleum Institute, and the National Association of Manufacturers all require public relations in dealing with

Percentage of consumers who agree

Companies must analyze and evolve their business practices to make their impact as positive as possible.
94%

I would buy a product that has environmental benefits.
94%

Companies must go beyond legal compliance to operate responsibly.
93%

I would buy a product associated with a cause.
93%

I would boycott a company for irresponsibility.
93%

It's OK if a company is not perfect, as long as it is honest about its efforts.
88%

I have researched a company's business practices or support of issues.
34.5%

◀ **Figure 11.2** Global Consumers' Attitudes toward Corporate Social Responsibility, 2011. *Source:* Kerkian, 2011.

their various publics. The goal is the maintenance and prosperity of the industry as a whole.

8. *Issues management.* Often an organization is as interested in influencing public opinion about some larger issue that will eventually influence its operation as it is in the improvement of its own image. Issues management typically uses a large-scale public relations campaign designed to move or shape opinion on a specific issue. Usually the issue is an important one that generates deep feelings. Death penalty activists, for example, employ a full range of communication techniques to sway people to their side. ExxonMobil frequently runs advertorials that address environmentalism and public transportation—important issues in and of themselves, but also important to the future of a leading manufacturer of gasoline.

9. *Media relations.* As the number of media outlets grows and as advances in technology increase the complexity of dealing with them, public relations clients require help in understanding the various media, in preparing and organizing materials for them, and in placing those materials. In addition, media relations requires that the public relations professional maintain good relationships with professionals in the media, understand their deadlines and other constraints, and earn their trust.

10. *Marketing communication.* This is a combination of activities designed to sell a product, service, or idea. It can include the creation of advertising; generation of publicity and promotion; design of packaging, point-of-sale displays, and trade show presentations; and design and execution of special events. It is important to note that PR professionals often use advertising but that the two are not the same. The difference is one of control. Advertising is controlled communication—advertisers pay for ads to appear in specific media exactly as they want. PR tends to be less controlled. The PR firm cannot control how or when its press release is used by the local paper. It cannot control how the media react to Nike's ongoing insistence that it has rectified reported worker abuses in its overseas shops. Advertising becomes a public relations function when its goal is to build an image or to motivate action, as opposed to the

usual function of selling products. The Smokey the Bear forest fire prevention campaign is a well-known successful public relations advertising campaign.

Advertising and public relations obviously overlap even for manufacturers of consumer products. Chevrolet must sell cars, but it must communicate with its various publics as well. Toyota, too, must sell cars. But in the wake of the involuntary acceleration recall, it needed serious public relations help. One result of the overlap of advertising and public relations is that advertising agencies increasingly own their own public relations departments or firms or associate closely with a PR company. For a close look at brand marketing in the Internet age, see the box, "Big but Silent No More: Protecting a Company's Good Name in the Era of Social Media."

Another way that advertising and public relations differ is that advertising people typically do not set policy for an organization. Advertising people *implement* policy after organization leaders set it. In contrast, public relations professionals usually are part of the policy decision process because they are the liaison between the organization and its publics. Effective organizations have come to understand that even in routine decisions the impact on public opinion and subsequent consequences can be of tremendous importance. As a result, public relations has become a management function, and a public relations professional typically sits as a member of a company's highest level of management. You'll soon read more about this.

11. *Minority relations/multicultural affairs.* Public affairs activities are directed toward specific racial minorities in this type of work. When the Denny's restaurant chain was beset by numerous complaints of racial discrimination during the 1990s, it undertook an aggressive campaign to speak to those who felt disenfranchised by the events. A secondary goal of its efforts, which were aimed largely at the African American community, was to send a message to its own employees and the larger public that this was the company line, that discrimination was wrong, that everybody was welcome in Denny's.

12. *Public affairs.* The public affairs function includes interacting with officials and leaders of the various power centers with whom a client must deal. Community and government officials and leaders of pressure groups are likely targets of this form of public relations. Public affairs emphasizes social responsibility and building goodwill, such as when a company donates money for a computer lab to the local high school.

13. *Special events and public participation.* Public relations can be used to stimulate interest in an organization, person, or product through a well-planned, focused "happening," an activity designed to facilitate interaction between an organization and its publics.

14. *Research.* Organizations often must determine the attitudes and behaviors of their various publics in order to plan and implement the activities necessary to influence or change those attitudes and behaviors.

▲ The fictitious Acme Fishhook Research Council in this Robotman & Monty cartoon is a good example of an organization that engages in industry relations activities.
MONTY: © Jim Meddick/Dist. by United Feature Syndicate, Inc.

An unfortunate incident between an airline and a celebrity thrust the issue of public relations in the Internet age into the cultural forum.

In February 2009, film director and self-admitted fat man Kevin Smith, after being seated on a Southwest Airlines flight, was asked to leave because he was too big. Known as Silent Bob in his screen roles, Smith was anything but quiet as he immediately began tweeting to his 1.6 million followers: "You [messed] with the wrong sedentary processed-foods eater! . . . I broke no regulation, offered no 'safety risk' (what, was I gonna roll on a fellow passenger?) . . . I saw someone bigger than me on THAT flight! But I wasn't about to throw a fellow Fatty under the plane as I'm being profiled. But he & I made eye contact, & he was like 'Please don't tell . . .'" (Meadows, 2009).

What quickly became known as "Fatgate" went global, but Smith refused all interviews, choosing to use social networking websites, podcasts, and his blog to turn his personal embarrassment into a discussion of society's alleged mistreatment of overweight people. Southwest responded in kind, tweeting and blogging an apology to Mr. Smith, but reiterating its policy on overweight passengers. Then Smith appeared on *The Daily Show* from where he tweeted, "Hey @SouthwestAir: you bring that same row of seats to the DailyShow, and I'll sit in 'em for all to see on TV. If I don't fit, I'll donate $10k to charity of your choice" and "But when I do (&

Big but Silent No More: Protecting a Company's Good Name in the Era of Social Media

buckle the belt as well)? 1) You admit you lied. 2) Change your policy, or at least re-train your staff to be a lot more human & a lot less corporate" (Hall, 2009). The airline never accepted the challenge.

This event occurred against a new reality for public relations professionals working to protect their brands' reputations—instant, immediate, unfiltered consumer commentary.

> "The public relations profession will have to take a stand with 'we the people' and counsel their clients as to how to better align their practices to foster the greater good of society."

"In 1985," wrote PR executive Howard Bragman, "it took five television commercials to get 85% penetration of the TV-viewing households. [Now], it takes 1,292 to achieve the same penetration" (2009, p. 28). But Mister Smith turned worldwide attention on Southwest with *zero* commercials. As a result, writes another industry professional, Len Stein, "Consumers (we the people) are becoming more demanding and discerning of corporate and product values. No longer does offering 'high-quality products and services' and displaying 'transparent and honest business practices' merit our trust. In increasing numbers, people want to know just what kind of behavior to expect from companies and how they are aligned with the greater good."

This is good news for consumers, argues Mr. Stein, because companies will have to react to this new situation by actually becoming better. "The public relations profession will have to take a stand with 'we the people' and counsel their clients as to how to better align their practices to foster the greater good of society" (2010). One way to make this happen, says Mike Swenson of PR firm Barklay, is to use the same new media "to engage in conversations directly with individual consumers. There are no filters and no buffers between brands and consumers in social media conversations. It's a two-way street that levels the playing field between brands and consumers" (in "PR in the Driver's Seat," 2009, p. S6). Adds another industry pro, Roxanne Taylor of Accenture, "I don't believe in PR. By this, I mean I don't believe in hype or spin. However, I believe in authentic communication" (in "Why I Believe in PR," 2009, p. S12).

Enter your voice. Are we seeing the end of **spin**, outright lying or obfuscation, as new, instant consumer media enforce candor? Do you think that companies will more openly engage their consumers in authentic communication about expectations, reputation, and service? If it took public battering at the hands of Twitter to involve Southwest in this discussion to better service, will that embarrassment always have to come first, or will the mere existence of social media encourage companies to proactively improve their products and services?

◀ Kevin Smith: Southwest Airline's big fat PR problem.

Public Relations' Management Function

We saw earlier that public relations people help *establish* communication strategies and advertising people *implement* them. This is public relations' management function, and it is critical to any organization's success. According to the Public Relations Society of America, this function encompasses the following:

- Anticipating, analyzing and interpreting public opinion, attitudes and issues that might impact, for good or ill, the operations and plans of the organization.
- Counseling management at all levels in the organization on policy decisions and courses of action and communication, taking into account their public ramifications and the organization's social or citizenship responsibilities.
- Researching, conducting and evaluating, on a continuing basis, programs of action and communication to achieve the informed public understanding necessary to the success of an organization's aims.
- Planning and implementing the organization's efforts to influence or change public policy.
- Setting objectives, planning, budgeting, recruiting and training staff, and developing facilities, in other words, managing the resources needed to perform all of the above (PRSA, 2012b).

Organization of a Public Relations Operation

Public relations operations come in all sizes. Regardless of size, however, the typical PR firm or department will have these types of positions (but not necessarily these titles):

Executive. This is the chief executive officer who, sometimes with a staff, sometimes alone, sets policy and serves as the spokesperson for the operation.

Account executives. Each account has its own executive who provides advice to the client, defines problems and situations, assesses the needs and demands of the client's publics, recommends a communication plan or campaign, and gathers the PR firm's resources in support of the client.

Creative specialists. These are the writers, graphic designers, artists, video and audio producers, and photographers—anybody necessary to meet the communication needs of the client.

Media specialists. Media specialists are aware of the requirements, preferences, limitations, and strengths of the various media used to serve the client. They find the right media for clients' messages.

Larger public relations operations may also have these positions as need demands:

Research. The key to two-way public relations communication rests in research—assessing the needs of a client's various publics and the effectiveness of the efforts aimed at them. Polling, one-on-one interviews, and **focus groups**, in which small groups of a targeted public are interviewed, provide the PR operation and its client with feedback.

Government relations. Depending on the client's needs, lobbying or other direct communication with government officials may be necessary.

Financial services. Very specific and sophisticated knowledge of economics, finance, and business or corporate law is required to provide clients with dependable financial public relations.

▼ The best public relations can serve both the client and the public, as demonstrated by the Ronald McDonald CareMobile program.

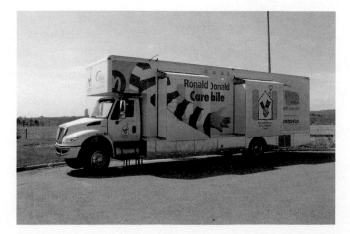

Trends and Convergence in Public Relations

Globalization, Concentration, and Specialization

As they have in the media industries themselves, globalization and concentration have come to public relations in the form of foreign ownership, reach of PR firms' operations into foreign countries, and the collection of several different companies into giant marketing organizations. For example, three of the world's top-10-earning PR firms, despite their U.S. roots, are owned by London-based WPP: Hill and Knowlton, Burson-Marsteller, and Ogilvy PR Worldwide. Hill and Knowlton alone has 2,000 employees working in 79 offices in 44 countries. New York–based independent Edelman PR has 3,100 employees in 51 offices around the world. Marketing giant Omnicom Group, also headquartered in New York, operates in 100 countries, has over 112,262 employees, and serves more than 5,000 clients. It accomplishes this with three of the world's top-seven-earning PR firms (Fleishman-Hillard, Ketchum, and Porter Novelli) and several specialty PR shops (for example, Brodeur Worldwide, Clark & Weinstock, Gavin Anderson & Company, and Cone). But Omnicom is also parent to several national and international advertising agencies, including three of the top 10 global earners (BBDO Worldwide, DDB Worldwide, and TBWA Worldwide); several media planning and buying companies; event branding and planning companies; outdoor, direct marketing, and online advertising specialty shops; and the global marketing company Diversified Agency Services, which itself is home to more than 160 companies offering services through its 700 offices in 71 countries. You can see the world's 10 largest marketing organizations in Figure 11.3.

Net fees in millions of dollars by firm rank and headquarters

Rank	Firm	Net fees
1	Dentsu, Tokyo	$3,577
2	Y & R Group, New York	$3,400
3	McCann Worldgroup, New York	$2,965
4	DDB Worldwide, New York	$2,655
5	Ogilvy & Mather, New York	$2,413
6	BBDO Worldwide, New York	$2,403
7	TBWA Worldwide, New York	$1,797
8	Publicis Worldwide, Paris	$1,524
9	Hakuhodo, Tokyo	$1,357
10	Havas Worldwide, New York	$1,327

▲ **Figure 11.3** World's 10 Largest Marketing Companies, 2012.
Source: Agency Report, 2013.

Another trend in public relations is specialization. We've seen the 14 activities of public relations professionals, but specialization can expand that list. This specialization takes two forms. The first is defined by issue. Environmental public relations is attracting ever-larger numbers of people, both environmentalists and industrialists. E. Bruce Harrison Consulting attracts corporate clients in part because of its reputation as a firm with superior **greenwashing** skills. That is, Harrison is particularly adept at countering the public relations efforts aimed at its clients by environmentalists. Health care and pharmaceuticals has also recently emerged as a significant public relations specialty.

Convergence

The second impetus driving specialization has to do with the increasing number of media outlets used in public relations campaigns that rely on new and converging technologies. Online information and advertising are a growing part of the total public relations media mix, as are **video news releases** (**VNRs**—preproduced reports about a client or its products distributed free of charge to television stations) and videoconferencing. We'll revisit video news releases near the end of this chapter. Television, in the form of the **satellite-delivered media tour**, in which spokespeople can be simultaneously interviewed by a worldwide audience connected to the on-screen interviewee via telephone, has further extended the reach of public relations. In addition, Web publishing has greatly expanded the number and type of available media outlets. All require professionals with quite specific skills.

The public relations industry is responding to the convergence of traditional media with the Internet in other ways as well. One is the development of **integrated marketing communications (IMC)**. We saw earlier how advertising and PR often overlap, but in IMC, firms actively combine public relations, marketing, advertising, and promotion functions into a more or less seamless communication campaign that is as at home on the Web as it is on the television screen and magazine page. The goal of this integration is to provide the client and agency with greater control over communication (and its interpretation) in an increasingly fragmented but synergized media environment. For example, a common IMC tactic is to employ **viral marketing**, a strategy that relies on targeting specific Internet users with a given communication and relying on them to spread the word through the communication channels with which they are most comfortable. This is IMC, and it is inexpensive and effective.

The industry has had to respond to the Internet in another way. The Net has provided various publics with a new, powerful way to counter even the best public relations effort, as we saw in Southwest Airlines' social media dust-up. Tony Juniper of the British environmental group Friends of the Earth calls the Internet "the most potent weapon in the toolbox of resistance." As Peter Verhille of PR giant Entente International explains, "One of the major strengths of pressure groups—in fact the leveling factor in their confrontation with powerful companies—is their ability to exploit the instruments of the telecommunication revolution. Their agile use of global tools such as the Internet reduces the advantages that corporate budgets once provided" (both quotes from Klein, 1999, pp. 395–396). For example, the Internet is central to United Students Against Sweatshops' ongoing efforts to monitor the child labor, safety, and working conditions of U.S. apparel and shoe manufacturers' overseas operations. USAS used the Net to build a nationwide network of students that organized protests and boycotts, resulting in several "victories"—for example, forcing Nike and Reebok to allow workers at one of its Mexican factories to unionize. Public

▼ This is a very successful, long-running advertising campaign. It is also a very successful, long-running public relations campaign.

Only you can prevent forest fires.

U.S. Department of Agriculture—Forest Service and Your State Forester 72-CFPP-96

relations agencies and in-house PR departments have responded in a number of ways. One is IMC. Another is the hiring of in-house Web monitors; a third is the growth of specialty firms such as eWatch, whose function is to alert clients to negative references on the Web and suggest effective countermeasures.

Smartphones, Tablets, and Social Networking Sites

We've already seen in this chapter how the Internet and social media are changing the PR landscape; industry professionals have also taken note. "The long-suffering, much-maligned press release, I'd argue, finally died," wrote *Advertising Age*'s Simon Dumenco, thanks to Twitter (2010, p. 28). Publics can Tweet, as did Kevin Smith, and so can agencies and their clients, making the press release, a PR staple since 1906, obsolete. "Welcome to a new wired world of empowered consumers," says Cone Communications' chief reputation officer Mike Lawrence (in Kerkian, 2011). Smartphones and tablets give PR's publics instant, on-the-spot opportunities to pan or praise its clients; that's obvious. But more important, they give people, especially young people, a greater sense of involvement with a company or organization. "Millennials demand fairness, transparency and clear, consistent rules in every aspect of life," writes Nick Shore, vice president of MTV's research group, "As consumers they feel comfortable leveraging their power (individually and collectively) to 'level the playing field.'" He offered a well-known example, "They more or less took down the record industry, demanding the right to buy and download single songs versus entire CDs" (in Goetzl, 2011).

Mobile technology and social networking also combine to grant publics "free megaphones that carry a customer's complaint around the world," writes *New York Times*' technology writer Randall Stross (2011, p. BU3). Gripe, for example, is a mobile app for smartphones and tablets that allows the instantaneous posting of a complaint or praise to people's Facebook friends and Twitter followers as well as to the named organization's customer service department. Naturally, some industry professionals worry about "social bullying" because a small number of critical customers, once connected to their friends and followers, can exert disproportionate influence. But Gripe's Farhad Mohit counters that because many others see the comments, it is unlikely that Facebook and Twitter will be abused. "You don't want to be viewed as a jerk by your friends and family" (in Stross, 2011, p. BU3).

Trust in Public Relations

We began our discussion of public relations with the industry's self-admission that the profession sometimes bears a negative reputation. Edward Bernays's call for greater sensitivity to the wants and needs of the various publics and Ivy Lee's insistence that public relations be open and honest were the industry's first steps away from its huckster roots. The post–World War II code of ethics and accreditation programs were a second and more important step. Yet Bernays himself was dissatisfied with the profession's progress. The father of public relations died in 1995 at the age of 103. He spent the greater part of his last years demanding that the industry, especially the PRSA, police itself. In 1986 Bernays wrote,

> Under present conditions, an unethical person can sign the code of the PRSA, become a member, practice unethically—untouched by any legal sanctions. In law and medicine, such an individual is subject to disbarment from the profession. . . . There are no standards. . . . This sad situation makes it possible for anyone, regardless of education or ethics, to use the term "public relations" to describe his or her function. (p. 11)

Many people in the profession share Bernays's concern, especially when the industry's own research shows that 85% of the American public thinks that PR practitioners "sometimes take advantage of the media to present misleading information that is favorable to their clients." That same Public Relations Society of America poll revealed that 79% of the general public believes that PR people "are only interested in disseminating information that helps their clients make money" (Burton, 2005). As a result,

▲ The father of public relations, Edward Bernays, used the last years of his long career and life to campaign for improved industry ethics.

Burson-Marsteller senior counselor Fraser Seitel (2004) is adamant about restoring trust in PR:

> The heart of public relations counsel is "to do the right thing." The cardinal rule of public relations is to "never lie." Nonetheless, in one bridling survey of 1,700 public relations executives, it was revealed that 25 percent of those interviewed admitted they had "lied on the job," 39 percent said they had exaggerated the truth, and another 44 percent said they had felt "uncertain" about the ethics of what they did. (p. 132)

Trust, too, is important to Fleishman-Hillard's executive vice president, John Saunders, who called on his colleagues to debate what their industry stands for. He told the 2005 annual meeting of the International Communications Consultancy Organisation,

> This is no longer the golden age of PR. We will need to change to get to where we want to be in the future. . . . We need to devote more energy to ethics. If we are to advise on reputation management, we must be above reproach. . . . We need to impose more rigorous standards on ourselves. (in Marriott, 2005)

Today in the United States there is nearly one person employed in PR for every 100,000 Americans, compared to .25 journalists for that same number of citizens, a "ratio of better than three-to-one, better equipped, better financed" (Sullivan, 2011). Estimates from both inside and outside the industry claim that from 50% to 90% of the stories we read in the paper or see on television originate entirely or in part from a public relations operation in the form of either a printed or a video news release. Critics further contend that 40% of what we read and see appears virtually unedited, leading PR professionals to boast that "the best PR is invisible" and "the best PR ends up looking like news" (Stauber & Rampton, 1995, p. 2).

But not all public relations professionals find comfort in the invisibility of their work or in the public's inability to distinguish between news and PR. In 2007, after Wal-Mart's and Sony's PR operations were discovered paying fake bloggers (**flogs**) to promote their brands (and attack competitors'), there were calls from **transparentists** who, according to PR executive Eric Webber (2007), demanded that the industry "adopt a position of full and total disclosure, driven by the innate openness and accessibility to information available on the Internet." If public relations is to hold consumer (and client) trust, he argued, its professionals must recognize that "it's too easy now for journalists, pro and amateur alike, to figure out when companies and their PR people lie, so we'd better tell the truth" (p. 8).

But if people *are* lied to by public relations, the cultural implications could not be more profound. What becomes of the negotiation function of culture, wherein we debate and discuss our values and interests in the cultural forum, if public relations gives some voices advantages not available to others? The remedy for this potential problem: Consumers must make themselves aware of the sources of information and the process by which it is produced. As we've seen throughout this book, we would expect nothing less of a media-literate person.

DEVELOPING MEDIA LITERACY SKILLS

Recognizing Video News Releases

The calls from PR professionals for ethics, accountability, and honesty were the result of the abuses noted earlier in this chapter. But another that caught the attention of the public and industry alike was the recent revelation that government agencies were making frequent use of video news releases (VNRs), presenting their favored public policy positions as actual news reports. In the uproar that followed, VNRs themselves became controversial. Congress's own General Accountability Office deemed their use by governmental agencies illegal. The FCC vowed to strengthen its rules on disclosure of the sources of VNRs and raised the maximum fine it could level at an offending station. The broadcast industry's Radio-Television News Directors Association clarified and strengthened its rules on VNR identification and disclosure.

But VNRs are still used in 90% of all American television newsrooms, primarily because even though many local stations have increased the amount of airtime they devote to news programming, few have the time or resources to produce a sufficient amount of original content to fill it. Moreover, despite the stricter FCC and industry-mandated disclosure rules, a recent Center for Media and Democracy study of 69 stations with a total audience of half the country found that while all made use of VNRs, not a single station identified them as such (Barstow, 2006) and a quarter of U.S. television news executives admit "a blurring of lines between advertising and news" (Farhi, 2012). So where the problem for broadcasters is identification and disclosure, the problem for media-literate viewers is recognizing VNRs, a somewhat difficult task because VNRs typically

- Look exactly like genuine news reports, employing the visual and aural conventions we typically associate with television news.
- Are narrated by a speaker whose voice, intonation, and delivery match those of a bona fide television news reporter.
- Carry the voice-over on a separate audio channel so the station can delete the original narration and have its own anchor or reporter narrate to give the appearance that the report originated locally.
- Are accompanied by a script in the event the local station wants its own personnel to do the narration but needs help in writing it.
- Come free of titles or other graphics because local stations have their own logos and video character typefaces.

VNRs can be used in their entirety or in part, and the companies that produce them consider even a five-second excerpt aired on a local news show a success. Many stations follow federal rules and industry ethics on disclosure, but often they do so in the "film and video provided by" scroll that flies by at the end of the broadcast, making the matching of source to content difficult. In the end, then, viewers must often depend on their own media literacy skills when confronting VNRs, although the FCC is trying to help, proposing new rules in 2012 that would require all commercial television stations to disclose on their websites any corporate interests behind the news they air.

In instances when a reporter or anchor acknowledges the outside source of a report while it airs, viewers must determine what level of trust they want to give the story. Not all VNRs are false or misleading. If we accept that they are created to further a particular individual's or organization's interests, they can provide useful information. In those cases where the source is not identified or is identified apart from the report, media-literate people should question not only the report but the value of a news operation that has such limited regard for its viewers.

The question remains, though, of how to identify a VNR when the station fails to do so. We are watching a VNR when

- The report is accompanied by visuals that are not from the station's broadcast area.
- No local station personnel appear in the report.
- There is no verbal or visual attribution (for example, "These scenes are from our sister station in Memphis" or a network logo in the corner of the screen).
- The report appears in the part of the newscast typically reserved for soft or feature stories.

An important component of media literacy is *possessing critical thinking skills that enable a person to develop independent judgments about media content*. Naturally, this encompasses *the ability to recognize when genre conventions are mixed*, in this case, public relations promotional material and television news. Challenge your media literacy skills, then, by watching one day's early and late editions of the local news from your favorite television station. Count the number of individual news reports, excluding weather and sports. How many of those reports were provided by a source other than the station itself? What were your clues? Did local station personnel appear as part of any of the stories? Was there verbal or visual attribution? Did the stories appear in the "soft news" segment of the news? Did the station acknowledge the outside source? If it did not, do you consider this deceptive? Why or why not? Can you explain your results and your reaction to those results in terms of your *expectations of local television news*, your *knowledge of local news and public relations genre conventions*, and your *ability to think critically about media messages, no matter how credible their sources*? You can take this challenge as either an opportunity for personal reflection, committing your thoughts to paper, or you can duel with classmates to see who can find the greatest number of VNRs or possibly the most egregious example of deception in the chosen broadcasts.

Resources for Review and Discussion

REVIEW POINTS: TYING CONTENT TO LEARNING OUTCOMES

▶ **Outline the history and development of the public relations industry.**

  ▶ The history of public relations can be divided into four stages: early public relations, the propaganda–publicity stage, early two-way communication, and advanced two-way communication.

  ▶ The evolution of public relations has been shaped by advances in technology, the growth of the middle class, growth of organizations, better research tools, and professionalization.

▶ **Describe how the organizational and economic nature of the contemporary public relations industry shapes the messages with which publics interact, especially in an increasingly converged media environment.**

  ▶ Public relations tells an organization's "story" to its publics (communication) and helps shape the organization and the way it performs (management).

  ▶ Advertising executes an organization's communication strategy; public relations provides several important management functions.

  ▶ Firms typically are organized around an executive, account executives, creative specialists, and media specialists. Larger firms typically include research, government relations, and financial service professionals.

▶ **Identify different types of public relations and the different publics each is designed to serve.**

  ▶ The publics served by the industry include employees, stockholders, communities, media, government, investment communities, and customers.

  ▶ Public relations firms provide all or some of these 14 services: community relations, counseling, development and fundraising, employee/member relations, financial relations, government affairs, industry relations, issues management, media relations, marketing communication, minority relations and multicultural affairs, public affairs, special events, and public participation and research.

▶ **Explain the relationship between public relations and its various publics.**

  ▶ Globalization, specialization, and convergence—in the form of video news releases, satellite-delivered media tours, integrated marketing communications, and viral marketing—are reshaping contemporary PR's relationships with its clients and its publics.

  ▶ Trust in public relations is essential if the industry is to perform its role for its clients and publics.

▶ **Apply key media literacy skills when consuming public relations messages, especially video news releases.**

  ▶ Recognizing video news releases is difficult, but media-literate viewers look for visuals from outside the station's area and the absence of station personnel, a lack of attribution, and the suspected VNR's presence in the soft news portion of the newscast.

KEY TERMS

flack, 265

astroturf, 266

pseudo-event, 267

public, 272

fixed-fee arrangement, 274

collateral materials, 274

cause marketing, 274

lobbying, 274

spin, 277

focus groups, 278

greenwashing, 280

video news release (VNR), 280

satellite-delivered media tour, 280

integrated marketing communications (IMC), 280

viral marketing, 280

flog, 282

transparentists, 282

QUESTIONS FOR REVIEW

1. What elements are essential to a good definition of public relations?

2. What are the four stages in the development of the public relations industry?

3. Who were Ivy Lee, George Creel, and Edward Bernays?

4. What is the difference between public relations and advertising?

5. What are some specific divisions of public relations' public affairs activities?

6. Who are public relations' publics? What are their characteristics?

7. What positions typically exist in a public relations operation?

8. How have new communication technologies influenced the public relations industry?

9. What is integrated marketing communications? What is its goal?

10. What is viral marketing? How does it work?

connect

For further review, go to the LearnSmart study module for this chapter.

QUESTIONS FOR CRITICAL THINKING AND DISCUSSION

1. Are you familiar with Mars Chocolate, the candy company in the opening vignette? What was your opinion of it before you read of its support for the fight against hunger in America? What is your opinion now? Does community relations such as this really work, or do most people see it as self-serving? Do you agree or disagree that a company's precrisis reputation can help it weather a crisis should one occur? Why or why not?

2. Have you ever been part of an Internet-fueled movement against the activities of an organization or in support of some good cause? If you were, you were engaged in public relations. Measure your experience against the lessons in this chapter. What kinds of public relations activities did you undertake? Who were your publics? Were you successful? Why or why not?

3. Were you aware of the Kevin Smith imbroglio? If so, how did you find out about it? Did you use the Internet to dig deeper into the story? Did your opinion of Southwest Airlines change as a result of the efforts of Mr. Smith? Were you satisfied with the company's response?

Advertising

Learning Objectives

Advertising is everywhere. As it becomes more ubiquitous, we tend to ignore it. But as we tend to ignore it, advertisers find new ways to make it more ubiquitous. As a result, and as with television, no one is neutral about advertising. We love it or we hate it. Many of us do both. After studying this chapter you should be able to

▶ Outline the history and development of the advertising industry.

▶ Evaluate contemporary criticisms and defenses of advertising.

▶ Describe how the organizational and economic nature of the contemporary advertising industry shapes the content of advertising, especially in an increasingly converged media environment.

▶ Identify different types of advertising and their goals.

▶ Explain the relationship between advertising content and its consumers.

▶ Apply key media literacy skills when consuming advertising, especially when interpreting intentional imprecision.

Does ambient advertising cut through the clutter or add to it?

287

YOUR ROOMMATES, BOTH ADVERTISING MAJORS, CHALLENGE YOU: "We bet you $10 that you can't go all of tomorrow without seeing an ad." You think, "I'll just stay away from radio and television—no problem, considering I have an MP3 player in my car and tons of homework to do." That leaves newspapers and magazines, but you can avoid their ads simply by not reading either for 24 hours. Online ads? You'll simply stay unlinked. Facebook and Twitter. You can survive a day friendless and unfollowed. "What about billboards?" you counter.

"We won't count them," your roomies graciously concede, "but everything else is in."

You shake hands and go to bed planning your strategy. This means no cereal in the morning—the Cheerios box has a McDonald's ad on it. There'll be no bus to school. Not only are the insides packed with ads, but a lot of buses are now covered in vinyl wrap ads that let riders see out the windows but turn buses into gigantic rolling commercials. Can't walk either. There are at least two ad kiosks on the way. It'll cost you more than $10 to take a cab, but this is about winning the bet, not about money. Cab it will be! You sleep well, confident victory will be yours.

The next evening, over pizza, you hand over your $10.

"What was it?" gloats one of your companions. "Sneak a peek at TV?"

"No," you say, and then you begin the list: The cab had an ad for a radio station on its trunk and a three-sided sign on its roof touting the pizza joint you're sitting in, a chiropractor, and Southwest Airlines. Inside, it had an electronic digital display hanging from the ceiling, pushing the lottery. The sidewalk near campus had the message "From here it looks like you could use some new underwear—Bamboo Lingerie" stenciled on it in water-soluble iridescent red paint. The restrooms on campus have Volkswagen ads pasted on their walls. Your ATM receipt carried an ad for a brokerage firm. You encountered a Domino's Pizza ad on the back of the cash register receipt you got at the grocery store; the kiwi you bought there had a sticker on it reminding you to buy Snapple. The shopping basket had a realtor's pitch pasted to the side; even the little

1800	1850

1625 ▲ First newsbooks with ads

1735 Ben Franklin sells ad space in *Pennsylvania Gazette*

1841 ▲ Palmer begins first ad agency

1869 Ayer begins first full-service ad agency

1880s ▲ Brands appear

rubber bar you used to separate your kiwi and mineral water from the groceries of the shopper in front of you had an ad on each of its four sides.

"Easiest $10 we ever made," smile your roommates.

In this chapter we examine the history of advertising, focusing on its maturation with the coming of industrialization and the Civil War. The development of the advertising agency and the rise of professionalism within its ranks are detailed, as is the impact of magazines, radio, World War II, and television.

We discuss the relationship between consumers and contemporary advertising in terms of how advertising agencies are structured, how various types of advertising are aimed at different audiences, and which trends—converging technologies, audience segmentation, globalization—promise to alter those relationships.

We study the controversies that surround the industry. Critics charge that advertising is intrusive, deceptive, inherently unethical when aimed at children, and corrupting of the culture. We look at industry defenses, too.

Finally, in the media literacy skills section, we discuss advertisers' use of intentional imprecision and how to identify and interpret it.

▲ Even in death, it's difficult to avoid advertising.

A Short History of Advertising

Your roommates had the advantage. They know that U.S. advertisers and marketers spend nearly $500 billion a year—half the world's total—trying to get your attention and influence your decisions. They also know that you typically encounter 5,000 commercial messages a day—as opposed to 560 a day in 1971 (Johnson, 2009). There are

...*Yank friendliness comes back to Leyte*

1900	**1950**	**2000**
1914 Federal Trade Commission established	**1957** Packard's *The Hidden Persuaders*	**2004** *Adbusters* Unbrand America
1922 First radio commercial	**1959** Quiz show scandal	**2005** MI4 initiated; chaos scenario
1923 *The Eveready Hour*, first regularly broadcast sponsored series	**1971** National Advertising Review Board established; TV cigarette commercial ban	**2008** Internet ad spending exceeds radio's
1936 Consumers Union established	**1980** ▲ Foreign ad spending first exceeds U.S. ad outlay	**2009** Internet ad spending exceeds magazines'
1938 Wheeler-Lea Act	**1994** First banner ad; spam appears	**2012** ▲ Internet ad spending exceeds all print advertising; Tobacco companies ordered to run corrective ads
1941 ▲ War Advertising Council (Ad Council) founded		
1948 Television to the public		

This narrow street in Salzburg, Austria, still exhibits evidence of early European advertising, which often took the form of artistically designed signs announcing the nature of the business below.

a lot of ads and a lot of advertisers. Almost everyone in the ad business complains about what has become commercial clutter, yet, in the words of *Advertising Age* writer Matthew Creamer (2007), "Like a fly repeatedly bouncing off a closed window, the ad industry is trying to fix the problem by doing more of the same. That is, by creating more ads" (p. 1). Some label it **ambient advertising**, others **360 marketing**, and by whatever name, these ads are showing up in some fairly nontraditional settings. This is because advertisers believe that "our susceptibility to marketing arises from our ignorance of its pervasiveness," what they call **murketing** (Manjoo, 2008, p. 7). Kentucky Fried Chicken paints municipal fire hydrants and other safety equipment in exchange for the right to display its logo; Sony hired graffiti artists in major cities to spray-paint commercials for its PlayStation Portable on walls and buildings. Officials in Brooklawn, New Jersey, sell naming rights to school facilities—the gym at the Alice Costello Elementary School is now the ShopRite of Brooklawn Center. Ad company GreenGraffiti "cleans" Domino Pizza logos into dirty sidewalks; InChairTV inserts commercials into specially licensed Disney/ABC programming for play on digital screens suspended above dental patients' heads; radio, concert promotion, and outdoor ad company Clear Channel maintains a separate Branded Cities division whose function is to "transform locations into destinations—places where consumers go for entertainment, dining, shopping, to work, and to live . . . and where brands are an integral part of that experience." Sony Ericsson hires actors to pose as tourists, walk up to people, and ask them to photograph them with its new line of smartphone cameras. We see ads on door hangers, on urinal deodorant cakes, in the mail, behind the batter at a baseball game, on basketball backboards in city parks. We hear **blinks**, one-second commercials between songs on the radio. We use digital adscreen hand driers in public restrooms and we find coupons on the toilet paper. It wasn't always like this, but advertising itself has been with us for a long time.

▶ Advertising everywhere—Sony hired graffiti artists in several major American cities to spray-paint commercials for its PlayStation Portable on walls and buildings.

Early Advertising

Babylonian merchants were hiring barkers to shout out goods and prices at passersby in 3000 B.C.E. The Romans wrote announcements on city walls. This ad was discovered in the ruins of Pompeii:

> The Troop of Gladiators of the Aedil
> Will fight on the 31st of May
> There will be fights with wild animals
> And an Awning to keep off the sun. (Berkman & Gilson, 1987, p. 32)

By the 15th century, ads as we know them now were abundant in Europe. **Siquis**—pinup want ads for all sorts of products and services—were common. Tradespeople promoted themselves with **shopbills**—attractive, artful business cards. Taverners and other merchants were hanging eye-catching signs above their businesses. In 1625 the first **newsbook** containing ads, *The Weekly News*, was printed in England. From the beginning, those who had products and services to offer used advertising.

Advertising came to the Colonies via England. British advertising was already leaning toward exaggeration and hyperbole, but colonial advertising was more straightforward. We saw in Chapter 4 that Ben Franklin was selling advertising space in his *Pennsylvania Gazette*. This 1735 ad is typical:

> A Plantation containing 300 acres of good Land, 30 cleared, 10 or 12 Meadow and in good English Grass, a house and barn & c. [creek] lying in Nantmel Township, upon French-Creek, about 30 miles from Philadelphia. Inquire of Simon Meredith now living on the said place. (Sandage, Fryburger, & Rotzoll, 1989, p. 21)

Advertising, however, was a small business before the Civil War. The United States was primarily an agricultural country at that time, with 90% of the population living in self-sufficiency on farms. Advertising was used by local retailers primarily to encourage area residents to come to their businesses. The local newspaper was the major advertising medium.

Industrialization and the Civil War

The Industrial Revolution and the Civil War altered the social and cultural landscape and brought about the expansion of advertising. By the 1840s the telegraph made communication over long distances possible. Railroads linked cities and states. Huge numbers of immigrants were welcomed to the United States to provide labor for the expanding factories. Manufacturers wanted access to larger markets for their goods. Advertising copywriter Volney B. Palmer recognized in 1841 that merchants needed to reach consumers beyond their local newspaper readership. He contacted several Philadelphia newspapers and agreed to broker the sale of space between them and interested advertisers. Within four years Palmer had expanded his business to Boston, and in 1849, he opened a branch in New York. The advertising agency had been invented.

The Civil War sped industrialization. More factories were needed to produce war material, and roads and railroads were expanded to move that material as well as troops. As farmworkers went to war or to work in the new factories, more farm machinery was needed to compensate for their departure. That meant that more factories were needed to make more machinery, and the cycle repeated.

▲ This early-18th-century tobacco label shows that the British had already mastered the use of celebrities in their advertising.

By the early 1880s the telephone and the electric light had been invented. That decade saw numerous innovations in manufacturing as well as an explosion in the type and availability of products. In the year 1880 alone, there were applications for more than 13,000 U.S. copyrights and patents. Over 70,000 miles of new railroad track were laid in the 1880s, linking cities and towns of all sizes. With more producers chasing the growing purchasing power of more consumers, manufacturers were forced to differentiate their products—to literally and figuratively take the pickle out of the barrel and put it in its own recognizable package. Brands were born: Quaker Oats, Ivory Soap, Royal Baking Powder, and many more. What advertisers now needed was a medium in which to tell people about these brands.

Magazine Advertising

We've seen in Chapter 5 how expansion of the railroads, the rise in literacy, and advantageous postal rates fueled the explosive growth of the popular magazine just before the end of the 19th century. The marriage of magazines and advertising was a natural. Cyrus H. K. Curtis, who founded the *Ladies' Home Journal* in 1883, told a group of manufacturers:

> The editor of the Ladies' Home Journal thinks we publish it for the benefit of American women. This is an illusion, but a very proper one for him to have. The real reason, the publisher's [Curtis's] reason, is to give you who manufacture things American women want, a chance to tell them about your product. (Sandage et al., 1989, p. 32)

By the turn of the century, magazines were financially supported primarily by their advertisers rather than by their readers, and aspects of advertising we find common today—creativity in look and language, mail-order ads, seasonal ads, and placement of ads in proximity to content of related interest—were already in use.

The Advertising Agency and Professionalism

In the years between the Civil War and World War I, advertising had rapidly become more complex, more creative, and more expensive, and it was conducted on a larger scale. Advertising agencies had to expand their operations to keep up with demand. Where Palmer offered merely to broker the sale of newspaper space, F. Wayland Ayer began his "full service" advertising agency in 1869. He named his firm N. W. Ayer and Sons after his father because, at only 20 years old, he felt that clients would not trust him with their business. Ayer (the son) provided clients with ad campaign planning, created and produced ads with his staff of artists and writers, and placed them in the most appropriate media. Several big agencies still operating today started at this time, including J. Walter Thompson, William Esty, and Lord & Thomas.

During this period, three factors combined to move the advertising industry to establish professional standards and to regulate itself. First was the reaction of the public and the medical profession to the abuses of patent medicine advertisers. These charlatans used fake claims and medical data in their ads to sell tonics that at best were useless and, at worst, deadly. The second was the critical examination of most of the country's important institutions, led by the muckrakers (Chapter 5). The third factor was the establishment in 1914 of the Federal Trade Commission (FTC), which had among its duties monitoring and regulating advertising. A number of leading advertising agencies and publishers mounted a crusade against gross exaggeration, false testimonials, and other misleading forms of advertising. The Audit Bureau of Circulations was established to verify circulation claims. The Advertising Federation of America (now the American Advertising Federation), the American Association of Advertising Agencies, the Association of National Advertisers, and the Outdoor Advertising Association all began operation at this time.

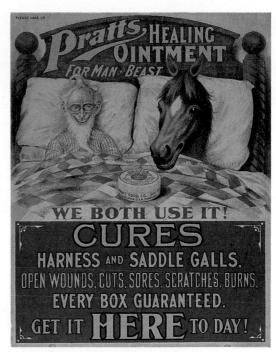

▲ Reaction to the deception and outright lies of patent medicine advertising—such as this 1880 piece for Pratts Healing Ointment—led to important efforts to professionalize the industry.

Advertising and Radio

The first radio ad, as we've seen in Chapter 7, was broadcast on WEAF in 1922 (the cost was $50 for a 10-minute spot). Radio was important to advertising in three major ways. First, although people both inside and outside government were opposed to commercial support for the new medium, the general public had no great opposition to radio ads. In fact, in the prosperous Roaring Twenties, many welcomed them; advertising seemed a natural way to keep radio "free." Second, advertising agencies virtually took over broadcasting, producing the shows in which their commercials appeared. The ad business became show business. The 1923 variety show *The Eveready Hour*, sponsored by a battery maker, was the first regularly broadcast sponsored series. Ad agency Blackett-Sample-Hummert even developed a new genre for its client Procter & Gamble—the radio soap opera. Third, money now poured into the industry. That income was used to expand research and marketing on a national scale, allowing advertisers access to sophisticated nationwide consumer and market information for the first time. The wealth that the advertising industry accrued from radio permitted it to survive during the Depression.

▼ A Plymouth hard-sell ad from 1931. The hard sell made its debut during the Depression as advertisers worked to attract the little consumer money that was available.

The Depression did have its effect on advertising, however. The stock market crashed in 1929, and by 1933 advertising had lost nearly two-thirds of its revenues. Among the responses were the hard sell—making direct claims about why a consumer *needed* a product—and a tendency away from honesty. At the same time, widespread unemployment and poverty bred a powerful consumer movement. The Consumers Union, which still publishes *Consumer Reports*, was founded in 1936 to protect people from unscrupulous manufacturers and advertisers. And in 1938 Congress passed the Wheeler-Lea Act, granting the FTC extended powers to regulate advertising.

World War II

The Second World War, so important in the development of all the mass media, had its impact on advertising as well. Production of consumer products came to a near halt during the war (1941–1945), and traditional advertising was limited. The advertising industry turned its collective skills toward the war effort, and the limited product advertising typically adopted a patriotic theme.

In 1941 several national advertising and media associations joined to develop the War Advertising Council. The council used its expertise to promote numerous government programs. Its best-known campaign, however, was on behalf of the sale of war bonds. The largest

USING MEDIA TO MAKE A DIFFERENCE
Effecting Positive Social Change

Advertising can often lead people to do good, and there is no better example of this than the work of the Ad Council. In fact, its mission is "Effecting Positive Social Change." Has it succeeded in making a difference? Who are Smokey Bear, Rosie the Riveter, McGruff the Crime Dog, the Crash Test Dummies, and the Crying Indian (Chief Iron Eyes Cody)? All are creations of the Ad Council. And with how many of these slogans are you familiar?

- Friends don't let friends drive drunk
- Only you can prevent forest fires
- A mind is a terrible thing to waste
- Just say no
- I am an American

All are from Ad Council campaigns. Can the ability of the Ad Council to make a difference be quantified? Consider the following:

- Applications for mentors rose from 90,000 a year to 620,000 in the first nine months after the start of its campaign for Big Brothers/Big Sisters.
- Sixty-eight percent of Americans say that they have personally stopped someone who had been drinking from driving. The old saying, "One More for the Road" has been replaced with "Friends Don't Let Friends Drive Drunk."
- The amount of waste Americans recycle has increased 385% since the start of the Environmental Defense campaign in the 1980s (www.adcouncil.org).

> "The Ad Council currently has more than 50 different public service campaigns on its docket, and it is able to secure about $2 billion a year in donated time and space from 28,000 different media outlets."

The Ad Council currently has more than 50 different public service campaigns on its docket, and it is able to secure about $2 billion a year in donated time and space from 28,000 different media outlets. Its primary focus today is kids' issues, devoting 80% of its resources to its 10-Year Commitment to Children: Helping Parents Help Kids campaign. But the Ad Council does not shy away from controversial issues. In the 1970s it took on sexually transmitted disease with its "VD Is for Everyone" campaign, an effort attacked by many religious groups, and many broadcasters refused to air its "Help Stop AIDS. Use a Condom" spots in 1987.

The Ad Council is able to make a difference because dozens of ad agencies, big and small, donate their time, energy, and creativity.

▲ The Ad Council has been using the skill of industry pros to effect positive social change for decades. Do you recognize either of these campaigns?

campaign to date for a single item, the war bond program helped sell 800 million bonds, totaling $45 billion. When the war ended, the group, now called the Advertising Council, directed its efforts toward a host of public service campaigns on behalf of countless nonprofit organizations (see the essay, "Effecting Positive Social Change"). Most of us have read or heard, "This message is brought to you by the Ad Council."

The impact of World War II on the size and structure of the advertising industry was significant. A high excess-profits tax was levied on manufacturers' wartime profits that exceeded prewar levels. The goal was to limit war profiteering and ensure that companies did not benefit too greatly from the death and destruction of war. Rather than pay the heavy tariff, manufacturers reduced their profit levels by putting income back into their businesses. Because the lack of raw materials made expansion or recapitalization difficult, many companies invested in corporate image advertising. They may not have had products to sell to the public, but they knew that the war would end someday and that stored-up goodwill would be important. One result, therefore, was an expansion in the number and size of manufacturers' advertising departments and of advertising agencies. A second result was a public primed by that advertising anticipating the return of consumer goods.

Advertising and Television

There was no shortage of consumer products when the war ended. The nation's manufacturing capacity had been greatly expanded to meet the needs of war, and now that manufacturing capability was turned toward the production of consumer products for people who found themselves with more leisure and more money (Chapter 1). People were also having more children and, thanks to the GI Bill, were able to think realistically about owning their own homes. They wanted products to enhance their leisure, please their children, and fill their houses.

◀ Consumer products go to war. Advertisers and manufacturers joined the war effort. These GIs are enjoying a Coke on Leyte Island in the Pacific in a 1945 *Collier's* ad.

...*Yank friendliness comes back to Leyte*

Naturally Filipinos thrilled when their Yankee comrades-in-arms came back to the Philippines. Freedom came back with them. Fair play took the place of fear. But also they brought back the old sense of friendliness that America stands for. You find it quickly expressed in the simple phrase *Have a Coke*. There's no easier or warmer way to say *Relax and be yourself*. Everywhere *the pause that refreshes* with ice-cold Coca-Cola has become a symbol of good will—an everyday example of how Yankee friendliness follows the flag around the globe.

*   *   *

Our fighting men meet up with Coca-Cola many places overseas, where it's bottled on the spot. Coca-Cola has been a globe-trotter "since way back when".

"Coke" = Coca-Cola
You naturally hear Coca-Cola called by its friendly abbreviation "Coke". Both mean the quality product of The Coca-Cola Company.

COPYRIGHT 1945, THE COCA-COLA COMPANY

Advertising was well positioned to put products and people together, not only because agencies had expanded during the war but also because of television. Radio's formats, stars, and network structure had moved wholesale to the new medium. Television soon became the primary national advertising medium. Advertisers bought $12 million in television time in 1949; two years later they spent $128 million.

Television commercials, by virtue of the fact that consumers could see and hear the product in action, were different from the advertising of all other media. The ability to demonstrate the product—to do the torture test for Timex watches, to smoothly shave sandpaper with Gillette Foamy—led to the **unique selling proposition (USP)**: that is, highlighting the aspect of a product that sets it apart from other brands in the same product category. Once an advertiser discovered a product's USP, it could drive it home in repeated demonstration commercials. Inasmuch as most brands in a given product category are essentially the same—that is, they are **parity products**—advertisers were often forced to create a product's USP. Candy is candy, for example, but M&Ms are unique: They melt in your mouth, not in your hand.

Some observers were troubled by this development. Increasingly, products were being sold not by touting their value or quality but by emphasizing their unique selling propositions. Ads were offering little information about the product, yet people were increasing their spending. This led to growing criticism of advertising and its contribution to the consumer culture (more on this controversy later in the chapter). The immediate impact was the creation of an important vehicle of industry self-regulation. In response to mounting criticism in books such as *The Hidden Persuaders* (Packard, 1957), and concern over increasing scrutiny from the FTC, the industry in 1971 established the National Advertising Review Board (NARB) to monitor potentially deceptive advertising. The NARB, the industry's most important self-regulatory body, investigates consumer complaints as well as complaints made by an advertiser's competitors.

Advertising and Its Audiences

The typical individual living in the United States will spend more than one year of his or her life just watching television commercials. It is a rare moment when we are not in the audience of some ad or commercial. This is one of the many reasons advertisers have begun to place their messages in many venues beyond the traditional commercial media, as we saw earlier, hoping to draw our attention. We confront so many ads every day that we overlook them, and they become invisible. As a result, many people become aware of advertising only when it somehow offends them.

Criticisms and Defenses of Advertising

Advertising does sometimes offend, and it is often the focus of criticism. But industry defenders argue the following:

- Advertising supports our economic system; without it new products could not be introduced and developments in others could not be announced. Competitive advertising of new products and businesses powers the engine of our economy, fostering economic growth and creating jobs in many industries.
- People use advertising to gather information before making buying decisions.
- Ad revenues make possible the "free" mass media we use not only for entertainment but also for the maintenance of our democracy.
- By showing us the bounty of our capitalistic, free enterprise society, advertising increases national productivity (as people work harder to acquire more of these products) and improves the standard of living (as people actually acquire more of these products).

The first defense is a given. Ours is a capitalistic society whose economy depends on the exchange of goods and services. Complaints, then, have less to do with the existence of advertising than with its conduct and content, and they are not new. At the 1941 founding meeting of the Advertising Council, J. Walter Thompson executive James Webb Young argued that such a public service commitment would go far toward improving the public's attitude toward his industry, one "rooted very deep. It is a sort of repugnance for the manifestations of advertising—or its banality, its bad taste, its moronic appeals, and its clamor" (quoted in "Story of the Ad Council," 2001). The second defense assumes that advertising provides information. But much—critics would say most—advertising is devoid of useful information about the product. Grant Leach, managing director of the ad agency The Revo Group, declares, "Consumers no longer buy products but rather lifestyles and the stories, experiences, and emotions products convey" (quoted in Williams, 2002, p. 17). The third defense assumes that the only way media can exist is through commercial support, but many nations around the world have built fine media systems without heavy advertiser support (see Chapter 15). To critics of advertising, the fourth defense—that people work hard only to acquire more things and that our standard of living is measured by what material things we have—draws an unflattering picture of human nature.

▲ Among the earliest demonstration ads, Timex took many a licking but kept on ticking.

Specific Complaints

Specific complaints about advertising are that it is often intrusive, deceptive, and, in the case of children's advertising, inherently unethical. Advertising is said to demean or corrupt the culture.

ADVERTISING IS INTRUSIVE Many critics fault advertising for its intrusiveness. Advertising is everywhere, and it interferes with and alters our experience. Giant wall advertisements change the look of cities. Ads beamed by laser light onto night skies destroy evening stargazing. School learning aids provided by candy makers that ask students to "count the Tootsie Rolls" alter education. Many Internet users complain about the commercialization of the new medium and fear advertising will alter its free, open, and freewheeling nature. Nearly 16% of online viewers, for example, will click away from a video site rather than watch a 15- or 30-second ad preceding the content they had initially selected (Learmonth, 2010b), and 67% of Americans find it unacceptable to receive unwanted advertising on their smartphones and tablets (Barron & Chowdhury, 2012). An Associated Press study of advertising and consumers demonstrated that although most "were eager to receive information that met their needs and just as eager to pass that information along to their personal networks . . . they were tired, even annoyed, by the current experience of advertising. And they lacked trust in most commercial messaging" (2010, p. 47). As for digital advertising, you can see how much users value them in Figure 12.1.

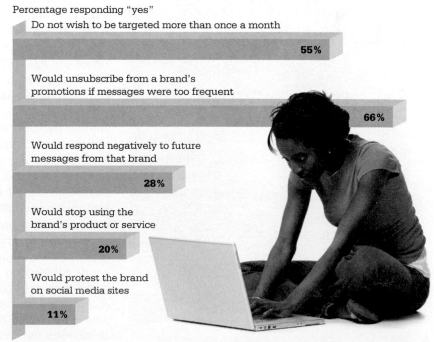

Percentage responding "yes"

Do not wish to be targeted more than once a month
55%

Would unsubscribe from a brand's promotions if messages were too frequent
66%

Would respond negatively to future messages from that brand
28%

Would stop using the brand's product or service
20%

Would protest the brand on social media sites
11%

▲ **Figure 12.1** Americans' Responses to Digital Advertising Overload, 2012.
Source: Barron & Chowdhury, 2012.

ADVERTISING IS DECEPTIVE Many critics say that much advertising is inherently deceptive in that it implicitly and sometimes explicitly promises to improve people's lives through the consumption or purchase of a sponsor's products. Jamieson and Campbell (1997) described this as the "If . . . then" strategy: "A beautiful woman uses a certain brand of lipstick in the ad, and men follow her everywhere. Without making the argument explicit, the ad implies that if you use this product you will be beautiful, and if you are beautiful (or use this product), you will be more attractive to men" (p. 242). They called the opposite strategy "If not . . . then not." When Hallmark says "When you care enough to send the very best," the implication is that when you do not send Hallmark, you simply do not care.

Advertising promises health, long life, sexual success, financial success, companionship, popularity, and acceptance. Industry defenders argue that people understand and accept these as allowable exaggerations, not as deception. Yet in 2012 fewer than half (47%) of consumers said they trust paid television, magazine, and newspaper ads, declines in confidence of 24%, 20%, and 25% respectively from three years earlier (Grimes, 2012).

ADVERTISING EXPLOITS CHILDREN The average American child, aged 2 to 11, is exposed to 25,600 television commercials, or 10,700 minutes of ads, a year; American kids see a quarter of a million television ads before their 13th birthday (Coates, 2009). Countries like Norway and Sweden, on the other hand, ban completely television ads aimed at kids, as does the Canadian province of Quebec. Ads and commercialism are increasingly invading the schools—the amount of sponsored educational material used in American schools rose 1,800% in the 1990s alone. Companies spend $17 billion a year marketing products to children, up from $100 million 20 years ago, and not only can a typical first grader recognize 200 logos, but kids from 3 to 5 show recognition rates as high as 92% for 50 different brands in 16 product categories—McDonald's was most recognizable—demonstrating that children as young as 3 can readily recognize the brands they see advertised (Skenazy, 2008; Andronikidis & Lambrianidou, 2010). Even 61% of youth marketers polled in a 2004 survey felt that "advertising to children starts too young" (Fonda, 2004, p. 52).

Critics contend that children are simply not intellectually capable of interpreting the intent of these ads, nor are they able before the age of 7 or 8 to rationally judge the worth of the advertising claims. This makes children's advertising inherently unethical. Television advertising to kids is especially questionable because children consume it in the home—with implicit parental approval, and most often without parental supervision. The question ad critics ask is, "If parents would never allow living salespeople to enter their homes to sell their children products, why do they allow the most sophisticated salespeople of all to do it for 20 minutes every hour every Saturday morning?" Rowan Williams, upon his installation as Britain's Archbishop of Canterbury in 2002, spoke not of the ethics of advertising to kids but of the morality. "If a child is a consumer, the child is an economic subject. And what economic subjects do is commit their capital, limit their options by doing so, take risks for profit or gratification." His argument, according to education writer Laura Barton (2002), is that "at a time in our lives when the future should be wide open (that is, childhood), we are increasingly encouraged to hem ourselves in, to define ourselves by the trainers [sneakers] we wear and the yogurts we eat. As such, advertising campaigns aimed

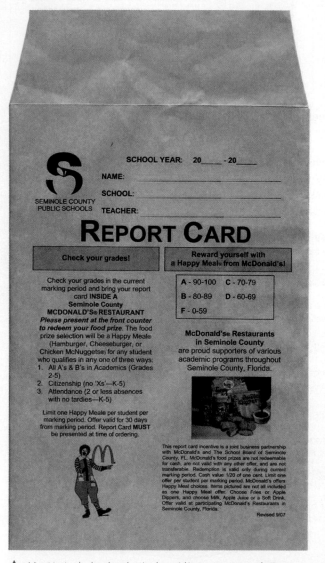

▲ Advertising in schools and on educational material is now common—and quite controversial. It took a parent uprising to end this practice of placing McDonald's ads on report cards in the Seminole County, Florida, schools.

There is no shortage of critics of advertising to children, especially advertising that promotes unhealthy diets. In 1983, companies spent $100 million on child-focused advertising; today they annually spend $17 billion, and the bulk of that money is for fast food, cereal, and snacks (Sirota, 2011). Opponents of advertising to kids point to social science evidence demonstrating a strong correlation between exposure to advertising and childhood obesity. One in six children and teens is obese, up threefold from a generation ago, leading the Federal Trade Commission to call childhood obesity the "most serious health crisis facing today's youth." The 65,000-member American Academy of Pediatrics has called for a ban on fast food commercials on kids' television shows (which the Disney Company agreed in 2012 to do). The U.S. Government Accountability Office has demanded greater FCC oversight of kids' television advertising.

The advertising and fast food industries have responded with a number of plans that they hope will help protect kids while maintaining their own freedom of expression. Television sponsors have promised to strictly adhere to commercial time limits set by the 1990 Children's Television Act, and the Better Business Bureau's Children's Food and Beverage Advertising Initiate said it would enforce voluntary nutritional standards among its member companies. The National Restaurant Association launched an initiative among its members, including companies such as Burger King and Denny's, to offer and promote healthful kids' meals (Neuman, 2011). The question in the cultural forum, however, is how to find the correct balance between freedom of commercial speech and the protection of children.

Advertisers and the fast food industry argue that they are entitled to First Amendment protection, so self-regulation is more than enough. Critics say the First Amendment offers no protection to advertising aimed at kids because children do not possess the ability to tell good messages from bad—the bedrock assumption of the First Amendment. Enter your voice.

> "One in six children and teens is obese, up threefold from a generation ago, leading the Federal Trade Commission to call childhood obesity the 'most serious health crisis facing today's youth.'"

▶ The ad and food industries have First Amendment protection. Who should protect kids like this from the ad and food industries?

directly at children amount to a perversion of innocence" (p. 2). The particular issue of fast-food and snack advertising to children is the subject of the essay, "Kids' Advertising: Is Self-Regulation Enough?"

ADVERTISING DEMEANS AND CORRUPTS CULTURE In our culture we value beauty, kindness, prestige, family, love, and success. As human beings we need food, shelter, and the maintenance of the species, in other words, sex. Advertising succeeds by appealing to these values and needs. The basis for this persuasive strategy is the **AIDA approach**—to persuade consumers, advertising must attract *attention*, create *interest*, stimulate *desire*, and promote *action*. According to industry critics, however, problems arise when important aspects of human existence are reduced to the consumption of brand-name consumer products. Freedom is choosing between a Big Gulp and a canned soda at 7-Eleven. Being a good mother is as simple as buying a bottle of Downy Fabric Softener. Success is drinking Chivas Regal. Love is giving your husband a shirt without ring-around-the-collar or your fiancée a diamond worth two months' salary.

Critics argue that ours has become a **consumer culture**—a culture in which personal worth and identity reside not in ourselves but in the products with which we surround ourselves. The consumer culture is corrupting because it imposes new definitions that

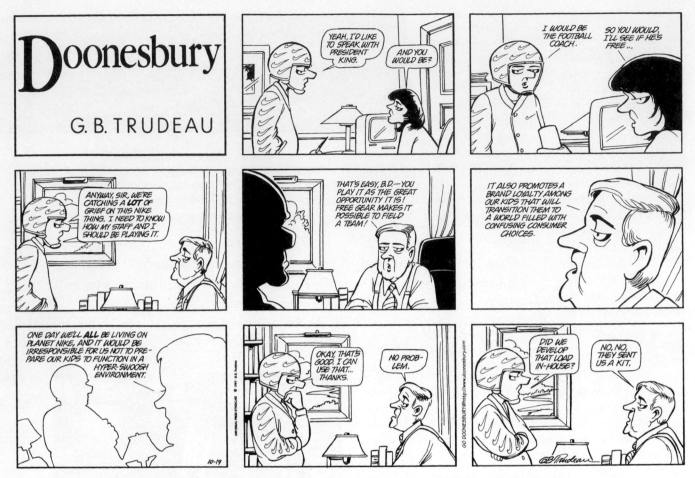

Large advertisers such as Nike have come under much criticism for their intrusion into virtually all aspects of people's lives. Here Garry Trudeau ponders life on Planet Nike.

serve the advertiser and not the culture on traditionally important aspects of our lives. If love, for example, can be bought rather than being something that has to be nurtured, how important can it be? If success is not something an individual values for the personal sense of accomplishment but rather is something chased for the material things associated with it, how does the culture evaluate success? Name the five most successful people you know. How many teachers did you name? How many social workers? How many wealthy or famous people did you name?

Critics further contend that the consumer culture also demeans the individuals who live in it. A common advertising strategy for stimulating desire and suggesting action is to imply that we are inadequate and should not be satisfied with ourselves as we are. We are too fat or too thin, our hair is in need of improvement, our clothes are all wrong, and our spouses don't respect us. Personal improvement is only a purchase away.

The ad-created consumer culture, according to former Wieden + Kennedy and Martin Agency executive Jelly Helm (his clients included Nike, Coke, and Microsoft), has produced an America that is "sick. . . . We work too hard so that we can buy things we don't need, made by factory workers who are paid too little, and produced in ways that threaten the very survival of the earth." It has produced an America that "will be remembered as the greatest wealth-producer ever. It will be a culture remembered for its promise and might and its tremendous achievements in technology and health. It also will be remembered as a culture of hedonism to rival any culture that has ever existed, a culture of materialism and workaholism and individualism, a culture of superficiality and disposability, of poverty and pollution and vanity and violence, a culture denuded of its spiritual wisdom" (Helm, 2002).

Scope and Nature of the Advertising Industry

The proliferation of the different types of sales pitches described in the opening vignette is the product of an avalanche of advertising. Advertisers are exploring new ways to be seen and heard, to stand out, to be remembered, and to be effective. With so many kinds of commercial messages, the definition of advertising must be very broad. For our purposes, advertising is mediated messages paid for by and identified with a business or institution seeking to increase the likelihood that those who consume those messages will act or think as the advertiser wishes.

The American advertising industry annually spends more than $360 billion to place commercial messages before the public. This amount does not include the billions of dollars spent in the planning, production, and distribution of those ads. An overwhelming proportion of all this activity is conducted through and by advertising agencies.

The Advertising Agency

There are approximately 6,000 ad agencies operating in the United States, employing roughly 500,000 people (Figure 12.2). Fewer than 500 agencies annually earn more than $1 million. Many agencies also produce the ads they develop, and virtually all buy time and space in various media for their clients. Production is billed at an agreed-upon price called a **retainer**; placement of advertising in media is compensated through **commissions**, typically 15% of the cost of the time or space. Commissions account for as much as 75% of the income of larger agencies.

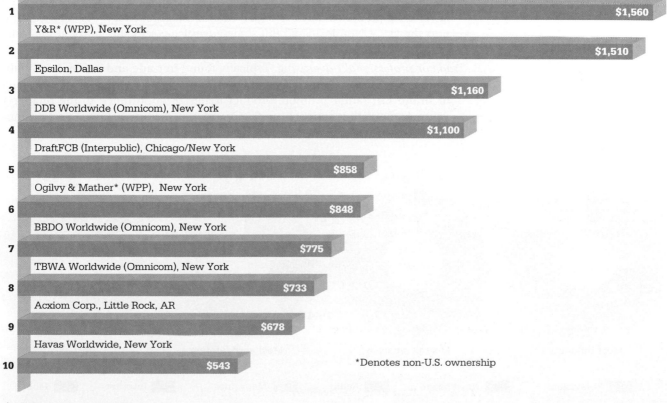

U.S. revenues in millions of dollars by agency rank, parent company if applicable, and headquarters

Rank	Agency	Revenue
1	McCann Worldwide (Interpublic), New York	$1,560
2	Y&R* (WPP), New York	$1,510
3	Epsilon, Dallas	$1,160
4	DDB Worldwide (Omnicom), New York	$1,100
5	DraftFCB (Interpublic), Chicago/New York	$858
6	Ogilvy & Mather* (WPP), New York	$848
7	BBDO Worldwide (Omnicom), New York	$775
8	TBWA Worldwide (Omnicom), New York	$733
9	Acxiom Corp., Little Rock, AR	$678
10	Havas Worldwide, New York	$543

*Denotes non-U.S. ownership

▲ **Figure 12.2** Largest U.S. Ad Agencies, 2012.
Source: World's 20 Largest Agency Networks, 2013.

Ad agencies are usually divided into departments, the number determined by the size and services of the operation. Smaller agencies might contract with outside companies for the services of these typical ad agency departments:

- *Administration* is the agency's management and accounting operations.
- *Account management* is typically handled by an account executive who serves as liaison between agency and client, keeping communication flowing between the two and heading the team of specialists assigned by the agency to the client.
- The *creative department* is where the advertising is developed from idea to ad. It involves copywriting, graphic design, and often the actual production of the piece—for example, radio, television, and Web spots.
- The *media department* makes the decisions about where and when to place ads and then buys the appropriate time or space (Figure 12.3). The effectiveness of a given placement is judged by its **cost per thousand (CPM)**, the cost of reaching 1,000 audience members. For example, an ad that costs $20,000 to place in a major newspaper and is read by 1 million people has a CPM of $20.
- *Market research* tests product viability in the market, the best venues for commercial messages, the nature and characteristics of potential buyers, and sometimes the effectiveness of the ads.
- As we saw in Chapter 11, many larger agencies have *public relations departments* as well.

Types of Advertising

The advertising produced and placed by ad agencies can be classified according to the purpose of the advertising and the target market. You may be familiar with the following types of advertising:

Institutional or corporate advertising. Companies do more than just sell products; companies also promote their names and reputations. If a company name inspires confidence, selling its products is easier. Some institutional or corporate advertising promotes only the organization's image, such as "FTD Florists support the U.S. Olympic Team." But some advertising sells the image at the same time it sells the product: "You can be sure if it's Westinghouse."

Trade or professional advertising. Typically found in trade and professional publications, messages aimed at retailers do not necessarily push the product or brand but rather promote product issues of importance to the retailer—volume, marketing support, profit potential, distribution plans, and promotional opportunities.

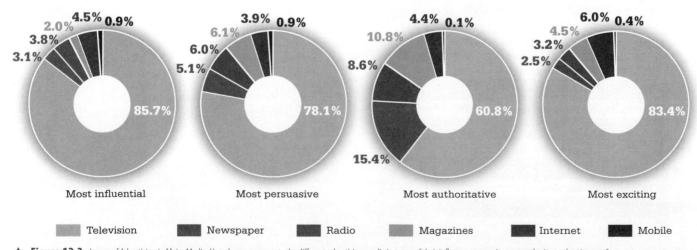

▲ **Figure 12.3** Image of Advertising in Major Media. How do consumers rate the different advertising media in terms of their influence, persuasiveness, authority, and excitement?
Source: Adapted from *Media Trends Track 2011, Television Bureau of Advertising Media Comparisons Study.* Used by permission. Reprinted by permission of the Television Bureau of Advertising, Inc.

Retail advertising. A large part of the advertising we see every day focuses on products sold by retailers like Sears and Macy's. Ads are typically local, reaching consumers where they live and shop.

Promotional retail advertising. Typically placed by retailers, promotional advertising focuses not on a product but on a promotion, a special event held by a retailer. "Midnight Madness Sale" and "Back to School Sale" are two promotions that often benefit from heavy advertising, particularly in newspapers.

Industrial advertising. Advertising of products and services directed toward a particular industry is usually found in industry trade publications. For example, *Broadcasting & Cable*, the primary trade magazine for the television industry, runs ads from program syndicators hoping to sell their shows to stations. It also runs ads from transmitter and camera manufacturers.

National consumer advertising. National consumer advertising constitutes the majority of what we see in popular magazines and on television. It is usually product advertising, commissioned by the manufacturer—McDonald's, Honda, Cheerios, Sony, Nike—aimed at potential buyers.

Direct market advertising. Product or service advertising aimed at likely buyers rather than at all consumers is called direct market advertising. These targeted consumers are reached through direct mail, catalogs, and telemarketing. This advertising can be personalized—"Yes, BRUCE FRIEDBERG, you can drive a Lexus for less than you think"—and customized. Computer data from credit card and other purchases, zip codes, telephone numbers, and organizational memberships are a few of the ways consumers are identified. Direct marketing accounted for 54.2% of all U.S. ad spending in 2010 and directly employed 1.4 million people (Direct Marketing Association, 2011).

Out-of-Home Advertising. As we saw in the opening vignette, advertising is inescapable. One reason is that we are exposed to advertising even when away from home and otherwise not actually engaged in media consumption. Out-of-home advertising, which accounts for more than $6.4 billion in annual spending, can include ads on billboards, street furniture, transit vehicles, and the digital screens we encounter everywhere from the gas pump to the DMV office (Hayes, 2012).

Public service advertising. Advertising that does not sell commercial products or services but promotes organizations and themes of importance to the public is public service advertising. The Heart Fund, the United Negro College Fund, and ads for MADD are typical of this form. They are usually carried free of charge by the medium that houses them.

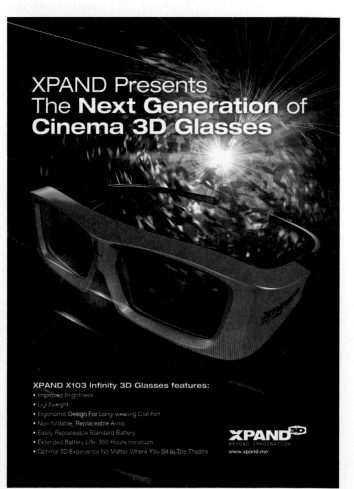

▼ Through this industrial ad appearing in *Variety*, Xpand hopes to attract movie theater owners to its brand of 3-D glasses.

The Regulation of Advertising

The FTC is the primary federal agency for the regulation of advertising. The FCC regulates the commercial practices of the broadcasting industry, and individual states can police deceptive advertising through their own regulatory and criminal bureaucracies. In the deregulation movement of 1980, oversight by the FTC changed from regulating unfair and deceptive advertising to regulating and enforcing complaints *against* deceptive advertising.

The FTC has several options for enforcement when it determines that an advertiser is guilty of deceptive practices. It can issue a **cease-and-desist order** demanding

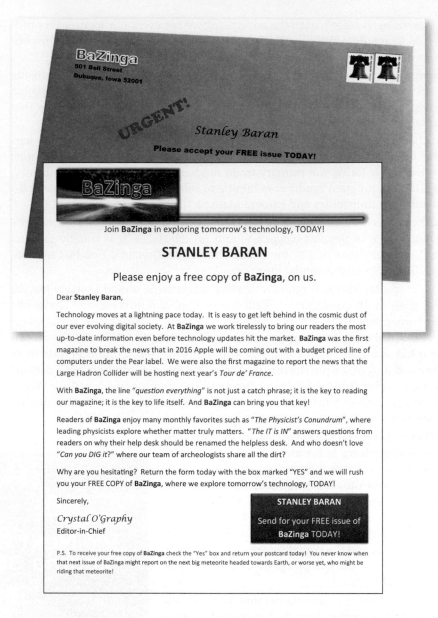

In this direct marketing piece, the advertiser has not only personalized the pitch—Dear Stanley Baran—but has also targeted this consumer's particular interests in the environment and technology based on its knowledge of his magazine subscriptions.

that the practice be stopped. It can impose fines. It can order the creation and distribution of **corrective advertising**. That is, a new set of ads must be produced by the offender that corrects the original misleading effort. For example, in 2012, U.S. tobacco companies were ordered to run corrective ads containing wording such as "Cigarettes cause cancer, lung disease, heart attacks, and premature death."

One of the greatest difficulties for the FTC is finding the line between false or deceptive advertising and **puffery**—that little lie that makes advertising more entertaining than it might otherwise be. "Whiter than white" and "stronger than dirt" are just two examples of puffery. On the assumption that the public does not read commercials literally—the Jolly Green Giant does not exist; we know that—the courts and the FTC allow a certain amount of exaggeration. Puffery may be allowed, but many in the ad industry dislike its slippery slope; puffery, says Keller & Heckman's Richard Leighton, means "never having to say you're sorry for untruths or exaggerated claims" (in Greenberg, 2009).

The FTC and courts, however, do recognize that an advertisement can be false in a number of ways. An advertisement is false if it does the following:

- Lies outright. Reebok claimed its EasyTone shoes produced 11% greater strength and tone in hamstring muscles than did regular walking shoes. The FTC said prove it. Reebok couldn't. Ads for POM Wonderful said its pomegranate juice is "backed

by $25 million in medical research" and is "proven to fight for cardiovascular, prostate, and erectile health." Not so, said the FTC.

- Does not tell the whole truth. Miller Lite's "new taste protector cap" does indeed better preserve the taste of the beer. But ads touting this feature do not tell the whole truth because Miller Lite's bottle caps are exactly the same as all other bottled beers' and have no taste-protecting characteristics beyond those of ordinary cans and bottles.

- Lies by implication, using words, design, production device, sound, or a combination of these. Television commercials for children's toys now end with the product shown in actual size against a neutral background (a shot called an **island**). This is done because production techniques such as low camera angles and close-ups can make these toys seem larger or better than they actually are.

Measuring the Effectiveness of Advertising

It might seem reasonable to judge the effectiveness of an ad campaign by a subsequent increase in sales. But many factors other than advertising influence how well a product fares, including changes in the economy, product quality, breadth of distribution, and competitors' pricing and promotion strategies. Department store magnate John Wanamaker is said to have complained in the late 1880s, "I know that fifty-percent of my advertising is wasted. I just don't know which fifty-percent." Today's advertisers feel much the same way, and as you might imagine, they find this a less-than-comforting situation. Agencies, therefore, turn to research to provide greater certainty.

A number of techniques may be used before an ad or ad campaign is released. **Copy testing**—measuring the effectiveness of advertising messages by showing them to consumers—is used for all forms of advertising. It is sometimes conducted with focus groups, collections of people brought together to see the advertising and discuss it with agency and client personnel. Sometimes copy testing employs **consumer juries**. These people, considered to be representative of the target market, review a number of approaches or variations of a campaign or ad. **Forced exposure**, used primarily for television advertising, requires advertisers to bring consumers to a theater or other facility (typically with the promise of a gift or other payment), where they see a television program, complete with the new commercials. People are asked their brand preferences before the show, and then after. In this way, the effectiveness of the commercials can be gauged.

Once the campaign or ad is before the public, a number of different tests can be employed to evaluate the effectiveness of the ad. In **recognition tests** people who have seen a given publication are asked, in person or by phone, whether they remember seeing specific ads. In **recall testing** consumers are asked, again in person or by phone, to identify which print or broadcast ads they most easily remember. This recall can be unaided, that is, the researcher offers no hints ("Have you seen any interesting commercials or ads lately?"), or aided, that is, the researcher identifies a specific class of products ("Have you seen any interesting pizza commercials lately?"). In recall testing, the advertisers assume that an easily recalled ad is an effective ad. **Awareness tests** make this same assumption, but they are not aimed at specific ads. Their goal is to measure the cumulative effect of a campaign in terms of "consumer consciousness" of a product. A likely question in an awareness test, usually made by telephone, is "What brands of laundry detergent can you name?"

What these research techniques lack is the ability to demonstrate the link that is of most interest to the client—did the ad move the consumer to buy the product? The industry hopes that that all-important connection can be better discovered using **neuromarketing research**—biometric measures such as brainwaves, facial expressions, eye-tracking, sweating, and heart rate monitoring. Because the unconscious accounts for the vast majority of the way peoples' brains process information, these methods tap consumers' subconscious reactions to marketing and advertising. This research is not without its critics, however, who argue that because neuromarketing appeals to the base level of human consciousness, it exploits consumers' nonreasoned, instinctual responses. Still, industry dissatisfaction with more traditional research methods continues to fuel work on neuromarketing research.

Trends and Convergence in Advertising

In the summer of 2005, the world's largest advertiser, Procter & Gamble, announced that it would cut $300 million from its television ad expenditures, a 15% drop from its typical annual spending on that medium. Said Jim Stengel, head of global marketing for the company, "I believe today's marketing model is broken. We're applying antiquated thinking and work systems to a new world of possibilities" (in Auletta, 2005, pp. 35–36). When the country's second-largest advertiser, General Motors, followed suit a year later, slashing its 2006 ad budget by $600 million to shift its marketing resources toward "channels such as direct marketing, websites, online video, event marketing, branded entertainment, and internet advertising," *Advertising Age*'s Jean Halliday (2007) called it "a drop so stunning it should convince even the staunchest doubters that the age of mass-media marketing is going the way of the horse and buggy" (p. 1). These public rebukes of the traditional advertising model demonstrated what most industry professionals already knew—their industry was in need of change in, some even said reinvention of, its *economics, creativity*, and *relationship with consumers*. The advertising business is facing its "chaos scenario," as media writer Bob Garfield called it, "a jarring media universe in which traditional forms of mass entertainment swiftly disappear and advertisers are left in the lurch" (in Klosterman, 2005, p. 63). This new, jarring media universe is forged by the interaction of converging technologies and the changes they drive in how, when, and why people consume them (and the ads they contain).

New and Converging Technologies

The production of advertising has inevitably been altered by computers. Computer graphics, morphing (digitally combining and transforming images), and other special effects are now common in national retail television advertising. And the same technology used to change the ads behind the batter in a televised baseball game is now employed to insert product placements into programs where no placement

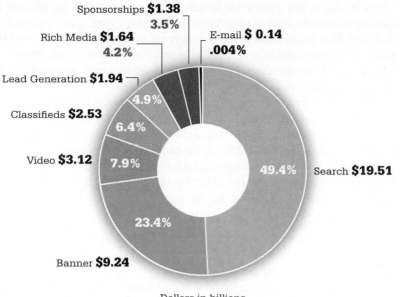

Sponsorships **$1.38**
3.5%

Rich Media **$1.64**
4.2%

E-mail **$ 0.14**
.004%

Lead Generation **$1.94**
4.9%

Classifieds **$2.53**
6.4%

Video **$3.12**
7.9%

Search **$19.51**
49.4%

23.4%

Banner **$9.24**

Dollars in billions
Total, $39.5 billion

◀ **Figure 12.4** U.S. Online Advertising, by Format, 2012.
Source: DigitalFastFacts, 2012.

originally existed—a character who was once eating an unbranded cookie can now munch an Oreo.

Computer databases and computerized printing have fueled the rapid growth of direct market advertising, and we saw in Chapter 5 that computerized printing has made possible zoned and other specialized editions of national magazines. But it is digital advertising, the convergence of all traditional forms of advertising with new digital technologies, that is attracting the most industry interest. In 2007 U.S. online ad spending was $19.5 billion; in 2012 it was $39.5 billion (Figure 12.4). Internet advertising exceeds that of radio, and in 2012 it surpassed that of magazines and newspapers combined (Ives, 2012).

Web advertising has matured since the first **banners**, static online billboards placed conspicuously somewhere on a Web page, appeared in May 1994 (D'angelo, 2009). Other forms are **search marketing**, advertising sold next to or in search results produced by users' keyword searches; **lead generation**, using Internet-created databases to collect names, addresses, e-mail addresses, and other information about likely clients or customers (Chapter 10); **rich media**, sophisticated, interactive Web advertising, usually employing sound and video; and **sponsorships**, Web pages "brought to you by," typically including a number of ad placements, advertorials, and other co-branded sections.

Smartphones, Tablets, and Social Networking Sites

Boosting all forms of digital advertising is their movement to mobile technologies like smartphones and tablets and the expansion of social networking sites. Mobile ad spending exceeded $2.6 billion in 2012 and is expected to grow to more than $10 billion by 2016, driven primarily by search and social network messaging (Olmstead, Sasseen, Mitchell, & Rosenstiel, 2012).

Industry data indicate that smartphone and tablet advertising encourages **e-commerce**, buying products and services online. Shopping with a smartphone or tablet in hand encourages impulse, on-the-spot buying, and 76% of mobile technology owners say they use their devices to conduct e-commerce (Patel, 2012). That's the good news for advertisers. The bad news is that because the smartphone is a "deeply personal medium," users are much less likely to welcome advertising that they would otherwise accept on a tablet, PC, or laptop; 66% say they are "turned off" by unwanted advertising on their phones (Barron & Chowdhury, 2012).

Social networking sites are clearly a boon to advertisers, as they can direct very specific messages to very specific users based on their freely provided information, a fact that does not make everyone happy as we saw in Chapter 10's discussion of privacy. Advertisers also take advantage of sites' interactivity, and virtually every company of any size has at the very least a Facebook and Twitter presence. In 2012, Facebook, already earning more than $5.7 billion a year in advertising revenue, added another $1.2 billion from mobile advertising alone (Whittaker, 2012; Lunden, 2012b). The annual figures for Twitter, $260 million, and LinkedIn, $226 million, are small by comparison, but they are growing at a rapid rate, 80% a year for Twitter and 46% a year for LinkedIn (Lunden, 2012a). Digital advertising in all its forms sits firmly at the center of the change buffeting today's ad industry because of its low cost (relative to traditional media), great reach, and, most important, interactivity, which gives it an accountability unparalleled in the traditional media.

NEW ECONOMICS Consumers are increasingly dissatisfied with hypercommercialism in other media and the lack of relevancy that much advertising has for them. They are becoming resistant to and resentful of much of the marketing they encounter, as you saw earlier in this chapter. As a result, many advertisers are now less interested in CPM, focusing instead on **return on investment (ROI)**, an accountability-based measurement of advertising success. After all, who cares how many thousands you are reaching if they reject your message? Industry professionals look at Internet and Web advertising and see that it is ideally suited for increased ROI, and have begun asking why all media can't offer some of that benefit. "As technology increasingly enables fine targeting and interaction between marketer and consumer," Garfield (2005) argued, "the old measurement and deployment standards are primitive almost to the point of absurdity" (p. 58).

Rather than simple brand exposure, measured by CPM, advertisers have begun to demand accountability. As such, the Web's **performance-based advertising**, for example, provides the ideal. The website carrying the ad gets paid only when the consumer takes some specific action, making a purchase or linking to the sponsor's site. This Web-inspired demand for accountability led to a 2005 call for the development of a new measure of the *effectiveness of all advertising*—**engagement**. The Association of National Advertisers, the American Association of Advertising Agencies, and the Advertising Research Foundation joined in a movement, dubbed MI4, to define exactly the psychological and behavioral aspects of engagement and how to measure it. Beyond moving advertising dollars to platforms promising greater engagement, demands for accountability can be seen in a number of innovations that threaten the traditional agency–brand relationship described earlier in this chapter: Clients are increasingly demanding from agencies—and receiving—agreements on campaign-specific outcomes and consensus on **accountability metrics**—that is, how the effectiveness of a specific ad or campaign will be judged. Some agencies now offer money-back guarantees if they cannot improve a brand's ROI and the introduction of **value-compensation programs** in which "all or at least a significant part" of the payment of an agency's fees "is predicated on meeting pre-established goals" (Fajen, 2008, p. 17).

NEW CREATIVITY "The traditional creative agencies have absolutely lost their way and their relevance," claims Joseph Jaffe, former ad agency executive (in Gross, 2005). Many have, but many others understand that the Internet-fueled fragmentation and democratization of media require a new type of appeal to consumers. If people are increasingly rejecting traditional *mass* media and the commercial messages they carry, the industry must become more creative in its messages and how it gets them to desired consumers. We've already seen many examples—product placement in all media; specially designed and targeted commercials delivered through cable or called up by DVR; online advergames; the sometimes annoying examples of ambient advertising that opened this chapter.

But the Internet has had its impact here as well. Much of advertising's creative community has learned to distinguish between typical, often unappreciated contextual

advertising on the Web and imaginative video advertising delivered by the Web, smartphones and tablets, MP3 players and iPods, and portable game devices. For example, traditional big-time television advertisers like BMW, IKEA, Lincoln-Mercury, Hidden Valley Ranch, and Burger King have moved significant amounts of their advertising dollars to the creation and distribution of short online films, sometimes episodic, often featuring well-known actors, to tout their products. Pen-maker Sharpie "took over" YouTube's homepage with an interactive mosaic made up of user-generated art. The page produced more than 62 million impressions in one day, leading to more than 72,000 visits to the company's website and 2 million new fans on its Facebook page (Sullivan, 2011).

NEW RELATIONSHIP WITH CONSUMERS The Internet, as we've seen throughout this text, makes mass communication less of a monologue and more of a conversation. Today's consumers are no longer passive media *receivers*, taking whatever the television networks and movie studios insist they should. Instead, they are empowered media *users*, increasingly free to control and shape the content they receive. "As all media becomes addressable, all media becomes refusable," said Ogilvy & Mather's vice chair, Steve Hayden. He argues that because the consumer now has the power to accept or reject content, an advertiser has to enter into a transaction with him or her, saying, "'I'll give you this content in exchange for your attention,' which has always been the model of mass advertising. But now, I've got to make that deal on a person-to-person basis" (in Kirsner, 2005).

This new **permission marketing**, of necessity, has led to a rethinking of the relationship between advertiser and consumer, one in which they act like partners, sharing information for mutual benefit. The new model of advertising will, as Hayden suggests, be a conversation between marketers and **prosumers**, proactive consumers who reject most traditional advertising and use multiple sources—traditional media, the Internet, product-rating magazines, recommendations from friends in the know—not only to research a product but also to negotiate price and other benefits. Economists call this *expressing disapproval*. Consumers now have two choices: *exit* (they simply do not buy the product) or *voice* (they explain exactly why they are dissatisfied and what they'd like instead). Active media users, who are at the same time skilled prosumers, who

Desempeño y estilo determinan emociones y comportamientos. Una nueva manera de ver y vivir la vida.

NISSAN

SHIFT_ inspiración

have access to interactive technologies, ensure that voice will, indeed, replace exit as the measure of advertisers' success.

Increased Audience Segmentation

Advertisers face other challenges as well. As the number of media outlets for advertising grows, and as audiences for traditional media are increasingly fragmented, advertisers have been forced to refine their ability to reach and speak to ever-narrower audience segments. Digital technology facilitates this practice, but segmentation exists apart from the new technologies. The ethnic composition of the United States is changing, and advertising is keeping pace. African Americans constitute just over 12% of the total U.S. population, and Hispanics, now the nation's largest minority, make up 18% (23% of all American kids are Hispanic). The Census Bureau reports that middle- and upper-income African Americans and Hispanics are indistinguishable from Whites in terms of such economic indicators as home ownership and consumer purchasing. In fact, by 2014, African Americans will account for 8.7% of all U.S. buying power; Hispanics will account for 10.2%, and Asians will account for 5.3% (Ethnic Buying, 2011); by 2015, Hispanic households alone will wield $1.5 trillion in buying power (Sass, 2012).

Psychographics

Demographic segmentation—the practice of appealing to audiences defined by varying personal and social characteristics such as race/ethnicity, gender, and economic level—has long been part of advertisers' strategy. But advertisers are making increased use of **psychographic segmentation**—that is, appealing to consumer groups with similar lifestyles, attitudes, values, and behavior patterns.

Psychographics entered advertising in the 1970s and is receiving growing attention as advertisers work to reach increasingly disparate consumers in increasingly segmented media. **VALS**, a psychographic segmentation strategy that classifies consumers according to values and lifestyles, is indicative of this lifestyle segmentation. Developed by SRI Consulting (2008), a California consulting company, VALS II divides consumers into eight VALS segments. Each segment is characterized by specific values and lifestyles, demographics, and, of greatest importance to advertisers, buying patterns. The segments, including some of their key demographic identifiers, are listed here:

Innovators: Successful, sophisticated, high self-esteem. Have abundant resources. Are change leaders and receptive to new ideas and technologies.

Thinkers: Motivated by ideals. Mature, satisfied, comfortable, reflective; value order, knowledge, and responsibility. Well educated, actively seek out information.

Achievers: Have goal-oriented lifestyles and deep commitment to career and family. Social lives structured around family, place of worship, and work.

Experiencers: Motivated by self-expression. Young and impulsive consumers; quickly become enthusiastic about new possibilities but equally quick to cool. Seek variety and excitement.

Believers: Motivated by ideals. Conservative, conventional, with concrete beliefs based on traditional, established codes: family, religion, community, and nation.

Strivers: Trendy, fun loving. Motivated by achievement; concerned about opinions and approval of others. Money defines success, but don't have enough to meet their desires. Favor stylish products.

Makers: Motivated by self-expression. Express themselves through work/projects. Practical, have constructive skills, and value self-sufficiency.

Survivors: Live narrowly focused lives. Have few resources. Comfortable with the familiar, primarily concerned with safety and security. Focus on meeting needs rather than fulfilling desires.

Globalization

As media and national economies have globalized, advertising has adapted. U.S. agencies are increasingly merging with, acquiring, or affiliating with agencies from other parts of the world. Revisit Figure 12.2. You'll see that two of the top 10 U.S. agencies are owned by foreign companies. In addition to the globalization of media and economies, a second force driving this trend is the demographic fact that today 80% of the world's population lives in developing countries, and by 2014 two-thirds of all the people in the world will live in Asia alone. The industry is already putting its clients in touch with these consumers. Foreign ad spending first exceeded U.S. totals in 1980, and today major media ad spending in America accounts for 33% of the world's total, down from 44% in 1986 (Johnson, 2011b). Ad spending in *developing* nations is growing at a faster rate than it is in the developed world. In fact, spending in the Asia-Pacific region will surpass North America as the world's biggest advertising market soon after 2014, and in 2012 60% of global marketers said they planned to shift their ad budgets to focus on emerging markets such as South Africa, Argentina, the "BRICS" (Brazil, Russia, India, China), and the "MIST" (Mexico, Indonesia, South Korea, Turkey; McClellan, 2012). Figure 12.5 shows the world's 10 biggest global advertisers.

DEVELOPING MEDIA LITERACY SKILLS

Interpreting Intentional Imprecision

Advertisers often use intentional imprecision in words and phrases to say something other than the precise truth, and they do so in all forms of advertising—profit and nonprofit, scrupulously honest and less so. There are three categories of intentional imprecision: unfinished statements, qualifiers, and connotatively loaded words and expressions.

We are all familiar with *unfinished statements,* such as the one for the battery that "lasts twice as long." Others include "You can be sure if it's Westinghouse," "Magnavox

Global advertising spending in billions of dollars by company rank and headquarters

Rank	Company	Spending
1	Procter & Gamble, Cincinnati, OH	$11.43
2	Unilever, London, UK and Rotterdam, Netherlands	$6.62
3	L'Oréal, Paris	$4.98
4	General Motors, Detroit, MI	$3.59
5	Nestlé, Vevey, Switzerland	$3.19
6	Toyota, Toyota City, Japan	$2.86
7	Coca-Cola, Atlanta, GA	$2.46
8	Reckitt Benckiser, Slough, UK	$2.43
9	Kraft Foods, Northfield, IL	$2.34
10	Johnson & Johnson, New Brunswick, NJ	$2.32

gives you more," and "Easy-Off makes oven cleaning easier." A literate advertising consumer should ask, "Twice as long as *what*?" "Of *what* can I be sure?" "Gives me more of *what*?" "Easier than *what*?" Better, more, stronger, whiter, faster—all are comparative adjectives whose true purpose is to create a comparison between two or more things. When the other half of the comparison is not identified, intentional imprecision is being used to create the illusion of comparison.

Qualifiers are words that limit a claim. A product *helps* relieve stress, for instance. It may not relieve stress as well as rest and better planning and organization. But once the qualifier "helps" appears, an advertiser is free to make just about any claim for the product because all the ad really says is that it helps, not that it does anything in and of itself. It's the consumer's fault for misreading. A product may *fight* grime, but there is no promise that it will win. In the statement "Texaco's coal gasification process could mean you won't have to worry about how it affects the environment," "could" relieves the advertiser of all responsibility. "Could" does not mean "will." Moreover, the fact that you *could stop worrying about the environment* does not mean the product does not harm the environment—only that you could stop worrying about it.

Some qualifiers are more apparent. "Taxes not included," "limited time only," "only at participating locations," "prices may vary," "some assembly required," "additional charges may apply," and "batteries not included" are qualifiers presented after the primary claims have been made. Often these words are spoken quickly at the end of radio and television commercials, or they appear in small print on the screen or at the bottom of a newspaper or magazine ad.

Other qualifiers are part of the product's advertising slogan. Boodles gin is "the ultra-refined British gin that only the world's costliest methods could produce. Boodles. The world's costliest British gin." After intimating that the costliest methods are somehow necessary to make the best gin, this advertiser qualifies its product as the costliest "British" gin. There may be costlier, and possibly better, Irish, U.S., Russian, and Canadian gins. Many sugared children's cereals employ the tactic of displaying the cereal on a

We regularly encounter intentional imprecision in advertising, although maybe not as bad as practiced by Dogbert.
DILBERT: © Scott Adams/Dist. by United Feature Syndicate, Inc.

table with fruit, milk, and toast. The announcer says or the copy reads, "Coco Yummies are *a part of* this complete breakfast"—so is the tablecloth. But the cereal, in and of itself, adds little to the nutritional completeness of the meal. It is "a part of" it. In December 2003, in order to forestall FTC action, KFC pulled television commercials claiming that its fried chicken was "part of" a healthy diet, a campaign characterized as "desperate and sleazy" by *Advertising Age* (MacArthur, 2003).

Advertising is full of words that are *connotatively loaded. Best-selling* may say more about a product's advertising and distribution system than its quality. *More of the pain-relieving medicine doctors prescribe most* means aspirin. *Cherry-flavored* products have no cherries in them. On the ecolabeling front, *no additives* is meaningless; the manufacturer decides what is and is not an additive. *Cruelty free;* again, the company decides. Other connotatively loaded ecolabels are *hypoallergenic* (advertiser-created, scientific-sounding, and meaningless), *fragrance free* (you can't smell the scent because of the chemicals used to hide it), *nontoxic* (won't kill you, but could cause other health problems), and *earth smart, green,* and *nature's friend*—all meaningless. Advertisers want consumers to focus on the connotation, not the actual meaning of these words.

Intentional imprecision is puffery. It is not illegal; neither is it sufficiently troubling to the advertising industry to warrant self-regulatory limits. But puffery is neither true nor accurate, and its purpose is to deceive. This means that the responsibility for correctly and accurately reading advertising that is intentionally imprecise rests with the media-literate consumer.

MEDIA LITERACY CHALLENGE
Finding Those Little White Lies

Finding intentional imprecision—those little white lies—in contemporary advertising can be a challenge, but one that a media-literate consumer should welcome. So, record all the commercials during one hour of either TV watching or radio listening. Then go through them carefully and identify ways in which they might have been intentionally imprecise. Did you find any *unfinished statements* like "It lasts twice as long"? List them and the questions you were left to ponder (Twice as long as what?). How many *qualifiers* like "helps relieve stress" or "this could be the last car you'll ever own" did you find? Were there examples of *connotatively loaded* words like "Coco Yummies are part of a complete breakfast"? How easy were these imprecisions to identify? Do you consider them deceptive or harmless? Why? Can you explain your results and your reaction to those results in terms of media literacy skills such as your *willingness to make an effort to understand ad content and filter out noise* and your *understanding of and respect for the power of commercial messages*?

Resources for Review and Discussion

REVIEW POINTS: TYING CONTENT TO LEARNING OUTCOMES

▶ **Outline the history and development of the advertising industry.**
- Advertising has been a part of commerce for centuries, but it became an industry in its own right with the coming of industrialization and the American Civil War.

▶ **Evaluate contemporary criticisms and defenses of advertising.**
- Advertising suffers from a number of criticisms—it is intrusive, it is deceptive, it exploits children, it demeans and corrupts culture.
- Advertising is also considered beneficial—it supports our economic system, it provides information to assist buying decisions, it supports our media system, it improves our standard of living.

▶ **Describe how the organizational and economic nature of the contemporary advertising industry shapes the content of advertising, especially in an increasingly converged media environment.**
- Advertising agencies typically have these departments: administration, account management, creative, media, market research, and public relations.
- There are several ways to measure an ad's effectiveness: copy testing, consumer juries, forced exposure, recognition tests, recall testing, awareness tests, and neuromarketing research.
- The interaction of converging technologies and the changes they drive in how, when, and why people consume them (and the ads they contain) is reshaping the economics and creativity of the advertising industry as well as its relationship with consumers.

▶ Reshaping of the industry has led to calls for better measures of effectiveness, such as engagement, return on investment (ROI), and performance-based advertising.

▶ **Identify different types of advertising and their goals.**
- There are different types of advertising: institutional or corporate, trade or professional, retail, promotional retail, industrial, national consumer, direct marketing, out-of-home, and public service.
- Advertisers must deal with consumers increasingly segmented not only by their media choices but also along demographic and psychographic lines.
- As with the media it supports, the advertising industry is increasingly globalized.

▶ **Explain the relationship between advertising content and its consumers.**
- Regulation of advertising content is the responsibility of the Federal Trade Commission, which recognizes that an ad can be false if it lies outright, does not tell the whole truth, or lies by implication. Puffery, the entertaining "little lie," is permissible.
- Largely because of the Internet, people have become proactive consumers who now have two options when dealing with marketers, exit and voice.

▶ **Apply key media literacy skills when consuming advertising.**
- Interpreting advertisers' intentional imprecision—unfinished statements, qualifiers, and connotatively loaded words—tests consumers' media literacy skills.

KEY TERMS

ambient advertising, 290

360 marketing, 290

murketing, 290

blinks, 290

siquis, 291

shopbills, 291

newsbook, 291

unique selling proposition (USP), 296

parity products, 296

AIDA approach, 299

consumer culture, 299

retainer, 301

commissions, 301

cost per thousand (CPM), 302

cease-and-desist order, 303

corrective advertising, 304

puffery, 304

island, 305

copy testing, 305

consumer juries, 305

forced exposure, 305

recognition tests, 305

recall testing, 306

awareness tests, 306

neuromarketing research, 306

banners, 307

search marketing, 307

lead generation, 307

rich media, 307

sponsorships, 307

e-commerce, 307

return on investment (ROI), 308

performance-based advertising, 308

engagement, 308

accountability metrics, 308

value-compensation program, 308

permission marketing, 309

prosumer, 309

demographic segmentation, 310

psychographic segmentation, 310

VALS, 310

QUESTIONS FOR REVIEW

1. Why are we seeing so many ads in so many new and different places?

2. Why do some people consider advertising to children unethical? Immoral?

3. In what ways can an ad be false?

4. What are the departments in a typical advertising agency? What does each do?

5. What are the different categories of advertising and the goal of each?

6. What is a cease-and-desist order? Corrective advertising? Puffery?

7. What are copy testing, consumer juries, forced exposure, recognition tests, recall testing, and awareness tests? How do they differ?

8. What is a prosumer? How do prosumers change the relationship between advertisers and their audience?

9. In what two ways do consumers express dissatisfaction? How does this affect contemporary advertising?

10. What are demographic and psychographic segmentation?

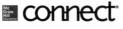

For further review, go to the LearnSmart study module for this chapter.

QUESTIONS FOR CRITICAL THINKING AND DISCUSSION

1. If you owned an advertising agency, would you produce advertising aimed at children? Why or why not?

2. If you were an FTC regulator, to what extent would you allow puffery? Where would you draw the line between deception and puffery? Give examples.

3. What do you think of the exit–voice dichotomy of consumer behavior? Can you relate it to your own use of advertising? If so, how?

Theories and Effects of Mass Communication

13

Learning Objectives

Media have effects. People may disagree about what those effects might be, but media do have effects. Advertisers would not spend billions of dollars a year to place their messages in the media if they did not have effects, nor would our Constitution, in the form of the First Amendment, seek to protect the freedoms of the media if the media did not have important consequences. We attempt to understand and explain these effects through mass communication theory. After studying this chapter you should be able to

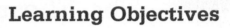 Outline the history and development of mass communication theory.

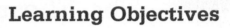 Explain what is meant by theory, why it is important, and how it is used.

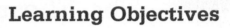 Describe influential traditional and contemporary mass communication theories.

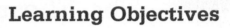 Analyze controversial effects issues, such as violence, media's impact on drug and alcohol consumption, and media's contribution to racial and gender stereotyping.

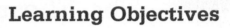 Apply mass communication theory to your own use of media.

The potential of powerful media effects provides a strong argument for increased media literacy.

"I KNOW THIS ISN'T LISTED ON THE SYLLABUS. But let's call it a pop quiz." Your instructor has surprised you. "Will this count in our final grade?" you ask. You are seared by the professor's stare.

"Put everything away except a piece of paper and a pen."

You do as instructed.

"Number your paper from 1 to 5. Items 1 through 3 are true–false. One. Most people are just looking out for themselves. Two. You can't be too careful in dealing with people. Three. Most people would take advantage of you if they got the chance. Now, number four. How much television do you watch each week?"

Not too tough, you think, you can handle this.

"Finally, number 5. Draw the outline of a dime as close to actual size as possible."

In this chapter we examine mass communication theory. After we define theory and discuss why it is important, we see how the various theories of mass communication that are prevalent today developed. We then study several of the most influential contemporary theories before we discuss the relationship between media literacy and mass communication theory. These theories and their application form the basis of our understanding of how media and culture affect one another, the effects of mass communication.

The Effects Debate

Whether the issue is online hate groups, televised violence, the absence of minority characters in prime-time television programming, or a decline in the quality of political discourse, the topic of the effects of mass communication is—and has always been—hotly debated. Later in this chapter we will take detailed looks at such effects issues as media's impact on violence, the use of drugs and alcohol, and stereotyping. But before we can examine specific effects issues, we must understand that there exists fundamental disagreement about the presence, strength, and operation of effects.

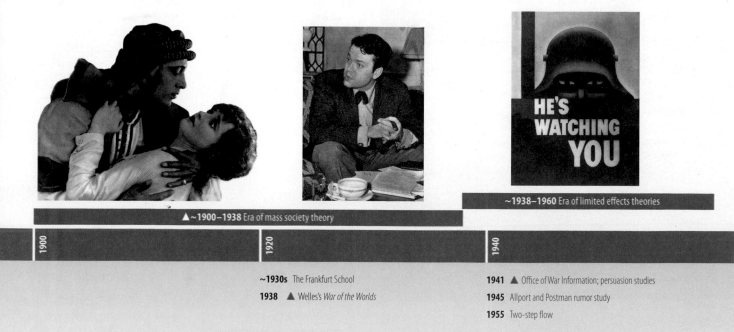

▲ ~1900–1938 Era of mass society theory

~1938–1960 Era of limited effects theories

| 1900 | 1920 | 1940 |

~**1930s** The Frankfurt School
1938 ▲ Welles's *War of the Worlds*

1941 ▲ Office of War Information; persuasion studies
1945 Allport and Postman rumor study
1955 Two-step flow

Many people still hold to the position that media have limited or minimal effects. Here are their arguments, accompanied by often made counterarguments.

1. *Media content has limited impact on audiences because it's only make-believe; people know it isn't real.*

The counterarguments: (a) News is not make-believe (at least it's not supposed to be), and we are supposed to take it seriously. (b) Most film and television dramas (for example, *CSI: Crime Scene Investigation* and *Modern Family*) are intentionally produced to seem real to viewers, with documentary-like production techniques such as handheld cameras and uneven lighting. (c) Much contemporary television is expressly *real*—reality shows such as *Cops* and *Real Housewives* and talk shows such as *The Jerry Springer Show* purport to present real people. (d) Advertising is supposed to tell the truth. (e) Before they develop the intellectual and critical capacity to know what is not real, children confront the world in all its splendor and vulgarity through television, what television effects researchers call the **early window**. To kids, what they see is real. (f) To enjoy what we consume, we **willingly suspend disbelief**; that is, we willingly accept as real what is put before us.

2. *Media content has limited impact on audiences because it is only play or just entertainment.*

The counterarguments: (a) News is not play or entertainment (at least it's not supposed to be). (b) Even if media content is only play, play is very important to the way we develop our knowledge of ourselves and our world. When we play organized sports, we learn teamwork, cooperation, the value of hard work, obedience to authority, and respect for the rules. Why should play be any less influential if we do it on the Internet or at the movies?

3. *If media have any effects at all, they are not the media's fault; media simply hold a mirror to society and reflect the status quo, showing us and our world as they already are.*

The counterargument: Media hold a very selective mirror. The whole world, in all its vastness and complexity, cannot possibly be represented, so media practitioners

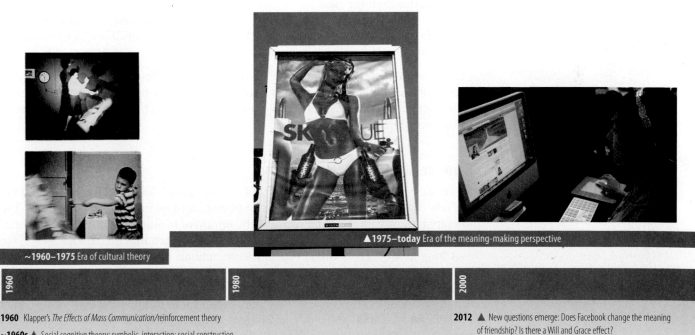

~1960–1975 Era of cultural theory

▲1975–today Era of the meaning-making perspective

1960

1980

2000

1960 Klapper's *The Effects of Mass Communication*/reinforcement theory

~1960s ▲ Social cognitive theory; symbolic interaction; social construction of reality; British cultural studies

~1970s Cultivation analysis

1972 Agenda setting; Surgeon General's Report on Television and Social Behavior

1975 Uses and gratifications; dependency theory

2012 ▲ New questions emerge: Does Facebook change the meaning of friendship? Is there a *Will and Grace* effect?

▲ The mirror that media hold up to culture is like a fun-house mirror—some things appear bigger than they truly are, some things appear smaller, and some disappear altogether.

must make choices. For example, in all the television shows and movies you've seen in your entire life, how many interracial marriages do you remember? Probably not very many. But in the real world, 10% of American marriages are interracial, a 28% increase over the last 10 years (U.S. Census, 2012a). And when was the last time you saw a car explode in an accident or police shoot it out with the bad guys on a city street? At best, media hold a fun-house mirror to society and distort what they reflect. Some things are overrepresented, others underrepresented, and still others disappear altogether.

4. *If media have any effect at all, it is only to reinforce preexisting values and beliefs. Family, church, school, and other socializing agents have much more influence.*

The counterarguments: (a) The traditional socializing agents have lost much of their power to influence in our complicated and fast-paced world. (b) Moreover, *reinforcement* is not the same as having no effects. If media can reinforce the good in our culture, media can just as easily reinforce the bad. Is racism eradicated yet? Sexism? Disrespect for others? If our media are doing no more than reinforcing the values and beliefs that already exist, then they are as empty as many critics contend. Former Federal Communications Commission member Nicholas Johnson has long argued of television in particular that the real crime is not what television is doing *to* us but what it could be doing *for* us, but isn't.

5. *If media have any effects at all, they are only on the unimportant things in our lives, such as fads and fashions.*

The counterarguments: (a) Fads and fashions are not unimportant to us. The car we drive, the clothes we wear, and the way we look help define us; they characterize us to others. In fact, it is media that have helped make fads and fashions so central to our self-definition and happiness. Kids don't kill other kids for their $150 basketball shoes because their mothers told them that Air Jordans were cool. (b) If media influence only the unimportant things in our lives, why are billions of dollars spent on media efforts to sway opinion about social issues such as universal health care, nuclear power, and global warming (Chapter 11)?

One reason these arguments about media power and effects continue to rage is that people often come to the issues from completely different perspectives. In their most general form, the debates over media influence have been shaped by three closely related dichotomies.

Micro- versus Macro-Level Effects

People are concerned about the effects of media. Does television cause violence? Do beer ads cause increased alcohol consumption? Does pornography cause rape? The difficulty here is with the word *cause*. Although there is much scientific evidence that media cause many behaviors, there is also much evidence that they do not.

As long as we debate the effects of media only on individuals, we risk remaining blind to what many believe is media's more powerful influence (both positive and negative) on the way we live. For example, when the shootings at the Littleton, Colorado, Columbine High School in 1999 once again brought public debate on the issue of media effects, USA Network copresident Steve Brenner was forced to defend his industry. "Every American has seen hundreds of films, hundreds of news stories, hundreds of depictions, thousands of cartoons," he said. "Millions don't go out and shoot people" (as quoted in Albiniak, 1999, p. 8).

Who can argue with this? For most people, media have relatively few *direct* effects at the personal or **micro level**. But we live in a culture in which people *have* shot people or are willing to use violence to settle disputes, at least in part because of the

cultural messages embedded in our media fare. The hidden, but much more important, impact of media operates at the cultural or **macro level**. Violence on television contributes to the cultural climate in which real-world violence becomes more acceptable. Sure, perhaps none of us have gone out and shot people. But do you have bars on the windows of your home? Are there parts of town where you would rather not walk alone? Do you vote for the "tough on crime" candidate over the "education" candidate?

The micro-level view is that televised violence has little impact because although some people may be directly affected, most people are not. The macro-level view is that televised violence has a great impact because it influences the cultural climate. You can read about a contemporary example of mass communication research on individuals in the box entitled "A Friend by Any Other Name: Research on Facebook and Relationships."

Administrative versus Critical Research

Administrative research asks questions about the immediate, observable influence of mass communication. Does a commercial campaign sell more cereal? Does an expanded Living Section increase newspaper circulation? Did video games inspire the killings of the 20 children at Sandy Hook Elementary School? For decades the only proofs of media effects that science (and therefore the media industries, regulators, and audiences) would accept were those with direct, observable, immediate effects. Seventy years ago, however, Paul Lazarsfeld (1941), the father of social science research and possibly the most important mass communication researcher of all time, warned of the danger of this narrow view. He believed **critical research**—asking larger questions about what kind of nation we are building, what kind of people we are becoming—would serve our culture better. Writing long before the influence of television and information access through the World Wide Web, he stated,

> Today we live in an environment where skyscrapers shoot up and elevateds (commuter trains) disappear overnight; where news comes like shock every few hours; where continually new news programs keep us from ever finding out details of previous news; and where nature is something we drive past in our cars, perceiving a few quickly changing flashes which turn the majesty of a mountain range into the impression of a motion picture. Might it not be that we do not build up experiences the way it was possible decades ago . . . ? (p. 12)

Administrative research concerns itself with direct causes and effects; critical research looks at larger, possibly more significant cultural questions. As the cartoon shows, Calvin understands the distinction well.

Transmissional Versus Ritual Perspective

Last is the debate that led Professor Carey to articulate his cultural definition of communication (Chapter 1). The **transmissional perspective** sees media as senders of information for the purpose of control; that is, media either have effects on our behavior or they do not. The **ritual perspective**, Carey (1975) wrote, views media not as a means of transmitting "messages in space" but as central to "the maintenance of society in time." Mass communication is "not the act of imparting information but the representation of shared beliefs" (p. 6). In other words, the ritual perspective is necessary to understand the *cultural* importance of mass communication.

Consider an ad for Skyy vodka. What message is being transmitted? Buy Skyy, of course. So people either do or do not buy Skyy. The message either controls or does not control people's alcohol-buying behavior. That is the transmissional perspective. But what is happening culturally in that ad? What reality about alcohol and socializing is shared? Can young people really have fun in social settings without alcohol? What constitutes a good-looking man or woman? What does success look like in the United States? The ritual perspective illuminates these messages—the culturally important content of the ad.

▼ The transmissional message in this liquor ad is obvious—buy Skyy. The ritual message is another thing altogether. What is it?

Defining Mass Communication Theory

Whether you accept the limited effects arguments or their counterarguments, all the positions you just read are based in one or more **mass communication theories**, explanations and predictions of social phenomena that attempt to relate mass communication to various aspects of our personal and cultural lives or social systems. Your responses to the five quiz questions that opened the chapter, for example, can be explained (possibly even predicted) by different mass communication theories.

The first four items are a reflection of **cultivation analysis**—the idea that people's ideas of themselves, their world, and their place in it are shaped and maintained primarily through television. People's responses to the three true–false items can be fairly accurately predicted by the amount of viewing they do (question 4). The more people watch, the more likely they are to respond "true" to these unflattering comments about others.

The solution to the dime-drawing task is predicted by **attitude change theory**. Almost everyone draws the dime too small. Because a dime is an inconsequential coin, we perceive it as smaller than it really is, and our perceptions guide our behavior. Even though every one of us has real-world experience with dimes, our attitudes toward that coin shape our behavior regarding it.

To understand mass communication theory, you should recognize these important ideas:

1. As we've just seen, *there is no one mass communication theory*. There is a theory, for example, that describes something as grand as how we give meaning to cultural symbols and how these symbols influence our behavior (symbolic interaction), and there is a theory that explains something as individual as how media influence people in times of change or crisis (dependency theory). Mass communication theorists have produced a number of **middle-range theories** that explain or predict specific, limited aspects of the mass communication process (Merton, 1967).

2. *Mass communication theories are often borrowed from other fields of science*. Attitude change theory (the dime question), for example, comes from psychology. Mass communication theorists adapt these borrowed theories to questions and issues in communication. People's behavior with regard to issues more important than the size of a dime—democracy, ethnicity, government, and gender roles, for example—is influenced by the attitudes and perceptions presented by our mass media.

3. *Mass communication theories are human constructions*. People create them, and therefore their creation is influenced by human biases—the times in which we live, the position we occupy in the mass communication process, and a host of other factors. Broadcast industry researchers, for example, have developed somewhat different theories to explain how violence is learned from television than have university researchers.

4. Because theories are human constructions and the environments in which they are created constantly change, *mass communication theories are dynamic*; they undergo frequent recasting, acceptance, and rejection. For example, theories that were developed before television and computer networks became mass media outlets have to be reexamined and sometimes discarded in the face of these new technologies.

A Short History of Mass Communication Theory

The dynamic nature of mass communication theory can be seen in its history. All disciplines' bodies of knowledge pass through various stages of development. Hypotheses are put forth, tested, and proven or rejected. Eventually a consensus develops that shapes a discipline's central ideas and, as such, the kinds of questions it asks and answers it seeks—and expects. However, over time some answers come to challenge those expectations. So new questions have to be asked, new answers are produced, and, eventually, a new consensus emerges. Mass communication theory is particularly open to evolving ideas for three reasons:

- *Advances in technology or the introduction of new media* fundamentally alter the nature of mass communication. The coming of radio and movies, for example, forced rethinking of theories based on a print-oriented mass communication system.
- *Calls for control or regulation* of these new technologies require, especially in a democracy such as ours, an objective, science-based justification.
- As a country committed to protecting *democracy and cultural pluralism*, we ask how each new technology or medium can foster our pursuit of that goal.

The evolution in thinking that resulted from these factors has produced four major eras of mass communication theory: the era of mass society theory, the era of the limited effects perspective, the cultural theory era, and the era of the meaning-making perspective. The first two may be considered early eras; the latter two best represent contemporary thinking.

The Era of Mass Society Theory

As we've seen, several important mass media appeared or flourished during the second half of the 19th century and the first decades of the 20th century. Mass circulation newspapers and magazines, movies, talkies, and radio all came to prominence at this time. This was also a time of profound change in the nature of U.S. society. Industrialization and urbanization spread, African Americans and poor southern Whites streamed northward, and immigrants rushed across both coasts in search of opportunity and dignity. People in traditional seats of power—the clergy, politicians, and educators—feared a disruption in the status quo. The country's peaceful rural nature was beginning to slip further into history. In its place was a cauldron of new and different people with new and different habits, all crammed into rapidly expanding cities. Crime grew, as did social and political unrest. Many cultural, political, educational, and religious leaders thought the United States was becoming too pluralistic. They

▶ Agnes Ayers swoons in Rudolph Valentino's arms in the 1921 movie *The Sheik*. Mass society theorists saw such common entertainment fare as debasing the culture through its direct and negative effects on helpless audience members.

charged that the mass media catered to the low tastes and limited reading and language abilities of these newcomers by featuring simple and sensationalistic content. The media needed to be controlled to protect traditional values.

The successful use of propaganda by totalitarian governments in Europe, especially Germany's National Socialist Party (the Nazis), provided further evidence of the overwhelming power of media. Media needed to be controlled to prevent similar abuses at home.

The resulting theory was **mass society theory**—the idea that the media are corrupting influences that undermine the social order and that "average" people are defenseless against their influence. To mass society theorists, "average" people were all those who did not hold their (the theorists') superior tastes and values. Walter Lippmann, a nationally syndicated columnist for the *New York Times* and one of the country's most important social commentators, was indicatively skeptical of average people's ability to make sense of the confusing world around them. Political essayist Eric Alterman quotes and summarizes Lippmann's thinking, expressed in his influential 1922 book *Public Opinion*:

> Writing in the early twenties, Lippmann famously compared the average citizen to a deaf spectator sitting in the back row. He does not know what is happening, why it is happening, what ought to happen. "He lives in a world he cannot see, does not understand and is unable to direct." Journalism, with its weakness for sensationalism, made things worse. Governance was better left to a "specialized class of men" with inside information. No one expects a steel-worker to understand physics, so why should he be expected to understand politics? (2008, p. 10)

The fundamental assumption of this thinking is sometimes expressed in the **hypodermic needle theory** or the **magic bullet theory**. The symbolism of both is apparent—media are a dangerous drug or a killing force against which "average" people are defenseless.

Mass society theory is an example of a **grand theory**, one designed to describe and explain all aspects of a given phenomenon. But clearly not all average people were mindlessly influenced by the evil mass media. People made consumption choices. They interpreted media content, often in personally important ways. Media did have effects, often good ones. No single theory could encompass the wide variety of media effects claimed by mass society theorists, and the theory eventually collapsed under its own weight.

The Emergence of the Limited Effects Perspective

Shifts in a discipline's dominant thinking usually happen over a period of time, and this is true of the move away from mass society theory. But media researchers often mark the emergence of the limited effects perspective on mass communication as occurring on the eve of Halloween 1938. On that night, actor and director Orson Welles broadcast his dramatized version of the H. G. Wells science fiction classic *The War of the Worlds* on the CBS radio network. Produced in what we would now call docudrama style, the realistic radio play in which Earth came under deadly Martian attack frightened thousands. People fled their homes in panic. Proof of mass society theory, argued elite media critics, pointing to a radio play with the power to send people into the hills to hide from aliens.

Research by scientists from Princeton University demonstrated that, in fact, 1 million people had been frightened enough by the broadcast to take some action, but the other 5 million people who heard the show had not, mass society theory notwithstanding. More important, however, these scientists determined that different factors led some people to be influenced and others not (Lowery & DeFleur, 1995).

The researchers had the benefit of advances in survey research, polling, and other social scientific methods developed and championed by Austrian immigrant Paul Lazarsfeld. The researchers were, in fact, his students and colleagues. Lazarsfeld (1941) argued that mere speculation about the impact of media was insufficient to

► **Figure 13.1** Model of Two-Step Flow of Media Influence. Media influence passes from the mass media through opinion leaders to opinion followers. Because leaders and followers share common personal and social characteristics, the potential influence of media is limited by their shared assumptions, beliefs, and attitudes. *Source:* After Katz & Lazarsfeld, 1955.

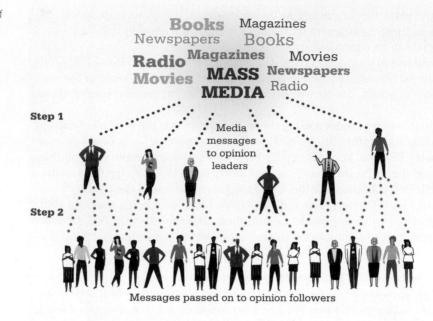

explain the complex interactions that mass communication comprised. Instead, well-designed, sophisticated studies of media and audiences would produce more valuable knowledge.

LIMITED EFFECTS THEORIES Using Lazarsfeld's work, researchers identified those individual and social characteristics that led audience members to be influenced (or not) by media. What emerged was the view that media influence was limited by *individual differences* (for example, in intelligence and education), *social categories* (such as religious and political affiliation), and *personal relationships* (such as friends and family). The theories that emerged from this era of the first systematic and scientific study of media effects, taken together, are now called **limited effects theories**.

TWO-STEP FLOW THEORY Lazarsfeld's own **two-step flow theory** of mass media and personal influence is a well-known product of this era and an example of a limited effects theory (Katz & Lazarsfeld, 1955). His research on the 1940 presidential election indicated that media influence on people's voting behavior was limited by **opinion leaders**—people who initially consumed media content on topics of particular interest to them, interpreted it in light of their own values and beliefs, and then passed it on to **opinion followers**, people like them who had less frequent contact with media (Figure 13.1).

Two-step flow theory has been rethought since Lazarsfeld's time. For example, television, virtually unavailable in 1940, has given everyone a more or less equal opportunity to consume media content firsthand. There is no doubt that opinion leaders still exist—we often ask friends what they've read or heard about a certain movie, book, or band—but their centrality to the mass communication process has diminished.

During and after World War II, the limited effects perspective and several theories it supported became more fully entrenched, controlling research and thinking about media until well into the 1960s. And as was the case with virtually all the media and support industries we've studied, the war itself was crucial to the development of mass communication theory during this era.

Memories of World War I were still very much alive, and not all Americans were enthused about entering another seemingly remote world conflict. Those who joined or were drafted into the armed forces apparently knew very little about their comrades-in-arms from different regions of the country and from different backgrounds. German propaganda seemed to prove the view of mass society theorists who claimed that mass media wielded remarkable power. The Office of War Information (OWI), therefore, set

Orson Welles directs *War of the Worlds*. The 1938 Halloween eve broadcast of this science fiction classic helped usher in the era of the scientific study of mass communication.

out to change public opinion about the wisdom of entering the war, to educate the military about their fellow soldiers and sailors, and to counter Nazi propaganda. Speeches and lectures failed. So, too, did informational pamphlets. The OWI then turned to filmmakers such as Frank Capra (see Chapter 11) and radio personalities such as Kate Smith for their audience appeal and looked to social scientists to measure the effectiveness of these new media campaigns.

The army established the Experimental Section inside its Information and Education Division, staffing it with psychologists who were expert in issues of attitude change. Led by Carl Hovland, these researchers tested the effectiveness of the government's mass communication campaigns. Continuing its work at Yale University after the war, this group produced some of our most influential communication research. Their work led to development of *attitude change theory*, which explains how people's attitudes are formed, shaped, and changed through communication and how those attitudes influence behavior (Hovland, Lumsdaine, & Sheffield, 1949).

ATTITUDE CHANGE THEORY Among the most important attitude change theories are the related ideas of dissonance and selective processes. **Dissonance theory** argues that when confronted by new or conflicting information people experience a kind of mental discomfort, a dissonance. As a result, we consciously and subconsciously work to limit or reduce that discomfort through three interrelated **selective processes**. These processes help us "select" what information we consume, remember, and interpret in personally important and idiosyncratic ways:

- **Selective exposure** (or **selective attention**) is the process by which people expose themselves to or attend to only those messages consistent with their preexisting attitudes and beliefs. How often do you read the work of an online pundit who occupies a different place on the political spectrum from you? You're more likely to read those pieces that confirm what you already believe. It's quite common for someone who buys a new car, electronic component, or other expensive item to suddenly start to see more of that product's advertising. You've spent a lot of money; that creates dissonance. The ads confirm the wisdom of your decision, reducing dissonance.

- **Selective retention** assumes that people remember best and longest those messages that are consistent with their preexisting attitudes and beliefs. Television viewers, for example, remember much more detail from the convention broadcasts of the political party to which they are philosophically closer than they do the broadcasts of competing parties.

- **Selective perception** predicts that people will interpret messages in a manner consistent with their preexisting attitudes and beliefs. When your favorite politicians change positions on an issue, they're flexible and heeding the public's will. When those you don't like do so, they're flip-flopping and have no convictions.

The dominant thinking at the time of the development of dissonance theory was limited effects theory; thus, the selective processes were seen as limiting media impact because content is selectively filtered to produce as little attitude change as possible. Contemporary mass communication theorists accept the power of the selective processes to limit the influence of media content when it is primarily informational. But because so much content is symbolic rather than informational, other theorists see the selective processes as relatively unimportant when it comes to explaining media's contribution to some important cultural effects. You will recognize these differing perspectives on media's power in the distinction made earlier in this chapter between the transmissional and ritual views of mass communication.

Here is an example of the distinction between informational and symbolic content and the way they relate to the selective processes. Few television stations would broadcast lecture programs by people who openly espouse the racist opinion that people of color are genetically more prone to commit crime. If we were to see such a show, however, the selective processes would likely kick in. We would change to another channel (selective exposure). If we did watch, we would interpret the ideas as loony or sick (selective perception); later we would quickly forget the arguments (selective retention).

Fortunately, the media rarely offer such overtly racist messages. The more likely situation in contemporary television is that the production conventions and economic and time demands of television news production lead to the common portrayal of certain people as more likely to be involved in violence and crime. It is easier and cheaper, for example, for stations to cover downtown violent crime—it's handy, it's visual, and it needs no significant research or writing—than to cover nonviolent crime, even though 90% of all felonies in the United States are nonviolent. As a result of these largely symbolic portrayals of crime, our selective processes do not have an opportu-

▶ Line drawing used in the 1945 Allport and Postman study of rumor. Psychologists Allport and Postman demonstrated the operation of the selective processes. When groups of White Americans were asked to whisper from one to another the subject of this drawing, the razor invariably shifted from the left hand of the White aggressor to that of the African American defender. Can you explain this result in terms of dissonance theory and the selective processes?
From "The Basic Psychology of Rumor," by Gordon W. Allport and Leo J. Postman from *Transactions of the New York Academy of Sciences*, Series II, VIII: 61–81. Reprinted by permission of Robert Allport.

nity to reshape the "information" in these news reports. There is little information, only a variety of interesting images.

Cultural theorists (we'll meet them later in this chapter) point to official government statistics as proof of the power of the media to shape attitudes toward race. Crime in the United States is committed by all races in near proportion to their presence in the population, yet African American males are disproportionately represented in the prison population and on death row. Why are Black and Hispanic drivers more likely to be stopped by police than are White drivers, and when stopped, why are they more likely to have their cars searched? Why are Black and Hispanic kids more likely to be suspended or expelled from school than are White kids who commit the same offenses (Hefling, 2012)? If our criminal laws and our justice and educational systems are racially neutral, they ask, why do these disparities exist? Does the razor still move to the hand of the young Black man?

REINFORCEMENT THEORY The selective processes, however, formed the core of what is arguably the most influential book ever published on the impact of mass communication. In *The Effects of Mass Communication*, written in 1960 by the eminent scientist and eventual head of social research for CBS Broadcasting Joseph Klapper, the core of the limited effects perspective is articulated firmly and clearly. Klapper's theory is based on social science evidence developed prior to 1960 and is often called **reinforcement theory**. It was very persuasive at a time when the nation's social fabric had yet to feel the full impact of the cultural change brought about by the war. In addition, flush with enthusiasm and optimism for the technology and science that had helped the United States defeat the Axis powers, the public could see little but good coming from the media technologies, and they trusted the work of Klapper and other scientists.

In retrospect, the value of reinforcement theory may have passed with the book's 1960 publication date. With rapid postwar urbanization, industrialization, and the increase of women in the workplace, Klapper's "nexus of mediating factors and influences" (church, family, and school) began to lose its traditional socializing role for many people. During the 1960s, a decade both revered and reviled for the social and cultural changes it fostered, it became increasingly difficult to ignore the impact of media. Most important, however, all the research Klapper had studied in preparation for his book was conducted before 1960, the year in which it is generally accepted that television became a mass medium. Almost none of the science he examined in developing his reinforcement theory considered television.

THE USES AND GRATIFICATIONS APPROACH Academic disciplines do not change easily. Limited effects researchers were unable to ignore obvious media effects such as the impact of advertising, the media's role in sustaining sentiment against the war in Vietnam and in spreading support for civil rights and the feminist movement, and increases in real-world crime that appeared to parallel increases in televised violence. They turned their focus to media consumers to explain how influence is limited. The new body of thought that resulted, called the **uses and gratifications approach**, claimed that media do not do things *to* people; rather, people do things *with* media. In other words, the influence of media is limited to what people allow it to be.

Because the uses and gratifications approach emphasizes *audience members'* motives for making specific consumption choices and the consequences of that intentional media use, it is sometimes seen as being too apologetic for the media industries. In other words, when negative media effects are seen as the product of audience members' media choices and use, the media industries are absolved of responsibility for the content they produce or carry. Media simply give people what they want. This approach is also criticized because it assumes not only that people know why they make the media content choices they do but also that they can clearly articulate those reasons to uses and gratifications researchers. A third criticism is that the approach ignores the fact that much media consumption is unintentional—when we go online for election news, we can't help but see ads. When we go to an action movie, we are presented with various representations of gender and ethnicity that have nothing to do with our choice of that film. A fourth criticism is that the approach ignores media's cultural role in shaping people's media choices and use.

Despite these criticisms, the uses and gratifications approach served an important function in the development of mass communication theory by stressing the reciprocal nature of the mass communication process. That is, scientists began to take seriously the idea that people are important in the process—they choose content, they make meaning, they act on that meaning.

AGENDA SETTING During the era of limited effects, several important ideas were developed that began to cast some doubt on the assumption that media influence on people and cultures was minimal. These ideas are still respected and examined even today. Among the most influential is **agenda setting**, a theory that argues that media may not tell us what to think, but media certainly tell us what to think *about*. In 1972, based on their study of the media's role in the 1968 presidential election, Maxwell McCombs and Donald Shaw (1972) wrote,

> In choosing and displaying news, editors, newsroom staff, and broadcasters play an important part in shaping political reality. Readers learn not only about a given issue, but how much importance to attach to that issue from the amount of information in a news story and its position. . . . The mass media may well determine the important issues—that is, the media may set the "agenda" of the campaign. (p. 176)

The agenda-setting power of the media resides in more than the amount of space or time devoted to a story and its placement in the broadcast or on the page. Also

DENNIS THE MENACE

"Boy! She sure has a lot of skin, huh, Dad?"

This Dennis the Menace cartoon demonstrates two criticisms of the uses and gratifications approach. Someone who chooses to read the newspaper may not intentionally select this cartoon but will see it nonetheless. In addition, someone who chooses to read this cartoon for its humor will still be confronted with its idealized cultural image of women. DENNIS THE MENACE® used by permission of Hank Ketcham Enterprises and © by North America Syndicate.

important is the fact that there is great consistency between media sources across all media in the choice and type of coverage they give an issue or event. This consistency and repetition signal to people the importance of the issue or event.

Researchers Shanto Iyengar and Donald Kinder (1987) tested the application of agenda-setting theory to the network evening news shows in a series of experiments. Their conclusions supported McCombs and Shaw. "Americans' views of their society and nation," they wrote, "are powerfully shaped by the stories that appear on the evening news" (p. 112). But Iyengar and Kinder took agenda setting a step or two further. They discovered that the position of a story affected the agenda-setting power of television news. As you might expect, the lead story on the nightly newscast had the greatest agenda-setting effect, in part because first stories tend to have viewers' full attention—they come before interruptions and other distractions can occur. The second reason, said the researchers, is that viewers accept the broadcasters' implicit categorization of the lead story as the most important. Iyengar and Kinder also tested the impact of vivid video presentations, discovering that emotionally presented, powerful images tended to undercut the agenda-setting power of television news because the images focused too much attention on the specific situation or person in the story rather than on the issue.

DEPENDENCY THEORY In 1975 Melvin DeFleur and Sandra Ball-Rokeach offered a view of potentially powerful mass media, tying that power to audience members' dependence on media content. Their **dependency theory** is composed of several assertions:

- The basis of media's influence resides in the "relationship between the larger social system, the media's role in that system, and audience relationships to the media" (p. 261).
- The degree of our dependence on media and their content is the "key variable in understanding when and why media messages alter audience beliefs, feelings, or behavior" (p. 261).

- In our modern industrial society we are increasingly dependent on media (a) to understand the social world; (b) to act meaningfully and effectively in society; and (c) to find fantasy and escape or diversion.

- Our level of dependency is related to (a) "the number and centrality (importance) of the specific information-delivery functions served by a medium"; and (b) the degree of change and conflict present in society (p. 263).

Limited effects theory has clearly been left behind here. Dependency theory argues that, especially in our complex and changing society, people become increasingly dependent on media and media content to understand what is going on around them, to learn how to behave meaningfully, and for escape. Think of a crisis, a natural disaster, for example. We immediately turn to the mass media. We are dependent on the media to understand what is going on around us, to learn what to do (how to behave), and even sometimes for escape from the reality of the situation. Now think of other, more personal crises—reaching puberty, attending high school, beginning dating, or having a child. Dependency theory can explain or predict our media use and its impact in these situations as well, as it can when we rely on media for aid in making a tough decision, such as voting or forming a decision on a complicated issue like war or health care reform.

SOCIAL COGNITIVE THEORY While mass communication researchers were challenging the limited effects perspective with ideas such as agenda setting and dependency theory, psychologists were expanding **social cognitive theory**—the idea that people learn through observation—and applying it to mass media, especially television.

Social cognitive theory argues that people model (copy) the behaviors they see and that **modeling** happens in two ways. The first is **imitation**, the direct replication of an observed behavior. For example, after seeing cartoon cat Tom hit cartoon mouse Jerry with a stick, a child might then hit his sister with a stick. The second form of modeling is **identification**, a special form of imitation in which observers do not copy exactly what they have seen but make a more generalized but related response. For example, the child might still be aggressive toward his sister but dump a pail of water on her head rather than hit her with a stick.

The idea of identification was of particular value to mass communication theorists who studied television's impact on behavior. Everyone admits that people can imitate what they see on television. But not all do, and when this imitation does occur in dramatic instances—for example, when someone beats a little girl to death after playing *Mortal Kombat* ("Teens Killed Girl," 2007)—it is so outrageous that it is considered an aberration. Identification, although obviously harder to see and study, is the more likely way that television influences behavior.

Social cognitive theorists demonstrated that imitation and identification are products of three processes:

Observational learning. Observers can acquire (learn) new behaviors simply by seeing those behaviors performed. Many of us who have never fired a handgun can do so because we've seen it done.

Inhibitory effects. Seeing a model, a movie character, for example, punished for a behavior reduces the likelihood that the observer will perform that behavior. In the media we see Good Samaritans sued for trying to help someone, and it reduces our willingness to help in similar situations. That behavior is inhibited by what we've seen.

Disinhibitory effects. Seeing a model rewarded for prohibited or threatening behavior increases the likelihood that the observer will perform that behavior. This, for example, is the basis for complaints against the glorification of crime and drugs in movies. Behaviors that people might not otherwise make, those that are inhibited, now become more likely to occur. The behaviors are disinhibited.

Cultural Theory—A Return to the Idea of Powerful Effects

The questions asked and the answers produced by the agenda-setting, dependency, and social cognitive theorists were no surprise to their contemporaries, the cultural theorists. These observers were primarily European social theorists and North American humanities scholars such as Marshall McLuhan and James Carey, both of whom we met earlier in this text. As America entered the 1960s, no one could remain unaware of the obvious and observable impact television was having on the culture; the increased sophistication of media industries and media consumers; entrenched social problems such as racial strife; the apparent cheapening of the political process; and the emergence of calls for controls on new technologies such as cable, VCR, satellite, and computer networks. Mass communication theorists were forced to rethink media's influence. Clearly, the limited effects idea was inadequate to explain the media impact they saw around themselves every day. But just as clearly, mass society theory explained very little.

It's important to remember that prominent theories never totally disappear. Joseph McCarthy's efforts to purge Hollywood of communists in the 1950s, for example, were based on mass society notions of evil media and malleable audiences, as were the late Reverend Jerry Falwell's attacks on the children's television show *Teletubbies* for its promotion of homosexuality (after all, Tinky Winky is purple—the gay color—his antenna is a triangle—the gay symbol—and he carries a purse), as were conservative groups' 2011 protests over clothier J. Crew's catalogue ad showing a mother spending weekend time with her son, whose favorite color is pink as evidenced by his painted toe nails: "Abandoning all trappings of gender identity . . . Blatant propaganda celebrating transgendered children" (Crary, 2011, p. B4). Social cognitive theory, limited effects, and uses and gratifications are regularly raised in today's debates over the regulation of video games (Chapter 9) and fast food advertising aimed at kids (Chapter 12).

But the theories that have gained the most support among today's media researchers and theorists are those that accept the potential for powerful media effects, a potential that is *either* enhanced or thwarted by audience members' involvement in the mass communication process. Important to this perspective on audience–media

interaction are **cultural theories**. Stanley Baran and Dennis Davis (2012) wrote that these theories share

> the underlying assumption that our experience of reality is an ongoing, social construction, not something that is only sent, delivered, or otherwise transmitted to a docile public. . . . Audience members don't just passively take in and store bits of information in mental filing cabinets, they actively process this information, reshape it, and store only what serves culturally defined needs. (p. 323)

This book's focus on media literacy is based in part on cultural theories, which say that meaning and, therefore, effects are negotiated by media and audiences as they interact in the culture.

CRITICAL CULTURAL THEORY A major influence on mass communication theory came from European scholarship on media effects. **Critical cultural theory**—the idea that media operate primarily to justify and support the status quo at the expense of ordinary people—is openly political and is rooted in **neo-Marxist theory**. "Old-fashioned" Marxists believed that people were oppressed by those who owned the factories and the land (the means of production). They called the factories and land the *base*. Modern neo-Marxist theorists believe that people are oppressed by those who control the culture, the *superstructure*—religion, politics, art, literature, and of course the mass media.

Modern critical cultural theory encompasses a number of different conceptions of the relationship between media and culture. But all share these identifying characteristics:

- *They tend to be macroscopic in scope.* They examine broad, culturewide media effects.
- *They are openly and avowedly political.* Based on neo-Marxism, their orientation is from the political Left.
- *Their goal is at the least to instigate change in government media policies; at the most, to effect wholesale change in media and cultural systems.* Critical cultural theories logically assume that the superstructure, which favors those in power, must be altered.

- *They investigate and explain how elites use media to maintain their positions of privilege and power.* Issues such as media ownership, government-media relations, and corporate media representations of labor and disenfranchised groups are typical topics of study for critical cultural theory because they center on the exercise of power.

THE FRANKFURT SCHOOL The critical cultural perspective actually came to the United States in the 1930s when two prominent media scholars from the University of Frankfurt escaped Hitler's Germany. Theodor Adorno and Max Horkheimer were at the heart of what became known as the **Frankfurt School** of media theory (Arato & Gebhardt, 1978). Their approach, centered in neo-Marxism, valued serious art (literature, symphonic music, and theater) and saw consumption of art as a means to elevate all people toward a better life. Typical media fare—popular music, slapstick radio and movie comedies, the soft news dominant in newspapers—pacified ordinary people while assisting in their repression.

Adorno and Horkheimer's influence on U.S. media theory was small during their lifetimes. The limited effects perspective was about to blossom, neo-Marxism was not well received, and their ideas sounded a bit too much like mass society theory claims of a corrupting and debasing popular media. More recently, though, the Frankfurt School has been "rediscovered," and its influence can be seen in two final examples of contemporary critical theory, British cultural theory and news production research.

BRITISH CULTURAL THEORY There was significant class tension in England after World War II. During the 1950s and 1960s, working-class people who had fought for their country were unwilling to return to England's traditional notions of nobility and privilege. Many saw the British media—with broadcasting dominated by graduates of the best upper-crust schools, and newspapers and magazines owned by the wealthy—as supporting long-standing class distinctions and divisions. This environment of class conflict produced theorists such as Stuart Hall (1980), who first developed the idea of media as a public forum (Chapter 1) in which various forces fight to shape perceptions of everyday reality. Hall and others in British cultural studies trusted that the media *could* serve all people. However, because of ownership patterns, the commercial orientation of the media, and sympathetic government policies toward media, the forum was dominated by the reigning elite. In other words, the loudest voice in the give-and-take of the cultural forum belonged to those already well entrenched in the power structure. **British cultural theory** today provides a home for much feminist research and research on popular culture both in Europe and in the United States.

NEWS PRODUCTION RESEARCH Another interesting strand of critical cultural theory is **news production research**—the study of how economic and other influences on the way news is produced distort and bias news coverage toward those in power. W. Lance Bennett (1988) identified four common news production conventions used by U.S. media that bolster the position of those in power:

1. *Personalized news.* Most news stories revolve around people. If a newspaper wants to do a report on homelessness, for example, it will typically focus on one person or family as the center of its story. This makes for interesting journalism (and increased ratings or circulation), but it reduces important social and political problems to soap opera levels. The two likely results are that these problems are dismissed by the public as specific to the characters in the story and that the public is not provided with the social and political contexts of the problem that might suggest avenues of public action.

2. *Dramatized news.* News, like other forms of media content, must be attractively packaged. Especially on television, this packaging takes the form of dramatization. Stories must have a hero and a villain, a conflict must be identified, and there has to be a showdown. Again, one problem is that important public issues take on the

character of a soap opera or a Western movie. But a larger concern is that political debate is trivialized. Fundamental alterations in tax law or defense spending or any of a number of important issues are reduced to environmental extremists versus greedy corporations or the White House versus Congress. This complaint is often raised about media coverage of campaigns. The issues that should be at the center of the campaign become lost in a sea of stories about the "horse race"—who's ahead; how will a good showing in New Hampshire help Candidate X in her battle to unseat Candidate Y as the front-runner?

3. *Fragmented news.* The daily time and cost demands of U.S. journalism result in newspapers and broadcasts composed of a large number of brief, capsulated stories. There is little room in a given report for perspective and context. Another contributor to fragmented news, according to Bennett (1988), is journalists' obsession with objectivity. Putting any given day's story in context—connecting it to other events of the time or the past—would require the reporter to make decisions about which links are most important. Of course, these choices would be subjective, and so they are avoided. Reporters typically get one comment from somebody on one side of the issue and a second comment from the other side, juxtapose them as if they were equally valid, and then move on to tomorrow's assignment.

4. *Normalized news.* The U.S. newswriting convention typically employed when reporting on natural or human-made disasters is to seek out and report the opinions and perspectives of the authorities. When an airplane crashes, for example, the report invariably concludes with these words: "The FAA was quickly on the scene. The cockpit recorder has been retrieved, and the reason for this tragedy will be determined soon." In other words, what happened here is bad, but the authorities will sort it out. Journalists give little independent attention to investigating any of a number of angles that a plane crash or flood might suggest, angles that might produce information different from that of officials.

The cultural effect of news produced according to these conventions is daily reassurance by the media that the system works if those in power are allowed to do their jobs. Any suggestions about opportunities for meaningful social action are suppressed as reporters serve the powerful as "stenographers with amnesia" (Gitlin, 2004, p. 31).

► West Virginia Governor Joe Manchin regularly manned the press conference microphones during the search and recovery efforts at the April 2010 Montcoal mining disaster that claimed nearly 30 lives. Here he talks to reporters. But why was he there in the first place? He did not direct the effort. He has no expertise in mine safety or rescue. News production researchers would argue that his presence was designed to normalize the news— to remind us that the system, as it is, works.

The Meaning-Making Perspective

A more micro-level-centered view of media influence, one paralleling cultural theories in its belief in the power of mass communication, is the **meaning-making perspective**, the idea that active audience members use media content to create meaning, and meaningful experiences, for themselves. Naturally, this use can produce important macro-level, or cultural, effects as well. Cultural and meaning-making theories, taken together, make a most powerful case for becoming media literate. They argue that who we are and the world in which we live are in large part of our own making.

SYMBOLIC INTERACTION Mass communication theorists borrowed **symbolic interaction** from psychology. It is the idea that cultural symbols are learned through interaction and then mediate that interaction. In other words, people give things meaning, and that meaning controls their behavior. The flag is a perfect example. We have decided that an array of red, white, and blue cloth, assembled in a particular way, represents not only our nation but its values and beliefs as well. The flag has meaning because we have given it meaning, and that meaning now governs certain behavior toward the flag. We are not free to remain seated when a color guard carries the flag into a room. We are not free to fold it any way we choose. We are not free to place it on the right side of a stage in a public meeting. This is symbolic interaction.

Communication scholars Don Faules and Dennis Alexander (1978) define communication as "symbolic behavior which results in various degrees of shared meaning and values between participants" (p. 23). In their view, symbolic interaction is an excellent way to explain how mass communication shapes people's behaviors. Accepting that these symbolic meanings are negotiated by participants in the culture, mass communication scholars are left with these questions: What do the media contribute to these negotiations, and how powerful are they?

Symbolic interaction theory is frequently used when the influence of advertising is being studied because advertisers often succeed by encouraging the audience to perceive their products as symbols that have meaning beyond the products' actual function. This is called **product positioning**. For example, what does a Cadillac mean? Success. A Porsche? Virility. General Foods International Coffees? Togetherness and intimacy.

SOCIAL CONSTRUCTION OF REALITY If we keep in mind James Carey's cultural definition of communication from Chapter 1—communication is a symbolic process whereby reality is produced, maintained, repaired, and transformed—we cannot be surprised that mass communication theorists have been drawn to the ideas of sociologists Peter Berger and Thomas Luckmann. In their 1966 book, *The Social Construction of Reality*, they never mention mass communication, but they offer a compelling theory to explain how cultures use signs and symbols to construct and maintain a uniform reality.

Social construction of reality theory argues that people who share a culture also share "an ongoing correspondence" of meaning. Things generally mean the same to me as they do to you. A stop sign, for example, has just about the same meaning for everyone. Berger and Luckmann call these things that have "objective" meaning **symbols**—we routinely interpret them in the usual way. But there are other things in the environment to which we assign "subjective" meaning. These things they call **signs**. In social construction of reality, then, a car is a symbol of mobility, but a Cadillac or Mercedes Benz is a sign of wealth or success. In either case the meaning is negotiated, but for signs the negotiation is a bit more complex.

Through interaction in and with the culture over time, people bring together what they have learned about these signs and symbols to form **typification schemes**—collections of meanings assigned to some phenomenon or situation. These typification schemes form a natural backdrop for people's interpretation of and behavior in "the major routines of everyday life, not only the typification of others . . . but typifications of all sorts of events and experiences" (Berger & Luckmann, 1966, p. 43). When you enter a classroom, you automatically recall the cultural meaning of its various elements: desks in rows, chalkboard or whiteboard, lectern. You recognize this as a classroom and impose your "classroom typification scheme." You know how to behave: address the person standing at the front of the room with courtesy, raise your hand when you have a question, talk to your neighbors in whispers. These "rules of behavior" were not published on the classroom door. You applied them because they were appropriate to the "reality" of the setting in your culture. In other cultures, behaviors in this setting may be quite different.

Social construction of reality is important to researchers who study the effects of advertising for the same reasons that symbolic interaction has proven valuable. But it is also widely applied when looking at how media, especially news, shape our political realities.

Crime offers one example. What do politicians mean when they say they are "tough on crime"? What is their (and your) reality of crime? It is likely that "crime" signifies (is a sign for) gangs, drugs, and violence. But the statistical (rather than the socially constructed) reality is that there is 10 times more white-collar crime in the United States than there is violent crime. Now think "welfare." What reality is signified? Is it big corporations seeking subsidies and tax breaks from the government? Or is it unwed, unemployed mothers, unwilling to work, looking for a handout? Social construction theorists argue that the "building blocks" for the construction of these "realities" come primarily from the mass media.

CULTIVATION ANALYSIS Symbolic interaction and social construction of reality provide a strong foundation for *cultivation analysis*, which says that television "cultivates" or constructs a reality of the world that, although possibly inaccurate, becomes meaningful to us simply because we believe it to be true. We then base our judgments about and our actions in the world on this cultivated reality provided by television.

Although cultivation analysis was developed by media researcher George Gerbner and his colleagues out of concern over the effects of television violence, it has been applied to countless other television-cultivated realities such as beauty, sex roles, religion, the judicial process, and marriage. In all cases the assumptions are the same—television cultivates realities, especially for heavy viewers.

Cultivation analysis is based on five assumptions:

1. *Television is essentially and fundamentally different from other mass media.* Unlike books, newspapers, and magazines, television requires no reading ability. Unlike the movies, television requires no mobility or cash; it is in the home, and it is free. Unlike radio, television combines pictures and sound. It can be consumed from people's very earliest to their last years of life.

2. *Television is the "central cultural arm" of U.S. society.* Gerbner and his colleagues (Gerbner, Gross, Jackson-Beeck, Jeffries-Fox, & Signorielli, 1978) wrote that television, as our culture's primary storyteller, is "the chief creator of synthetic cultural patterns (entertainment and information) for the most heterogeneous mass publics in history, including large groups that have never shared in any common public message systems" (p. 178). The product of this sharing of messages is the **mainstreaming** of reality, moving individual and different people toward a shared, television-created understanding of how things are.

3. *The realities cultivated by television are not necessarily specific attitudes and opinions but rather more basic assumptions about the "facts" of life.* Television does not teach facts and figures; it builds general frames of reference. Return to our earlier discussion of the portrayal of crime on television. Television newscasts never say, "Most crime is violent, most violent crime is committed by people of color, and you should be wary of those people." But by the choices news producers make, television news presents a broad picture of "reality" with little regard for how its "reality" matches that of its audience.

4. *The major cultural function of television is to stabilize social patterns.* That is, the existing power relationships of the culture are reinforced and maintained through the meaning-making television images encourage. Gerbner and his colleagues (1978) made this argument:

> The repetitive pattern of television's mass-produced messages and images forms the mainstream of the common symbolic environment that cultivates the most widely shared conceptions of reality. We live in terms of the stories we tell—stories about what things exist, stories about how things work, and stories about what to do—and television tells them all through news, drama, and advertising to almost everybody most of the time. (p. 178)

Because the media industries have a stake in the political, social, and economic structures as they exist, their stories rarely challenge the system that has enriched them.

5. *The observable, measurable, independent contributions of television to the culture are relatively small.* This is not a restatement of limited effects theory. Instead, Gerbner and his colleagues explained its meaning with an "ice-age analogy":

> Just as an average temperature shift of a few degrees can lead to an ice age . . . so too can a relatively small but pervasive influence make a crucial difference. The "size" of an effect is far less critical than the direction of its steady contribution. (Gerbner, Gross, Morgan, & Signorielli, 1980, p. 14)

In other words, even though we cannot always see media effects on ourselves and others, they do occur and eventually will change the culture, possibly in profound ways.

The Effects of Mass Communication—Four Questions

Scientists and scholars use these theories, the earliest and the most recent, to form conclusions about the effects of mass communication. You are of course familiar with the long-standing debate over the effects of television violence. But there are other media effects questions that occupy thinkers' interest beyond that and the others highlighted here.

Does Media Violence Lead to Aggression?

No media effects issue has captured public, legislative, and industry attention as has the relationship between media portrayals of violence and subsequent aggressive behavior. Among the reasons for this focus are the facts that violence is a staple of both television and movies and that the United States experienced an upsurge in real violence in the 1960s, just about the time television entrenched itself as the country's dominant mass medium, and that movies turned to increasingly graphic violence to differentiate themselves from and to compete with television.

The prevailing view during the 1960s was that *some* media violence affected *some* people in *some* ways *some* of the time. Given the dominance of the transmissional perspective of communication and the limited effects theories, researchers believed that for "normal" people—that is, those who were not predisposed to violence—*little* media violence affected *few* people in *few* ways *little* of the time. However, increases in youth violence, the assassinations of Robert F. Kennedy and the Reverend Martin Luther King Jr., and the violent eruption of cities during the civil rights, women's rights, and anti–Vietnam War movements led to creation of the Surgeon General's Scientific

Advisory Committee on Television and Social Behavior in 1969. After two years and $1 million worth of research, the committee (whose members had to be approved by the television networks) produced findings that led Surgeon General Jesse L. Steinfield to report to the U.S. Senate:

> While the . . . report is carefully phrased and qualified in language acceptable to social scientists, it is clear to me that the causal relationship between televised violence and antisocial behavior is sufficient to warrant appropriate and immediate remedial action. The data on social phenomena such as television and violence and/or aggressive behavior will never be clear enough for all social scientists to agree on the formulation of a succinct statement of causality. But there comes a time when the data are sufficient to justify action. That time has come. (Ninety-Second Congress, 1972, p. 26)

Despite the apparent certainty of this statement, disagreement persists over the existence and extent of the media's contribution to aggressive behavior. Few would argue that media violence *never* leads to aggressive behavior. The disagreement is about what circumstances are needed for such effects to occur, and to whom.

UNDER WHAT CIRCUMSTANCES? A direct causal relationship between violent content and aggressive behavior—the **stimulation model**—has been scientifically demonstrated in laboratory experiments. So has the **aggressive cues model**—the idea that media portrayals can suggest that certain classes of people, such as women or foreigners, are acceptable targets for real-world aggression, thereby increasing the likelihood that some people will act violently toward people in these groups.

Both the stimulation and aggressive cues models are based on social cognitive theory. Fueled by the research of psychologists such as Albert Bandura, social cognitive theory has made several additional contributions to the violence debate.

Social cognitive theory deflated the notion of **catharsis**, the idea that watching violence in the media reduces people's innate aggressive drive. Social scientists were already skeptical: Viewing people eating does not reduce hunger; viewing

► Ernest Borgnine in Sam Peckinpah's *The Wild Bunch* (1969). In trying to differentiate itself from the television industry, the movie industry turned to graphic violence, fueling the debate over media violence and subsequent real-world aggression.

▲ These scenes from Albert Bandura's media violence research are typical of the laboratory response to portrayals of media violence that social learning researchers were able to elicit from children.

people making love does not reduce the drive to reproduce. But social cognitive theory provided a scientific explanation for the research that did show a reduction in aggression after viewing violence. This phenomenon was better explained not by some cathartic power of the media but by inhibitory effects. That is, as we saw in our discussion of social cognitive theory, if media aggression is portrayed as punished or prohibited, it can indeed lead to the reduced likelihood that that behavior will be modeled.

Some people, typically media industry practitioners, to this day defend catharsis theory. But over 40 years ago, respected media researcher and theorist Joseph Klapper, who at the time was the head of social research for CBS television, told the U.S. Senate, "I myself am unaware of any, shall we say, hard evidence that seeing violence on television or any other medium acts in a cathartic . . . manner. There have been some studies to that effect; they are grossly, greatly outweighed by studies as to the opposite effect" (Ninety-Second Congress, 1972, p. 60).

Social cognitive theory introduced the concept of **vicarious reinforcement**—the idea that observed reinforcement operates in the same manner as actual reinforcement. This helped direct researchers' attention to the context in which media violence is presented. Theoretically, inhibitory and disinhibitory effects operate because of the presence of vicarious reinforcement. That is, seeing the bad guy punished is sufficient to inhibit subsequent aggression on the part of the viewer. Unfortunately, what researchers discovered is that in contemporary film and television, when the bad guys are punished, they are punished by good guys who out-aggress them. The implication is that even when media portray punishment for aggressive behavior, they may in fact be reinforcing that very same behavior.

Social cognitive theory introduced the concept of **environmental incentives**—the notion that real-world incentives can lead observers to ignore the negative vicarious reinforcement they have learned to associate with a given behavior.

In 1965 Bandura conducted a now-classic experiment in which nursery school children saw a video aggressor, a character named Rocky, punished for his behavior. The children subsequently showed lower levels of aggressive play than did those who

Television's ability to serve prosocial ends is obvious in the public service messages we see sprinkled throughout the shows we watch. For example, NBC's *The More You Know* series has been running short, clever PSAs mixed among its regular commercials for more than 20 years. They feature the network's biggest stars, cover issues like quitting smoking, good parenting, remembering to take prescriptions, and good exercise, but you probably remember them from their iconic shooting star and rainbow tail.

But television writers and producers also more aggressively use their medium to produce prosocial effects by embedding important cultural messages in the entertainment they create. The relationship between the Centers for Disease Control and Prevention (CDC) and several popular programs is indicative. Aware that 88% of Americans learn about health issues from television, experts at the CDC work with the writers of series like *House*, *Grey's Anatomy*, *ER*, *Private Practice*, *Law & Order*, and *Desperate Housewives* to include important health information in their scripts. If

you watched the episodes of *24* in which Los Angeles suffered a terrorist attack you learned, from this partnership, how infectious agents can be spread by physical contact, how to handle a government-mandated quarantine, and the civil liberty issues involved in such a quarantine. If you are a fan of *Raising Hope*, *The Vampire Diaries*, *Glee*, or *Parenthood*, you've viewed stories written in conjunction with the National Campaign to Prevent Teen and Unplanned Pregnancy designed to promote safe sex.

This "prime-time activism" can be traced to Harvard professor Jay Winsten and his 1988 campaign to get Hollywood to push his novel "designated driver" idea. You know what a designated driver is—he or she is the person among a group of friends who is selected to remain alcohol-free during a get-together and then to drive

> "In the four network television seasons that followed these meetings, designated drivers were part of the story lines of 160 different prime-time shows seen by hundreds of millions of viewers."

everyone else home. The concept, much less the term, did not even exist until Professor Winsten, through the intervention of CBS executive Frank Stanton, contacted Stanton's friend Grant Tinker, then chair of NBC, to ask for help. Intrigued by Winsten's plan to develop a new social norm, Tinker put his considerable clout behind the effort, writing letters to the heads of the 13 production companies that did the most business with the networks. Tinker personally escorted Professor Winsten, director of Harvard's Center for Health Communication, to meetings with all 13 producers.

In the four network television seasons that followed these meetings, designated drivers were part of the story lines of 160 different prime-time shows seen by hundreds of millions of viewers. Professor Winsten was successful in placing his message in entertainment programming, but did his message make a difference? Absolutely. Within one year of the introduction of the idea of the designated driver in these television shows, 67% of U.S. adults said they were aware of the concept, and by 1991, 52% of adults under 30 years old said they had served as a designated driver.

◀ Story lines revolving around contemporary social issues are frequently embedded in prime-time shows after consultation with experts. Episodes of *24* offered information on how to deal with health and civil liberty issues in the event of a terrorist biological attack.

had seen Rocky rewarded. This is what social cognitive theory would have predicted. Yet Bandura later offered "sticker-pictures" to the children who had seen Rocky punished if they could perform the same actions they had seen him perform. They all could. Vicarious negative reinforcement may reduce the likelihood that the punished behavior will be performed, but that behavior is still observationally learned. It's just that, at the same time it is observed and learned, observers also learn not to make it. When the real world offers sufficient reward, the originally learned behavior can be demonstrated.

FOR WHOM? The compelling evidence of cognitive learning researchers aside, it's clear that most people do not exhibit aggression after viewing film or video violence. There is also little doubt that those predisposed to violence are more likely to be influenced by media aggression. Yet viewers need not necessarily be predisposed for this link to occur, because at any time anyone can become predisposed. For example, experimental research indicates that frustrating people before they view media violence can increase the likelihood of subsequent aggressive behavior.

But the question remains, who, exactly, is affected by mediated violence? If a direct causal link is necessary to establish effects, then it can indeed be argued that some media violence affects some people in some ways some of the time. But if the larger, macro-level ritual view is applied, then we all are affected because we live in a world in which there is more violence than there might be without mass media. We live in a world, according to cultivation analysis, in which we are less trusting of our neighbors and more accepting of violence in our midst. We experience **desensitization**. This need not be the case. As researcher Ellen Wartella (1997) said, "Today, we find wide consensus among experts that, of all the factors contributing to violence in our society, violence on television may be the easiest to control" (p. 4). And in a clear sign of that wide consensus, the American Medical Association, the American Academy of Pediatrics, the American Psychological Association, and the American Academy of Child & Adolescent Psychiatry issued a joint report in summer 2000 offering their combined view that the effects of violent media are "measurable and long lasting" and that "prolonged viewing of media violence can lead to emotional desensitization toward violence in real life" (as quoted in Wronge, 2000, p. 1E).

Do Portrayals of Drugs and Alcohol Increase Consumption?

Concern about media effects reaches beyond the issue of violence. The claims and counterclaims surrounding media portrayals of drugs and alcohol parallel those of the violence debate.

The wealth of scientific data linking media portrayals of alcohol consumption, especially in ads, to increases in youthful drinking and alcohol abuse led the U.S. Department of Health and Human Services' National Institute of Alcohol Abuse and Alcoholism to report, "The preponderance of the evidence indicates that alcohol advertising stimulates higher consumption of alcohol by both adults and adolescents" and "There is sufficient evidence to say that alcohol advertising is likely to be a contributing factor to overall consumption and other alcohol-related problems in the long term" (Center for Science in the Public Interest, 2002, p. 2). The Center on Alcohol Marketing and Youth (2012) reports the following:

- More youth in the United States drink alcohol than smoke tobacco or marijuana, making it the drug most used by America's young people.
- Every day, 4,750 people under 16 take their first drink of alcohol.
- The average age at which young people 12 to 17 begin to drink is 13 years old.
- Underage drinking is estimated to account for between 11% and 20% of the U.S. alcohol market. Even the lower estimate of 11% represents 3.6 billion drinks each year.
- Youth who start drinking before the age of 15 are five times more likely to develop alcohol dependence or abuse in their lifetimes than are those who begin drinking at age 21 years or later.
- Programming popular with teens is filled with alcohol advertising. Every year since 2001, alcohol ads have appeared on 13 or more of the 15 programs most popular with teens ages 12 to 17.
- The neuroscience, psychology, and marketing scientific literature concludes that adolescents, because of how the human brain develops, may be particularly attracted to branded products such as alcohol that are associated with risky behavior and that provide, in their view, immediate gratification, thrills, and/or social status.
- Long-term studies have shown that youth who see, hear, and read more alcohol ads are more likely to drink and drink more heavily than their peers.

BE FABULOUS*

MOËT & CHANDON

▲ What does this magazine ad say about drinking? About attractiveness? About having fun? About women? Are you satisfied with these representations of important aspects of your life?

Yet there is a good deal of scientific research—typically from alcohol industry scientists—that discounts the causal link between media portrayals and real-world drinking. Again, researchers who insist on the demonstration of this direct causal relationship will rarely agree on media's influence on behavior. The larger cultural perspective, however, suggests that media portrayals of alcohol, both in ads and in entertainment fare, tell stories of alcohol consumption that predominantly present it as safe, healthy, youthful, sexy, necessary for a good time, effective for dealing with stress, and essential to ceremonies and other rites of passage.

The same scenario exists in the debate over the relationship between media portrayals of nonalcohol drug use and behavior. Relatively little contemporary media content presents the use of illegal drugs in a glorifying manner. In fact, the destructive power of illegal drugs is often the focus of television shows such as *CSI: Miami* and *Breaking Bad* and a central theme in movies such as *Adventureland* and *Maria Full of Grace*. Scientific concern has centered therefore on the impact of commercials and other media portrayals of legal over-the-counter drugs. Again, impressive amounts of experimental research suggest a causal link between this content and subsequent abuse of both legal and illegal drugs; however, there also exists research that discounts the causal link between media portrayals and the subsequent abuse of drugs. It cannot be denied, however, that media often present legal drugs as a cure-all for dealing with that pesky mother-in-law, those screaming kids, that abusive boss, and other daily annoyances. Prescription drug advertising is enough of a public health issue that the Food and Drug Administration on several occasions has considered banning it. Nonetheless, it is illegal in every other country in the world except in the United States and New Zealand.

What Is Media's Contribution to Gender and Racial/Ethnic Stereotyping?

Stereotyping is the application of a standardized image or concept to members of certain groups, usually based on limited information. Because media cannot show all realities of all things, the choices media practitioners make when presenting specific people and groups may well facilitate or encourage stereotyping.

Numerous studies conducted over the last 70 years have demonstrated that women, people of color, older people, gays and lesbians—in fact, all of our nation's "out-groups"—are consistently underrepresented in our mass media. Media effects research over that same period has consistently demonstrated the impact of this underrepresentation:

> Media use has been determined to play a meaningful role in the development of racial/ethnic cognitions and intergroup behaviors. Indeed, research has consistently revealed modest but significant associations between viewing media portrayals of race/ethnicity and outcomes concerning outgroup members' competence . . . socioeconomic status . . . group status . . . social roles . . . and judgments regarding a variety of race-based attributions and stereotypes. (Mastro, 2009, p. 325)

Any of a number of theories, especially cultivation analysis, symbolic interaction, and social construction of reality, can explain these effects. This underrepresentation influences people's perceptions, and people's perceptions influence their behaviors. Examine your own perceptions not only of women and people of color but of older people, lawyers, college athletes, and people sophisticated in the use of computers. What images or stereotypes come immediately to mind?

▲ These images (clockwise from top left) from *The L Word*, *Will & Grace*, *Queer as Folk*, and *Modern Family* offer samples of contemporary television's portrayals of gay people and homosexuality. Researchers believe that repeated and frequent exposure to representations such as these influence people's perceptions of gays and issues relating to homosexuality. Some call this the *Will & Grace* effect, "the single most important indicator of one's support for gay rights is whether one knows someone who is gay, [and a gay person] on TV will do" (Lithwick, 2012, p. 77). Today, having "met" many gay people in real and media life, a large majority of Americans favor gay rights and more than half favor gay marriage (Langer, 2013). The question, then—as it typically is when discussing media stereotypes—is, Which came first, the culture's perceptions of gay people or gay people's representation in the media? Clearly, television's presentation of gays has matured over time—from invisible to realistic and sympathetic. But was television's "evolution" in its representation of homosexuality a *mirror* of culture's already changing attitudes, or did the medium *lead* that change?

Sure, maybe you were a bit surprised at the data on race and school discipline described earlier; still, you're skeptical. You're a smart, modern, college-educated individual. Use the following quiz to test yourself on your stereotypes of crime, marriage, and family:

1. Which of these states has the highest divorce rate: Arkansas, Oklahoma, or Massachusetts?

2. Which category of Americans—White, Hispanic, or African American—has the highest rate of substance abuse?

3. Which two states have the higher rates of teenage pregnancy: New Hampshire, Mississippi, or Texas?

4. Rank these cities in order of their crime rates, highest to lowest: Atlanta, New York, Memphis.

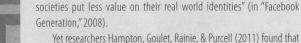

CULTURAL FORUM

A Friend by Any Other Name: Research on Facebook and Relationships

Mass communication researchers often examine issues in the cultural forum, for example, the fast food advertising / childhood obesity link or the effects of violent video games. But sometimes their work fuels discussion in the cultural forum. That's the case with media researchers' examination of people's use of Facebook. They want to know if social network sites are changing the nature of friendship. Does social networking allow people to become more connected to and supportive of their friends, or does it diminish friendship because it lacks the intimacy of face-to-face contact? In exchange for more and a wider network of friends, do people give up the kind of personal relationships that fuel the development of empathy and understanding of emotional nuance that comes from "reading" others' faces and bodies when communicating? Explains media researcher Julian Kiker, "Our notion of what a 'friend' is is shifting, and I think if you talk to people of different demographics—particularly different ages—you'll find, if you ask them the definition of 'friend,' they have very different notions of that" (in Przybys, 2011).

British psychiatrist Himanshu Tyagi offers the view that in the social networking world "everything moves fast and changes all the time . . . Relationships are quickly disposed at the click of a mouse . . . You can delete your profile if you don't like it and swap an unacceptable identity in the blink of an eye for one that is more acceptable . . . It may be possible that young people who have no experience of a world without online

societies put less value on their real world identities" (in "Facebook Generation," 2008).

Yet researchers Hampton, Goulet, Rainie, & Purcell (2011) found that Facebook users not only use the social networking site to keep up with close social ties, but compared to non-Facebookers, they are more likely to be trusting of others and have more "core ties" among their real-world social networks. As for the nature of friendship, Facebookers get more social and emotional support as well as more companionship from others than do non-Facebookers: "For Facebook users, the additional boost is equivalent to about half the total support that the average American receives as a result of being married." Their

> "Contrary to studies done earlier in the decade, the Internet is not linked to social isolation. Rather, it can lead to larger, more diverse social networks."

conclusion is that "contrary to studies done earlier in the decade, the Internet is not linked to social isolation. Rather, it can lead to larger, more diverse social networks."

Enter your voice. Are you on Facebook? What is your definition of friendship? What do you think is lost and gained as a result of your use of the social networking site? What do you make of the fact that the number of users who are "unfriending" others grows every year, up to 63% in 2011 (Madden, 2012). Does this mean that they find these friendships unsatisfying, or does it suggest that users are refining and redefining for themselves just what a friend really is? Is this the kind of question that mass communication researchers can answer to your satisfaction? Why or why not?

◀ Is a Facebook friend really a friend?

Are you surprised to learn that the divorce rate is lowest in liberal, northeast Massachusetts (2.2 out of every 1,000 marriages), far lower than heartland states Arkansas (5.7 per 1,000) and Oklahoma (4.9 per 1,000; U.S. Census Bureau, 2012b)? Drug users? Substance abusers? African Americans have a lower rate of drug abuse (5%) than do White (9%) and Hispanic (7.7%) Americans (Szalavitz, 2011). Teenage pregnancy rates are higher in Texas (88 per 1,000 teenage girls) and Mississippi (85 per 1,000), again regions typically viewed as socially conservative. New Hampshire (33/1,000) has the lowest, joined by two other New England states, Vermont (40/1,000) and Maine (43/1,000), with teen pregnancy rates well below the national average of 70 births per 1,000 teen women

(Guttmacher Institute, 2010). New York City, "Gomorrah of the North," is the safest big city in America, with a per capita crime rate of 4.2%, compared to Memphis (18%) and Atlanta (16%; Ott, 2009). How did you develop your stereotypes of these people and places? Where did you find the building blocks to construct your realities of their lives?

Do Media Have Prosocial Effects?

Virtually every argument that can be made for the harmful or negative effects of media can also be applied to the ability of media to do good. A sizable body of science exists that clearly demonstrates that people, especially children, can and will model the good or prosocial behaviors they see in the media, often to a greater extent than they will the negative behaviors. Research on the impact of media portrayals of cooperation and constructive problem solving (Baran, Chase, & Courtright, 1979) and other "good" behaviors indicates that much more than negative behavior can be socially learned from the media (see the essay, "Television and the Designated Driver").

DEVELOPING MEDIA LITERACY SKILLS

Applying Mass Communication Theory

There are many more theories of mass communication and effects issues than we've covered here. Some apply to the operation of media as part of specific social systems. Some examine mass communication at the most micro level; for example, How do viewers process individual television scenes? This chapter has focused on a relatively small number of theories and effects that might prove useful to people trying to develop their media literacy skills. Remember Art Silverblatt's (2008) elements of media literacy in Chapter 1. Among them were understanding the process of mass communication and accepting media content as a "text" providing insight into ourselves and our culture. Among the media literacy skills we identified was an understanding of and respect for the power of media messages. Good mass communication theory speaks to these elements and skills. Good mass communication theorists understand media effects. Media-literate people, then, are actually good mass communication theorists. They apply the available conceptions of media use and impact to their own content consumption and the way they live their lives.

MEDIA LITERACY CHALLENGE
Be a News Production Researcher

An awareness of the impact of media on individuals and society is an important component of media literacy, and as you've read, news production research suggests that media do indeed have a powerful effect on people and culture. This work examines economic and other influences on the way news is produced and how these influences distort coverage in favor of society's elites. Like much of critical cultural theory, this is a controversial perspective, but your challenge is to test its validity for yourself. First, choose one of the following media outlets (or if you want to compete against your classmates, divide them between yourselves): a daily newspaper, a local television news broadcast, a national news magazine, and a network television news broadcast. Then, identify as many examples of the four common news production conventions as you can find—personalized, dramatized, fragmented, and normalized news—and discuss their "slant." Once you've completed this exercise, explain why you are more or less likely to accept the arguments of the news production research perspective.

Resources for Review and Discussion

REVIEW POINTS: TYING CONTENT TO LEARNING OUTCOMES

▶ **Outline the history and development of mass communication theory.**
- ► Developments in mass communication theory are driven by advances in technology or the introduction of new media, calls for their control, and questions about their democratic and pluralistic use.

▶ **Explain what is meant by theory, why it is important, and how it is used.**
- ► In understanding mass communication theory we must recognize that:
  - There is no one mass communication theory.
  - Theories are often borrowed from other fields of science.
  - Theories are human constructions and they are dynamic.
- ► Three dichotomies characterize the different sides in the effects debate:
  - Micro- versus macro-level effects.
  - Administrative versus critical research.
  - Transmissional versus ritual perspective on communication.
- ► In the media effects debate, these arguments for limited media influence have logical counters:
  - Media content is make-believe; people know it's not real.
  - Media content is only play or entertainment.
  - Media simply hold a mirror to society.

- If media have any influence, it is only in reinforcing preexisting values and beliefs.
- Media influence only the unimportant things like fads and fashions.

▶ **Describe influential traditional and contemporary mass communication theories.**
- ► The four major eras of mass communication theory are mass society theory, limited effects theory, cultural theory, and the meaning-making perspective. The latter two mark a return to the idea of powerful media effects.

▶ **Analyze controversial effects issues.**
- ► Despite lingering debate, the media violence/viewer aggression link is scientifically well established.
- ► The same holds true for the relationship between media portrayals of drug and alcohol use and their real-world consumption.
- ► The stories carried in the media can and do contribute to stereotyping of a wide array of people and phenomena.
- ► The same scientific evidence demonstrating that media can have negative effects shows that they can produce prosocial effects as well.

▶ **Apply mass communication theory to your own use of media.**
- ► Media-literate individuals are themselves good mass communication theorists because they understand media effects and how and when they occur.

KEY TERMS

early window, 319
willing suspension of disbelief, 319
micro-level effects, 320
macro-level effects, 321
administrative research, 321
critical research, 321
transmissional perspective, 322
ritual perspective, 322
mass communication theories, 322
cultivation analysis, 323
attitude change theory, 323
middle-range theories, 323
mass society theory, 325
hypodermic needle theory, 325
magic bullet theory, 325
grand theory, 325

limited effects theory, 326
two-step flow theory, 326
opinion leaders, 326
opinion followers, 326
dissonance theory, 327
selective processes, 327
selective exposure (attention), 327
selective retention, 327
selective perception, 328
reinforcement theory, 329
uses and gratifications approach, 330
agenda setting, 330
dependency theory, 331
social cognitive theory, 332
modeling, 332
imitation, 332

identification, 332
observational learning, 332
inhibitory effects, 332
disinhibitory effects, 332
cultural theory, 334
critical cultural theory, 334
neo-Marxist theory, 334
Frankfurt School, 335
British cultural theory, 335
news production research, 335
meaning-making perspective, 337
symbolic interaction, 337
product positioning, 337
social construction of reality, 337
symbols, 337
signs, 337

QUESTIONS FOR REVIEW

1. What are the four eras of mass communication theory?

2. What are dissonance theory and the selective processes?

3. What is agenda setting?

4. What is the distinction between imitation and identification in social cognitive theory?

5. What assumptions about people and media are shared by symbolic interaction and social construction of reality?

6. What are the five assumptions of cultivation analysis?

7. What four common news production conventions shape the news to suit the interests of the elite?

8. What are the characteristics of critical cultural studies?

9. What are the early window and willing suspension of disbelief?

10. What are the stimulation and aggressive cues models of media violence? What is catharsis?

For further review, go to the LearnSmart study module for this chapter.

QUESTIONS FOR CRITICAL THINKING AND DISCUSSION

1. Do media set the agenda for you? If not, why not? If they do, can you cite examples from your own experience?

2. Can you find examples of magazine or television advertising that use ideas from symbolic interaction or social construction of reality to sell their products? How do they do so?

3. Do you pay attention to alcohol advertising? Do you think it influences your level of alcohol consumption?

Media Freedom, Regulation, and Ethics

14

Learning Objectives

Our democracy exists on a foundation of self-governance, and free and responsible mass media are essential to both democracy and self-governance. But media, because of their power and the often conflicting demands of profit and service under which they operate, are (and should be) open to some control. The level and sources of that control, however, are controversial issues for the media, in the government, and in the public forum. After studying this chapter you should be able to

▶ Outline the history and development of our contemporary understanding of the First Amendment.

▶ Explain the justification for and exercise of media regulation.

▶ Distinguish between a media system that operates under a libertarian philosophy and one that operates under a social responsibility philosophy.

▶ Define and discuss media ethics and how they are applied.

▶ Describe the operation and pros and cons of self-regulation.

▶ Assess your personal commitment to media reform.

Bradley Manning, whistle-blower or traitor?

UP UNTIL NOW, EVERYTHING HAD BEEN RIGHT ABOUT THE JOB. Editor of a major college daily newspaper makes a great resumé entry, you are treated like royalty at school events, you get to do something good for your campus, and, if you do your job well, even for the larger world out there. But as the tension around you grows, you start to wonder if it's all worth it.

First there was the blow-up over your Bradley Manning editorial. Manning is the soldier who, in 2010, provided scores of documents concerning the war in the Middle East to the website WikiLeaks which, in turn, made them available to the world. Among the classified materials were memos and cables indicating that officials knew of but ignored torture in Iraq and had covered up evidence of child abuse by contractors in Afghanistan. There was evidence that the official military count of civilian deaths in Iraq and Afghanistan was much higher than publicly revealed. Most dramatically, there was video footage of a 2007 incident in which an Apache helicopter fired on civilians in Baghdad. It showed American soldiers shooting and killing 11 individuals, including two Reuters journalists, none of whom returned fire. Because the material was classified, Manning was arrested, charged with treason, a crime punishable by death, and held in solitary confinement for more than a year. After three years in jail he was on trial and you wanted to editorialize in favor of a speedy and fair outcome.

No way, argued your assistant editor. "He's a traitor and a criminal. Let him rot. The government made those documents secret for a reason." You were prepared for this: "It's illegal for officials to classify material if the goal is to hide violations of the law, governmental inefficiency, or administrative error. It's also not allowed if the intent is to merely prevent embarrassment to an official or agency or to prevent the release of information that does not pose a threat to national security." But she was ready for you, too: "Revealing those secrets cost American lives!" You countered, "They never should have been secrets in the first place, and besides, the Secretary of Defense said no lives were lost as a result of the leaks and even the country's foreign policy was unaffected. And tell me this, what's the difference between Daniel Ellsberg, who released the equally classified Pentagon Papers to the *New York Times* and Bradley Manning who gave materials to WikiLeaks? Why is Ellsberg considered a whistle-blower and hero and Manning a traitor?"

1900

1925

1644   Milton's *Areopagitica*

1791 ▲ Bill of Rights ratified

1919 ▲ "Clear and present danger" ruling

1931   *Near v. Minnesota* prior restraint ruling

1935 ▲ Hauptmann/Lindbergh trial

1943   NBC "traffic cop" decision

1947   Social responsibility theory of the press

Then there's your commentary on Edward Snowden, the whistle-blower (although most of your staff said traitor), who in May 2013 revealed the existence of a top-secret National Security Agency (NSA) program that collected the Internet data of all Americans through access to the servers of all the major Internet companies, Web giants like Verizon, Google, Facebook, and Apple. The Prism program, as it was called, was officially aimed at detecting foreign terrorists, but the materials Snowden provided to England's *Guardian* newspaper and the *Washington Post* made it clear that *all* Americans' Net activity was being collected and stored. Moreover, the documents showed that the secret Foreign Intelligence Surveillance Court had approved the NSA's use of information on Americans "inadvertently" collected, even in the absence of a warrant. Snowden willingly revealed his identity. "I have no intention of hiding who I am because I know I have done nothing wrong," he said. Nonetheless, the government charged Snowden with espionage, bringing with it a possible death sentence. Snowden fled first to Hong Kong and then to Russia as politicians from all political stripes called for his arrest, even assassination. Many journalists also condemned him, most publicly NBC's David Gregory, who accused *Guardian* reporter Glenn Greenwald of "aiding and abetting a crime" and asked him why he himself should not be charged with a crime for publishing Snowden's materials. "I think it's pretty extraordinary," replied Mr. Greenwald, "that anybody who would call themselves a journalist would publicly muse about whether or not other journalists should be charged with felonies" (in Carr, 2013).

While your fellow students at the paper and on campus were debating the whistle-blower/traitor issue, you wanted to write that the revelations were as valuable as those in Ellsberg's release of the Pentagon Papers. They had generated what you believed to be a much needed public discussion about the balance between liberty and security, as well as important questions about the relationship between journalism and the government.

In both instances you've argued in favor of more, rather than less, media freedom and public knowledge. This is America; who can have a problem with that? Both columns run as above-the-fold editorials. You get 61 angry phone calls and e-mails, nine longtime advertisers pull their regular weekly buys, and your assistant editor and two other staffers quit the paper.

These dilemmas, routinely faced by real college and professional editors, highlight two important lessons offered in this chapter. First, what is legal may not always be

what is right. Second, when media practitioners do try to do the right thing, they have to consider the interests, needs, and values of others besides themselves.

In this chapter we look at how the First Amendment has been defined and applied over time. We study how the logic of a free and unfettered press has come into play in the area of broadcast deregulation. We also detail the shift in the underlying philosophy of media freedom from libertarianism to social responsibility theory. This provides the background for our examination of the ethical environment in which media professionals must work as they strive to fulfill their socially responsible obligations.

A Short History of the First Amendment

The U.S. Constitution mentions only one industry by name as deserving special protection—the press. Therefore, our examination of media regulation, self-regulation, and ethics must begin with a discussion of this "First Freedom."

As we saw in Chapter 4, the first Congress of the United States was committed to freedom of the press. The First Amendment to the new Constitution expressly stated that "Congress shall make no law . . . abridging the freedom of speech, or of the press." As a result, government regulation of the media must be not only unobtrusive but also sufficiently justified to meet the limits of the First Amendment. Media industry self-regulation must be sufficiently effective to render official restraint unnecessary, and media practitioners' conduct should be ethical in order to warrant this special protection.

Early Sentiment for a Free Press

Democracy—government by the people—requires a free press. The framers of the Bill of Rights understood this because of their experience with the European monarchies from which they and their forebears had fled. They based their guarantee of this privileged position to the press on **libertarianism**, the philosophy that people cannot govern themselves in a democracy unless they have access to the information they need for that governance. Libertarian philosophy is based on the **self-righting principle**, which was forcefully stated in 1644 by English author and poet John Milton in his book *Areopagitica*. Milton argued from two main points:

- The free flow or trade of ideas serves to ensure that public discourse will allow the truth to emerge.
- Truth will emerge from public discourse because people are inherently rational and good.

But as we also saw in Chapter 4, even the First Amendment and libertarian philosophy did not guarantee freedom of the press. The Alien and Sedition Acts were passed a scant eight years after the Constitution was ratified. And Milton himself was to become the chief censor of Catholic writing in Oliver Cromwell's English government.

Defining and Refining the First Amendment

Clearly, the idea of freedom of the press needed some clarification. One view was (and is) housed in the **absolutist position**, which is expressed succinctly by Supreme Court Justice Hugo Black:

> No law means no law. . . . My view is, without deviation, without exception, without any ifs, buts, or whereases, that freedom of speech means that government shall not do anything to people, either for the views they have or the views they express, or the words they speak or write. (in McMasters, 2005, p. 15)

Yet the absolutist position is more complex than this would suggest. Although absolutists accept that the First Amendment provides a central and fundamental wall of protection for the press and free expression, several questions about its true meaning remained to be answered over time. You can read about a recent controversial Supreme Court First Amendment ruling in the box entitled, "First Amendment Protection for Violence but Not for Sex." But for now, let's look at some of history's answers.

WHAT DOES "NO LAW" MEAN? The First Amendment said that the U.S. Congress could "make no law," but could state legislatures? City councils? Mayors? Courts? Who has the power to proscribe the press? This issue was settled in 1925 in a case involving the right of a state to limit the publication of a socialist newsletter. The Supreme Court, in *Gitlow v. New York*, stated that the First Amendment is "among the fundamental personal rights and 'liberties' protected by the due process clause of the Fourteenth Amendment from impairment by the states" (Gillmor & Barron, 1974, p. 1). Given this, "Congress shall make no law" should be interpreted as "government agencies shall make no law." Today, "no law" includes statutes, laws, administrative regulations, executive and court orders, and ordinances from government, regardless of locale.

WHAT IS "THE PRESS"? Just what "press" enjoys First Amendment protection? The Supreme Court, in its 1952 *Burstyn v. Wilson* decision, declared that movies were protected expression. In 1973 Justice William O. Douglas wrote in *CBS v. Democratic National Committee*,

> What kind of First Amendment would best serve our needs as we approach the 21st century may be an open question. But the old fashioned First Amendment that we have is the Court's only guideline; and one hard and fast principle has served us through days of calm and eras of strife, and I would abide by it until a new First Amendment is adopted. That means, as I view it, that TV and radio . . . are all included in the concept of "press" as used in the First Amendment and therefore are entitled to live under the laissez faire regime which the First Amendment sanctions. (Gillmor & Barron, 1974, pp. 7–8)

Advertising, or commercial speech, enjoys First Amendment protection. This was established by the Supreme Court in 1942. Despite the fact that the decision in *Valentine v. Christensen* went against the advertiser, the Court wrote that just because expression was commercial did not necessarily mean that it was unprotected. Some justices argued for a "two-tiered" level of protection, with commercial expression being somewhat less worthy of protection than noncommercial expression. But others argued that

First Amendment Protection for Violence but Not for Sex

In 2006 California passed a law that would have required the labeling of violent video games and banned their sale to children under 18 years old. The gaming industry sued, and the case, *Brown v. Entertainment Merchants Association* (2011), eventually made its way to the U.S. Supreme Court, where in a 7-2 decision, Justices ruled that "a state possesses legitimate power to protect children from harm, but that does not include a free-floating power to restrict the ideas to which children may be exposed." In his dissent, Justice Stephen Breyer, citing the scientific evidence linking viewing violent games and aggression, argued that he found "sufficient

grounds in these studies and expert opinions for this court to defer to an elected legislature's conclusion that the videogames in question are *particularly likely to* harm children."

The issues of free speech and the possible harmful effects of violent video games were of sufficient interest to thrust this decision firmly into the cultural forum, but it was Justice Antonin Scalia's assertion— "Because speech about violence is not obscene," it cannot be regulated even when children are involved and even when it involves sexually assaulting an image of a human being; but speech about sex has long been restricted, especially when children are involved, so therefore it is censorable—that drew the most attention. The

> "A state possesses legitimate power to protect children from harm, but that does not include a free-floating power to restrict the ideas to which children may be exposed."

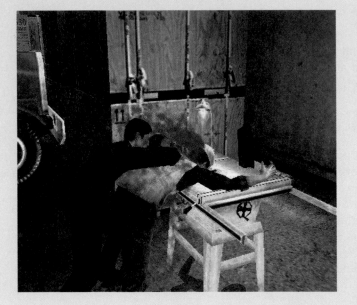

◀ Videogame violence is protected expression.

decision's critics saw this as "violence is normal but sex, even nonviolent and consensual, is not." Employing as an example a gruesome game sequence from *Mortal Kombat II* in which a young woman is ripped in two by freakishly large combatants, Jon Stewart (2011) explained the decision to his *Daily Show* viewers, "The state has no interest in restricting the sale of [violent video games] to children, but if while being disemboweled, this woman were to [expose her breast], regulate away." Enter your voice. Is this a "win" for the First Amendment, a loss, or a split decision? Why, in our culture, does media violence merit greater free speech protection than mediated sex?

this was illogical because almost all media are, in fact, commercial, even when they perform a primarily journalistic function. Newspapers, for example, print the news to make a profit.

In its 1967 *Time, Inc. v. Hill* decision, the Supreme Court applied similar logic to argue that the First Amendment grants the same protection to entertainment content as it does to nonentertainment content. Is an entertainingly written news report less worthy of protection than one that is dully written? Rather than allow the government to make these kinds of narrow and ultimately subjective judgments, the Supreme Court has consistently preferred expanding its definition of protected expression to limiting it.

WHAT IS "ABRIDGMENT"? Even absolutists accept the idea that limits can be placed on the time, place, and manner of expression—as long as the restrictions do not interfere with the substance of the expression. Few, for example, would find it unreasonable to limit the use of a sound truck to broadcast political messages at 4:00 a.m. But the Supreme Court did find unconstitutional an ordinance that forbade all use of sound amplification except with the permission of the chief of police in its 1948 decision in *Saia v. New York*. The permissibility of other restrictions, however, is less clear-cut.

CLEAR AND PRESENT DANGER Can freedom of the press be limited if the likely result is damaging? The Supreme Court answered this question in 1919 in *Schenck v. United States.* In this case involving the distribution of a pamphlet urging resistance to the military draft during World War I, Justice Oliver Wendell Holmes wrote that expression could be limited when "the words used are used in such circumstances and are of such a nature as to create a clear and present danger that they will bring about the substantive evils that Congress has a right to prevent." Justice Holmes added, "Free speech would not protect a man in falsely shouting fire in a theater and causing panic." This decision is especially important because it firmly established the legal philosophy that there is no absolute freedom of expression; the level of protection is one of degree.

BALANCING OF INTERESTS This less-than-absolutist approach is called the **ad hoc balancing of interests**. That is, in individual First Amendment cases several factors should be weighed in determining how much freedom the press is granted. In his dissent to the Court's 1941 decision in *Bridges v. California*, a case involving a *Los Angeles Times* editorial, Justice Felix Frankfurter wrote that free speech and press is "not so absolute or irrational a conception as to imply paralysis of the means for effective protection of all the freedoms secured by the Bill of Rights. . . . In the cases before us, the claims on behalf of freedom of speech and of the press encounter claims on behalf of liberties no less precious."

FREE PRESS VERSUS FAIR TRIAL One example of the clash of competing liberties is the conflict between free press (First Amendment) and fair trial (Sixth Amendment). This debate typically takes two forms: (1) Can pretrial publicity deny citizens judgment by 12 impartial peers, thereby denying them a fair trial? (2) Should cameras be allowed in the courtroom, supporting the public's right to know, or do they so alter the workings of the court that a fair trial is impossible?

Courts have consistently decided in favor of fair trial in conflicts between the First and Sixth Amendments. But it was not until 1961 that a conviction was overturned because of pretrial publicity. In *Irvin v. Dowd* the Court reversed the death sentence

► Media intrusion during the 1935 Bruno Hauptmann kidnapping trial led to the banning of radio transmissions and photographers from the courtroom. Hauptmann is seated in the center, hands crossed.

conviction of confessed killer Leslie Irvin because his right to a fair trial had been hampered by press coverage that labeled him "Mad Dog Irvin" and reported crimes he had committed as a juvenile, his military court-martial, his identification in a police lineup, his failure to pass a lie detector test, his confession to six killings and numerous robberies, and his willingness to trade a guilty plea for a life sentence. Of 430 potential jurors screened before the trial by attorneys, 370 said they were already convinced Irvin was guilty. Nonetheless, although "tainted" by pretrial publicity, four of the 370 were seated as jurors. The Court determined that Irvin's trial was therefore unfair.

Print reporters have long enjoyed access to trials, but broadcast journalists have been less fortunate. In 1937, after serious intrusion by newspaper photographers during the 1935 trial of Bruno Hauptmann, accused of kidnapping the baby of transatlantic aviation hero Charles Lindbergh, the American Bar Association (ABA) adopted canon 35 as part of its Code of Judicial Ethics. This rule forbade cameras and radio broadcasting of trials. In 1963 the ABA amended the canon to include a prohibition on television cameras. This, however, did not settle the issue of cameras in the courtroom.

Texas was one of three states that did not subscribe to canon 35. When the conviction for theft, swindling, and embezzlement of Texas financier Billy Sol Estes was overturned by the Supreme Court because of "the insidious influence" (Justice William Douglas's words) of cameras on the conduct of the trial, the wisdom of banning television seemed settled. But Justice Clark counseled, "When advances in [broadcast journalism] permit reporting . . . by television without their present hazards to a fair trial we will have another case" (*Estes v. State of Texas*, 1965). In other words, cameras were back in if they posed no hazard to the principle of fair trial.

In 1972 the ABA replaced canon 35 with canon 3A(7), allowing some videotaping of trials for specific purposes but reaffirming its opposition to the broadcast of trial proceedings. But in 1981 the Supreme Court, in *Chandler v. Florida*, determined that television cameras in the courtroom were not inherently damaging to fairness. Today, all 50 states allow cameras in some courts—47 permit them in trial courts—and the U.S. Congress is debating opening up federal courts, including the Supreme Court, to cameras. For now, photography and broadcast of federal trials is banned by Federal Rule of Criminal Procedure 53. Still, so common has the televising of court proceedings become that Court TV, a cable channel programming nothing but real trials and commentary on them, was launched in 1991 (it's now called truTV and carries much more varied programming).

LIBEL AND SLANDER Libel, the false or malicious publication of material that damages a person's reputation, and **slander**, the oral or spoken defamation of a person's character, are not protected by the First Amendment. The distinction between libel and slander, however, is sufficiently narrow that "published defamation, whether it is in a newspaper, on radio or television, in the movies, or whatever, is regarded since the 1990s as libel. And libel rules apply" (Pember, 1999, p. 134). Therefore, if a report (1) defames a person, (2) identifies that person, and (3) is published or broadcast, it loses its First Amendment protection.

A report accused of being libelous or slanderous, however, is protected if it meets any one of three tests. The first test is *truth*. Even if a report damages someone's reputation, if it is true, it is protected. The second test is *privilege*. Coverage of legislative, court, or other public activities may contain information that is not true or that is damaging to someone's reputation. The press cannot be deterred from covering these important news events for fear that a speaker's or witness's comments will open it to claims of libel or slander. The third test is *fair comment;* that is, the press has the right to express opinions or comment on public issues. For example, theater and film reviews, however severe, are protected, as is commentary on other matters in the public eye.

For public figures, however, a different set of rules applies. Because they are in the public eye, public figures are fair game for fair comment. But does that leave them open to reports that are false and damaging to their reputations? The Supreme Court faced this issue in 1964 in *New York Times v. Sullivan*. In 1960 the Committee to Defend Martin Luther King bought a full-page ad in the *New York Times* asking people to contribute to Dr. King's defense fund. The ad detailed abuse of Dr. King and other civil rights workers at the hands of the Montgomery, Alabama, police. L. B. Sullivan, one of three elected commissioners in that city, sued the *Times* for libel. The ad copy was not true in some of its claims, he said, and because he was in charge of the police, he had been "identified."

The Supreme Court ruled in favor of the newspaper. Even though some of the specific facts in the ad were not true, the *Times* had not acted with **actual malice**. The Court defined the standard of actual malice for reporting on public figures as *knowledge of its falsity or reckless disregard* for whether or not it is true.

PRIOR RESTRAINT There is much less confusion about another important aspect of press freedom, **prior restraint**. This is the power of the government to *prevent* the publication or broadcast of expression. U.S. law and tradition make the use of prior restraint relatively rare, but there have been a number of important efforts by government to squelch content before dissemination.

In 1931 the Supreme Court ruled in *Near v. Minnesota* that freedom from prior restraint was a general, not an absolute, principle. Two of the four exceptions it listed were in times of war when national security was involved and when the public order would be endangered by the incitement to violence and overthrow by force of orderly government. These exceptions were to become the basis of two landmark prior restraint decisions. The first, involving the *New York Times*, dealt with national security in times of war; the second, focusing on protecting the public order, involved publishing instructions for building an atomic bomb.

On June 13, 1971, at the height of the Vietnam War, the *New York Times* began publication of what commonly became known as the Pentagon Papers. The papers included detailed discussion and analysis of the conduct of that unpopular war during the administrations of Presidents Kennedy and Johnson. President Nixon's National Security Council (NSC) had stamped them Top Secret. Believing that this was an improper restriction of the public's right to know, NSC staff member Daniel Ellsberg gave copies to the *Times*. After the first three installments had been published, the Justice Department, citing national security, was able to secure a court order stopping further publication. Other newspapers, notably, the *Washington Post* and *Boston Globe*,

began running excerpts while the *Times* was silenced until they, too, were enjoined to cease.

On June 30 the Supreme Court ordered the government to halt its restraint of the *Times*'s and other papers' right to publish the Pentagon Papers. Among the stirring attacks on prior restraint written throughout its decision was Justice Hugo Black's:

> In the First Amendment the Founding Fathers gave the free press the protection it must have to fulfill its essential role in our democracy. The press was to serve the governed, not the governors. The Government's power to censor the press was abolished so that the press would remain forever free to censure the Government. The press was protected so that it could bare the secrets of government and inform the people. Only a free and unrestrained press can effectively expose deception in government. (*New York Times v. United States*, 1971)

Then came the case of the magazine *The Progressive*. In 1979 the magazine announced its intention to publish instructions on how to make a hydrogen bomb. President Jimmy Carter's Justice Department successfully obtained a court order halting publication, even though the article was based on information and material freely obtained from public, nonclassified sources. Before the case could come to court, several newspapers published the same or similar material. The Justice Department immediately abandoned its restraint, and six months later *The Progressive* published its original article.

OBSCENITY AND PORNOGRAPHY Another form of press expression that is not protected is **obscenity**. Two landmark Supreme Court cases established the definition and illegality of obscenity. The first is the 1957 *Roth v. United States* decision. The Court determined that sex and obscenity were not synonymous, a significant advance for freedom of expression. It did, however, legally affirm for the first time that obscenity was unprotected expression. The definition or test for obscenity that holds even today was expressed in the 1973 *Miller v. State of California* decision. Chief Justice Warren Burger wrote that the basic guidelines must be

> (a) whether the average person, applying contemporary community standards, would find that the work, taken as a whole, appeals to the prurient interest, (b) whether the work depicts or describes, in a patently offensive way, sexual conduct specifically defined by the applicable state law, and (c) whether the work, taken as a whole, lacks serious literary, artistic, political, or scientific value.

The problem for the courts, the media, and the public, of course, is judging content against this standard. For example, what is patently offensive to one person may be quite acceptable to others. What is serious art to one may be serious exploitation to another. And what of an erotic short story written online by an author in New York City but accessed and read by people in Peoria, Illinois? Whose community standards would apply?

An additional definitional problem resides in **pornography**, expression calculated solely to supply sexual excitement. Pornography is protected expression. The distinction between obscenity and pornography may, however, be a legal one. Sexually explicit content is pornography (and protected) until a court rules it illegal; then it is obscene (and unprotected). The difficulty of making such distinctions can be seen in Justice Potter Stewart's famous declaration in *Jacobellis v. Ohio* (1964), "I may not be able to come up with a definition of pornography, but I certainly know it when I see it," and his dissent two years later in *Ginzburg v. United States* (1966), "If the First Amendment means anything, it means that a man cannot be sent to prison merely for distributing publications which offend a judge's sensibilities, mine or any others." Clearly, the issues of the definition and protection of obscenity and pornography may never be clarified to everyone's satisfaction.

Other Issues of Freedom and Responsibility

The First Amendment has application to a number of specific issues of media responsibility and freedom.

INDECENCY Obscenity and pornography are rarely issues for broadcasters. Their commercial base and wide audience make the airing of such potentially troublesome programming unwise. However, broadcasters frequently do confront the issue of **indecency**. According to the FCC, indecent language or material is that which depicts sexual or excretory activities in a way that is offensive to contemporary community standards.

The FCC recently modified, much to broadcasters' dissatisfaction, its way of handling indecency complaints, making it easier for listeners and viewers to challenge questionable content. Stations must now prove they are innocent; in other words, a complaint has validity by virtue of having been made. To broadcasters, this "guilty until proven innocent" approach is an infringement of their First Amendment rights, as it requires them to keep tapes of all their content in the event they are challenged, even in the absence of evidence that a complaint has merit.

The debate over indecency, however, has been confounded by several events. First, a huge surge in complaints (from 111 in 2000 to more than a million in 2004) followed two specific broadcast events: the split-second baring of Janet Jackson's breast at the 2004 Super Bowl football game and rocker Bono's spontaneous award show utterance of an expletive later that year. And even though the FCC's own data revealed that 99.9% of the complaints, most with identical wording, originated with one group, the conservative Christian Parents Television Council, it still boosted indecency fines by 100% (Rich, 2005; Soundbites, 2005). Just how widespread and real, asked broadcasters, was outrage over indecent content? Then there were a series of high-profile incidents of self-censorship. Faced with FCC-mandated penalties of up to $325,000 for every single station airing "offensive" content, several PBS member stations refused to show a documentary on Marie Antoinette because it discussed King Louis XVI's impotence and depicted some of the queen's suggestive etchings. Several other PBS outlets passed on director Martin Scorsese's musical documentary *The Blues* because many of the older blues players spoke a bit "naturally" on camera. Because some on-screen rescuers uttered curses as they fought through the inferno, several CBS affiliates refused to broadcast, four years after it had first aired without a single complaint, *9/11 Camera at Ground Zero*, an award-winning documentary honoring the New York City police, firefighters, and other rescue personnel who lived and died on that horrible day. Citing examples such as these, NBC and Fox eventually challenged the FCC's indecency rules, scoring a federal court of appeals victory in 2007. But when the Commission appealed

In 2006, worried about heavy FCC indecency fines, several CBS affiliates chose not to run a documentary honoring the 9/11 rescue effort because several of the police officers and firefighters in it cursed as they fought smoke, debris, and fear. The award-winning movie had aired four years earlier without complaint.

that decision, a second federal court again sided with the broadcasters, finding that the FCC's rules were so vague, they fostered unconstitutional self-censorship (Neumeister, 2010). That decision was eventually upheld by the Supreme Court in its unanimous *FCC v. Fox* decision in 2012.

DEREGULATION The difficulty of balancing the public interest and broadcasters' freedom is at the heart of the debate over deregulation and the relaxation of ownership and other rules for radio and television. Changes in ownership rules have always been controversial, but relaxation of the regulation of broadcasters' public service obligations and other content controls have provided just as much debate.

The courts have consistently supported the FCC's right to evaluate broadcasters' performance in serving the public interest, convenience, and necessity. Naturally, that evaluation must include some judgment of the content broadcasters air. Broadcasters long argued that such "judgment" amounted to unconstitutional infringement of their First Amendment freedom. Many listeners and viewers saw it as a reasonable and quite small price to pay for the use of their (the public's) airwaves.

The Supreme Court resolved the issue in 1943 in *National Broadcasting Co. v. United States*. NBC argued that the FCC was no more than a traffic cop, limited to controlling the "flow of traffic." In this view, the regulation of broadcasters' frequency, power, times of operation, and other technical matters was all that was constitutionally allowable. Yet the Court turned what is now known as the **traffic cop analogy** against NBC. Yes, the justices agreed, the commission is a traffic cop. But even traffic cops have the right to control not only the flow of traffic but its composition as well. For example, drunk drivers can be removed from the road. Potentially dangerous "content," like cars with faulty brakes, can also be restricted. It was precisely this traffic cop function that required the FCC to judge content. The commission was thus free to promulgate rules such as the **Fairness Doctrine**, which required broadcasters to cover issues of public importance and to be fair in that coverage, and **ascertainment**, which required broadcasters to ascertain or actively and affirmatively determine the nature of their audiences' interest, convenience, and necessity.

The Fairness Doctrine, ascertainment, and numerous other regulations, such as rules on children's programming and overcommercialization, disappeared with the coming of deregulation during the Reagan administration. License renewal, for example, was once a long and difficult process for stations, which had to generate thousands of pages of documents to demonstrate that they not only knew what their audiences

◀ Broadcast deregulation produced a rush of toy-based children's television shows such as *Pokemon*, which critics contend are inherently unfair to children who cannot recognize them as program-length commercials.

wanted and needed but had met those wants and needs. The burden of proof in their efforts to keep their licenses rested with them. Had they been fair? Had they kept commercial time to acceptable levels? What was their commitment to news and public affairs? Now deregulated, renewal is conducted through a much less onerous process. Broadcasters simply file brief quarterly reports with the commission indicating compliance with technical and other FCC rules. Then, when their licenses are up for renewal (every eight years), they file a short, postcardlike renewal application.

The deregulation drive began in earnest with President Reagan's FCC chair, Mark Fowler, in the 1980s. Fowler rejected the trustee model of broadcast regulation. He saw many FCC rules as an unconstitutional infringement of broadcasters' rights and believed that "the market" was the audience's best protector. He said that special rules for the control of broadcasting were unnecessary, likening television, for example, to just another home appliance. He called television no more than "a toaster with pictures."

The first FCC chair under President George W. Bush, Michael Powell, was also a strong advocate of deregulation. Of the public interest, he has said that he "has no idea" what it is. "It is an empty vessel," he added, "in which people pour whatever their preconceived views or biases are" (quoted in Hickey, 2002, p. 33). In another press conference he called regulation of telecommunications "the oppressor" (Coen & Hart, 2002, p. 4).

This view of deregulation is not without its critics. Republican and Democratic congressional leaders, liberal and conservative columnists, and numerous public interest groups from across the political spectrum continue to campaign against such fruits of deregulation as concentration, conglomeration, overcommercialization, the abandonment of children, the lowering of decency standards, and the debasement of news. Their argument for rolling back the deregulation of broadcasting rests in the philosophy of noted First Amendment scholar Alexander Meiklejohn (1960), who argued half a century ago that regulation limiting the media's freedom is, indeed, forbidden,

> *but not legislation to enlarge and enrich it.* The freedom of mind which benefits members of a self-governing society is not a given and fixed part of human nature. It can be increased and established by learning, by teaching, by the unhindered flow of accurate information, by giving men [*sic*] health and vigor and security, by bringing them together in activities of communication and mutual understanding. And the federal legislature is not forbidden to engage in that positive enterprise of cultivating the general intelligence upon which the success of self-government so obviously depends. On the contrary, in that positive field the Congress of the United States has a heavy and basic responsibility to promote the freedom of speech. (pp. 19–20; italics added)

COPYRIGHT The First Amendment protects expression. *Copyright*—identifying and granting ownership of a given piece of expression—is designed to protect the creator's financial interest in that expression. Recognizing that the flow of art, science, and other expression would be enhanced by authors' financial interest in their creation, the framers of the Constitution wrote Article I, Section 8 (8), granting authors exclusive rights to their "writings and discoveries." A long and consistent history of Supreme Court decisions has ensured that this protection would be extended to the content of the mass media that have emerged since that time.

The years 1978 and 1998 saw extensive rewritings of U.S. copyright law. Copyright now remains with creators (in all media) for the span of their lives, plus 70 years. During this time, permission for the use of the material must be obtained from the copyright holder, and if financial compensation (a fee or royalty) is requested, it must be paid. Once the copyright expires, the material passes into the **public domain**, meaning it can be used without permission.

The exception to copyright is *fair use*, instances in which material can be used without permission or payment. Fair use includes (1) limited noncommercial use, such as photocopying a passage from a novel for classroom use; (2) use of limited portions of a work, such as excerpting a few lines or a paragraph or two from a book for use in a magazine article; (3) use that does not decrease the commercial value of the original, such as videotaping a daytime football game for private, at-home evening viewing; and (4) use in the public interest, such as a *Consumer Reports'* use of pieces of drug company television commercials to highlight its media literacy efforts.

Two specific applications of copyright law pertain to recorded music and cable television. Imagine the difficulty cable companies would have in obtaining permission from all the copyright holders of all the material they import and deliver to their subscribers. Yet the cable operators do make money from others' works—they collect material from original sources and sell it to subscribers. The solution to the problem of compensating the creators of the material carried by cable systems was the creation of the Copyright Royalty Tribunal, to which cable companies paid a fee based primarily on the size of their operations. These moneys were then distributed to the appropriate producers, syndicators, and broadcasters. Congress abolished the Copyright Royalty Tribunal in 1993, leaving cable copyright issues in the hands of several different arbitration panels under the auspices of the Library of Congress.

Now imagine the difficulty songwriters would have in collecting royalties from all who use their music—not only film producers and radio and television stations, but bowling alleys, supermarkets, and restaurants. Here the solution is the **music licensing company**. The two biggest are the American Society of Composers, Authors and Publishers (ASCAP) and Broadcast Music Inc. (BMI). Both collect fees based on the users' gross receipts and distribute the money to songwriters and artists.

THE INTERNET AND EXPANDING COPYRIGHT The Internet, as we saw in Chapter 7 with MP3 and in Chapter 10 with file-sharing, is forcing a significant rethinking of copyright, one that disturbs many advocates of free expression. They fear that efforts to protect the intellectual property rights of copyright holders are going too far. The expansion of copyright, argues technology writer Dan Gillmor (2000), gives "the owners of intellectual property vast new authority, simultaneously shredding users' rights" (p. 1C).

For example, in January 2000, a California Superior Court, citing the Digital Millennium Copyright Act (Chapter 10), ruled the posting of DVD decryption software to be illegal. The defendants argued that they did not violate copyright. The court ruled against them because they posted "tools" on the Web that would allow others to violate copyright. Tech writer Gillmor (2000) scoffed, "Let's ban cars next. Were you aware that bank robbers use them for getaways?" (p. 6C). In August of that same year, a New York court reaffirmed the ban on posting decryption software, adding that even posting links to sites offering the software was a violation of copyright. And we've already seen the controversy surrounding MP3 and file-sharing, neither of which copies anybody's intellectual property, but both of which allow the sharing of copyrighted material.

Copyright exists, say critics of its expansion, to encourage the flow of art, science, and expression, and it grants financial stake to creators, not to enrich those creators but to ensure that there is sufficient incentive to keep the content flowing. "It's always important to remember that copyright is a restriction on free speech, and it's a constitutionally granted restriction on free speech. Therefore, we need to be careful when we play with copyright, because it can have some serious effects on public discourse and creativity," argued copyright expert Siva Vaidhyanathan (as quoted in Anderson, 2000, p. 25). In other words, tightening copyright restrictions can have the effect of inhibiting the flow of art, science, and expression.

Some free-expression champions see the tightening of copyright, or **digital rights management (DRM)**, as something other than the justifiable protection of intellectual property. Rather, they argue, it is the drive for more control over and therefore profit from the distribution of content. Technology writer Gillmor (2002) argues that new copy-protected digital content and copyright rules combine to "help the entertainment cartel grab absolute control over customers' reading, viewing, and listening" (p. F1).

The DRM debate escalated with the Supreme Court's 2005 *Grokster* decision (Chapter 7). The entertainment industries were heartened by the ruling that a technology was illegal if it "encouraged" copyright infringement; digital rights activists and technologists were appalled. The Court had disallowed Hollywood's 1984 challenge to videotape (*Sony Corp. v. Universal City Studios*, the so-called *Betamax* decision) because VCR, even if some people used it to violate copyright, had "substantial non-infringing uses." But *Grokster* "relies on a new theory of copyright liability that measures whether manufacturers created their wares with the 'intent' of inducing consumers to infringe. It means that inventors and entrepreneurs will not only bear the costs of bringing new products to market, but also the costs of lawsuits if consumers start using their products for illegal purposes." Who, ask critics, can judge an innovation's intent? Is copyright infringement the *primary* use of P2P networks like Grokster, or is their intent to bring together people making fair use sharing of already purchased material (Gibbs, 2005, p. 50)? What is actually at play here, say *Grokster* critics, is the entertainment industries' dual goal of undoing the Betamax decision and eradicating all fair use of their content (Howe, 2005b). Not to worry, say others, because technology always overruns copyright law. And as we've seen at several junctures of this text, this reassessment of DRM and copyright may well already be under way.

Despite the fact that the copyright holders have recently had some victories (2009's jailing of file-sharing site Pirate Bay's Swedish founders) and losses (a lawsuit revealed that Viacom had been paying marketing companies and its own employees to upload poor-quality, fake-pirated versions of its content to YouTube from untraceable computers in order to promote its television shows while simultaneously suing the video site for infringement; Boulton, 2010), most parties seem to be seeking accommodation. One effort is Creative Commons, a nonprofit corporation founded in 2001 as an easy way for people to share and build on the work of others, consistent with the rules of copyright. Creative Commons provides users with free licenses and other legal tools to mark (copyright) their creative work with the level of freedom they wish it to carry, granting to others specific rights to share, remix, or even use it commercially. Among more traditional media companies, all four major record labels now sell much of their catalogs with limited or no DRM, or as *Wired*'s Frank Rose (2008) put it, "Music execs are trying to turn back the clock, remove DRM, and finally give us what we should have had in 1999" (p. 34). All the television and most of the cable channels provide free or low-cost downloads either without DRM or with limited copyright control. Most of the world's books will soon find themselves living online with quite robust reader access. Most big media companies are embracing websites like YouTube and Facebook, willing to forfeit a bit of DRM control in exchange for exposure for their content. The future of copyright and DRM, then, is being negotiated in the culture right now. You and other media consumers sit on one side of the table; the media industries are on the other. You will be in a stronger position in these cultural negotiations if you approach these developments as a media-literate person.

Social Responsibility Theory

As we saw at the beginning of this chapter, the First Amendment is based on the libertarian philosophy that assumes a fully free press and a rational, good, and informed public. But we have also seen in this and earlier chapters that the media are not necessarily fully free. Government control is sometimes allowed. Corporate control is assumed and accepted. During the 1930s and 1940s, serious doubts were also raised concerning the public's rationality and goodness. As World War II spread across Europe at the end of the 1930s, libertarians were hard-pressed to explain how Nazi propaganda could succeed if people could in fact tell right from wrong. As the United States was drawn closer to the European conflict, calls for greater government control of press and speech at home were justified by less-than-optimistic views of the "average American's" ability to handle difficult information. As a result, libertarianism came under attack for being too idealistic.

Time magazine owner and publisher Henry Luce then provided money to establish an independent commission of scholars, politicians, legal experts, and social activists who would study the role of the press in U.S. society and make recommendations on how it should best operate in support of democracy. The Hutchins Commission on Freedom of the Press, named after its chairperson, University of Chicago chancellor Robert Maynard Hutchins, began its work in 1942 and, in 1947, produced its report "The Social Responsibility Theory of the Press" (Pickard, 2010).

Social responsibility theory is a **normative theory**—that is, it explains how media should *ideally* operate in a given system of social values—and it is the standard against which the public should judge the performance of the U.S. media. Other social and political systems adhere to different normative theories, and these will be detailed in Chapter 15.

Social responsibility theory asserts that media must remain free of government control, but in exchange media must serve the public. The core assumptions of this theory are a cross between libertarian principles of freedom and practical admissions of the need for some form of control on the media (McQuail, 1987):

- Media should accept and fulfill certain obligations to society.
- Media can meet these obligations by setting high standards of professionalism, truth, accuracy, and objectivity.
- Media should be self-regulating within the framework of the law.
- Media should avoid disseminating material that might lead to crime, violence, or civil disorder or that might offend minority groups.
- The media as a whole should be pluralistic, reflect the diversity of the culture in which they operate, and give access to various points of view and rights of reply.
- The public has a right to expect high standards of performance, and official intervention can be justified to ensure the public good.
- Media professionals should be accountable to society as well as to their employers and the market.

In rejecting government control of media, social responsibility theory calls for responsible, ethical industry operation, but it does not free audiences from their responsibility. People must be sufficiently media literate to develop firm yet reasonable expectations and judgments of media performance. But ultimately it is practitioners, through the conduct of their duties, who are charged with operating in a manner that obviates the need for official intrusion.

Media Industry Ethics

A number of formal and informal controls, both external and internal to the industry, are aimed at ensuring that media professionals operate in an ethical manner consistent with social responsibility theory. Among the external formal controls are laws and regulations, codified statements of what can and can't be done and what content is permissible and not permissible, and industry codes of practice. Among the external informal controls are pressure groups, consumers, and advertisers. We have seen how these informal controls operate throughout this text. Our interest here is in examining media's internal controls, or ethics.

Defining Ethics

Ethics are rules of behavior or moral principles that guide our actions in given situations. The word comes from the Greek *ethos,* which means the customs, traditions, or character that guide a particular group or culture. In our discussion, ethics specifically refer to the application of rational thought by media professionals when they are deciding between two or more competing moral choices.

For example, it is not against the law to publish the name of a rape victim. But is it ethical? It is not illegal to stick a microphone in a crying father's face as he cradles the broken body of his child at an accident scene. But is it ethical?

The application of media ethics almost always involves finding the *most morally defensible* answer to a problem for which there is no single correct or even best answer. Return to the grieving father. The reporter's job is to get the story; the public has a right to know. The man's sorrow is part of that story, but the man has a right to privacy. As a human being he deserves to be treated with respect and to be allowed to maintain his dignity. The reporter has to decide whether to get the interview or leave the grief-stricken man in peace. That decision is guided by the reporter's ethics.

Three Levels of Ethics

Because ethics reflect a culture's ideas about right and wrong, they exist at all levels of that culture's operation. **Metaethics** are fundamental cultural values. What is justice? What does it mean to be good? Is fairness possible? We need to examine these questions to know ourselves. But as valuable as they are for self-knowledge, metaethics provide only the broadest foundation for the sorts of ethical decisions people make daily. They define the basic starting points for moral reasoning.

Normative ethics are more or less generalized theories, rules, and principles of ethical or moral behavior. The various media industry codes of ethics or standards of good practice are examples of normative ethics. They serve as real-world frameworks within which people can begin to weigh competing alternatives of behavior. Fairness is a metaethic, but journalists' codes of practice, for example, define what is meant by fairness in the world of reporting, how far a reporter must go to ensure fairness, and how fairness must be applied when being fair to one person means being unfair to another.

Ultimately, media practitioners must apply both the big rules and the general guidelines to very specific situations. This is the use of **applied ethics**, and applying ethics invariably involves balancing conflicting interests.

Balancing Conflicting Interests

In applying ethics, the person making the decisions is called the **moral agent**. For moral agents, sticky ethical issues invariably bring together conflicting interests—for example, those of the editor, readers, and advertisers in this chapter's opening vignette.

Media ethicist Louis Day (2006) identified six sets of individual or group interests that often conflict:

- The interests of the moral agent's *individual conscience;* media professionals must live with their decisions.
- The interests of *the object of the act;* a particular person or group is likely to be affected by media practitioners' actions.

- The interests of *financial supporters;* someone pays the bills that allow the station to broadcast or the newspaper or magazine to publish.
- The interests of *the institution;* media professionals have company loyalty, pride in the organization for which they work.
- The interests of *the profession;* media practitioners work to meet the expectations of their colleagues; they have respect for the profession that sustains them.
- The interests of *society;* media professionals, like all of us, have a social responsibility. Because of the influence their work can have, they may even have greater responsibilities than do many other professionals.

In mass communication, these conflicting interests play themselves out in a variety of ways. Some of the most common, yet thorniest, require us to examine such basic issues as truth and honesty, privacy, confidentiality, personal conflict of interest, profit and social responsibility, and protection from offensive content.

TRUTH AND HONESTY Can the media ever be completely honest? As soon as a camera is pointed at one thing, it is ignoring another. As soon as a video editor combines two different images, that editor has imposed his or her definition of the truth. Truth and honesty are overriding concerns for media professionals. But what is truth? Take the case of Chicago television station WBBM. In its coverage of a 2011 night of violence in that city, anchor Steve Bartelstein introduced the story, "Kids on the street as young as four were there to see it all unfold, and had disturbing reactions." The report then ran video of an interview with a four-year-old African American boy. Asked by a reporter, "What are you going to do when you get older?" the boy responded, "I'm going to have me a gun!" On camera back at his news desk Bartelstein exclaimed, "That is very scary indeed." WBBM, however, did not air the remainder of the interview, which went like this: "You are! Why would you want to do that?" asked the startled reporter. "I'm going to be the police!" insisted the boy. But the boy had indeed said he was going to get a gun, so all the station did was report the truth (Butler, 2011).

PRIVACY Do public figures forfeit their right to privacy? In what circumstances? Are the president's marital problems newsworthy if they do not get in the way of the job? Who is a public figure? When are people's sexual orientations newsworthy? Do you report the names of women who have been raped or the names of juvenile offenders? What about sex offenders? How far do you go to interview grieving parents? When is secret taping permissible?

▶ Senator Larry Craig's arrest for solicitation was news. Absent that event, how newsworthy would you have considered his sexual orientation?

Our culture values privacy. We have the right to maintain the privacy of our personal information. We use privacy to control the extent and nature of interaction we have with others. Privacy protects us from unwanted government intrusion. The media, however, by their very nature, are intrusive. Privacy proves to be particularly sensitive because it is almost a metaethic, a fundamental value. Yet the applied ethics of the various media industries allow, in fact sometimes demand, that privacy be denied.

The media have faced a number of very important tests regarding privacy over the last few years. Media pursuit of celebrities is one.

High-profile stories such as the 2004 rape investigation of basketball player Kobe Bryant and the 2007 arrest of Senator Larry Craig highlight the difficult ethical issues surrounding privacy. Kobe Bryant is a celebrity, a public figure. He therefore loses some right to privacy. But what about the woman accusing him of rape? Was it an invasion of her privacy when several publications released her name and photograph after they appeared on the Web? Craig's arrest for soliciting sex from an undercover police officer in an airport restroom was certainly news; the arrest of a senator is certainly newsworthy. Most people would also consider the arrest of an ardent anti–gay rights legislator for allegedly seeking gay sex in a public place to be newsworthy as well. But what about Senator Craig's homosexuality in the first place? Many reporters in his home state of Idaho and in Washington knew of his sexual orientation (despite his protestations to the contrary). Should they have reported on it, especially as the senator was an outspoken anti–gay rights crusader? Or did they consider his, anyone's, sexual orientation a matter of privacy? Before the arrest, many bloggers had revealed Craig's "secret." Only after the arrest did his local paper, the *Idaho Statesman*, report it (Strupp, 2007).

CONFIDENTIALITY An important tool in contemporary news gathering and reporting is **confidentiality**, the ability of media professionals to keep secret the names of people who provide them with information. Without confidentiality, employees could not report the misdeeds of their employers for fear of being fired; people would not tell what they know of a crime for fear of retribution from the offenders or unwanted police attention. The anonymous informant nicknamed "Deep Throat" would never have felt free to divulge the Nixon White House involvement in the Republican break-in of the Democratic Party's Watergate campaign offices were it not for the promise of confidentiality from *Washington Post* reporters Carl Bernstein and Bob Woodward.

But how far should reporters go in protecting a source's confidentiality? Should reporters go to jail rather than divulge a name? Every state in the Union, except Wyoming, and the District of Columbia has either a **shield law**, legislation that expressly protects reporters' rights to maintain sources' confidentiality in courts of law, or court precedent upholding that right. There is no shield law in federal courts, and many journalists want it that way. Their fear is that once Congress makes one "media law" it may want to make another. For example, media professionals do not want the government to legislate the definition of "reporter" or "journalist."

The ethics of confidentiality are regularly tested by reporters' frequent use of quotes and information from "unnamed sources," "sources who wish to remain anonymous," and "inside sources." Often the guarantee of anonymity is necessary to get the information, but is this fair to those who are commented on by these nameless, faceless newsmakers? Don't these people—even if they are highly placed and powerful themselves—have a right to know their accusers?

PERSONAL CONFLICT OF INTEREST As we've seen, ethical decision making requires a balancing of interests. But what of a media professional's own conflicts of interest? Should media personalities accept speaking fees, consulting contracts, or other compensation from groups that may have a vested interest in issues they may someday have to cover? Must media organizations disclose any and all possible conflicts of the commentators who appear in their news shows?

Consider these recent controversies. During the 2012 presidential race, the *Wall Street Journal* failed to disclose that 10 of its editorial writers who produced dozens of pro-Romney and anti-Obama pieces also served as official advisers to the Romney campaign (Strupp, 2012). CNN's Bill Schneider is Distinguished Senior Fellow and Resident Scholar at Third Way, a Washington think tank that lobbies against health care reform. Civil rights activist Reverend Al Sharpton hosts MSNBC's nightly current affairs program, *Politics Daily*, which gave considerable coverage to the 2012 shooting death of unarmed African American teen Trayvon Martin and the controversial Florida "stand your ground" law that rendered the shooter blameless . . . all the while leading vigils in support of the boy's family and protests against the law. The Pentagon enlists more than 75 retired generals as "message force multipliers" in support of the wars in the Middle East. Although the generals had financial ties to more than 150 military contractors, and despite the fact that the *New York Times* won a Pulitzer Prize for its reporting on the Pentagon's PR operation, none was ever identified in any of the 4,500 appearances they made on news outlets ranging from ABC to NPR from January 2002 to mid-2008 (Media Matters, 2008).

▶ Reverend Al Sharpton, hands-on social advocate or plain-speaking MSNBC current affairs host?

Other conflict-of-interest issues bedevil media professionals. The war in the Middle East raised the problem of **embedding**, reporters accepting military control over their output in exchange for close contact with the troops. The interests in conflict here are objectivity and access—do reporters pay too high a price for their exciting video or touching personal interest stories? This **access journalism**—reporters acting deferentially toward news sources in order to ensure continued access—was at the core of the American media's disastrous performance in "both of the major catastrophes of our time" (G. Mitchell, 2009, p. 16). The first, the unnecessary war in Iraq, is personified by Judith Miller and her *New York Times* coverage that hastened the invasion. In exchange for continued access to influential newsmakers like Vice President Dick Cheney and his chief of staff, Scooter Libby, she granted these powerful players anonymity "for the purpose of stomping on exactly the kind of dissent" for which such grants of confidentiality are intended (McKelvey, 2009, p. 59). She went to jail in 2005 to protect that relationship. The second is the press's failure to anticipate and warn citizens about the disastrous economic slide that hit the country in late 2008. "How could 9,000 business reporters blow it?" asked financial writer Dean Starkman. Pulitzer Prize–winning Wall Street reporter Gretchen Morgenson faulted the media's own bad economics. "Low morale, lost expertise, and constant cutbacks, especially in investigative reporting—these are not conditions that produce an appetite for confrontation and muckraking" (in Starkman, 2009). McClatchy Newspapers' Washington Bureau chief John Walcott (2008) was a bit harsher, accusing reporters of seeking personal gain in their stenography of Wall Street's false optimism, saying, "Instead of being members of the Fourth Estate, too many . . . reporters have been itching to move up an estate or two, to become part of the Establishment or share the good times." The box entitled "Journalists as Truth Vigilantes?" offers a look at another ethical issue facing journalists and how well or poorly they deal with the issue.

PROFIT AND SOCIAL RESPONSIBILITY The media industries are just that, industries. They exist not only to entertain and inform their audiences but also to make a profit for their owners and shareholders. What happens when serving profit conflicts with serving the public?

The conflict between profit and responsibility was the subject of the Academy Award–nominated 1999 movie *The Insider*. In late 1995, CBS executives killed an exclusive *60 Minutes* interview with Jeffrey Wigand, a former Brown & Williamson tobacco company executive, who told anchor Mike Wallace that cigarette manufacturers manipulated nicotine levels and had lied under oath before Congress. Many observers at the time—and many moviegoers four years later—believed that the company's real fear was that a threatened lawsuit from Brown & Williamson would reduce the value

▲ Is embedding's trade of increased access in exchange for increased official control ethical?
DOONESBURY © 2003 G. B. Trudeau. Reprinted with permission of Universal Uclick. All rights reserved.

USING MEDIA TO MAKE A DIFFERENCE
Journalists as Truth Vigilantes?

New York Times public editor Arthur Brisbane wanted to use his blog to make a difference. With a 2012 post entitled "Should the *Times* be a Truth Vigilante?" he hoped to create a discussion with his readers about the proper role of journalists when the people they cover express obvious falsehoods. "If the newspaper's overarching goal is truth, oughtn't truth be embedded in its principal stories? In other words, if a candidate repeatedly utters an outright falsehood, shouldn't the *Times* coverage nail it right at the point where the article quotes it?" (2012).

What had moved him to ask the question was criticism from his own paper's Paul Krugman who complained that *Times* reporters had repeatedly allowed Republican Presidential candidate Mitt Romney to claim that President Obama "has a habit of apologizing for America." Not a habit; never happened even once, said Krugman, and Brisbane agreed. The paper's reporters, however, never said so in their coverage of candidate Romney. But here Brisbane was not sure whether they should. "Is it possible to be objective and fair when the reporter is choosing to correct one fact over another?" he asked.

The post did indeed make a difference, but not quite the one Mr. Brisbane had anticipated. In the words of *Salon's* Glen Greenwald, it "sparked such intense reaction because it captured and inflamed long-standing anger toward media outlets for mindlessly amplifying statements without examining whether they're true . . . [It's] basically the equivalent of pondering in a medical journal whether doctors should treat diseases, or asking in a law review article whether lawyers should defend the legal interests of their clients, etc.: reporting facts that conflict with public claims (what Brisbane tellingly demeaned as being "truth vigilantes") is one of the defining functions of journalism" (2012). Press critic Jay Rosen added, "Something happened in our press over the last 40 years or so that never got acknowledged and to this day would be denied by a majority of newsroom professionals. Somewhere along the way, truth-telling

> "It's basically the equivalent of pondering in a medical journal whether doctors should treat diseases."

was surpassed by other priorities the mainstream press felt a stronger duty to. These include such things as 'maintaining objectivity,' 'not imposing a judgment,' 'refusing to take sides' and sticking to what I have called the 'view from nowhere'" (2012).

But did Mr. Brisbane really make a difference? Journalist Clay Shirky says yes, "Having asked, in a completely innocent way, whether the *Times* should behave like an advocate for the readers, rather than a stenographer to politicians, the question cannot now be unasked. Every day in which the *Times* (and indeed, most US papers) fail at what has clearly surfaced as their readers' preference on the matter will be a day in which that gap remains uncomfortably visible" (2012).

◄ © 2012 – www.someguywithawebsite.com. Reprinted Courtesy of August I. Pollack.

of the executives' CBS stock. More recently, in February 2010, 173 Toyota dealers, primarily in the southeastern United States, shifted their advertising from ABC affiliates to non-ABC stations "as punishment" for the aggressive coverage of Toyota's safety problems by that network and its chief investigative reporter Brian Ross. To its credit, ABC refused to soften its reporting (Rhee & Schone, 2010).

◄ Everyone's for freedom of speech . . . except when they're not.

Concentration and conglomeration raise serious questions about media professionals' willingness to choose responsibility over profit. Media law expert Charles Tillinghast (2000) commented,

> One need not be a devotee of conspiracy theories to understand that journalists, like other human beings, can judge where their interests lie, and what risks are and are not prudent, given the desire to continue to eat and feed the family. Nor does one have to be possessed of such theories to understand that wealthy media corporations often share outlooks common to corporations in many different fields, as a result of their status, not of any "agreements." It takes no great brain to understand one does not bite the hand that feeds—or that one incurs great risk by doing so. (pp. 145–146)

Balancing profit and social responsibility is a concern not just for journalists. Practitioners in entertainment, advertising, and public relations often face this dilemma. Does an ad agency accept as a client the manufacturer of sugared children's cereals even though doctors and dentists consider these products unhealthy? Does a public relations firm accept as a client the trade office of a country that forces prison inmates to manufacture products in violation of international rules? Does a production company distribute the 1950s television show *Amos 'n' Andy* knowing that it embodies many offensive stereotypes of African Americans?

Moreover, balancing profit and the public interest does not always involve big companies and millions of dollars. Often, a media practitioner will face an ethical dilemma at a very personal level. What would you do in this situation? The editor at the magazine where you work has ordered you to write an article about the 14-year-old daughter of your city's mayor. The girl's addiction to amphetamines is a closely guarded family secret, but it has been leaked to your publication. You believe that this child is not a public figure. Your boss disagrees, and the boss *is* the boss. By the way, you've just put a down payment on a lovely condo, and you need to make only two more installments to pay off your new car. Do you write the story?

OFFENSIVE CONTENT Entertainment, news, and advertising professionals must often make decisions about the offensive nature of content. Other than the particular situation of broadcasters discussed earlier in this chapter, this is an ethical rather than a legal issue.

Offensive content is protected. Logically, we do not need the First Amendment to protect sweet and pretty expression. Freedom of speech and freedom of the press exist expressly to allow the dissemination of material that *will* offend. But what is offensive? Clearly, what is offensive to one person may be quite satisfactory to another. Religious leaders on the political Right have attacked the cartoon show *SpongeBob Squarepants* for supposedly promoting homosexuality, and critics from the political Left have attacked just about every classic Disney cartoon for racial stereotyping. Television stations and networks regularly bleep cusswords that are common on cable television and in the schoolyard but leave untouched images of stabbings, beatings, and shootings. Critics mounted two national protests against CBS and its 2010 Super Bowl broadcast. From the Left, there were objections to a spot sponsored by conservative group Focus on the Family; from the Right, there were objections to an ad for a gay dating site. Where do we draw the line? Do we consider the tastes of the audience? Which members of the audience—the most easily offended? These are ethical, not legal, determinations.

Codes of Ethics and Self-Regulation

To aid practitioners in their moral reasoning, all major groups of media professionals have established formal codes or standards of ethical behavior. Among these are the Society of Professional Journalists' *Code of Ethics*, the American Society of Newspaper Editors' *Statement of Principles*, the Radio–Television Digital News Association's *Code of Broadcast News Ethics*, the American Advertising Federation's *Advertising Principles of American Business*, and the Public Relations Society of America's *Code of Professional Standards for the Practice of Public Relations*. These are prescriptive codes that tell media practitioners what they should do.

To some, these codes are a necessary part of a true profession; to others, they are little more than unenforceable collections of clichés that restrict constitutional rights and invite lawsuits from outsiders. They offer at least two important benefits to ethical media practitioners: They are an additional source of information to be considered when making moral judgments, and they represent a particular media industry's best expression of its shared wisdom. To others, however, they are meaningless and needlessly restrictive. Ethicists Jay Black and Ralph Barney (1985/86),

▶ To Focus on the Family's James C. Dobson, the friendship between SpongeBob and Patrick is offensive, crossing "a moral line." Others might disagree. Where you draw the line on offensive content is an ethical, not a legal, issue.

for example, argue, "The fact should be evident that the First Amendment has a primary purpose of protecting the distribution of ideas . . . from restriction efforts by legions of 'regulators.' Ethics codes should be considered among those 'regulators'" (p. 28). They continue, "It is indeed not difficult to find examples of codified professional ethics that ultimately become self-serving. That is, they tend to protect the industry, or elements of the industry, at the expense of individuals and other institutions, even of the full society" (p. 29).

In addition to industry professional codes, many media organizations have formulated their own institutional policies for conduct. In the case of the broadcast networks, these are enforced by **Standards and Practices Departments**. Local broadcasters have what are called **policy books**. Newspapers and magazines standardize behavior in two ways: through **operating policies** (which spell out standards for everyday operations) and **editorial policies** (which identify company positions on specific issues). Many media organizations also utilize **ombudsmen**, practitioners internal to the company who serve as "judges" in disputes between the public and the organization. Sometimes they have titles such as public editor or reader advocate. Despite data indicating that having an ombudsman fosters increased credibility among readers and audiences, only 30 American newspapers and two networks (ESPN and PBS) maintain the role (Farhi, 2011b). Some outlets—the *Washington Post,* for example—use a **readers' representative**, who regularly responds to outside criticism.

These mechanisms of normative ethics are a form of self-regulation, designed in part to forestall more rigorous or intrusive government regulation. In a democracy dependent on mass communication, they serve an important function. We are suspicious of excessive government involvement in media. Self-regulation, however, has certain limitations:

- *Media professionals are reluctant to identify and censure colleagues who transgress.* To do so might appear to be admitting that problems exist; whistle-blowers in the profession are often met with hostility from their peers.

- *The standards for conduct and codes of behavior are abstract and ambiguous.* Many media professionals see this flexibility as a necessary evil; freedom and autonomy are essential. Others believe the lack of rigorous standards renders the codes useless.

- *As opposed to those in other professions, media practitioners are not subject to standards of professional training and licensing.* Again, some practitioners view standards of training and licensing as limiting media freedom and inviting government control. Others argue that licensing has not had these effects on doctors and lawyers.

- *Media practitioners often have limited independent control over their work.* Media professionals are not autonomous, individual professionals. They are part of large, hierarchically structured organizations. Therefore, it is often difficult to punish violations of standards because of the difficulty in fixing responsibility.

Critics of self-regulation argue that these limitations are often accepted willingly by media practitioners because the "true" function of self-regulation is "to cause the least commotion" for those working in the media industries (Black & Whitney, 1983, p. 432). True or not, the decision to perform his or her duties in an ethical manner ultimately rests with the individual media professional.

◀ When Children's Healthcare of Atlanta, one of the largest pediatric hospitals in the country, launched its Strong4Life movement to fight childhood obesity, it used several uncompromising ads featuring overweight kids. With Georgia having the second highest rate of obesity in the country, Children's stood by the need for an in-your-face approach. But many people, even some in the public health community, saw the images they used as offensive (Teegardin, 2012). The overriding message—the need for families to recognize that obesity is a widespread public health problem—certainly is not offensive. Why do you think the campaign was so controversial? Children's did not give into the pressure to pull the ads and to this day remains committed to bring Georgia out of the top 10 when it comes to childhood obesity. What would you have done?

As Black and Barney (1985/86) explain, an ethical media professional "must rationally overcome the status quo tendencies . . . to become the social catalyst who identifies the topics and expedites the negotiations societies need in order to remain dynamic" (p. 36).

DEVELOPING MEDIA LITERACY SKILLS

Media Reform

What do these groups and people have in common—Common Cause, the National Rifle Association, the National Organization for Women, Code Pink: Women's Preemptive Strike for Peace, the National Association of Black and Hispanic Journalists, the Leadership Conference on Civil Rights, the AFL–CIO, the Consumer Federation of America, the Chicago City Council, the Christian Coalition, the Traditional Values Coalition, the National Association of Broadcasters, the Center for Digital Democracy, Communication Workers of America, MoveOn.org, the Writer's Guild, the Rainbow/PUSH Coalition, Global Exchange, the Parents Television Council, the Catholic Conference, the Screen Actors Guild, the Association of Christian Schools, rockers Bonnie Raitt, Billy Joel, Pearl Jam, Patti Smith, and Don Henley, country singers Naomi Judd, George Jones, and Porter Wagoner, media moguls Ted Turner and Barry Diller, Republicans John McCain, Olympia Snowe, Jesse Helms, Kay Bailey Hutchinson, Ted Stevens, and Trent Lott, Democrats John Kerry, John Edwards, Ernest Hollings, Byron Dorgan, and Edward Markey? They all publicly oppose the FCC's weakening of the country's media ownership rules.

"Take the force of right-wingers upholding community standards who are determined to defend local control of the public airwaves," wrote conservative newspaper columnist William Safire. "Combine that with the force of lefties eager to maintain diversity of opinion in local media; add in independent voters' mistrust of media manipulation; then let all these people have access to their representatives by e-mail and fax, and voilà! Congress awakens to slap down the power grab" (in "Two Cents," 2003, p. 46). The FCC's "drive to loosen the rules," echoed liberal commissioner Michael Copps, "awoke a sleeping giant. American citizens are standing up in never-before-seen numbers to reclaim their airwaves and to call on those who are entrusted to use them to serve the public interest" (in Trigoboff, 2003, p. 36). Those never-before-seen numbers totaled 2 million communications to the Commission just before and soon after its 3-to-2 vote to relax ownership restrictions designed to encourage diversity of opinion in broadcasting. Congress received more comment on the decision that summer than on any other issue besides the invasion of Iraq.

The people had spoken against greater media concentration and for media reform, and they were heard. Over the objections of a Republican-controlled FCC and Republican president George W. Bush, the Republican-controlled House voted 400 to 21 to revoke the FCC's actions. The Republican-controlled Senate followed suit, 55 to 40. Upon entering the White House, President Obama expressed his support for media reform: "I'm committed to having the FCC review what our current policies are in terms of media diversification," he said. "And part of what I want to do is to expand the diversity of voices in media or have policies that encourage that." FCC Commissioner Michael Copps reiterated the president's commitment: "Today, a new spirit of change is abroad in the land. The question is whether we can have media capable of covering the issues that real Americans—not just Wall Street and Madison Avenue—care about. A media environment dominated by the established interests, unwilling or unable to reflect the concerns of ordinary citizens, is the natural enemy of change" (2008, p. 18).

We have seen throughout this text that culture is created and maintained through communication, and that mass communication is increasingly central to that process. Media-literate citizens, then, demand the most robust communication, for it is through our cultural conversations that we create and re-create ourselves, that we know ourselves,

the world around us, and others in it. Because media-literate people know that media content is a text that provides insight into our culture and our lives, they insist on more voices, not fewer. The active and growing media reform movement—the sleeping giant—is driven by the desire to make our media more responsive, more integral to how we live our personal, social, and cultural lives. In truth, then, the media reform movement is rooted in media literacy.

If you revisit the diverse cast of activists that opened this section, you'll see that they find wisdom in the words of former FCC commissioner Nicholas Johnson and Pope John Paul II. Johnson said that in our pursuit of a "viable self-governing society . . . whatever your first issue of concern, media [reform] had better be your second, because without change in the media, progress in your primary area is far less likely" (in McChesney, 2004, p. 24). Shortly before the death of Pope John Paul II in 2005, the Vatican released the popular religious leader's January 24 letter "to those responsible for communications." "The mass media," wrote the pontiff, "can and must promote justice and solidarity according to an organic and correct vision of human development by reporting events accurately and truthfully, analyzing situations and problems completely, and providing a forum for different opinions. An authentically ethical approach to using powerful communication media must be situated within the context of a mature exercise of freedom and responsibility, founded upon the supreme criteria of truth and justice" (2005, p. 54).

Resources for Review and Discussion

REVIEW POINTS: TYING CONTENT TO LEARNING OUTCOMES

▶ **Outline the history and development of our contemporary understanding of the First Amendment.**
  - ▶ The First Amendment is based on libertarianism's self-righting principle.
  - ▶ The absolutist position—no law means no law—is not as straightforward as it may seem. Questions have arisen over the definition of the press, what is abridgement, balancing of interests, the definition of libel and slander, the permissibility of prior restraint, and control of obscenity and pornography.

▶ **Explain the justification for and exercise of media regulation.**
  - ▶ Media professionals face other legal issues, such as how to define and handle indecent content, the impact of deregulation, and the limits of copyright.

▶ **Distinguish between a media system that operates under a libertarian philosophy and one that operates under a social responsibility philosophy.**
  - ▶ Libertarianism assumes a good and rational public with full access to all ideas; social responsibility theory, favoring responsible self-interest over government regulation, is the norm against which the operation of the American media system should be judged.

▶ **Define and discuss media ethics and how they are applied.**
  - ▶ Ethics, rules of behavior or moral principles that guide our actions, are not regulations, but they are every bit as important in guiding media professionals' behavior.
  - ▶ There are three levels of ethics—metaethics, normative ethics, and applied ethics.
  - ▶ Ethics require the balancing of several interests—the moral agent's individual conscience, the object of the act, financial supporters, the institution itself, the profession, and society.
  - ▶ Ethics, rather than regulation, influence judgments about matters such as truth and honesty, privacy, confidentiality, personal conflict of interest, the balancing of profit and social responsibility, and the decision to publish or air potentially offensive content.

▶ **Describe the operation and pros and cons of self-regulation.**
  - ▶ There is divergent opinion about the value and true purpose of much industry self-regulation.

▶ **Assess your personal commitment to media reform.**
  - ▶ The media reform movement generated in response to government plans to further relax industry regulation shows that a media-literate public understands the necessity of a free and democratic media system.

KEY TERMS

QUESTIONS FOR REVIEW

1. What are the basic tenets of libertarianism? How do they support the First Amendment?

2. What is the absolutist position on the First Amendment?

3. Name important court cases involving the definition of "no law," "the press," "abridgment," clear and present danger, balancing of interests, and prior restraint.

4. Define obscenity, pornography, and indecency.

5. What is the traffic cop analogy? Why is it important in the regulation of broadcasting?

6. What is copyright? What are the exceptions to copyright? What is DRM?

7. What are the basic assumptions of social responsibility theory?

8. What are ethics? What are the three levels of ethics?

9. What is confidentiality? Why is confidentiality important to media professionals and to democracy?

10. What are some forms of media self-regulation? What are the strengths and limitations of self-regulation?

connect

For further review, go to the LearnSmart study module for this chapter.

QUESTIONS FOR CRITICAL THINKING AND DISCUSSION

1. How much regulation or, if you prefer, deregulation do you think broadcasters should accept?

2. Of all the groups whose interests must be balanced by media professionals, which ones do you think would have the most influence over you?

3. In general, how ethical do you believe media professionals to be? Specifically, print journalists? Television journalists? Advertising professionals? Public relations professionals? Television and film writers? Direct mail marketers?

Global Media

15

Learning Objectives

Satellites and the Internet have made mass media truly global. Earth has become a global village. But not all countries use mass media in the same ways. Moreover, many people around the world resent the "Americanization" of their indigenous media systems. After studying this chapter you should be able to

▶ Outline the development of global media.

▶ Explain the practice of comparative analysis.

▶ Identify different media systems from around the world.

▶ Describe the debate surrounding the New World Information Order and other controversies raised by the globalization of media.

The BBK Music Phone Supergirl Contest—China's version of American Idol.

HENRI AND YOU HAVE BEEN PEN PALS SINCE SEVENTH GRADE. He's visited you here in the United States, and you've been to his house in the small, walled village of Alet, near Carcassonne in southern France. You treat each other like family. Which means you sometimes fight. But unlike siblings living under the same roof, you have to carry on your dispute by e-mail.

Dear Henri,

What's with you guys and your language police? For everyone else it's *e-mail*. For you it's *courriel*. People around the world are innovating with Internet *start-ups*. You have *jeune-pousses*. My French isn't as good as yours, but doesn't that mean little flower or something? And *mot-dièse* instead of *hashtag*. Sharp-word, really?

Mon ami,

Close, *mais pas de cigare* (but no cigar, my linguistically challenged friend). I admit that we may seem a little foolish to the rest of you, but the Académie Française (what you called the language police) is simply trying to protect our language because it represents the deepest expression of our national identity. The French speak French, our popular culture reflects and is reflected in French, and our history and literature are preserved in French. Maybe as an American speaking another country's language (English from England) you don't understand. We French will not be stripped of our *patrimoine*, our cultural heritage.

Dear Henri,

Too late! English is the first language of 500 million people and the second of another billion (Baron, 2011). The world's air traffic control systems all use English for their communication. Three-quarters of all the world's mail is written in English. English is the primary language for the publication of scientific and scholarly reports and for many international organizations such as the European Union and the Association of Southeast Asian Nations. Protecting the culture of a country that reveres Jerry Lewis is one thing, but keeping up with the rest of the planet is another.

Mon ami,

Sacre bleu, we do keep up with the rest of the world! In fact, we are the globe's cultural leaders, the avant garde. Surely you've recently seen *Le Fabuleux Destin d'Amélie*

Voice of America

1900 | 1925

1901 ▲ Marconi sends wireless signal transatlantic

mid-1920s European colonial powers use shortwave radio to connect holdings

1923 Radio comes to China

1928 Baird sends television image from London to New York

1940 ▲ Voice of America goes on air

Poulain and *Un Long Dimanche de Fiançailles* at your local cinema. I think in America they were called *Amélie* and *The Very Long Engagement*. They were worldwide hits. And I'm sure you saw *The Artist*, a little French production that won your Academy Award a little while ago.

Dear Henri,

Say what you will, my friend, but 31 of the 32 most-viewed dramatic TV shows in France last year were episodes of American programs: *House, Criminal Minds, The Mentalist*, and *CSI: Miami*. Another American show, *Castle*, is Number 1 with young adults. And if you're wondering about that lone non-American entry in the Top 32, it's *Doc Martin*, from England . . . yeah, where English comes from (Bunk, 2012).

Not only are American programs like these overseas hits (*House* is watched by 82 million people in 66 foreign countries), but American formats are also sold abroad to become local productions. Foreign-language *Hollywood Reporter, Dr. Oz, Wheel of Fortune, Law & Order*, and *Desperate Housewives* clones exist all over the world. *The Apprentice* is another format that has been sold globally. In China it's called *Wise Man Takes All*. China also has a version of *American Idol—The BBK Music Phone Supergirl Contest*. Local versions of foreign shows also travel the other way. *America's Funniest Home Videos* and *Hole in the Wall* originated in Japan; *The Killing* comes from Denmark; and of course, *American Idol* comes to the United States via England.

Throughout this text we have seen how globalization is altering the operation of the various mass media industries, as well as the process of mass communication itself. In this chapter, we focus specifically on this globalization and its impact.

In doing so we will look at the beginnings of international media and their development into a truly global mass media system. To study today's global media we will use comparative analyses to see how different countries establish media systems consistent with their specific people, cultures, and political systems. Naturally, we will discuss the programming available in other countries. And because global media influence the cultures that use them both positively and negatively, we visit the debate over cultural imperialism. Finally, our media literacy discussion deals with contrasting the way other countries handle different media issues with the way we do things here in America.

1950

1975

2000

1960s ▲ British pirate broadcasters go on air

1980 MacBride Report calls for New World Information Order

1984 German RTL goes on air

1985 Radio Martí goes on air

1989 ▲ Fall of European communism

1990 TV Martí goes on air

1996 Al Jazeera

2006 Al Jazeera International

2007 Al Jazeera English in U.S.

2009 UK okays/limits product placement

2010 Sweden says TV movie commercial breaks may be finable offense; Spain limits TV beauty ads

2011 ▲ Arab Spring

2013 Al Jazeera America

A Short History of Global Media

In Chapters 7 and 8 we saw that radio and television were, in effect, international in their earliest days. Guglielmo Marconi was the British son of an Italian diplomat, and among his earliest successes was the 1901 transmission of a wireless signal from England to Newfoundland. American inventors, in the persons of Philo Farnsworth and Russian immigrant Vladimir Zworykin, met and eventually overcame the challenge posed by Scotland's John Logie Baird, among whose greatest achievements was the successful transmission of a television picture from London to New York in 1928. But both the Marconi and the Baird transmissions were experimental, designed to attract attention and money to their infant technologies. However, it was not much later in the development of radio and television that these media did indeed become, if not truly global, at least international.

The Beginning of International Mass Media

Almost from the very start, radio signals were broadcast internationally. Beginning in the mid-1920s, the major European colonial powers—the Netherlands, Great Britain, and Germany—were using **shortwave radio** to connect with their various colonies in Africa, Asia, and the Middle East, as well as, in the case of the British, North America (Canada) and the South Pacific (Australia). Shortwave was (and still is) well suited for transmission over very long distances, because its high frequencies easily and efficiently reflect—or **skip**—off the ionosphere, producing **sky waves** that can travel vast distances.

CLANDESTINE STATIONS It was not only colonial powers that made use of international radio. Antigovernment or antiregime radio also constituted an important segment of international broadcasting. These **clandestine stations** typically emerged "from the darkest shadows of political conflict. They [were] frequently operated by revolutionary groups or intelligence agencies" (Soley & Nichols, 1987, p. vii). In World War II, for example, stations operating from Britain and other Allied nations encouraged German soldiers and sailors to sabotage their vehicles and vessels rather than be killed in battle. Allied stations, such as the Atlantic Station and Soldiers' Radio Calais, also intentionally broadcast misleading reports. Posing as two of the many official stations operated by the German army, they frequently transmitted false reports to confuse the enemy or to force official Nazi radio to counter with rebuttals, thus providing the Allies with exactly the information they sought.

But it was in the Cold War that clandestine broadcasting truly flowered. In the years between the end of World War II and the fall of European communism in 1989, thousands of radio, and sometimes television, pirates took up the cause of either revolutionary (pro-communist) or counterrevolutionary (anti-communist) movements. In addition, other governments tangentially related to this global struggle—especially the growing anticolonial movements in South and Central America and in Africa—made use of clandestine broadcasting.

During the Cold War unauthorized, clandestine opposition stations typically operated outside the nations or regions to which they broadcast to avoid discovery, capture, and imprisonment or death. Today the relatively few clandestine operations functioning inside the regions to which they transmit can be classified as **indigenous stations**, and they can make use of technologies other than radio. For example, al-Zawraa (The Gate) is an antigovernment Sunni-operated satellite television station transmitting from constantly changing locations inside Iraq to beam anti-American and anti-Shiite content to Sunni insurgents and other Iraqis involved in that war-torn country's ongoing civil war. Opposition stations transmitting to the regions they hope to influence from outside those areas are **exogenous stations**. FreeNK is an example of an exogenous (or international) station. It broadcasts from South Korea in opposition to the despotic rule of North Korea's Kim Jong Un. But because radios sold in North Korea are pretuned to receive nothing but official government stations and cannot be changed, only radios smuggled into the country can deliver FreeNK. FreeNK's response, therefore, is heavier reliance on the Internet. Naturally, many other clandestine operations have migrated to the Internet. Even al-Qaeda produces a weekly Web newscast, *Sout al-Khilafa* (*Voice of the Caliphate*). But because the difficult terrain in many embattled nations makes telephone lines an impossibility and poverty renders wireless Internet a rarity, radio remains the medium of choice for many out-groups.

PIRATE BROADCASTERS Another type of broadcast operation transmitting from outside its desired audience's geographic location involved something a bit more benign than war and revolution. These were stations that began broadcasting into Great Britain in the 1960s. Called **pirate broadcasters**, they were illegally operated stations broadcasting to British audiences from offshore or foreign facilities. Among the more notable were Radio Caroline, which reached a daily audience of a million listeners with its signal broadcast from the MV *Frederika* anchored 3½ miles off the Isle of Man, and Radio Veronica, broadcasting from a ship off the coast of the Netherlands.

These pirates, unlike their politically motivated clandestine cousins, were powerful and well subsidized by advertisers and record companies. Moreover, much like the commercial radio stations with which we are now familiar, they broadcast 24 hours a day, every day of the year. These pirates offered listeners an alternative to the controlled and low-key programming of the British Broadcasting Corporation's (BBC) stations. Because the BBC was non-commercial, pirate stations represented the only opportunity for advertisers who wanted to reach British consumers. Record companies intent on introducing Britain's youth to their artists and to rock 'n' roll also saw the pirates as the only way to reach their audience, which the staid BBC all but ignored.

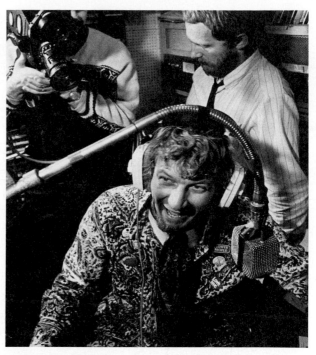

▲ Disc jockey Robby Dale broadcasts from pirate station Radio Caroline aboard the MV *Frederika*, anchored off Great Britain's Isle of Man.

Enterprising broadcasters also made use of foreign locales to bring commercial television to audiences otherwise denied. The top-rated network in Germany today, for example, is RTL. Now broadcasting from the German city of Cologne, it began operations in January 1984 in Luxembourg, transmitting an American-style mix of children's programming, sports, talk shows, and action–adventure programming into Germany to compete with that country's two dominant public broadcasters, ARD and ZDF.

THE UNITED STATES AS INTERNATIONAL BROADCASTER World War II brought the United States into the business of international broadcasting. Following the lead of Britain, which had just augmented its colonial broadcast system with an **external service** called the BBC World Service, the United States established in 1940 what would eventually be known as the Voice of America (VOA) to counter enemy propaganda and disseminate information about America. The VOA originally targeted countries in Central and South America friendly to Germany, but as the war became global, it quickly began broadcasting to scores of other nations, attracting, along with Britain's World Service, a large and admiring listenership, first in countries occupied by the Axis powers, and later by those in the Soviet sphere of influence.

It was this Cold War with the Soviets that moved the United States into the forefront of international broadcasting, a position it still holds today. To counter the efforts of the Soviet Union's external service, Radio Moscow, the United States established three additional services. Radio in the American Sector (RIAS), broadcasting in German, served people inside East Berlin and East Germany; Radio Free Europe (RFE) broadcast to all of the other Communist-bloc Eastern European countries in their native languages; and Radio Liberty (RL) was aimed at listeners in the Soviet Union itself. When these services were initiated, people both in the United States and abroad were told that they were funded by contributions from American citizens. However, as a result of the furor

▼ The Voice of America logo.
Reprinted by permission of Voice of America.

Al Jazeera America: Coming to Your Town?

As pro-democracy protests exploded across Egypt in January 2011, millions of Americans were glued to their video screens. They watched in real time as a spontaneous people's uprising in a Muslim country toppled an oppressive dictator, a despot, Hosni Mubarak, who enjoyed the support of the United States.

Night after night, day after day, viewers saw video of violent clashes, peaceful demonstrations, warm greetings between soldiers and protestors, and official pronouncements. They heard reporters and commentators, well versed in Egyptian culture and politics, offer expert accounts and analyses aimed squarely at English-speaking audiences. The drama was inescapable.

Most of those Americans, however, did not see these historic events on their television sets. They saw them unfold online because the only television news operation with a fully staffed operation in Egypt capable of this depth and breadth of coverage was Al Jazeera, and cable channel Al Jazeera English was almost invisible on American television.

Al Jazeera was founded in 1996 by Sheikh Hamad bin Khalifa Al-Thani, the Emir of Qatar. Al Jazeera means "the island" or "the peninsula," referring to the shape of Qatar, a small, oil-rich country on the Persian Gulf and an American ally. Al-Thani's goal was to create a news channel that would serve as "a beacon for democracy in the highly censored world of state-controlled Arabic media." As a result, Al Jazeera quickly angered most of the neighboring Middle Eastern regimes because an independent news organization "was a major departure from anything done before and was truly shocking for the Arab public . . . some in the Arab world even accused [the channel] of being a mouthpiece for American ideas" (Dahl, 2011). Al Jazeera has been banned in Algeria, Morocco, Iraq, Bahrain, and Tunisia. When democracy protests erupted in Egypt, president Mubarak shuttered Al Jazeera's offices, took its equipment, arrested its reporters, and booted it from the state-owned satellite carrier (Al Jazeera took to Facebook to tell people how to find it on 10 other regional satellite operations that replaced regular programming with Al Jazeera's video feed). "I am proud to say," writes the channel's director general Wadah Khanfar, "the Al Jazeera Network has been reporting from the region's hot spots well before they 'mattered' in January, 2011" (2011).

> "The only television news operation with a fully staffed operation in Egypt capable of this depth and breadth of coverage was Al Jazeera, and cable channel Al Jazeera English was almost invisible on American television."

In fact, many observers argue that the democratic movements now sweeping the Middle East could rightly be called "The Al Jazeera Revolution."

Naturally, then, when Al Jazeera English was launched in November 2006, American cable companies should have been excited to offer their viewers this additional perspective on a part of the world that so thoroughly dominates U.S. foreign policy and where the country was fighting two wars. After all, 120 million households in more than 100 countries in Europe, Asia, and Africa tune in every day; it's only proper that in an ever-interconnected world Americans would want to tune in as well. In fact, only a few small community operators in Ohio, Vermont, and the District of Columbia and satellite providers Dish and DirecTV elected to carry the world's fastest-growing news channel.

But there was indeed American demand for the channel (40% of Al Jazeera English's Web traffic comes from the U.S.; Vivarelli, 2013). So, in 2013, Al Jazeera bought cable channel Current TV for $500 million, renamed it Al Jazeera America, and staffed it with a host of high-profile U.S. journalists like CNN's Soledad O'Brien and NBC's Michael Viqueira. Al Jazeera America maintains 12 domestic and 65 foreign news bureaus, employs more than 800 journalists, focuses on "news of substance to everyday Americans rather than celebrity fare and partisan bickering," and has access to more than 50 million American TV households (Littleton, 2013).

Enter your voice. How comfortable are you with Al Jazeera America on your home's television screen? Even if you might not watch it, do you think it's important that the channel is available to more Americans? Do you think it will succeed? Why or why not?

◀ Soledad O'Brien, one of the many high-profile U.S. journalists now working for Al Jazeera America.

that arose when it was revealed in 1971 that they were in fact paid for by the Central Intelligence Agency, they were brought openly under government control and funded and administered by the International Broadcasting Bureau, whose members were appointed by the president.

The communist nations targeted by these services attempted to jam their signals by broadcasting on the same frequencies at higher powers, but they were only minimally successful in keeping their people from listening to these Western broadcasts. It was the success of these **surrogate services**—broadcast operations established by one country to substitute for another's own domestic service—that prompted President Ronald Reagan in 1985 to establish a special division of the VOA, Radio Martí, to broadcast into Communist Cuba. Radio Martí, still in operation, was joined by TV Martí in 1990.

A final United States external service established during World War II and the Cold War, Armed Forces Radio and Television Service (AFRTS), remains active today under its new name, American Forces Radio and Television Service. Maintained by the American military, its stated mission is "to deliver Department of Defense internal information and radio and television programming services which provide 'a touch of home' to Department of Defense personnel and their families serving overseas" (AFRTS, 2012). It employs shortwave radio, seven Earth-orbiting satellites, and MP3 technology to reach listeners and viewers in 175 countries and aboard U.S. ships with commercial-free fare.

▲ Radio Martí's logo.

THE VOA TODAY Today, 125 million listeners a day tune in to VOA broadcasts in 45 languages, and another 20 million people in 23 developing countries listen to its surrogate operations, RFE, RL, Radio Martí, and the recently added Radio Free Asia, Arabic-language Radio Sawa, and Radio Sila, broadcasting in Arabic and French into Darfur from Chad. Throughout its history, the VOA has frequently vacillated between two roles in response to world events and political pressures at home: (1) disseminating Western propaganda and (2) providing objective information. With the threat of communist world domination now nonexistent, it attempts to meet the far less contradictory goals of spreading American culture and disseminating health and social information.

The VOA's commitment to the spread of American culture is evidenced by the establishment in 1992 of a 24-hour top 40–style service, VOA Europe, and in 1998 of a 24-hour, all-news English-language worldwide radio service characterized by a snappy style reminiscent of domestic commercial stations. The VOA's focus on transmitting health and other practical information can be seen in the increased efforts it devotes to programs aimed at Third World nations on AIDS prevention, nutrition, and vaccination.

◄ The television drama *Touch* simultaneously premiered in 100 different countries.

In pursuit of this humanitarian goal, the VOA now frequently strikes agreements with local stations in these countries to broadcast its programs over their AM and FM stations, making them accessible to people who listen outside the shortwave band. You can read more about a different surrogate service, Qatar's attempt at openness in the closed world of state-controlled Arabic media, in the essay, "Al Jazeera America: Coming to Your Town?"

Global Media Today

In 2012 the drama *Touch*, starring Kiefer Sutherland, premiered on America's Fox Television Network. It debuted simultaneously in 100 other countries, all with the same sponsor, Unilever. The Cartoon Network is satellite- and cablecast in 145 countries in 14 languages. The Discovery Channel has 63 million subscribers in Asia, 35 million in Europe, the Middle East, and Africa, 30 million in India, and 18 million in Latin America. Nickelodeon is the globe's most distributed kids channel, viewable in more than 320 million households worldwide. Although *24*, *Prison Break*, and *Desperate Housewives* have long been available on the Iranian black market, religious and political leaders in that conservative country have given official approval to the broadcast of *Lost*. Disney runs 35 subscription services for Japanese mobile phone users, attracting 38 million subscribers in its first year. CBS maintains six "branded" cable channels in the United Kingdom. *SpongeBob Squarepants* is the favorite television show among Chinese kids. There is a Chinese production of *Cellular*, a Hindi remake of *Bride Wars*, and Chinese, Brazilian, Russian, Mexican, and Argentinean productions of *High School Musical*. And although you might have heard American voices in the 2009 movie *Astro Boy* (Nicholas Cage, Nathan Lane, and Kristen Bell, for example), it is actually a U.S. version of a Japanese *anime* (cartoon). Britain's Channel 4 *alone* pays Fox Television $1 million per episode for *The Simpsons*, and satellite channel BSkyB pays $814,000 an episode for *Glee*.

Downton Abbey, a hit on America's PBS television network and broadcast in more than 200 countries, originally airs on England's ITV1 and is produced by British production company Carnival Films, which is owned by U.S. media giant NBC-Universal. American Spanish-language network Telemundo, owned by NBC, has programming offices in Tokyo; Mexican media conglomerate Televisa has offices in China and coproduction deals with state-run China Central Television, as does Venezuela's Venevision; and Brazil media company Globo produces content for a number of India's television networks. If you're in the right place, you can join the nearly 400 million households worldwide that watch one of MTV's international channels. TV France International, that country's umbrella distribution organization, has partnerships with Fox, Warner Brothers, the Discovery and Sundance channels, and Bravo. Its all-French channel is available to viewers in the United States on DirecTV. Close to 200 nations receive CNN by satellite. Radio Beijing broadcasts to a worldwide audience in 40 languages; the Chinese also maintain the China Xinhua News Network, a 24-hour global English-language television service, and publish *China Daily USA Weekly*, an English-language newspaper, in eight major American cities. Hundreds of millions of Internet users spread throughout scores of countries can tune in to thousands of Web radio stations originating from every continent except Antarctica. AT&T, the United States' largest telecommunications and cable company, and British Telecom, Britain's biggest telecommunications provider, have merged their international operations into a single $10 billion unit. Media know few national borders.

But the global flow of expression and entertainment is not welcomed by everyone. French law requires that 40% of all music broadcast by its radio stations be in French. Iran bans "Western music" altogether from radio and television. Turkey forbids the use of the letters Q and W, punishable by fine, because they do not belong to the Turkish alphabet. Jamaica's Broadcasting Commission bans American hip-hop music to, it says, guard against underage sex and juvenile delinquency. America's northern neighbor mandates that all television programming contain at least 15% "Canadian-made

content." While *The Simpsons* is widely distributed across the Middle East by Saudi Arabian DBS provider MBC, all references to Duff Beer have been changed to soda, and Moe's Bar does not appear at all. The Germans and Austrians are wary of *The Simpsons* as well, refusing to air episodes that include the topic of a nuclear accident at the plant where Homer works. To ensure that its people do not access "foreign" or otherwise "counterrevolutionary" Internet content, the Chinese government requires all Internet accounts to be registered with the police. It employs 40,000 "e-police" to enforce its dozens of Net-related laws (dissidents call it the Great Firewall). Media may know few national borders, but there is growing concern that they at least respect the cultures within them.

One traditional way to understand the workings of the contemporary global media scene is to examine the individual media systems of the different countries around the world. In doing so, we can not only become familiar with how different folks in different places use media but also better evaluate the workings of our own system. Naturally, not every media system resembles that of the United States. As a result, such concepts as audience expectations, economic foundations, and the regulation of mass media differ across nations. The study of different countries' mass media systems is called **comparative analysis** or **comparative studies**.

Comparative Analyses

Different countries' mass media systems reflect the diversity of their levels of development and prosperity, values, and political systems. That a country's political system will be reflected in the nature of its media system is only logical. Authoritarian governments need to control the mass media to maintain power. Therefore, they will institute a media system very different from that of a democratic country with a capitalistic, free economy. The overriding philosophy of how media ideally operate in any given system of social values is called a normative theory (Chapter 14).

William Hachten (1992) offered "five concepts" that guide the world's many media systems—Western, development, revolutionary, authoritarianism, and communism. We'll examine each and provide a look at examples that exemplify them.

THE WESTERN CONCEPT: GREAT BRITAIN The **Western concept** is an amalgamation of the original libertarian and social responsibility models (Chapter 14). It recognizes two realities: There is no completely free (libertarian) media system on Earth, and even the most

You can enjoy *The Simpsons* just about everywhere in the Middle East, but if you do catch it there, you'll never see Homer drink a beer or visit Moe's Bar.

commercially driven systems include the expectation not only of public service and responsibility but also of meaningful government oversight of mass communication to ensure that media professionals meet those responsibilities.

Great Britain offers a good example of a media system operating under the Western concept. The BBC was originally built on the premise that broadcasting was a public trust (the social responsibility model). Long before television, BBC radio offered several services—one designed to provide news and information, another designed to support high or elite culture such as symphony music and plays, and a third designed to provide popular music and entertainment. To limit government and advertiser control, the BBC was funded by license fees levied on receivers (currently about $215 a year), and its governance was given over to a nonprofit corporation. Many observers point to this goal-oriented, noncommercial structure as the reason that the BBC developed, and still maintains, the most respected news operation in the world.

Unlike U.S. media, British media do not enjoy First Amendment protections, but as their notorious tabloids demonstrate, they nonetheless operate with a great deal of freedom.

Eventually, Britain, like all of western Europe, was forced by public demand to institute more American-style broadcasting. Fueled by that demand and advances in digital broadcasting, there are now many hundreds of radio stations in the United Kingdom. Most prominent are the 10 domestic BBC networks. The BBC also maintains 40 local stations that program a combination of local news and music, primarily for older listeners. There are also three national commercial radio networks, Virgin Radio, Classic FM, and talkSPORT, and a growing number of local commercial stations. As in the United States, most belong to larger chains.

The BBC also maintains eight television networks, all digital, each having its own character; for example, BBC One carries more popular fare, while BBC Two airs somewhat more serious content. Commercial television exists, too. ITV programs six digital networks; Channel 4 maintains four; and Five runs three. These commercial operations accept limits on the amount of advertising they air and agree to specified amounts of public affairs and documentary news programming in exchange for their licenses to broadcast. This is referred to as their **public service remit**.

In terms of other regulation, the media in Great Britain do not enjoy a First Amendment–like guarantee of freedom. Prior restraint does occur, but only when a committee of government officials and representatives of the media industry can agree on the issuance of what is called a **D-notice**. British media are also forbidden to report on court trials in progress, and Parliament can pass other restrictions on the media whenever it wishes—for example, the ban, imposed in 1988 and maintained for several years, on broadcasting the voice of anyone associated with the Irish Republican Army or other paramilitary movements.

THE DEVELOPMENT CONCEPT: HONDURAS The media systems of many Third World or developing African, Asian, Latin and South American, and eastern European nations formerly part of the Soviet bloc best exemplify the **development concept**. Here government and media work in partnership to ensure that media assist in the planned, beneficial development of the country. Content is designed to meet specific cultural and societal needs—for example, teaching new farming techniques, disseminating information on methods of disease control, and improving literacy. This isn't the same as authoritarian control. There is less censorship and other official control of content, but often marginally so.

Honduras offers one example. This small Central American country of 6.4 million people is one of the poorest in the Western Hemisphere; 85% of its population lives in poverty. As a result, the people own only half a million television sets and 2.5 million radio receivers. All of Honduras's 11 television stations are commercial; 290 of its radio stations are commercial and the government network, Radio Honduras, operates about 20 stations. Radio and printed leaflets have been particularly successful in reducing the number of infant deaths in Honduras caused by diarrheal dehydration and helping people with issues of family planning.

The 1982 Honduras Constitution guarantees freedom of the press, but there is significant control of media content. All the major newspapers are owned by powerful business executives or politicians with allegiances to different elites. Because the media in Honduras are constitutionally mandated to "cooperate with the state in the fulfillment of its public functions," journalists must be licensed and adhere to the Organic Law of the College of Journalists of Honduras. As such, they are forbidden to produce reports that "preach or disseminate doctrines that undermine the foundation of the State or of the family." Nor can journalists produce content that "threatens, libels, slanders, insults, or in any other way attacks the character of a public official in the exercise of his or her function." These were the "decrees" invoked by the Honduran military government when it ordered the National Commission of Telecommunications (Conatel), the official body that regulates the country's media, to close down television station Canal 36 and Radio Globo after they broadcast messages from ousted president Manuel Zelaya during a 2009 coup. The international press freedom organization Reporters Without Borders ranked Honduras 135th in its annual world press freedom index (if you're curious, the U.S. was 47th). Honduras, "marked by a culture of violence towards the media . . . has languished at the bottom of the list since the coup in June 2009" and earned its poor rating because of the "deaths of five journalists in 2011, two as a direct result of their work, as well as the regular persecution of opposition media and community radio stations" (Reporters Without Borders, 2012).

THE REVOLUTIONARY CONCEPT: POLAND No country "officially" embraces the **revolutionary concept** as a normative theory, but this does not mean that a nation's media will never serve the goals of revolution. Stevenson (1994) identified four aims of revolutionary media: ending government monopoly over information, facilitating the organization of opposition to the incumbent powers, destroying the legitimacy of a standing government, and bringing down a standing government. The experience of the Polish democracy movement Solidarity is a well-known example of the use of media as a tool of revolution.

▲ The Polish workers' and democracy movement, Solidarity, was greatly aided by media, both official outlets from beyond Poland's borders and its own extensive network of clandestine new and old communication technologies.

By the first years of the 1980s, the Polish people had grown dissatisfied with the domination of almost all aspects of their lives by a national Communist Party perceived to be a puppet of the Soviet Union. This frustration was fueled by the ability of just about all Poles to receive radio and television signals from neighboring democratic lands (Poland's location in central Europe made it impossible for the authorities to block what the people saw and heard). In addition, Radio Free Europe, the Voice of America, and the BBC all targeted Poland with their mix of Western news, entertainment, and propaganda. Its people's taste for freedom thus whetted, Solidarity established an extensive network of clandestine revolutionary media. Much of it was composed of technologies traditionally associated with revolution—pamphlets, newsletters, audiotapes and videocassettes—but much of it was also sophisticated radio and television technology used to disrupt official broadcasts and disseminate information. Despite government efforts to shut the system down, which went as far as suspending official broadcasting and mail services in order to deny Solidarity these communication channels, the revolution was a success, making Poland the first of the Eastern-bloc nations to defy the Party apparatus and install a democratically elected government. You can read about how new media have added new muscle to the revolutionary concept in the box titled "Social Media and the Middle East Democracy Movement."

THE AUTHORITARIANISM AND COMMUNISM CONCEPTS: CHINA Because only three communist nations remain and because the actual operation of the media in these and other **authoritarian systems** is quite similar, we can discuss authoritarianism and communism as a single concept. Both call for the subjugation of media for the purpose of serving the government. China is not only a good example of a country that operates its media according to the authoritarian/communist concepts, it also demonstrates how difficult it is becoming for authoritarian governments to maintain strict control over media and audiences.

The Chinese media system is based on that of its old ideological partner, the now-dissolved Soviet Union. For a variety of reasons, however, it has developed its own

peculiar nature. China has more than 1.3 billion people living in more than a million hamlets, villages, and cities. As a result, in the early 2000s, the government undertook an extensive program called *Cuncun Tong*, designed to bring at least radio, but preferably radio and television, to every one of those million locales. At the same time, it closed down hundreds of local newspapers and broadcast stations to solidify its control over content through its central and provincial government operations, primarily China Central Television. There are now 2,416 radio and 1,279 television stations in operation. But because of China's immense size, 66,000 relay or repeater stations are employed to reach its many viewers and listeners. Ninety-eight percent of all Chinese homes have television (*CIA World Factbook*, 2008).

Only relatively recently has the newspaper become an important medium. Widespread rural illiteracy and the lack of good pulpwood restricted the newspaper to the larger cities. Cities and towns were dotted with hundreds of thousands of reading walls where people could catch up on the official news. But when China embarked on its Open Door Policy in the late 1970s, it committed itself to developing the newspaper as a national medium. As a result, most reading walls are now gone, the few remaining used primarily by older people.

The media exist in China to serve the government. Chairman Mao Zedong, founder of the Chinese Communist Party, clarified the role of the media very soon after coming to power in 1949. The media exist to propagandize the policies of the Party and to educate, organize, and mobilize the masses. These are still their primary functions.

Radio came to China via American reporter E. C. Osborn, who established an experimental radio station in China in 1923. Official Chinese broadcasting began three years later. Television went on the air in 1958, and from the outset it was owned and controlled by the Party in the form of Central China Television (CCTV), which in turn answers to the Ministry of Radio and Television. Radio, now regulated by China People's Broadcasting Station (CPBS), and television stations and networks develop their own content, but it must conform to the requirements of the Propaganda Bureau of the Chinese Communist Party Central Committee.

Financially, Chinese broadcasting operates under direct government subsidy. But in 1979 the government approved commercial advertising for broadcasting, and it has evolved into an important means of financial support. Coupled with the Chinese government's desire to become a more active participant in the international economy, this commercialization has led to increased diversity in broadcast content. It has also led to increased corruption as major media, despite its illegality, openly sell news

USING MEDIA TO MAKE A DIFFERENCE
Social Media and the Middle East Democracy Movement

Tens of thousands of Iranians from all walks of life took to the streets in the summer of 2009 to protest what they saw as the illegitimate reelection of President Mahmoud Ahmadinejad. The government, already skilled at slowing the Internet and shutting down opposition websites, immediately expelled or placed under house arrest all foreign journalists, closed opposition newspapers, and used its own state-run radio and television stations to first ignore the protests and then blame them on outside Western agitators hostile to Iran. The protesters responded by using the Internet and social media to make a difference for their Green Revolution and democracy.

Only a few decades before, the Polish Solidarity movement's communication tools were pamphlets, newspapers, and loudspeaker trucks. But in 2009, Iran's police and army, as they had ever since the 1979 Islamic revolution, easily silenced these outlets. However, rather than stop the insurrection in a country where a third of the population is linked to the Internet and 60% have cell phones, this crushing of dissent pushed the protesters to those very same media where they made dramatically effective use of Twitter and YouTube. Protest organizers used cell phones to direct people to Twitter, where thousands of dissidents could be instantly mobilized into hundreds of daily demonstrations and nightly rooftop protests, shouting "Alaho Akbar" (God is Great) in defiance of the government. Hours of violent and bloody cell phone video were uploaded onto YouTube, none more famous than the image of Neda Aga Soltan's death, migrating from there to media outlets across the world.

Did the Green Revolution's use of social media make a difference? After all, Ahmadinejad's repressive regime remained in power despite weeks of violent protest. Evidence that it did

◄ Cell phone video of the murder of Neda Aga Soltan, seen worldwide on the Internet, not only galvanized Iran's Green Revolutionaries, but earned them global support.

was to come soon, as satellite and Web video of the revolt fueled democratic hopes across the region.

On December 17, 2010, Tunisian street vendor Mohamed Bouazizi set himself afire to protest mistreatment by corrupt government police. Demonstrations erupted immediately, and protestors uploaded cell phone video of their rallies to Facebook, YouTube, and local broadcasters. These images of defiance sped electronically around the country, and the revolution swept into all parts of Tunisian society. Twenty-eight days after Bouazizi's sacrifice, Tunisia's dictator of 23 years, Zine el-Abidine Ben Ali, fled into exile in Saudi Arabia.

Those images also made their way to Egypt, where anger at the brutal June 6, 2010 beating of Khaled Said at the hands of corrupt Alexandria police had been simmering for

> "Rather than stop the insurrection in a country where a third of the population is linked to the Internet and 60% have cell phones, this crushing of dissent pushed the protesters to those very same media where they made dramatically effective use of Twitter and YouTube."

months. Said's crime was that he had used his blog to post video of cops sharing the loot from a drug bust. Within five days of the 24-year-old businessman's death, demonstrators created a Facebook page, We Are All Khaled Said, to galvanize anger against the authoritarian government of Hosni Mubarak. Within a week, the page had 130,000 friends; by year's end, in a country of 5 million Facebook users, it had 473,000 (Preston, 2011).

By March 2011 these images of oppressed people fighting for freedom and dignity in Iraq, Tunisia, and Egypt had spawned an "Arab Spring"—democracy movements in Yemen, Libya, Bahrain, Algeria, Morocco, Jordan, Oman, Iraq, Syria, and Saudi Arabia. Some, for example in Libya and Bahrain, were met with government brutality, but others produced "voluntary" reform on the part of once-powerful rulers who saw that new media were a growing, uncontrollable check on their authority. "While it is almost impossible to isolate the impact of social media tools from the general swirl of events that set off the popular uprisings across the Middle East," wrote the *New York Times*'s Jennifer Preston, "there is little doubt that they provided a new means for ordinary people to connect with human rights advocates trying to amass support against police abuse, torture and . . . permanent emergency laws allowing people to be jailed without charges. Facebook and YouTube also offered a way for the discontented to organize and mobilize. . . . Far more decentralized than political parties, the strength and agility of the networks clearly caught [Middle Eastern] authorities . . . by surprise, even as [these governments] quickly attempted to shut them down" (2011, p. A10).

coverage to Western companies, for example, $20,000 a page in the Chinese version of *Esquire* and $4,000 a minute on state-run China Central Television (Barboza, 2012). For several decades, only the state's China TV Programming Agency could buy foreign content, and it was limited to purchasing no more than 500 hours a year. Rules also restricted stations to programming no more than 25% of their time to imported fare. *The Teletubbies* (*Antenna Babies* in China) is a longtime favorite. Restrictions on *foreign* content still exist, but there is now an emphasis on *domestic* coproduction with

Only 50 foreign movies a year can be exhibited in China. *Harry Potter* made the cut in 2011.

foreign programmers. In 2005, the central government "encouraged" the Ministry of Culture, the State Administration of Radio, Film and TV, and the General Administration of Press and Publications to develop procedures to open "foreign investment in cultural products and media in China," as long as all programming remained "at least 51% state-owned" (Goldkorn, 2005). This is why, as you saw earlier in this chapter, producers from across the globe have set up shop in China and why local versions of Western fare like *American Idol* and *Ugly Betty* now flourish there.

Basic government control over major media and the Internet remains, however. For example, only 50 foreign movies are permitted exhibition in China each year (20 by flat-fee arrangement and another 30 through profit-sharing with the government). In December 1997, anticipating the explosive growth of the Internet (China today, home to 50 million blogs and with more than 485 million users, has the world's largest and fastest-growing online population), the Party began enforcing criminal sanctions against those who would use the Net to "split the country," "injure the reputation of state organs," "defame government agencies," "promote feudal superstitions," or otherwise pose a threat to "social stability." Internet accounts have to be registered with the police. The state has established a 24-hour Internet task force to find and arrest senders of "counterrevolutionary" commentary. Popular bulletin boards are shut down when their chat becomes a bit too free. Websites such as Human Rights Watch, the *New York Times*, and publications about China that are independent of government control, such as *China News Digest*, are officially blocked, but not very successfully, as skilled Internet users can easily traverse the Web by routing themselves through distant servers such as DynaWeb and FreeGate or from one of the country's nearly 200,000 unlicensed Internet cafés (Stewart, 2010; Stone & Barboza, 2010).

Programming

Regardless of the particular concept guiding media systems in other countries, those systems produce and distribute content, in other words, programming. In most respects, radio and television programming throughout the world looks and sounds much like that found in the United States. There are two main reasons for this situation: (1) The United States is a world leader in international distribution of broadcast fare, and (2) very early in the life of television, American producers flooded the world with their programming at very low prices. Foreign operators of emerging television systems were delighted to have access to this low-cost content, because they typically could not

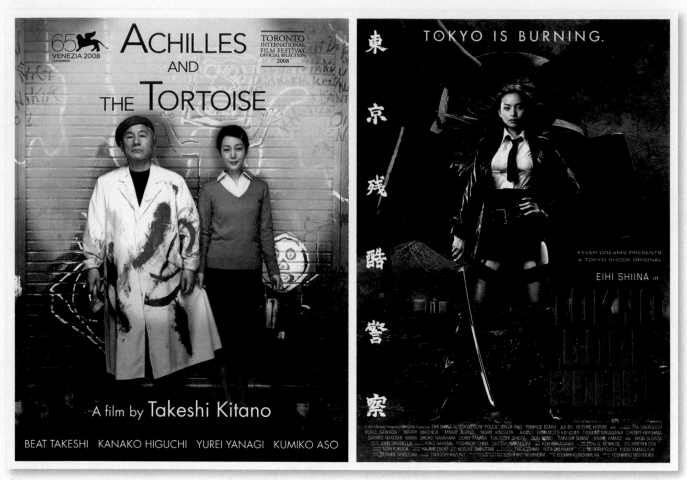

▲ Many countries hope their fare will find a worldwide audience, especially an American one. Here are two posters from Japanese films hoping to make their way to American screens.

afford to produce their own high-quality domestic material. For American producers, however, this strategy served the dual purpose of building markets for their programming and ensuring that foreign audiences would develop tastes and expectations similar to those in the United States, further encouraging future sales of programs originally produced for American audiences (Barnouw, 1990).

Naturally, programming varies somewhat from one country to another. The commercial television systems of most South American and European countries are far less sensitive about sex and nudity than are their counterparts in the United States. In Brazil, for example, despite a constitutional requirement that broadcasters respect society's social and ethical values, television networks such as SBT, TV Record, and TV Globo compete in what critics call the *guerra da baixaria*, the war of the lowest common denominator. Guests on variety shows wrestle with buxom models dressed only in bikinis and eat sushi off other women's naked bodies. On game shows, male contestants who give wrong answers can be punished by having patches of leg hair ripped out, while those who answer correctly are rewarded by having a nearly naked model sit in their laps. European commercial operations regularly air shows featuring both male and female nudity, sometimes because it is integral to the plot, sometimes simply for titillation.

Another difference between American programming and that of its global neighbors is how that content is utilized in different places. Naturally, broadcasting systems relying on the sale of commercial time find most value in programming that attracts the greatest number of viewers or a large number of viewers with the desired demographics. Commercial channels are just that, commercial. But many broadcast systems, those relying on license fees or other public support, frequently offer programming specifically designed to have educational, social, or political value. Many nations, even those with commercially supported systems, use a particular genre, the soap opera, for educational and social purposes.

The Debate over Cultural Imperialism

There are few physical borders between countries in a globally mediated world. Governments that could once physically prohibit the introduction and distribution of unwanted newspapers, magazines, and books had to work harder at jamming unwanted radio and television broadcasts. But they could do it, until satellite came along. Governments cannot disrupt satellite signals. Only lack of the necessary receiving technology can limit their reach. Now, with the Internet, a new receiving technology is cheap, easy to use, and available to more and more millions of people in every corner of the world . . . and because of the universal availability of free translation software like Google Translate, its content is readable to those millions of people wherever they live. As a result, difficult questions of national sovereignty and cultural diversity are being raised anew.

The MacBride Report and the NWIO

The debate over these questions reached its height with the 1980 release of the MacBride Report by the United Nations Educational, Scientific, and Cultural Organization (UNESCO). The report was named after the chair of the commission set up to study the question of how to maintain national and cultural sovereignty in the face of rapid globalization of mass media. At the time, many Third World and communist countries were concerned that international news coverage was dominated by the West, especially the United States, and that Western-produced content was overwhelming the media of developing countries, which lacked sufficient resources to create their own quality fare. The fear was that Western cultural values, especially those of the United States, would overshadow and displace those of other countries. These countries saw this as a form of colonialization, a **cultural imperialism**—the invasion of an indigenous people's culture by powerful foreign countries through mass media.

The MacBride Report, endorsed by UNESCO, called for the establishment of a New World Information Order (NWIO) characterized by several elements problematic to Western democracies. In arguing that individual nations should be free to control the news and entertainment that entered their lands, it called for monitoring of all such content, monitoring and licensing of foreign journalists, and requiring that prior government permission be obtained for direct radio, television, and satellite transmissions into foreign countries. Western nations rejected these rules as a direct infringement on the freedom of the press.

Western allies of the United States may have agreed that the restrictions of the NWIO were a threat to the free flow of information, yet virtually every one had in place rules (in the form of quotas) that limited U.S. media content in their own countries. Canada, our closest cultural neighbor, required that specific proportions of all content—print and broadcast—either be produced in Canada or reflect Canadian cultural identity. Canadian law forbids foreign (read: American) ownership in its commercial broadcasting channels. The French made illegal the printing of certain U.S. words, including "hamburger" and "cartoon" (France maintains an official office to prosecute those who would "debase" its language, the Académie Française in our opening vignette). The European Union's Television Without Frontiers Directive requires member countries' broadcasters to dedicate a majority of their airtime to European-produced programming and to commission at least 10% of all their shows from local, independent producers. South Korean law mandates that movie houses show native films at least 146 days out of each year. In October 2005, UNESCO approved the *Convention on the Protection and Promotion of the Diversity of Cultural Expressions* by a

▼ When introducing its McItaly burger, McDonald's proclaimed that it "spoke Italian." But most Italians deemed their government's endorsement of the new line of fast foods a "monstrous act of national betrayal."

▲ The two most popular English-language magazines on the European continent are *Time* and *Newsweek*, both published in the Netherlands. Do these American-born publications pose a threat to European nations' "cultural integrity," or do they bring divergent peoples closer together?

vote of 148 to 2. The two dissenters were the United States and Israel (UNESCO, 2005). The convention permits countries to treat "cultural products" such as movies, books, music, and television shows differently than they do other, more durable commodities. That is, countries can legally establish quotas and subsidies to protect their local media industries. And while the convention's text argued that the defense of every country's cultural heritage is "an ethical imperative, inseparable from respect for human dignity," it was clear from the debate preceding its passage that its true goal was protecting other countries' "cultural heritage" specifically from American media ("How They See Us," 2005).

The resistance to U.S. media would not exist among our international friends if they did not worry about the integrity of their own cultures. It is folly, then, to argue that non-native media content will have no effect on local culture—as do many U.S. media content producers. The question today is, How much influence will countries accept in exchange for fuller membership in the global community? In light of instant, inexpensive, and open computer network communication, a parallel question is, Have notions such as national sovereignty and cultural integrity lost their meaning? For example, ESPN is carried on 20 networks in 21 languages to 155 million television households in 183 different countries. *The Simpsons* is drawn in South Korea. The BBC broadcasts daily to a worldwide audience in 40 languages, as does Radio Beijing from China. CNN uses its satellites to transmit to a billion viewers in almost 200 countries. *The Simpsons Movie* premiered simultaneously in 100 countries and in 50 languages. Its summer 2007 opening weekend box office in the United States was $72 million. Elsewhere, it topped $100 million. Two of the three largest U.S. record companies have international ownership. Hollywood's Columbia Pictures is owned by Japanese Sony, and 20th Century Fox is owned by Rupert Murdoch's Australian corporation. As Thomas Middelhoff, former CEO of Bertelsmann, a German company that controls a large proportion of the U.S. book publishing market and earns more money from the United States than from any other nation, including its homeland, explained, "We're not foreign. We're international. I'm an American with a German passport" (as quoted in McChesney, 1999, p. 104).

The Case for the Global Village

There are differing opinions about the benefits of this trend away from nation-specific cultures. Global village proponents see the world community coming closer together as a common culture is negotiated and, not incidentally, as we become more economically interconnected. There should be little fear that individual cultures and national identities will disappear, because the world's great diversity will ensure that culture-specific, special-interest fare remains in demand. Modern media technology makes the delivery of this varied content not only possible but profitable. Not only do native-language versions of U.S. television shows like *Jeopardy* exist in virtually every western European country, but other "translations" are taking place. For example, hot on the heels of the success of the Spider-Man movies, Marvel Comics and an Indian company announced the birth of *Spider-Man India*, in which a young Bombay lad, Pavitr Prabhakar, inherits powers from a sacred yogi and accessorizes his Spidey suit with a traditional dhoti while dealing with local problems and challenges (Bal, 2004). As a result of these cultural exchanges, argue proponents of globalization, "a global culture is created, piece by piece, but it grows more variegated and complex along the way. And even as geographically based identities blur and fade, new subcultures, based on shared tastes in music or literature or obscure hobbies, grow up" (Bennett, 2004, p. 62).

The Case against the Global Village

The global village is here, say those with a less optimistic view, and the problem is what it looks like. *Time* media writer James Poniewozik (2001, p. 69) calls it "the new cold

war—between the Hollywood/Mickey D's axis and every other world culture." When in 2010, for example, Mickey D's introduced its new line of McItaly fast foods to that nation, it announced that "McDonald's Speaks Italian." The Italian government even sent its minister of agriculture to the product launch in Rome. But "real Italians" reacted angrily, denouncing the government's actions as a "monstrous act of national betrayal" (Fort, 2010).

Proponents of the global flow of communication find value in the local adoption of varied cultures. In Indonesia, *Sesame Street* becomes *Jalan Sesama* and counts among its residents the book-reading orangutan Tantan.

Media critic Robert McChesney (1997) fears for worldwide democracy. "The present course," he writes, "is one where much of the world's entertainment and journalism will be provided by a handful of enormous firms, with invariably pro-profit and pro-global market political positions on the central issues of our times. The implications for political democracy, by any standard, are troubling" (p. 23).

There is no simple answer to the debate over protecting the integrity of local cultures. As we've just seen, there is even disagreement over the wisdom of doing so. Media-literate people should at least be aware of the debate and its issues, and they may also want to consider the paradox of what Josef Joffe (2006), editor of Germany's weekly *Die Zeit*, calls the "soft power" of America's exported culture. It "does not bend hearts" as cultural imperialism's critics contend. Rather, "it twists minds in resentment and rage." He points to data collected by the Pew Global Attitudes Project. When asked if they "like American music, movies, and television," large percentages of citizens in England (62%), France (65%), Germany (67%), and Italy (69%) said "yes." But when asked if "it's good that American ideas and customs are spreading," other large percentages of people in England (33%), France (27%), Germany (24%), and Italy (43%) said "no" (p. 15). Like most debates over mass communication, the simple answers aren't always the correct answers.

DEVELOPING MEDIA LITERACY SKILLS

Making the Invisible Visible: Comparative Analysis

While comparative analysis offers us a glimpse of other countries' media systems, it also helps us understand our own. This is because we tend to think that the characteristics of our own media system are "natural," the way it is. Those aspects of media become so familiar that we don't see or perceive them at all. But comparative analysis,

► These Malaysian female students are encouraged to "Makan" (eat) at their local Kuala Lumpur McDonald's. Although critics of cultural imperialism see this as an intrusion of Western culture into the lives of these people, defenders of globalization of culture see the expansion of opportunity for both the "sending" and the "receiving" cultures.

comparing the way our media operate to the workings of another country's media, can help us identify aspects of our own system that might require a little more thought. Comparative analysis has the "capacity to render the invisible visible," to draw attention to aspects of any media system, including our own, "that may be taken for granted and difficult to detect when the focus is on only one national case" (Blumler & Gurevitch, 1975, p. 76).

We've seen elsewhere in this text that with New Zealand, the United States is the only country in the world that permits advertising of prescription drugs, that America is alone among industrialized nations in permitting advertising in children's television programming, and that as opposed to here at home, European nations require that Internet users opt-in before their personal data can be shared, but here are a number of other aspects of foreign media systems that differ from our own:

- The Spanish government bans airing television commercials for beauty products and services before 10 p.m. "Broadcasters cannot carry advertisements for things that encourage the cult of the body and have a negative impact on self-image—such as slimming products, surgical procedures, and beauty treatments—which are based on ideas of social rejection as a result of one's physical image or that success is dependent on factors such as weight or looks" (Hall, 2010a, p. 6).

- The Spanish government also bans advertising on its noncommercial channels, relying instead on public subsidies. Since they became *sin public*, these outlets have seen all-time ratings highs and regularly top the commercial channels (Hopewell & de Pablos, 2010).

- Sweden's Supreme Court ruled that inserting commercial breaks into televised movies at particularly dramatic moments "violates the integrity and value of the film" and is punishable by fine (Rehlin, 2010).

- The British government is considering a ban on Photoshopped models in publications aimed at people younger than 16; the French government is considering requiring warning labels on print ads that have been retouched; the French version of *Marie Claire* magazine runs 100% unretouched issues; the German magazine *Brigitte* no longer uses models on its covers or inside on editorial pages, relying instead on staffers and "real women" from its readership (Hall, 2010a).

- British law, which only began permitting product placement in television shows in 2009, still bans it from children's programming (Hall, 2010b).

- With more than 12 million residents, São Paulo, Brazil, is the seventh most populous city in the world. Its Clean City Law places a total ban on outdoor business signage of any kind. No billboards, no logos, no posters on bus stops. None. More than 70% of its citizens say the law is "beneficial" (Jefferson, 2011).

- Mexico, Bolivia, and France make free newspapers available to young readers (Fitzgerald, 2010).

- Annual government funding for noncommercial media in the United States amounts to $1.35 per person. In Canada it is $22.48; in Slovenia, $51.57; in the United Kingdom, $80.36; in Denmark, $101.00; and in Finland, $101.01 (Naureckas, 2009).

Can you explain why these differences might exist? Would any of these rules or practices seem "natural" in our American media system? Why or why not? Are there any that you would like to see adopted by our homegrown system? Why or why not? The hallmarks of a media-literate individual are critical thinking, analysis, and reflection. As such, you should have ready answers to these questions. Do you?

MEDIA LITERACY CHALLENGE
Do Your Own Comparative Analysis

As a media-literate individual you know that *media content is a text providing insight into contemporary culture*, and as you've just read, comparative analysis is one way to "make visible" aspects of your own culture's media by looking at the media of other places. Here are several facts about other countries' media activities. What do they say to you about those specific countries and their media systems? How do these facts compare to the same situation in the United States? What do any differences say about our media? About us as a culture? Take this challenge either by offering your responses in a brief essay or in debate with one or more classmates.

1. People in Serbia watch more television per day, 5 hours, 39 minutes, than people in any other country.

2. The proportion of Indian homes with television rose from less than one-third in 2001 to 50% today, correlating with a decrease in the country's birth rate.

3. In Madagascar, barely one in six households has a television.

4. More Peruvian homes have televisions than have electricity—people use batteries to run their sets (numbers 1-4 in Global Media Habits, 2011).

5. South Korea has nearly universal broadband access, yet newspaper circulation has fallen only minimally.

6. European daily newspapers have the largest newspaper circulation declines in the world.

7. Japan's biggest newspaper, *Yomiuri Shimbun*, with 10 million daily readers, has a larger circulation than the *Wall Street Journal*, *New York Times*, *USA Today*, and the *Los Angeles Times* combined (numbers 5-7 in Global Media, 2011).

Resources for Review and Discussion

REVIEW POINTS: TYING CONTENT TO LEARNING OUTCOMES

▶ **Outline the development of global media.**
- ▸ For decades, international mass media took the form of shortwave radio broadcasts, especially in the form of clandestine stations, both exogenous and indigenous.
- ▸ Other exogenous operations are pirate broadcasters and many countries' external services such as the BBC and VOA.

▶ **Explain the practice of comparative analysis.**
- ▸ Different countries rely on different media systems to meet their national needs. The study of these varying models is called comparative analysis.
- ▸ Naturally, different systems make varying use of different programming as their nations' needs demand.

▶ **Identify different media systems from around the world.**
  ▶ There are five main models or concepts: Western, development, revolutionary, authoritarianism, and communism.

▶ **Describe the debate surrounding the New World Information Order and other controversies raised by the globalization of media.**
  ▶ There is serious debate about the free and not-so-free flow of mass communication across borders. The conflict is between those who want the free flow of information and those who worry about the erosion of local culture.
  ▶ Much of this controversy, however, has more to do with protecting countries' media systems from American influence than it does with protecting all countries' cultural integrity.

KEY TERMS

shortwave radio, 384	pirate broadcasters, 385	D-notice, 391
skip, 384	external service, 385	development concept, 391
sky waves, 384	surrogate service, 386	revolutionary concept, 391
clandestine stations, 384	comparative analysis (studies), 389	authoritarian system, 392
indigenous stations, 384	Western concept, 389	cultural imperialism, 397
exogenous stations, 384	public service remit, 391	

QUESTIONS FOR REVIEW

1. What are clandestine broadcast stations? Differentiate between indigenous and exogenous stations.

2. What are pirate broadcasters? What differentiates them from traditional clandestine operators?

3. How did World War II and the Cold War shape the efforts of the United States in terms of its external and surrogate services?

4. What is comparative analysis?

5. What are the main characteristics of media systems operating under Hachten's Western concept?

6. What are the main characteristics of media systems operating under Hachten's development concept?

7. What are the main characteristics of media systems operating under Hachten's revolutionary concept?

8. What are the main characteristics of media systems operating under Hachten's authoritarianism and communism concepts?

9. What is cultural imperialism? What two telecommunications technologies fuel current concern over its operation?

10. What was the MacBride Report? Why did most Western nations reject it?

Mc Graw Hill Education **connect**

For further review, go to the LearnSmart study module for this chapter.

QUESTIONS FOR CRITICAL THINKING AND DISCUSSION

1. Britain's external service, the BBC, is available on shortwave radio, the Internet, and American cable and satellite television. Listen to or watch the BBC. How does its content compare to the homegrown radio and television with which you are familiar? Think especially of news. How does its reporting differ from that of cable networks such as CNN and from broadcast networks such as ABC, CBS, and NBC? Why do you think differences exist? Similarities?

2. Do you have experience with another country's media? If so, which one? Can you place that system's operation within one of the concepts listed in this chapter? Describe how that system's content is similar to and different from that with which you are familiar in the United States. Do you favor one system's fare over another's? Why or why not?

3. Do you think countries, especially developing nations, should worry about cultural imperialism? Would you argue that they should use low-cost Western fare to help their developing system get "off the ground," or do you agree with critics that this approach unduly influences their system's ultimate content?

Glossary

absolutist position regarding the First Amendment, the idea that no law means no law

access journalism reporters acting deferentially toward news sources in order to ensure continued access

accountability metrics agreement between ad agency and client on how the effectiveness of a specific ad or campaign will be judged

Acta Diurna written on a tablet, account of the deliberations of the Roman senate; an early "newspaper"

actual malice the standard for libel in coverage of public figures consisting of "knowledge of its falsity" or "reckless disregard" for whether or not it is true

addressable technology technology permitting the transmission of very specific content to equally specific audience members

ad hoc balancing of interests in individual First Amendment cases, several factors should be weighed in determining how much freedom the press is granted

ad-pull policy demand by an advertiser for an advance review of a magazine's content, with the threat of pulled advertising if dissatisfied with that content

administrative research studies of the immediate, practical influence of mass communication

advergames video games produced expressly to serve as brand commercials

advertorials ads in magazines and newspapers that take on the appearance of genuine editorial content

advocacy games primarily online games supporting an idea rather than a product

affiliate a broadcasting station that aligns itself with a network

agenda setting the theory that media may not tell us what to think but do tell us what to think about

aggressive cues model of media violence; media portrayals can indicate that certain classes of people are acceptable targets for real-world aggression

AIDA approach the idea that to persuade consumers advertising must attract *attention*, create *interest*, stimulate *desire*, and promote *action*

à la carte pricing charging cable subscribers by the channel, not for tiers

Alien and Sedition Acts series of four laws passed by 1798 U.S. Congress making illegal the writing, publishing, or printing of "any false scandalous and malicious writing" about the president, the Congress, or the U.S. government

aliteracy possessing the ability to read but being unwilling to do so

all-channel legislation 1962 law requiring all television sets imported into or manufactured in the United States to be equipped with both VHF and UHF receivers

alternative press typically weekly, free papers emphasizing events listings, local arts advertising, and "eccentric" personal classified ads

ambient advertising advertising content appearing in nontraditional venues

app abbreviation for application; software for mobile digital devices

applied ethics the application of metaethics and normative ethics to very specific situations

appointment consumption audiences consume content at a time predetermined by the producer and distributor

ascertainment requires broadcasters to ascertain or actively and affirmatively determine the nature of their audiences' interest, convenience, and necessity; no longer enforced

astroturf fake grassroots organization

attitude change theory theory that explains how people's attitudes are formed, shaped, and changed and how those attitudes influence behavior

audience fragmentation audiences for specific media content becoming smaller and increasingly homogeneous

audion tube vacuum tube developed by DeForest that became the basic invention for all radio and television

augmented reality (AR) permits users to point phones at things in the real world and be instantly linked to websites containing information about those things superimposed over the screen image

authoritarian/communism system a national media system characterized by authoritarian control

awareness tests ad research technique that measures the cumulative effect of a campaign in terms of a product's "consumer consciousness"

bandwidth a communication channel's information-carrying capacity

banners online advertising messages akin to billboards

basic cable television channels provided automatically by virtue of subscription to a cable provider

billings total sale of broadcast airtime

Bill of Rights the first 10 amendments to the U.S. Constitution

binary code information transformed into a series of digits 1 and 0 for storage and manipulation in computers

bitcasters "radio stations" that can be accessed only over the World Wide Web

BitTorrent file-sharing software that allows users to create "swarms" of data as they simultaneously download and upload "bits" of a given piece of content

blinks one-second radio commercials

block booking the practice of requiring exhibitors to rent groups of movies (often inferior) to secure a better one

blockbuster mentality filmmaking characterized by reduced risk taking and more formulaic movies; business concerns are said to dominate artistic considerations

blogs regularly updated online journals

B-movie the second, typically less expensive, movie in a double feature

bounded cultures (co-cultures) groups with specific but not dominant cultures

brand entertainment when commercials are part of and essential to a piece of media content

branding films sponsor financing of movies to advance a manufacturer's product

brand magazine a consumer magazine published by a retail business for readers having demographic characteristics similar to those consumers with whom it typically does business

British cultural theory theory of elites' domination over culture and its influence on bounded cultures

broadband a channel with broad information-carrying capacity

broadsides (sometimes **broadsheets**) early colonial newspapers imported from England, single-sheet announcements or accounts of events

browsers software programs loaded on personal computers and used to download and view Web files

bundling delivering television, VOD, audio, high-speed Internet access, long-distance and local phone service, multiple phone lines, and fax via cable

C3 rating measure of viewing of commercials that appear in a specific program within 3 days of its premiere telecast

calotype early system of photography using translucent paper from which multiple prints could be made

casual games classic games most often played in spurts and accommodated by small-screen devices

catalogue albums in record retailing, albums more than three years old

catharsis theory that watching mediated violence reduces people's inclination to behave aggressively

cause marketing PR in support of social issues and causes

cease-and-desist order demand made by a regulatory agency that a given illegal practice be stopped

cinématographe Lumière brothers' device that both photographed and projected action

circulation the number of issues of a magazine or newspaper that are sold

clandestine stations illegal or unlicensed broadcast operations frequently operated by revolutionary groups or intelligence agencies for political purposes

clear time when local affiliates carry a network's program

click stream the series of choices made by a user on the Web

cloud computing storage of all computer data, including personal information and system-operating software, on distant computers

cloud-music services sites allowing users to store all their digital music online and stream it to any computer or digital device anywhere

coaxial cable copper-clad aluminum wire encased in plastic foam insulation, covered by an aluminum outer conductor, and then sheathed in plastic

collateral materials printing, research, and photographs that PR firms handle for clients, charging as much as 17.65% for this service

commissions in advertising, placement of advertising in media is compensated, at typically 15% of the cost of the time or space, through commissions

common carrier a telecommunications company required to carry others' messages with no power to restrict them—for example, a phone company

communication the process of creating shared meaning

community antenna television (CATV) outmoded name for early cable television

commuter papers free dailies designed for younger commuters

comparative analysis the study of different countries' mass media systems

comparative studies see **comparative analysis**

complementary copy newspaper and magazine content that reinforces the advertiser's message, or at least does not negate it

concentration of ownership ownership of different and numerous media companies concentrated in fewer and fewer hands

concept films movies that can be described in one line

confidentiality the ability of media professionals to keep secret the names of people who provide them with information

conglomeration the increase in the ownership of media outlets by nonmedia companies

consumer culture a culture in which personal worth and identity reside not in the people themselves but in the products with which they surround themselves

consumer juries ad research technique in which people considered representative of a target market review a number of approaches or variations of a campaign or ad

consumption-on-demand the ability to access any content, anytime, anywhere

controlled circulation a magazine provided at no cost to readers who meet some specific set of advertiser-attractive criteria

conventions in media content, certain distinctive, standardized style elements of individual genres

convergence the erosion of traditional distinctions among media

cookie an identifying code added to a computer's hard drive by a visited website

copyright identifying and granting ownership of a given piece of expression to protect the creators' financial interest in it

copy testing measuring the effectiveness of advertising messages by showing them to consumers; used for all forms of advertising

corantos one-page news sheets on specific events, printed in English but published in Holland and imported into England by British booksellers; an early "newspaper"

cord-cutting viewers leaving cable and DBS altogether and relying on Internet-only television

corporate independent studio specialty or niche division of a major studio designed to produce more sophisticated—but less costly—movies

corrective advertising a new set of ads required by a regulatory body and produced by the offender that correct the original misleading effort

cost of entry amount of money necessary to begin media content production

cost per thousand (CPM) in advertising, the cost of reaching 1,000 audience members, computed by the cost of an ad's placement divided by the number of thousands of consumers it reaches

cottage industry an industry characterized by small operations closely identified with their personnel

cover rerecording of one artist's music by another

critical cultural theory idea that media operate primarily to justify and support the status quo at the expense of ordinary people

critical research studies of media's contribution to the larger issues of what kind of nation we are building, what kind of people we are becoming

crowdfunded journalism journalists pitch stories to readers who can contribute small amounts of money to those they want to see completed

crowdsource outsourcing tasks to an online network of people, the crowd, for cooperative problem-solving and production

cultivation analysis idea that television "cultivates" or constructs a reality of the world that, although possibly inaccurate, becomes the accepted reality simply because we as a culture believe it to be the reality

cultural definition of communication communication is a symbolic process whereby reality is produced, maintained, repaired, and transformed; from James Carey

cultural imperialism the invasion of an indigenous people's culture, through mass media, by outside, powerful countries

cultural theory the idea that meaning and therefore effects are negotiated by media and audiences as they interact in the culture

culture the world made meaningful; socially constructed and maintained through communication, it limits as well as liberates us, differentiates as well as unites us, defines our realities and thereby shapes the ways we think, feel, and act

custom publishing publications specifically designed for an individual company seeking to reach a narrowly defined audience

daguerreotype process of recording images on polished metal plates, usually copper, covered with a thin layer of silver iodide emulsion

dataveillance the massive electronic collection and distillation of consumer data

day-and-date release simultaneously releasing a movie to the public in some combination of theater, cable, DVD, and download

decoding interpreting sign/symbol systems

democracy government by the people

demographic segmentation advertisers' appeal to audiences composed of varying personal and social characteristics such as race, gender, and economic level

dependency theory idea that media's power is a function of audience members' dependency on the media and their content

deregulation relaxation of ownership and other rules for radio and television

desensitization the idea that viewers become more accepting of real-world violence because of its constant presence in television fare

development concept of media systems; government and media work in partnership to ensure that media assist in the planned, beneficial development of the country

digital audio radio service (DARS) direct home or automobile delivery of audio by satellite

digital cable television delivery of digital video images and other information to subscribers' homes

digital computer a computer that processes data reduced to a binary code

digital divide the lack of technological access among people of color, people who are poor or disabled, and those in rural communities

digital natives people who have never known a world without the Internet

digital recording recording based on conversion of sound into 1s and 0s logged in millisecond intervals in a computerized translation process

digital rights management (DRM) protection of digitally distributed intellectual property

digital video disc (DVD) digital recording and playback player and disc, fastest-growing consumer electronic product in history

digital video recorder (DVR) video recording device attached to a television, which gives viewers significant control over content

dime novels inexpensive late 19th- and early 20th-century books that concentrated on frontier and adventure stories; sometimes called **pulp novels**

disinhibitory effects in social cognitive theory, seeing a model rewarded for prohibited or threatening behavior increases the likelihood that the observer will perform that behavior

dissonance theory argues that people, when confronted by new information, experience a kind of mental discomfort, a dissonance; as a result, they consciously and subconsciously work to limit or reduce that discomfort through the selective processes

diurnals daily accounts of local news printed in 1620s England; forerunners of our daily newspaper

DMX (Digital Music Express) home delivery of audio by cable

D-notice in Great Britain, an officially issued notice of prior restraint

domain name on the World Wide Web, an identifying name, rather than a site's formal URL, that gives some indication of the nature of a site's content or owner

dominant culture (mainstream culture) the culture that seems to hold sway with the large majority of people; that which is normative

double feature two films on the same bill

duopoly single ownership and management of multiple radio stations in one market

early window the idea that media give children a window on the world before they have the critical and intellectual ability to judge what they see

e-book a book that is downloaded in electronic form from the Internet to a computer or handheld device

e-commerce buying products and services online

economies of scale concept that relative cost declines as the size of the endeavor grows

editorial policy newspapers' and magazines' positions on certain specific issues

e-mail (electronic mail) function of Internet allowing communication via computer with anyone else online, anyplace in the world, with no long-distance fees

embedding war correspondents exchanging control of their output for access to the front

encoding transforming ideas into an understandable sign/symbol system

encryption electronic coding or masking of information on the Web that can be deciphered only by a recipient with the decrypting key

engagement psychological and behavioral measure of ad effectiveness designed to replace CPM

environmental incentives in social learning theory, the notion that real-world incentives can lead observers to ignore negative vicarious reinforcement

e-publishing the publication and distribution of books initially or exclusively online

e-reader digital book having the appearance of a traditional book but with content that is digitally stored and accessed

ethics rules of behavior or moral principles that guide actions in given situations

ethnic press papers, often in a foreign language, aimed at minority, immigrant, and non-English readers

exergame video game designed to encourage beneficial physical activity

exogenous stations clandestine broadcast operations functioning from outside the regions to which they transmit

expanded basic cable in cable television, a second, somewhat more expensive level of subscription

external service in international broadcasting, a service designed by one country to counter enemy propaganda and disseminate information about itself

factory studios the first film production companies

Fairness Doctrine requires broadcasters to cover issues of public importance and to be fair in that coverage; abolished in 1987

fair use in copyright law, instances in which material may be used without permission or payment

feature syndicates clearinghouses for the work of columnists, cartoonists, and other creative individuals, providing their work to newspapers and other media outlets

feedback the response to a given communication

fiber optics signals carried by light beams over glass fibers

First Amendment Congress shall make no law respecting an establishment of religion, or prohibiting the free exercise thereof; or abridging the freedom of speech, or of the press; or the right of the people peacefully to assemble, and to petition the Government for a redress of grievances

first-person perspective game video game in which all action is through the eyes of the player

first-run syndication original programming produced specifically for the syndicated television market

fixed-fee arrangement the arrangement whereby a PR firm performs a specific set of services for a client for a specific and prearranged fee

flack a derogatory name sometimes applied to public relations professionals

flash mobs (sometimes **smart mobs**) large, geographically dispersed groups connected only by communications technology, quickly drawn together to perform collective action

flog fake blog; typically sponsored by a company to anonymously boost itself or attack a competitor

focus groups small groups of people who are interviewed, typically to provide advertising or public relations professionals with detailed information

forced exposure ad research technique used primarily for television commercials, requiring advertisers to bring consumers to a theater or other facility where they see a television program, complete with the new ads

format a radio station's particular sound or programming content

fraction of selection graphic description of how individuals make media and content choices based on expectation of reward and effort required

franchise films movies produced with full intention of producing several sequels

Frankfurt School media theory, centered in neo-Marxism, that valued serious art, viewing its consumption as a means to elevate all people toward a better life; typical media fare was seen as pacifying ordinary people while repressing them

freemium games video games in which advertising serves as in-game virtual currency

gamification use of video game skills and conventions to solve real-world problems

genre a form of media content with a standardized, distinctive style and conventions

Global Television Audience Metering meter (GTAM meter) video ratings technology that will actively and passively measure viewing across all platforms

global village a McLuhan concept; new communication technologies permit people to become increasingly involved in one another's lives

globalization ownership of media companies by multinational corporations

grand theory a theory designed to describe and explain all aspects of a given phenomenon

green light process the process of deciding to make a movie

greenwashing public relations practice of countering the public relations efforts aimed at clients by environmentalists

hard news news stories that help readers make intelligent decisions and keep up with important issues

home page entryway into a website, containing information and hyperlinks to other material

hosts computers linking individual personal computer users to the Internet

hypercommercialism increasing the amount of advertising and mixing commercial and noncommercial media content

hyperlink connection, embedded in Internet or website, allowing instant access to other material in that site as well as to material in other sites

hypodermic needle theory idea that media are a dangerous drug that can directly enter a person's system

iconoscope tube first practical television camera tube, developed in 1923

identification in social cognitive theory, a special form of imitation by which observers do not exactly copy what they have seen but make a more generalized but related response

imitation in social cognitive theory, the direct replication of an observed behavior

importation of distant signals delivery of distant television signals by cable television for the purpose of improving reception

in-band-on-channel (IBOC) digital radio technology that uses digital compression to "shrink" digital and analog signals, allowing both to occupy the same frequency

indecency in broadcasting, language or material that depicts sexual or excretory activities in a way offensive to contemporary community standards

indigenous stations clandestine broadcast operations functioning from inside the regions to which they transmit

inferential feedback in the mass communication process, feedback is typically indirect rather than direct; that is, it is inferential

information gap the widening disparity in amounts and types of information available to information haves and have-nots

information service legal designation allowing a telecommunication service provider to maintain control over what passes over its lines

inhibitory effects in social cognitive theory, seeing a model punished for a behavior reduces the likelihood that the observer will perform that behavior

instant books books published very soon after some well-publicized public event

instant messaging (IM) real-time e-mail, allowing two or more people to communicate instantaneously and in immediate response to one another

integrated audience reach total numbers of the print edition of a newspaper plus unduplicated Web readers

integrated marketing communications (IMC) combining public relations, marketing, advertising, and promotion into a seamless communication campaign

Internet a global network of interconnected computers that communicate freely and share and exchange information

Internet service provider see **ISP**

interpersonal communication communication between two or a few people

island in children's television commercials, the product is shown simply, in actual size against a neutral background

ISP (Internet service provider) company that offers Internet connections at monthly rates depending on the kind and amount of access needed

joint operating agreement (JOA) permits a failing paper to merge most aspects of its business with a successful local competitor, as long as editorial and reporting operations remain separate

kinescope improved picture tube developed by Zworykin for RCA

kinetograph William Dickson's early motion picture camera

kinetoscope peep show devices for the exhibition of kinetographs

knowledge gap growing differences in knowledge, civic activity, and literacy between better-informed and less-informed Americans

LAN (local area network) network connecting two or more computers, usually within the same building

LCD (liquid crystal display) display surface in which electric currents of varying voltage are passed through liquid crystal, altering the passage of light through that crystal

lead generation using Internet-created databases to collect names, addresses, e-mail addresses, and other information about likely clients or customers

LED (light-emitting diode) light-emitting semiconductor manipulated under a display screen

libel the false and malicious publication of material that damages a person's reputation (typically applied to print media)

libertarianism philosophy of the press that asserts that good and rational people can tell right from wrong if presented with full and free access to information; therefore, censorship is unnecessary

limited effects theory media's influence is limited by people's individual differences, social categories, and personal relationships

linotype technology that allowed the mechanical rather than manual setting of print type

liquid barretter first audio device permitting the reception of wireless voices; developed by Fessenden

literacy the ability to effectively and efficiently comprehend and utilize a given form of communication

lobbying in public relations, directly interacting with elected officials or government regulators and agents

location-based mobile advertising technology allowing marketers to send targeted ads to people where they are in the moment

Low Power FM (LPFM) 10- to 100-watt nonprofit community radio stations with a reach of only a few miles

macro-level effects media's widescale social and cultural impact

magalogue a designer catalogue produced to look like a consumer magazine

magic bullet theory the idea from mass society theory that media are a powerful "killing force" that directly penetrates a person's system

mainframe computer a large central computer to which users are connected by terminals

mainstreaming in cultivation analysis, television's ability to move people toward a common understanding of how things are

mass communication the process of creating shared meaning between the mass media and their audiences

mass communication theories explanations and predictions of social phenomena relating mass communication to various aspects of our personal and cultural lives or social systems

massively multiplayer online role-playing game (MMO) interactive online game where characters and actions are controlled by other players, not the computer; also called **virtual worlds games**

mass medium (pl. **mass media**) a medium that carries messages to a large number of people

mass society theory the idea that media are corrupting influences; they undermine the social order, and "average" people are defenseless against their influence

master antenna television (MATV) connecting multiple sets in a single location or building to a single, master antenna

meaning-making perspective idea that active audience members use media content to create meaning, and meaningful experiences, for themselves

media literacy the ability to effectively and efficiently comprehend and utilize mass communication

media multitasking simultaneously consuming many different kinds of media

medium (pl. media) vehicle by which messages are conveyed

metaethics examination of a culture's understanding of its fundamental values

metering Internet use charged "by the byte"; heavier users pay more, more-modest users pay less

microcomputer a very small computer that uses a microprocessor to handle information (also called a **personal computer** or **PC**)

microcinema filmmaking using digital video cameras and desktop digital editing machines

micro-level effects effects of media on individuals

microwave relay audio and video transmitting system in which super-high-frequency signals are sent from land-based point to land-based point

middle-range theories ideas that explain or predict only limited aspects of the mass communication process

minicomputer a relatively large central computer to which users are connected by terminals; not as large as a mainframe computer

modeling in social cognitive theory, learning through imitation and identification

modem a device that translates digital computer information into an analog form so it can be transmitted through telephone lines

montage tying together two separate but related shots in such a way that they take on a new, unified meaning

moral agent in an ethical dilemma, the person making the decision

MP3 file compression software that permits streaming of digital audio and video data

muckraking a form of crusading journalism that primarily used magazines to agitate for change

MUD (multiuser dimension) online text-based interactive game

multimedia advanced sound and image capabilities for microcomputers

multiple points of access ability of a media-literate consumer to access or approach media content from a variety of personally satisfying directions

multiple system operator (MSO) a company owning several different cable television operations

murketing making advertising so pervasive consumers are ignorant of its presence

music licensing company an organization that collects fees based on recorded music users' gross receipts and distributes the money to songwriters and artists

narrowcasting aiming broadcast programming at smaller, more demographically homogeneous audiences

neo-Marxist theory the theory that people are oppressed by those who control the culture, the superstructure, as opposed to the base

network centralized production, distribution, decision-making organization that links affiliates for the purpose of delivering their viewers to advertisers

network neutrality granting equal carriage over phone and cable lines to all websites

neuromarketing research biometric measures (brain waves, facial expressions, eye-tracking, sweating, and heart rate monitoring) used in advertising research

newsbook early weekly British publication that carried ads

newspaper chains businesses that own two or more newspapers

news production research the study of how economic and other influences on the way news is produced distort and bias news coverage toward those in power

news staging re-creation on television news of some event that is believed to have happened or which could have happened

NFC (near-field communication) chip tag embedded in a magazine page that connects readers to advertisers' digital content

niche marketing aiming media content or consumer products at smaller, more demographically homogeneous audiences

nickelodeons the first movie houses; admission was one nickel

Nipkow disc first workable device for generating electrical signals suitable for the transmission of a scene

noise anything that interferes with successful communication

nonlinear TV watching television on our own schedules, not the programmer's

normative ethics generalized theories, rules, and principles of ethical or moral behavior

normative theory an idea that explains how media should ideally operate in a given system of social values

obscenity unprotected expression determined by (1) whether the average person, applying contemporary community standards, would find that the work, taken as a whole, appeals to the prurient interest, (2) whether the work depicts or describes, in a patently offensive way, sexual conduct specifically defined by the applicable state law, and (3) whether the work, taken as a whole, lacks serious literary, artistic, political, or scientific value

observational learning in social cognitive theory, observers can acquire (learn) new behaviors simply by seeing those behaviors performed

off-network broadcast industry term for syndicated content that originally aired on a network

offset lithography late 19th-century advance making possible printing from photographic plates rather than from metal casts

oligopoly a media system whose operation is dominated by a few large companies

ombudsman internal arbiter of performance for media organizations

O&O a broadcasting station that is owned and operated by a network

open source software freely downloaded software

operating policy spells out standards for everyday operations for newspapers and magazines

operating system the software that tells the computer how to work

opinion followers people who receive opinion leaders' interpretations of media content; from **two-step flow theory**

opinion leaders people who initially consume media content, interpret it in light of their own values and beliefs, and then pass it on to opinion followers; from **two-step flow theory**

opt-in/opt-out consumers giving permission to companies to sell personal data, or consumers requesting that companies do not sell personal data

parity products products generally perceived as alike by consumers no matter who makes them

pass-along readership measurement of publication readers who neither subscribe nor buy single copies but who borrow a copy or read one in a doctor's office or library

payola payment made by recording companies to DJs to air their records

paywall making online content available only to those visitors willing to pay

penny press newspapers in the 1830s selling for one penny

performance-based advertising Web advertising where the site is paid only when the consumer takes some specific action

permission marketing advertising that the consumer actively accepts

persistence of vision images our eyes gather are retained by our brains for about 1/24 of a second, producing the appearance of constant motion

personal computer (PC) see **microcomputer**

personal peoplemeter ratings technology; a special remote control with personalized buttons for each viewer in the household

pilot a sample episode of a proposed television program

piracy the illegal recording and sale of copyrighted material

pirate broadcasters unlicensed or otherwise illegally operated broadcast stations

pixel the smallest picture element in an electronic imaging system such as a television or computer screen

platform the means of delivering a specific piece of media content

platform agnostic having no preference in where media content is accessed

platform agnostic publishing digital and hardcopy books available for any and all reading devices

platform rollout opening a movie on only a few screens in the hope that favorable reviews and word-of-mouth publicity will boost interest

playlist predetermined sequence of selected records to be played by a disc jockey

podcasting recording and downloading of audio files stored on servers

policy book delineates standards of operation for local broadcasters

pornography expression calculated solely to supply sexual excitement

premium cable cable television channels offered to viewers for a fee above the cost of their basic subscription

print on demand (POD) publishing method whereby publishers store books digitally for instant printing, binding, and delivery once ordered

prior restraint power of the government to *prevent* publication or broadcast of expression

production values media content's internal language and grammar; its style and quality

product placement the integration, for a fee, of specific branded products into media content

product positioning the practice in advertising of assigning meaning to a product based on who buys the product rather than on the product itself

prosumer a proactive consumer

protocols common communication rules and languages for computers linked to the Internet

pseudo-event event that has no real informational or issue meaning; it exists merely to attract media attention

psychographic segmentation advertisers' appeal to consumer groups of varying lifestyles, attitudes, values, and behavior patterns

P2P peer-to-peer software that permits direct Internet-based communication or collaboration between two or more personal computers while bypassing centralized servers

public in PR, any group of people with a stake in an organization, issue, or idea

public domain in copyright law, the use of material without permission once the copyright expires

public service remit limits on advertising and other public service requirements imposed on Britain's commercial broadcasters in exchange for the right to broadcast

puffery the little lie or exaggeration that makes advertising more entertaining than it might otherwise be

pulp novels see **dime novels**

put agreement between a television producer and network that guarantees that the network will order at least a pilot or pay a penalty

QR (quick response) code small, black-and-white squares that appear on many media surfaces that direct mobile device users to a specific website

radio frequency identification (RFID) chip grain-of-sand–sized microchip and antenna embedded in consumer products that transmit a radio signal

rating percentage of a market's total population that is reached by a piece of broadcast programming

readers' representative media outlet employee who regularly responds to outside criticism

recall testing ad research technique in which consumers are asked to identify which ads are most easily remembered

recent catalogue albums in record retailing, albums out for 15 months to three years

recognition tests ad research technique in which people who have seen a given publication are asked whether they remember seeing a given ad

reinforcement theory Joseph Klapper's idea that if media have any impact at all, it is in the direction of reinforcement

remainders unsold copies of books returned to the publisher by bookstores to be sold at great discount

retainer in advertising, an agreed-upon amount of money a client pays an ad agency for a specific series of services

retransmission fee money a local cable operation pays to a broadcast station to carry its signal

return on investment (ROI) an accountability-based measure of advertising success

reverse compensation fee paid by a local broadcast station for the right to be a network's affiliate

revolutionary concept normative theory describing a system where media are used in the service of revolution

rich media sophisticated, interactive Web advertising, usually employing sound and video

ritual perspective the view of media as central to the representation of shared beliefs and culture

RSS (really simple syndication) aggregators allowing Web users to create their own content assembled from the Internet's limitless supply of material

satellite-delivered media tour spokespeople can be simultaneously interviewed by a worldwide audience hooked to the interviewee by telephone

search engines Web- or Net-search software providing on-screen menus

search marketing advertising sold next to or in search results produced by users' keyword searches

secondary service a radio station's second, or nonprimary, format

selective attention see **selective exposure**

selective exposure the idea that people expose themselves to or attend to those messages that are consistent with their pre-existing attitudes and beliefs

selective perception the idea that people interpret messages in a manner consistent with their preexisting attitudes and beliefs

selective processes people expose themselves to, remember best and longest, and reinterpret messages that are consistent with their preexisting attitudes and beliefs

selective retention assumes that people remember best and longest those messages that are consistent with their existing attitudes and beliefs

self-righting principle John Milton's articulation of libertarianism

share the percentage of people listening to radio or of homes using television tuned in to a given piece of programming

shield laws legislation that expressly protects reporters' rights to maintain sources' confidentiality in courts of law

shopbills attractive, artful business cards used by early British tradespeople to promote themselves

shortwave radio radio signals transmitted at high frequencies that can travel great distances by skipping off the ionosphere

signs in social construction of reality, things that have subjective meaning

siquis pinup want ads common in Europe before and in early days of newspapers

skip ability of radio waves to reflect off the ionosphere

sky waves radio waves that are skipped off the ionosphere

slander oral or spoken defamation of a person's character (typically applied to broadcasting)

smart mobs see **flash mobs**

smartphone a cell phone containing an advanced operating system such as Apple's iOS or Android.

social cognitive theory idea that people learn through observation

social construction of reality theory for explaining how cultures construct and maintain their realities using signs and symbols; argues that people learn to behave in their social world through interaction with it

social networking sites Websites that function as online communities of users

social responsibility theory (or **model**) normative theory or model asserting that media must remain free of government control but, in exchange, must serve the public

soft news sensational stories that do not serve the democratic function of journalism

spam unsolicited commercial e-mail

spectrum scarcity broadcast spectrum space is limited, so not everyone who wants to broadcast can; those who are granted licenses must accept regulation

spin in PR, outright lying to hide what really happened

split runs special versions of a given issue of a magazine in which editorial content and ads vary according to some specific demographic or regional grouping

sponsored content online articles paid for by advertisers

sponsorships in Web advertising, pages "brought to you by," typically including ad placements, advertorials, and other co-branded sections

spot commercial sales in broadcasting, selling individual advertising spots on a given program to a wide variety of advertisers

spyware identifying code placed on a computer by a website without permission or notification

Standards and Practices Department the internal content review operation of a television network

stereotyping application of a standardized image or conception applied to members of certain groups, usually based on limited information

sticky an attribute of a website; indicates its ability to hold the attention of a user

stimulation model of media violence; viewing mediated violence can increase the likelihood of subsequent aggressive behavior

streaming the simultaneous downloading and accessing (playing) of digital audio or video data

stripping broadcasting a syndicated television show at the same time five nights a week

subscription TV early experiments with over-the-air pay television

subsidiary rights the sale of a book, its contents, even its characters to outside interests, such as filmmakers

surrogate service in international broadcasting, an operation established by one country to substitute for another's own domestic service

sweeps periods special television ratings times in February, May, July, and November in which diaries are distributed to thousands of sample households in selected markets

symbolic interaction the idea that people give meaning to symbols and then those symbols control people's behavior in their presence

symbols in social construction of reality, things that have objective meaning

syndication sale of radio or television content to stations on a market-by-market basis

synergy the use by media conglomerates of as many channels of delivery as possible for similar content

targeting aiming media content or consumer products at smaller, more specific audiences

taste publics groups of people or audiences bound by little more than their interest in a given form of media content

technological determinism the idea that machines and their development drive economic and cultural change

technology gap the widening disparity between communication technology haves and have-nots

telecommunications service legal designation rendering a telecommunication service provider a common carrier, required to carry the messages of others and with no power to restrict them

tentpole an expensive blockbuster around which a studio plans its other releases

terminals user workstations that are connected to larger centralized computers

terrestrial digital radio land-based digital radio relying on digital compression technology to simultaneously transmit analog and one or more digital signals using existing spectrum space

theatrical films movies produced primarily for initial exhibition on theater screens

third-party publishers companies that create video games for existing systems

third-person effect the common attitude that others are influenced by media messages, but we are not

360 marketing see **ambient advertising**

tiers groupings of channels made available by a cable or satellite provider to subscribers at varying prices

time-shifting taping a show on a VCR for later viewing

Total Audience Measurement Index (TAMi) measure of viewing of a single television episode across all platforms

trade books hard- or softcover books including fiction and most nonfiction and cookbooks, biographies, art books, coffee-table books, and how-to books

traffic cop analogy in broadcast regulation, the idea that the FCC, as a traffic cop, has the right to control not only the flow of broadcast traffic but its composition as well

transmissional perspective the view of media as senders of information for the purpose of control

transparentists PR professionals calling for full disclosure of their practices—transparency

trustee model in broadcast regulation, the idea that broadcasters serve as the public's trustees or fiduciaries

two-step flow theory the idea that media's influence on people's behavior is limited by opinion leaders—people who initially consume media content, interpret it in light of their own values and beliefs, and then pass it on to opinion followers, who have less frequent contact with media

typification schemes in social construction of reality, collections of meanings people have assigned to some phenomenon or situation

unique selling proposition (USP) the aspect of an advertised product that sets it apart from other brands in the same product category

URL (uniform resource locator) the designation of each file or directory on the host computer connected to the Internet

uses and gratifications approach the idea that media don't do things *to* people; people do things *with* media

VALS advertisers' psychographic segmentation strategy that classifies consumers according to values and lifestyles

value-compensation program ad agency/brand agreement that payment of the agency's fees is predicated on meeting pre-established goals

vast wasteland expression coined by FCC chair Newton Minow in 1961 to describe television content

vertical integration a system in which studios produced their own films, distributed them through their own outlets, and exhibited them in their own theaters

vicarious reinforcement in social cognitive theory, the observation of reinforcement operates in the same manner as actual reinforcement

video game a game involving action taking place interactively on-screen

video news release (VNR) preproduced report about a client or its product that is distributed free of charge to television stations

video-on-demand (VOD) service allowing television viewers to access pay-per-view movies and other content that can be watched whenever they want

viral marketing PR strategy that relies on targeting specific Internet users with a given communication and relying on them to spread the word

virtual worlds games se **massively multiplayer online role-playing games**

Voice over Internet Protocol (VoIP) phone calls transferred in digital packets over the Internet rather than on circuit-switched telephone wires

WAN (wide area network) network that connects several LANs in different locations

Web radio the delivery of "radio" over the Internet directly to individual listeners

webisode Web-only television show

Western concept of media systems; normative theory that combines libertarianism's freedom with social responsibility's demand for public service and, where necessary, regulation

Wi-Fi wireless Internet

willing suspension of disbelief audience practice of willingly accepting the content before them as real

wire services news-gathering organizations that provide content to members

World Wide Web a tool that serves as a means of accessing files on computers connected via the Internet

yellow journalism early 20th-century journalism emphasizing sensational sex, crime, and disaster news

zero-TV homes homes with sets but receive neither over-the-air nor cable/satellite television

zipping fast-forwarding through taped commercials on a VCR

zonecasting technology allowing radio stations to deliver different commercials to specific neighborhoods

zoned editions suburban or regional versions of metropolitan newspapers

zoopraxiscope early machine for projecting slides onto a distant surface

References

Adams, M. (1996). The race for radiotelephone: 1900–1920. *AWA Review, 10,* 78–119.

Advertising mediums that most influence product purchases. (2011, April). *Editor & Publisher,* p. 18.

AFRTS. (2012). Mission statement. Online: http://afrts.dodmedia.osd.mil/.

Agency report 2013. (2013, April 9). *Advertising Age,* pp. 32–38.

Aguilar, R. (2012, February 1). What does the activism surrounding SOPA reveal about the future of online organizing? *Truthout.* Online: http://www.truth-out.org/what-does-activism-surrounding-sopa-reveal-about-future-online-organizing/1327952848.

Albiniak, P. (1999, May 3). Media: Littleton's latest suspect. *Broadcasting & Cable,* pp. 6–15.

Albiniak, P. (2002, April 29). Railing—but no derailing. *Broadcasting & Cable,* p. 7.

Alford, H. (2012, April 22). Watch every click you make. *New York Times,* p. ST2.

Allport, G. W., & Postman, L. J. (1945). The basic psychology of rumor. *Transactions of the New York Academy of Sciences, 8,* 61–81.

Alpert, J., & Hajaj, N. (2008, July 25). We knew the Web was big. *Google Blog.* Online: http://googleblog.blogspot.com/2008/07/we-knew-web-was-big.html.

Alterman, E. (2005, March 14). The pajama game. *The Nation,* p. 10.

Alterman, E. (2008, February 24). The news from Quinn-Broderville. *The Nation,* pp. 11–14.

Ambrose, J. (2007, January 12). Newspapers going, but not yet gone. *Providence Journal,* p. B5.

Anderson, A., Guskin, E., & Rosenstiel, T. (2012). Alternative weeklies: At long last, a move toward digital. *State of the news media 2012.* Online: http://stateofthemedia.org/2012/native-american-news-media/alternative-weeklies-at-long-last-a-move-toward-digital/.

Anderson, C. A., Berkowitz, L., Donnerstein, E., Huesmann, L. R., Johnson, J. D., Linz, D., et al. (2003). The influence of media violence on youth. *Psychological Science in the Public Interest, 4,* 81–110.

Anderson, M. (2011, December 13). Lowe's stands by its decision to pull ads from TV show. *Providence Journal,* p. B8.

Anderson, M. K. (2000, May/June). When copyright goes wrong. *Extra!,* p. 25.

Anderson, S. (2012, April 8). Just one more game. *New York Times Magazine,* pp. 28–33, 55.

Andrews, L. (2012, February 5). Facebook is using you. *New York Times,* p. SR7.

Andronikidis, A. I., & Lambrianidou, M. (2010). Children's understanding of television advertising: A grounded theory approach, *Psychology and Marketing, 27,* 299–332.

Angell, R. (2002, March 11). Read all about it. *The New Yorker,* pp. 27–28.

Arango, T., & Carter, B. (2009, November 21). An unsteady future for broadcast. *New York Times,* p. B1.

Arato, A., & Gebhardt, E. (1978). *The essential Frankfurt School reader.* New York: Urizen Books.

Arbitron. (2012). Radio station formats. Online: http://www.arbitron.com/home/formats.htm.

Associated Press. (2010, March). *A new model for communication: Studying the deep structure of advertising and news consumption.* Baltimore: Carton Donofrio Partners.

Associated Press et al. v. United States, 326 U.S. 1, 89 L. Ed. 2013, 65 S. Ct. 1416 (1945).

Association of Magazine Media. (2011, November 21). MAA releases benchmark magazine mobile media study. Online: http://magazine.org/association/press/mpa_press_releases/mag-mobile-reader-study.aspx.

Association of Magazine Media. (2012a). Magazine media factbook 2011–2012. Online: http://www.magazine.org/advertising/magazine-media-factbook/keyfacts.html.

Association of Magazine Media. (2012b, January 10). 2011 overall magazine advertising revenue flat. Online: http://www.magazine.org/advertising/revenue/by_ad_category/pib-4q-2011.aspx.

Atkinson, C. (2004, September 27). Press group attacks magazine product placement. *AdAge.com.* Online: http://www.adage.com/news.cms?newsid=41597.

The Atlantic. (2013, February). Sponsored content guidelines. Online: http://cdn.theatlantic.com/static/front/docs/ads/TheAtlanticAdvertisingGuidelines.pdf.

Attenberg, J. (2012, March 6). Jonathan Franzen comments on Twitter. *Whatever-Whatever.net.* Online: http://www.whatever-whenever.net/blog/2012/03/delilloness/.

Audit Bureau of Circulations. (2011, November 16). Going mobile: How publishers are maturing and monetizing their offerings. Online: http://www.accessabc.com/gomobile/.

Auletta, K. (2001, December 10). Battle stations. *The New Yorker,* pp. 60–67.

Auletta, K. (2005, March 28). The new pitch. *The New Yorker,* pp. 34–39.

Auletta, K. (2012, June 25). Paper trail. *New Yorker,* pp. 36–41.

Ault, S. (2009, October 16). Studios adjust to digital distribution. *Variety.* Online: http://www.variety.com/article /VR1118010062.html?categoryid=3766&cs=1.

Avlon, J. (2012, March 10). Rush Limbaugh scandal proves contagious for talk-radio advertisers. *Daily Beast.* Online: http://www.thedailybeast.com/articles/2012/03/10 /rush-limbaugh-scandal-proves-contagious-for-talk-radio -advertisers.html.

Baar, A. (2011, February 28). Survey finds phones revolutionize video games. *MediaPost.* Online: http://www.mediapost .com/publications/article/145761/survey-finds-phones -revolutionize-video-games.html.

Baar, A. (2012, January 21). Video rental stores on "life support." *MediaPost.* Online: http://www.mediapost .com/publications/article/166190/video-rental -stores-on-life-support.html?print.

Bagdikian, B. (2004, March). Print will survive. *Editor & Publisher,* p. 70.

Bal, S. (2004, July 9). India ink. *Entertainment Weekly,* p. 19.

Ball, S., & Bennett, J. (2010, January 15). Heidi Montag, Version 3.0. *Newsweek.* Online: http://www.newsweek.com /id/231093.

Ball, S., & Bogatz, G. A. (1970). *The first year of* Sesame Street: *An evaluation.* Princeton, NJ: Educational Testing Service.

Banfield, A. (2003, April 29). MSNBC's Banfield slams war coverage. *AlterNet.* Online: http://www.alternet.org/print .html?storyid=15778.

Banning bad news in Iraq. (2004, August 10). *New York Times,* p. A20.

Baran, S. J., Chase, L. J., & Courtright, J. A. (1979). *The Waltons:* Television as a facilitator of prosocial behavior. *Journal of Broadcasting, 23,* 277–284.

Baran, S. J., & Davis, D. K. (2012). *Mass communication theory: Foundations, ferment and future* (6th ed.). Boston: Wadsworth Cengage.

Barnes, B. (2013, February 12). Tiny price increase for movie tickets. *New York Times,* p. C4.

Barboza, D. (2012, April 4). In China press, best coverage cash can buy. *New York Times,* p. 1.

Barlow, J. P. (1996). Selling wine without bottles: The economy of mind on the global Net. In L. H. Leeson (Ed.), *Clicking in: Hot links to a digital culture.* Seattle, WA: Bay Press.

Barnes, B. (2008, March 23). At cineplexes, sports, opera, maybe a movie. *New York Times,* pp. A1, A15.

Barnouw, E. (1966). *A tower in Babel: A history of broadcasting in the United States to 1933.* New York: Oxford University Press.

Barnouw, E. (1990). *Tube of plenty: The evolution of American television.* New York: Oxford University Press.

Baron, D. (2011, October 10). Resistance may be futile: Are there alternatives to global English. *OUPBlog.* Online: http://blog.oup.com/2011/10/global-english/.

Barron, G., & Chowdhury, P. (2012, March 7). The consequences of digital ad bombardment. *Upstream Systems.* Online: http://cache.upstreamsystems.com /wp-content/uploads/pdf/YouGov2012n.pdf.

Barstow, D. (2006, April 6). Report faults video reports shown as news. *New York Times,* p. A17.

Bart, P. (2000, January 3–9). The big media blur. *Variety,* pp. 4, 95.

Bart, P. (2007, June 11–17). And now, a scene from our sponsor. *Variety,* pp. 4, 58.

Barton, L. (2002, July 30). Cereal offenders. *Guardian Education,* pp. 2–3.

Bazelon, E. (2011, October 16). The young and the friended. *New York Times Magazine,* pp. 15–16.

Bennett, D. (2004, February). Our mongrel planet. *American Prospect,* pp. 62–63.

Bennett, W. L. (1988). *News: The politics of illusion.* New York: Longman.

Berger, P. L., & Luckmann, T. (1966). *The social construction of reality: A treatise in the sociology of knowledge.* Garden City, NY: Doubleday.

Berkman, H. W., & Gilson, C. (1987). *Advertising: Concepts and strategies.* New York: Random House.

Bernays, E. L. (1986). *The later years: Public relations insights, 1956–1988.* Rhinebeck, NY: H & M.

Berners-Lee, T., & Fischetti, M. (1999). *Weaving the Web: The original design and ultimate destiny of the World Wide Web by its inventor.* New York: HarperCollins.

Bing, J. (2006, January 2–8). Auds: A many-splintered thing. *Variety,* pp. 1, 38–39.

Bittner, J. R. (1994). *Law and regulation of electronic media.* Englewood Cliffs, NJ: Prentice Hall.

BitTorrent. (2012, January 9). Bittorrent and μTorrent software surpass 150 million user milestone; announce new consumer electronics partnerships. Online: http://www.bittorrent.com /intl/es/company/about/ces_2012_150m_users.

Black, J. (2001). Hardening of the articles: An ethicist looks at propaganda in today's news. *Ethics in Journalism, 4,* 15–36.

Black, J., & Barney, R. D. (1985/86). The case against mass media codes of ethics. *Journal of Mass Media Ethics, 1,* 27–36.

Black, J., & Whitney, F. C. (1983). *Introduction to mass communications.* Dubuque, IA: William C. Brown.

Blow, C. M. (2009, June 27). The purient trap. *New York Times,* p. A19.

Blumenauer, E. (2009, November 15). My near death panel experience. *New York Times,* p. WK12.

Blumler, J. G., & Gurevitch, M. (1975). Towards a comparative framework for political communication research. In S. H. Chaffee (Ed.), *Political communication. Issues and strategies for research.* Beverly Hills, CA: Sage.

Bogle, D. (1989). *Toms, coons, mulattos, mammies, & bucks: An interpretive history of Blacks in American films.* New York: Continuum.

Bosman, J. (2010, November 10). Times will rank e-book best sellers. *New York Times,* p. C3.

Boss, S. (2007, May 13). The greatest mystery: Making a best seller. *New York Times,* pp. 3.1, 3.6.

Boulton, C. (2010, March 20). YouTube brand may be an advantage in Viacom copyright case. *eWeek.* Online: http://www.eweek.com/c/a/Search-EnginesYouTube -Brand-May-Be-an-Advantage-in-Viacom-Copyright -Case-572764/.

Boyce, J. C. (2010, September 7). Americans don't burn books. *Salon.* Online: http://www.huffingtonpost.com/james -boyce/americans-dont-burn-books_1_b_707187.html.

Boylan, J. G. (2010, January 11/18). End of the century. *The Nation,* pp. 31–34.

Bradbury, R. (1981). *Fahrenheit 451.* New York: Ballantine. (Originally published in 1953.)

Bragman, H. (2009, January 19). A cynical world could use a little PR. *Broadcasting & Cable,* p. 28.

Braverman, S. (2010, August 26). Would Americans rather be younger, thinner, richer or smarter? *Harris Poll.* Online: http://www.harrisinteractive.com/vault/HI-Harris-Poll -Adweek-Would-You-Rather-2010-08-26.pdf.

Bray, H. (2006, January 28). Google China censorship fuels calls for US boycott. *Boston Globe,* p. A10.

Bridges v. California, 314 U.S. 252 (1941).

Brisbane, A. S. (2012, January 12). Should the *Times* be a truth vigilante? *New York Times.* Online: http://publiceditor.blogs .nytimes.com/2012/01/12/should-the-times-be-a-truth -vigilante/?scp=1&sq=Should%20the%20Times%20be%20 a%20Truth%20Vigilante&st=cse.

Brodesser-Akner, C. (2008, January 7). How Ford snared starring role in *Knight Rider* TV movie, *Advertising Age,* p. 22.

Brodsky, J. (1987, December 8). *Nobel lecture.* Online: http:// nobelprize.org/nobel_prizes/literature/laureates/1987 /brodsky-lecture-e.html.

Brown v. Entertainment Merchants Association, U. S. No. 08-1448 (2011).

Brubach, H. (2007, April 15). Starved to perfection. *New York Times Style Magazine,* p. 42.

Bunk, B. (2012, January 5). What were the top shows in France in 2011? *Spoilertv.com.* Online: http://www.spoilertv. com/2012/01/what-were-top-shows-in-france-in-2011 .html.

Burnham, V. (2001). *Supercade: A visual history of the videogame age 1971–1984.* Cambridge: MIT Press.

Burton, B. (2005, November 15). Fake news: It's the PR industry against the rest of us. Online: http://www.prwatch.org /node/4174/print.

Busbee, J. (2011, August 11). Don't believe what you see: More staged news. *Yahoo Sports.* Online: http://www .redicecreations.com/article.php?id=16299.

Butler, B. (2011, July 20). Young guns. *Maynard Institute for Journalism Education.* Online: http://mije.org/health /young-guns.

Byrne, D. (2008a, January). The fall and rise of music. *Wired,* pp. 124–129.

Byrne, D. (2008b, January). The Radiohead revolution. *Wired,* pp. 120–123.

A candid conversation with the high priest of popcult and metaphysician of media. (1969, March). *Playboy,* pp. 53–74, 158.

Carey, J. W. (1975). A cultural approach to communication. *Communication, 2,* 1–22.

Carey, J. W. (1989). *Communication as culture.* Boston: Unwin Hyman.

Carmichael, M. (2011, November 14). New necessities: What consumers can't live without. *Advertising Age,* pp. 6, 8.

Carnevale, D. (2005, December 9). Books when you want them. *Chronicle of Higher Education,* p. A27.

Carr, D. (2004, August 2). Publish till you drop. *New York Times,* p. C1.

Carr, D. (2011, January 9). Media savant. *New York Times Book Review,* pp. 9–10.

Carr, D. (2013, June 24). The other Snowden drama: Impugning the messenger. *New York Times.* Online: http://www .nytimes.com/2013/06/25/business/media/the-other -snowden-drama-impugning-the-messenger.html?_r=0.

CBS v. Democratic National Committee, 412 U.S. 94 (1973).

Center on Alcohol Marketing and Youth. (2012). Fact sheets: Underage drinking in the United States. Online: http:// camy.org.

Center for Science in the Public Interest. (2002). Booze news. Online: http://www.cspinet.org/booze/alcad.htm.

Chandler v. Florida, 449 U.S. 560 (1981).

Chang, R. (2009b, July 13). Virtual goods give brands a new way to play in gaming. *Advertising Age,* p. 12.

Chin, F. (1978). *Cable television: A comprehensive bibliography.* New York: IFI/Plenum.

Chmielewski, D. C. (2012, March 20). 100 million TVs will be Internet-connected by 2016. *Los Angeles Times.* Online: http://latimesblogs.latimes.com/entertainmentnewsb uzz/2012/03/100-million-tvs-will-be-internet-connected -by-2016.html.

Chozick, A. & Rohwedder, C. (2011, March 18). The ultimate reality show. *Wall Street Journal.* Online: http://online.wsj .com/article/SB100014240527487038997045762044434334 87336.html?mod=wsj_share_twitter.

CIA world factbook. (2008). China. Online: https://www.cia .gov/library/publications/the-world-factbook.

Cieply, M. (2010, January 27). He doth surpass himself; *Avatar* outperforms *Titanic. New York Times,* p. C1.

Cisco Systems. (2013, May 29). Cisco visual networking index: Forecast and methodology, 2012–2017. *Cisco.com.* Online: http://www.cisco.com/en/US/solutions/collateral/ns341 /ns525/ns537/ns705/ns827/white_paper_c11-481360 _ns827_Networking_Solutions_White_Paper.html.

CJR Comment. (2003, September/October). 9/11/03. *Columbia Journalism Review,* p. 7.

Coates, D. (2009, November 13). Ad infinitum. *MediaPost.* Online: http://www.mediapost.com/publications/?art _aid=117174&fa=Articles.showArticle.

Coen, R., & Hart, P. (2002, April). Last media ownership limits threatened by judicial action. *Extra! Update,* p. 4.

Condé Nast says it expects to introduce new print products to grow retail sales. (2010, March 4). *Supermarket News.* Online: http://supermarketnews. com/news/conde_nast_0304/.

Consumer Electronics Association. (2008, November 24). How Americans plan to make do. *Broadcasting & Cable,* p. 18.

Cook, J. (2010, March 5). How ABC News' Brian Ross staged his Toyota death ride. *Gawker.* Online: http://gawker .com/5486666/how-abc-news-brian-ross-staged-his-toyota -death-ride.

Cook, T. D., Appleton, H., Conner, R. F., Shaffer, A., Tamkin, G., & Weber, S. J. (1975). *Sesame Street revisited.* New York: Russell Sage Foundation.

Copps, M. J. (2008, April 7). Not your father's FCC. *The Nation,* p. 18.

Copps, M. J. (2011, June 9). Statement of Commissioner Michael J. Copps on release of FCC staff report "The Technology and Information Needs of Communities." *Federal Communications Commission.* Online: http://www.fcc.gov/document /copps-information-needs-communities-report.

Cox, A. M. (2005, March). Howard Stern and the satellite wars. *Wired,* pp. 99–101, 135.

Cox, C. (1999, September/October). Prime-time activism. *Utne Reader,* pp. 20–22.

Cox, C. (2000, July/August). Plugged into protest? *Utne Reader,* pp. 14–15.

Crary, D. (2011, May 8). Ad reaction creates debate about gender stereotypes for boys. *Providence Journal,* p. B4.

Creamer, M. (2007, April 2). Caught in the clutter crossfire: Your Brand. *Advertising Age,* pp. 1, 35.

The crisis in publishing. (2003, February 21). *The Week,* p. 22.

Cuban knows what's wrong with newspapers. (2006, November 20). *Advertising Age,* p. 10.

Czitrom, D. J. (2007). Twenty-five years later. *Critical Studies in Media Communication,* 24, 481–485.

D'angelo, F. (2009, October 26). Happy birthday, digital advertising! *Advertising Age.* Online: http://adage.com /digitalnext/article?article_id=139964.

Daniels, E. A. (2009). Sex objects, athletes, and sexy athletes: How media representations of women athletes can impact adolescent girls and college women. *Journal of Adolescent Research,* 24, 399–422.

Data Page. (2011a, October). Percentage of moms whose children used devices by age 2. *Editor & Publisher,* p. 18.

Data Page. (2011b, October). Reasons for local newspaper subscriptions. *Editor & Publisher,* p. 18.

Data Page. (2011c, April). How gen Y access newspaper content. *Editor & Publisher,* p. 18.

Davis, R. E. (1976). *Response to innovation: A study of popular argument about new mass media.* New York: Arno Press.

Day, L. A. (2006). *Ethics in media communications: Cases and controversies* (6th ed.). Belmont, CA: Wadsworth.

DeFleur, M. L., & Ball-Rokeach, S. (1975). *Theories of mass communication* (3rd ed.). New York: David McKay.

deGraf, B. (2004, May 5). Smart mobs vs. Amway. *AlterNet.* Online: http://www.alternet.org/print.html?storyid=18605.

delia Cava, M. R. (2012, March 16–18). Books, CDs, photos, going, going . . . *USA Today,* pp. 1A–2A.

Dellamere, D. (2009, August 19). Lessons from the Birmingham Eccentric. *Columbia Journalism Review.* Online: http:// www.cjr.org/behind_the_news/lessons_from_the _birmingham_ec.php?page=all.

Delo, C. (2012, October 4). Facebook hits billionth user, reveals first major ad from global agency of record. *Advertising Age.* Online: http://adage.com/article/digital/facebook-serves-1 -billion-makes-a-video-ad-celebrate/237571/.

Deloitte. (2011, February 1). "State of the media democracy" survey: TV industry embraces the Internet and prospers. Online: http://www.deloitte.com/us/mediademocracy.

DeMaria, R., & Wilson, J. L. (2004). *High score: The illustrated history of electronic games.* New York: McGraw-Hill.

Depillis, L. (2013, June 7). Google's latest product isn't free: It's called 'The Internship.' *New Republic.* Online: http://www .newrepublic.com/article/113405/internship-movie-review -google-wants-be-loved#.

Dibbell, J. (2007, June 17). The life of the Chinese gold farmer. *New York Times Magazine,* pp. 36–41.

Digital Fast Facts. (2012, February 27). *Advertising Age,* insert.

Direct Marketing Association. (2011). *2011 statistical factbook.* New York: Author.

Dougherty, H. (2012, February 2). 10 key statistics about Facebook. *Hitwise.com.* Online: http://weblogs.hitwise .com/heather-dougherty/2012/02/10_key_statistics_about _facebo_1.html.

Dove Research. (2011). *The real truth about beauty: Revisited.* Online: http://www.dove.us/social-mission/self-esteem -statistics.aspx.

Drucker, P. E. (1999, October). Beyond the information revolution. *Atlantic Monthly,* pp. 47–57.

Duggan, M., & Brenner, J. (2013, February 14). The demographics of social media users—2012. *Pew Internet & American Life Project.* Online: http://www.pewinternet.org /Reports/2013/Social-media-users/The-State-of-Social -Media-Users.aspx.

Dumenco, S. (2006, January 16). Oh please, a blogger is just a writer with a cooler name. *Advertising Age,* p. 18.

Dumenco, S. (2008, June 23). Th-th-th-that's all, folks! No more talk of media end-times. *Advertising Age,* p. 48.

Dumenco, S. (2010, September 13). In non-loving memory: RIP, press releases (1906–2010)—long live the Tweet. *Advertising Age,* p. 28.

Dumenco, S. (2011, December 4). Even the FTC can't stop Facebook's mad rush toward total information awareness. *Advertising Age.* Online: http://adage.com/article/the-media -guy/ftc-stop-facebook-s-rush-total-info-awareness/231337/.

Dunham, W. (2009, January 7). Mississippi has highest teen birth rate. *Reuters.* Online: http://www.reuters.com/article /idUSTRE50679220090107.

E&P Staff. (2010, July 2). L. A. county supervisors to 'L.A. Times': Knock off the fake ad sections! *Editor & Publisher.* Online: http://www.editorandpublisher.com/ Headlines/l-a-county-supervisors-to-l-a-times-knock-off -the-fake-ad-sections-61888-.aspx.

E-book sales now outstrip print books, says Amazon. (2011, May 29). *Providence Journal,* p. F4.

E-books outsell paper books on Barnes & Noble online store. (2010, December 30). *Huffington Post.* Online: http://www .huffingtonpost.com/2010/12/30/ebooks-paper-books -barnes-noble-nook_n_802835.html.

Ebenkamp, B. (2009, August 1). The monetization of Mimi: Mariah CD to have ads. *Billboard.* Online: http://www .billboard.biz/bbbiz/content_display/industry /e3i8b177543696059c9f49d0a5a16866ba4.

Eddy, M. (2011, October 26). Austrian law student takes on Facebook over possible data privacy violations in Europe. *Newsday.* Online: http://www.newsday.com/news /austrian-student-takes-on-facebook-over-privacy -1.3274291.

Edison not "the father of sound"? (2008, March 28). *Providence Journal,* p. A5.

Edison Research. (2011). The infinite dial: Navigating digital platforms. Online: http://www.edisonresearch.com /Infinite_Dial_2011.pdf.

Edmonds, R. (2013a, May 7). Newspapers: Stabilizing, but still threatened. *The State of the News Media 2013*. Online: http://stateofthemedia.org/2013/newspapers-stabilizing -but-still-threatened/.

Edmonds, R. (2013b, January 2). For newspaper stocks, 2012 was a surprisingly good year. *Poynter.org*. Online: http:// www.poynter.org/latest-news/business-news/the-biz -blog/199403/for-newspaper-stocks-2012-was-a -surprisingly-good-year/.

Edmonds, R., Guskin, E., & Rosenstiel, T. (2011). Newspapers: Missed the 2010 media rally. *State of the news media 2011*. Online: http://stateofthemedia.org/2011/newspapers-essay/.

Edmonds, R., Guskin, E., Rosenstiel, T., & Mitchell, A. (2012). Newspapers: Building digital revenues proves painfully slow. *State of the news media 2012*. Online: http:// stateofthemedia.org/2012/newspapers-building-digital -revenues-proves-painfully-slow/.

Eggerton, J. (2007, November 12). Net neutrality back in spotlight. *Broadcasting & Cable*, pp. 19–23.

Eggerton, J. (2009, May 14). Copps pushes localism, non-discrimination principle. *Broadcasting & Cable*. Online: http://www.broadcastingcable.com/article/232512-Copps _Pushes_Localism_Non_Discrimination_Principle.php.

Electronic Frontier Foundation. (2012, March). Stop the Internet blacklist bills. Online: https://wfc2.wiredforchange .com/o/9042/p/dia/action/public/?action_KEY=8173.

Elias, P. (2010, December 27). Spam fighter brings home the bacon. *Providence Journal*, p. B2.

Ellis, J. (2012, December 11). Young-adult readers may have abandoned print, but they'll take news in their pockets. *NiemanLab.org*. Online: http://www.niemanlab.org/2012 /12/young-adult-readers-may-have-abandoned -print-but-theyll-take-news-in-their-pockets/.

eMarketer Staff. (2010, January 27). Boomers log some serious TV time. *Adweek*. Online: http://www.adweek .com/aw/content_display/news/media/ e3i888f5f58648771050980256a519cf4cb.

Entertainment Software Association. (2013). Essential facts. Online: http://www.theesa.com/facts/pdfs/ESA_EF _2013.pdf.

Epstein, Z. (2012, January 16). Video game sales fall 21% in December, down 8% for full-year 2011. *BGR.com*. Online: http://www.bgr.com/2012/01/16/video-game-sales-fall-21 -in-december-down-8-for-full-year-2011/.

Erard, M. (2004, July 1). In these games, the points are all political. *New York Times*, p. G1.

Estes v. State of Texas, 381 U.S. 532 (1965).

Ethnic Buying Power. (2011, December). *Television Advertising Bureau*. Online: http://www.tvb.org/media/file/TV_Basics.pdf.

Ewen, S. (2000). Memoirs of a commodity fetishist. *Mass Communication & Society*, 3, 439–452.

"Facebook Generation" faces identity crisis. (2008, July 4). *Medical News Today*. Online: http://www .medicalnewstoday.com/releases/113878.php.

Factsheet: The U. S. Media Universe. (2011, January 5). *Nielsen Wire*. Online: Nielsen Wire http://blog.nielsen.com /nielsenwire/online_mobile/factsheet-the-u-s-media -universe/.

Fagbire, O. J. (2007, July 17). Product placement just keeping it real claims Michael Bay. *Product Placement News*. Online: http://www.product-placement.biz/200707172269/News /Product-Placement/product-placement-just-keeping-it -real-claims-michael-bay.html.

Fajen, S. (2008, July 7). The agency model is bent but not broken. *Advertising Age*, p. 17.

Falk, W. (2005, November 29). The trouble with newspapers. *Providence Journal*, p. B7.

Fallows, J. (2010, June). How to save the news. *Atlantic*, pp. 44–56.

Farago, P. (2013, January 2). Holiday 2012 delivers historical worldwide app downloads. *Flurry Blog*. Online: http://blog .flurry.com/bid/92809/Holiday-2012-Delivers-Historical -Worldwide-App-Downloads.

Farhi, P. (2005, June/July). Under siege. *American Journalism Review*, pp. 26–31.

Farhi, P. (2009, May 17). Click, change. *Washington Post*, p. E1.

Farhi, P. (2011a, March 29). On NBC, the missing story about parent company General Electric. *Washington Post*. Online: http://www.washingtonpost.com/lifestyle/style/on-nbc -the-missing-story-about-parent-company-general -electric/2011/03/29/AFpRYJyB_story.html.

Farhi, P. (2011b, Winter). Speak no evil. *American Journalism Review*, pp. 22–27.

Farhi, P. (2012, January 3). FCC seeks to change regulation of corporate interests disclosure on TV news. *Washington Post*. Online: http://www.washingtonpost.com/lifestyle /style/fcc-seeks-to-change-regulation-of-corporate interests-disclosures-on-tv-news/2012/01/03 /gIQAEhQBZP_story.html.

Faules, D. F., & Alexander, D. C. (1978). *Communication and social behavior: A symbolic interaction perspective*. Reading, MA: Addison-Wesley.

Feldman, G. (2001, February 12). Publishers caught in a Web. *The Nation*, pp. 35–36.

Federal Communications Commission. (2012). Low power broadcast radio stations. Online: http://www.fcc.gov /guides/low-power-broadcast-radio-stations.

Finally, 21st century phone service. (2004, January 6). *Business Week*. Online: http://www.businessweek.com/technology /content/jan2004/tc2004016.

Fischer, M. (2011, October 19). Your phone knows more about you than your mom. *Advertising Age*. Online: http://adage .com/article/digitalnext/phone-mom/230507/.

Fitzgerald, M. (1999, October 30). Robert Sengstake Abbott. *Editor & Publisher*, p. 18.

Fitzgerald, M. (2010, February). Growing young readers. *Editor & Publisher*, p. 16.

Fitzsimmons, J. (2013, January 9). What nightly news shows can learn from PBS' climate coverage. *Media Matters*. Online: http://mediamatters.org/blog/2013/01/09 /what-nightly-news-shows-can-learn-from-pbs-clim /192127.

Fleming, M. (2005, June 6–12). H'wood's new book club. *Variety*, p. 3.

Fonda, D. (2004, June 28). Pitching it to kids. *Time,* pp. 52–53.

Forbes, T. (2011, June 27). "Cars 2": Entertainment or merchandise mover? *MediaPost.* Online: http://www .mediapost.com/publications/article/153120/cars-2 -entertainment-or-merchandise-mover.html.

Forbes, T. (2012, January 20). Anti-SOPA campaign: An instant case history in the new PR. *MediaPost.* Online: http://www .mediapost.com/publications/article/166193/anti-sopa -campaign-an-instant-case-history-in-the.html.

Fort, M. (2010, January 28). McDonald's launch McItaly burger. *Guardian.* Online: http://www.guardian.co.uk/lifeandstyle /wordofmouth/2010/jan/28/mcdonalds-launch-mcitaly -burger.

Francis, T. (2011, December 26). The Humble Bundle guys—PC Gamer's community heroes of the year. *PC Gamer.* Online: http://www.pcgamer.com/2011/12/26/the-humble-bundle -guys-pc-gamers-community-heroes-of-the-year/.

Franzen, C. (2012, March 2). Why Facebook shouldn't worry about Znyga's new platform. *IdeaLab.* Online: http:// idealab.talkingpointsmemo.com/2012/03/why-facebook -shouldnt-worry-about-zyngas-new-platform .php?ref=fpnewsfeed.

Friedman, W. (2012, September 6). Premium video viewing soars. *MediaPost.* Online: http://www.mediapost.com /publications/article/182487/premium-video-viewing -soars.html#axzz2XWXMXtKq.

Friedman, W. (2013a, March 25). Movies could screen tough 2013. *MediaPost.* Online: http://www.mediapost.com /publications/article/196590/movies-could-screen -tough-2013.html#axzz2TwiVkBmj.

Friedman, W. (2013b, March 15). Digital video usage grows on gaming consoles. *MediaPost.* Online: http://www .mediapost.com/publications/article/195899/digital -video-usage-grows-on-gaming-consoles .html#axzz2XpWblyWL.

Friedman, W. (2013c, March 11). 'Zero TV' trend rejects trad TV viewing. *MediaPost.* Online: http://www.mediapost.com /publications/article/195487/zero-tv-trend-rejects-trad-tv -viewing.html#axzz2XWXMXtKq.

Friend, T. (2000, April 24). Mickey Mouse Club. *The New Yorker,* pp. 212–214.

Friend, T. (2009, January 19). The Cobra. *The New Yorker,* pp. 40–49.

Garchik, L. (2000, July 25). Death and hobbies. *San Francisco Chronicle,* p. D10.

Gardner, E. (2009, November 6). Forty years of sunny days. *USA Today,* p. 1D.

Gardner, T. (2010, November). When haters are best ignored. *Extra!,* p. 3.

Garfield, B. (2005, April 4). The chaos scenario. *Advertising Age,* pp. 1, 57–59.

Garfield, B. (2007, March 26). The post-advertising age. *Advertising Age,* pp. 1, 12–14.

Garofoli, J. (2012, January 26). Obama's speech echoes Occupy movement themes. *San Francisco Chronicle,* p. A1.

Garrett, D. (2007, December 17–23). Disc biz seeks new spin in '08. *Variety,* pp. 9, 14.

Garside, J., & Power, H. (2008, January 13). EMT managers will have to sing for their super. *Telegraph.co.uk.* Online: http:// www.telegraph.co.uk/money/main.;html?xml=/money /2008/01/13/cnemi113.xml.

Genoways, T. (2007, September/October). Press pass. *Mother Jones,* pp. 79–81, 84.

Gerbner, G., Gross, L., Jackson-Beeck, M., Jeffries-Fox, S., & Signorielli, N. (1978). Cultural indicators: Violence profile no. 9. *Journal of Communication, 28,* 176–206.

Gerbner, G., Gross, L., Morgan, M., & Signorielli, N. (1980). The "mainstreaming" of America: Violence profile no. 11. *Journal of Communication, 30,* 10–29.

Germain, D. (2005, December 14). Hollywood sees biggest box office decline in 20 years. *AOL News.* Online: http://aolsvc.news.aol.com/movies/article.adp?id =20051214130609990010.

Gertner, J. (2005, April 10). Our ratings, ourselves. *New York Times Magazine,* pp. 34–46.

GfK Roper. (2008, December 1). What people do during commercials. *Advertising Age,* p. 6.

Gibbs, M. (2005, July 18). A new theory with consequences. *Network World,* p. 50.

Gillespie, E. M. (2005, August 20). Small publishers, big sales. *Providence Journal,* pp. B1–B2.

Gillespie, N. (2007, June). Kiss privacy goodbye—and good riddance, too. *Reason.* Online: http://www.reason.com /news/29166.html.

Gillmor, D. (2000, August 18). Digital Copyright Act comes back to haunt consumers. *San Jose Mercury News,* pp. 1C, 6C.

Gillmor, D. (2002, July 21). Hollywood, tech make suspicious pairing. *San Jose Mercury News,* pp. 1F, 7F.

Gillmor, D. M., & Barron, J. A. (1974). *Mass communication law: Cases and comments.* St. Paul, MN: West.

Gilson, D. (2011, March/April). Wii shall overcome. *Mother Jones,* pp. 55–57.

Ginsberg, T. (2002, January/February). Rediscovering the world. *American Journalism Review,* pp. 48–53.

Ginzburg v. United States, 383 U.S. 463 (1966).

Gitlin, T. (2004, July). It was a very bad year. *American Prospect,* pp. 31–34.

Gitlin, T. (2013, April 25). The tinsel age of journalism. *Tom Dispatch.org.* Online: http://www.tomdispatch.com /post/175692/.

Gitlow v. New York, 268 U.S. 652 (1925).

Global media: Emerging market dailies. (2011, October 3). *Advertising Age,* p. 34.

Global media habits: A TV in every house. (2011, October 3). *Advertising Age,* p. 8.

Goetzl, D. (2011, December 23). MTV Research: It's (video) game time for marketers. *MediaPost.* Online: http://www .mediapost.com/publications/article/164789/mtv-research -its-video-game-time-for-marketers.html.

Goldkorn, J. (2005, August 10). Media regulation in China: Closed open closed open for business. Online: http:// www.danwei.org/media_and_advertising/media _regulation_in_china_clos.php.

Graser, M. (2011, February 14–20). Pic biz brandwagon. *Variety*, pp. 1, 25.

Greenberg, K. (2009, March 10). ANA discusses line between falsehood, puffery. MediaPost. Online: http://www.mediapost.com/publications/article/101890/

Greenberg, K. (2011, September 16). Consumers more critical of cause marketing. *MediaPost*. Online: http://www.mediapost.com/publications/article/158743/consumers-more-critical-of-cause-marketing.html.

Greenwald, G. (2012, January 13). Arthur Brisbane and selective stenography. *Salon*. Online: http://www.salon.com/2012/01/13/arthur_brisbane_and_selective_stenography/.

Greider, W. (2005, November 21). All the king's media. *The Nation*, pp. 30–32.

Grimes, M. (2012, April 10). Nielsen: Global consumers' trust in "earned" advertising grows in importance. *Nielsen.com*. Online: http://www.nielsen.com/us/en/insights/press-room/2012/nielsen-global-consumers-trust-in-earned-advertising-grows.html.

Gross, D. (2005, July 25). Innovation: The future of advertising. *Fortune*. Online: http://www.fortune.com/fortune/0,15935,1085988,00.html.

Guskin, E., & Mitchell, A. (2011). Hispanic media: Faring better than the mainstream media. *State of the news media 2011*. Online: http://stateofthemedia.org/2011/hispanic-media-fairing-better-than-the-mainstream-media/.

Guthrie, M. (2010, April 26). Is network TV's model lost? *Broadcasting & Cable*, pp. 10–11.

Guttmacher Institute. (2010, January). U.S. teenage pregnancies, births and abortions: National and state trends and trends by race and ethnicity. Online: http://www.guttmacher.org/pubs/USTPtrends.pdf.

Hachten, W. A. (1992). *The world news prism* (3rd ed.). Ames: Iowa State University Press.

Hafner, K., & Lyon, M. (1996). *Where wizards stay up late: The origins of the Internet*. New York: Simon & Schuster.

Hall, E. (2010a, January 25). Beauty riskier than booze on Spanish TV. *Advertising Age*, p. 6.

Hall, E. (2010b, February 15). U.K. tightens rules on newly approved TV product placement. *Advertising Age*, pp. 4, 22.

Hall, E. T. (1976). *Beyond culture*. New York: Doubleday.

Hall, J. (2010, October 7). Branded-entertainment lessons courtesy of a Quebec TV show. *Advertising Age*. Online: http://adage.com/article_id=146334.

Hall, K. (2009, February 16). Kevin Smith challenges Southwest: Bring airline seat to Daily Show and I'll sit in it. *Huffington Post*. Online: http://www.huffingtonpost.com/2010/02/16/kevin-smith-challenges-so_n_463886.html.

Hall, S. (1980). Cultural studies: Two paradigms. *Media, Culture and Society, 2*, 57–72.

Halliday, J. (2007, February 12). GM cuts $600M off ad spend—yes, really. *Advertising Age*, pp. 1, 25.

Hamilton, A. (2000, August 21). Meet the new surfer girls. *Time*, p. 67.

Hamilton, A. (2005, January 10). Video vigilantes. *Time*, pp. 60–63.

Hampp, A. (2010, January 4). *Avatar* soars on fat ad spending, mass marketing. *Advertising Age*, pp. 1, 20.

Hampton, K. N., Goulet, L. S., Rainie, L., & Purcell, K. (2011, June 16). Social networking sites and our lives. *Pew Internet & American Life Project*. Online: http://pewinternet.org/~/media//Files/Reports/2011/PIP%20-%20Social%20networking%20sites%20and%20our%20lives.pdf.

Hansell, S. (2005, June 28). Cable wins Internet-access ruling. *New York Times*, p. C1.

"Hard Numbers." (2012, November/December). *Columbia Journalism Review*, p. 11.

Hardt, H. (2007, December). Constructing photography: Fiction as cultural evidence. *Critical Studies in Media Communication*, pp. 476–480.

Harris, M. (1983). *Cultural anthropology*. New York: Harper & Row.

Harris, S. D. (2009, December 20). More and more consumers turn to e-readers. *Providence Journal*, E4.

Havrilesky, H. (2010, January 30). "Digital Nation": What has the Internet done to us? *Salon*. Online: http://www.salon.com/entertainment/tv/frontline/index.html?story=/ent/tv/iltw/2010/01/30/frontline_digital_nation.

Hayes, C. (2007, November 12). The new right-wing smear machine. *The Nation*, pp. 11–13.

Hayes, D. (2003, September 15–21). H'wood grapples with third-act problems. *Variety*, pp. 1, 53.

Hayes, N. (2012, February 22). Out-of-home advertising grows in 2011. *Outdoor Advertising Association of America*. Online: http://www.oaaa.org/press/news/news.aspx?NewsId=1367.

Hedges, C. (2011, June 27). Gone with the papers. *Truthdig.com*. Online: http://www.truthdig.com/report/item/gone_with_the_papers_20110627/.

Hefling, K. (2012, March 7). Minority students punished more harshly by schools. *Providence Journal*, p. B3.

Helm, J. (2002, March/April). When history looks back. *Adbusters*.

Hendricks, M. (2012, February 1). Growth trend continues for newspaper websites; more visitors stayed longer in Q4 2011 vs. 2010. *Newspaper Association of America*. Online: http://www.naa.org/News-and-Media/Press-Center/Archives/2012/Growth-Trend-Continues-For-Newspaper-Websites.aspx.

Herskowitz, J. E. (2011, August 18). Journalism schools: Surviving or thriving? *Editor & Publisher*. Online: http://www.editorandpublisher.com/Features/Article/Journalism-Schools--Surviving-or-Thriving-.

Hickey, N. (2002, May/June). Media monopoly Q&A. *Columbia Journalism Review*, pp. 30–33.

Hightower, J. (2004a, May). The people's media reaches more people than Fox does. *Hightower Lowdown*, pp. 1–4.

Hightower, J. (2004b, May 15). Grand larceny of pin-striped thieves. *Progressive Populist*, p. 3.

Hinchey, M. (2006, February 6). More media owners. *The Nation*, p. 15.

Hirschberg, L. (2007, September 2). The music man. *New York Times Magazine*, pp. 28–33, 46–49.

Hogan, M. (2011, November 20). In an iTune age, do we need the record store? *Salon*. Online: http://www.salon

.com/2011/11/20/in_an_itunes_age_do_we_need_the _record_store/.

Hopewell, J., & de Pablos, E. (2010, February 1–7). Spanish auds flock to pubcaster's ad-free pix. *Variety,* p. 13.

Hovland, C. I., Lumsdaine, A. A., & Sheffield, F. D. (1949). *Experiments on mass communication.* Princeton, NJ: Princeton University Press.

How they see us. (2005, November 4). *The Week,* p. 19.

Howe, J. (2005a, November). The hit factory. *Wired,* pp. 200–205, 218.

Howe, J. (2005b, August). The uproar over downloads. *Wired,* p. 40.

Iezzi, T. (2007, January 29). A more-targeted world isn't necessarily a more civilized one. *Advertising Age,* p. 11.

Ifill, G. (2007, April 10). Trash talk radio. *New York Times,* p. A21.

Internet Movie Database. (2012). Top grossing movies of all time at the USA box office. Online: http://www.imdb.com /boxoffice/alltimegross.

Internet World Statistics. (2013, January 1). Internet users in the world. Online: http://www.internetworldstats.com/stats.htm.

Internet World Stats. (2012, February 8). World Internet usage and population statistics. Online: http://www .internetworldstats.com/stats.htm.

Irvin v. Dowd, 366 U.S. 717 (1961).

Italie, H. (2007, November 18). Government study: Americans reading less. Online: http://www.chron.com/disp/story .mpl/ap/politics/5312713.html.

Ives, N. (2006a, February 13). Print buyers search for real-time ad metrics. *Advertising Age,* p. S-2.

Ives, N. (2006b, April 17). Magazines shape up for digital future. *Advertising Age,* pp. 3, 46.

Ives, N. (2007a, April 23) Mags march calmly into face of chaos. *Advertising Age,* pp. 3, 44.

Ives, N. (2007b, May 28). All the mag stats you can handle. *Advertising Age,* p. 4.

Ives, N. (2008, November 17). As ASME fortifies ad/edit divide, some mags flout it. *Advertising Age,* 3.

Ives, N. (2010, April 2). Ads venturing further into magazines' editorial pages. *Advertising Age.* Online: http://adage.com /article/mediaworks/ads-venturing-magazines-editorial -pages/143111/.

Ives, N. (2011a, January 31). Look, up in the air: It's a bird, a plane, captive affluent print readers. *Advertising Age,* p. 3.

Ives, N. (2011b, February 21). "The Greatest Movie Ever Sold" is buying in. *Advertising Age.* Online: http://adage.com /article/mediaworks/product-placement-explored-bashed -spurlock-film/148991/.

Ives, N. (2011c, June 22). American Medical Association pushes end to photoshopped body images in ads. *Advertising Age.* Online: http://adage.com/article/mediaworks/ama-end -ads-unrealistic-body-images/228354/.

Ives, N. (2012, January 19). Online ad spending to pass print for the first time, forecast says. *Advertising Age.* Online: http:// adage.com/article/mediaworks/emarketer-online-ad -spending-pass-print-time/232221/.

Iyengar, S., & Kinder, D. R. (1987). *News that matters: Television and American opinion.* Chicago: University of Chicago Press.

Jackson, J. (2001, September/October). Their man in Washington. *Extra!,* pp. 6–9.

Jackson, J. (2012, April). 12th annual fear & favor review. *Extra!,* pp. 7–9.

Jackson, J., & Hart, P. (2002, March/April). Fear and favor 2001. *Extra!,* pp. 20–27.

Jacobellis v. Ohio, 378 U.S. 184, 197 (1964).

James, M. (2011, December 8). Cable TV networks feel pressure of programming costs. *Los Angeles Times.* Online: http:// articles.latimes.com/2011/dec/08/business/la-fi-ct-cable -economics-20111208.

James, M. (2013, April 8). Digital subscriptions boost newspaper circulation revenue in 2012. *Los Angeles Times.* Online: http://articles.latimes.com/2013/apr/08/business /la-fi-ct-newspaper-industry-20130408.

Jamieson, K. H., & Campbell, K. K. (1997). *The interplay of influence: News, advertising, politics, and the mass media.* Belmont, CA: Wadsworth.

Jardin, X. (2005a, April). The Cuban revolution. *Wired,* pp. 119–121.

Jardin, X. (2005b, December). Thinking outside the box office. *Wired,* pp. 256–257.

Jarvis, J. (2013, May 28). In the end was the word and the word was the sponsor's. *Buzz Machine.com.* Online: http:// buzzmachine.com/2013/05/29/in-the-end-was-the-word -and-the-word-was-the-sponsors/.

Jefferson, C. (2011, December 22). Happy, flourishing city with no advertising. *Good Cities.* Online: http://www.good.is /post/a-happy-flourishing-city-with-no-advertising/.

Joffe, J. (2006, May 14). The perils of soft power. *New York Times Magazine,* pp. 15–17.

John Paul II. (2005, April 11). Two cents: Letter to commemorate the Feast of Saint Francis DeSales. *Broadcasting & Cable,* p. 54.

Johnson, B. (2011a, October 3). Leading media companies. *Advertising Age,* pp. 44–45.

Johnson, B. (2011b, December 5). Where's the growth? Follow the BRIC road. *Advertising Age,* pp. 1, 8.

Johnson, C. (2012, Spring). Second chance. *American Journalism Review,* pp. 18–25.

Johnson, C. A. (2009, February 11). Cutting through advertising clutter. *CBS News.* Online: http://www.cbsnews.com/2100 -3445_162-2015684.html.

Johnson, S. (2009, June 15). How Twitter will change the way we live. *Time,* pp. 32–37.

Justices scrap Internet child porn law. (2002, April 17). *Providence Journal,* p. A3.

Kalet, H. (2007, May 15). Imus shocked at grassroots reaction. *Progressive Populist,* p. 21.

Kamiya, G. (2009, February 17). The death of news. *Salon.* Online: www.salon.com/opinion/kamiya/2009/02/17 /newspapers/print.html.

Kantar Media. (2011, March 17). Branded entertainment. Online: http://kantarmediana.com/insight-center /news/us-advertising-expenditures-increased-65 -percent-2010.

Kato, M. (2012, January). Arrested development. *Game Informer,* pp. 10–12.

Katz, E., & Lazarsfeld, P. F. (1955). *Personal influence: The part played by people in the flow of communications.* New York: Free Press.

Keller, B. (2011, July 17). Let's ban books. *New York Times Magazine*, pp. 9–10.

Kelly, C. (2010, June 11). Female athletes almost invisible on television—except Abby Sunderland. *True Slant.* Online: http://trueslant.com/caitlinkelly/2010/06/11/female -athletes-almost-invisible-on-television-except-abby -sunderland/.

Kelly, K. (2008, November 23). Becoming screen literate. *New York Times Magazine*, pp. 48–53.

Kennedy, D. (2004, June 9). Mad as hell at the FCC. *Boston Phoenix.* Online: http://www.alternet.org/print .html?storyid=16116.

Kennedy, L. (2002, June). Spielberg in the Twilight Zone. *Wired,* pp. 106–113, 146.

Kent, S. L. (2001). *The ultimate history of video games.* New York: Three Rivers Press.

Kerkian, S. (2011, October 4). Global consumers voice demand for greater corporate responsibility. *Cone Communications.* Online: http://www.coneinc.com/2011globalcrrelease.

Kern, T. (2005, December 5). Convergence makes a comeback. *Broadcasting & Cable,* p. 32.

Khanfar, W. (2011, February 1). US viewers seek Al Jazeera coverage. *Al Jazeera.* Online: http://english.aljazeera.net /indepth/opinion/2011/02/201121121041735816.html.

Kirchner, L. (2013, May/June). Turn on, log in, opt out? *Columbia Journalism Review,* pp. 49–53.

Kirsner, S. (2005, April). Hayden's planetarium. *CMO Magazine.* Online: http://www.cmomagazine.com/read/040105 /planetarium.html.

Klaassen, A. (2005a, December 5). Local TV nets try pay to play. *Advertising Age,* pp. 1, 82.

Klaassen, A. (2005b, December 5). Want a gold record? Forget radio, go online: *Advertising Age,* p. 12.

Klapper, J. T. (1960). *The effects of mass communication.* New York: Free Press.

Klein, N. (1999). *No logo: Taking aim at the brand bullies.* New York: Picador.

Klosterman, C. (2005, August). What we have here is a failure to communicate. *Esquire,* pp. 62–64.

Knopper, S. (2011, November 24). Rock radio takes another hit. *Rolling Stone,* p. 19.

Konner, J. (1999, March/April). Of Clinton, the Constitution & the press. *Columbia Journalism Review,* p. 6.

Kristula, D. (1997, March). *The history of the Internet.* Online: http://www.davesite.com/webstation/net-history.shtml.

Kulicke, H. (2011, October). Quest for success. *Editor & Publisher,* pp. 48–52.

Kuralt, C. (1977). *When television was young* (videotape). New York: CBS News.

Kurtz, H. (2009, August 24). Death panels smite journalism. *Washington Post.* Online: http://www.washingtonpost.com /wp-dyn/content/article/2009/08/24/AR2009082400996.html.

Kuttner, R. (2007, March/April). The race. *Columbia Journalism Review,* pp. 24–32.

Langer, G. (March 18). Poll tracks dramatic rise in support for gay marriage. *ABC News.* Online: http://abcnews.go.com /blogs/politics/2013/03/poll-tracks-dramatic-rise-in -support-for-gay-marriage/.

Lardinois, F. (2012, October 29). Comscore: U.S. Internet users watched 39 billion online videos in September, number of viewers down slightly from August. *Tech Crunch.* Online: http://techcrunch.com/2012/10/29/comscore-u-s-internet -users-watched-39-billion-online-videos-in-september -number-of-viewers-down-slightly-from-august/.

Lasswell, H. D. (1948). The structure and function of communication in society. In L. Bryson (Ed.), *The communication of ideas.* New York: Harper.

Lawless, J. (2008, January 2). US near bottom of Global Privacy Index. *Washington Post.* Online: http://www .washingtonpost.com/wp-dyn/content/article/2008/01/02 /AR2008010201082_pdf.

Lazarsfeld, P. F. (1941). Remarks on administrative and critical communications research. *Studies in Philosophy and Social Science, 9,* 2–16.

Leading national advertisers. (2010, June 21). *Advertising Age,* pp. 10–11.

Learmonth, M. (2010a, January 18). Thinking outside the box: Web TVs skirt cable giants. *Advertising Age,* pp. 1, 19.

Learmonth, M. (2010b, February 2). For some consumers, online video ads still grate. *Advertising Age.* Online: http:// adage.com/article_id=141860.

Lemann, N. (2009, November 15). Journalism schools can push coverage beyond breaking news. *Chronicle of Higher Education,* pp. B8–B9.

Lemire, C. (2011, May 20). Spurlock sells out and has a great time doing it. *Providence Journal,* p. D3.

Leonard, A. (2013, April 10). Google's war against fake news. *Salon.* Online: http://www.salon.com/2013/04/10/googles _war_against_fake_news/.

Lepore, J. (2009, January 26). Back issues. *The New Yorker,* pp. 68–73.

Lester, J. (2002, Spring). Carved runes in a clearing. *Umass,* pp. 24–29.

Lewis, P. (2005, July 25). Invasion of the podcast people. *Fortune,* pp. 204–205.

Lithwick, D. (2012, March 12). Extreme makeover. *New Yorker,* pp. 76–79.

Littleton, C. (2013, June 20). Al Jazeera won't stoop to score with U.S. channel. *Variety,* p. 27.

Littleton, C., & Schneider, M. (2009, December 7–13). Turn on tune in. *Variety,* pp. 1, 62.

Loechner, J. (2011a, March 2). Play it again, Sam. *Mediapost.* Online: http://www.mediapost.com/publications /?fa=Articles.showArticle&art_aid=14573.

Loechner, J. (2011b, June 23). Teen media behavior; texting, talking, socializing, TV watching, mobiling. *MediaPost.* Online: http://www.mediapost.com/publications /article/152661/.

Lowenstein, D. (2005, May). 2005 state of the industry speech. *Entertainment.Software Association.* Online: http://www .theesa.com/archives/2005/05/e3_state_0_1.php.

Lowrey, A. (2011, July 20). Readers without Borders. *Slate*. Online: http://www.slate.com/articles/business /moneybox/2011/07/readers_without_borders.html.

Lowery, S. A., & DeFleur, M. L. (1995). *Milestones in mass communication research*. White Plains, NY: Longman.

Lowman, S. (2010, March 21). The future of children's book publishing. *Washington Post*, p. BW8.

Lukovitz, K. (2013, January 25). Super Bowl: 39% prefer ads over game. *MediaPost*. Online: http://www.mediapost.com /publications/article/191847/super-bowl-39-prefer-ads -over-game.html#axzz2XWXMXtKq.

Lunden, I. (2012a, January 31). Social network ads: LinkedIn falls behind Twitter; Facebook biggest of all. *PaidContent*. Online: http://paidcontent.org/article/419-social-network -ads-linkedin-falls-behind-twitter-facebook-biggest-of-al/.

Lunden, I. (2012b, February 17). Analyst: Facebook will make $1.2 billion annually from mobile ads. *TechCrunch*. Online: http://techcrunch.com/2012/02/17/analyst-facebook-will -make-1-2-billion-annually-from-mobile-ads/.

Lunden, I. (2012c, February 24). First look: Survey warns of consumers turning off from digital ads. *TechCrunch*. Online: http://techcrunch.com/2012/02/24/first-look-survey -warns-of-consumers-turning-off-from-digital-ads/.

Lyons, D. (2005, November 14). Attack of the blogs. *Forbes*, pp. 128–138.

MacArthur, K. (2003, November 18). KFC pulls controversial health-claim chicken ads. *AdAge.com*. Online: http://www .adage.com/news.cms? newsid=39220.

MacMillan, R. (2009, February 11). In DC media, newspapers sink, niche outlets swim. *Reuters*. Online: http://blogs .reuters.com/mediafile/2009/02/11/in-dc-media -newspapers-sink-niche-outlets-swim/.

Madden, M. (2012, February 24). Privacy management on social media sites. *Pew Internet & American Life Project*. Online: http://pewinternet.org/Reports/2012/Privacy -management-on-social-media-aspx.

Madrak, S. (2009, October 31). The Senate announces deal on reporters' shield law; bloggers included. *Crooks and Liars*. Online: http://crooksandliars.com/susie-madrak/senate -announces-deal-reporters-shiel.

Mahler, J. (2010, January 24). James Patterson Inc. *New York Times Magazine*, pp. 32–39, 46–48.

Mandese, J. (2009, July 8). Forrester revises interactive outlook, will account for 21% of marketing by 2014. *MediaPost*. Online: http://www.mediapost.com/publications /?fa=Articles.showArticle&art_aid=109381.

Manjoo, F. (2008, July 27). Branded. *New York Times Book Review*, p. 7.

Manjoo, F. (2011, July 26). How Netflix is killing piracy. *Slate*. Online: http://www.slate.com/articles/technology /technology/2011/07/how_netflix_is_killing_piracy.html.

Marche, S. (2012, May). Is Facebook making us lonely? *Atlantic*. Online: http://www.theatlantic.com/magazine /archive/2012/05/is-facebook-making-us-lonely/8930/.

Marich, R. (2011, October 17–23). VOD's vigor gives H'wood new hope. *Variety*, pp. 1, 12.

Marriott, H. (2005, October 27). ICCO president Saunders calls for "ethical" approach. *PRWeek*. Online: http:// www.prweek.com/uk/news/article/524519.

Martin, C. E. (2007, April 18). The frightening normalcy of hating your body. Online: http://www.truthout.org /issues_06/printer_041807WA.shtml.

Masnick, M. (2013, April 8). Authors Guild's Scott Turow: The Supreme Court, Google, e-books, libraries & Amazon are all destroying books. *Techdirt*. Online: http://www.techdirt. com/articles/20130408/01345422620/authors-guilds-scott -turow-supreme-court-google-ebooks-libraries-amazon -are-all-destroying-authors.shtml.

Masnick, M., & Ho, M. (2012, January). *The sky is rising*. *Techdirt*. Online: http://www.techdirt.com/skyisrising/.

Mast, G., & Kawin, B. F. (1996). *A short history of the movies*. Boston: Allyn & Bacon.

Mastro, D. (2009). Effects of racial and ethnic stereotyping. In J. Bryant & M. B. Oliver (Eds.), *Media effects: Advances in theory and research*. New York: Routledge.

Matsa, K., Rosenstiel, T., & Moore, P. (2011). Magazines: A shake-out for news weeklies. *State of the news media 2011*. Online: http://stateofthemedia.org/2011/magazines-essay/.

Matsa, K., Sasseen, J., & Mitchell, A. (2012). Magazines: Are hopes for tablets overdone? *State of the news media 2012*. Online: http://stateofthemedia.org/2012/magazines-are -hopes-for-tablets-overdone/.

McAdams, D. D. (2010, March 22). Broadcast nets own 80% of prime-time shows. *Television Broadcast*. Online: http:// www.televisionbroadcast.com/article/96866.

McChesney, R. W. (1997). Corporate media and the threat to democracy. New York: Seven Stories Press.

McChesney, R. W. (1999). *Rich media, poor democracy*. Urbana: University of Illinois Press.

McChesney, R. W. (2004, July). Waging the media battle. *American Prospect*, pp. 24–28.

McChesney, R. W. (2007). *Communication revolution*. New York: New Press.

McClellan, S. (2002, May 27). Winning, and losing too. *Broadcasting & Cable*, pp. 6–7.

McClellan, S. (2011, October 19). Public more worried about privacy loss than terrorism. *MediaPost*. Online: http://www .mediapost.com/publications/article/160709/public-more -worried-about-privacy-loss-than-terror.html.

McClellan, S. (2012, March 14). Global ad budgets shift to emerging markets. *MediaPost*. Online: http://www .mediapost.com/publications/article/170166/global-ad -budgets-shift-to-emerging-markets.html.

McCombs, M. E., & Shaw, D. L. (1972). The agenda-setting function of mass media. *Public Opinion Quarterly, 36*, 176–187.

McCullagh, D. (2005, June 27). DSL providers hope to mimic cable's win. Online: http://news.com.com/2102-1034_3 -5765085.html.

McGonigal, J. (2011, February 15). Video games: An hour a day is key to success in life. *Huffington Post*. Online: http://www.huffingtonpost.com/jane-mcgonigal /video-games_b_823208.html.

McKelvey, T. (2009, June). Keeping secrets. *American Prospect*, pp. 58–59.

McKenna, K. (2000, August). John Malkovich interview. *Playboy*, pp. 65–78.

McLuhan, M. (1962). *The Gutenberg galaxy: The making of typographic man.* London: Routledge.

McLuhan, M. (1964). *Understanding media: The extensions of man.* New York: McGraw-Hill.

McLuhan, M., & Fiore, Q. (1967). *The medium is the massage.* New York: Random House.

McLuhan, M., & Stern, G. E. (1967). A dialogue: Q & A. In M. McLuhan & G. E. Stern (Eds.), *McLuhan: Hot and cool: A primer for the understanding of McLuhan and a critical symposium with a rebuttal by McLuhan.* New York: Dial Press.

McMasters, P. K. (2005, March 27). Censorship is alive and well, deadly to free expression. *Providence Journal,* p. I5.

McQuail, D. (1987). *Mass communication theory: An introduction.* Beverly Hills, CA: Sage.

Meadows, B. (2009, February 14). Kevin Smith "too fat" to fly Southwest. *People.* Online: http://www.cnn.com/2010/SHOWBIZ/02/15/kevin.smith.southwest/index.html.

Media Matters. (2008, May 14). Military analysts named in *Times* exposé appeared or were quoted more than 4,500 times on broadcast nets, cables, NPR. Online: http://mediamatters.org/research/200805130001.

Meehan, M. (2004, January 20). The ratings game: System has its flaws, one of which is lax oversight. *Knight Ridder Tribune News Service,* p. 1.

Meikeljohn, A. (1960). *Political freedom.* New York: Harper.

Melber, A. (2008, October 30). Web puts dog-whistle politics on a leash. *The Nation.* Online: http://www.thenation.com/doc/20081117/melber.

Menaker, D. (2009, September 14). Redactor agonistes. *Barnes & Noble Review.* Online: http://bnreview.barnesandnoble.com/t5/Reviews-Essays/Redactor-Agonistes/ba-p/1367.

Merton, R. K. (1967). *On theoretical sociology.* New York: Free Press.

Mieszkowski, K. (2008, February 2). Young voters are stoked. *Salon.* Online: http://www.salon.com/news/feature/2008/02/02/youth_vote_2008.html.

Miller v. State of California, 413 U.S. 15 (1973).

Mindlin, A. (2009, January 5). Web passes papers as news source. *New York Times,* p. B3.

Mirkinson, J. (2012, February 29). Rush Limbaugh: Sandra Fluke, woman denied right to speak at contraception hearing, a "slut." *Huffington Post.* Online: http://www.huffingtonpost.com/2012/02/29/rush-limbaugh-sandra-fluke-slut_n_1311640.html.

Mitchell, A., Rosenstiel, T., & Christian, L. (2012). Mobile devices and news consumption: Some good signs for journalism. *State of the news media 2012.* Online: http://stateofthemedia.org/2012/mobile-devices-and-news-consumption-some-good-signs-for-journalism/.

Mitchell, B. (2011, October 19). It's time: 5 reasons to put up a metered paywall. *Poynter.* Online: http://www.poynter.org/latest-news/business-news/newspay/149953/its-time-5-reasons-for-taking-the-plunge-into-a-metered-paywall/.

Mitchell, G. (2009, April). Watchdogs failed to bark on economy. *Editor & Publisher,* p. 16

Mnookin, S. (2007, December). The angry mogul. *Wired,* pp. 202–212.

Mobile Marketing 2011. (2011, October 10). *Advertising Age,* Insert.

Molina, B., & Swartz, J. (2013, May 28). Forecast: Tablet shipments to outpace PCs by 2015. *USA Today.* Online: http://www.usatoday.com/story/tech/personal/2013/05/28/idc-tablets-pcs/2365667/.

Morozov, E. (2012, January 23). Warning: This site contains conspiracy theories. *Slate.* Online: http://www.slate.com/articles/technology/future_tense/2012/01/anti_vaccine_activists_9_11_deniers_and_google_s_social_search_.html.

Morrisey, J. (2011, September 4). O.K., downloaders, let's try this song again. *New York Times,* p. BU1.

Morrison, M. (2013, June 3). Superman reboot 'Man of Steel' snares $160M in promotions. *Advertising Age.* Online: http://adage.com/article/news/superman-reboot-man-steel-snares-160m-promotions/241822/.

Morrison, P. (2011, October). Media monopoly revisited. *Extra!* pp. 13–15.

Moses, A. (2007, August 7). New life for Afterworld on Web and phone. Online: http://www.smh.com.au/news/afterworld-series-hits-tv-web-and-phone/207/08/07.htm.

Moyers, B. (2004, September 11). Journalism under fire. *AlterNet.* Online: http://www.alternet.org/module/19918.

Moyers, B. (2007, February 12). Discovering what democracy means. Online: http://www.tompaine.com/discovering_what_democracy_means.php.

Muller, J. (2011, September 13). Where newspapers thrive. *Los Angeles Times.* Online: http://articles.latimes.com/2011/sep/13/opinion/la-oe-muller-weeklies-20110913.

Mutual Film Corp. v. Industrial Commission of Ohio, 236 U.S. 230 (1915).

National Broadcasting Co. v. United States, 319 U.S. 190 (1943).

National Cable and Telecommunications Association (NCTA). (2012). Industry statistics. Online: http://www.ncta.com/statistics/aspx.

Naureckas, J. (2009, November). Public media and the democratification of news. *Extra!,* pp. 12–13.

Near v. Minnesota, 283 U.S. 697 (1931).

Neuman, W. (2011, April 29). U.S. seeks new limits on food ads for children. *New York Times,* p. B1.

Neumeister, L. (2010, July 7). "Bad words" ban for TV struck down. *Providence Journal,* p. B4.

The new imperative. (2005, September 26). *Advertising Age,* pp. M1–M24.

Newport, F. (2011, August 29). Americans rate computer industry best, federal gov't worst. *Gallup.com.* Online: http://www.gallup.com/poll/149216/americans-rate-computer-industry-best-federal-gov-worst.aspx.

Newspaper Association of America. (2011, August 26). Newspaper readership & audience by age and gender. Online: http://www.naa.org/Trends-and-Numbers/Readership/Age-and-Gender.aspx.

New York Times v. Sullivan, 376 U.S. 254 (1964).

New York Times v. United States, 403 U.S. 713 (1971).

Nichols, J. (2007, January 29). Newspapers . . . and after? *The Nation,* pp. 11–17.

Nichols, J. (2009, May 18). Public firms' greed fueled papers' woes. *Providence Journal,* p. C5.

Nichols, J. (2010, February 22). Obama's neutrality. *The Nation*, p. 5.

Nielsen Company. (2011, January 6). *U. S. audiences & devices.* Online: http://blog.nielsen.com/nielsenwire/wp-content/uploads/2011/01/nielsen-media-fact-sheet-jan-11.pdf.

Ninety-Second Congress. (1972). *Hearings before the Subcommittee on Communications on the Surgeon General's Report by the Scientific Advisory Committee on Television and Social Behavior.* Washington, DC: U.S. Government Printing Office.

Norsigian, J., Diskin, V., Doress-Worters, P., Pincus, J., Sanford, W., & Swenson, N. (1999). The Boston Women's Health Book Collective and *Our bodies, ourselves:* A brief history and reflection. *Journal of the American Medical Women's Association.* Online: http://www.ourbodiesourselves.org.

NPD Group. (2011, October 19). According to The NPD Group, Americans still listen to music on AM/FM radio more than any other choice, but streaming music via smartphones is gaining ground. Online: http://npdgroup.com/wps/portal/npd/us/news/pressreleases/pr_111019a.

O2. (2012, June 29). Making calls has become fifth most frequent use for a smartphone for newly-networked generation of users. *All About You.* Online: http://news.o2.co.uk/?press-release=making-calls-has-become-fifth-most-frequent-use-for-a-smartphone-for-newly-networked-generation-of-users.

O'Brien, T. L. (2005, February 13). Spinning frenzy: P. R.'s bad press. *New York Times,* p. 3.1.

Obst, L. (2012, June 15). Hollywood's completely broken. *Salon.* Online: http://www.salon.com/2013/06/15/lynda_obst_hollywoods_completely_broken/.

Olmstead, K., Sasseen, J., Mitchell, A., & Rosenstiel, T. (2012). Digital: News gains audience but loses ground in chase for revenue. *State of the news media 2012.* Online: http://stateofthemedia.org/2012/digital-news-gains-audience-but-loses-more-ground-in-chase-for-revenue/.

100 global marketers, 2011. (2011, December 5). *Advertising Age,* pp. 6–7.

O'Malley, G. (2012, June 1). Online movie spend surpasses DCD, Blu-ray. *MediaPost.* Online: http://www.mediapost.com/publications/article/175994/#axzz2WyRPevOP.

O'Malley, G. (2013, March 15). Nearly 4 billion minutes of video ads streamed in February. *MediaPost.* Online: http://www.mediapost.com/publications/article/195903/nearly-4-billion-minutes-of-video-ads-streamed-in.html#axzz2Nuo6zptn.

Online video business. (2012, January 2). *Broadcasting & Cable,* pp. 30–31.

Online video market 2011. (2011, September 19). *Advertising Age,* Insert.

Open Mobile Video Coalition. (2012, January 6). Mobile digital TV expands nationwide to 120 stations. Online: http://www.openmobilevideo.com/_assets/docs/press-releases/2012/OMVC-at-CES-2012-FINAL.pdf.

Oppelaar, J. (2003, May 12–18). Will Apple for pay keep doldrums away? *Variety,* p. 42.

Oremus, W. (2012, April 13). Hell phone. *Slate.* Online: http://www.slate.com/articles/technology/technology/2012/04/how_to_stop_text_spam_why_cellphone_spam_is_on_the_rise_and_what_you_can_do_about_it_.2.html.

Oreskovic, A. (2012, January 23). YouTube video views hit 4 billion per day. *Huffington Post.* Online: http://www.huffingtonpost.com/2012/01/23/youtube-video-views_n_1223070.html.

Ortutay, B. (2012, January 23). Pew report finds tablet, e-book ownership nearly doubled over the holidays. *Minneapolis Star-Tribune.* Online: http://www.startribune.com/lifestyle/137878993.html.

Osnos, P. (2009, March/April). Rise of the reader. *Columbia Journalism Review,* pp. 38–39.

Ott, B. (2009, June 5). America's safest cities. *Real Clear Politics.* Online: http://www.realclearpolitics.com/articles/2009/06/05/americas_safest_cities_96815.html.

Outing, S. (2005, November 16). Investigative journalism: Will it survive? *Editor & Publisher.* Online: http://www.editorandpublisher.com/eandp/columns/stopthepresses_display.jsp?vnu_content_id=1001523690.

Owen, L. H. (2013, April 11). Ebooks made up 23 percent of US publisher sales in 2012, says the AAP. *Paid Content.* Online: http://paidcontent.org/2013/04/11/ebooks-made-up-23-percent-of-us-publisher-sales-in-2012-says-the-aap/.

Packard, V. O. (1957). *The hidden persuaders.* New York: David McKay.

Palast, G. (2003, July 31). Silence of the media lambs. *AlterNet.* Online: http://www.alternet.org/print.html?storyid=16524.

Palser, B. (2011, Winter). Apple's gift to publishers. *American Journalism Review,* p. 52.

Patel, S. (2012, February 29). Inmobi releases first wave of mobile media consumption Q4 survey—global results. *Inmobi.* Online: http://www.inmobi.com/inmobiblog/2012/02/29/inmobi-releases-first-wave-of-mobile-media-consumption-q4-survey-%E2%80%93-global-results/.

Pearlstein, S. (2005, November 9). Prime time gets redefined. *Washington Post,* p. D1.

Pegoraro, R. (2005, August 14). Broadband is too important to be left to cable-phone duopoly. *Washington Post,* p. F7.

Pelli, D. G., & Bigelow, C. (2009, October 20). A writing revolution. *Seed Magazine.* Online: http://seedmagazine.com/content/article/a_writing_revolution/.

Pember, D. (1999). *Mass media law.* Boston: McGraw-Hill.

Perez-Pena, R. (2007, December 8). Success without ads. *New York Times,* p. C1.

Pew Research Center. (2011, September 22). *Press widely criticized, but trusted more than other sources.* Online: http://www.people-press.org/2011/09/22/press-widely-criticized-but-trusted-more-than-other-institutions/.

Pfanner, E. (2013, February 26). Music industry sales rise, and digital revenue gets the credit. *New York Times,* p. B3.

Phillips, B. (2010, September 9). U.S. Department of Transportation announces record-low level of drunk-driving fatalities. *Beer Institute.* Online: http://www.beerinstitute.org/BeerInstitute/files/ccLibraryFiles/Filename/000000001089/Dept%20of%20Transportation%20Data%202010%20-%20FINAL%209-9-10.pdf.

Pickard, V. (2010). "Whether the giants should be slain or persuaded to be good": Revisiting the Hutchins Commission and the role of media in a democratic society. *Critical Studies in Media Communication, 27,* 391–411.

Pincus, J. (1998). Introduction. In Boston Women's Health Book Collective (Eds.), *Our bodies, ourselves for the new century* (pp. 21–23). New York: Touchstone.

Plambeck, J. (2010, February 25). 10 billionth download for iTunes. *New York Times,* p. C5.

Plate, T. (2003, January 23). Media giantism and the IHT crisis. *Providence Journal,* p. B4.

Pollak, C. (2009, December 18). Video games in play. *NielsenWire.* Online: http://blog.nielsen.com/nielsenwire /consumer/video-games-in-play/.

Pollack, J. (2011, May 30). Sympathy for the devil: Why the major labels might be right this time. *Huffington Post.* Online: http://www.huffingtonpost.com/jeff-pollack /sympathy-for-the-devil-wh_b_865887.html.

Pomerantz, D. (2009, August 6). The Web auteur. *Forbes.* Online: http://www.forbes.com/2009/08/06/online-video -innovation-technology-e-gang-09-whedon.html.

Poniewozik, J. (2001, Fall). Get up, stand up. *Time,* pp. 68–70.

Poniewozik, J. (2004, September 27). The age of iPod politics. *Time,* p. 84.

PopCap. (2011, December 2). 2011 PopCap games social gaming research. *Information Solutions Group.* Online: http://www.infosolutionsgroup.com/pdfs/2011_PopCap _Social_Gaming_Research_Results.pdf.

Popova, M. (2012, January 10). Network: The secret life of your personal data, animated. *Brainpicking.org.* Online: http:// www.brainpickings.org/index.php/2012/01/10/network -michael-rigley/.

PR in the driver's seat. (2009, October 26). *Advertising Age,* p. S6.

Preston, J. (2011, February 6). Movement began with outrage and a Facebook page that gave it an outlet. *New York Times,* p. A10.

Project for Excellence in Journalism. (2004). *The state of the news media 2004.* Online: www.stateofthemedia .org./2004/.

Project for Excellence in Journalism. (2006). *The state of the news media 2005.* Online: http://www.stateofthenewsmedia .org/2005/.

PRSA. (2012a, March). Industry facts and figures. *Public Relations Society of America.* Online: http://media.prsa.org /prsa+overview/industry+facts+figures/.

PRSA. (2012b, March, 2012). What is public relations? *Public Relations Society of America.* Online: http://www.prsa.org /aboutprsa/publicrelationsdefined/.

Przybys, J. (2011, January 30). Facebook changing the meaning of friendship. *Las Vegas Review-Journal.* Online: http:// www.lvrj.com/living/facebook-changing-the-meaning-of -friendship-114891819.html.

Purcell, K., & Rainie, L. (2010, March 1). Understanding the participatory news consumer. *Pew Internet and American Life Project.* Online: http://pewinternet.org/Reports/2010 /Online-News.aspx.

Purcell, K., Rainie, L., Mitchell, A., Rosenstiel, T., & Olmstead, K. (2010). Understanding the participatory news consumer.

Pew Internet & American Life Project. Online: http:// pewinternet.org/Reports/2010/Online-News.aspx.

PQ Media. (2012). Global product placement spending forecast 2012–2016. *PQmedia.* Online: http://www.pqmedia.com /about-press-201212.html.

Quantcast. (2012, March). Top sites for United States. Online: http://www.quantcast.com/top-sites/US.

Quindlen, A. (2000, July 17). Aha! Caught you reading. *Newsweek,* p. 64.

Radio Broadcasters Attract Another 2.1 Million Weekly Listeners According to Radar 108. (2011, March 16). *Arbitron.* Online: http://arbitron.mediaroom.com/index .php?s=43&item=750.

Rainie, L. (2011, May 30). Internet phone calls. *Pew Internet and American Life Project.* Online: http://pewinternet.org /Reports/2011/13--Internet-phone-calls--Skype/Main -report.aspx.

Rainie, L., & Duggan, M. (2012, December 27). E-book reading jumps; print book reading declines. *Pew Internet & American Life Project.* Online: http://libraries.pewinternet .org/2012/12/27/e-book-reading-jumps-print-book -reading-declines/.

Rainey, J. (2011, December 5). NBC stations will use content from nonprofit news outlets. *Los Angeles Times.* Online: http://latimesblogs.latimes.com/entertainmentnewsbuzz /2011/12/nbc-stations-will-share-content-from-non-profit -news-outlets.html.

Recording Industry Association of America. (2011). 2010 year-end shipment statistics. Online: http://www .RIAA.com.

Rehlin, G. (2010, March 1–7). Swedish court takes un-commercial break. *Variety,* p. 4.

Reporters Without Borders. (2012, January 25). 2011–2012 world press freedom index. Online: http://en.rsf.org/IMG /CLASSEMENT_2012/C_GENERAL_ANG.pdf.

Rhee, J., & Schone, M. (2010, February 8). Toyota dealers pull ABC TV ads; anger over "excessive stories." *ABC News.* Online: http://abcnews.go.com/Blotter/toyota-dealers-pull -abc-tv-ads-anger-excessive-toyota-safety-recall /story?id=9776474.

Ricchiardi, S. (2007, August/September). Distorted picture. *American Journalism Review,* pp. 36–43.

Rich, F. (2004, March 28). Real journalism's in trouble, while fake stuff flourishes. *Providence Journal,* pp. E1, E2.

Rich, F. (2005, February 6). The year of living indecently. *New York Times,* p. 2.1.

Rich, M. (2007, July 22). A magical spell on kids' reading habits? *Providence Journal,* p. J2.

Rideout, V. J., Foehr, U. G., & Roberts, D. F. (2010). *Generation M^2: Media in the lives of 8- to 18-year-olds.* Menlo Park, CA: Kaiser Family Foundation.

Romenesko, J. (2012, April 16). Editor: We'll cover advertisers' staged events. *JimRomenesko.com.* Online: http:// jimromenesko.com/2012/04/16/newspaper-will-cover -advertisers-staged-events/.

Rosaldo, R. (1989). *Culture and truth: The remaking of social analysis.* Boston: Beacon Press.

Rose, F. (2008, March). Let my video go. *Wired,* pp. 33–34.

Rosen, J. (2012, January 12). So whaddaya think: should we put truthtelling back up there at number one? *Press Think.* Online: http://pressthink.org/2012/01/so-whaddaya-think-should-we-put-truthtelling-back-up-there-at-number-one/.

Rosenberg, R. S. (1992). *The social impact of computers.* Boston: Harcourt Brace Jovanovich.

Rosenstiel, T., & Mitchell, A. (2011). Overview. *State of the news media 2011.* Online: http://stateofthemedia.org/2011/overview-2/.

Roth v. United States, 354 U.S. 476 (1957).

Saia v. New York, 334 U.S. 558 (1948).

Sampson, H. T. (1977). *Blacks in black and white: A source book on Black films.* Metuchen, NJ: Scarecrow Press.

Sandage, C. H., Fryburger, V., & Rotzoll, K. (1989). *Advertising theory and practice.* New York: Longman.

Sanders, L., & Halliday, J. (2005, May 24). BP institutes "ad-pull" policy for print publications. *AdAge.com.* Online: http://www.adage.com/news.cms?newsId=45132.

Sanders, S. (2010, February 19). This ain't your mother's Farmville—well, actually it is. *National Public Radio.* Online: http://www.npr.org/blogs/alltechconsidered/2010/02/this_aint_your_mothers_farmvil.html.

Santhanam, L., Mitchell, A., & Rosenstiel, T. (2012). Audio: How far will digital go? *State of the news media 2012.* Online: http://stateofthemedia.org/2012/audio-how-far-will-digital-go/.

Saroyan, S. (2011, June 17). Storyseller. *New York Times Magazine,* pp. 26–29.

Sass, E. (2009, April 10). "Custom publishing" chugs along. *MediaPost.* Online: http://www.mediapost.com/publications/?fa=Articles.showArticle&art_aid=103849.

Sass, E. (2011a, July 27). 56% of Americans check online news daily. *MediaPost.* Online: http://www.mediapost.com/publications/article/154841/.

Sass, E. (2011b, October 28). Clear Channel Radio lays off DJs. *MediaPost.* Online: http://www.mediapost.com/publications/article/161330/clear-channel-radio-lays-off-djs.html.

Sass, E. (2011c, December 14). 239 magazines launched in 2011. *MediaPost.* Online: http://www.mediapost.com/publications/article/164252/239-magazines-launched-in-2011.html.

Sass, E. (2012, April 17). Hispanics wield $1 trillion+ buying power. *MediaPost.* Online: http://www.mediapost.com/publications/article/172672/hispanics-wield-1-trillion-buying-power.html.

Sass, E. (2012, December 13). Magazine launches outpace closures in 2012. *Media Daily News.* Online: http://www.mediapost.com/publications/article/189250/#axzz2VARlJWwN.

Sass, E. (2013a, May 31). Magazine audiences grow in print, digital. *Media Daily News.* Online: http://www.mediapost.com/publications/article/201555/magazine-audiences-grow-in-print-digital.html#axzz2VARlJWwN.

Sass, E. (2013b, May 22). Newspaper, magazine ad fortunes continue to decline. *Media Daily News.* Online: http://www.mediapost.com/publications/article/200960/newspaper-magazine-ad-fortunes-continue-to-declin.html#axzz2UcI4ekMF.

Schechner, S., & Peers, M. (2011, December 6). Cable-TV honchos cry foul over soaring cost of ESPN. *Wall Street Journal.* Online: http://online.wsj.com/article/SB10001424052970204083204577080793289112260.html.

Schenck v. United States, 249 U.S. 47 (1919).

Schwartzman, A. J. (2004, December 3). Media Access Project issues statement on Supreme Court order granting certiorari in *Brand X v. FCC.* Online: http://www.mediaaccess.org.

Schweizer, K. (2010, September 13). Asia-Pacific to pass North America as biggest ad market in 2014. *Bloomberg.* Online: http://www.bloomberg.com/news/2010-09-12/asia-pacific-to-pass-north-america-as-biggest-ad-market-in-2014.html.

Scribner, S. (2001, February 7). Conspiracy to limit the films we see. *Hartford Courant,* pp. D1, D3.

Seabrook, J. (2003, July 7). The money note. *The New Yorker,* pp. 42–55.

Seabrook, J. (2012, January 16). Streaming dreams. *New Yorker,* pp. 24–30.

Scola, N. (2011, November 20). Congress seeks to tame the Internet. *Salon.* Online: http://www.salon.com/2011/11/20/congress_seeks_to_tame_the_internet/.

Seipp, C. (2002, June). Online uprising. *American Journalism Review,* pp. 42–47.

"Seismic Changes Rock Worldwide B.O. Picture." (2013, April 16). *Variety,* pp. 82–83.

Seitel, F. P. (2004). *The practice of public relations.* Upper Saddle River, NJ: Pearson.

Sellers, J. (2001). *Arcade fever.* Philadelphia: Running Press.

Shame on BP and Morgan Stanley ad pull policies. (2005, May 24). *AdAge.com.* Online: http://www.adage.com/news.cms?newsId=45141.

Shane, S. (2012, February 8). Radical U.S. Muslims little threat, study says. *New York Times,* p. A10.

Sheehy, A. (2011, October). E-book publishing & e-reading devices 2011 to 2015. *Generatorresearch.com.* Online: http://www.giiresearch.com/report/gs220581-ebook-publishing-ereading-devices-2011-2015.html.

Shenk, D. (1997). *Data smog: Surviving the information glut.* New York: Harper Edge.

Sherman, S. (2004, March 15). Floating with the tide. *The Nation,* pp. 4–5.

Shields, R. (2009, November 1). Illegal downloaders "spend the most on music," says poll. *The Independent,* p. 6.

Shirky, C. (2010). The shock of inclusion. *Edge.* Online: http://www.edge.org/q2010/q10_1.html.

Shirky, C. (2012, January 12). The *New York Times* public editor's very public utterance. *Guardian.* Online: http://www.guardian.co.uk/commentisfree/cifamerica/2012/jan/13/new-york-times-public-editor?CMP=twt_gu.

Should Comcast buy Disney? (2004, February 27). *The Week,* p. 39.

Sigmund, J. (2010, October 20). Newspapers reach nearly three-in-four adult consumers with buying power every week. *Newspaper Association of America.* Online: http://www.naa.org/PressCenter/SearchPressReleases/2010/NEWSPAPERS-REACH-NEARLY-THREE-IN-FOUR-ADULT-CONSUMERS-WITH-BUYING-POWER-EVERY-WEEK.aspx.

Silverblatt, A. (2008). *Media literacy* (3rd ed.). Westport, CT: Praeger.

Sirota, D. (2011, May 27). Kid-baiting ads have gone too far. *Salon.* Online: http://www.salon.com/2011/05/27/snoop _dogg_ronald_mcdonald_advertising/.

Sisario, B. (2012, August 22). The new rise of a summer hit: Tweet it maybe. *New York Times,* p. A1.

Skenazy, L. (2008, May 19). Keep targeting kids and the parents will start targeting you. *Advertising Age,* p. 20.

Sloan, W., Stovall, J., & Startt, J. (1993). *Media in America: A history.* Scottsdale, AZ: Publishing Horizons.

Smith, L. D. (2011, May 25). 2011 Edelman value, engagement and trust in the era of social entertainment survey. *Edelman. com.* Online: http://www.edelman.com/news/ShowOne .asp?ID=274.

Smith, S. (2011a, December 29). Facebook reaches 300 million active mobile app users. *MediaPost.* Online: http://www .mediapost.com/publications/article/164958/facebook -reaches-300-million-active-mobile-app-use.html.

Smith, S. (2011b, November 29). "Economist" reports 1 million app readers. *MediaPost.* Online: http://www.mediapost .com/publications/article/163170/economist-reports-1 -million-app-readers.html.

Smith, S. (2012a, March 1). Pew claims smartphone tipping point passed. *MediaPost.* Online: http://www.mediapost .com/publications/article/169171/pew-claims-smartphone -tipping-point-passed.html.

Smith, S. (2012b, March 23). End of an age: Netflix, Hulu, Amazon will beat physical video viewing in 2012. *MediaPost.* Online: http://www.mediapost.com/publications/article /170863/end-of-an-age-netflix-hulu-amazon-will-beat -phy.html.

Smith, S. (2013a, March 26). Tablet gaming is hacking and slashing other platforms. *MediaPost.* Online: http://www .mediapost.com/publications/article/196638/tablet-gaming -is-hacking-and-slashing-other-platfo.html#axzz2XpWblyWL.

Smith, S. (2013b, March 1). Is that ringtone you hear the death knell for console gaming? *MediaPost.* Online: http://www .mediapost.com/publications/article/194604 /#axzz2XpWblyWL.

Smolkin, R. (2004, April/May). The next generation. *American Journalism Review,* pp. 20–28.

Snider, M. (2012, September 5). NPD: Total number of U.S. video game players drops. *USA Today.* Online: http:// content.usatoday.com/communities/gamehunters /post/2012/09/npd-total-number-of-us-video-game -players-drops/1.

Soderbergh, S. (2013, April 30). Steven Soderbergh's state of the cinema talk. *Deadline.com.* Online: http://www.deadline .com/2013/04/steven-soderbergh-state-of-cinema-address/.

Soley, L. C., & Nichols, J. S. (1987). *Clandestine radio broadcasting: A study of revolutionary and counterrevolutionary electronic communication.* New York: Praeger.

Sony Corp. v. Universal City Studios, 464 U.S. 417 (1984).

SoundBites. (2005, December). A better mousetrap. *Extra! Update,* p. 2.

SoundBites. (2011, August). Driven by profits, not quality. *Extra!,* p. 3.

SRI Consulting. (2008, January). *Understanding U.S. consumers.* Menlo Park, CA: Author.

Stampler, L. (2013, June 5). Swiffer pulls ad showing 'Rosie the Riveter' icon doing chores. *Business Insider.* Online: http://www.businessinsider.com/swiffer-pulls-rosie -the-riveter-ad-2013-6.

Stanley, T. L. (2005, December 19). Reasons people skip movies. *Advertising Age,* p. 20.

Starkman, D. (2009, January 14). How could 9,000 business reporters blow it? *Mother Jones.* Online: http://www .motherjones.com/print/19947.

Stars diss Hollywood: Clooney, Edgerton & more swipe at commercial movie bombs. (2012, January 23). *Huffington Post.* Online: http://www.huffingtonpost.com/2012/01/23 /stars-diss-hollywood-clooney-edgerton_n_1223315.html.

Stauber, J. C., & Rampton, S. (1995). *Toxic sludge is good for you: Lies, damn lies and the public relations industry.* Monroe, ME: Common Courage Press.

Stein, L. (2010, February 12). Where has all the trust gone? *MediaPost.* Online: http://www.mediapost.com /publications/?fa=Articles.showArticle&art_aid=122357.

Steinberg, B. (2011, October 3). Are video-on-demand viewers Big Media's next great hope? *Advertising Age,* p. 16.

Steinberg, S. H. (1959). *Five hundred years of printing.* London: Faber & Faber.

Stelter, B. (2012, February 2). Youths are watching, but less often on TV. *New York Times,* p. B1.

Sterling, C. H., & Kitross, J. M. (1990). *Stay tuned: A concise history of American broadcasting.* Belmont, CA: Wadsworth.

Sternberg, J. (2012, September 25). The Atlantic tries native ads. *Digiday.com.* Online: http://www.digiday.com/publishers /the-atlantic-tries-native-ads/.

Stevenson, M. (2008, June 27). Trying to parse the new radio daze. *Providence Journal,* p. B4.

Stevenson, R. L. (1994). *Global communication in the twenty- first century.* New York: Longman.

Stewart, A. (2013, January 7–13). 2012: A tough act to follow. *Variety,* pp. 9, 33.

Stewart, A., & Cohen, D. S. (2013, April 16). The end. *Variety,* pp. 40–47.

Stewart, C. S. (2010, February). The lost boys. *Wired,* pp. 68–73, 107.

Stewart, Jon. (2011, June 30). Moral combat. *The Daily Show.* Online: http://www.thedailyshow.com/watch/thu-june -30-2011/moral-kombat.

St. George, D. (2009, April 20). Study finds some youth "addicted" to video games. *Washington Post.* Online: http://www .washingtonpost.com/wp-dyn/content/article/2009/04/19 /AR2009041902350.html.

Stone, B. (2009, March 29). Is Facebook growing up too fast? *New York Times,* pp. BU1, 6–7.

Stone, B., & Barboza, D. (2010, January 16). Scaling the digital wall. *New York Times,* p. B1.

The story of the Ad Council. (2001, October 29). *Broadcasting & Cable,* pp. 4–11.

Streisand, B., & Newman, R. J. (2005, November 14). The new media elites. *U.S. News & World Report,* pp. 54–63.

Stross, R. (2011, May 29). Consumer complaints made easy. Maybe too easy. *New York Times,* p. BU3.

Strupp, J. (2007, October). When is it appropriate to "out" polls? *Editor & Publisher,* pp. 12–13.

Strupp, J. (2012, September 27). Editorial page editors: WSJ lack of Romney advisers disclosure "inexcusable" and "shameless." *Media Matters.* Online: http://mediamatters .org/blog/2012/09/27/editorial-page-editors-wsj-lack-of -romney-advis/190152.

Sullivan, A. (2002, May). The blogging revolution. *Wired,* pp. 43–44.

Sullivan, A. (2013, February 24). Guess which Buzzfeed piece is an ad, ctd. *The Dish.* Online: http://dish.andrewsullivan .com/?s=native+advertising+derek+thompson.

Sullivan, J. (2011, May/June). True enough. *Columbia Journalism Review,* pp. 34–39.

Sullivan, L. (2009, June 16). In-game ads in the ad game. *MediaPost.* Online: http://www.mediapost.com /publications/?fa=Articles.showArticle&art_aid=108089.

Sullivan, L. (2011, September 7). Home run: Sharpie YouTube ad grabs 62 million impressions. *MediaPost.* Online: http:// www.mediapost.com/publications/article/158097/.

Survey: Readers prefer community paper for news. (2011, December 1). *National Newspaper Association.* Online: http://www.nnaweb.org/?/nnaweb/content01/2475/.

Swing, E. L., Gentile, D. A., Anderson, C. A., & Walsh, D. A. (2010). Television and video game exposure and the development of attention problems. *Pediatrics,* 126, 214–221.

Szalavitz, M. (2011, November 7). Study: Whites more likely to abuse drugs than blacks. *Time.* Online: http://healthland .time.com/2011/11/07/study-whites-more-likely-to-abuse -drugs-than-blacks/.

Szatmary, D. P. (2000). *Rockin' in time: A social history of rock-and-roll* (4th ed.). Upper Saddle River, NJ: Prentice-Hall.

Taylor, C. (2003, March 10). Day of the smart mobs. *Time,* p. 53.

Taylor, D. (1991). Transculturating TRANSCULTURATION. *Performing Arts Journal, 13,* 90–104.

Teague, D. (2005, May 24). U.S. book production reaches new high of 195,000 titles in 2004; fiction soars. Online: http://www .bowker.com/press/bowker/2005_0524_bowker.htm.

Tebbel, J. (1987). *Between covers: The rise and transformation of American book publishing.* New York: Oxford University Press.

Tebbel, J., & Zuckerman, M. E. (1991). *The magazine in America 1741–1990.* New York: Oxford University Press.

Teegardin, C. (2012, January 1). Grim childhood obesity ads stir critics. *Atlanta Journal Constitution.* Online: http://www.ajc .com/news/grim-childhood-obesity-ads-1279499.html.

Teens killed girl using *Mortal Kombat* moves: Police. (2007, December 20). Online: http://www.thewest.com.au /ContentID=51798.

Television Bureau of Advertising. (2011). TV basics. Online: http://www.tvb.org/tvfacts/tvbasics.html.

Tessler, J. (2010, February 23). FCC says broadband education needed. *TVNewsCheck.* Online: http://www.tvnewscheck .com/articles/2010/02/23/daily.2/.

Thompson, B. (2007, November 19). A troubling case of readers' block. *Washington Post,* p. C1.

Thompson, B. (2009, June 1). At publishers' convention, is writing on the wall? *Washington Post.* Online: http://www .washingtonpost.com/wp-dyn/content/article/2009/05/31 /AR2009053102119.html.

Thornton, L. (2009, February/March). Can the press fix itself? *American Journalism Review,* p. 2.

Thorp, B. K. (2011, April 1). Terry Jones burns Qur'an; Mob kills ten UN workers. *Broward/Palm Beach New Times.* Online: http://blogs.browardpalmbeach.com/pulp/2011/04/terry _jones_afghan_riot.php.

Tillinghast, C. H. (2000). *American broadcast regulation and the First Amendment: Another look.* Ames: Iowa State University Press.

Time, Inc. v. Hill, 385 U.S. 374 (1967).

Timpane, J. (2010, March 30). Google's vast digital library. *Providence Journal,* pp. D1–D2.

Top 50 global marketers. (2009, December 28). Annual 2010. *Advertising Age,* p. 15.

Traffic stats. (2010, March 2). Pogo.com. *Alexa.* Online: http:// www.alexa.com/siteinfo/pogo.com.

Trench, M. (1990). *Cyberpunk.* Mystic Fire Videos. New York: Intercon Production.

Trigoboff, D. (2003, June 9). Copps: Dereg foes will be back. *Broadcasting & Cable,* p. 36.

Tsukayama, H. (2012a, January 17). SOPA: Twitter will not join Wikipedia, Reddit in blackout. *Washington Post.* Online: http://www.washingtonpost.com/business/technology /sopa-twitter-will-not-join-wikipedia-reddit-in-blackout /2012/01/17/gIQAvDta5P_story.html.

Tsukayama, H. (2012b, March 28). Xbox adds HBO Go, MLB.TV, Xfinity, as it evolves from game console. *Washington Post.* Online: http://www.washingtonpost.com/business /technology/xbox-adds-hbo-go-mlbtv-xfinity-as-it-evolves -from-game-console/2012/03/28/gIQASdAWgS_story .html?wpisrc=nl_tech.

Tsukayama, H. (2012c, April 3). Consumers concerned about online data sharing, sales. *Washington Post.* Online: http:// www.washingtonpost.com/blogs/post-tech/post /consumers-concerned-about-online-data-sharing -sales/2012/04/03/gIQAWwpOtS_blog.html?wpisrc=nl_tech.

Tsukayama, H. (2013, April 16). Snapchat processes 150 million images per day. *Washington Post.* Online: http://articles. washingtonpost.com/2013-04-16/business/38573186 _1_snapchat-evan-spiegel-instagram.

25 banned books that you should read today. (2011, March 3). *DegreeDirectory.org.* Online: http://degreedirectory.org /articles/25_Banned_Books_That_You_Should_Read_Today .html.

Two cents: William Safire on re-reg vote. (2003, July 21). *Broadcasting & Cable,* p. 46.

UNESCO. (2005, October 20). General Conference adopts Convention on the Protection and Promotion of the Diversity of Cultural Expressions. Online: http://portal.unesco.org.

USA Today. (2000, July 9). The *Potter* phenomenon: It's just magic. *Honolulu Advertiser,* p. E4.

U.S. Census Bureau. (2012a, April 25). 2010 census shows interracial and interethnic married couples grew by 28 percent over decade. Online: http://www.census.gov /newsroom/releases/archives/2010_census/cb12-68.html.

U.S. Census Bureau. (2012b, August). Marriage and divorces— number and rate by state: 1990–2009. Online: http://www .census.gov/compendia/statab/2012/tables/12s0133.pdf.

Valentine v. Christensen, 316 U.S. 52 (1942).

Vane, S. (2002, March). Taking care of business. *American Journalism Review,* pp. 60–65.

Vega, T. (2013, April 8). Sponsors now pay for online articles, not just ads. *New York Times,* p. BU1.

Virgin, B. (2004, March 18). We've become instant billboards. *Seattle Post-Intelligencer,* p. E1.

Vivarelli, N. (2013, February 11–17). Al Jazeera's (r)evolution. *Variety,* pp. 14–15.

Vorhaus, M. (2009, February 9). Ad presence in console games has little effect on purchase. *Advertising Age,* p. 18.

Walcott, J. (2008, October 9). Truth is not subjective. *McClatchy Newspapers.* Online: http://www.mcclatchydc.com/257/story/53716.html.

Walker, R. (2009). Reality bytes. *New York Times Magazine,* p. 32.

Wallenstein, A. (2012, April 16). Survey: A la carte could fetch $1.50 per channel. *Variety.* Online: http://www.variety.com/article/VR1118052724.html?cmpid=RSS.

Walsh, M. (2011, January 26). Stop the presses, mobile surpasses print time spent. *MediaPost.* Online: http://www.mediapost.com/publications/article/164050/stop-the-presses-mobile-surpasses-print-time-spen.html.

Walsh, M. (2012a, April 3). Online radio moving up the charts. *MediaPost.* Online: http://www.mediapost.com/publications/article/171672/online-radio-moving-up-the-charts.html?edition=45319.

Walsh, M. (2012b, April 5). Pandora hits 1 billion listening hours, revs lag. *MediaPost.* Online: http://www.mediapost.com/publications/article/171883/pandora-hits-1-billion-listening-hours-revs-lag.html?edition=45447.

Walsh, M. (2012c, May 1). Mobile to become top email platform. *MediaPost.* Online: http://www.mediapost.com/publications/article/173702/#axzz2Y0dA8xnn.

Walsh, M. (2013, April 26). Smartphones overtake feature phones, consumers want all services. *MediaPost.* Online: http://www.mediapost.com/publications/article/199019/#axzz2Y0dA8xnn.

Ward, E., Stokes, G., & Tucker, K. (1986). *Rock of Ages: The* Rolling Stone *history of rock & roll.* New York: Rolling Stone Press.

Wartella, E. A. (1997). *The context of television violence.* Boston: Allyn & Bacon.

Wasik, B. (2012, January). Crowd control. *Wired,* pp. 76–83, 112–113.

Wasserman, E. (2009, February 23). Press travails need Web-wide response. *Providence Journal,* p. B6.

Webber, E. (2007, April 30). No need to bare all: PR should strive for translucence. *Advertising Age,* p. 8.

Wedemeyer, J. (2010, January 29). Christina Hendricks and her husband defend her controversial Golden Globes dress. *People.* Online: http://stylenews.peoplestylewatch.com/2010/01/29/christina-hendricks-and-her-husband-defend-her-controversial-golden-globes-dress/.

Whitney, D. (2011, November 23). A chaos theorist on video guides: Maybe we need them, but maybe we have outgrown them. *MediaPost.* Online: http://www.mediapost.com/publications/article/162952/a-chaos-theorist-on-video-guides-maybe-we-need-th.html.

Whitney, D. (2012, February 22). Machima's one billion views and counting come from a strong POV. *MediaPost.* Online: http://www.mediapost.com/publications/article/168255/machinimas-one-billion-views-and-counting-come-fr.html.

Whitney, L. (2010, January 13). Poll: Most won't pay to read newspapers online. Online: http://news.cnet.com/8301-1023_3-10433893-93.html.

Whittaker, Z. (2012, June 22). Facebook could see ad revenue hit in "Sponsored Stories" lawsuit. *ZDNet.* Online: http://www.zdnet.com/blog/btl/facebook-could-see-ad-revenue-hit-in-sponsored-stories-lawsuit/80613.

Why Elvis still lives. (2002, August 9). *The Week,* p. 9.

Why I believe in PR. (2009, October 26). *Advertising Age,* p. S12.

Williams, M. E. (2009, August 12). This is your brain on retouching. *Salon.* Online: http://www.salon.com/mwt/broadsheet/feature/2009/08/12/kelly_clarkson/index.html.

Williams, M. E. (2011, March 30). Why are parents defending a kids' push-up bra? *Salon.* Online: http://www.salon.com/2011/03/30/abercrombie_fitch_pushup_bikinis_for_children/.

Williams, T. (2002, January/February). Dream society. *Adbusters,* p. 17.

Winslow, G. (2009, January 5). Delivery dilemmas. *Broadcasting & Cable,* pp. 15–16.

World's 20 Largest Agency Networks. (2013, April 29). *Advertising Age,* supplement.

Wronge, Y. S. (2000, August 17). New report fuels TV-violence debate. *San Jose Mercury News,* pp. 1E, 3E.

Yarow, J. (2012, March 27). iPad users are spending $70,000 a day on iPad newspapers and magazines. *Business Insider.* Online: http://www.businessinsider.com/ipad-users-are-spending-70000-a-day-on-newspapers-and-magazines-2012-3.

Young, B. (2009, December 10). Human capacity for information is massive but finite. *TechNewsWorld.* Online: http://www.technewsworld.com/perl/search.pl?query=Human+capacity+for+information+is+massive+but+finite.

Younge, G. (2010, October 11). Islamophobia, European-style. *Nation,* p. 10.

Zeller, T. (2006, January 15). China, still winning against the Web. *New York Times,* p. A4.

Zickuhr, K. (2010, December 16). Craigslist and online classifieds. *Pew Internet & American Life Project.* Online: http://pewinternet.org/Reports/2010/Generations-2010/Trends/Classifieds.aspx.

Zickuhr, K. (2011, February 13). Generations and their gadgets. *Pew Internet & American Life Project.* Online: http://www.pewinternet.org/Reports/2011/Generations-and-gadgets.aspx.

Zickuhr, K., & Smith, A. (2012, April 13). Digital differences. *Pew Internet & American Life Project.* Online: http://pewinternet.org/Reports/2012/Digital-differences/Overview.aspx#.

Zinn, H. (1995). *A people's history of the United States, 1492–present.* New York: HarperPerennial.

Zipp, Y. (2013, March 17). The novel resurgence of independent bookstores. *Christian Science Monitor.* Online: http://www.csmonitor.com/USA/Society/2013/0317/The-novel-resurgence-of-independent-bookstores.

Zittrain, J. (2009, July 20). Lost in the cloud. *New York Times,* p. A19.

Credits

RF; p. 153 (right): © Masterfile RF; p. 154: © AP Images; p. 155 (both): The Granger Collection, NY; p. 156: Courtesy of Culver Pictures; p. 157: The Granger Collection, NY; p. 159 (top): © Bettmann/Corbis; p. 159 (bottom): Courtesy of Broadcasting & Cable; p. 160: © Stockbyte/PunchStock RF; p. 162: © RubberBall Productions RF; p. 163 (top): © Michael Ochs Archives/Getty Images; p. 163 (bottom): © Alexander Tamargo/Getty Images; p. 165: © P. Ughetto/PhotoAlto RF; p. 167 (all): © Bettmann/Corbis; p. 168 (left): © Chris Polk/WireImage/Getty Images; p. 168 (right): © Kyrre Lien/AFP/Getty Images; p. 168 (bottom): photo: Adam Rose/© Fox/Courtesy Everett Collection; p. 169 (left): © Steve Jennings/WireImage/Getty Images; p. 169 (right): © Kevin Mazur/WireImage/Getty Images; p. 171: © L. Mouton/PhotoAlto RF; p. 172: © Jason Squires/WireImage/Getty Images; p. 174: Courtesy of Apple; p. 175: © Dave Hogan/Getty Images; p. 176: © Alex Wong/Getty Images.

Chapter 8 Opener: © HBO/Courtesy: Everett Collection; p. 182 (left): © Division of Work and Industry National Museum of American History, Smithsonian Institution; p. 182 (middle): The Granger Collection, NY; p. 182 (right): © Ingram Publishing RF; p. 183 (top): © West High Drama/Llc/The Kobal Collection; p. 183 (left TV): © Classic PIO/Fotosearch RF; p. 183 (left Lucy): © CBS/Photofest; p. 183 (middle): © Handout/KRT/Newscom; p. 183 (right): McGraw-Hill Education/Mark A. Dierker; p. 184: © Division of Work and Industry National Museum of American History, Smithsonian Institution; p. 185 (left): Courtesy of Culver Pictures; p. 185 (right): The Granger Collection, NY; p. 186 (all): The Kobal Collection/Picture Desk; p. 187: © CBS/Photofest; p. 189: © AP Images; p. 190: © Ryan McVay/Getty Images RF; p. 191: © The Barco Library of The Cable Center, Denver, CO; p. 192: © Children's Television Network/Jim Hensen/Courtesy Everett Collection; p. 194 (left): © CBS/Photofest; p. 194 (right): © NBC/Courtesy Everett Collection; p. 194 (bottom): © Courtesy Everett Collection; p. 195: © Jason Reed/Getty Images RF; p. 196: © Jeff Greenberg/PhotoEdit; p. 197: © Kevin Jordan/Getty Images RF; p. 198: © Mike Ehrmann/Getty Images; p. 199 (Spartacus): © USA Network/Courtesy Everett Collection; p. 199 (Newsroom): photo: John P. Johnson/© HBO/Courtesy Everett Collection; p. 199 (Girls): © HBO/Photofest; p. 199 (Homeland): © Showtime Networks/Photofest; p. 203: © Tim Pannell/Corbis RF; p. 205: © David Silverman/Getty Images.

Chapter 9 Opener: © Anatolii Babii/Alamy; p. 210 (left, middle): Wayne Namerow Collection, photograph Courtesy of Wayne Namerow; p. 210 (right): © Brand X Pictures/PunchStock RF; p. 211 (left): © Roger Ressmeyer/Corbis; p. 211 (middle): © BananaStock/PunchStock RF; p. 211 (right): ©

Toy Alan King/Alamy; p. 212 (left, right): Wayne Namerow Collection, photograph Courtesy of Wayne Namerow; p. 212 (bottom): Courtesy of the Computer History Museum; p. 213 (top): © Roger Ressmeyer/Corbis; p. 213 (bottom): © Mike Derer/AP Images; p. 215 (all): © Susan Baran; p. 219 (top): © Chris Ratcliffe/Bloomberg via Getty Images; p. 223: © Allan Shoemake/Getty Images RF.

Chapter 10 Opener: © Khaled Desouki/AFP/Getty Images; p. 232 (left): Library of Congress; p. 232 (middle, right): © AP Images; p. 233 (top): © Robbie McClaran; p. 233 (left): © Dynamic Graphics/Jupiterimages RF; p. 233 (middle): © Jason Reed/Getty Images RF; p. 233 (right): © Creatas/PictureQuest RF; p. 234 (top): © Bernard Gutfryd/Woodfin Camp & Associates; p. 234 (bottom): From the MIT Museum, © Koby-Antupit Studio, Cambridge/Belmont, MA; p. 235, p. 236 (top): © AP Images; p. 236 (bottom): © Agence France Presse/Getty Images; p. 237 (left): © Apple Inc./AP Images; p. 237 (bottom): Courtesy of Apple; p. 237 (right): © PSL Images/Alamy; p. 239 (left): © Doug Wilson/Corbis; p. 239 (right): © Paul Sakuma/AP Images; p. 239 (bottom): © Roger Ressmeyer/Corbis; p. 240: © Catrina Genovese/WireImage/Getty Images; p. 242: © Brand X/JupiterImages/Getty Images RF; p. 245 (left): © 1962 University of Toronto Press. Reproduced by permission of the publisher. Photo by Alan Gallegos/AG Photograph; p. 245 (right): Courtesy of MIT Press; p. 247: © Emmanuel Dunand/AFP/GettyImages; p. 249: © Mario Tama/Getty Images.

Chapter 11 Opener: © McGraw-Hill Education/Mark Dierker, photographer; p. 264 (left): The Granger Collection, NY; p. 264 (middle, right): Library of Congress; p. 265 (left): Courtesy of Culver Pictures; p. 265 (middle): © Tony Freeman/PhotoEdit; p. 265 (right): Courtesy of Toyota; p. 266: © Bill Coons/UPI/Newscom; p. 267: © Tony Freeman/PhotoEdit; p. 268 (top): Courtesy of Toyota; p. 268 (bottom): The Granger Collection, NY; p. 269: © Getty Images; p. 270: Courtesy of Culver Pictures; p. 271, p. 272: © Courtesy Everett Collection; p. 277: © Peter Kramer/AP Images; p. 278: © Hand-out/Ronald McDonald House Charities/Newscom; p. 280: Courtesy Cambridge Consulting Corporation/USDA; p. 282: © Bettmann/Corbis.

Chapter 12 Opener: © Andy Kropa/Getty Images; p. 288 (left, right): The Granger Collection, NY; p. 288 (middle): Library of Congress; p. 289 (top): © Susan Baran; p. 289 (left): Courtesy of Culver Pictures; p. 289 (middle): © Brand X Pictures/PunchStock RF; p. 289 (right computer): © iStockvectors/Getty Images RF; p. 289 (right magazines): © Creative Crop/Digital Vision/Getty Images RF; p. 290 (top): © Adam Woolfitt/Woodfin Camp & Associates; p. 290 (bottom): © Rusty Kennedy/AP Images; p. 291: The Granger

Collection, NY; p. 292: © 2012 Hasbro, Inc. Used with permision; p. 293 (top): The Granger Collection, NY; p. 294 (bottom): Courtesy of Brown Brothers; p. 294 (left): © The Martin Advertising Agency/Getty Images; p. 294 (right): McGruff the Crime Dog appears Courtesy of the National Crime Prevention Council—The nation's focal point for crime prevention; p. 295: Courtesy of Culver Pictures; p. 297 (top): Courtesy of The Advertising Archives; p. 297 (bottom): © Mike Kemp/Rubberball/Getty Images RF; p. 298: Courtesy Campaign for a Commercial-Free Childhood; p. 299: © Christina Kennedy/PhotoEdit; p. 303: Courtesy of Definition Branding & Marketing; p. 304: © Brand X/Superstock RF; p. 305: From "Public Service Announcement Posters" by the National Sexual Violence Resource Center, 2012. Available from http://www.nsvrc.org. Copyright 2012 by the National Sexual Violence Resource Center. Reprinted with permission; p. 310: © Bill Aron/PhotoEdit; p. 312: © Brand X Pictures/PunchStock RF.

Chapter 13 Opener: © Byron Peter/Photo Researchers; p. 318 (left): © Famous Players/Paramount/The Kobal Collection; p. 318 (middle): © Ingram Publishing RF; p. 318 (right): Office of War Information Photograph Collection/Library of Congress; p. 319 (left): Courtesy of Professor Albert Bandura, Stanford University; p. 319 (middle): © Bill Aron/PhotoEdit; p. 319 (right): McGraw-Hill Education/Mark A. Dierker; p. 320: © Susan Baran; p. 321: © CW/Courtesy Everett Collection; p. 322: © Bill Aron/PhotoEdit; p. 324: © Famous Players/Paramount/The Kobal Collection; p. 327: © CBS Radio/Photofest; p. 329: © Brand X Pictures RF; p. 333: © Comedy Central/Courtesy Everett Collection; p. 334: © Ragdoll Ltd./Courtesy Everett Collection; p. 336: © Mark Wilson/Getty Images; p. 340: © Warner Brothers/Photofest; p. 341: Courtesy of Professor Albert Bandura, Stanford University; p. 342: photo: Kelsey McNeal/TM and Copyright © 20th Century Fox Film Corp. All rights reserved, Courtesy Everett Collection; p. 344: Courtesy of The Advertising Archives; p. 345 (L Word): photo: Liane Hentscher/© Showtime/Courtesy Everett Collection; p. 345 (Will & Grace): © NBC/Courtesy Everett Collection; p. 345 (Modern Family): The Kobal Collection/Picture Desk; p. 345 (Queer as Folk): © SHOWTIME/Courtesy Everett Collection; p. 346: McGraw-Hill Education/Mark A. Dierker.

Chapter 14 Opener: © Jose Luis Magana/AP/Corbis; p. 352 (left): National Archives and Records Administration; p. 352 (middle): © Photodisc/Punchstock RF; p. 352 (right): Courtesy of Culver Pictures; p. 353 (left): © Bettmann/Corbis; p. 353 (middle): © Getty Images RF; p. 353 (right): Courtesy of the United States Government; p. 354: © Getty Images; p. 356: © Splash News/Newscom; p. 357: © Don Heupel/AP Images; p. 358:

Index